Shadows of Progress

Shadows of Progress:

Documentary Film in Post-War Britain

Edited by Patrick Russell & James Piers Taylor

A BFI book published by Palgrave Macmillan

First published in 2010 by
PALGRAVE MACMILLAN

on behalf of the

BRITISH FILM INSTITUTE
21 Stephen Street, London W1T 1LN
www.bfi.org.uk

PALGRAVE MACMILLAN in the UK is an imprint of Macmillan Publishers Limited, registered in England, company number 785998, of Houndmills, Basingstoke, Hampshire RG21 6XS. Palgrave Macmillan in the US is a division of St Martin's Press LLC, 175 Fifth Avenue, New York, NY 10010. Palgrave Macmillan is the global academic imprint of the above companies and has companies and representatives throughout the world. Palgrave® and Macmillan® are registered trademarks in the United States, the United Kingdom, Europe and other countries.

Cover design: couch
Cover images: *Faces of Harlow* (Derrick Knight, 1964), Derrick Knight & Partners; *Stone Into Steel* (Paul Dickson, 1960), Wallace Productions

Designed by couch

Set by Cambrian Typesetters, Camberley, Surrey
Printed in China

This book is printed on paper suitable for recycling and made from fully managed and sustained forest sources. Logging, pulping and manufacturing processes are expected to conform to the environmental regulations of the country of origin.

British Library Cataloguing-in-Publication Data
A catalogue record for this book is available from the British Library
A catalog record for this book is available from the Library of Congress
10 9 8 7 6 5 4 3 2 1
19 18 17 16 15 14 13 12 11 10

ISBN 978-1-84457-321-9 (pbk)
ISBN 978-1-84457-322-6 (hbk)

Contents

Acknowledgments

Thank you to Rebecca Barden for commissioning the book and Sophia Contento and Joy Tucker for their editing of the manuscript, and to all for their patience and good humour. We would like to thank Robin Baker, Head Curator (BFI National Archive), for his support of the project from the outset, and our immediate colleagues, particularly Jez Stewart and Sue Woods, for coping with its effect on the curatorial team's day-to-day workload skilfully and cheerfully.

For providing access to research materials with unfailing courtesy and enthusiasm, a huge vote of thanks should go to everyone at the BFI National Library, but particularly to Sarah Currant, Sean Delaney, David Sharp and Emma Smart, and the BFI Special Collections curators Carolyne Bevan and Nathalie Morris. For their irreplaceable help with scanning illustrations, we should like to thank Nigel Arthur and Mike Caldwell of BFI Stills, Posters and Designs, Ian O'Sullivan of the BFI National Library and particularly Cristina Pia, Curatorial Intern at the BFI National Archive. We are grateful to colleagues at the National Library of Scotland (particularly Janet McBain and Kay Foubister) and the National Screen and Sound Archive of Wales (especially Iola Baines and John Reed) for access to collections and/or illustrations. We are grateful to our colleagues at the BP Video Library (Steve Croston and Elena Adams) for access to materials relating to BP's film history, and for their collegial enthusiasm for the project.

While thanking all of the book's contributors, we should especially like to acknowledge Tim Boon, Steve Foxon and Bert Hogenkamp for their interest and input. Scott Anthony made an essential contribution to the latter stages of the project in the form of significant assistance with editing the manuscript as deadlines loomed – making creative and stylistic as well as technical contributions all of which improved the text. Other friends and colleagues who provided valuable information, comment or support include Shona Barrett, Christophe Dupin, Jon Hoare and Tom Rice. Over the years, or in specific connection with the writing of this book, we have benefited from the recollections and insights of many of those involved in post-war documentary-making. As well as some of those whose careers are discussed in Part II of this book, we are particularly grateful to Anne Balfour-Fraser, Kevin Brownlow, Sheila Dickson, Rodney Giesler, Euan Pearson, Roly Stafford, Wolfgang Suschitzky and Ray Townsend. We owe particular thanks to Ken Gay, whose collection of papers, donated to the BFI in 2009, became an invaluable source for the writing of this book. Our debt to the Broadcasting Entertainment Cinematography and Theatre Union (BECTU) History Project, one of the great under-sung initiatives in preserving British film history, should be equally obvious from the text.

Other essential contributions to the BFI's post-war documentary project, of which this book is part, were made by: Sam Dunn and all at BFI DVD, James Blackford, Margaret Deriaz, Helen

Edmunds and Fiona Grimes, Maggi Hurt, Scott Starck, Paul Hexter and the Dry Lab team, Lynn McVeigh and the Business Support Unit, Ben Thompson and the Film Lab team. The BFI is grateful for the restoration funding generously supplied by the Esmee Fairbairn Foundation and the Anker-Petersen Charity.

The writing of this book was touched by sadness, when one of its contributors, Dave Berry, died a few days after completing the final draft of his chapter. He is much missed.

The writing of this book would have been impossible without the support and forbearance of those closest to us. Patrick Russell thanks Aileen, Clementine – and new arrival Laurie, to whom he dedicates this book. James Piers Taylor thanks and dedicates this book to Claire White.

Notes on Contributors

DAVE BERRY, formerly Research Officer of the National Screen and Sound Archive of Wales, was author of *Wales and Cinema: The First Hundred Years* (1996). He died in January 2010.

TIMOTHY BOON is Chief Curator, the Science Museum, and author of *Films of Fact: A History of Science in Documentary Films and Television* (2008).

MICHAEL BROOKE is a Curator (*screenonline*), BFI National Archive.

ROS CRANSTON is a Curator (Non-Fiction), BFI National Archive, and leader of the BFI project This Working Life, which celebrates Britain's industrial heritage on film.

LEO ENTICKNAP is Director of Learning and Teaching and Lecturer in Cinema at the Institute of Communications Studies, University of Leeds, and author of *Moving Image Technology: From Zoetrope to Digital* (2005).

STEVEN FOXON is a freelance documentary historian and moving-image archive consultant, and programmer of the BFI's British Transport Films DVD collection. He is currently researching a PhD on Anstey, Elton and their contribution to films for industry.

ERIK HEDLING is Professor of Film Studies, Lund University. His books include *British Fictions* (2001), *Lindsay Anderson: Maverick Film-Maker* (1998) and *Filmanalys: en introduktion* (1999).

BERT HOGENKAMP is media historian at the Netherlands Institute for Sound and Vision and a professor at the Free University, Amsterdam. His books include *Deadly Parallels: Film and the Left in Britain: 1929–39* (1986) and *Film, Television and the Left in Britain: 1950–1970* (2000).

KATY McGAHAN is a Curator (Non-Fiction), BFI National Archive, and produced the BFI DVD release *The Joy of Sex Education* (2009).

PATRICK RUSSELL is Senior Curator (Non-Fiction), BFI National Archive, author of the BFI Screen Guide *100 British Documentaries* (2007) and co-editor of *The Lost World of Mitchell and Kenyon* (2004).

JAMES PIERS TAYLOR is a freelance Curator who has worked across the moving-image archive sector.

REBECCA VICK is a Curator (Non-Fiction), BFI National Archive.

Introduction: Whatever Happened to the Documentary Movement?

Grierson got it moving with his drifters
Others followed on with social ills
Legge & Harry Watt
Helped it on a lot.
Rotha showed us dark satanic mills.

Wartime gave us fires that Jennings started
And Features-vérité like 'Next of Kin'.
With the Welfare State
Those mills began to date
And Prestige Films for Industry were in.

Pipelines, aircraft, oil-rigs were the subjects.
They treated them from every sort of slant.
Chairmen in Rolls-Royces
Cartoons with funny voices
And Helicopter shots of foundry plant.

Now 50 years have drifted since it started.
What's left of all those hopes and dreams and more?
Commercials made for Schweppes
And Training films for reps
And films about pollution by the score.

These twenty lines were published in 1977, on the back page of the in-house newssheet of a busy industrial film unit[1] – a wistfully comic ode that, it's easy to imagine, was penned on a Friday afternoon, after a long lunch. Or on a Monday morning, before a looming deadline. Its unnamed author is unlikely to win any prizes for verse. He even misspells a name ('Legge' should be 'Legg'). What he's casually voicing, however, is one of those profound, profoundly normal, questions that adult life often poses. What's left of all those hopes and dreams?

We can trust his answer. He isn't out to impress; he isn't grinding axes; he's not expecting academics or journalists to be reading his lines in 1977; he's not expecting you to be reading them now. He assumes his readers know what he's talking about, fellow working stiffs with a self-effacing love of film, a pragmatic intelligence and a lugubrious sense of humour in working order. Our anonymous scribe is probably Gordon Begg, known in the business for waggish turns of phrase and the head of the film unit in question: Millbank Films, a producer of promotional, recruitment and staff communication films for its parent company, ICI. By now, Millbank had branched out into making 16mm films for use across British industry, so famously flagging in the run-up to the Winter of Discontent. The makers of these 'training films for reps' knew exactly what their heritage was, and needed no reference books to tell them so (which was lucky: none did). They were the direct, immediate descendents of the 'great generation' of British documentary film-makers, that of Grierson, and of Legg and Watt, Rotha and Jennings.

They knew they were fated to be less feted. To judge by the textbooks, theirs is less a great generation than a lost generation: lost, unfairly, to most accounts of documentary's history. By 1977, it's true, their industry was experiencing decline, but it was a decline setting in only after many vibrant years. In the intervening decades it had turned out thousands of films, seen by millions of people. It's a credible supposition that it wasn't the perennially crisis-ridden British feature film but the documentary film, of exactly the kind our anonymous poet has anatomised, that constituted the *real* British film industry – the production line that kept the labs open. Its surviving work offers us, casual viewers and scholars alike, countless pleasures and fascinations. Its creative standards are high, and it abounds with historical interest. Post-war pipelines and pollution have as real a presence in history as pre-war mills and social ills, and a presence that looms larger in the history being made now, in our own times. Themselves products of history, these films, like all films, should be understood in the circumstances under which they came to be made, circumstances that prompted their best and their worst characteristics alike. They had plenty of both. Their undeniable limitations often prove as interesting as their underrated strengths. They should not be exempted from social or artistic critique – quite the opposite. What they do at least deserve is more attention than the short shrift they've received.

This volume, intended for general as well as specialist readers, is an introduction to Britain's lost post-war generation of documentary film-makers. Part I sets out the context, briskly surveying the territory on which they worked. Part II, the bulk of the book, samples their career stories, and the absorbing issues they raise.

Before getting to the history, a quick detour through the historiography is unavoidable. How did this post-war generation come, in the first place, to be 'lost'?

NOTES

1. 'Afterthoughts: Whatever Happened to the Documentary Movement?', *Take 22*, Millbank Films Ltd, December 1977, back page (unpaginated).

PART ONE:
Between the Tides: Mapping Post-War Documentary

1 The Long Tail

Britain's post-war documentarists have been thrice overshadowed. First, by the towering presence of what came before them, the 'Documentary Movement' of John Grierson and others. Second, in the field of film criticism, they were elbowed aside by a short-lived contemporary development: the 'Free Cinema'. Finally, as the fortunes of the documentary film gradually fell the status of television documentary increasingly rose.

In contrast to the post-war documentarists, the 'original' British Documentary Movement has been generously supplied with memoirists and chroniclers, cultists and critics. These writers did much to maintain its profile in the cultural memory of its own century: an analogue epoch in which printed texts played a larger role in the maintenance of general knowledge, and the establishment of canons, than they do in the digital epoch in which this book is published. Although far from unanimous in their judgments, most studies of the Movement share a common chronological frame of reference. In one such influential history, Elizabeth Sussex's *The Rise and Fall of British Documentary*, the 'rise' begins in 1929, when John Grierson, under the guidance of Stephen Tallents, made *Drifters* for the Empire Marketing Board Film Unit.[1] The 'fall' sets in during the late 1940s, leading to the demise of the Crown Film Unit, the EMB Unit's direct descendent, in 1952. In such texts, if later documentaries get referred to at all, then it's briefly and apathetically.[2]

A problem with the story of the 'fall' is that it can't be a quantitative one: a slight dip in documentary production in the late 1940s was soon followed by twenty years of huge growth. The biographical story of fall is only superficially more persuasive. The careers of some of the early Movement's most influential leaders – notably Grierson's and Paul Rotha's – stumbled in the late 1940s, while film-makers like Harry Watt and Pat Jackson were largely departing documentary altogether. However, other members of the Movement – Arthur Elton and Edgar Anstey are the salient examples – went on to have remarkably stable, successful post-war careers. More to the point, the second generation of documentarists upon whom this book is focused were but a heartbeat from the first: variously inspired by the Movement or reacting against it. In terms of personnel, there is more evidence for continuity than collapse, so many post-war documentarists having been either trained by or working under their immediate predecessors. On one or two occasions, even sacked by them.

Has the 'fall' been measured qualitatively, then – are the later films, however numerous or closely linked to what came before, simply inferior? Any answer is necessarily subjective and begs further questions. Are the two periods' outputs to be compared via the best examples, by the worst, or by the median? On all three counts, the post-war documentary at least holds its own, and on the last it is arguably far superior. Technical competence increased; talent did not precipitously decline. If post-war documentary certainly failed to yield a single film-maker of the stature of a Humphrey Jennings, nevertheless many of the directors discussed in Part II of this book were no less gifted than many of their more famous predecessors.

While both generations of documentary film-making were financed in much the same way, by state bodies, private industry and other institutions, for this very reason the second generation tends to be treated more sceptically. A great deal of documentary history is animated by a slightly whiggish tendency to be written in terms of 'progress'. The word 'movement' itself suggests progression and has both political and artistic connotations. Politically, progress is usually taken to mean travel on a left-ish path. Artistically, 'progress' is defined in romantic terms – those of autonomy and originality. These judgmental tendencies coalesce with the aforementioned biographical orientation of general histories of the Movement. The story of film-makers like Rotha, for instance, is easily told as a heroic bottom-up struggle by artists, scorning the commercial film trade, to secure alternative forms of patronage for documentary films with a political or artistic cutting edge. World War II saw such documentary come into unprecedented sums of money for production, in the form of state sponsorship for films at one with national purpose but consistent with collective ideals. This undoubtedly encouraged the more politically inclined in the Movement to hope that a similar relationship could blossom post-war, whereby backing from a state more closely aligned with socialistic ideals would usher in a new era of official funding for artistically fresh films allied to radical social purpose. From this perspective, the late 1940s fall is indeed a palpable one, as the cash-strapped Attlee government had bigger things on its mind than the plight of the Documentary Movement. To likeminded historians, having traced the central line of the Movement's relationship with the state from the EMB, through the GPO, to the Crown Film Unit, its closure will indeed represent a terminus.

For many admirers of the British Documentary Movement, its 1930s reliance on sponsorship is judged a progressive one, by comparison with alternative models. During the post-war period, however, the balance of influence over form and content shifted somewhat from the 'artist' to the sponsor. This process was inevitable (and indeed legitimate, insofar as it was the sponsor's money that was being spent), but for such Movement admirers it is easily equated with stagnation. As for ideology: although the entire national consensus had moved to the left, on screen the vague 'politics' of the documentary film at the very least moved no further left than that new consensus. For ideological *critics* of the Documentary Movement, already sceptical of the extent of the radicalism of Grierson and his colleagues, this lack of progression is presumably to be equated not just with stagnation but also with reaction. In any case, as they turn to the 1950s the focus of intellectual debates about documentary moves offshore to America and to France, or, if remaining at home, to the anomalous Free Cinema, and to the subsequent rise of TV documentary. It moves sharply away from the sponsored film, apparently of huge interest in its 1930s context, but in the 1950s of almost none.[3]

This consensus on British documentary's fallen state begs plenty more questions. How else could anyone entering the industry of the 1940s or early 1950s have made documentaries other than through sponsorship? Had there been no sponsorship, how many documentaries would have been made at all? Though the 'balance of power' shifted, did it shift all the way, and to the same extent in every case? Why should we automatically characterise the relationship of artist to sponsor as a power struggle? Why should we automatically take one side against the other? Is it not in any case of considerable interest to examine the process of documentary sponsorship becoming mainstream at almost all society's major institutions within the context of the mixed economy, at the same time affording a detailed survey of how the story of the Documentary Movement plays out over many years beyond the late 1940s?

All film-makers were not alike, and all sponsors were not alike: these statements apply equally to documentary before the war and after it. For some of the second-generation film-makers profiled in Part II of this book, sponsorship was a prison, for others a playground; for some a partnership, for others a battleground, or a site of deep dilemmas. And if the pre-war Movement had indeed had its leftist and avant-garde strands, these were never the whole story. At least as robust a strand of the Movement was a conception of documentary as an *applied art*, whose big political idea was less to critique society from without than to aid its humane and effective functioning, by illuminating the interconnections on which it is built from within. For such documentary, sponsorship is more than a mere means to funds: it is a means of participation in society through its myriad institutions. If we take this strand of British documentary as seriously as the more iconoclastic one, then the late 1940s begin to look very different, a period of transition and flux between two more stable periods of growth. What comes out the other end may no longer be a 'movement' in the continental sense. Instead, in pragmatic Anglo-Saxon style, it was a *school* of British documentary that synthesised much of the Movement's ethos, and certainly a great deal of its aesthetic, with the documentary-making that had contemporaneously taken place outside its blurred boundaries: the educational films made at Gaumont-British Instructional, say, or the interest films made by commercial film companies, and especially the sponsored industrial films produced outside the Movement.[4]

State sponsorship eventually went on the increase again, though admittedly its creative scope was more tightly constrained than most of its beneficiaries wished. Even more significant was the extraordinary increase in sponsorship by industry, which played perfectly to a blending of the 'documentary' and the 'industrial film' into a single robust form. It put Grierson and Tallents' basic proposition into practice on a larger scale in post-war Britain than anywhere at any time before or since: the idea that the interests of the documentary-maker *coincided* with the enlightened public relations and the day-to-day practical needs of institutions (industry often proving a more relaxed sponsor than the state).

If this was but the tail end of the great British documentary, then it was, in a fashionable twenty-first-century phrase, a *long tail*. In fact, the true fall of the British documentary film tradition came not in the late 1940s but over the course of the 1970s, as British industry, under recessionary financial pressures, began reducing investment in film, and tightening its criteria for it. The 'prestige film' – the broader sort of documentary produced under sponsorship – rapidly disappeared. The practical film remained, as it does to this day, but its hitherto stable identity as a form of documentary cinema gradually faded as several coincidental developments kicked in. A generation of film-makers and public relations officers (PROs) were beginning to retire. Video was beginning to replace film: audiovisual communications began to be thought of as a separate specialised discipline. Before long, of course, the post-war consensus itself – in which the documentary film had flourished – collapsed.

Feeding into that collapse had been a growing distrust of institutions in general, an ever more prominent feature of post-war public life. The critical reputation of the British school of documentary undoubtedly suffered from this budding cynicism. By, say, 1979, the belief that 'documentary' and 'public relations' were compatible was as anachronistic as in 1945 it had been obvious. As early as the 1950s, the state-corporatist and capitalist basis for so much of the second generation's sponsorship had fallen out of intellectual fashion, which had so embraced the first generation's exploitation of the same in the 1930s. Enter Free Cinema, which played up the romantic artistry, and added a hint of political rebellion, ensuring it would fall on the correct side of a new critical consensus. Free Cinema's leaders, Lindsay Anderson and Karel Reisz, were probably more interested in breaking into the feature film world than in making statements about documentary as such. However, they found it easier to get documentary shorts financed. They therefore felt obliged not just to assault the staid feature industry of the day, but the orthodox documentary, as practised by the late Movement (Jennings, being its sole 'artist', exempted from the critique) and by the present school descended from it. A bold venture, Free Cinema is often characterised as plucky underdog, and in industrial terms that's largely what it was. In terms of critical coverage, however, it was top dog: the underdog was the mainstream documentary that it attacked. In the documentary industry at large, Free Cinema caused many reactions, including bemusement, indifference, distaste, admiration, jealousy – and no little hurt.[5] Most documentary histories written since have followed the critical pattern set in the 1950s. A characteristic and telling example is Jim Hillier and Alan Lovell's *Studies in Documentary*.[6] There are only two studies: one of the Movement, defined by the usual chronological boundaries; the other of Free Cinema. Lovell quotes Reisz's critique (originally published in *Universities and Left Review*) of the Shell Film Unit's *Song of the Clouds*.[7] Reisz's attack ensured that Shell's film, and other documentaries from the presumably 'unFree' cinema, are only ever seen in the shadow of such attacks rather than in their own light.

Although Free Cinema rapidly secured chattering-class recognition out of all proportion to its size (and, some would argue, to its merits) before disappearing, much more damaging to the film documentary were the boxes busily planting themselves in the living rooms of ordinary members of the public. By the late 1950s, television documentary was beginning to find its own distinctive voice. Over the course of the 1960s its prevalence grew, and by the 1970s it had firmly eclipsed the film documentary in public impact. The boundaries between the large and small screen documentary industries were not completely impermeable but they *were* separate industries.[8] Their rivalry played out slowly, and only in hindsight does the small screen's triumph seem predestined. Thus, most of those who had entered the documentary film industry in the early post-war period were still there in the 1970s: on the wrong side of the fence perhaps, and certainly on the wrong side of history.

It was the effect of television on distribution as much as on cultural criticism that eventually did for the documentary film: still worth seeing, but was it worth *going* to see? Today, the history of documentary television is deeper in the dark ages than that of its film counterpart: beyond a handful of names of (probably atypical) television auteurs, like Denis Mitchell and Philip Donnellan, and a few well-remembered series and current affairs slots, the vast majority of post-war TV documentaries have remained unseen and unknown for many years, while in recent years much of post-war documentary film has become increasingly available in digital form.[9] For whig histories, however, television documentary as a *concept* can clearly be taken to represent progress in comparison with the continuation of the sponsored documentary because of its apparently greater independence of institutional influence and its willingness to tackle political controversy. However, it often suffered from artistic limitations that the best of sponsored film-making easily avoided. This was a direct legacy of the tradition of craftsmanship, and the mastery of syntax, that the second documentary generation had inherited from the first, whose stylistic template they tended to refine and perfect. Drama-documentary descended from wartime 'story documentary' remained a significant part of the palate as did the 'essay' film of lyrical commentary or blank verse over well-shot images. Other films favouring the primacy of the visual dispense with words altogether and consist of image and music only, taking documentary in a more abstract, formalist direction. Often the post-war manifestations of such forms took on a more domesticated, middlebrow, middle-aged flavour than in their youthful 1930s incarnation (again, not an *automatically* bad thing), but they also sometimes updated them in keeping with the temper of the times. Geoffrey Jones's are probably the most best-known examples of the 'pure' visual documentary, though there are many one-off examples. The drama-documentary often acquired greater psychological sophistication than it had enjoyed before. A frequent curiosity of the post-war documentary is its tendency to corrupt the 'story documentary' into 'comedy documentary' – 'docu-farce' – especially when dealing with the quintessentially post-war subject of strained industrial relations.

Cinematographers of Movement pedigree, like Wolfgang Suschitzky and Fred Gamage, contributed their considerable pictorial talents throughout the post-war decades. While television documentary directors became increasingly adept with 16mm *vox pops*, their film peers, often shooting mute on 35mm and dubbing sound later, continued to blend commentary, effects and music in pursuit of the harmonious total effect. Scores by such composers as Malcolm Arnold, Elisabeth Lutyens, Wilfred Josephs and the particularly prolific Edward Williams make as fine an aural contribution to the post-war documentary, often in an English romantic style, as the likes of Britten, William Alwyn and Muir Mathieson had to its precursor. Less often, documentary made use of more experimental soundtracks, or of folksongs or music hall instead of orchestras. The falling off in quality of its musical accompaniments was one of the most painful signs of the 1970s' decline of the documentary tradition.

Until then, TV may have possessed greater immediacy and editorial independence than film, but, its own inheritance being less from cinema than from radio journalism, it often demonstrated less impressive formal qualities – or at least different ones. Conversely, if the film documentarists often faced greater constraints on their subjects and viewpoints, they more often brought to their work the rich texture and the assured poise that make it such a delight to revisit.

Gross generalisations these may be, but it's certainly true to say that the major pity of the post-war period was not that it began with documentary's unambiguous, ignominious and rapid decline. The real pity was that as the period progressed it was less often possible than it might have been (though not always *im*possible) for the inherited strengths of documentary cinema to be combined with those of newly emerging documentary television. On the film side, post-war documentary had many of the virtues and the faults of the society it was part of: constructive, capable, humane and (contrary to the cynicism) largely sincere, but with limits placed on the free exercise of its imagination, and the free roam of its critical gaze, and its internal tensions suppressed. The post-war generation consolidated and built upon what, it must be admitted, are the more innovatory achievements of the preceding one, but were unable, in the end, to pass their own achievements on. The apparent stability of the British documentary school was in reality a precarious one, like that of post-war Britain itself. However, it was in the 1970s, not in the 1940s, that these became indisputable cultural and industrial facts.

Up until then, in their separate ways, both documentary film *and* documentary television had done their share of great, good and downright interesting things that media history has a duty to acknowledge, to explain and to learn from.

NOTES

1. Elizabeth Sussex, *The Rise and Fall of British Documentary* (Berkeley and London: University of California Press, 1975).

2. Later key books included Paul Swann's *The British Documentary Film Movement, 1926–1946* (Cambridge: Cambridge University Press, 1989), Ian Aitken's *The Documentary Movement: An Anthology* (Edinburgh: Edinburgh University Press, 1998). Studies of Grierson including ones by Aitken and Jack C. Ellis, and Grierson associate Forsyth Hardy, and books by Movement adherents (Paul Rotha, Basil Wright and Harry Watt among them) and fellow travellers (Roger Manvell) also played a part in canonising the Movement. Books by Rachel Low and Eva Orbauz are also noteworthy.
3. Brian Winston, particularly in his book *Claiming the Real* (London: BFI, 1995), is one of the Movement's most trenchant, iconoclastic critics. Less a history than a commentary on history, Winston's book stands 'whig' docu-history on its head: sharing largely the same objects of scrutiny as other writers but reversing judgments on them (critiquing films and film-makers praised by many other authors). The post-war manifestation of the Griersonian tradition, whose 1930s manifestation Winston enthusiastically knocks, is conspicuously absent.
4. As marked by the recent publication of Vinzenz Hediger and Patrick Vonderau, *Films that Work: Industrial Film and the Productivity of Media* (Amsterdam: Amsterdam University Press, 2009), sponsored and industrial films are gradually getting some overdue international attention as rich sources of study – as well as nostalgic enjoyment. Their championing and digitisation by American collector Rick Prelinger has played a particular role in familiarising internet users with the concept, and much of the content, of American sponsored film-making. The peculiarity of the British situation is the close association between the sponsored film, in its period of greatest scale and reach, with the documentary film, so soon after the latter had enjoyed such enormous influence on national film culture. Prelinger refers to much of his field as 'ephemeral' film-making, but a great deal of what was produced under British sponsorship is anything but. Eynon Smart noted that: 'In this country business interprets the purpose of the medium rather more widely than industry on the Continent. An industrialist who considers that it will be good for his business to sponsor a film unconnected with that business will sometimes make an industrial film. Some of the most active companies in the field have through the years produced a range of enlightened and (at least at first sight) disinterested work. It is of course not disinterested; but enlightened is an entirely proper adjective for such films as BP's *The Shadow of Progress*.' Eynon Smart, 'Ever-widening Scope for Industrial Films', *The Times*, 25 April, 1972, p. 17. It is true that in the post-war period sponsored industrial film-making also took place outside the London-based documentary sector; often produced on 16mm for small industrial concerns, and frequently by tiny production units based outside London. These films fall outside the scope of this book other than, like Free Cinema or documentary television, as a point of comparison. Well worthy of attention, their lineage is more from industrial photography than from documentary film-making.
5. A sample of reactions is worth quoting at length:

   In the film union's journal:

   Ralph Bond: 'Lindsay Anderson's film ... is an impressive if much over-long exercise in a style of documentary film-making which was once fashionable but has recently been out of favour. Its impact owes much to the brilliant, uninhibited camera movements of Walter Lassally and it is a pity that the sound track does not have the same mastery ... The only positive affirmation in *Every Day Except Christmas* is that the workers in the Market are splendid people, warm, expert at their craft, the Salt of the Earth ... Grierson and his group proved the same thing in other fields twenty years ago, often with much keener penetration ... I hope Lindsay Anderson will go on trying.' Ralph Bond, 'Not So Free Cinema', *Film & TV Technician*, June/July 1957, p. 92.

   Arthur Elton: 'For all its solid elegance, *Every Day Except Christmas* displays a sense neither of social nor of economic reality. Lindsay Anderson parades his engaging and ebullient cast like a missionary showing off converted cannibals to a visiting bishop.' Arthur Elton, 'Twenty-Five Years of Documentary', *Film & TV Technician*, May 1958, pp. 262–3;

Lewis McLeod and Elizabeth Russell (juniors at British Transport Films): 'Free Cinema has resulted in a few individuals each making individual films and insisting on full blown-up credits, but all these individuals seem to express a surprising lack of individual comment in their films. One may well ask where they would have been without the excellent photography of one of their number ... To their very great credit they have desired to carry on the tradition of British Social Documentary, despite their frequent abuse of old documentary trail-blazers whom they now accuse of helping to prop up the Establishment. Let us hope the sins of the father, etc.! ... It is a thousand pities that Free Cinema is announcing its decease without ever really meeting the challenge ...' Lewis McLeod and Elizabeth Russell, 'The End of Free Cinema', *Film & TV Technician*, April 1959, p. 61.

Ken Gay, the documentary correspondent of *Films & Filming*, observed that 'to make unusual subjects without financial backing in scarce leisure time, by definition limits the field to those with rich fathers or a taste for bohemian living' (Ken Gay, 'How Free Can We Be?', *Films & Filming*, September 1957, p. 33); a year later, giving a middling review to a British Transport production (*The Land of Robert Burns*) he observed: 'it is professional film-making like this, given a mastery of the sponsorship, that will out-do the over-feted Free Cinema time and time again'. Ken Gay, 'Regaining the Poetry of the Cinema', *Films & Filming*, December 1958, p. 33.

Peter Hopkinson wrote in the same publication that: 'There is really nothing in these so self-conscious efforts that was not done years and years ago ... Ambling round with a hand held camera snatching unobserved shots of unaware people, and then creating a pattern and spurious unity in their editing is the most facile and meretricious form of film-making possible. Nevertheless these films of Free Cinema do concentrate to a degree on an element that certainly is disappearing from documentary films – the human being ... (and) do attempt to show the current lives of individual people in this country of ours at this time, even if on the screen they tend to mirror more the attitudes and psychology of the film-makers themselves than what is really going on in the minds and hearts of the subjects photographed.' Peter Hopkinson, 'Facts Out of Focus', *Films and Filming*, January 1958, p. 34.

Sarah Erulkar and Peter de Normanville, in a BECTU History Project interview, recall the slamming of Shell films by Anderson and Reisz, and recall the Free Cinema films having had great merit but, Erulkar observed, 'they were also doing all the commercials ... which we all envied and wanted to do', de Normanville adding: 'That group was kicking at everything. They were trying to make a name for themselves by knocking everything else down.'

6. Alan Lovell, and Jim Hillier, *Studies in Documentary* (London: Secker & Warburg, 1972).
7. *Song of the Clouds* was something of a straw man, as not everyone who admired documentaries of its type considered it an outstanding example. Casting his net wider, Reisz wrote: 'there are half a dozen pubs around Soho Square where, any evening of the week, you can meet the writers, directors and technicians who make their living out of film "shorts". Here they find some comfort in bewailing the timidity of producers, the bureaucracy of Government departments, the wilfulness of commercial sponsors.
   There are excellent craftsmen among them who work on scientific and training films – they are relatively contented; there are well-paid hacks who never really cared, or if they once did, no longer do; and there are – the most talented among them – those who make colour films with immaculately photographed landscapes, expensive-sounding commentaries and symphonic musical backgrounds. These are the prestige merchants, gifted people who have so long been in the position of the poet making a living in the advertising agency that they have come to discuss their advertiser's copy as poetry.' Karel Reisz, 'A Use for Documentary', *Universities & Left Review* no. 3, Winter 1958, pp. 23–4.
8. That they weren't impermeable is demonstrated by the several occasions in Part II of this book, in which second-generation figures find themselves making films for the small screen. There are several other examples. To give just two: the talented Associated-Redifussion documentary-maker Peter Morley had

started at Technical & Scientific Films; Stephen Peet, who later made his name with the BBC's pioneering oral history series *Yesterday's Witness*, had a background in sponsored film.

9. Essential websites for study of post-war documentary include the BFI's *screenonline* and *InView* sites, accessible to educational institutions (which include large and growing representative selections from across the documentary field); British Pathé's website (which includes Pathé Documentary Unit productions as well as newsreels); and the BP Video Library's site (which includes most of BP's superb catalogue of post-war films); as well as the currently planned (subject to funding) *Portrait of Britain* website which will make available many highlights from the collections of Britain's public-sector moving-image archives relating to British locations. On DVD, the BFI has published a four-disc anthology tying in with the publication of this book, as well as ongoing series of titles representing the work of the three major post-war public sector sponsors: British Transport Films, the National Coal Board and the COI.

The starkest illustration of the relative weight and depth of insight accorded the British documentaries of the 1930s and '40s in comparison to those of the 1950s and '60s comes from the pioneering American histories of documentary which remained standard works long after publication: Erik Barnouw's *Documentary: A History of the Non-fiction Film* (New York: Oxford University Press, 1974); Richard Barsam's *Non Fiction Film: A Critical History* (Indiana: Indiana University Press, 1992) and Jack C. Ellis's *The Documentary Idea* (New Jersey: Prentice Hall, 1989) (later much revised and expanded, with Betsy MacLaine, as *A New History of Documentary Film* [New York: Continuum, 2005]). These authors were writing in an age in which the international dissemination of documentary knowledge heavily depended on the distribution of 35mm and 16mm film prints. The imbalance in American coverage reflects, entirely reasonably, indeed usefully, the history of which British films were distributed to arthouse audiences in the USA (for instance, at the Museum of Modern Art). Post-war documentaries received some US distribution but not as a coherent body of work and not, for the most part, to this viewership. Of the three authors just mentioned, Barsam tries creditably hard to take the story of the British Movement past 1945, which gets his account into the biggest tangle via an extremely arbitrary list of key films sketchily related to their production background. Other books tend to jump straight from Movement 'fall' to Free Cinema 'rise'. The exponential growth in digital access to archival films would seem likely to widen many canons – but as post-war documentary illustrates, canons are products of cultural psychology as well as access.

2 Documentary Culture: Groupings, Gatherings and Writings

The notion of a 'movement' implies some degree of internal cohesion assisted by organisational structures. The need for a body serving the Documentary Movement had been identified pre-war, with Paul Rotha establishing the Associated Realist Film Producers in 1935 as a cooperative body for documentary film-makers. In 1937 it ceded many of its functions as consultant and advisory body to the newly formed Film Centre and had effectively dissolved by 1940 as its members were dispersed into the many facets of war work.

Towards the end of the war, however, there was enthusiasm for a new body 'to express the documentary outlook' and in 1945 Rotha, R. K. Neilson-Baxter and Donald Alexander forged the Federation of Documentary Film Units (FDFU), operating from the address of Basic Films.[1] The FDFU represented eight of the leading independent documentary production units: Neilson-Baxter's Basic, Alexander's DATA, Rotha's Films of Fact, animators Halas & Batchelor, Merlin Film Co., the Realist Film Unit, Seven League Productions and World Wide Pictures. This list of companies effectively defined the contours of the self-selecting Movement (outside the Crown and Shell Film units). Rotha wrote that the government 'should plan a number of feature-length documentary films through the appropriate members of the Federation of Documentary Film Units and the Crown Film Unit', and furthermore that it should introduce a training scheme in documentary production in conjunction with the Association of Cine-Technicians (ACT) (the film technicians' union) and FDFU.[2]

Such aspirations were out of step with both the reality of Britain's economic position after the war and actual levels of enthusiasm for film production within government. In 1947 Rotha's own company, Films of Fact, went into liquidation. The same year, however, he (together with Edgar Anstey, Ralph Bond and Basil Wright) attended an international conference of individual documentary film-makers in Brussels which concluded with the decision to establish the World Union of Documentary (WUD).

A British chapter of the World Union of Documentary, named British Documentary was launched in January 1948. Its first meeting was attended by 150 people, introduced by Stephen Tallents and addressed by John Grierson. However, the solidarity of British Documentary was also short lived. Alexander and Wright returned from the 1948 WUD conference in Czechoslovakia espousing the wonders of film sponsorship in socialist countries. They were publicly shot down by Grierson, who in his new role as Controller of Films at the Central Office of Information (COI) had a contrary position to promote. At the autumn 1948 meeting of British Documentary, Grierson tried to prevent ratification of the WUD constitution. The situation worsened the following year as Cold War tensions made association with communist nations more difficult. The decision to hold the 1949 WUD meeting at the 'Paris Peace Conference', an event widely seen as the product of Soviet propaganda, made any engagement by British officialdom impossible. In 1950 the World Union of Documentary collapsed and British Documentary (the organisation) was no more. As early as 1947 Ronald Tritton, as Head of Films Division at the COI, had been dismissing the documentary old guard and their 'pompous conclaves'.[3] With the end of 'British Documentary' they lost their last such conclave. The shape of documentary film-making in the post-war world would be necessarily different (not least, the internationalism of post-war documentary turned out to be a matter more of the globalisation of industrial ventures than the spreading of international citizenship by the United Nations). However, the list of members of British Documentary is a fascinating personification of what a post-war Movement might have looked like – alongside the 1930s' great and the good were younger people, mostly junior employees of FDFU units, Crown or Shell. Many survived the post-war years by alternating employment at such units with those that had, a few high-profile 'political' invitees aside, pointedly been excluded from these conclaves, and by leaving such crusades behind: to some a relief, for others a cause for regret.

(Reproduced courtesy of the National Library of Scotland)

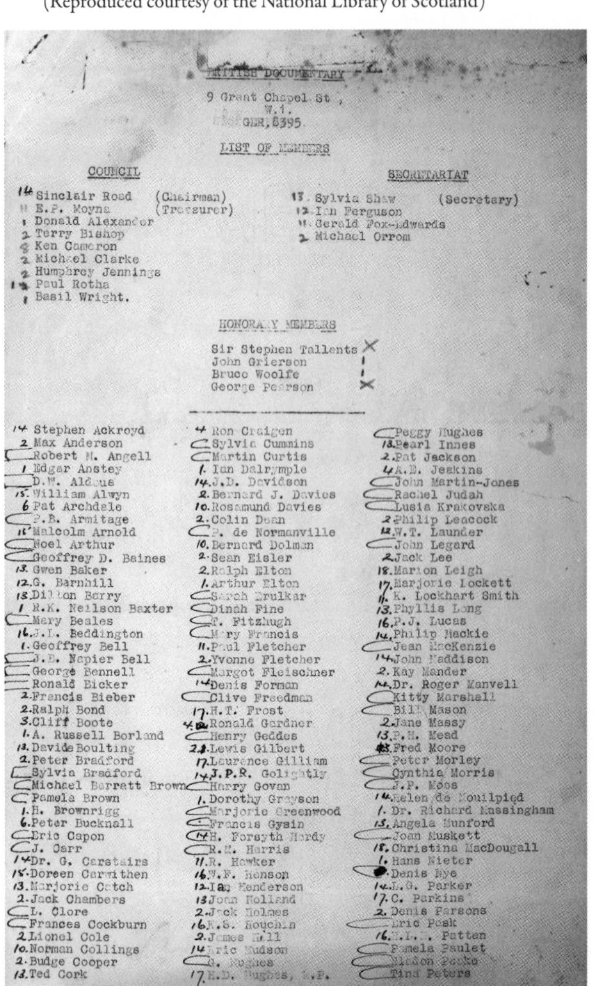

BRITISH DOCUMENTARY

9 Great Chapel St,
W.1.
GER. 8395.

LIST OF MEMBERS

COUNCIL

Sinclair Road (Chairman)
E.P. Moyne (Treasurer)
Donald Alexander
Terry Bishop
Ken Cameron
Michael Clarke
Humphrey Jennings
Paul Rotha
Basil Wright.

SECRETARIAT

Sylvia Shaw (Secretary)
Ian Ferguson
Gerald Fox-Edwards
Michael Orrom

HONORARY MEMBERS

Sir Stephen Tallents
John Grierson
Bruce Woolfe
George Pearson

Stephen Ackroyd
Max Anderson
Robert M. Angell
Edgar Anstey
D.W. Aldous
William Alwyn
Pat Archdale
P.B. Armitage
Malcolm Arnold
Noel Arthur
Geoffrey D. Baines
Gwen Baker
G. Barnhill
Dillon Barry
R.K. Neilson Baxter
Mary Beales
J.L. Beddington
Geoffrey Bell
J.E. Napier Bell
George Bennell
Ronald Bicker
Francis Bieber
Ralph Bond
Cliff Boote
A. Russell Borland
David Boulting
Peter Bradford
Sylvia Bradford
Michael Barratt Brown
Pamela Brown
H. Brownrigg
Peter Bucknall
Eric Capon
J. Carr
Dr. G. Carstairs
Doreen Carwithen
Marjorie Catch
Jack Chambers
L. Clore
Frances Cockburn
Lionel Cole
Norman Collings
Budge Cooper
Ted Cork

Ron Craigen
Sylvia Cummins
Martin Curtis
Ian Dalrymple
J.D. Davidson
Bernard J. Davies
Rosamund Davies
Colin Dean
P. de Normanville
Bernard Dolman
Sean Eisler
Ralph Elton
Arthur Elton
Sarah Erulkar
Dinah Fine
T. Fitzhugh
Mary Francis
Paul Fletcher
Yvonne Fletcher
Margot Fleischner
Denis Forman
Clive Freedman
H.T. Frost
Ronald Gardner
Henry Geddes
Lewis Gilbert
Laurence Gilliam
J.P.R. Golightly
Harry Govan
Dorothy Grayson
Marjorie Greenwood
Francis Gysin
H. Forsyth Hardy
R.M. Harris
R. Hawker
W.F. Henson
Ian Henderson
Joan Holland
Jack Holmes
K.S. Houchin
James Hill
Eric Hudson
G. Hughes
H.D. Hughes, M.P.

Peggy Hughes
Pearl Innes
Pat Jackson
A.E. Jeakins
John Martin-Jones
Rachel Judah
Lusia Krakovska
Philip Leacock
W.T. Launder
John Legard
Jack Lee
Marion Leigh
Marjorie Lockett
K. Lockhart Smith
Phyllis Long
P.J. Lucas
Philip Mackie
Jean MacKenzie
John Maddison
Kay Mander
Dr. Roger Manvell
Kitty Marshall
Bill Mason
Jane Massy
P.H. Mead
Fred Moore
Peter Morley
Cynthia Morris
J.P. Moss
Helen de Mouilpied
Dr. Richard Massingham
Angela Munford
Joan Muskett
Christina MacDougall
Hans Nieter
Denis Nye
L.G. Parker
C. Parkins
Denis Parsons
Eric Pask
[illegible] Patten
Pamela Paulet
Bladon Peake
Tina Peters

A harder-headed alternative grouping was the Association of Short Film Producers (ASFP). This had been formed by Gaumont-British Instructional supremo H. Bruce Woolfe in 1938. In 1947 the ASFP changed its name but kept its acronym, becoming the Association of Specialised Film Producers. The ASFP, slammed by the doctrinaire documentarists as a 'bosses' union', represented the producers of cinema shorts, documentaries, sponsored industrial films and government films: thus, ASFP interests extended from the documentary into the short entertainment film and advertising. In 1964 the ASFP as was became the Federation of Specialised Film Associations – consisting of three quasi-autonomous groups: the British Animation Group (BAG), the Advertising Film Producers Association (AFPA) and, confusingly, a new ASFP – still serving documentaries, sponsored industrial and government films. In 1947, Woolfe was succeeded as chairman by Frank Hoare, himself succeeded much later by K. Lockhart-Smith. Both were senior executives of the Film Producers Guild, the largest of the post-war documentary producers. Although smaller companies often felt their interests were being crowded out in the ASFP, by the early 1950s it was the only game in town: producers like Basic, World Wide and even the socialistically inclined DATA were now among its members.

Across the table from the ASFP sat the Association of Cine-Technicians (ACT, later ACTT, standing for Association of Cinema and Television Technicians, and now BECTU). The ACT was formed in 1933 as the independent trade union for those working in film. Its offices at 2 Soho Square were right at the centre of London's documentary production. Several documentary specialists were, at various points, involved in the ACT's administration. Notably, senior union leader and committed socialist Ralph Bond had had one foot in the Documentary Movement. In the post-war period, the younger film-maker Max Anderson (a noted director of documentaries at Crown, Basic and elsewhere) was, until his untimely death in 1958, another well-known firebrand. The union included a Shorts and Documentary Branch, which held monthly screenings of new work for its members. Among the active participants in the branch, crossing generations, were Wright, Neilson-Baxter and Geoffrey Bell, Peter de Normanville, Tony Thompson and Derrick Knight. The union journal *Ciné-Technician* (later called *Film & TV Technician*), carried a column on the branch and frequently ran articles reflecting on the contemporary state of the documentary form.[4]

(Reproduced courtesy of the National Library of Scotland)

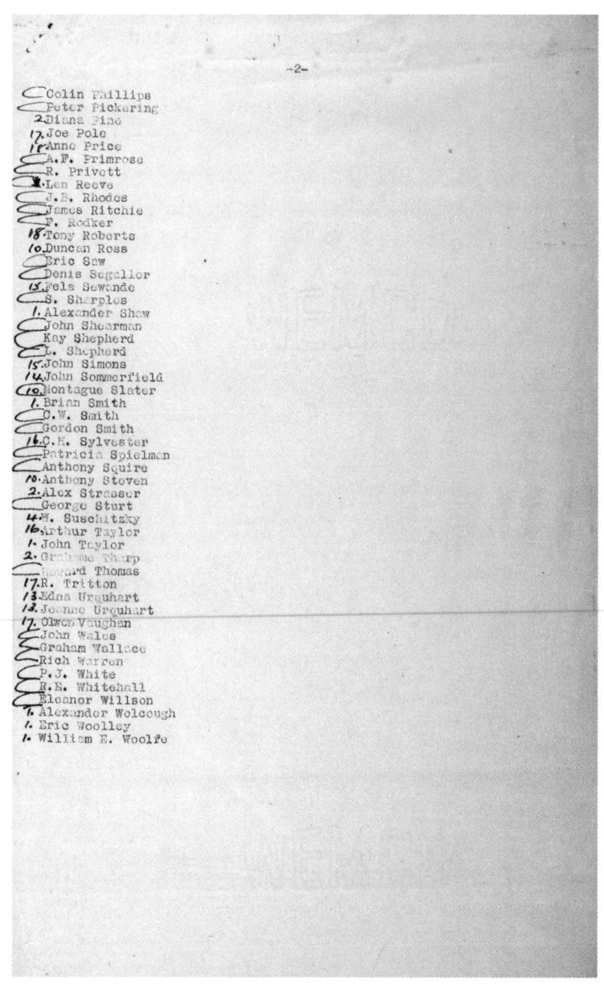

-2-

Colin Phillips
Peter Pickering
2. Diana Pine
17. Joe Pole
18. Anne Price
A.F. Primrose
R. Privett
Len Reeve
J.B. Rhodes
James Ritchie
F. Rodker
18. Tony Roberts
10. Duncan Ross
Eric Saw
Denis Segaller
15. Fela Sewande
S. Sharples
1. Alexander Shaw
John Shearman
Kay Shepherd
L. Shepherd
15. John Simons
14. John Sommerfield
10. Montague Slater
1. Brian Smith
C.W. Smith
Gordon Smith
16. C.H. Sylvester
Patricia Spielman
Anthony Squire
10. Anthony Steven
2. Alex Strasser
George Sturt
4. W. Suschitzky
16. Arthur Taylor
1. John Taylor
2. Grahame Tharp
Howard Thomas
17. R. Tritton
13. Edna Urquhart
13. Jeanne Urquhart
17. Olwen Vaughan
John Wales
Graham Wallace
Rich Warren
P.J. White
R.E. Whitehall
Eleanor Willson
1. Alexander Wolcough
1. Eric Woolley
1. William E. Woolfe

The ACT had two major practical effects upon the documentary business. First, it was responsible every five years for negotiating its members' terms with the ASFP (sometimes said to be among the best in the business). Much more controversially, it operated a closed shop, which meant that the union effectively controlled employment. Max Anderson, for instance, apparently sought to block his unrelated namesake Linsday Anderson's entry into the ACT, but it was not only those associated with deviant developments such as Free Cinema who had ambivalent relationships with their union.[5]

Beyond the world of trade bodies, there was still scope for interest groups, encompassing debate and the sharing of news without the ideological edge of the failing late 1940s bodies. In 1947, building on similar pre-war organisations, Edgar Anstey and Arthur Elton were instrumental in setting up the Scientific Films Association (SFA), in turn affiliated to the International Scientific Film Association (ISFA). The SFA's goal was to encourage the making and use of scientific and industrial film, and to bring together interested organisations and individuals. With an office and a small permanent staff, the SFA published specialised catalogues, and the journal *Scientific Film Review*, while ISFA simultaneously published (from London) *Science and Film*; in 1960 the periodicals were merged as *Scientific – Film – Scientifique*. Anstey and Elton, and many of the younger film-makers working in this field, were frequent contributors. In 1953, the previously unincorporated body was registered under the Companies Act. By 1960, the SFA had 168 individual, forty corporate and twenty-one non-corporate bodies as members.

The SFA did not limit itself to a narrow definition of 'scientific'. Many of the conferences it put on over the course of the late 1940s and early 1950s were concerned with the relationship of documentary film-making to industry. The SFA came up with the idea of a national competitive festival of films from this field. This came to fruition in 1957, although by then the ASFP was in the driving seat of organising it. Between 8 and 12 October 1957, Britain's first Festival of Films in the Service of Industry was held in Harrogate, with 600 attendees, under the presidency of Lord Godber, Chairman of the Shell Group. In many ways this event symbolised the settled state of the documentary sector, with the factionalism of the 1940s behind it. Of the 320 films entered, 131 were selected for screening. Among the entrants, the largest number, 30 per cent of the total, were in the Public Relations and Prestige category – an interesting indication of its pre-eminence as well as its prevalence.[6]

An issue of the Film Producers Guild journal focuses on the Festival of Film in the Service of Industry

The event (followed by another, also in Harrogate, in 1959), led to the establishment of the British Industrial Films Association (BIFA). This organisation was chaired by Tritton, by now well established as head of public relations at British Petroleum. BIFA's president was Sir Peter Runge, head of the Federation of British Industries (FBI), which was very much the film organisation's godfather. BIFA had some 120 organisational members (the commercial film units were excluded from membership on the grounds that they already had the

ASFP). It was under BIFA's auspices that, from 1964, an annual national festival of sponsored films commenced, a suggestion that came from the Council of European Industrial Foundations (CEIF), the chief organising body for the International Industrial Film Festivals that were also now taking place. As the CEIF's British chapter, the FBI (now merged with other employers' organisations as the Confederation of British Industries [CBI]) delegated to BIFA its representation on the CEIF committee responsible for the international festivals – where Britain (followed by West Germany) tended to win more awards than any other country. BIFA, too, organised innumerable conferences, including several on the use of film for training, addressed by such luminaries as Richard Beeching, Lord Robens and Richard Costain. BIFA strongly promoted the use of film as an aid to exports. It also started a series of 'Monthly Newcomers' screenings for members of new documentary releases, mirroring those being run concurrently by the ACT's shorts branch.

In 1967, encouraged by the inducement of further government funding, the SFA and BIFA were merged to create the British Industrial and Scientific Films Association (BISFA), with Elton as its first chairman and Runge as president. Tritton and Anstey both later occupied the chair; on his 1974 retirement from British Transport Films, Anstey later became president, succeeding from World Wide Pictures stalwart Clifford Parris.

Though billed as a sensible tidying-up operation, the new group was not without conceptual flaws: BIFA having been mainly made up of sponsors, the SFA primarily of producers, there was always a risk of conflict of interest. Even the film labs were eligible to join and, keen to boost business, most did. BISFA represented the coming together of all facets of what was still referred to as the documentary film industry. When government funding dried up, BISFA continued, with some financial problems, though the SFA was reconstituted in 1973 as a separate body (with a narrower 'scientific' focus than before). Among many other activities (publications, including a monthly journal; continuing 'Monthly Newcomers'), BISFA inherited from BIFA the running of the increasingly huge annual festival of sponsored films, normally taking place in Brighton, an essential fixture on the calendar of many in the industry at which a great deal of viewing, debating and heavy drinking was done. At the same time, documentaries, whether produced under sponsorship or in other ways, also had plenty of other such outlets, at the documentary, short film and general film festivals that took place internationally (Venice being the most prestigious, and others, including those at Leipzig and Oserhausen). At home, the British Film Academy (subsequently the Society for Film and Television Arts and now BAFTA) awarded annual prizes that testify to the importance of documentaries and shorts to the UK film industry (at various times, these awards included Best Documentary, Best Short Film and Best Specialised Film, and the Robert Flaherty Award).

Who was writing about documentary? In the 1930s and '40s, the Movement had its own semi-official house journals: *World Film News*, *Documentary News Letter* and then *Documentary Film News*. At the same time, the BFI-published journals *Sight & Sound* (containing general commentary on film) and *Monthly Film Bulletin* (containing reviews of new releases) also followed British documentary closely. Post-war documentary, as we have seen, was to have a lower profile among cinema intellectuals, not least because the post-war generation were much less fervent polemicists (Free Cinema again to the contrary: Lindsay Anderson had more in common with Grierson and Rotha than he might have liked to admit, including his enthusiasm for use of the written word – skilfully composed and propitiously placed – as a form of cultural self-promotion). After the closure of *Documentary Film News* in 1949, there were no direct equivalents. *Monthly Film Bulletin*

continued to review short films, though the number of them it covered slowly fell through the 1950s, until by the late 1960s, only a small minority of documentaries were still being included. As for *Sight & Sound*, it published a substantial two-part enquiry by David Robinson, 'Looking for Documentary', in 1957: a fair-minded account, praising the Free Cinema films (Robinson was well acquainted with their makers), showing respect for Shell and for the best of the sponsored film world, and noticing, too, the arrival of television talents like Denis Mitchell. But this was an exception. Interestingly enough, the big sponsored film libraries heavily *advertised* in *Sight & Sound* but their films received little coverage from its journalists, its post-war editors having largely lost interest in any aspect of British documentary other than Free Cinema.

However, beyond these narrow horizons, the total coverage of documentary was growing, not shrinking. An important post-war publication was the widely read independent monthly *Films and Filming*, pitched at a less exclusive film-buff clientele than *Sight & Sound*. From its inception *Films and Filming* included a regular documentary column written by Ken Gay. In these columns, the most specialised of sponsored films rubbed shoulders with 'art' documentaries from Britain and abroad.[7]

Just as significant were the journals catering to the market in non-theatrical film exhibition. The documentary short was highly visible in *Film*, the journal of the British Federation of Film Societies, for it was one of the staples of their programming. Extending into more specialised areas, *Film User* (initially *16mm Film User* and later *Audio Visual*) was directed towards organisers of non-theatrical screenings, including those in industry and education as well as entertainment. *Film User* included a reviews section covering almost all significant non-theatrical releases (including 16mm releases of feature films), preceded by news and articles covering everything from sponsors' activities to detailed projection advice. Similar, shorter-lived publications included *Film Sponsor* and *Industrial Screen* (eventually incorporated into *Film User*). Alongside these sat the yet more specialist educational audiovisual (AV) press: journals like *Visual Education* and *Look and Listen*. *The Times Educational Supplement*, no less, often reviewed films with an educational dimension.

The most outstanding neglected fact about documentary's post-war media presence is that, over many years, it was reported on in detail in several national newspapers – not in their arts sections but rather on their business pages. All of the national broadsheets retained a modicum of interest in documentary, peaking in the 1960s and early 1970s when the *Financial Times*, *The Times* and the *Guardian* each kept a designated industrial films correspondent on their books (the *Glasgow Herald* also published on the topic regularly). Correspondents included Robinson P. Rigg, then John Chittock at the *FT*, Ken Roberts, Gordon Davis and latterly Eynon Smart at *The Times*, and John Roberts and Kenneth Myer at the *Guardian*. The commissioners and makers of sponsored documentary were doubtless their most avid readers, but such national media attention to post-war documentary shouldn't be dismissed.[8]

By 1966, media interest in the sponsored documentary was judged extensive enough to warrant the formation of an Industrial Film Correspondents Group (later the Film and Video Press Group). Alongside these film journal and newspaper correspondents were representatives from publications like *Industry Week*, *British Industry* and *Industrial Training International*. The PR and advertising press also carried coverage of the longer sponsored film: *IPR Journal*, *Advertisers Weekly*, *Advertising Management*, *Industrial Advertising & Marketing* and *Worlds Press News* (at these last two, Jane Senior and Gloria Tessler were the long-serving 'film' correspondents). Alec Hughes, the AV officer of the British Association for the Advancement of Science, contributed film writing to such publications as *Discovery*, *New Scientist* and *Science Journal*, as well as *Industrial & Commercial Training* and *The Supervisor*. At one point, even Peter Cowie, a much-respected post-war critic of cinema (well-known for his writings about the likes of Bergman and Welles) was a member. The group became responsible for some special BISFA awards. Its Critics' Award was for 'the director of the film which most imaginatively communicates its message' (winners included Richard Need, Sarah Erulkar and Eric Marquis). Later, the Clifford Wheeler Memorial Award went to whichever of the previous year's BISFA award-winners was deemed to have been most effectively distributed to its intended audience.

We shouldn't read too much into such a small, low-voltage organisation. Post-war Britain was full of voluntary organisations, and this one, like most, was as much social club as professional body. But it's reasonable to assume that its members' columns were sharpened by pooling their knowledge and thinking. Since their articles were read by films officers, this could in turn have inflected output. Most of the pieces by most of these writers have yet to be researched. There must be hundreds, perhaps thousands, more in the many publications of the countless organisations for whom documentaries were made.

The groupings, gatherings and writings circulating around post-war documentary demonstrate that, for both good and ill, a culture of pragmatic professionalism had largely replaced one of sectarian zeal. Never let it be said, however, that the passion that had fuelled documentary culture was ever entirely extinguished.

NOTES

1. See Paul Rotha, *Rotha On The Film: A Selection Of Writings About The Cinema* (London: Faber, 1958), p. 231, and Federation of Documentary Film Units, 'Documentary Films and Present Needs', *FDFU Bulletin* no. 1, January 1946.
2. Paul Rotha, 'The Government and the Film Industry' (1945), in Rotha, *Rotha On The Film*, pp. 270–1.
3. Letter from Ronald Tritton to B. C. Sendall, Head of COI Home Division, 1 July 1947, TNA INF 12/564.
4. See for example: Basil Wright, 'Documentary Today', *Film & TV Technician*, May 1959, pp. 78–9; Richard Cawston, 'Documentary A Review', *Film & TV Technician*, August 1963, pp. 226–7; Terry Trench, 'Documentary in the Doldrums', *Film & TV Technician*, October 1963, pp. 275–6.
5. The case of the Andersons is mentioned by Leon Clore in his BECTU History Project interview. Derek Williams remembers the closed shop as: 'A policy which Basil Wright described to me as "seemingly intended to break young men's hearts" ... Young people bent on film careers, like Eric Marquis and me, came from random directions, with the zeal of religious converts. Once through the pearly gates we found the typical film technician to be a cynical Londoner ... who had often chanced to be born near a studio or laboratory ... the best of them made creditable film-makers, but we called the other half "the deadbeats", whose existence blocked the creative young for a generation. The harm can only be guessed ... it made our union membership a source of sarcasm and extreme reluctance.' (Comments supplied to the authors.)

   Williams's contemporary Derrick Knight, who had his own difficulties getting in, later became a shop steward as well as committee member and offers a more positive assessment: 'I understood that the rule might ... stand in the way of talented young hopefuls who did not know how to manoeuvre themselves into the line at the right moment but protecting the employment conditions of union members seemed to me at the time to be the right decision. I was one of the lucky ones ... In my case there was no difficulty in getting my union membership. I came to appreciate the strength of the ACT in defending its members and getting the best possible conditions and rates for them in an industry which was notorious for its hiring and firing and for the low rates it sought to pay. [At the ACT Shorts and Documentary Committee] we debated the application forms of would be new members. We held the tap of recruitment into the shorts section in our hands. Our decisions determined the fate of all potential newcomers. It felt a bit weird but in the circumstances seemed very practical. When I became a producer and employer in later years, I knew how the system worked and was able to help many such young hopefuls jump over the hurdles.' (From Knight's draft memoirs, extract supplied to the authors.)
6. The full list of categories and winners is an interesting one: Public Relations and Prestige, won by *Oil Harbour – Aden* (made by World Wide Pictures for Wimpey); Sales Promotion: *Introducing Telex* (RHR Productions for Creed & Co.); Training Inside Industry: *Successful Instruction* (RHR for the Army Kinema Corporation); Technical and Technological: *High Speed Flight – Approaching the Speed of Sound* (Shell Film Unit); Schools: *Mirror in the Sky* (Realist Film Unit for Mullard and the Educational Foundation for Visual Aids); Sales and Dealer Training: *Golden Minutes* (United Motion Pictures for Wolf Electric Tools); Health and Safety: *Don't Be a Dummy* (Verity Films for the Central Electricity Authority); Careers: *Golden Future* (World Wide for the Transvaal and Orange Free State Chamber of Mines); Productivity: *Introducing Work Study* (World Wide for the British Productivity Council); Human Relations in Industry: *Men on the Mend* (British Transport Films; reflecting its scope and

eminence, BTF was the only producer or sponsor to have a film nominated in every category, as again in the 1959 festival).

The 1957 festival was opened by the junior government minister Lord Mancroft who stated: 'I believe that it is of the utmost importance that all members of the industrial orchestra should know what parts the other players are attempting to play, why and how the whole opera of industry goes. I believe that films have an enormous future in that respect.'

7. Gay was, for instance, an early UK enthusiast for Frederick Wiseman, but as his day job was administering the National Coal Board's film activities (at the right hand first of Donald Alexander and then of Francis Gysin), his columns took a sympathetic interest also in the use of films by industrial and other sponsors, warmly reviewing the best examples. While *Films and Filming* was respectful of British documentary's present course, on balance its regret for its decline as a cultural force was evident.
8. The most influential was Chittock, a fixture of post-war film culture, whose love of cinema (reflected in his chairmanship of the British Federation of Film Societies) was, unusually, combined with a fascination with economics (reflected in Chittock's publishing and editing of the facts-and-figures-heavy *Screen Digest*, covering the film and TV industry in general). In the industrial film, both interests combined well, as Chittock's work on the journals *Film and Video Communication* and *Training Digest* further demonstrates.

3 Films Nobody Sees?: Distribution and Exhibition

> What began in Grierson's day as an invited local group moving into a neighbourhood hall to be educated, informed and, hopefully, entertained by a mobile 16mm projector, has grown and diversified into innumerable areas of special interest – as he predicted it would.
>
> Edgar Anstey[1]

> FILMS on the SHELF = MONEY WASTED; a film only fulfils its purpose if it reaches the audiences for which it is made.
>
> Advertisement for Sound-Services Ltd[2]

Distribution has always been fundamental to the success or failure of British films no matter what their genre, and in this the documentary and the sponsored film were no different. There were three main routes to getting a film seen: theatrical exhibition, non-theatrical exhibition and television broadcast. Although all three were used, it was the second method that proved the principal route for getting most of the documentaries discussed in this book seen.

THEATRICAL EXHIBITION

At the beginning of the post-war era, sponsors and producers were understandably interested in cinema distribution. As well as offering a mass audience, the cinema programme of the period also featured space for short films alongside the main feature, trailers and ads. That such a space existed, and that it was desirable to sponsors, did not easily equate to sponsors' films obtaining that space, however. World War II had brought documentary to cinema screens more often than it had been there before. In the early post-war period, fuller cinema bills, with their opportunity for shorts, remained. Opportunity diminished as the 1950s wore on, while mechanisms designed to protect British product paradoxically hindered the advancement of most sponsored and independent documentary.

One problem, increasingly intractable by the early 1960s, was that the two companies dominating the exhibition circuits, the Rank Organisation and the Associated British Picture Corporation, also maintained their own interests in production and distribution. The weekly cinemagazines produced by their respective associates *Look at Life* (1959–69) and the *Pathé Pictorial* (1918–69) happily filled the short slot in the majority of their cinema programmes. The United Artists studio had a deal with the (generally reviled) company Harold Baim Films for accompanying shorts. Between these tied deals there remained opportunities for exhibition, but diminished ones that did not match the hopes of sponsors or producers.

The 'cinemagazines' produced by many industrial sponsors rarely featured in actual cinemas, although there were major exceptions: most prominently the National Coal Board's *Mining Review*, for which wide distribution claims were made.[3] Others such as *Ingot Pictorial* (the cinemagazine of steel company Richard Thomas & Baldwins) played in cinemas local to the works but not elsewhere in the country. Prestige documentaries on subjects of general interest had the best chance of reaching cinema screens. British Petroleum and British Transport Films (BTF) had the most notable success in finding their travelogues, natural history and general interest documentaries in supporting programmes. Such exceptions tended to prove the rule, however. For a sponsored documentary, cinema release was usually seen as a luxury.

TELEVISION

The expansion of television in the post-war era, especially after commercial TV began in 1955, appeared to offer new screening opportunities. In fact the perceived proximity of these films to advertising made TV broadcasting difficult. Ironically, it was only in Britain, whose mastery of the sponsored documentary form was so internationally respected, that it found such difficulty in being placed on the small screen.

Again, however, certain sponsors' products fitted more easily into the TV schedules – once more, the prestige films of BTF and of the oil companies were examples of documentaries that could interest and entertain a general audience without contravening advertising guidelines. For example,

Non-theatrical dissemination, as delineated by *Film User*

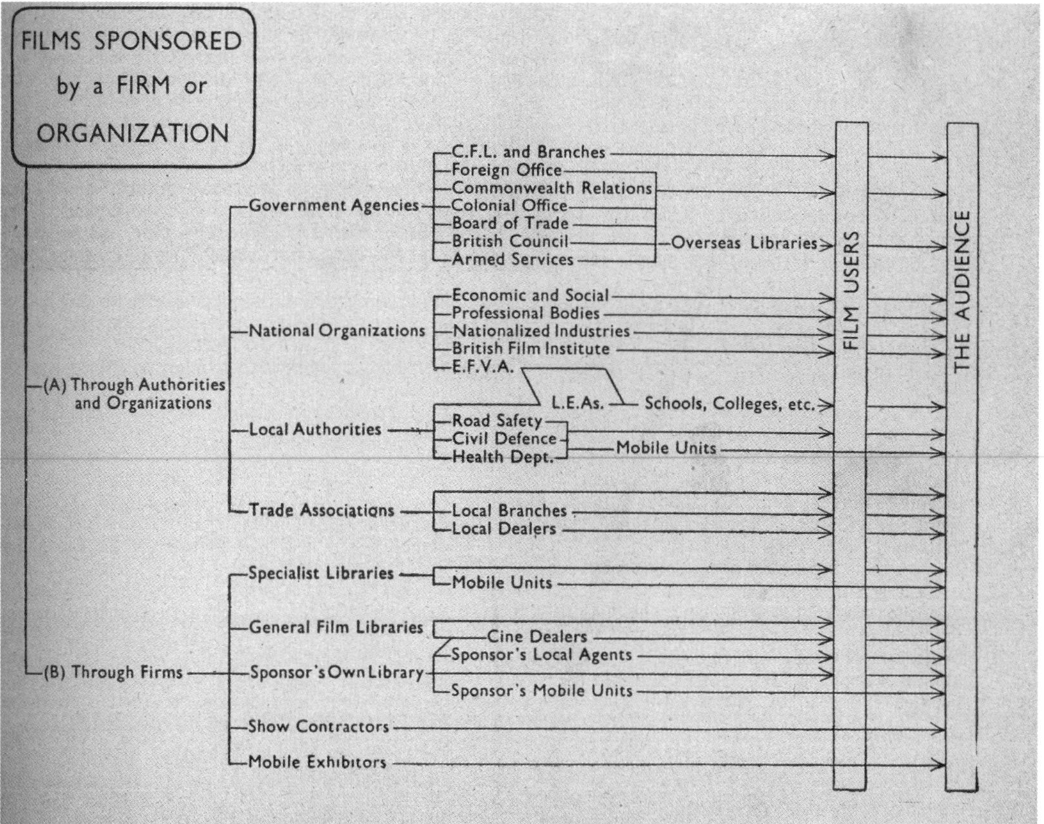

Shell's *The Rival World* (1955) was shown on BBC primetime in its year of release. The COI, with its government imprimatur, could also effect public service broadcasts as well as securing commercial advertising space: in the 1950s, in particular, a large number of documentaries that were part of major government campaigns appear to have been shown on the BBC. Between 1964 and 1966 Associated-Rediffusion broadcast some sponsored documentaries in a late-night Tuesday slot called *Camera Eye*. For obvious reasons, films on charity and social welfare also frequently evaded the strictures on television broadcasting of sponsored productions.

From the mid-1950s, the BBC began colour tests on television and needed films of high photographic quality in order to enable their engineers to assess successful picture transmission. They turned to the readily available sponsored documentaries shot on 35mm in colour stocks, available from organisations like BTF, BP and Shell, ICI, Unilever and others. It's a peculiar but important fact that these films were among the *most repeatedly broadcast* of any content on post-war British television. Many titles, of a pool of around 150, were shown dozens or even hundreds of times, and some such as Shell's *Coupe des Alpes* (1958), BP's *Giuseppina* (1959) and BTF's *Overhaul* (1958) gained a genuine cult following. The films were initially shown unscheduled, but between 1967 and 1972 they began being listed, allowing retailers of colour television sets to demonstrate the new technology in their dealerships. By this point, the trade-tests were being shown six times per day, five days per week.

NON-THEATRICAL EXHIBITION

Exhibition of films outside television and the cinema circuit could take many forms, as indicated by a 1950s diagram from the pages of *Film User*. By far the widest technique, however, was the use of a film library. The deployment of film libraries for the purpose of non-theatrical exhibition began before World War II, but continued, operating on a larger scale than ever before, until the widespread availability of home video. It was sometimes, indeed, said that the non-theatrical circuit was the *exception* to the general rule that 'cinema' was in decline.[4] As late as the early 1970s, films booked from these libraries were seen by around 17 million people every year.[5] To give just a sample: the Gas Council claimed an annual non-theatrical audience of 5 million in 1955;[6] the Shell Film Unit claimed a European audience for its films of over 10 million in 1965 (based on 196,000 screenings);[7] the Shell-Mex and BP Film Library claimed to be

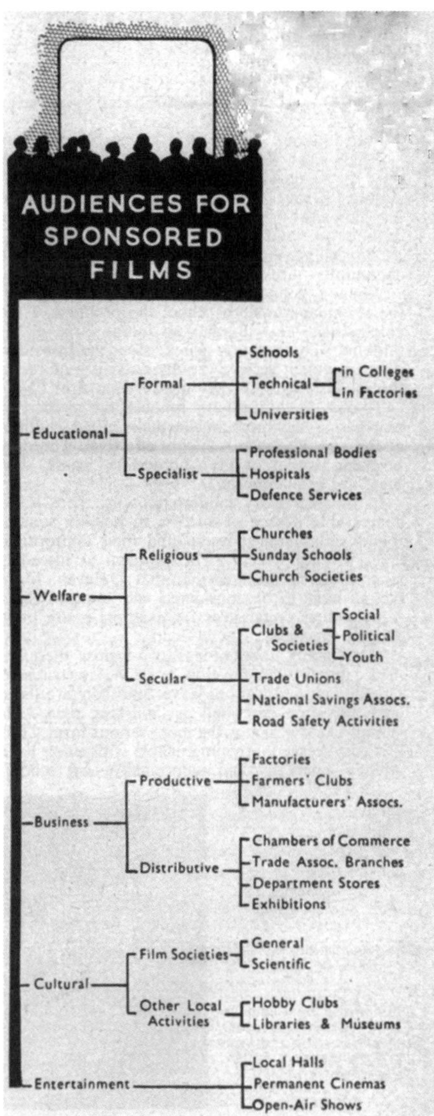

Non-theatrical audiences, as profiled by *Film User*

sending out 35,000 prints a year in 1969;[8] Sound-Services claimed to be shipping 2,000 films *a day, every day* in 1968.[9] The figures are difficult to verify, and true quantification impossible – but browsing the film journals and the distribution catalogues repeatedly confirms the overall impression of an extremely sizeable operation. The number of film libraries alone was massive. In August 1961 *The Times* began listing the details of libraries, a different one each week: six years later the 290th was listed.[10]

The hirers of films from these libraries were separable into several categories. Social and political groups and clubs included unions, sports clubs, women's organisations, religious groups and so on. Government-sponsored groups included the Armed Forces, emergency services and local authorities. Among industrial and business audiences were chambers of commerce, professional associations and individual companies. Educational viewers – in schools and colleges – were a core target for many sponsors and their libraries, and indeed the classroom audience for the sponsored documentary available on 16mm was the very last to go. Not to be forgotten were the film societies, vibrant through the 1950s, '60s and '70s, whose passion was for the medium itself: they were a continuing source of support for quality documentary shorts throughout the post-war period, as marked by the British Federation of Film Societies' initiation of an annual award for best sponsored film.[11]

The documentary film-maker whose work was disseminated through such channels was in a paradoxical position. On one hand, not only might his film be seen by many viewers, its shelf-life could be extremely long (certainly compared with the many television documentaries which, whatever their immediate impact, then promptly and permanently disappeared from view). On the other, this slow-burn effect inhibited any likelihood of really influential journalistic coverage, and his own reputation as a film-maker was unlikely to be enhanced by the impressive statistics claimed by the film libraries carrying his work. Moreover, if the audience for documentary was apparently very sizeable, it was not, perhaps, the *right* audience from the viewpoint of cinema intelligentsia. With the exception of the educational groups, non-theatrical audiences probably tended towards the middle-aged rather than the young, and to the rural and small-town middle classes more than their metropolitan counterparts. Some audience groups were overwhelmingly female and some overwhelmingly male, and programming tailored accordingly. Others were mixed. Autumn and winter, with their darker nights, constituted the 'peak' non-theatrical season.

While it's impossible here to cover the full gamut of film libraries supplying these hirers, a survey of the major players gives a sense of the field.

THE COI'S LIBRARIES (1940–2000)

The Central Film Library (CFL) was established in London in 1940 as the successor and inheritor of the Imperial Institute Film Library set up in 1927 and the GPO Film Library. During the war it was the distribution agency for films produced or acquired by the Ministry of Information. Post-war it continued this role for the Central Office of Information. Officially produced films were also distributed by affiliated bodies: the Scottish Central Film Library in Glasgow and the Central Film Library of Wales in Cardiff.[12]

The Central Film Library offered around 2,000 films for hire through its main catalogue. Over time the list of films distributed was increased by a selection of films sponsored by organisations other than government departments and requested by ministerial departments or members of their industrial advisory panel. Also included were the film libraries of the British Productivity Council, the National Savings Committee, the United States Information Service and a large selection from the National Film Board of Canada.

Hire of prints from the Central Film Library, as with its predecessors, was initially on the basis of free loans. In 1952, government austerity measures within the information services (the same ones that saw the abolition of the Crown Film

Unit) led to the implementation of charges, much to the chagrin of the CFL's user base. (Films deemed to be of great national importance, such as those associated with major health or public safety campaigns, were exempted on a case-by-case basis.) The number of films borrowed fell instantly by nearly half; however, the service continued to be used and the number of borrowers soon began to climb again. In 1966 it was generating an income from the hire and sale of films of over £100,000 a year.

From 1953 onwards, a separate *Catalogue of Films For Industry* was also issued, crossing over in content with the main catalogue but consisting mainly of titles made for private industrial and commercial organisations, rather than the government, and also featuring American- and European-produced material of industrial use. While the Central Film Library excluded films containing advertising, this restriction was eased for those titles carried in the industrial catalogue.

The distribution of films outside the United Kingdom was dealt with separately. These films were supplied by the COI and listed in the catalogue of their Overseas Film Library. They could reach audiences via several agencies, such as branches of British Information Services and the British Council. Films produced for industrial sponsors were considered an extremely important part of the overseas library and the COI acquired copies of titles for distribution under the guidance of the Board of Trade. In 1967 the COI claimed a global non-theatrical audience of over 20 million for the films it distributed.

THE PETROLEUM FILMS BUREAU (PFB) (1939–74)

The Petroleum Films Bureau was established in 1939 to support the non-theatrical distribution of films made for oil industry sponsors. All the major oil companies with film output supported it, but its origination was largely attributable to Shell. In 1939 it only had 150 prints of fifteen films, but by 1957 it had 5,800 prints of 224 films and claimed to have serviced 500,000 screenings in the intervening period.[13]

The oil companies didn't limit themselves to the PFB. The Shell-Mex and BP film library also distributed the films that the Shell-Mex and BP organisation had sponsored directly, together with films from its parent companies Shell and BP. Some films produced for BP, Esso, National Benzole and Shell-Mex and BP also appeared in COI catalogues. The PFB appears to have been enormously popular with non-theatrical hirers across the country.

"And what do the words 'Sound-Services' mean in your languages?"

"They mean the same thing, old chap, in any language spoken in Europe, North Africa or the Middle East. Everyone understands 'Sound-Services' to be the largest sponsored film library in Europe and the only one in the world operating under complete computer control. It has audiences of millions, connections everywhere, unrivalled international conference facilities including the use of closed circuit TV and, of course, we all admire the excellent road show service they run in Britain. To summarise, I understand the words 'Sound-Services' to be synonymous with experience and expertise in communications."

"Well, thank you. And may I compliment you all on your perfect English?"

"Oh, we're not speaking English. Sound-Services are dubbing our dialogue. They dub into 42 languages, you know. And they do it awfully well."

KINGSTON ROAD, MERTON PARK, LONDON SW19 TEL: 01-542 7201

Members of INFORFILM — the international association of informational film distributors

SOUND-SERVICES (1936–71)

Sound-Services regularly promoted itself as the largest documentary film distributor in Europe, which all available evidence appears to support. Although it was unique in its size, in its operation it was similar to other independent distributing libraries such as the Random Film Library, the Argus Film Library and the later Golden Films.

The company was formed in 1936 by the US Western Electric Company to take over the distribution business of their Industrial and Educational Department, the Western Electric School Hiring Service and their road show service. Using mobile cinema vans they could take the films out practically anywhere and played a large role in developing and supporting the non-theatrical circuit. In 1947 Sound-Services became an associate part of the Film Producers Guild, issuing its first library catalogue of forty films in 1948.

From their sponsored film library they distributed films for a wide range of sponsors, numbering around 500, and including at various times clients as diverse as Air India, Babcock & Wilcox Ltd, the British Electrical Development Association, the Consumer Council, Dunlop, Ford, Kodak and the Royal Institute of Chemistry. Some, like Dunlop and Ford, were presented as if they were independent libraries and issued separate catalogues; most used the cheaper service of simply appearing in the Sound-Services listings. Sound-Services also operated an Educational Film Library (from 1963) and a Management Training Film Library (from 1965).

In 1962, Sound-Services claimed that over 200,000 16mm prints were loaned out. By 1968 they claimed to be reaching an audience of 23 million, 3 million more than the previous year and to be lending to 50,000 organisations from their list of nearly 2,000 titles.[14]

OTHERS

The Gebescope Library, established in 1933, became the GB Film Library in 1947 and the Rank Film Library in 1962. It was primarily an entertainment film distribution library but it also offered sponsored documentary titles on free loan. Alongside Sound-Services it was the major commercial film library, and Rank billed itself as 'No. 1 in Sponsored Films'. The UK sponsors serviced included Unilever, Wimpey and Costain, but they also carried a range of films sponsored by US firms, including a large number of management training titles.

Alongside these mainstream libraries were more unorthodox alternatives. For example, Contemporary Films was a major player on the post-war distribution scene, supplying both independent cinemas and non-theatrical renters with a mixture of art-cinema repertory, and left-wing or merely left-field British and international productions. In the 1960s and later the Concord Film Council existed to distribute 16mm films concerned with social issues that came from many sources, including the sponsored documentary field. The several film-makers in Part II of this book who maintained an interest in independent as well as sponsored production were likely to find some of their work being distributed by the large, mainstream libraries, and some by these alternative ones. Certain films (for example, COI productions with a social welfare theme) might find themselves in both.

THE END OF NON-THEATRICAL DISTRIBUTION

Despite the fact that most of the films discussed in this book were shown to most of their viewers on 16mm projectors, until well into the 1960s, and often beyond, a distinguishing feature of the British sponsored film – at least insofar as it was synonymous with 'British documentary' – was that it was produced on 35mm to the highest cinematic standards. As the 1960s turned into the 1970s the high-quality sponsored documentary film appeared to be in rude health, but the new decade proved much more difficult than was expected. The Petroleum Films Bureau closed in 1974 with the British oil companies announcing new film libraries: the BP Film Library, the National Benzole Film Library and the Shell Film Library. These were sham identities disguising the fact that the companies were actually cost-cutting. The Shell Film Library's address in Hendon was actually that of the Random Film Library. The address of the 'BP Film Library' and the 'National Benzole Film Library' in Willesden was that of a new distributor called the Argus Film Library, which already ran the ICI Film and Electricity Council libraries.[15] The shuffling of film libraries reflected a deeper uncertainty; fewer companies were offering free loans of their films and many began giving up on the idea of reaching large audiences on film.

Sound-Services began the 1970s by implementing a new membership scheme for borrowers that offered limited new benefits and demanded an annual fee. The reaching for new revenue opportunities preceded restructuring in their parent company. In 1971 the name Guild Sound & Vision Ltd was applied to all the activities of Guild Holdings Ltd and Sound-Services Ltd. They remained engaged in the industrial and educational market with Guild Learning distributing and Guild Sponsored Services running a film library. The library moved from London to Peterborough in 1973. Between 1979 and 1982 film sales plummeted from 98 per cent to 60 per cent of their business and continued to fall as video replaced the earlier medium.

The Central Film Library changed its name to CFL Vision in 1983, eventually closing in March 2000. For a while, a limited library of its titles continued to be operated by a private company called Euro View Management Services, now a dead website. The Rank Film Library lasted longer than most, but its main business was never the sponsored documentary film: it was bought by Carlton International in 1997 and is now owned by ITV Global Entertainment.

The causes of the end of non-theatrical distribution matched many of the causes of the decline of the sponsored documentary film. Businesses were looking for economies, public relations were moving resources towards other media, the rise of video for home and business use was causing the available audience to decrease and the established non-theatrical audience was aging. What is most curious is not that non-theatrical 'cinema' ended when it did, but that it carried on for so long, providing opportunities for so many people to see so many films that theatre-owners and television schedulers showed so much less interest in. A dependence on non-theatrical distribution has been one of the sticks used by critics to beat the 1930s Documentary Movement, from what is arguably a metrocentric, even elitist perspective. The question of how wide such non-theatrical distribution actually went, or how great was its impact, hangs on the deeper question of what place community gatherings and voluntary organisations had in pre-war and post-war provincial life. Theirs was surely a bright presence, though the glowing glare of television eventually outshone it.[16]

NOTES

1. Edgar Anstey, 'Skill, Time and Money Needed if Audience is to be Impressed', *The Times*, 27 June 1974, p. 16.
2. Text from full-page advertisement for Sound-Services in *Film Sponsor* vol. 1 no. 8, November 1948, p. 256.
3. Until 1955 its cinema distribution was handled by National Screen Services, and subsequently by DATA Film Distributors.
4. As late as 1974, more or less exactly the point at which non-theatrical went into sharp decline, Ken Gay wrote that 'it is apparent that audiences for non theatrical showings are larger than those achieved in cinemas even for features ... and as cinemas close or get smaller the trend goes on'. Ken Gay, 'Past and Present', *Films and Filming*, June 1974, p. 72.
5. John Burder, *The Work of the Industrial Film Maker* (London: Focal Press, 1973), p. 12.
6. R. J. Gregg, 'On Being a Sponsor', *Film User*, October 1955, pp. 500–2.
7. Shell Oil statistics quoted in Rudmer Canjels, 'From Oil to Celluloid: A History of Shell Films', in Jan Luiten van Zanden, *A History of Royal Dutch Shell; Appendices. Figures and Explanations, Collective Bibliography, and Index* (Oxford: Oxford University Press, 2007), p. 22.
8. Godfrey Jennison films officer at Shell-Mex and BP quoted in Gloria Tessler, 'Talking to Sponsors', *Film User*, January 1969, pp. 25–6.
9. Robinson P. Rigg, 'World in Focus', *Business Screen Magazine* vol. 29 no. 1, 1968, p. 50.
10. The first listed was the Unilever Film Library in Anon., 'Common Market Discussion; Main Differences Covered', *The Times*, 8 August 1961, p. 14; the last was that of the public relations department within British United Airways in Anon., 'Bank Clerks the New Box Office Stars', *The Times*, 26 June, 1967, p. 22.
11. Having run screenings of the annual best for several years, the award – which later became the Grierson – was initiated in 1970. Nominees on this first occasion included *The Shadow of Progress*, *GIGO* and *Let There Be Light*. The Federation was at this time chaired by John Chittock, of *Financial Times* and *Screen Digest* fame. In 1975, as part of the '50 Years of Film Societies', Chittock made a personal selection of 'The Best Sponsored Films of All Time' shown at Shell's theatre (the selected titles were *Night Mail*, *The River Must Live*, *Snow*, *Opus*, the NCB's safety cartoon *The Self-Rescuing Breathing Apparatus*, a selection of Barclays Bank commercials and, from abroad, Bert Haanstra's *Glas* and the American union film *The Inheritance*).
12. Paul Nugat, 'The Central Film Library', *Film Sponsor*, April 1950, pp. 245–6.
13. Brian Watkinson, 'Another Record Year', *Film User*, February 1958, p. 55. Watkinson was editor of *Film User*.
14. KD, 'Sponsored Film Audience Tops 23 Million', *Sound Services News*, 6 May 1969.
15. These libraries had previously been run in-house by the organisations.
16. Last word to the Gas Council's films officer, who, tongue slightly in cheek, advised that his films were 'made primarily for non-theatrical distribution ... shown on 16mm projectors whenever and wherever a group of people can be cajoled or coerced into giving up their leisure to see them. An exception to this definition is the considerable use of films in schools. Here the pupils are to regard a film as a welcome relief from proving Pythagoras' Theorem by the long method – only to regret it

when they have to write an essay on the film. Every individual is potentially a member of the audience. Belonging to a youth club, the Girl Guides or a Mothers' Union practically ensures seeing 16mm films at some time or other. Her Majesty's Prisons, through the efforts of the welfare officers, provide a regular clientele, and incarceration in any of them is a virtual guarantee of seeing some Gas Council films; indeed, a six-months' sentence at Wormwood Scrubs is a convenient way of seeing *all* of them, for they are booked *en bloc* over that period.' Stanley Irving, 'Audience of 600,000', *Film User*, May 1963, p. vii.

4 Production

War expanded, energised and momentarily stabilised documentary production: it also sowed the seeds of its destruction as a narrowly based film movement. The very scale of official demand for propaganda necessitated diversity of supply: steady work for Crown and the independent film units associated with the Documentary Movement; plenty too for producers without their background or affiliations.

Thus was the basis for post-war documentary production laid. This would, like the national economy itself, be a mixed one. Despite the short shelf life of post-war Crown, the tradition of the internal film unit tied to state sponsorship was maintained by the emergence of a film unit for nationalised transport shortly before Crown's demise, and of a unit for nationalised coalmining shortly afterwards. On the free enterprise side, the Shell Film Unit went from strength to post-war strength. Being so closely tied to their industrial sponsors, these production units are covered in the next chapter. (Internal units, it should be noted, also materialised at ICI and Ford, and inside varied organisations from Dunlop and the Richard Costain and John Laing & Sons construction companies, through to the Royal Society for the Protection of Birds.)

Otherwise, the story of post-war documentary production is that of the independent sector so enlarged by the war effort. The various success and failure stories that this sector saw are among the fascinations of post-war documentary. Idealists and chancers, sharp dealmakers and posh patrons, warhorses and workhorses: what follows is a selective survey of some of post-war documentary's most significant independent producers.

MOVEMENT REMNANTS: REALIST, ANVIL AND DATA

> For the first time we have a Labour Government in Britain with a clear Parliamentary majority and the people are beginning to inherit the earth. We at DATA stand in a key position to give the people some of the information they need to reconstruct their inheritance.[1]

Not only did Rotha's Films of Fact collapse into insolvency early in the post-war period; the Strand Film Company also fizzled out. A few years later, two untimely deaths, of Richard Massingham and of Humphrey Jennings respectively, caused Massingham's Public Relationship Films to close, and the proportion of documentary output from Ian Dalrymple's Wessex Films to be curtailed. However, other companies deeply rooted in Documentary Movement history continued. The post-war story of the Realist Film Unit well illustrates how the eminence of documentary in the literature of cinema fell in inverse proportion to rising levels of production and of the practical use of film by society that had been one of the Movement's stated aims. In Movement chronicles, Realist is usually cited alongside Strand as the key independent producer of the 1930s, but it's frequently forgotten that it continued in active business until the early 1970s, eventually clocking up over 200 productions, often highly appreciated in the expanding fields of science education and social welfare.

Founded in 1937 by Basil Wright, with his father Major Lawrence Wright, Realist expanded through World War II under the direction of John Taylor. During Taylor's wartime stewardship, a few productions augured society's post-war reform: films like Taylor's officially suppressed *Goodbye Yesterday* (1941) and Maxwell Anderson's *The Harvest Shall Come* (1942). However, these were outnumbered by smaller films, better foreshadowing Realist's own post-war experience. There were two significant strands. One, particularly associated with director Alex Strasser, was technical films on science and medicine.[2] A fruitful wartime relationship with Imperial Chemical Industries paid off in early post-war commissions like *Salt* (1947) and *The Story of Penicillin* (1947). This success was built on with work for the Ministry of Health (a six-part series on *Some Aspects of Accessible Cancers*, 1951), Glaxo (*A Vitamin Emerges*, 1957), the World Health Organisation (*We Have the Cure*, 1956) and schools films sponsored by the Gas Council and Mullards. The Unit's second emerging wartime specialism, associated with director Brian Smith (who headed Realist in the early post-war years, following Taylor's departure to run Crown), were films dealing with the upbringing of children. The *Your Children* (1945–51), series became Realist's post-war calling card: far more relevant to most contemporary film renters than such official pre-war classics as Wright's *Children at School* (1937). Aimed mainly at trainee teachers, Margaret Thomson's *Children Learning by Experience* and *Children Growing Up with Other People* (both 1947) were groundbreaking experiments in unmediated observational film-making, albeit for instrumental purposes. Very much reflecting broader patterns, social concern had supplanted social critique.

Wright came back to head the company following his father's death in 1954. He had been concentrating on the sister company International-Realist (I-R), which, though legally separate used the same address and resources, and some of the same staff. For Wright, I-R was evidently in part a vehicle for the more

. . . the people who made the YOUR CHILDREN *series*

REALIST

FILM UNIT LIMITED

58 OF OUR FILMS ARE NOW IN DISTRIBUTION BY THE CENTRAL FILM LIBRARY

9 GREAT CHAPEL STREET
LONDON W.1 GERrard 1958

Children Learning by Experience

ambitious pet projects of the sort squeezed by the post-war settlement. I-R's two best-known films make it into most Movement histories as late hurrahs: Wright's gorgeous, if fey, *Waters of Time* (1951) and the UNESCO-funded Wright–Rotha film *World Without End* (1953). Far more popular and lucrative than either, however, was *Bernard Miles on Gun Dogs* (1949), circuit released as the short accompanying *Scott of the Antarctic* (1948).

Back at Realist's helm, Wright's own late films, often on arts and crafts subjects, are tired late works. In the 1960s J. B. Holmes, another Movement veteran, joined Realist and oversaw production of several of its better late films, in support of some of that decade's iconic public information campaigns: *The Smoking Machine* (1964) and *Traffic in Towns* (1963). Following Holmes's departure, the Unit became less active. Its last documented project was a series of shortened versions of Gilbert and Sullivan operettas released for educational distribution in 1973 (made in collaboration with the education company Seabourne Enterprises). While Realist had always had stability of personnel, its one constant had been Adrian Jeakins, chief cameraman ever since 1937.

TEN YEARS OF ACHIEVEMENT

A Full programme of film production—and world fame for sound recording for films of all types, from major features to commercials.

Member of the Association of Specialised Film Producers
ANVIL FILMS LTD., BEACONSFIELD STUDIOS, BEACONSFIELD, BUCKS.
BEACONSFIELD 557

If the Realist Film Unit may well have been kept afloat by the Wright family fortune, the Anvil Film and Recording Group underwrote its documentary output by selling post-production expertise. Anvil was established on the Crown Film Unit's closure by three of its staffers, Ken Cameron, Richard Warren and Ralph Nunn May. Operating from Crown's former Beaconsfield Studios base, it provided audio facilities (and Cameron's skills – he was the great sound recordist of his generation) to large swathes of the documentary and feature film industries alike.[3] In parallel, Anvil's own production programme eventually ran to some 350 shorts. In 1956, Anvil acquired the controlling interest in Realist, as part of a group of affiliated units that also included the side projects Anvil Films (Scotland) and World Mirror Productions and Hans Nieter's small Seven League Productions.

Anvil's documentary work, largely steered by Warren, was versatile, competent and largely unexceptional. Reflecting Cameron's sound interests, there was a musical education strand in some of the output (Muir Mathieson ended up on the board of Anvil and Realist), as well as science films in similar vein to Strasser's at Realist. For the Foreign and Colonial Offices, Anvil became the go-to producer for a raft of films presenting overseas audiences with a cosy view of contemporary British life. These smoothly blend the socialist and conservative, masculine and feminine elements of post-war consensus, as their very titles suggest: *Mr Jenkins Pays His Rates* (1956) and *An English Village* (1957); *A British Trade Union* (1954) and *Getting Together: A Story of Co-Operatives* (1955). Anvil was markedly the most prolific producer of films for the British Productivity Council, turning out over twenty BPC films: to take just two made the same year, *A Case for Shiftwork?* (1961) and *Change and Employment* (1961), the latter dealing with management and workforce responses to job insecurity caused by technological advance. Anvil also took many Ministry of Defence contracts, alongside which came work for innumerable small-scale sponsors. The company even ended up something of a specialist in petcare, Pedigree Petfoods having become a regular sponsor in the 1970s. The last recorded production by Warren was *Pet Feeding – a Shared Responsibility* (1981). Back in Crown days, he had been a unit manager for Humphrey Jennings on *A Diary for Timothy*.

For intriguing contrast we may turn to the idealism of the Documentary and Technicians Alliance (DATA Film Productions). While Realist and Anvil settled into amiable compromise, DATA stridently strode into an unhappily uncooperative future. DATA's story started with a mutiny in Rotha's wartime ranks, whereby employees left Paul Rotha Productions (which then became Films of Fact [FoF]). They included directors J. D. Chambers and Budge Cooper, cameraman Wolfgang Suschitzky and, their ringleader, Cooper's husband, the director Donald Alexander. They were mostly staunch left-wingers (some of them, including Alexander and Chambers, Communist Party members), and set DATA up as Britain's first film-makers' cooperative.[4] The break-up with Rotha had not been entirely acrimonious: DATA now occupied offices at 21 Soho Square (which had once housed the GPO Film Unit), while FoF initially had offices at both 21 and 17. Staff were sometimes 'exchanged' between the companies to help out with certain projects. When FoF folded, DATA took on many of its staff (such as Michael Orrom, Michael Clarke and James Ritchie). At its height, DATA had about fifty employees, though usually half that (with freelancers frequently brought in as workflow required).

Early DATA films show the company's preference for films of 'social significance', chiming with the earliest stages of the social democratic experiment. For the Economic Information Unit, *All Eyes on Britain* (1947) presents an optimistic outlook for post-war prospects, while Cooper's *Birth-Day* (1945) encouraged mothers to use maternity services. Mary Beales made some of DATA's most interesting films: *Fair Rent* (1946) explained Aberdeen's rent tribunal system and *Dover, Spring 1947* covered the town's post-war replanning.[5] Another ongoing DATA project was to film the New Town development at Hemel Hempstead, while *The Bridge* (1947) covered reconstruction in Yugoslavia. Financed by the Ministry of Labour, *Code Name: Westward Ho!* (1949) dealt with displaced people – European Volunteer Workers – arriving in Britain to join the mining and cotton industries, with both of which, thanks to Alexander, DATA was developing close relationships. These relationships proved helpful as growing anxieties about state sponsorship were compounded in DATA's case by Grierson's appointment at the COI (he and Alexander being uneasy bedfellows).

On the back of *Cotton Come Back* (1946), for the Board of Trade, Alexander persuaded the Cotton Board to appoint him as films adviser, resulting in DATA's delightfully experimental *Chasing the Blues* (1946) and the stolid *Science Joins an Industry* (1946), both cheerleading a spike in cotton's fortunes which proved painfully brief. He pulled the same trick with the Steel Company of Wales, for ongoing coverage of its development of the Margam and Trostre sites, in turn bringing work from the British Iron and Steel Federation. A similar 'coverage' project was initiated with Anglo-Iranian Oil, building a Kentish refinery. The pragmatist in Alexander knew that keeping the unit in credit meant actively courting such industrial sponsorship, though the ideologue in him hoped DATA's presence in the cooperative movement would kick-start its interest in film as a tool for political education. Unfortunately, his optimism was misplaced, and his pragmatism internally controversial, as was the strong-willed Alexander himself, having some of the same autocratic tendencies as his old boss Rotha.[6] Alexander departed, reappearing at the National Coal Board, to be replaced first by Terrick Fitzhugh then by the ubiquitous Holmes.[7] Holmes had occupied similar 'caretaker' roles at the GPO and Crown: universally liked, he may have been less effective than Alexander in moulding the cooperative to a focused plan of activity.

In 1948 the cooperative had began making the NCB's *Mining Review* newsreel. By the turn of the 1950s, DATA was deriving three-quarters of its income from this series.[8] As the decade wore on, what had started as a niche production line increasingly became DATA's total programme,

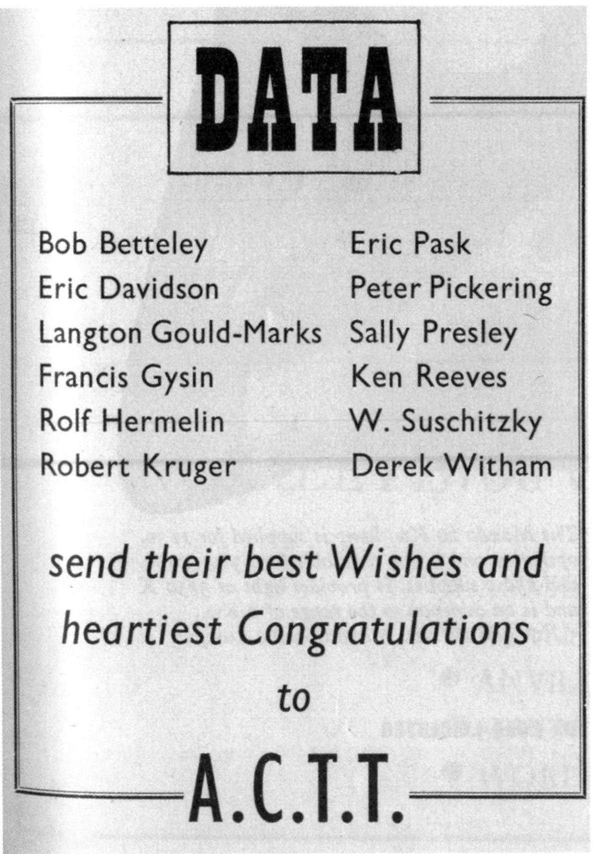

subsidising all other overheads despite the fact that the series' sponsor now had its own increasingly experienced unit in-house.[9] Hence, in 1961, it was the NCB's films officer – Donald Alexander – who effectively pulled the plug on his former charges, on undeniably sensible economic grounds, by not renewing DATA's rolling contract for *Mining Review*, instead bringing the series, and many of the cooperative's staff, into the NCB's film unit. DATA soon wound itself up.[10]

DATA can be credited with forging a longer-term relationship with a working-class community – the mining community – than any other offshoot of the mostly middle-class Documentary Movement had yet managed, and the resulting films are immensely enjoyable as well as historically significant. But it's retrospectively interesting how similar DATA's films now feel to other documentaries made at the time by production companies with none of the same political motives. Stylistically, DATA's early films are reminiscent of those made by the likes of Alexander, Cooper and Chambers at Rotha's during the war. Politically, few DATA films veer very far left of the contemporary consensus. Some even appear embarrassingly dated today (see, for example, Holmes' well-meaning but excruciatingly class-bound recruitment film *Probation Officer* [1950]). As such, DATA is a classic illustration of the post-war gap between ambitions off the screen, and what it was possible to project onto it.

BASIC FILMS AND THE LEON CLORE STABLE

> What's wrong with a good cliché?[11]
>
> Leon Clore

At first glance Leon Clore was a Jewish impresario with a gold Rolls Royce and an eye for talent, running a suite of companies from a single address with one phone number. A closer look belies the stereotype and reveals something substantial and unique. If the cliché can't entirely be shaken off, Clore might have wanted it that way.

Lindsay Anderson later recalled, 'I am quite conscious of my extraordinary luck in having been able to work like this, and of my debt to Leon Clore.'[12] Under Clore's management, experimental, commercial and industrial documentarists mingled together. Veterans like John Taylor and Margaret

Leon Clore

Thomson mixed with young Turks like Anderson, and Americans like avant-gardist James Broughton and blacklist exile Joseph Losey. Clore's generous, protective patronage attracted film-makers like Anderson, Karel Reisz and John Fletcher, Anthony Simmons, John Krish and Stephen Frears. Clore supported the careers of cinematographers like Walter Lassally and Larry Pizer.[13] He was to be described as 'something of a "Diaghilev"' to young British documentary film-makers. As he put it himself, with characteristic self-effacement, 'I'd got a name for helping people. I provided cameras, cutting rooms and equipment free if I thought the people had something.'[14] While the idealism of some companies had led them into financial difficulties, and others had shifted to a more commercially driven agenda necessitating careful sponsor relations, Clore's own financial security seems to have kept Basic Films, and the companies that were to follow, solvent while allowing their film-makers unusual creative latitude.[15]

Basic Films had come out of much the same ferment as Realist and DATA. The company was started in 1944 by the husband and wife team R. K. (Rod) Neilson-Baxter and Kay Mander, in collaboration with J. B. (Sam) Napier-Bell, as a John Lewis-style 'co-partnership'. All had worked at the Shell Film Unit. Their company name reflected a vision of lucid communication inherited from Shell. Basic's technical film-making included several productions on radar and sonar. Formal education was also a strength: Mander's *La Famille Martin* (1948) and two successor films were (for the time) highly innovative aids to French teaching. However, political disagreements and financial problems led to the acrimonious departure of Neilson-Baxter and Mander, and to the recruitment of Clore, along with John Taylor and Max Anderson, all fresh from the Crown Film Unit.[16] One of Basic's most ambitious projects, directed by Napier-Bell soon after Clore's arrival, was the Festival of Britain film *Forward a Century* (1951), sponsored by the Petroleum Films Bureau. A comparison of the Britain of 1851 and 1951, its political line was reputedly softened at sponsor request. However, despite the standard leftist sympathies of Basic's bosses, the co-partnership structure was now abandoned.[17]

COI projects, including more than averagely creative ones like Anderson's *Foot and Mouth* (1955) and Krish's *Return to Life* (1960), provided Basic with its bedrock. Commissions also came from the Gas Council, the NCB and the British Productivity Council, for whom the important titles *Company of Men* (1959), *Dispute* (1961) and *Words are Not Enough* (1963) were all directed by Fred Moore. As well as charity films for the NSPCC and corporate work for Shell Chemicals, the British Iron and Steel Federation and the British Nylon Spinners, for whom Napier-Bell directed the gorgeously kitsch *Everything But Everything in Bri-Nylon* (1960), Basic also made a handful of children's entertainment films for the Rank group.

Clore obviously had his eye out for opportunities outside the sponsored film world, and was always quick to form new companies that didn't meet Basic's 'explanatory' brief. At the same time as Basic was labouring on *Forward a Century*, under the production company name of Tresco, Clore was producing the unofficial *Festival, 1951*, a freeform semi-documentary of a young boy's wanderings on the South Bank, directed by Derek York. In 1952, Clore formed Countryman Films, with

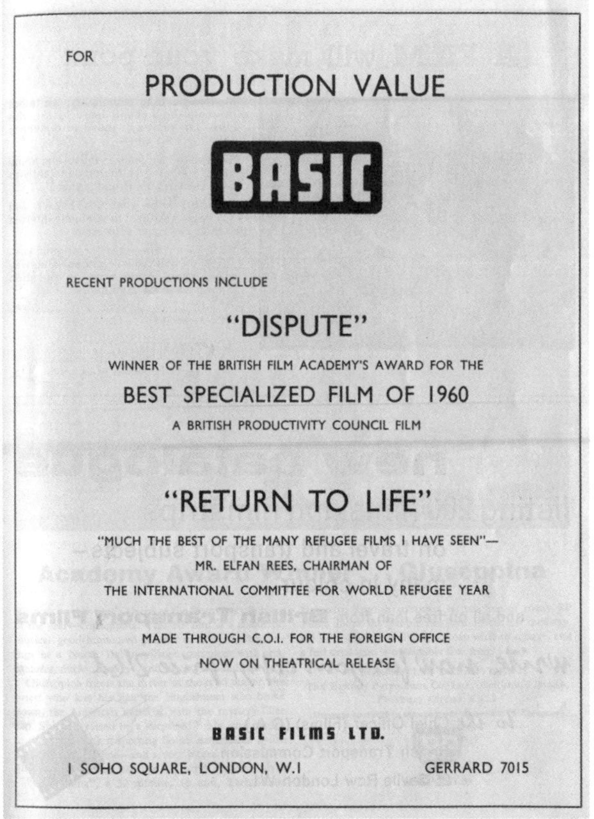

Grahame Tharp and John Taylor, in order to make *The World of Life* series about nature and the countryside, distributed theatrically by Columbia. Countryman's biggest success was *The Conquest of Everest* (1953) – Oscar nominated for the Best Documentary Feature of 1953. While the Everest film seems an obvious winner now, the difficulties of filming were immense and director Tom Stobart felt that the producers were taking a real risk.[18] Later it produced ex-documentarist Pat Jackson's *Virgin Island* (1958). In 1953, there had been a change of address from 18 to No. 1 Soho Square as another company joined the fold.[19] Harlequin Productions, set up that year by Clore, Simmons and John Arnold, was to be a more speculative venture for making documentary shorts and low-budget feature films. It made no films after 1957, but in its few years of operation it produced Simmons's *Sunday by the Sea* (1953) and *Bow Bells* (1954), backed the fledgling Free Cinema with Lorenza Mazzetti's film *Together* (1956) and provided work for Joseph Losey with *Time Without Pity* (1957).

In the mid-1950s, Clore started using the name Graphic Films in parallel with Basic's.[20] While Clore and Napier-Bell jointly ran Basic, Napier-Bell was uninvolved in any of Graphic's productions. Several key creative staff – cameramen Lassally and Pizer, directors Krish, Fletcher and Simmons – worked on both Graphic and Basic films, but Moore only on Basic projects, and Arnold produced many Graphic but few Basic films. The second difference was that the two companies tilled different fields of sponsorship. COI and BPC work was always handled by Basic. The connection with Graphic's formative sponsor, Ford, was effected in 1956 through their newly appointed films officer Karel Reisz. Ford's contributions to Free Cinema, together with some of the sponsor's more conventional films, were made under the Graphic label, as were films for other off-the-beaten-track clients. Less well-known films were made at Graphic in parallel with Free Cinema – in entirely different but equally creative style – including John Krish's *I Want to Go To School* (1959), for the National Union of Teachers, and *They Took Us to the Sea* (1961), for the NSPCC. As the two companies' names suggest, Graphic was in general a more innovative producer, while a meat-and-potatoes approach predominated at Basic.

In 1961 Arnold and Clore formed another company with several of their directors, Film Contracts, solely for the purpose of making advertisements.[21] Film Contracts allowed directors from other spheres to make commercials and thus cover expenses in fallow periods. Joseph Losey was one of those to benefit from the opportunities it offered.[22] Charitable intentions were tempered by exclusive contracts, lest these skills and contacts be taken elsewhere. Film Contracts' first advertisement was for the socialist paper *Daily Herald*; clients that followed included Persil, Kellogg's, Kraft, Campari, Guinness and Rowntree.

In 1966, disharmony returned to Basic Films. For reasons that are unclear, but were probably financial, Napier-Bell and Clore fell out. Finances were disentangled and Basic left the Clore nest, remaining as Napier-Bell's project, indeed eventually relocating to the Napier-Bells' semi in Richmond. *Communicate to Live* (1972), a film for the Post Office directed by Ronnie Whitehouse, won BAFTA Gold and a small but steady stream of sponsored work kept the company going until, in 1974, Napier-Bell announced his retirement and with it the end of Basic Films. The company's swansong was *Carpets in Acrilan*, a promo for Monsanto carpets.[23]

The separation of Basic from the Clore companies encouraged Graphic to seek COI contracts in competition with its former stablemate. Throughout the 1970s, Clore and Arnold produced a range of solid output for government and the Armed Forces, using freelance directors including Krish, Pearson, Bill Mason, Derek Williams, Sarah Erulkar and John MacKenzie. Clore simultaneously pursued features production: Karel Reisz's cult hit *Morgan – A Suitable Case for Treatment* (1966) was followed in 1969 by *All Neat in Black Stockings* (directed by Christopher Morahan) and in 1981 by the greatest success of Clore's career, Reisz's *French Lieutenant's Woman*. While Graphic Films continued producing into the 1980s, its output gradually diminished then ceased in 1986, as production on film, even 16mm for schools, was slowing down.

Leon Clore is remembered by associates as a rough diamond, his abrasive exterior concealing great kindness. In his way, he was as much a godfather to innovative film-making as Grierson had once been. The resemblance ends there: Clore engaged little in personal self-promotion or in industry politics, and did not seek to promulgate any particular ideological or aesthetic position through the extremely varied films he enabled to be made. For these reasons, his name is less familiar than it should be.

WORLD WIDE PICTURES

> Carr is essentially a film man, energetic and shrewd.[24]

As the 1930s Movement was still in full swing, LSE graduate James Carr was completing studies in film technique at the Regent Street Polytechnic. He had one film under his belt, *Waterways of London* (1934), about life on canal boats. It was distributed theatrically, and some legal requirement must have necessitated an organisational structure because in April 1935 Carr purchased 'off the shelf' a dormant company, Sidney Olcott Productions Ltd, and changed its name to World Wide Pictures.[25] A grandiose title for a twenty-four-year-old student, it wouldn't appear in any film's credits for another seven years.

Waterways of London yielded little income. Carr began freelancing for established production companies, including Strand and Sydney Box's Verity Films. Changes at Verity in 1942, combined with the opportunities offered by wartime production, led Carr to take a chance on retrieving the World Wide name and starting his own company – for real this time. With a rented office, rented camera and a single prospective contract from the Army Kinema Corporation, as well as support from Box and the exhibitor Lou Morris, Carr got going. Twenty years later he was Managing

Director of a group of companies with a state-of-the-art production centre in the City, a separate animation studio, offices, cutting-rooms and more than 170 staff.

In the immediate post-war period, Carr had pinned his colours to the Documentary Movement establishment by joining the Federation of Documentary Film Units. This was despite his on-record irritation at Movement cliquiness.[26] Carr's own leanings, like most in the FDFU, were leftwards. His recruitment of staunch communist Ralph Bond as a producer/director in 1945 brought trade union sponsorship for Bond to direct *Unity is Strength* (1945), made for the Amalgamated Engineering Union, and *The Power in the Land* (1947), sponsored by the Electrical Trades Union and directed by Terry Bishop, also of socialist views. World Wide's offices in 10a Soho Square (1948) were in the same building as Halas & Batchelor. Across the square was the old GPO/Crown base at No. 21, then hosting the Colonial Film Unit (downstairs) and DATA (upstairs). For a while Film Centre occupied No. 34, Basic was at 18, Realist was round the corner on Great Chapel Street. Here was the workplace and playing field of the 'Soho Square Boys', the documentary gang that Lindsay Anderson and others would later disparage.

Like several of these neighbours, Carr was a legendarily heavy drinker but in every other respect he was rather different: a self-made pragmatist of small physical stature, humble Northern origins (a Cumbrian coalminer's son) and pugnacious, plain-speaking personality. Unlike some of these better-bred peers, Carr fully appreciated the necessity of solvency. In 1946 he was joined by Vincent Llewellyn 'Johnny' Price, an accountant with a background in furniture and experience as a Colonel in the Eighth Army, who brought World Wide invaluable business acumen. Whatever his own personal allegiances, Carr's company was unencumbered by the socialist politics or cooperative structures of other FDFU members. Ralph Bond left in 1948, his time increasingly taken up with activities at the ACT. From henceforth, World Wide would work with industry rather than its unions.

James Carr

Responsive to the emerging realities of documentary's post-war economics, World Wide wasn't afraid to flatter potential clients, to advertise for work from them, to focus tightly on their stated needs. Typical of Carr's writing was his 1953 appeal in the *Public Relations* journal for a 'creative partnership' between industrial sponsor and film producer.[27] In 1950 Carr and Price appointed the public relations executive Gerald Fox-Edwards to the role of 'sponsor liaison'. A contemporary article noted that 'there is a marked absence of the "long haired" approach among these people'.[28]

World Wide's early contracts initially had come from the Armed Forces and the COI. Spectacular critical success came with two government-sponsored films directed by briefly rising star Paul Dickson: *The Undefeated* (1950) and *David* (1951). Mary Francis's municipally themed films *Every Drop to Drink* (1948, about London's water supply) and *Bristol, British City* (1951) were equally well received. Far more exotic, *They Planted a Stone* (1953), directed by the interesting itinerant documentarist Robin Carruthers, was Oscar-nominated. Although a COI film, its international subject (the Blue Nile dam scheme) resonated with the sort of foreign location work increasingly valued by private-sector sponsors. With films like *The New Explorers* (1955), *Oil Harbour – Aden* (1955) and the educational *Your Skin* (1957) lucrative associations with three major sponsors – BP, Wimpey and Unilever – were initiated. These companies (and others including Phillips, Merck and the banking industry) would remain clients for decades.

Clifford Parris, a film director at World Wide at the time, then producer and later Company Chairman, recalled: 'in the mid-1950s, films paid for by industry began to change. Films had to have a specific purpose – not just simply, "wouldn't it be a good idea to make a film about Waterloo Station."'[29] World Wide's output in fact had a mixed character. Although the company's success was dependent on salesmanship and good customer relations, it wasn't entirely reducible to them. Production quality was also part of the mix, and Carr's feelings for his medium were genuine; however, as time went on the running-to-stand-still personality of the company certainly precluded the more freewheeling atmosphere of, say, Graphic. Some of Carr's directors felt an oppressive 'give-the-punters-what-they-want' ethos, as well as a sense that getting the next commission was more important than executing the current one.

Accordingly, World Wide attracted a mixed workforce of cinephiles and Soho lifers. Among the former passing through the staff ranks were Peter Hopkinson, John Krish, John Schlesinger, Kevin Brownlow (who directed the Wimpey-sponsored *Ascot – A Race Against Time* [1961]) and Peter Watkins (famous for *Culloden* and *The War Game* at the BBC, he made World Wide's 1963 COI/Ministry of Aviation short *The Controllers*). Reliable producers and directors busy at the more professionalised World Wide of the 1960s and '70s included the likes of Glyn Jones, Peter Bradford,

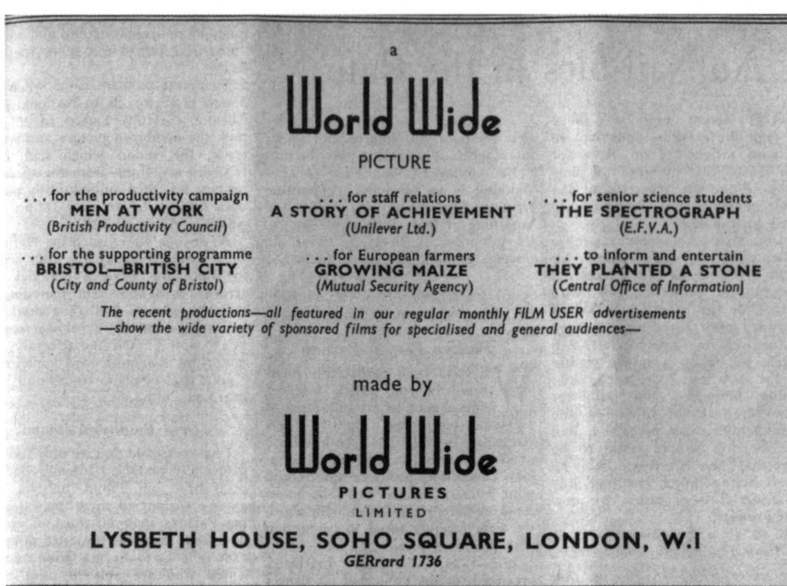

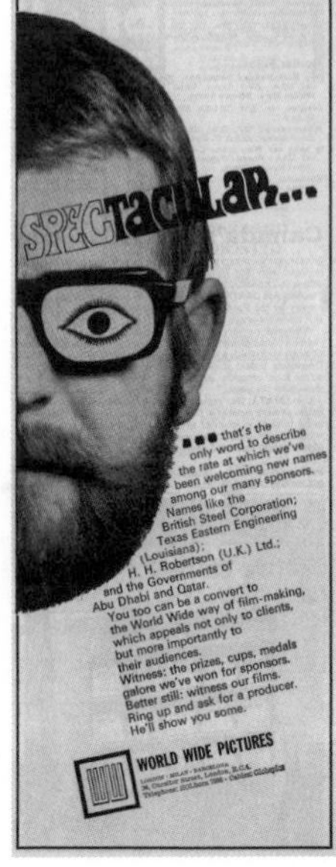

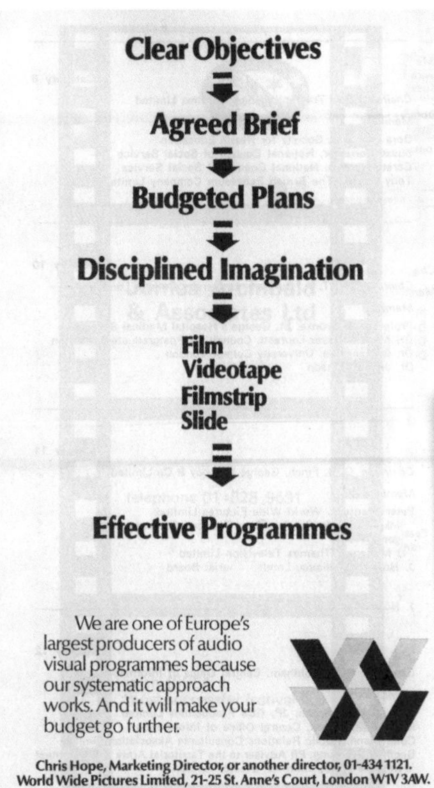

Changing personae of World Wide Pictures

David Morphet and Philip Harland. Longstanding senior cameramen Ronnie Anscombe and ex-DATA member Kenneth Reeves were also mainstays. Additionally, World Wide employed freelancers. One of the most notable was Harry Watt who, with Wolfgang Suschitzky photographing, made *People Like Maria* (1958) for the World Health Organisation at Carr's company.

In the 1950s and early '60s, World Wide films were frequently celebrated at awards ceremonies in the wider cinema world. *The Undefeated* won the BAFTA for best Documentary of 1950, *David* was nominated for the same award the following year. An Oscar was won by Lindsay Anderson and Guy Brenton's *Thursday's Children* (1954), though World Wide's role was essentially that of subsidising its post-production. *Foothold on Antarctica* (1956) and *Antarctic Crossing* (1958) were nominated for short and feature documentary Oscars respectively. Such success was not just gratifying recognition, but also among the best coverage a company could acquire as publicity for its services.

Like Anvil, World Wide generated extra income through the provision of technical services. In 1959 Peter Gilpin joined World Wide and developed their World Wide Sound division, which made post-synchronised foreign-language versions of feature films, documentaries and television programmes, eventually becoming the largest such facility in the UK. The same year, Chartered Accountant Ronald Aylott was appointed as Company Secretary, a typical kind of appointment for many companies but seemingly atypical for documentary film producers. A further mark of both the company's financial success and its client focus came with the opening of film studios at Cursitor Street off Chancery Lane in 1962. The location placed World Wide close to the headquarters of major corporations, the richest potential client base for industrial films. An article in the business pages of *The Times* noted the advantages of the location over the 'remote suburban studios that cluster on London's west side', less convenient for industrialists and the advertising agents to travel to.[30]

Further markers of financial success came in 1964, with more company expansion. A production unit, World Wide Pictures Srl, was set up in Milan. The same year Carr joined a consortium led by his old employer Sidney Box seeking, ultimately unsuccessfully, to take over Associated-Rediffusion's London Weekend Television.[31] World Wide's new studios and production centre formed an important part of the bid. In 1970 a new basement sound studio was added featuring CinemaScope-equipped screening rooms capable of seating a hundred people, high-end facilities that again impressed sponsors.

In 1972 80 per cent of World Wide's production remained on film, but much had already switched to 16mm, a move that had been resisted by many competitors who saw the abandonment of 35mm as tantamount to abandoning cinematic tradition and quality. As early as 1974 World

Wide formed a Video Division, gambling that the new medium would 'make a vital contribution across the whole spectrum of employee relations, as well as to training, marketing communication, etc.'.[32] This new division allowed World Wide a considerable market advantage. It was a typically astute move; by 1980 work on film had slipped to 50 per cent of World Wide's production, with video making up 30 per cent and the widely forgotten tape and slide programmes accounting for the remaining 20 per cent.[33]

The change in medium paralleled a change in the balance of content as potentially award-winning prestige films were reduced to a trickle. In August 1977 Carr and Price stepped down from their roles as chairman and joint managing director, but continued as company directors. They were succeeded by Clifford Parris (combining chairman and executive producer roles) and Peter Gilpin as managing director.[34] In 1979, World Wide announced the official retirement of Carr and Price as directors of the company. In many ways, their departure, breaking a continuity of personnel dating back to the war, marked a moment that had already passed. In the 1980s World Wide fully redefined its products from sponsored films to 'corporate' or 'commissioned programmes'.[35] To read this as failure would mean ignoring unparalleled business success. Each time, just before the wind changed World Wide Pictures had moved its sail. It was thus the only member of Soho's Federation of Documentary Film Units that made it into the 1980s: in 1984, it grossed £2 million. Today, under the chairmanship of Ray Townsend, who was an editor under Carr back in the 1960s, it remains Britain's longest-running independent production company. Much of its work now comes from longstanding clients like the European Space Agency, and from the Middle East – the one part of the world where the concept of prestige documentary-making remains vibrantly alive.

THE FILM PRODUCERS GUILD

Small Team Talent, Big Firm Facilities.[36]

If any single company can be said to have dominated the production of sponsored film in the post-war era then it is the many-headed hydra that was the Film Producers Guild (FPG), the operational name for Guild Holdings Ltd, based at Guild House, Upper St Martins Lane.[37] On its initial association the Guild consisted of seven subsidiary companies; twenty years later it numbered twenty-one subsidiary companies and employed 600 permanent staff. In 1968, the FPG claimed to have, for the fourth consecutive year, 'made more films for commerce and industry than any other organisation in the world'.[38] Among an enormous client base sat various arms of the UK state (from the Colonial Office to the United Kingdom Atomic Energy Authority [UKAEA]), the governments of the Federal Republic of Germany, Northern Ireland and Saudi Arabia, the OECD, banking, pharmaceuticals and the motor industry. The Guild also served a raft of leading advertising agencies. Guild companies' output was seen theatrically, non-theatrically and on television in the UK, in Europe and around the world.

The FPG came out of the tying together of several companies that worked out of Merton Park Studios. During World War II, the studio was used by several producers making Ministry of Information (MOI) propaganda films. Prominent among them was Sidney Box's Verity Films. Verity's strategy was continually to undercut competitors' prices, a risky plan that secured a constant stream of work but kept the company perpetually on the brink of economic failure. Bankruptcy was avoided when Box turned to his old employers Publicity Films for financial support, eventually leaving the company in the hands of his colleague A. T. Burlinson. The resulting stability allowed Verity to manoeuvre itself into a supervisory role for the neighbouring Greenpark, Gryphon and Technique film units.

Merton Park Studios were owned by Sound-Services Ltd, an independent business, run by E. P. L. Pelly, that had once been part of the US Western Electric Company. Sound-Services distributed educational and sponsored films and ran film shows combining educational material and advertising, often using their fleet of mobile cinema vans. The combination of production units and creative staff from the Verity alliance with the studios, production facilities and distribution service of the Sound-Services group offered a formidably integrated business proposition

In 1944 the affiliation between the production companies at Merton Park Studios was sealed by the creation of a coordinating company named the Film Producers Guild Ltd, wholly owned by Sound-Services (known as Guild Holdings from 1947). The Guild represented the association of seven film companies: Verity Films, Publicity Films, Merton Park Studios, Technique Film Productions, Greenpark Productions, Gryphon Films and Sound-Services. Sound-Services' Pelly and Verity's A. T. Burlinson were joint managing directors, but Sound-Services' ascendancy was indicated by Pelly's position as chairman and the appointment of Sound-Services' staff F. A. Hoare and K. Lockhart Smith as director and secretary of the company.

While the FDFU was a grouping of affinity based on ideological inclination and an intellectualised conception of the documentary form, the FPG association was a matter of economics. While the Movement was lobbying Labour for enhanced government funding for film, the FPG adroitly addressed itself to private finance, advertising in *The Economist* to promote films in the service of industry.[39] While internal disputes over commercial work haunted Basic and DATA, and Films of Fact went to the wall, the Guild was attracting – and generating – the lion's share of the work and the financial security which it bestowed. Five months before the Guild's formation, Hoare had a letter published in *The Times* in which he expressed his support for vertical integration within business. Looking to his own industry, he stressed that 'without the financial strength and the large technical and other resources associated with great

THE FILM PRODUCERS GUILD LTD

GUILD HOUSE, UPPER ST. MARTIN'S LANE, LONDON, W.C.2

Telephone: TEMPLE BAR 5420 (13 Lines) *Telegrams:* FILMICITY, LONDON

Chairman and Joint Managing Director: E. P. L. PELLY
Joint Managing Director: A. T. BURLINSON
Director: F. A. HOARE
Secretary: K. LOCKHART SMITH

An Association of Producers and Distributors of Documentary, Industrial, Educational and National Propaganda Films.

ASSOCIATES:

GUILD HOLDINGS LTD.
Managing Director: E. P. L. PELLY

VERITY FILMS LTD.
Managing Director: A. T. BURLINSON

PUBLICITY FILMS LTD.
Managing Director: EDWARD BECKETT

GREENPARK PRODUCTIONS LTD.
Managing Director:
RALPH KEENE

MERTON PARK STUDIOS LTD.
Joint Managing Directors:
F. A. HOARE A. T. BURLINSON

TECHNIQUE FILM PRODUCTIONS
Director of Production:
RONALD H. RILEY

THE HORIZON FILM UNIT
Director of Production:
MAXWELL MUNDEN

SOUND-SERVICES LTD.
Managing Director: F. A. HOARE

General Production Manager: A. C. SNOWDEN
Studio Manager: W. H. WILLIAMS
Director of Animation Unit: T. R. THUMWOOD
Supervising Editor: JULIAN WINTLE
Scenario Editor: OSWALD SKILBECK
Music Editor: JOHN BATH
Operating Manager of Non-Theatrical Distribution: H. S. HIND
Commercial Manager of Non-Theatrical Distribution: E. S. MORDEN
Director of Cinema Distribution (Advertising Films): EDWARD BECKETT
Manager of Cinema Distribution (Advertising Films): R. THOMSON

combinations, the prospect for British films in the world market is poor indeed'.[40] Such business wisdom saw the FPG attract outside financial interest and investment. In 1955 the merchant bank Charterhouse took a 38 per cent share in Guild Holdings, which it increased to 92.5 per cent in 1969.[41]

Now, not only would it would be wrong to dismiss the Guild (as most of the Soho Square boys did to their cost) as merely a money-making enterprise of more interest to business historians than to film buffs. It would also be a misunderstanding of the business model itself: it was predicated on the partition of business and creative functions, thus freeing the creatives of many of the financial and administrative burdens that weighed down their counterparts in so many other documentary companies. Each of the FPG units had a different identity and clientele, and was further orientated by the individuals who acted as managing director and producers. Across a vast output, there was as much worthwhile documentary work made by film-makers deployed by companies within the Guild as without.

Verity Films remained by far the FPG's most prolific producer, with an output of at least 400 titles in the post-war period. In the range and quality of its work, Verity is best compared with World Wide: it marketed itself as a producer of industrial public relations and training films, and provided a safe pair of hands for the bigger-budget end of the sponsored-film spectrum. Verity's varied work ranges from steelmakers Richard Thomas & Baldwins' *Ingot Pictorial* cinemagazine through to Eric Marquis's *Time out of Mind* (1968) for Roche, and the diminutive *Divertimento* (1968) setting a Malcolm Arnold piece to the strange images visible through the microscopes of BP's Sunbury-on-Thames research station. Verity's successful commissions for the MOI during World War II paid dividends post-war with continuing contracts for the Ministry of Defence, the Army Kinema Corporation and the Admiralty. They also made many films for the Gas Council, including their *The Story of Gas* series (1954), and for the General Post Office. For much of the period the company was run by Oswald Skilbeck and, latterly, by Seafield Head, also a talented director.

Without question, Greenpark Productions, responsible for some 200 titles, was the Guild's 'Rolls Royce' service, the plushest and artiest of the companies: *the* quintessential prestige documentary unit.[42] Greenpark's earliest managing director, Ralph Keene, was a veteran of Strand, in many ways the closest of the 1930s Movement units to Greenpark aesthetics and Guild business thinking. Keene's *Cyprus is an Island* (1946) and *A String of Beads: A Tea Garden Idyll* (1948) and former Strand colleague John Eldridge's *Three Dawns to Sydney* (1948) set the pattern for Greenpark's post-war production: lyrical and literate, award-winning, international and essentially apolitical.

Produced by Keene's successor Paul Fletcher, Eldridge's *Waverley Steps* (1948) was an Edinburgh city symphony, feted by critics and festivals, but hated by the COI who had sponsored it. Given the lushness of its films, Greenpark was on occasion the Guild's loss-leader. Also produced by Fletcher, *West of England* (1951) was sponsored by the Board of Trade through the COI. Although its ostensible subject was the Gloucestershire cloth trade, typically its director Humphrey Swingler, with regular scriptwriter Laurie Lee, broadened it to a luxuriant Technicolor essay on the scenery, people and traditions of the Stroud valley. On Fletcher's departure, Swingler became Greenpark Productions' long-time post-war head, and a much-loved fixture of the documentary film industry. Humphrey was a scion of a wealthy, slightly bohemian family whose brothers were the communist poet Randall Swingler and the Labour MP Stephen Swingler. A former teacher, he had worked at Merton Park

Humphrey Swingler

Studios, at *March of Time* and with Jennings in Crown's cutting-rooms. Said to be somewhat unworldly (and another of documentary's famously heavy drinkers), he was able, as producer and sometime director at Greenpark, to indulge his aesthetic tastes without having to deal with the business issues that beset his counterparts outside the Guild.

Not everyone was convinced by Greenpark's pastoral poetry. Michael Clarke, a prominent director of sponsored films for BTF, Shell and others, remarked disparagingly that Greenpark's principle was to 'shoot a slum against the light and call it art', the broader argument being that the style epitomised a picturesque corruption of the British documentary film form.[43] It was undoubtedly an aesthetic that could fall into cliché but at its best – as in the better films by Derek Williams, the most talented of Greenpark's many contracted and freelancing directors – it was impressive. As in many of Williams's films, Greenpark was favoured by BP, its key post-war client. However, the company should not be typecast. For instance, a series of 1960s Midland Bank films, like *Meet the Midland* (1963) and *A Letter from Liz* (1965), both directed by Daniel Ingram, are free of lyricism and were considered some of the freshest films on the sponsored-film scene at the time.

Technique Film Productions was led by producer-director Ronald H. Riley; on its demise he moved to Verity but later founded, within the Guild, RHR Productions. Many of Riley's sponsors crossed over with those of Verity and Greenpark: success came with films like *Tribute to Fangio* (1959, directed by Riley) for BP, *Understanding Aggression* (1960) for the Ministry of Health and a series of novel and popular films sponsored by the British Insurance Association: *Six Candles* (1960), *Suspects All* (1964) and *The Stable Door*, the latter directed by none other than Pat Jackson. Another novelty hit was *Jam Session* (1962), a musical fantasy sales promo for Robertsons. The company also secured civil defence film contracts for the MoD, and produced a number of curiousities for Northern Ireland's Stormont government, such as *The Ulster Covenant* (1962). In 1965, Riley split from the FPG, forming Ronald H. Riley and Associates as a separate company that continued into the 1980s surviving Riley's own death in 1968 (one of its oddest associations was with Ken Loach, on the unhappy 1971 COI production *Talk About Work*, from which Loach withdrew his credit). The FPG, meanwhile, tried to switch RHR contracts to the newly formed Guild House Films headed by Anthony Pelissier and David Cobham.

Maxwell Munden, a Verity staffer, formed the Horizon Film Unit as a Guild associate in 1945; there he directed *Song of the People* (1945) for the Cooperative Wholesale Society, a remarkable film, and a socialist anomaly in the FPG credits. The company only lasted until 1947, when Munden formed Film Workshop with Dennis Shand. Film Workshop aimed for a 'practical, craftsmanship approach to the making of "films for a purpose"' aimed at the smaller-pocketed sponsor and the lower-budgeted productions of larger sponsors.[44]

Technical & Scientific Films (T&S), formed by Dr Denis Ward in 1949, and after Verity and Greenpark the third mainstay of the Guild, did exactly what it said on the tin. Much of Ward's output was commissioned for training purposes. *The Man Who Stops Accidents* (1954) trailblazed the concept of a safety film sponsored by one industry (steel firm Richard Thomas & Baldwins) that became widely distributed through industry at large. Generally, from the series *Practical Aspects of Farm Equipment Maintenance* (1949) for Esso, through to *Field Investigation Techniques* (1976) for the Central Water Planning Unit, T&S (nicknamed 'tickle and scratch' in the biz) skilfully and honestly ploughed its particular furrow of dry practicality, yielding some 250 productions all told.

In later years, T&S was headed by former DATA chairman Terrick Fitzhugh. Advertising and short promotional films were dealt with by Publicity Films and Merton Park Productions and later the Guild Television Service. Animated films were made by W. M. Larkins and the Larkins Studio, Britain's major producer of sponsored cartoons after Halas & Batchelor. The Interfilm unit, headed by a former Greenpark producer G. Buckland-Smith, specialised in productions with overseas sponsorship or foreign-location shoots. In 1959, the Guild was joined by Films of Today (FoT), who represented the 'mini market' dealing with smaller companies that could only afford 16mm production, the opposite end of the spectrum to Greenpark's 35mm top-drawer service.[45] The former niche expanded, however, as the latter slowly shrank. FoT's Managing Director Geoff Busby, later became MD of the Film Producers Guild itself and by 1972 was managing director of the holding company.

Despite such diversity of approach and marketplace dominance, the Guild was far from immune to the changing fortunes of sponsored film-making. In January 1975 it rationalised operations in a major reorganisation that saw the activities of its best-known subsidiaries – Verity, Greenpark and T&S – absorbed into the remaining five. Busby said at the time that the changes and their concomitant redundancies were 'sad but we are convinced that this reorganisation will provide a solid foundation for future developments in line with the requirements of the industry today'.[46] Greenpark had become too costly – the prestige documentary, though the most highly regarded type of sponsored film, was perhaps inevitably the first casualty of the industry's downturn. The following year saw further rationalisation when the Film Producers Guild merged with another production company, Cygnet Films (which had made generally undistinguished educational and sponsored documentaries since the early 1950s), to form Cygnet Guild Communications, wholly owned by Guild Sound and Vision.[47]

Owners, the Charterhouse Group, were evidently becoming less convinced by the value of the company and expressed a wish to decrease their interest in Cygnet Guild.[48] In November 1976 an opportunity to do so arose, and Esselte AB acquired the majority share in Guild Sound and Vision.[49] The Greenpark name was resurrected in 1979 for a film about a royal visit to the Middle East, *The Queen in Arabia*, for the Foreign and Commonwealth Office, but fewer and fewer companies were interested in such prestige product.[50] Guild Sound and Vision were still engaged in the industrial and educational market with a subsidiary, Guild Learning, distributing and occasionally producing material, and Guild Sponsored Services running a film library. But the game was up, really: between 1979 and 1982 film sales plummeted from 98 per cent to 60 per cent of Guild's business and continued falling thereafter.[51] Guild Sound and Vision moved into the lucrative new home video market, supplying cassettes to the new video-rental stores through subsidiary Guild Home Video.[52] It made valuable distribution deals with 20th Century-Fox and merged with Pathé in 1997. For a year it was known as Guild Pathé Cinema before simply becoming Pathé distribution in 1998, the Guild name finally making a quiet exit. Its former contribution to the best of British documentary, seen by millions worldwide, went unremarked.

MINORS AND MAJORS, IDEALISTS AND ADVERTISERS

> The 'film' has many faces – features, television, adverts and us, the documentary or short film producers. But are we considered as part of a 'something' because we use directors, writers, laboratories and cameras and are thought to be part of the eternal financial crises prevalent among the big boys? Are we looked upon by industry as a conglomerate of specialist individuals, each particularly weird in his own way, and consequently not considered as seriously as we think we should be? The short-film producers are, in fact, collectively geared to the making of films for and about the whole community: housing, environment, training, sales aids, trade and commerce, education etc., etc. *ad nauseam*. But what we do need is finance! We do not – perhaps unfortunately – make 'porn' films.
>
> Antony Barrier[53]

A number of the other small production companies that survived (even thrived) through the 1950s would, if pressed to define themselves, probably have said they were in the business of making short films. Their Documentary Movement connections were scant, and their doctrinal commitment to documentary small. They were not averse to dabbling in fictional shorts.

On the factual film side, their work was often with non-sponsored 'interest films', aimed at cinemas, exhibitors having a greater tolerance for independently produced supporting shorts in the early post-war than in the later. However, simple economics demanded these firms began to compete in the 'sponsored-film' market: those that survived into the 1960s did so by eventually making sponsorship the basis of their business. By this point the distinction between their work and that of self-styled 'documentary' companies was irrelevant. For sponsors, these businesslike producers delivered solid, generally unexceptional films to budget and schedule. They often achieved business stability by hooking up with one or two regular, small-scale sponsors, occasionally winning more commissions from swisher sponsors like the oil companies. Typically, these companies had entrepreneurs in charge, and a skeleton staff of in-house creatives and technicians, frequently supplemented with freelance hires.

Increasingly these hires were high-profile ones, often drawn from the core school of British documentary. Three examples – Rayant Pictures, Wallace Productions and British Films – suffice to illustrate this branch of the business.

Rayant Pictures turned out some 300 works between 1947 and 1979. At first, under the creative stewardship of producer Anthony Gilkison, Rayant concentrated on anonymous, enjoyable non-sponsored shorts, frequently directed by William Pollard, theatrically released through 20th Century-Fox.[54] Rayant's most notable interest films were the *Spotlight* series of two-reelers. Narrated by Robert Beatty, each edition informatively but breezily covered a single subject; for example, *Spotlight on Crime* (1947) detailed the workings of Scotland Yard.

From the mid-1950s, the balance of Rayant's productions altered and by the mid-1960s sponsored productions dominated workload. Pollard, having moved to the Film Producers Guild, was replaced as resident director by John Durst (himself formerly at the Guild), and after Gilkison's departure in 1964, Durst took over production duties. As Rayant's portfolio and budgets grew, highly rated directors were brought in: Margaret Thomson on one occasion, Sarah Erulkar and BTF mainstay Kenneth Fairbairn on several more. Benefiting from an established reputation for economical location work, Rayant became one of the British Travel Association's favourite producers. For industry, alongside sporadic film-making for BP, Unilever, the Gas Council and the United Steel Companies, Rayant shot a sequence of films following the trail of the Burmah Oil Company's surveying programme and became principal film-maker for major engineering firm GKN. Early Rayant/COI projects were simple records of royal visits abroad, but led to slightly more expensive commissions for home departments, like *Atomic Achievement* (1956), about Calder Hall. The company's biggest boost came from the GPO's revitalised interest in film. This first brought simple films like *Right from the Start* (1965), part of a campaign to recruit clerical staff, but culminated in *Picture to Post* (1969), the most celebrated GPO film made since Film Unit days. Unfortunately, the onset of the sector's general decline meant that Rayant would never again make such a prestigious production, though work for much the same range of sponsors continued through the 1970s, the company's last documented productions, in 1979, being for a business on the brink of growth: Barratt Homes.

By pursuing sponsorship in parallel with other sources of income, Wallace Productions made a range of solid and occasionally inspired contributions to documentary. The company's first resident producer was A. V. Curtice, later joined and then superseded by Frank Bundy, an industry veteran who had photographed scores of Gaumont-British Instructional films in the 1930s (including Rotha's *The Face of Britain*, 1935). In fact, an important basis of the company's work was a contractual arrangement made with Gaumont-British Instructional in 1945, whereby Wallace made films in the *Our Club Magazine* series for Rank's Children's Educational Film Department. Concurrently, Wallace made a short-lived series of children's natural history films, *Tales of the Woodland*, based on Enid Blyton stories. Later, and up until the late 1960s, Wallace was a regular contributor of short features and serials to the Children's Film Foundation. The company also actively pursued contracts for short advertising films. Simply put, documentary was just another line of business.

The company alternated cheaper films directed by the likes of Bundy or fellow staff member J. E. Ewins, with more expensive ones headed by bought-in documentary film-makers of wider reputation. John Taylor, Brian Salt and Paul Dickson all made at least one Wallace film each; Max Anderson, Bill Mason and Stephen Cross made several. Wallace had two long-term client relationships. One was United Dairies, but far more notable was Wallace's work for the United Steel Companies: relatively costly documentaries, commendably attentive to aesthetic form. An earlier example of the company's

willingness to experiment in this direction had been Taylor's Ford Motors film, *Opus 65* (1952). This was one of several one-off industrial commissions taken on by Wallace in the 1950s and '60s: other sponsors included Courtaulds, Massey Ferguson and Whitbread. For the public sector, Wallace made the earliest British Productivity Council films, at least one internal training film each for the NCB and BTF, and some COI/Ministry of Agriculture films on beef production. Mysteriously, the last recorded credit to Wallace Productions is for a film called *I Want to Be Happy* (1972), an off-beat short about the day in the life of a London busker – directed by Patrick, Lord Lichfield, better known as a photographer and minor royal.

Before gaining independence in 1930, British Films had been the production unit of the Conservative and Unionist Film Association. The core of British's business was film exhibition. Its patented 'Filmobile' (Landrovers converted into mobile projection units) were supplied – 2,000 of them – to eighty-six countries (this success was recognised with a Queen's Award for Export Achievement in 1977). But British doubled as a busy if low-rent production company. Alongside its stolid resident film-maker William Hammond, some notable names occasionally fetched up at the firm, usually out of financial necessity. They included Jack Howells, ex-Massingham associate Michael Law and, late in his career, J. B. Holmes. Following the demise of his own short-lived company (GBS Films) former Film Producers Guild man G. Buckland-Smith joined British Films, running its production programme for ten years from 1970 until his death. British continued for a few more years, sustained by such varied fare as alcohol-concern films for the RAF, campaign films for anti-vivisection groups and BP-sponsored North Sea films.

Among the other companies more or less fitting the same profile as Rayant, Wallace and British are: Anglo-Scottish (prolific with early COI and later Films of Scotland commissions), Holdsworth

Films/Gerard Holdsworth Productions (whose clients included Whitbread and the MoD as well as Unilever and Ford, Esso and BP), United Motion Pictures (COI and Ford) and Random Film Productions, who worked for the less prestigious oil sponsors, notably National Benzole.

The short-film interests of the big boys of commercial cinema also deserve mention. Pathé and Rank both sporadically invested in the documentary film. In the case of Associated British Pathé, the early post-war creation of the Pathé Documentary Unit was a significant development, arising from head producer Howard Thomas's intention to break with the frivolity of the pre-war newsreel and develop Pathé's post-war output in a more sober new direction. The Documentary Unit's personnel included a senior producer, Peter Baylis, who had been both at *March of Time* and at the Shell Film Unit; Gerard Bryant who had been at Crown and would later spend many years in the NCB Film Unit; and Peter Bradford and Jack Howells, who had come from Rotha and DATA respectively. While initiating some of its own productions – compilation films drawing on Pathé's archive, theatrically released – the Unit took on work from similar sponsors to those of the other documentary producers (including the COI, the British Travel Association, the Gas Council and various charities and oil companies), whose quality matched the best of their competitors'. From the mid-1950s 'Pathé Documentary Unit' was no longer used on screen but under the label of the parent company, and now overseen by Terry Ashwood, documentaries continued to be made until 1970 and the demise of Pathé as a stand-alone company.

Rank's relationship with non-fiction was more fickle. J. Arthur Rank was behind the *This Modern Age* series (1946–50), which, under the influence of *March of Time*, brought documentary sobriety and serious subject matter to the cinemagazine; and documentary features like Jill Craigie's *The Way We Live* (1946). These were short-lived experiments, however. On the educational front, the venerable Gaumont-British Instructional was effectively closed by attrition, as the result of a series of mergers beginning in 1953. For the most part, Rank's successor, John Davis, showed little interest in documentary until the launch of the full-colour *Look at Life* (1959–69) cinemagazine series. At first well received, *Look at Life* developed a reputation for bland glibness, especially compared to the increasing maturity of television current affairs; however, its range of subjects is quite impressive (everything from change in Africa, to the modern jazz scene to current breeds of cats). Its greater significance of was its stranglehold on the supporting slot at Rank's cinemas, resented in the documentary business for preventing others getting near these screens. However, the Rank Organisation Short Films Group brought Rank closer to the documentary world by taking commissions from many of the established sponsors, including the British Productivity Council, BP and the COI. The Group's *Revolutions for All* (1967), made by regular director Jeff Inman for Churchmans cigar manufacturers (featuring Denis Norden on an amusing tour round their factory), was a non-theatrical novelty hit. At the same time, the Group pioneered the practice of making training films which were produced speculatively rather than under sponsorship, then made commercially available to employers: for example, a series of films entitled *The Customer and You*, the most famous being *Who Killed the Sale?* (1970), directed by Michael Tuchner (better known as a television, and later feature, director). This business model, spreading in the 1970s (most famously at Video Arts), was part and parcel of the decline of the short documentary by making a distinct discipline of film as a training tool.

In the meantime, however, beyond these small corners of big empires, from the late 1950s onwards came a spurt of new producers. In common with the Rayants and Wallaces, these were often companies with tiny core staffs, supplemented by freelancers. Unlike those older firms, they were driven less by honest commercialism than a desire for independence.

First, there were firms set up by producers and directors who had been at bigger production companies and now sought greater autonomy or a larger slice of the financial cake. Examples include Jack Howells Productions, Michael Orrom's Film Drama, Ray Elton & Partners (set up by a veteran of *March of Time*, the Film Producers Guild and the Rank Short Films Group) and David Cobham Productions (headed by a former Guild film-maker later best known for the family feature film *Tarka the Otter* ([1978] and many TV productions thereafter). One of the most significant was Anthony Gilkison Associates, headed by the veteran former producer at Rayant Pictures. Describing itself both as a production consultancy and as a production company, it made around seventy films between 1960 and 1975. Moving away from formulaic solutions to familiar briefs, Gilkison's films evidence an awareness that the tastes of the 'general audience' were becoming more sophisticated. They increasingly commanded decent budgets, enabling him to bring in good directors, including Sarah Erulkar, her husband Peter de Normanville, Stephen Cross and John Armstrong.

A particularly fruitful relationship was with the Gas Council, who, having been pleased by several cookery films produced by Gilkison with Erulkar directing, entrusted to the same team *The Air My Enemy* (1971), the gas industry's most costly and successful film ever. Turning to the smaller-scale sponsors, projects for the Jersey, Irish and Israeli tourist authorities made Gilkison's firm something of a specialist in promoting overseas travel to British viewers. In a very different register, de Normanville made, for the OECD, *Co-Operation is our Business* (1970). Regular work came from Castrol and from Vauxhall Motors.

Through films for the food and drinks industries, alongside their work for the Gas Council, Gilkison's filmography took on an Epicurean flavour, as in *Sugar in Your Kitchen* (1969), *Bread – Something of a Miracle* (1974), *Wine* (1967), *A Round of Bass* (1972) and *This is your Guinness* (1975). It's tempting to assume these films to be naff dispatches from the culinary dark ages – and that isn't entirely untrue. Yet they do have a certain interest as signs, alongside the growth in cookery programming on television, of our national Puritanism in plodding retreat. Their high production values also reflect an attempt to think the subject through in cinematic rather than televisual terms: perhaps a fool's errand. If nothing else, Anthony Gilkison and Associates' films provide a good gauge of what counted as modern, tasteful documentary of broad non-theatrical appeal during the final heyday of industrial sponsorship.

In the late 1960s, John Armstrong a former Shell staffer, formed Pelican Films, which transcended its small size to establish a reputation for polished, 35mm location film-making, confirmed by an Oscar nomination for *The End of the Road* (1976). Armstrong worked closely with Alan Pendry and hired film-makers like Peter de Normanville, Michael Clarke and Derek Williams to write, produce or direct on a freelance basis. Edward Williams contributed several characteristically good scores. Above all, it was admirable photography by such varied veterans as Adrian Jeakins, Walter Lassally, Billy Williams, Charles Stewart (better known for his television work, with Roger Graef and others) and, frequently, Ron Bicker, that furnished Pelican's superior house style. Deployment of multiple cameras was, incidentally, a signature Pelican technique.

The new company's first release was *Raceday* (1967), a Le Mans film for Shell International. The Shell group went on to sponsor several other early productions, but Armstrong was meanwhile attracting significant mid-budget industrial clients such as the British Steel Corporation, Joseph Lucas Ltd (a household name as a leading manufacturer of motorcar and aerospace components) and the Cement and Concrete Association. From the mid-1970s, Pelican's core sponsor was BP, via its new films officer Ian Brundle who, like Armstrong and Pendry, had a Shell background. Pelican became a prodigious chronicler of the planning, development, oil recovery and pipelining associated with BP's Forties and Buchan fields in the North Sea. Pelican's last major production was directed by Pendry for the Abu Dhabi Gas Liquefaction Company. *The Flame Moves East* (1978) commemorated the building of an energy-saving new plant, and the incongruous Arab-Japanese partnership behind it. *The Flame* was designed for screening to politicians and civil servants as well as to the public, a tribute to Britain's enduring reputation for prestige film-making – if only among overseas clients. Pelican's last work, a sporadically released BP series called *This Earth* (1984–93), was a far cry from Academy glory. Distributed to schools on video, these programmes were latter-day contributions to the oil sponsors' longstanding educational mission: to encourage younger viewers' awareness of geology, environmental science and some ecological considerations, while effacing the sponsors' own presence. Pelican Films ceased activity on Armstrong's retirement, when this solid but less than earth-shattering series came to an end.

Antony Barrier was an ex-Ranker who struck out on his own with the enterprising Antony Barrier Productions in 1969. He too attracted film directors of good calibre such as Erulkar, de Normanville, Joe Mendoza, David Eady, Richard Taylor, Philip Owtram and Robin Jackson.[55] Eventually making a partial switch to video, Barrier stayed in business until 1984. He scored an early try with Taylor's *William Webb Ellis – Are You Mad?* (1970), commissioned by the Rugby Union for its centennial celebrations, very popular on the non-theatrical circuit. However, the breadth and variety of his work suggests a genuine interest in integrating business skills with sincere mainstream (apolitical) film-making. Barrier Productions' filmography thus includes Post Office documentaries, good industrial films for Esso and the electricity and nuclear industries, several shorts for the GLC and French-teaching aids for Mary Glasgow Publications (for whom Ray Elton & Partners produced English-teaching films).

Several provocative charity films produced by Barrier deserve a special mention. Owtram's *A Man's World* (1973) and *Men Apart* (1973), respectively sponsored by industry (Esso) and by charity (the Royal National Mission to Deep Sea Fishermen), were commendably dour portraits of the East Coast fishing life with a little of the *Drifters* inheritance in them. Mendoza's film *Out of the Darkness* (1972), sponsored by Christian Aid, stands out merely by being one of pitifully few sponsored documentaries directly tackling racism against non-white immigrants to Britain and (most of the film being shot on the India-Pakistan border) drawing attention to the poverty from which many of them had come. Erulkar and de Normanville made of *The Living City* (1977), another Christian Aid film, an effective and moving portrait of Calcutta. On the debit side, the company was not above contributions to the ignoble art of saddling documentaries about already unpromising subjects with heroically bad titles. To whit: *Sludge – An Asset to Agriculture* (1978).

In contrast to these more-or-less conventional business ventures, an intriguing 1960s development was the brief re-emergence of the youthful, politically conscious documentary producer. The key name here is that of Derrick Knight, a former employee of Realist and the Film Producers Guild. Heading his own company, Derrick Knight & Partners, from 1958, Knight became one of the most interesting figures in 1960s British film culture. Bert Hogenkamp tells the story of Knight and his firm in this book's final chapter, so full details need not be repeated here. DATA offers an interesting comparison, Knight's being a later attempt at reconciling leftish idealism with running a business efficiently. Although both cases reveal a gap between aims and outcomes, Knight & Partners were arguably more successful, in respect of producing a more varied, more contemporary body of work for a wider sponsor group, while yet managing to make a few genuinely independent productions.

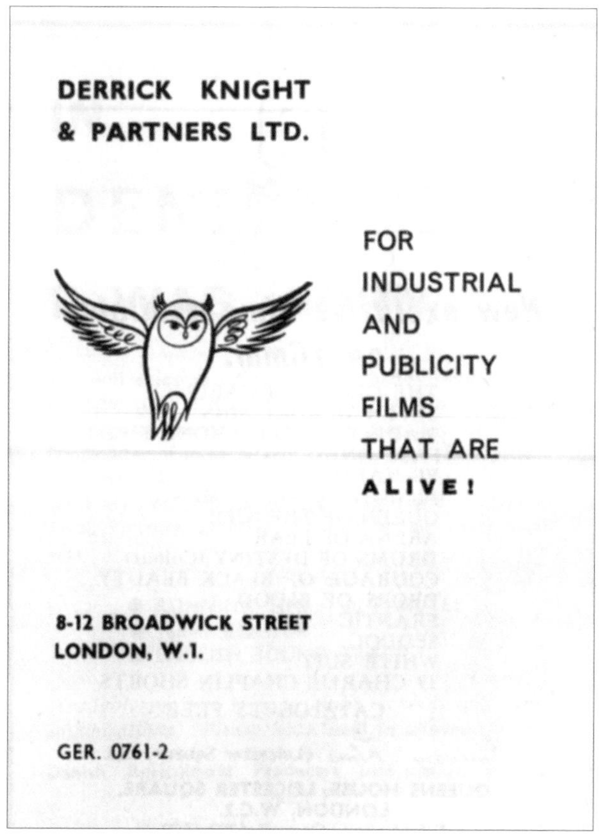

(Comparable contemporaries – Mithras Films and its offshoot David Naden Associates – had less sustained impact on mainstream documentary, partly because they did not confine themselves to factual film-making, and partly because, positioning themselves further to the left, they engaged less enthusiastically with standard sponsorship.)

Sensitive to the modern scene, Knight's company applied a Direct Cinema-influenced technique to British industrial documentary in its most important film *A Time to Heal* (1963); and also took serious interest in the television medium, the best of several productions for the BBC being *Travelling for a Living* (1965). Of course, compared to Direct Cinema in the USA, or to 1930s Griersonianism, Knight & Partners' influence was small, their achievements were limited and their experiment, ultimately, financially unsustainable.[56] Politically they were soon to be dated by the emergence of hard-left film cooperatives who decried the compromise of mediation and for whom the concept of industrial patronage was unconscionable.[57]

A non-political, but socially conscious and artistically engaged, film production company was that owned by Anne Balfour-Fraser, which produced about a hundred documentaries between 1958 and 1983. Though running a permanently low-budget outfit, Balfour-Fraser was in a secure enough financial position for the character of its output to be informed by her humanitarian and artistic interests. (It also benefited from the producer's good connections; for instance, Elisabeth Lutyens, a cousin, composed the music for several productions.) Directors were always hired freelance, and Balfour employed some very good ones. Some notable names, like David Muir, Peter Jessop, Kevin Brownlow and Mamoun Hassan, worked at the company as cinematographers or editors.

Balfour-Fraser came from the distinguished Balfour family (she was the granddaughter of Gerald, brother of Arthur) and had graduated from the Royal Academy of Music. Her first film work was under the trading name of Inca, applied to a series of *Music in Miniature* films distributed to cinemas, and miscellaneous other productions including the short fiction film *Simon* (1956), popular at international festivals. On securing several commissions for sponsored films on medical subjects, Balfour-Fraser renamed the company Samaritan Films. Having significantly broadened its output and wary of being typecast, in 1970 she renamed Samaritan Balfour Films. The name Inca was also revived when Balfour-Fraser began making films for sponsors or audiences in the Middle East – the family name being anathema there.

Besides medical and Middle Eastern films, Balfour-Fraser had three areas of activity. Charities that commissioned work from Samaritan/Balfour included the Royal Commonwealth Society for the Blind, the Spastics Society and the Leprosy Relief Association. Films on planned parenthood were translated into many languages. Samaritan's outstanding production was *I Think They Call Him John* (1964), a study of old age directed with piercing intensity by John Krish. On the same subject, another excellent and moving short was *Cast Us Not Out* (1969), directed by Richard Bigham. Funded, unusually, by the Jewish Welfare Board, it framed its account of the homes run by the sponsor in a general indictment of society's attitudes to the aged.

A second strand, probably Balfour-Fraser's favourite, was films about visual art. She became one of the Arts Council's favourite producers, and one of the few that made mainstream sponsored films as well as Arts Council productions. Most of these arts films were made by two directors. One was Dudley Shaw Aston, who had attracted notice for his 1950s BFI-funded films about Barbara Hepworth and Coventry Cathedral. The other was the much younger David Thompson, who directed many titles including *The Pre-Raphaelite Revolt* (1967) and *Monet in London* (1974).

Finally, Balfour-Fraser, like Gilkison and Barrier, made films financed by major documentary sponsors, including the COI and BP. The COI films allocated to her were often documentaries about the caring professions commissioned by the Ministry of Health and its successor the DHSS. Erulkar's award-winning Home Office film for children, *Never Go with Strangers* (1970), was one of the most socially significant of the COI's 1970s use of the documentary sector. Samaritan/Balfour also made around ten BP films, directed by highly rated oil documentary specialists including de Normanville, Williams and Owtram. Williams's *Turkey – The Bridge* (1966) is well off the beaten track, being almost entirely focused on archaeology and the history of ancient civilisations. Later, Balfour-Fraser was a beneficiary of BP's increasing interest in films about energy and the environment, as in de Normanville's *Energy in Perspective* (1976). Williams's exceptionally attractive *The Shetland Experience* (1977), sponsored by the Sullom Voe Environmental Advisory Group, was Oscar-nominated (as had been *Turkey – The Bridge*). The company also took on work for smaller sponsors. Balfour-Fraser also even did some films for the Children's Film Foundation: the short feature *Junket 89* (1970) and a series of shorts, *The Trouble with 2B* (1972).

A very different manifestation of the 1960s' spirit of independence were the growing links between the advertising industry and the documentary shorts business. For instance, Charles Barker Films was an offshoot of the well-established advertising agency of that name, and became a fixture on the BISFA festival scene from the mid-1960s (as did successor company Wadlow Grosvenor Productions). Cammell Hudson Associates was a partnership between Donald Cammell and Hugh Hudson (later famed for making *Chariots of Fire*). Among their half dozen sponsored films, *The Tortoise and the Hare* (1966), directed by Hudson and photographed by Wolfgang Suschitzky, was one of the most crowd-pleasing sponsored films of the decade, though not for the documentary purist: it was a flashy modern vehicle for Pirelli tyres resetting Aesop's fable on the Italian motorways and 'starring' a goods lorry and an E-type Jaguar. James Garrett and Partners was one of London's most successful and influential advertising production companies, in business for forty years from 1963. Its main excursion into sponsored shorts came in a sequence in the mid-1970s for the COI.

The most important, James Archibald & Associates, was the creation of the former head of film and television at J. Walter Thompson. At JWT, James Archibald had pioneered the practice of bringing in established film directors most of whom, hitherto, had shunned commercials. Reflecting Archibald's background, the new company sought to invigorate sponsored shorts with the youthful contemporary inspiration and stimulating, stylish techniques of modern advertising while responsibly documenting serious subjects. Archibald's speciality proved to be government films given, by the COI's admittedly staid standards, a slightly experimental edge; and films for NGOs, especially in the arts field. *Opus* (1967) and *Music!* (1968) had fair claim to being the most ambitious British-sponsored films of their moment, subconsciously filtering the 'state-of-the-nation' perspective of 1940s documentary through the spirit of the late 1960s. COI officials were conscious that *Opus*, a documentary impression of contemporary arts and culture in Britain, was their most important production of recent times, commissioned by the Foreign Office for continuous projection in the British Pavilion at Expo 67 in Montreal prior to worldwide distribution. Archibald made an unusual choice of director in experimental film-maker Don Levy, who turned out a frenetic montage piece whose vision of Swinging London, beneath the strains of both The Beatles and electronic composition, embraces Marat/Sade and Mary Quant alike. *Music!* updated the *Listen to Britain* concept by encapsulating a day in the nation's life with counterpointed documentary vignettes of its musical culture, from pub sing-alongs to the Proms via brass bands and The Beatles. A rare piece of film sponsorship by the National Music Council of Great Britain, this was directed by Michael Tuchner. Because the freelance crews Archibald brought in to make his films were not usually drawn from the 'usual suspects' of documentary production, his company is easily neglected. It remained active until his untimely death in 1983. Though some of his films have inevitably dated, as a body of work they stand up well and deserve further exploration.

NOTES

1. DATA appeal (undated) for support-shareholders and investment, Donald Alexander collection, National Library of Scotland: SSA 4/20/12.
2. Strasser, officially billed in his later Realist years as 'producer of scientific and educational films' subsequently wrote the manual *The Work of the Science Film Maker* (London: Focal Press, 1972). He remained with Realist into the 1960s. The other key directors working under Taylor during World War II were Brian Smith, Margaret Thomson and Philip Leacock, all of whom left at earlier stages.
3. Ken Cameron was the brother of famed journalist and author James Cameron, whose writing and speech graces not a few sponsored documentaries, as well as television broadcasts. Examples include Philip Leacock's Crown film *Festival in London* (1951), several BP and Unilever films, and the aforementioned *Traffic in Towns* (1963).
4. Alexander and Chambers were among those who resigned their membership of the Communist Party of Great Britain following the Soviet crushing of Hungarian rebellion in 1956. On its establishment, DATA was quickly accepted as a member of the Cooperative Productive Federation. It was only after persistent lobbying that in 1949 the most prestigious cooperative organisation, the Cooperative Union, welcomed DATA in its midst. Under DATA's constitution, all permanent employees could become members, on a one member one vote basis, whatever their function or seniority, and elected the management committee, initially chaired by Alexander, which ran the company day-to-day and reported back to them.
5. Beales was married at the time to fellow DATA member Francis Gysin, and later to Michael Orrom. She later became a sculptor.
6. The cooperative movement was already becoming less stridently political: it proved too difficult to shift its ingrained assumption that film was essentially a minor sales aid. DATA made a handful of undistinguished films in this vein: a more ambitious planned film for the Cooperative Production Federation had to be cancelled (while the only trade union that was willing to commission any films

was the minor National Union of Tailors and Garment Workers). On industrial sponsorship DATA's administrator, and soon-to-be-chairman Terrick Fitzhugh advised in a memo: 'there are within Data, two different schools of thought ... ranging from those to whom we are an ordinary film unit, more scrupulous and with higher purposes than others, but still prepared to trim our sails to economic gales, and operating in the same sphere as, and in competition with, for example, the various components of the Film Producers Guild; up to those to whom our higher purpose sets us quite apart from such units and involve a corresponding difference in methods of operation; we are more reserved, we stand on our reputation and choose our sponsors carefully, we do not solicit work but invite consultation.' Terrick Fitzhugh, 'Promotion' SSA: 4/20/1.3. Regarding Alexander's leadership, one of the cooperative's youngest members remembers: 'there were rumblings of discontent, usually to be heard in the café below 21 Soho Square ... or in Victor's café virtually next door to the *Mining Review* offices in Greek Street ... Jack Chambers was – although never aggressively seeking to be – the popular alternative leader sought by the younger generation'. Peter Pickering, 'A Brief & Very Subjective History of DATA' (2009, Word Document supplied to the authors by Pickering), p. 2.

7. Interestingly, Alexander wrote to the committee that 'I am exhausted with the futility of attempting to make middle-class young men either into co-operators or into social film-makers ... who have been brought up with all the usual middle-class advantages ... They are inhibited utterly by their upbringing and by the nature of the film industry from belonging to the class struggle or understanding it.' SSA: 4/20/10.
8. 'The Economic Plan as at August 10th 1949', SSA: 4/10/9, predicted turnover for next six months – £9,600 out of £14,767 to come from *Mining Review*.
9. *Mining Review* was at first run by Leslie Shepherd and Terrick Fitzhugh reporting to Alexander (with Dick Storey editing) within DATA's total programme (overseen by Alexander). Francis Gysin produced the series between 1952 and 1958. Following his departure, Peter Whale was brought in to run the series along with Budge Cooper, together with Robert Kruger, who had taken over from Dick Storey as editor. Whale and Cooper were both employed by the NCB rather than DATA, and a decidedly odd couple: Cooper a fiery feminist, Whale a conservative ex-Movietone man.
10. 'DATA reached the zenith/nadir of democratic operation in the late 50s when the committee itself – with no single overall executive producer "running" the unit – became virtual general manager and executive producer in one ... It petered out somewhat nastily, as being a co-operative the (few) remaining assets had somehow to be fairly shared among the members. There is some doubt as to whether they were!', Pickering, 'A Brief & Very Subjective History of DATA', p. 4.
11. 'Leon always had the last word. I once rejected a suggestion from him on the grounds it was an "old cliché". "What's wrong with a good cliché?" It should be engraved on his tombstone.' Euan Pearson, 'Leon Clore – A Memoir', 24 November 2009, unpublished document supplied by Pearson to the authors.
12. Lindsay Anderson, 'Free Cinema', *Universities & Left Review* vol. 1 no. 2, Summer 1957, p. 52.
13. Clore gave Lassally his first lighting cameraman job on a short for the COI. Lassally and the equally talented Pizer became mainstays of Basic and Graphic Films.
14. Anon., 'The Times Diary; A Clore with a Diaghilev Touch', *The Times*, 18 April 1968, p. 10.
15. Leon was the nephew of Sir Charles Clore, the financier and property magnate. Charles reputedly gave his nephew a block of flats in Chelsea as a wedding gift.
16. Basic's staff apparently wanted to make cinema commercials, which ran counter to how Neilson-Baxter saw the company. Napier-Bell sided with the staff, out-voting Neilson-Baxter who resigned in disgust,

the idealism of the unit's purpose having failed to match the idealism of its democratic structure. It was a tension comparable to that at DATA, the socialised mixed economy paradoxically confusing the role and intentions of the politically aware documentarian. Clore had first entered the film industry in the 1930s as a clapperboy, at Stoll Pictures then at Gaumont-British. He worked on the second unit of Hitchcock's *Sabotage*. At Crown, Clore had directed one film, *Beet Sugar* (1949), from which he concluded that directing was not his own forté. Despite this, he was in effect a convinced auteurist long before the term was popularised, believing that the director was creatively responsible for the film, and that the producer's job was to support the director in achieving his vision for it.

17. Besides Anderson's well-known left-wing sympathies, Napier-Bell was a Communist Party member (albeit the sort of communist who sends his sons to public school) until 1956. In 1950 he and camera assistant Clement Gayton were arrested in London; they and other socialist film-makers had been out in force to record police action at the banned May Day demonstrations. Anon., 'May Day Demonstrations: Convictions and Acquittals', *The Times*, 17 May 1950, p. 3. This was the event filmed by Anthony Simmons, as described by Michael Brooke in his piece on Simmons in Part II. In his BECTU History Project interview, Clore claims to have been left-wing when young, and to have become right-wing once mature.
18. Tom Stobart, *I Take Pictures For Adventure* (New York: Doubleday, 1957), p. 204.
19. Where the company remained until 1 Soho Square was bought by Paul McCartney (McCartney Productions Ltd [MPL]) in the 1970s, and Clore relocated across Soho to Golden Square.
20. The company was registered at Companies House on 25 June 1949. It was originally used as a vehicle for making filmstrips.
21. The company was registered earlier on 7 September 1955. A 1960s publicity handout declared that: 'Film Contracts Limited ... with its consistent high level of talent in its group of film-makers, is a guarantee of quality product. Although accustomed to feature film work, where action may be developed in leisurely fashion to be reckoned in minutes, they have evolved new techniques to compress mood, scene-setting, action and sales punch cinematically into a 30-second or even 15-second spot. Continually to refresh creative talent is always a problem: Film Contracts Limited tackles it by encouraging its film-makers to alternate their work on commercials with feature and documentary films.' This eventually proved the firm's undoing, its directors too often unavailable due to those prior commitments.
22. Losey made television advertisements for Horlicks and Fray Bentos at Film Contracts in the 1960s.
23. The film used the device of bored salesmen in reverie and combined gorillas and ex-circus elephants from Twycross Zoo, a stripper from Paul Raymond's Revue bar, a commentary by children's TV favourite Johnny Morris and the sponsor's carpets. (The film, sadly, like many industrially sponsored titles, is lost to time.)
24. R. S. [Ronald Strode], 'They Make Your Films: No. 3 World Wide Pictures Ltd', *Film Sponsor*, August 1950, p. 376.
25. The authors are grateful to Ray Townsend of World Wide Pictures for providing information on the company's incorporation and registration.
26. Carr let out his frustrations in a letter to the editor of *Documentary News Letter* vol. 3 no. 2, February 1942, p. 29, complaining of 'discrimination between those who are within a small, self-appointed coterie of "leaders of documentary" and those who are not'.
27. James Carr, 'Sponsor and Producer; A Creative Partnership', *Public Relations*, April 1953.
28. R. S., Ibid.

29. Quoted in Graham Wade, 'Big Budget Clients Not After Cheapos', *Broadcast*, 28 June 1985, pp. 14–15. Whether or not this is a conscious dig at John Schlesinger whose brief career at World Wide Pictures overlapped with Parris's long one, the dates are out: *Terminus* was released in 1961. Amusingly Schlesinger believed that World Wide had little time for him, because he had ideas 'above my station', recalled in William J. Mann, *Edge of Midnight: The Life of John Schlesinger* (London: Hutchinson, 2004), p. 134.
30. Anon. [Our Industrial Staff], 'Film-Making in the City', *The Times*, 4 April 1962, p. 17.
31. Anon., 'Show Business Group Seek An ITV Contract "Marrying Creative Ability With Management"', *The Times*, 12 December 1963, p. 4.
32. Ken Roberts [press release on behalf of World Wide Pictures Ltd], 19 August 1974, Oxford Public Relations, BFI Special Collections, Ken Gay collection Box 52.
33. Derek Harris, 'Growth is in Industry and Commerce', *The Times*, 25 January 1980, Audio-Visual Supplement, p. I.
34. Parris had been a managing director of the company since 1965, see Anon., 'A New Team Takes Over at Top', *World Wide News* (1977), Ken Gay collection, Box 59.
35. Christopher Courtney Taylor, marketing director of World Wide Pictures, quoted in Wade, 'Big Budget Clients Not After Cheapos'.
36. Inside headlines to Film Producers Guild publicity leaflet c. 1965.
37. Until 1947 the company in ownership was known as Sound-Services Ltd. Upon becoming Guild Holdings, the brand name of Sound-Services was retained for the Guild's film distribution activity. The name changed officially on 20 January 1947. See 'Production Companies; Feature Films and Documentaries', in Peter Noble (ed.), *The British Film Yearbook 1949–1950* (London: Skelton Robinson, 1949), p. 263.
38. The Film Producers Guild Ltd, *British Film Production Company Leads World* (The Film Producers Guild Ltd, 26th April 1968), Ken Gay collection, Box 16 File 28.
39. The Film Producers Guild placed advertisements for its services in eleven separate editions of *The Economist* between 17 February 1945 and 11 January 1947.
40. F. A. Hoare, 'State and Industry; Letters to the Editor', *The Times*, 23 March 1944, p. 5.
41. Guild Holdings Limited, *Staff Benefits No.2: An Explanatory Booklet for Employees of Guild Holdings Ltd* (Guild Holdings Ltd, 1971), Ken Gay collection Box 26. The major investors prior to 1969 were the London Press Exchange, the Charterhouse Industrial Development Co. and the Ambrose Investment Trust.
42. Derrick Knight refers to the 'plushy-prestige or Rolls Royce filming of Greenpark' in a 1966 draft of his book 'A Long Look at Short Films' (unpublished, supplied to the authors). Incidentally, it was other Guild companies RHR Productions and Verity Films that produced films *for* Rolls Royce.
43. Michael Clarke, 'Notes on the Shell Film Unit and Film Centre', January 1994, (unpublished) (held by BFI National Library).
44. Ronald Strode, 'They Make Your Films: No. 5 Film Workshops Ltd', *Film Sponsor*, October 1950, pp. 13, 30.
45. 'mini-market': Knight, 'A Long Look at Short Films'.
46. The Film Producers Guild Limited, press release (27 January 1975), Ken Gay collection Box 44.
47. Cygnet Guild Communications Limited 'Cygnet Guild Communications – Background Information', press release (20 February 1979), Ken Gay collection Box 58.
48. Anon., 'Briefly: Business and Finance', *The Times*, 10 January 1976, p. 19.

49. The Charterhouse Group, 'Swedish Company to Acquire Major Stake in Guild Sound And Vision', news release (4 November 1976), BFI Special Collections Ken Gay collection Box 49.
50. Greenpark Productions Limited, Greenpark Productions, press release, n.d. (1979), Ken Gay collection Box 59.
51. Anon., 'Guild-ing the Video Libraries', *Audio Visual* no. 129, September 1982, p. 32.
52. Ibid., p. 31.
53. Antony Barrier, 'Goodbye To All Fat', *Ad Weekly*, 5 May 1972, Films supplement, p. 3.
54. A loss to posterity particularly to be regretted is 1952's *Dark London*, a short about the capital city's burgeoning black community, which has apparently not survived.
55. Barrier even once secured Pat Jackson for a rare return to documentary (*Beajamar* [1970], a Bahamas tourist promotion for BOAC).
56. A comparison with Grierson is not absurd. Knight similarly gathered a group of young talents around him to turn out a variety of films, and pursued sponsorship with faith in its benevolent potential, as an aid to the increasing self-awareness of an industrial society very differently structured than in Grierson's time. Knight wrote, for instance: 'I envisage a completely fresh approach to the use of film which will give it a vital role in the dialogue between company and customer, management and worker; between industrial complex as a living organism and the society in which it exists.'
57. An exception was Liberation Films, which become a fertile producer of health and sex education 'trigger' films in the 1970s.

5 Sponsorship

As diverse as producers, sponsors were at least as complex. Documentary had a range of uses, more or less broad, defined and determined by the mechanics and costs of production and distribution, and by motives that varied but were almost never financial. Sponsoring a documentary, unlike backing a feature film, was rarely a speculative investment. That it was a loss leader was more or less a given: 'No sponsor would ever, twice, expect his films to pay.'[1]

Over the long term, quality documentary production, particularly of the prestige variety, depended on business and public administration sharing a broader vision than pure profit or target-driven efficiency. Over the shorter term, sponsors trusted their films officers to guide them between the extremes of utilitarianism and irrelevance. People like Edgar Anstey at British Transport and Donald Alexander at the National Coal Board are usually referred to, using familiar filmographic terminology, as producers or executive producers. In fact, as those organisations' 'films officers', their roles extended from policy to distribution as well as production. This was a job title with lineage: films officer had been John Grierson's designation at the Empire Marketing Board. Post-war, the title proliferated, though the quality of personnel varied. Here it is worth quoting John Chittock of the *Financial Times* at some length:

> The precise responsibilities of a films officer are by no means universally established. In some cases – too many – he is a glorified clerical officer who knows a little about photography. In rare instances, he may be a mainly armchair executive with an administrative background in films ... Occasionally he may be a practical film-maker ... A really good films officer must have many talents, usually apparently incompatible ones. First, above all, he must have a thorough experience of film production; this is essential so that he talks the same language as producers and thereby safeguards his company's interests when films are commissioned ... The films officer also needs to have a keen film sense (and) a thorough knowledge of the film industry and the personalities within it – so that he is good at choosing the right production companies; but he must also have a good general knowledge of business and industry at large ... This broad range of talents is rarely to be found in one man ... In those cases where a films officer falls into this exceptional group, the rewards for his company are great. Ford, Unilever, Shell, British Transport Films and British Petroleum are some which come immediately to mind as trail blazers who have benefited by outstanding films officers.[2]

The films officer's struggle was played out across a post-war boom in documentary film-making of such scale and complexity that any exhaustive survey of its sponsors is impossible. Mullard, George Wimpey and Richard Costain are just three of the more cinematically active industrialists not profiled in the following pages. Less regular film-making originated from fields as varied as banking and

Have You a Films Officer?

A FILMS OFFICER is a necessity for the larger sponsors. He is expected to see beyond the " smart salesman " approach, to understand film jargon, to be able to relate a script to a budget and, above all, to make the best use of a film when it is delivered by the production company.

But not every company or association which uses film has occasion to employ a Films Officer. World Wide takes particular care of these sponsors' interests. We are always glad to give advice, to show films we have made, and to explain how the finished film was followed up. We consider this " after-sales-service " to be of very great importance.

Sponsors include

CENTRAL OFFICE OF INFORMATION
NATIONAL COAL BOARD
BRITISH TRANSPORT COMMISSION
ADMIRALTY
ARMY KINEMA CORPORATION
ROYAL AIR FORCE
MIDDLESEX COUNTY COUNCIL
METROPOLITAN WATER BOARD
VAUXHALL MOTORS
ROYAL NATIONAL LIFEBOAT INSTITUTION
BANKERS INFORMATION SERVICES
COTTON BOARD
LINTAS LTD.
S. H. BENSON LTD.

WORLD WIDE PICTURES LTD.

LYSBETH HOUSE SOHO SQUARE LONDON W.1

Telephone: GERRARD 1736-7-8

brewing, and from trade bodies as well as individual firms. In the all-important field of energy, significant (public-sector) sponsors not discussed here included the various electricity bodies and the UK Atomic Energy Authority. Among national agencies, alongside its role as a film distributor, the British Council directly sponsored films promoting British culture abroad. The British Tourist Authority (in its various guises) sponsored films promoting travel to Britain. The post-war revival of the Films of Scotland Committee paid for further national projection, some of it entrusted to London as well as to Glasgow producers. In a specialist field, direct funding from the Educational Foundation for Visual Aids supplemented the making of classroom films by mainstream sponsors. The Arts Council of Great Britain represented the most freethinking sponsor of the period (other than the BFI), though relatively few of its films were made by 'documentary' producers. Given the nature of their financing, charities were inevitably the source for a smaller total number of films than official or industrial concerns, but their impact on audiences was disproportionate, and likewise their attraction for film-makers since they guaranteed serious subjects.

What follows is an introduction to some of the most important and interesting players in three of the major sectors – government and other arms of the state, traditional industries and newer ones. These documentary sponsors were among Europe's largest employers.

THE UNDEFEATED: GOVERNMENT AND THE COI

> A good film is seldom cheap to design and make, but its appeal is direct and universal.[3]

> Mental straight-jackets encourage mediocrity and get it.[4]

On 1 April 1946, the day the first post-war financial year began, the Central Office of Information came into being, replacing the wartime Ministry of Information and in most histories of British documentary signalling the beginning of the end of that great national tradition, the final demise being marked eight years later with the closure of the government's Crown Film Unit.[5] It's an appealing generalisation but one which has a significant problem: far from signifying the end of government film production the creation of the COI ultimately marked its acceleration. In fact, in the post-war era, government was responsible for the commissioning of thousands of films and television items, a magnitude dwarfing that of the 1930s and World War II. While the Crown Film Unit was lost in 1952, government (through the COI) continued to provide work for independent production companies as the nation's largest single commissioner of documentary and informational film.

Unlike its wartime predecessor, however, the COI was a service rather than a ministerial department. As individual government departments resumed responsibility for their information policy, the COI was to become the state's default public-sector advertising agency. It was a political compromise that few enthusiastically favoured at the time. The COI lost some of its power to shape its editorial policy artistically; the government departments were often frustrated at having to work through a middle man; the documentary old guard believed that the state should be producing its own films; independent production companies found the economics of working with officialdom unprofitable; writers and directors often found government an interfering and miserly sponsor.[6]

That all sides found the process frustrating is indicated in a Cabinet Office enquiry into relations with the documentary film business in 1947.[7] The question of delays and their associated costs appeared again in a 1949 report on the government information service.[8] In 1957 the ASFP suggested the formation of an interdepartmental planning board to consider the reorganisation of government film production. This proposal was rejected but the COI did begin having quarterly liaison meetings with the ASFP, leading to the joint production of a paper on improving communications between sponsoring departments, the COI and their film contractors.[9] However, when a Select Committee investigated the Central Office of Information in 1959/60 they found that little had actually changed in the film production process since 1947.[10] The COI was evidently a muddled and frustrating compromise, but a compromise that, in typically British fashion, proved more politically, socially and economically tenable than more efficient alternatives.

Philip Mackie, a civil servant and an officer of the COI Films Division, presented the internal take on film production in an article clearly not intended for outside eyes. In his icy record he lays out how the 'Ministry of Help' in need of a short film on 'Industrial Exteriosis' approaches the COI Films Division who decided that 'Nadir Films' would be the perfect company to produce, with 'Hector Bathos' to direct.[11]

It has been convincingly argued that the wartime experience of running the Ministry of Information influenced the post-war development of government information services.[12] Indeed, the post-war structure of film sponsorship had been initiated right at the start of war, when the MOI decided to use independent production companies to make the bulk of government propaganda – a decision thought to lessen 'unacceptable' bias and draw a distinction between 'Allied' and 'Axis' methods.[13] With the onset of the Cold War, the arms-length process of film commissioning and production changed little over time, although the fortunes of government information and the COI itself did fluctuate across the post-war period.

The COI Films Division was part of the bureaucratic machinery of government and working apolitically for several ministries under successive administrations. As such it never benefited from the type of singular vision achieved by many of the corporate PROs and films officers. The various heads of COI Films Division never had the authority of BP's Ronald Tritton, say, or Shell's Alex Wolcough to set the direction of a film programme.

Early on, however, there seemed to be another route it could have taken. In 1948 the COI appointed John Grierson as Controller of Films, a role above that of the Head of Films Division in the established civil servant structure. Grierson would be ultimately responsible both for Crown and for relations with the independent contractors. It seemed on the face of it to be a move towards re-establishing the sort of public film-making that Grierson had supervised as films officer at the Empire Marketing Board and GPO or even to establish the model of state patronage he had introduced at the National Film Board of Cananda. Many expected a new era of documentary production to be ushered in.

Grierson set about reorganising Crown and improving relations with the independents by establishing a forward plan of work that would speed production and allow for better budgeting. At the core was the idea that the Films Division would concentrate on making feature documentaries for theatrical release. But the post-war economic situation in Britain was simply unfavourable to the types of budgets these films required. The situation wasn't helped by Conservative Party sniping that the COI was churning out propaganda for the Labour government at the taxpayer's expense, nor by Grierson's ineffective Macchiavellianism.[14] The COI became subject to a series of inquiries and reports.

The French Report of 1949 endorsed the post-war reorganisation of the home information services but made recommendations for reduction in expenditure.[15] The key saving identified was a decrease in the amount of paid publicity the COI produced, an area clearly affecting film production. It further, more specifically, decried the expense of the Crown Film Unit's studio at Beaconsfield. Even Crown's staff accepted that maintaining a studio, with all its concomitant overheads, represented substantial expense.[16] Placed in competition for work with independent producers who had become government contractors during the war, most of them maintaining lower overheads and, unlike Crown, able to tout for more lucrative contracts from private-sector sponsors, the internal unit was doubly undermined. The Crown studios often sat idle, accruing costs while work went outside.[17] The ASFP realised its advantage and reported to the French Committee that production costs were lower with its members.[18] Frustrated by the entire experience, Grierson resigned from the COI in 1950, seeking other opportunities for state sponsorship. He moved on to Group 3, a project of the National Film Finance Corporation to produce socially purposive feature films (those that it oversaw proved to be far from radical), leaving public-information documentary behind.

While the ASFP managed to help hasten the demise of the Crown Film Unit that its members were in direct competition with, it proved less successful in growing the government film budget. When the Conservatives gained power in 1951 seeking new economies in state expenditure, Crown lost what little official support it could muster. In 1952 the Unit was closed, an event conventionally considered the formal end of Documentary Movement history. Nowadays even Crown's own post-war existence is little celebrated but it was extant as long after the war as it was during it, and around 75 per cent of its output was actually produced in that later period. Crown was an Oscar winner with *Daybreak in Udi* (1949) and was nominated for another with *Royal Scotland* (1952). Its passing was decried at the time, with the Labour Party opposing the decision, which was also the focus of a concerted campaign by various film luminaries. *The Economist* offered a fair and sober analysis of Crown's fate, but even it felt there might be some value in keeping a smaller internal unit, salvaging the best of what it had to offer.[19] There were to be repeated calls for the re-establishment of government film-making, Labour MPs raised the prospect in the House in 1953 and 1957, John Grierson pondered on the formation of a 'Group 4' producing documentaries alongside Group 3's features, and the COI itself mooted the idea of a 'rapid news' unit.[20] For decades, governmental film enthusiasts remained wedded to the idea of an internal production unit.

If Conservatives were less interested in the COI's films of social concern, the Drogheda Report in 1954 emphasised the importance of directing information resources into projecting Britain abroad, reflecting the needs of a nation that was both post-war and increasingly post-imperial.[21] In 1961 the COI Films division was split into four parts in response to an increasing use of media, especially for the Commonwealth and overseas.[22] The new divisions were 1) a redefined and smaller Films Division responsible only for making films for theatrical and non-theatrical showings, at home and abroad, for TV 'fillers' aimed at the domestic audience and for the COI production library, 2) Television and Newsreels which serviced the increasing overseas demand for this material, 3) Radio and 4) a Film Services Unit to operate the Central Film Library and to provide common distribution, publicity and technical services.

The reorganisation marked the changing fortunes of the COI's formal output too. The longer 'documentary' became a much smaller part of COI output as fillers, magazine programmes and items for TV grew in importance. The COI's main activity was becoming the publicising of Britain overseas.[23] The COI contributed to the Overseas Information Service, and worked for the FCO serving its embassies, consulates and commissions. In 1970 work for the overseas services accounted for 75 per cent of the COI's staff time, and 37 per cent of spending on overseas work was for documentary films, newsreels and television material.[24] The 1960s had marked a general increase in expenditure on the production of film, television and radio and away from printed books, magazines and pamphlets. Outside Britain, the COI did not buy advertising or publicity space in the press or on radio or television, thus it was seen as paramount that the material they produced would be palatable to broadcasters. Alongside rapidly produced ephemeral items, this was also the era of prestige presentations of the nation in films such as Peter Hopkinson's *Today in Britain* and Don Levy's *Opus*, both redolent of their very different moments of their decade (1964 and 1967 respectively).

In the production of material for overseas, priority was given to the promotion of trade and industrial publicity to support British exporters, and Britain's position in world affairs, her foreign and commonwealth relationships and British policy on defence, economic and financial issues. The concentration on these areas, which accounted for about 80 per cent of COI's overseas output by 1969, followed the recommendations of the Plowden Committee that overseas information work should support clear policy objectives.[25] The remaining 20 per cent was part of a more general programme of national projection and included subjects such as parliamentary and local government and educational and social services.

Overseas publicity did in fact prompt direct government production. Within the television and newsreel division a small production unit was formed with a film crew 'In Britain Now' shooting background news material.[26] In 1970 the COI's director general wrote that 'the COI has no camera teams of its own' indicating the film crew was no more, while later revealing how other film-making functions had shifted back into the COI realm. The COI's in-house technicians were cut off from the 'documentary' sector. For documentaries, the situation remained that independent companies made the film to the sponsoring department's brief, under the supervision of a COI production control officer. It was cinemagazines for overseas use, and all television magazine programmes, not 'documentaries', that were scripted and supervised within the COI. For the television news service all the staff would be provided except for a camera team.[27]

The 1970s saw a wide-ranging government reorganisation that entailed the COI being subject to a series of reviews and investigations, beginning with the Newton Report in 1970.[28] Some suspected that Prime Minister Edward Heath wanted to close the COI down.[29] Newton's review considered the breaking up of the COI but eventually rejected the idea; however, it did question the tying of departments' information needs to the work of the COI. A further review of COI activities was requested by Heath and conducted by Sir Ronald Melville in 1972.[30] Melville's report recommended a 10 per cent reduction in COI staff, with particular attention towards making savings in the area of overseas information work. Further critical analyses followed. In 1978 there was both another review of national projection and another investigation into COI expenditure.[31] With the UK facing new economic constraints at the end of the decade and the political mood swinging towards free market approaches, the COI was again threatened.

Two elements of COI working practice perceived as contrary to the cost-saving benefits of competition came under the spotlight: the production of material in house for overseas use and the principle of ministerial information work going through the COI, with costs made against the relevant Ministry's budget allocation. The reviews indicated that both processes should cease.

The end of the 'allied service' principle of covering information costs and a movement towards a repayment model resulted in a weakening of the COI's position, as it made it easier for departments to opt out of using COI services.[32] A review of home departments in 1979 made it clear that many of them would do so. While the MOD remained happy there were less contented noises from others, especially when it came to film. The DHSS thought that the on-costs for film were too high at 30 per cent and the MSC considered that the COI's estimates for film productions 'flew in the face of reason'.[33]

Meanwhile, in an echo of 1952 and the closure of the Crown Film Unit by a previous Conservative administration, plans were afoot to terminate the remaining film production staff employed by the COI for overseas work. In 1981 as these services were about to be outsourced, MP Bob Cryer asked the Minister for the Civil Service about the effects of closing the 'Central Office of Information film unit'.[34] In written answers to his questions in October his appellation was unremarked upon, but answers to a subsequent enquiry to the Chancellor in December reminded Mr Cryer that there was 'no COI film unit as such'.[35] The nature of the COI's engagement in film production clearly remained a mystery to some in government.

For all the romance associated with the idea of the internal unit and despite the frustrations expressed by film-makers, a good proportion of the films produced by the independent contractors had proved to be fine pieces of work. From strong social films like Paul Dickson's *The Undefeated* (1950) and John Krish's *Return to Life* (1960) through such exciting communications as Hugh Hudson's *Design for Today* (1965) and John MacKenzie's *Apaches* (1977), the COI's post-war output includes many films worthy of rediscovery, as well as others whose historical content is more interesting than their artistic form.

The COI was frequently an unpopular sponsor with production companies and film-makers, but no government agency is short of criticism and regular gripes did not preclude long-running associations. The Treasury's eagle eye over the COI ensured that it held fast to contracts that limited commissioned companies' profits to 2.5 per cent of the production costs and left them to cover any overruns.[36] However, it was regular business: companies like Basic, Greenpark, Verity and World Wide established relationships early which led to a stream of work lasting decades. If only for turnover, the COI remained a valuable client to keep. For the film-makers the COI commissioning process, departmental interference and a disinterest in their personal artistic vision were inhibiting factors. However, work for the COI offered more varied opportunities than all but the largest corporate sponsors could provide, especially in 'social documentary' fields like welfare and education. How happy a COI project would be was often down to the chemistry between the representatives of the sponsoring department, their COI intermediary and the producers.

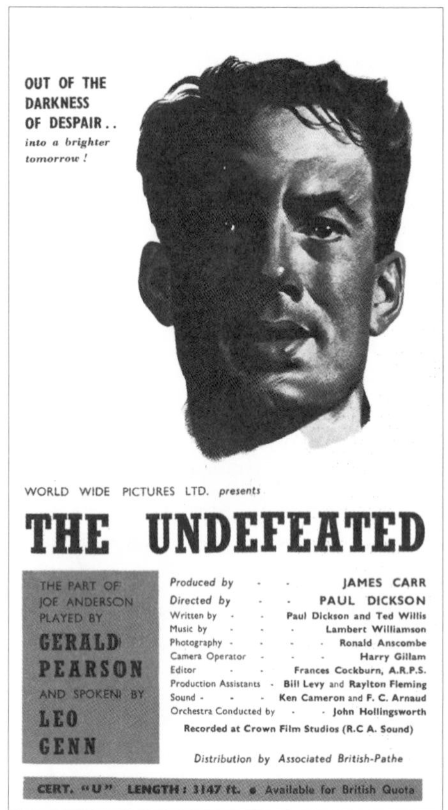

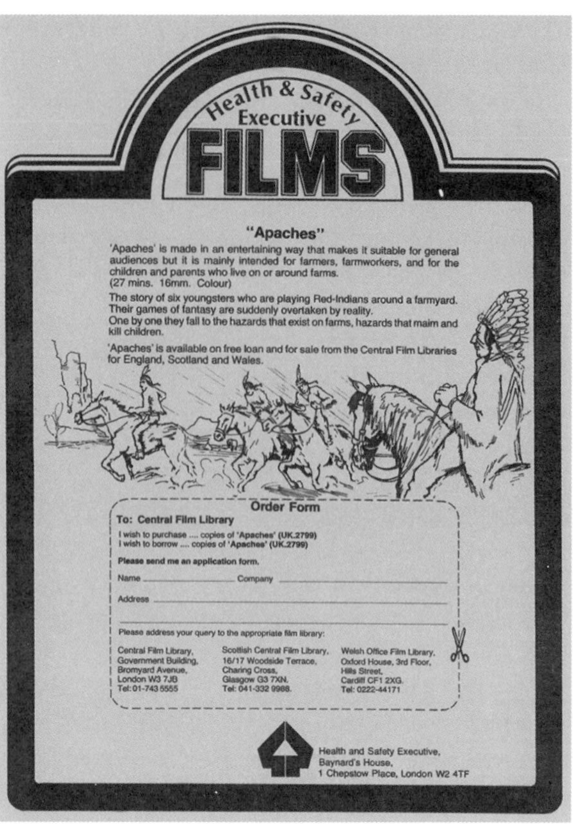

The Undefeated and *Apaches*: cutting-edge official film-making for the targeted campaigns of two different eras

The Central Office of Information continues to fund moving-image production in the service of government's information aims. But where government sponsored film-making had begun in the documentary form, in the post-war era it often increasingly became something else: advertisement for careers in the military, the NHS and in schools, or fillers on everything from the Green Cross Code and TV licensing to the Aids epidemic. If COI output was sometimes 'mediocre' or middling, then it was often because it served ordinary purposes and not grand social aims. Because of the association of the 1930s Movement with government bodies the EMB and GPO, the shadow of its reputation fell longest and darkest over the government-sponsored film of the post-war era. It is a shadow from which the latter has only rarely stepped out, but one that has hidden decades of state communication through the medium of the moving image and the agency of the COI, which has outlasted most of the government departments and agencies it was first set up to serve.

STUDIES IN CHANGE: PUBLIC BODIES (GPO, GAS COUNCIL, BRITISH PRODUCTIVITY COUNCIL)

> A very few years ago the word 'productivity' was a technical term unfamiliar to all except economists and a handful of up-to-date industrialists. Now it is in common use.
>
> Paul Fletcher, 1955[37]

The General Post Office had provided the hub for the pre-war Movement, in the form of its GPO Film Unit, before the latter mutated to wartime Crown; the GPO entered post-war life as just another COI client. Internal responsibility for film commissioning fell to GPO information officers Sid Baskerville and John Groves, for whom documentary film was never of great import. Many commercials for postal services were made (some of them by Crown) in the late 1940s, then through the 1950s small batches of training and promotional films were turned out, mostly by low-rent producers. From the end of the decade, the GPO began sponsoring more broadly based and expensive documentary productions, notably the enjoyably glossy Oscar-nominated featurette *Thirty Million Letters* (1963, directed by James Ritchie), a conscious homage to *Night Mail*, produced for the GPO by British Transport Films. Another popular title was *Ship to Shore* (1965), the first of several made by Rayant Pictures, detailing the work of the twelve GPO radio stations linking ships anywhere in the world to land communication systems.

Renewed institutional enthusiasm for film resulted in PRO Toby O'Brien recruiting the GPO's first post-war films officer in 1966. Aubrey Jones was tasked with planning a discrete film production and distribution programme that bypassed the COI. He initially focused the GPO's output on staff information and recruitment films, such as Rayant's *Liz and Sally* (1967), a lighthearted look at the training and work of a telephonist, aimed at female school leavers. Increasingly, however, the films were placed into wider non-theatrical distribution through the Random Film Library and others. Another successful title was *Over the Counter* (1968), directed by Sam Napier-Bell at Basic, looking towards the services and sophisticated machinery of post offices at the end of the twentieth century, presented through the device of two Post Office workers reminiscing in 1997. Later the GPO began enterprisingly exploiting opportunities for theatrical distribution. The Rank group, stung by the monopoly

accusations surrounding the placement of *Look at Life*, decided to approach the GPO as a co-sponsor. Rank's film *The Post Office Tower of London* (1967) presented a tour of the famous new building.

The GPO was proving a remarkable late developer among post-war sponsors. Gerald Boarer continued the momentum built up by Jones when his predecessor was promoted in 1968. Since being appointed as Jones's assistant in 1966, Boarer had made his mark with a series of cinema commercials introducing the two-tier postal service, starring magician David Nixon. *Picture to Post* (1969), a documentary on stamp design and production for which Boarer negotiated a cinema distribution partnership with MGM, became one of the biggest theatrical successes in British short-film history. This cemented the GPO/MGM relationship, which saw further cinema exhibition for *The First and the Fastest* (1969), an Antony Barrier production about the 1969 *Daily Mail* Air Race, and *After the Arrow* (1971), a World Wide film using commemorative stamps to trace British heritage from the Norman Conquest to Concorde. The philatelic audience was treated again with Balfour Films' *The Rainbow Verdict* (1971), directed by David Thompson (bringing the same attention to pictorial detail as to his Arts Council documentaries at Balfour).

By now, the GPO name was no more: government department turned state corporation, it was redesignated the 'Post Office' and began rationalising its activities. Post Office Telecommunications, set up as a separate division of the Post Office in October 1969, now had its own film library, and for a period its own films officer, Michael Capon. It sponsored some forty productions during the 1970s. Within the main Post Office, films had been moved from the PR to the Marketing department whose new director George White moved to axe documentary production. Boarer managed to hang on with a less ambitious programme through to his own retirement in 1985. His final production was *Men of Letters* (1985), an elegiac commemoration of 350 years of the world's first public postal service. Boarer commissioned Eric Marquis to write and direct, but a falling out over money left Marquis's script being realised at World Wide Pictures: the director's career, and the films officer's, both ending on a flat note.

When the gas industry was brought under full public control in 1948, it too brought documentary baggage into the post-war settlement. Between the wars it had been a byword for liberal sponsorship thanks to its patronage of *Enough to Eat?* (1936), *The Smoke Menace* (1937), *Children at School* (1937) and *The Londoners* (1939) and above all its sponsorship of *Housing Problems* (1935). The payoff had been an infinitely less celebrated string of films – by card-carrying Movement documentarists – like 1935's *Men Behind the Meters* and *How Gas Is Made*, or 1937's *Pots and Plans* and *How to Cook*. Post-war nationalisation ironically led to the number of 'progressive' films produced by the gas industry waning, although not entirely evaporating.

The Gas Council sponsored 200 post-war films. These, they declared, were 'produced for the purpose of making better known the services of the gas industry in providing a modern labour saving fuel for the home, the office and the factory', but also to 'depict the contribution made by the gas industry to the national economy and to the welfare of the community as a whole'.[38] The extent of the continuity between the gas industry's interwar and post-war film programmes mirrors the relative modesty of the changes wrought on the industry itself. 'Nationalisation' of gas production and supply resembled neither the transformative takeover of coalmining and health services, nor the tentative nationalisation of steel. Instead, the formation of twelve Area Boards that collectively formed the Gas Council represented a measured reorganisation. The primary architect of its post-war films policy was Stanley Irving, films officer from 1951 to 1967. Irving (a film director at Gaumont-British Instructional in the 1930s, then films officer at the Ministry of Works) claimed studiously to have avoided favouring particular producers (let alone setting up an internal unit) precisely to evade a house style.[39]

While treatments varied, the production programme's rolling contribution to social documentary became tightly focused on one topic: the cleanliness of the air. For all the sponsor's self-interest, this was, incontestably, a prominent issue in post-war public affairs. *Guilty Chimneys* (1954) played at least as big role in the national debate as *The Smoke Menace* had in the 1930s. Intensively screened by the National Smoke Abatement Society, it was frequently mentioned in the national press, and even cited in parliamentary debates preceding the passage of the 1956 Clean Air Act. Alex Strasser's films *Window to the Sky* (1959) and *Clearing the Air* (1965) further updated the story, documenting the Act's municipal implementation and the setting up of smoke control zones. *The Air My Enemy* (1971), which ended the sequence, belongs as much to the wider cycle of ecology documentaries then emerging from across the spectrum of film sponsorship (the smoke menace long since trounced, the new airborne threat is sulphur dioxide, and beyond that humanity itself).

Air pollution aside, social documentary was attenuated. In contrast with the innovatory *Housing Problems*, Realist's *Gas In Modern Housing* (1964) unemotively documents gas's contribution to post-war construction, evidencing living standards that had risen beyond recognition in thirty years. Made as late as 1984, *Housing Solutions* is a historically knowing piece of titling and sponsorship. Made on the verge of *re*privatisation, it observes that the slum clearances and utopian planning championed by its forebear had had some disastrous effects. These films had professional audiences – notably, Housing Committees – particularly in mind. For lay viewers, productions like World Wide's *Summer in Winter* (1964), promoting gas-fired central heating, are pure marketing tools (and few escape the kitsch trappings of the period).

Gas Council heirs to *Enough to Eat?* also proved scarce. Post-war, there generally *was* enough to eat, and British documentary's concern with malnutrition moved abroad, as in Shell's *Food or Famine*. No, it was the menu of cooking-by-gas films that continued to grow: some, it must be said, more appetising than others. *A Scratch Meal with Marcel Boulestin* (1936) had been one of Arthur Elton's less feted films. Its post-war counterparts were such as *Pride and Joy* (1952), with Philip Harben, and *Cookery Carnival* (1957), featuring the Craddocks. These were followed by a succession of later colour films like *Something Nice to Eat* (1967) and *Cooking for the Family* (1970) which had in their sights both a 'general' audience of housewives and the particular audience of schoolgirls in domestic science classes.

There was no post-war *Children at School* from this sponsor either: none of the Gas Council's business. However, explicitly aimed at secondary schools were three films released under the series heading *The Transference of Heat* (1947) and fourteen making up *The Story of Gas* (1954), with accompanying teaching booklets, filmstrips and wallcharts. For adults, *What's in a Flame* (1962) and *The Four Seasons* (1962) are cut-price public-sector equivalents to the Shell Film Unit's magisterial popular science treatises. Film Workshop also produced two short-lived cinemagazines *Behind the Scenes* (1953), and its colour successor *Mr Therm's Review* (1955).

Considered as documentary records, the most valuable Gas Council films are accounts of the British industry's development. The symbolic symbiosis of coal and gas had long been stressed in the films (even the clean air films were at pains to stress that the *mis*use of coal was the problem). Where *Saharan Venture* (1965) shows gas being liquefied and imported, the proposed change from coal to oil-based gas, rapidly superseded by the switch to natural gas, brought films like *Sea Born Treasure* (1968) and *Natural Gas for Britain* (1970), charting the discovery and exploitation of North Sea reserves. The North Sea project coloured all the industry's documentary output, from films covering advances in pipelining to those reflecting changing systems of distribution and supply to both industrial and domestic consumers. Irving's 1967 replacement, Bob Sullivan, oversaw the transition of this programme into the British Gas era and, while he himself died in 1977, an active catalogue of films, available in both 16mm and video form, was maintained until privatisation was implemented in 1986.

In contrast to the tight focus of most of these films, the definitive post-war gas film, if measured by reach and by longevity, was *Family Album* (1948), an attractive half-hour Technicolor production, written by Roy Plomley and performed by professional actors with wry but gentle humour. A mini-*Cavalcade*, charting the story of four generations of a family living in the same house, it weaves (very lightly) the changing role of gas in heating the building into a kindly social history of a century. An iconic fixture on the non-theatrical circuit, so great was *Family Album*'s durability that it had to be revised with new material in 1966: the final 'contemporary' sequence was itself becoming outdated, though 2,000 bookings per year were still reportedly being made. Schoolteachers were part of an apparently vast fanbase. For some adult societies, a showing was said to be an annual ritual which, in itself, says something about post-war Britain.

'British productivity', post-war at that, may sound like a contradiction in terms. The British Productivity Council (BPC) has been the most rapidly forgotten of post-war documentary sponsors, probably because the organisation itself has left so few visible traces, and its films (never revived) are not the easiest for later viewers to relate to. It deserves extended treatment, not only for being an important fixture on the documentary scene, and commissioning over a hundred films from an array of production companies, but for judging them mission-critical. No other sponsor accorded film production a greater importance in the meeting of core organisational objectives, nor wove film-making so tightly into its administrative structure.

The British Productivity Council came into being in 1952, successor to the UK section of the Anglo-American Council on Productivity. A prototypical quango, the BPC sought to make virtues of its disadvantages by emphasising its independence of government, its dearth of executive powers and its neutrality about the appropriate structures of industrial ownership and management. Its stated purpose was simply 'to stimulate the improvement of productivity in every sector of the national economy by every possible means'.

In the summer of 1953, the Council set up a Visual Aids department, headed by full-time films officer Paul Fletcher. In the late 1930s and early '40s, Fletcher had freelanced as a writer for various producers (including Strand, Merton Park and the APFU) before moving to Greenpark, where, on Ralph Keene's departure, he took over as managing director of the unit.[40] Immediately prior to taking up his BPC position, he had been producing film items at the BBC. Overseeing Fletcher's work was a committee constituted of formal representatives of the Federation of British Industry, the British Employers Confederation, the TUC and the nationalised industries – the latter represented by Edgar Anstey.

Being one of only six such BPC steering groups, the existence of the Visual Aids Committee indicates the significance that the parent body invested in its work. The Council's 1956 publication *Visual Aids* summarised its thinking about the topic:

> The film is by far the most versatile of all visual methods. It can provide, among other things, a record of an operation, an inspection of a process, a demonstration of a product, an explanation of a balance sheet or of a technique, an encouragement to progress or an epic of an enterprise. Alone among the visual techniques it is a medium of expression in its own right, as distinct from a mere means of transmission or reproduction.[41]

Fletcher rolled out the BPC's films in distinct phases. The first films would, in the words of FBI head Sir Norman Kipping, instil in general viewers 'an interest in the up-to-date', an 'impatience with the old-fashioned' and 'a pride in good industrial achievement'.[42] To these ends, two four-minute pilot films were commissioned from Wallace Productions in 1953, followed by a series of six half-hour films. Fletcher succeeded in placing these with the BBC for nationwide broadcast, under a series title: *There's Always A Better Way*. The BPC hailed the initiative as simultaneously a 'pioneer experiment in sponsored television'[43] and an auspicious start to 'the most ambitious film-propaganda scheme yet undertaken in Britain by a single organisation'.

Public consciousness somewhat raised, the BPC's next set of films, advertised under the umbrella title of *Better Ways*, was concerned with introducing Work Study, the pet subject of the productivity expert. At this time, a BPC work-study unit was touring the UK, giving courses in which the films were used as teaching aids. *Better Ways* was intended to sell the concept to managers, for action and to keep their operatives informed. The third phase of production moved from the merits and theory of work study to its implementation, often within particular fields like agriculture and office work (which represented a shift from the BPC's initial emphasis on heavy industry).

The fourth wave of BPC films, in which an expanded variety of productivity topics received coverage, extended throughout the whole of the 1960s. *Variety Reduction* (1958) was an unusual film that picked up some of the sponsor's best-ever reviews. The esoteric-sounding topic of whether industrial firms should consider reducing their product range is made compelling by a dialogue-heavy *Twelve Angry Men*-style dramatisation. Other films covered training practices, ergonomics and quality and stock control, together with novel practices such as network analysis (later termed critical path analysis), organisation and methods (O&M) and value analysis (a system for costs scrutiny and reduction). All yield intriguing primary-source material for specialist historians.

Of broader interest in picturing post-war industry is the suite of BPC films dealing explicitly with human relations in the workplace. Apart from *Men at Work*, most early BPC films dealt gingerly with the productivity impact of faulty industrial relations. With the 1959 release of Basic's *A Company of Men* the Council began sustained release of industrial relations films, two of the best – 1960's *Dispute* and 1970's *A Study in Change* – being recognised by the Society of Film and Television Arts. As with the work-study films, management and workforces were both considered target audiences, the former to inform action, the latter to provide context. This was, the BPC admitted, 'a very sensitive area of film-making. Audiences who may readily accept a film on an industrial technique tend to be less receptive, even cynical, about a film on management–worker relations.'[44] Films in this strand, more than other BPC productions, often took the form of drama – *A Study in Change* is a particularly intriguing low-key reinvention of 'story documentary' that reconstructs an actual consultation process employing those involved in the dispute as performers.

Financing of BPC films is unusually noteworthy. The Council's own income came partly from the Treasury, drawing on Mutual Security Agency counterpart funds. But Britain was also affiliated to the European Productivity Agency (EPA), itself paid out of a combination of member contributions and Economic Cooperation Administration funds: the Marshall Plan. The EPA had its own mind-bogglingly elaborate arrangements for film production in place, which resulted in many BPC films receiving EPA funding.[45]

Fletcher claimed that the BPC rejected cinema exhibition because cinematic entertainment values would conflict with the rigour and sobriety of the organisation's messaging. After the early experiment with television (the 1954 transmissions claiming an average audience of 3.5 million people per broadcast), the BPC's distribution was fundamentally non-theatrical. It is impossible to quantify the absolute scale of BPC distribution confidently, but it's clear that its *relative* scale was unusually high. For several years the BPC provided the most heavily booked prints in the CFL's 2,000-strong catalogue: in one twelve-month period, World Wide's production *Introducing Work Study* (1955), directed by Clifford Parris, reportedly received 34 per cent more bookings than the next most popular CFL title. *Men at Work* and *Raising the Standard* (both 1954) were the next most popular BPC titles, both also booked several hundred times each year. The CFL felt it necessary, in 1964, to announce it was adding a premium to hire charges for popular BPC titles because of the high demand. Overseas bookings, not limited to EPA members, were also reported.

The Council was a pioneer in popularising the 'trigger films' concept, claiming that research proved that the documentaries' messages would be dissipated *unless* followed by group dialogue. Therefore the BPC produced accompanying notes for every film despatched by the CFL with every loan print. Besides drawing attention to particular aspects of each film, these brochures emphasised certain golden rules: the discussion leader should always see the film first; he shouldn't synopsise it before the screening; above all, the discussion should take place straightaway.

The twelve months commencing November 1962 were designated National Productivity Year, whose negligible impact reflected the BPC's increasingly muted public presence. In fact, the story of the British Productivity Council illustrates how film history often goes out of synch with history itself. It was under the Attlee government, under Stafford Cripps's influence, that labour productivity came to prominence, the technocratic enthusiasms of Britain's social democrats coincidentally aligning with those of the capitalist USA. But at this point, a mere handful of films were addressing the question directly: rather, a glut of American films was being imported into Europe. By the time of the BPC's formation, under the Conservatives, official enthusiasm had already cooled, just as

Fletcher's department was firing up. For all its associations with managerialism, and although it had its left-wing detractors, scepticism tended to be greater on the right. Accordingly, enthusiasm was revitalised in the Wilson era, but by this point the BPC itself was being written off: yet in film terms it was still delivering more productivity propaganda than any other source. Finally, the Council's state funding was pulled by the Heath government: over the next few years the BPC tottered to a standstill, but its film production activities chimed with the newfound popularity of management training. By its 1975 demise (aptly enough, the last BPC film was named *Cash Flow Crisis*) the film programme was the only visible reminder of its sponsor's continued existence.

In this light, the relationship of the BPC's films to Britain's better-known documentary history emerges clearly. The head of the Council's work-study unit stated that it was 'the intention of the British Productivity Council to hold a mirror up to industry':[46] by definition, a documentary project. Allied to the Council's bipartisan national propaganda function, it thus represents a continuation of documentary's wartime role. More so than their MOI forebears, however, BPC films had a patchy rate of intellectual and emotional conversion but they were impressively disseminated. Moreover, as a part of documentary's ongoing chronicle of what it means to be British they should not be overlooked. The usual questions of class, culture and ideology surface quickly enough. In 1958, Sir Charles Norris (the British Productivity Council's director) wrote of

> a need for filmmakers to become more familiar with industry and its needs ... The members of an industrial audience, of whatever level, live on a different planet from that inhabited by many film people. Their interests are different; their values are different; and unless a scriptwriter or director can learn to understand them, and understand them with sympathy, the effectiveness of the film as a means of communication is bound to suffer.[47]

Looking at the problem from the opposite end, at a premiere of three BPC films the same year Norris advised his audience to remember that their purpose was 'to appeal to, and gain the attention of, audiences who are more or less complete strangers to the subjects with which they deal. They are not normally enlightened and expert chaps like you.'[48]

MAKING TRACKS: BRITISH TRANSPORT

> The opportunity offered in 1949 was to practise Grierson's creative interpretation of actuality in the area of public transport and to bring it alive on the screen. As Tallents phrased it, 'the spirit that must animate any public service'.
>
> Edgar Anstey[49]

> Public relations is more difficult in an organisation in trouble than in one riding the crest of success. The Railways have been in trouble for so long that people are inclined wearily to expect shortcomings, be suspicious of promises, and to be most impolitely incredulous when promises are fulfilled. People almost expect the Railway to have shortcomings. They also expect to have their newspapers and their letters in time each morning.
>
> Richard Beeching[50]

Edgar Anstey, OBE, Chief Officer (Films) for the British Transport Commission, had been one of Grierson's well-known pre-war protégés. An urbane clubman and paragon of the liberal establishment,

Edgar Anstey (S. Foxon collection)

Anstey occupied innumerable chairmanships and board memberships, and his voice and byline were familiar to a wider educated public as *The Spectator*'s film critic, and as a panel member on the BBC radio programme *The Critics*.[51] A link between new documentary and old, between the British-sponsored film and its overseas peers, between specialised film production and the British film industry at large, it's hard to believe that Anstey also had time to run a film unit.

Indeed, some of the hands-on production of British Transport Films he delegated to trusted colleagues: in earlier years to Stewart McAllister, of Crown renown, and Ian Ferguson; latterly to John Shearman and James Ritchie. Anstey claimed 'little conflict between those considerations which lead to high technical and imaginative film qualities and those considerations which yield large audiences at minimum cost'.[52] He was looked up to by many, and by some reviled – but none could gainsay his political skills. His accomplishment as a films officer was to prove the financial value and maintain the political position of the documentary film within a complex national organisation, while upholding its cultural standing, in the film industry and among a wider public.

Under the 1947 Transport Act, the British Transport Commission (BTC) was created to implement the Attlee government's vision of integrated, publicly owned transport – controlling all nationalised transportation with the exception of airways. In aggregate, these concerns employed 900,000 staff, exceeding even the collieries'. In practice, perhaps unsurprisingly, they never overcame their origins as rival baronies which, incidentally, inherited public relations practices with widely varying levels of sophistication (London Transport at the top end, road haulage at the bottom). Following the BTC's formation, its Public Relations and Publicity Office, under Jack Brebner and Christian Barman (important exponents of interwar public relations in the Tallents/Beddington vein) commissioned two investigations into the use of film. One, carried out internally, collated the film work of BTC's pre-nationalised components. The other, by Film Centre, studied the use of film at comparable organisations: Shell, ICI and the Gas Council. The combined outcome was the formation of a new BTC films service, including its own production unit, with Anstey in charge. Apparently, he would have preferred to remain at Film Centre, advising Transport on the same basis that Elton advised Shell, but the BTC's personnel rules didn't allow for this. So, from 1949, reporting initially to Brebner, Anstey set up the service, soon named British Transport Films, at whose helm he would remain until 1974. The plan also involved requisitioning film-related staff and equipment inherited from the private railway companies and London Transport (LT). So BTF represented, at least in personnel terms, an amalgam of the documentary-making of the Movement and the pre-war industrial film-making that had subsisted outside its orbit. Among Anstey's closest BTF associates would be administrator Charles Potter, who had been at the London Midland and Scottish railway since 1930;

one of the most famous creative graduates of BTF would be cinematographer David Watkin, who came in from the Southern Railways film unit and later became a famed feature films director of photography.

BTF's established complement of permanent employees was kept very small (around ten people) though augmented by long rolling contracts and replenished by freelance directors. Between employees and contractors, Anstey drew on two generations of directorial talent: the likes of J. B. Holmes, John Taylor, Rod Neilson-Baxter, Alex Shaw and Ralph Keene from the older generation, of John Krish, Joe Mendoza, Michaels Orrom and Clarke, and Bill Mason from the younger. Long-term BTF directors included Kenneth Fairbairn, Tony Thompson and later film-makers like Gloria Sachs and David Lochner. The mainstays were technical staff, such as cinematographer Ron Craigen and editor John Legard. BTF's initial policy, maintained through the 1950s, was to regulate workflow by mixing in-house with outsourced productions: many of the major 1950s units, like DATA, Greenpark and Wallace, made at least one British Transport film. BTF's core budget was met by annual submission to the Commission, often claimed by Anstey to have been less than the cost of one locomotive. Specialised productions could be requested from anywhere within the internecine Commission. To come up with broader subjects, Anstey chaired an *ad hoc* BTC film programme committee, on which each region of British Railways, and all other Commission divisions, were represented: its ideas for films were in turn referred to the BTC's coordinating committee for public relations and publicity. In practice, within the financial year Anstey had fair room for manoeuvre and was usually able to keep some special projects on the go alongside the requested items.

The majority of BTF's work was for the railways, followed by London Transport. During these years, virtually all BTF's film-making fell into three distinct types: films that encouraged the public to use the network; training and communication films aimed at employees; and films that sought to update both public and staff on progress in investment, technology and services. The travelogues are much the best known, though the internal films were by some distance more numerous. The BTF of the 1950s, as both an industrial and an artistic project, most fascinates when all three categories are considered together. Three of the best-remembered individual BTF productions, all directed by freelancers – John Taylor's *Holiday* (1957), very much in the first category, and John Schlesinger's *Terminus* (1961) and Geoffrey Jones's *Snow* (1963), both in the third – illustrate BTF's diversity, all three being stylistically atypical of the general output. It's such films as *This is York* (1953), *Journey into History* (1952), *Any Man's Kingdom* (1956), *The Land of Robert Burns* (1956) and *Journey Into Spring* (1957) that epitomised a recognisable BTF house style of documentary classicism. Lushly textured, skilfully and sometimes imaginatively rendered, gentle, warm – though oftentimes haunted by a certain longing – these films were sometimes accused of representing a betrayal by journeymen of the Movement's earlier radicalism. They can equally be taken as key cinematic expressions of much of the 1950s project of reconciliation: having banked social reform, Britain was now ready for more harmonious pleasures. BTF's soothing visions of Britain as reachable by rail marry their inbuilt socialist commitment to public ownership and investment to small 'c' conservative feelings. A valued sense of the past is a repeated theme of these films: 'the present like a vein of the past', 'dusk and dawn are banks of the one river and time is only a bridge'.[53]

At worst conformist and twee, at best quite magical, with these travelogues BTF became a byword for quality and, among innumerable awards, vied with BP as the British sponsor most often nominated for an Oscar. These travelogues effectively fell into both the (soft) selling and the prestige categories at once. Their direct purpose was to boost ticket sales. The clearest circumstantial

Modern comforts in *Blue Pullman*; heritage and romance in *Every Valley*

evidence of BTC faith in them doing so is that commercial reps were frequently despatched to introduce non-theatrical showings, accompanied by brochures about the places seen in the films. Usually filmed in pleasing light in spring or summer, but shown in the darker, colder months, such introduced showings were aimed particularly at boosting off-peak group bookings for rail, bus or other journeys. At the same time, other audiences, thinking little of travel, enjoyed these films instead as classy, tasteful entertainments: the best ones remained in popular distribution for many years after their sales relevance had receded. Nationalised transport, and railways especially, were all this time struggling to regain pre-war standards in the face of unstable finances, depreciating assets, skilled-labour shortages, productivity battles and vacillating government policies. If it's difficult to prove how much BTF improved the prestige of the system, it's quite clear that BTF was more prestigious *than* the system.

The internal films inevitably have a lot less gloss on them ... As for those films aimed at staff and public alike, many detailed communications, including the ongoing *Report on Modernisation* series about the investment programme (initiated from the mid-1950s and big on shiny new locos and vast marshalling yards), were alternated with lustrous celebrations of major new services. Perhaps BTF's most famous productions were *Elizabethan Express* (1954) and *Blue Pullman* (1960; referring to the 90mph service with diesel engines at both ends, the film's West End premiere timed to coincide with its maiden journey). Meanwhile, BTF came closer than any 1950s sponsor to that decade's *Night Mails*. Films like *Train Time* (1950) and the gorgeous *Every Valley* (1957) respectively knit the operations and the social implications of public transport's running into the tapestry of a society in which industries and communities interconnect in innumerable ways. The public, it was hoped, would be more understanding of the transport system, including its defects, if so informed and stimulated, and employees would become more resilient and prouder of their achievements. Potter recalled, of screenings for staff, families and friends: 'When attending these shows, I definitely felt in the auditorium the effect on staff morale of films such as *Blue Pullman* and the *Modernisation* series.'[54]

Distribution, internal and external, was another BTF success story. A discipline instilled in the service, that many sponsors lacked, was the planning of each title's distribution ahead of its production. Indeed, BTF was unusual in not infrequently making back its investment. Around the early 1960s, BTF claimed to be receiving an aggregate audience of 6 million viewers per annum in UK cinemas, that 1.5 million were seeing BTF films across the peak non-theatrical season, that each title had a total average non-theatrical viewership of over 3 million and that over 1,000 copies of staff films were in constant internal circulation. For screenings to staff, besides the use of some 150 mobile projectors, BTF had two travelling film projection trains. Through the mid-1960s BTF also had success in placing its progress report films on television (their presence in BBC schedules easily justified by their public-information content). Aware of their prestige quality and subjects, the COI snapped up prints of major BTF productions, and the British Council also took some for overseas distribution. British Rail also had its own European and US offices in which it placed prints; some level of paid theatrical distribution was apparently achieved in all the major English-speaking countries.

The substantial structural change in BTF's history was the result of the 1962 breaking up of the BTC, which had largely failed to implement true integration. BTF was henceforth housed within the British Railways Board (BRB), with Anstey now reporting to the BRB's chief PRO Eric Merrill, a logical development as the railway network had provided the bulk of its work. BTF continued to be deployed by other parts of the former BTC, on the basis of paid contracts. Its work for London Transport remained particularly prodigious. This included two major prestige films – *All That Mighty Heart* (1963), a day-in-the-life of London and the whole vast LT undertaking; and *A Hundred Years Underground* (1964), co-produced and transmitted by the BBC – as well as a sequence of films documenting the construction of the Victoria Line across the decade.

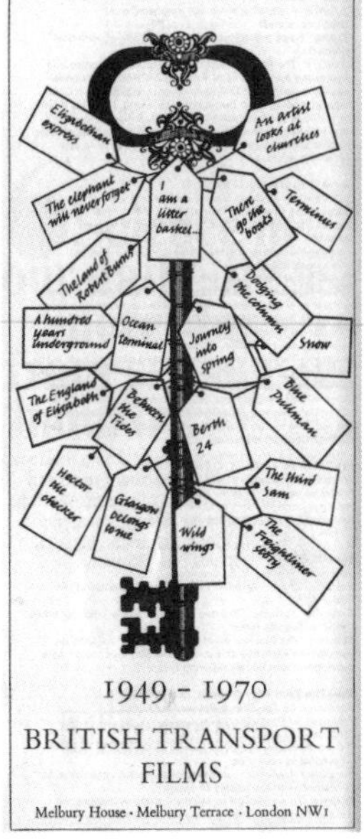

BTF moves with the times

The BRB's head was Dr Richard Beeching, infamously seconded from ICI to rationalise the railways, and shift the balance from social service to business, investment to downsizing. BTF could no longer entirely evade close association with its patron. Anstey personally directed *Reshaping British Railways* (1963), the film version of Beeching's report, shown on television as well as to staff. Beeching's regime would necessitate BTF becoming 'more functional in its aim – films aim at creating interest and getting traffic, and are more directly aimed at appropriate sections of business than they used to be', for example by being projected to invited audiences such as the representatives of possible freight custom.[55] It also meant stricter budgetary control, and encouragement of BTF taking on outside sponsorship and making facilities available for hire. It was in the midst of these changes, in 1966, that BTF won an Oscar for *Wild Wings* (1965), a lyrical natural history film and the sort of prestige effort the unit would get the chance to make fewer of in future.

From the late 1960s, BTF increasingly moved from broad 'documentary' to specialised 'communication'. The off-the-beaten-track exceptions – like the delightful *The Scene from Melbury House* (1973) – prove the rule. BTF even produced some of British Rail's TV commercials, having competitively tendered for them against other producers. In a useful illustration of the fact that on-screen and off-screen realities often ran to different timetables, the successful introduction of Advanced Passenger Trains prompted plenty of skilled technical film-making but no evergreen audience favourites like *Blue Pullman* – whose own subject had proved prone to breakdowns and only lasted a decade and a half. In the 1970s, when BR was really getting on track, BTF, though far from slowing down, was in relative retrenchment.

John Shepherd, formerly a Ministry of Defence films officer, guided BTF through its declining years. The 700-odd British Transport Films were always more popular with the public than with critics. Documentary film writers tend to damn them with faint praise, or to ignore or dismiss them altogether. Yet it's arguable that the spirit of the dying Crown Film Unit had been channelled into BTF and the films service of the National Coal Board. In these state units, the notion of national public service documentary persisted, though its boundaries had retreated to that of 'nation' as state corporation.[56] Therein, they're as fascinating a barometer of the *state* of the nation as anything from the 1940s.

UNDER THE SURFACE: THE NATIONAL COAL BOARD

> I believe that it has been to the credit of the Board, and to the policies of successive Chairmen, that we have come to be regarded as enlightened sponsors and that from the beginning we have given encouragement to our film-makers to interpret the briefs to which they have worked in the most imaginative ways open to them.
>
> Sir Derek Ezra[57]

> It cannot be stressed too strongly that a large industrial firm, or even a Government department, does not naturally turn to the full use of film and other audio-visual material in information and instruction. Unless the documentary film-makers themselves put up correct ideas, and fight for them, very little will ever be done ... unless someone trained in the documentary school had gone in and begun to plan, the wide use of films by the Coal Board would have remained a daydream.
>
> Donald Alexander[58]

Fellow servants of a state corporation, with similar ties to the pre-war Movement, the film-makers deployed by the post-war coal industry were very much on a parallel track (albeit a grittier one) to those at BTF. While BTF's history is presided over by a single eminent figure, the National Coal Board's screen history loosely divides into three phases, corresponding to the tenures of three films officers (reporting in turn to the NCB's Head of Public Relations – initially Sir Noel Newsome, then Sir Guy Nott-Bower, Noel Gee and, for many years, Geoffrey Kirk). Onto these three phases, the economic cycles weathered by nationalised coal itself were imprecisely superimposed.

Between 1947 and 1951, the National Coal Board's first (part-time) films officer Kurt Lewenhak ran a programme that included a recruitment campaign and, to no great success, 'silent' investment in feature films with a loosely pro-nationalisation message, such as Jill Craigie's *Blue Scar* (1949). A few one-off documentaries were also commissioned by Lewenhak, notably *Nines Was Standing* (1950), directed by Humphrey Swingler at Greenpark, and *The Miner* (1950), made by J. B. Holmes at World Wide. Much more propitiously, Lewenhak oversaw in 1947 the set-up of *Mining Review*, a series of one-reel reports and magazine stories from collieries and their communities released monthly into cinemas, then available on 16mm to non-theatrical audiences. Lewenhak and Newsome had dexterously grabbed for *Mining Review* the cinema slot that *Britain Can Make It* (and *Worker in Warfront* before it) had previously occupied.

At its gentlest, *Mining Review* was about helping bind coalfields, with distinct economic and cultural histories, to a new national family, while boosting the good image of mineworkers among the wider cinemagoing public. At its harder core, the series was also about convincing the public that this was no longer the industry that had surfaced bitter, exhausted and inefficient from depression and war – and convincing miners themselves that they were no longer a depressed class. *Mining Review*'s first edition, *1st Year No. 1*, was released nine months after the NCB's establishment; its last,

36th Year No. 5, four months before the Thatcher government's 1983 re-election. They make an exceptionally poignant double-bill. NCB spokesmen would later, repeatedly, assert that the series reached 50 per cent of UK cinemas every month – claiming in the late 1950s a national audience of 13 million people per issue. Though these figures should be treated with scepticism, the oft-overlooked fact remains that *no* offshoot of the Documentary Movement ever had quite such theatrical reach over so long a period.

However, it was the 1951 appointment of former DATA chairman Donald Alexander as Lewenhak's replacement that decisively deepened the Coal Board's commitment to the medium. While continuing to keep an eye on *Mining Review*, Alexander proposed that the Board implement an ambitious programme of film-making for internal distribution in support of the industry's revolutionary plans (announced by the government's 1950 Plan for Coal) for pit modernisation and work mechanisation. He further argued that it could most economically, and with greatest technical accuracy, be delivered by an internal unit. The NCB Technical Film Unit was established on a three-year trial basis in 1953. The arrangement was made permanent once its value was proven: over seventy films went into production over those three years, demand rapidly outstripped supply and about 10 per cent of the industry's total training budget was going on film. Alexander also oversaw the professionalisation of distribution: the setting up of a central library, supplemented by libraries under a designated regional liaison officer in each NCB division. These arrangements had been based on a study of the operation of the Petroleum Films Bureau and of the Gas Council's library. For NCB films as a whole, excluding *Mining Review*, a 1961 report claimed a UK reach of 829,727 people.[59] In time, the NCB even achieved overseas distribution, the result of sales to countries with substantial coal interests: Australia, India, the Middle East and North America (incongruously, *Mining Review* items were often run on Canadian television). As so often with post-war

Donald Alexander at far left (Reproduced courtesy of the National Library of Scotland)

documentary, however, influence cannot be measured by width of distribution alone, but also by effective targeting. A technical training film seen by a tiny audience of divisional planning engineers could have a greater effect on the industry's running than one seen by every employee and many outside.

Donald Alexander is one of post-war documentary's most fascinating figures, an unbending idealist quite unlike the smooth Anstey, but also shrewder in the art of the post-war possible than his erstwhile boss Paul Rotha. A sincere left-winger, he shared with other 1930s intellectuals a fascination with the concrete, practical world of masculine manual work. It's reasonable to suppose that, having failed to make of DATA any sort of vehicle for radical social change, by taking over from Lewenhak, and setting up the Unit, he was consciously embracing this half of his personality. In time-honoured documentary fashion, Alexander now gathered around him a mixture of freelancers and core staff, enthusiastic youth (including Alun Falconer, Rodney Giesler, Bob Kingsbury and Philip Owtram) and experienced old hands (like Ralph Elton, Geoffrey Bell, Brian Salt).[60]

In these lights, it's particularly intriguing to note that while the Unit became fully established as a section of the NCB, Alexander himself was paid not by the Board but by Film Centre – which, therefore, was simultaneously advising both coal and petroleum! Such films as Kingsbury's *Flight Loading* (1956), about a colliery's conversion to cutter-loading, Salt's *Coal Preparation* (1956) about the work of surface washeries, Bell's *Keep Your Diesels Running* (1956) and Giesler's *Watch That Trailing Cable!* (1957) can be enjoyed today as spare monochrome counterparts to Shell's plush coloured hymns to technicality: clear instructions that are also crisply fluent little movies, often costing just a few hundred pounds each. The Unit's catalogue rapidly grew to a visual compendium of all aspects of coal-getting: sinking and installation, support systems, ventilation, shot-firing, machinery use, transport, tunnelling, surface preparation and maintenance, as well as safety and first aid.

An annual films budget was received by the PR department from the Board, and a working group prioritised the needs of departmental heads. Films not requested at the start of the year, but urgently needed during it, had to be met by departments' own budgets. It was also possible for a regional division of the Board to sponsor a film (a 1955 film on the all-important *Anderton Shearer-Loader* was the first of these, requested by the North Western division). *Mining Review* priorities were set entirely separately, by a weekly editorial committee, drawn from the Board, the National Union of Mineworkers, and the producers and distributors. Directors and crews were generally spared these processes, and able to get on with the film-making.

Shooting on the surface

Beyond letting *Mining Review* tick over, films for a wider public were limited to those for schools, technical colleges and universities, institutions that contained the miners and managers, theoreticians and engineers of the future, and to whom private-sector employers like ICI, Unilever and BP were simultaneously targeting many of their films. Most of the NCB's classroom films were outsourced by Alexander to Basic, including *Nine Centuries of Coal* (1958), a historical reconstruction directed by Sam Napier-Bell and probably the most widely distributed single film in the NCB's history (said within a year of release to have received 30,000 external bookings). However, in the second half of Alexander's reign the character of the output began changing.

It's probably no coincidence that it was 1957 – the year in which coal's fortunes, vis-à-vis oil's, most dramatically changed – that efforts to make films for an adult, non-mining public were stepped up. Three of the more ambitious internal films were recut that year in shorter, more accessible forms in the hope of securing cinema release. *Fire Underground* (1955) became *Pit Incident* (1957), *Rawdon Reborn* (1954) became *Holiday Shift* (1957) and *Bevercotes New Mine* (1957) became *Deep Dig* (1957). *New Power in Their Hands* (1959), a compilation film based on the previous six years' accumulation of technical footage, and a more generalised, and artily rendered, statement about the industry, received national television broadcast. This memorable film anxiously pitches the imminent revolution promised by the comprehensive introduction of power loading; its edgy mood matches that of an industry dislodged from the secure knowledge that national economic fortunes rested upon its own. Internally, the introduction of work study brought with it many films calling for a modicum of emotional as well as technical intelligence, the most notable being Elton's *Shaft Survey* (1957) and Alexander's *Experiment* (1958).

In 1961, Alexander brought *Mining Review*, and much of its staff, in house to the NCB Film Unit – so renamed because of its broadened scope. After a wealth of achievements, Alexander's sudden resignation in 1963 surprised everyone except himself.[61] Explaining his timing, he cited the availability of former *Mining Review* producer Francis Gysin to replace him, and a newly sympathetic climate at the Board, thanks to the appointment of Kirk, and the media-savvy Lord Robens as chairman.[62] For several years, Alexander took on occasional freelance contracts with Gysin, notably directing the sales tool *People Like Us* (1963) and the major industrial relations film *The 4 M's* (1964), exactly the sort of productions necessitated by the industry's new predicaments.[63] But in his last working decade this legend of the 1930s Documentary Movement earned his living as head of the AV department of the University of Dundee.

Gysin's background was in several respects similar to Alexander's – Cambridge, Rotha, DATA – but his character was very different, avuncular where Alexander's was intense.[64] In some respects, Robens was the Board's counterpart to Beeching, presiding over his industry's contraction in the face of rationalist economics, but in their day they were often contrasted in the national press. Robens was a less desiccated character and his PR strategy janus-faced: cheerleading the industry in public while talking tough and plainly to his staff. For film, the two chairmen had opposite effects: BTF came under pressure to narrow its compass while the NCB Unit's was widened and its position consolidated. Under Gysin, the NCB Film Unit became perhaps the biggest industrial film unit in the world, with some fifty staff, plus freelancers. Such legendary veterans as Jack Ellitt, Cyril Arapoff, Fred Gamage and Robin Carruthers were deployed; so were ex-DATA (and Rotha) people like Peter Pickering, John Reid (producer of *Mining Review* in the early post-DATA years) and Robert Kruger (the series' producer from 1964 until its closure). So too were younger film-makers such as Ean Wood, Euan Pearson, David Pitt and Sean Hudson. Across their output, a greater variety of content and style became evident. As well as films targeted towards domestic and industrial customers, shorts like *The Big Meeting* (1963), about the Durham Miners Gala, or *Coals! Coals!* (1967), about the dying practice of horse-and-cart coal delivery (set to folksinging by Steve Benbow), were agreeable social documentaries intended for general non-theatrical distribution. *The Master Singers* (1965), a fine piece of South Welsh social history by Robert Vas (ex-Free Cinema and soon to become a great talent in poetic television documentary) was a co-production with the BBC. *King George V* (1970), a self-conscious attempt to beat BTF at its own filming-of-locomotives game, got cinema release on the strength of its use as the supporting item for the royal film performance of *Love Story*!

The 1970s were an equally busy but less creative period, though notable for the 1972 rebranding of *Mining Review* as *Review*, following which half of all issues were made for sponsors other than the NCB. For clients as diverse as the Brewers Society, the Metropolitan Police and numerous charities, the opportunity of cinema exposure was unusual. The Coal Board had meanwhile made early incursions into video production, turning out quick, ephemeral safety communications. These were produced by a separate group of technicians but, by the late 1970s, the ratio of video to film production was growing. Eventually, of course, the cost-effective attractions of the newer technology became irresistible. Such fine late film productions as *Miners* (1976) and *Forty Years On* (1978) exude, today, a valedictory quality. The last NCB Film Unit productions were released in 1983: for several months thereafter its staff, no longer producing anything, were engaged in their own tensely negotiated local exit strategy just as much bigger storms were descending upon the mining industry itself. The Unit was quietly closed in 1984, while the national miners' strike raged before a rapt nation.

The 900-odd films the NCB had made were taken for granted in the film industry of their day, and their value is only now beginning to be fully understood. To base an argument for their importance on their artistic contribution to the documentary form would clearly be beside the point of the film-makers' main intentions. Two other things are more important. One is the films' value as documentary record: they are now much the most reachable route, certainly for Britons born since their coal industry's demise, into a cavernous world that was once so heavily peopled. The other is the pivotal position of the NCB in the British documentary story. While (using state-of-the-art cameras and colour film stocks) BTF was conjuring verdant cinema daydreams, and another breed of documentary-maker was traversing the globe following the oil industry's odysseys, the NCB documentarists were burrowing deep underground with the most iconic of domestic workforces and traditional documentary equipment. Compared to the pre-war documentaries inspired by similar subject matter, the NCB films were skilfully made and addictively enjoyable, but more modest, and arguably more honest, in intent. Through sheer experience brought by long exposure, the NCB's official film-makers undoubtedly acquired a better grasp of the economics and technology of mining than their predecessors, and, perhaps, an increasingly warmer, less lofty view of its practitioners. As Lee Hall, acclaimed for his creative writing about mining culture, argues of the men who people *Mining Review*:

> Very little about the British miner seen here is Stakhanovite. They are slight, mellow chaps; what distinguishes them is their culture rather than brute force ... The idea of these films is to bring all that is hidden into the light, show us what we rely on, what we owe. These films are not really about venerating the men who do the dirty work, but about celebrating the notion of the national machine.[65]

MOLTEN MOVIES: THE STEEL INDUSTRY

Emerging from World War II, the steel industry prompted one of the most promising early post-war documentary releases though under British Council sponsorship: the still-impressive *Steel* (released in July 1945). An account of the whole process of manufacture from ore mining to ingot forging made by Ronald Riley at Technique Film Productions, it was ambitiously shot (by Jack Cardiff) in Technicolor and established the post-war relationship between steel and celluloid. The manufacture of steel yielded a uniquely visual drama that was the industry's cinematic trump card. However, while several unusually memorable films were fabricated from its source material, they were products of fragmented sponsorship: an industry of complicated structure and unsettled governance, whose screen oeuvre would be correspondingly disjointed.

Steel's position in the mixed economy was a shifting one, and its film-making shifted with it. Public ownership, augured by Labour's 1945 manifesto, sat lower down the priority list than other nationalisations, complicated by the numerous interests in other fields of industry held by most steel firms. Moreover, they had in the British Iron and Steel Federation (BISF), a single strong trade body imposed on them in the 1930s as a cautiously centralising measure, now an obstacle to further state interference. To minimise difficulty, 1949's legislation, implemented in 1951, pursued not the lock-stock-and-barrel approach taken to the nationalisation of coalmining, but a state buy-up of shares in all the individual firms, which remained intact as components of the new Iron and Steel Corporation of Great Britain. The incoming Churchill government suspended the Corporation and, over the next decade, sixteen of its seventeen main companies were successfully reprivatised.

The short-lived Iron and Steel Corporation sponsored no films, but collectively the industry initiated many films to meet perceived industry-wide needs through the BISF while many of its individual members sponsored their own documentaries. The smaller ones usually turned to local and internal 16mm units, while major ones turned to the London documentary school.

The Steel Company of Wales was a post-war pooling of the established steel manufacturers in South Wales. Its focus was investment in new or expanded operations in Llanelli, Swansea and Margam, Port Talbot. The company's investment in film-making exactly reflected this industrial strategy: a sequence of half a dozen documentary records, mostly produced by DATA and released between 1950 and 1956, chronicling the progress of construction and redevelopment of these sites.

Richard Thomas & Baldwins, a steel and tinplate manufacturer strong in Wales and the Midlands, sponsored a smattering of stand-alone films, such as *Forward Together* (1954, a history of the company). Its major contribution to the cinema of steel was the engaging magazine series *Ingot Pictorial*, released three times a year between 1949 and 1959, an intriguing parallel on-screen world to that of *Mining Review*. RT&B was the odd man out, the steel firm that remained in public ownership following the reprivatisation, employing about 10 per cent of the industry's workforce.

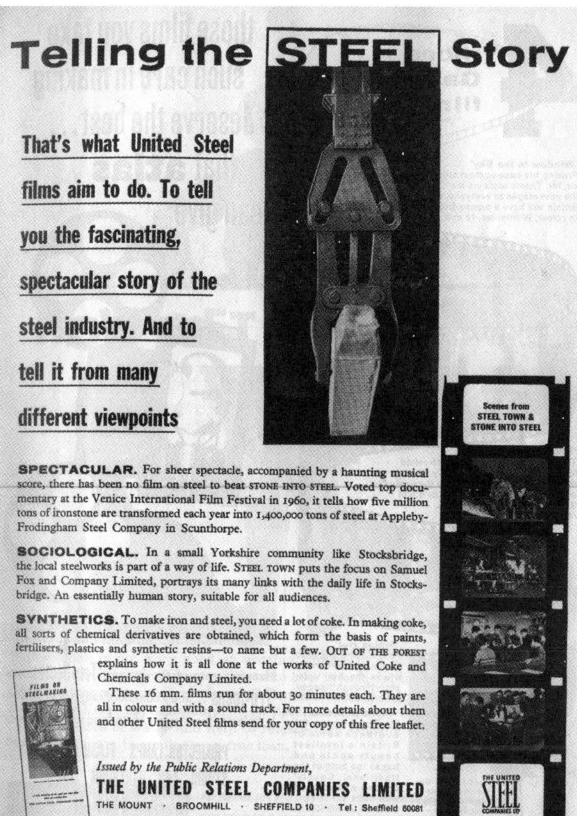

Operating across Yorkshire and Lincolnshire from its Sheffield base, United Steel Companies Ltd made relatively few post-war films, but those of greatest quality and scope. They forged a fruitful relationship with Wallace Productions, who put their wealthy sponsor's generous budgets to good use, hiring freelance directors such as Max Anderson, Paul Dickson and Bill Mason. Reviewing Mason's film *Project Spear*, *Monthly Film Bulletin* felt able, as late as 1964, not only to praise 'an excellent example of how to make an industrial film which combines information with social relevancy', but to suggest that the company's enterprising screen work 'warrants comparison with the classic school of documentary'.[66] Also, in 1959, the most ambitious of the company's films to that date, *Steel Town* and *Steel Rhythm*, opened at the Leicester Square Odeon before touring towns selected for their proximity to the company's 38,000 shareholders.

Pictorially, these films fuse the elemental to the futuristic, emphasising mechanised and increasingly automated modernisation of an ancient craft. Thematically, they make another quintessential link, of man with machine, implying a progressive company with twin commitments to investing in hardware and in workforces. The use of cinema to influence opinion is made clearer by the screen work of the British Iron and Steel Federation itself. The BISF films, of which there were eventually more than fifty, fell into two categories. About half of them reflected the practical side of the Federation's work: a programme of instructional film-making, rooted in the 1952 BISF publication, *Plan for Training*.

For the public, following several pleasant 1950s films entrusted to such units as British Films, came highly budgeted, memorable works such as Interfilm's assured *Listen to Steel* (1963), directed by Daniel Ingram, and the same production company's memorably odd curio *Men of Consett* (1961), by Tom Stobart. Pride and paranoia supplied the background to these. In the first, modernity is repeatedly emphasised: new converters and furnace types, continuous casting and tonnage oxygen-based techniques sure to increase efficiency and capacity. In the second, in a breach of the 'rules' of prestige documentary, a political line is easily detected alongside weird class tensions, cringeworthy non-professional acting and a stunningly filmed evocation of the night shift. The industry's continued insecurity about its political position was heightened by rising economic tides: easy access to raw materials (abundant indigenous iron ore and cheap coal) now a thing of the past, while an international surplus was kicking in. Unable to cushion itself against economic cycles, enthusiasm for investment, on the part of individual BISF members, duly flagged. In its collegiate form the industry grasped the opposite risk, of stirring public, political and staff suspicions. These films were intended to mitigate this predicament.

Listen to Steel proved to be the last major documentary funded by steel while still in private hands. The Wilson government renationalised the industry in 1967, merging the independent companies into the British Steel Corporation, which became overnight the largest steel-producing organisation in the non-communist world. The BSC inherited film prints from its predecessors, keeping in circulation those which hadn't been outdated by the ownership change or subsequent technical developments. At the same time, BSC initiated its own course of film sponsorship, whose basic mix (technology updates, accident prevention and general interest) remained much the same as in the private-sector era. World Wide's solid *Study in Steel* (1968), directed by Alan Pendry, had by far the greatest longevity of non-theatrical distribution, but films such as Anthony Gilkison and Associates' *Wonderful World* (1970) also made theatrical release. As in nationalised transport (and the NCB), numerous individual departments of BSC initiated their own films, but the difference is that all production was not channelled through, and budgeted by, a central films division.

After the first few years BSC rarely matched the higher budgets allocated to prestige films by United Steel or the BISF. In the 1970s, beset by losses, rationalisation became the core business stratagem, with steelmaking concentrated in ever fewer regions. The state company would not casually pay for films unlikely to win friends or influence people the way its private predecessors had envisaged.

Steel and coal teach contrasting lessons in post-war documentary's use. Mining films benefited from sponsorship applied systematically over many years by a single service of a single nationalised organisation, while steel's most interesting screen moments were functions of private ownership in a particularly apprehensive phase. Steelworks, like collieries, were no easy places to film in. Here, the problem was not so much coping with confined space as with finite time: 'You can't very well ask a huge ingot in the 8,000 ton press to please go back and do it again – the angle wasn't quite right. And, of course, it is precisely this element that makes "filming steel" so tough on the film-maker.'[67] Filming steel was also not without dangers. In 1962, a Technical & Scientific crew helmed by respected director David Villiers was filming in RT&B's Spencer Steelworks. An explosion in a steel retort showered them with molten metal, injuring cameraman Fred Gamage, his assistant George Gill and Villiers himself. Gill and Villiers both died in hospital.[68]

RIVAL WORLDS: THE OIL INDUSTRY

> Art and oil are both three letter words. To most minds the connection ends there. Not to BP. Their search for oil is a relentless, adventurous, always risky occupation and provides fascinating material for films. So where the BP oil rig goes, there go the BP cameras.
>
> BP Advertisement[69]

> It is good business for the petrol-peddler to hide his opulence behind the livery of art.
>
> Article from 1939[70]

Throughout much of the twentieth century the association between the cottage industry of British documentary film, and the colossal corporations of the oil industry ran surprisingly deep and flowed abundantly. The first five years of the Shell Film Unit, between 1934 and the outbreak of war, is the most familiar part of the story, but it was in post-war Britain that the relationship's apex was reached. In large measure, petroleum sustained and powered post-war society. Plastics and pesticides, air travel and artificial fibres, globalisation and growing populations, all and more were predicated on the increasing availability of the most versatile of the fossil fuels. Corporations involved in discovering and exploiting its global reserves became among the world's most dynamic organisations – transnationals with revenues higher than some nation states. Multinational operation based on developing the natural resources of numerous dispersed territories, with no guarantee of success, placed a premium on well-honed public relations. Oil's meteoric rise, at the partial expense of older domestic industries, also made it imperative that it be understood at home as something more than a product for sale. The vast post-war film work of Shell and BP, supplemented by the less copious output of other companies, is impressive in its quality and fascinating in its contrasts.[71] No sector of society made more enthusiastic use of the sponsored film than the oil companies; no medium was more enthusiastically embraced by them than the documentary film, and so nobody interested in the relationship of media to society can afford to leave the post-war oil documentary out of its history.

Shell and BP were the only non-American businesses among the 'seven sisters' that dominated their industry. Inevitably, both made films documenting the principal stages, upstream and downstream, of searching for, drilling and refining oil. Both also fashioned creative corporate self-portraiture in films from Shell's *The Oilmen* (1955) and BP's *Oil for the 20th Century* (1951) to *This is Shell* (1970) and *This is BP* (1972). Another common subject was motor racing, yielding such popular titles as Shell's *Grand Prix* (1949) and BP's *Tribute to Fangio* (1959) (by Bill Mason and Ronald H. Riley respectively; Mason was the pre-eminent exponent of this genre). The similarities, however, concealed substantial differences of approach, traceable to those who shaped these film programmes. At the formative stages the key individuals were, at Shell, Alex Wolcough and Arthur Elton; at BP, Ronald Tritton.[72]

Tritton claimed that 'films can evoke feelings in an audience: they can make people feel well disposed towards a company or an industry and realise that it is a decent, honest, well-run and efficient organisation',[73] while Elton observed that his films 'have publicised Shell Petroleum's reputation as a great international commercial company, but one with a lively sense of international responsibility and a leader in the fields of science and technology'.[74] Tritton's appeal was to the emotions, Elton's to the intellect.

Both companies were keen that their films should maintain an impression of independence. Shell's derived from two main precepts: references to Shell should be strictly limited to the film credits; and while films might be made by Shell employees, oversight should be in the purview of a third party. Both tactics dated back to the pre-war period. The first was traceable to the strategic vision of Shell's interwar PR pioneer, Jack Beddington, and was carried forward by Arthur Elton in his 'First Law of Industrial Sponsorship': 'the impact of a sponsored film upon its audience will be in inverse ratio to the number of times the sponsor insists on having his name mentioned'.[75] The second was serviced by the appointment and use of Film Centre, Elton's independent production consultancy. Film Centre and Elton had first been contracted by Shell in 1937 and their relationship would continue until Elton's death in 1973. During most of this period, 'the Shell Film Unit' was a mixture of Shell employees and freelancers, both of them committed to individual projects by Film Centre. Among the many film-makers associated with fine work at the Unit were Peter de Normanville, Denis Segaller and Ramsay Short, John Armstrong, Michael Clarke, Michael Heckford, Philip Owtram, Alan Pendry and Robin Jackson. For directors with a technical bent, the appeal of Shell was great. By definition free of baser qualities, and shot on the highest budgets in the documentary business, the best films – 'expository psalms', as David Robinson termed them at the time – are creatively executed and austerely beautiful in their precision.

BP was less concerned with concealing its identity but Tritton did appreciate the value of the independent voice. Going further than Shell, he bypassed the idea of maintaining a film unit, instead using independent producers. BP made contracts with companies right across the documentary spectrum, from Greenpark and World Wide through the smaller Guild companies and even DATA, to several of the new units that emerged in the 1960s and '70s. For BP's film-makers, too, oil was an attractive sponsor. Eynon Smart reported that BP 'rate the success of their work as resulting in part from the freedom their top management has allowed them (and) in part from the similar creative freedom they have allowed the production companies': a sharp contrast with, say, the COI. [76]

The two global competitors had common domestic interests. Between 1932 and 1975 they shared a joint marketing operation in the UK through the company Shell-Mex and BP.[77] This had been one of the very prompts for Beddington's initiative in setting up the Shell Film Unit (which reflected Shell's dominance of the joint body; BP's lower profile was, in turn, a prompt for Tritton's launch of BP's film-making programme). Post-war, however, Shell-Mex and BP sponsored films independently, and rarely used Shell's unit. Shell-Mex and BP's film library carried both Shell and BP films alongside its own independent sponsored product, as did the Petroleum Films Bureau, which Shell had been instrumental in setting up. Films sponsored by the Shell-Mex and BP films officer Geoffrey de Gruchy Barkas differed markedly from those initiated by Shell or BP separately. He made the distinction clear: 'public relations or prestige subjects concerned with exploration for oil, drilling, refining and research would clearly be outside our province, for this field is excellently covered by our parent groups'.[78] Instead, working mainly with minor production companies, Barkas covered industrial subjects related to products made from oil: farming films, motor enthusiasts' films and films aimed at service station owners. In many respects, the film programmes of Shell and BP competitors like Esso and Mobil were more analogous to Barkas's than to Elton's or Tritton's. Like Shell-Mex and BP these were the UK marketing arms of global (American) firms, as opposed to the Head Offices of global firms based in London.[79]

Leaving salesmanship to Shell-Mex and BP, films officers at the parent companies were able to pursue two dissimilar corporate strategies for achieving similar aims through documentary film. Shell entered the post-war period famed for its science and technical films, permeated with what Elton termed the 'aesthetics of clarity', exemplified by the work of directors such as de Normanville, Segaller and Short.[80] The Unit's famous pre-war film *Transfer of Power* (1939, directed by Geoffrey Bell), about gears, provided the model for much of what would follow (it was even remade, expertly by Robin Jackson, as *Acting in Turn* in 1975). The return to peacetime production was marked by further technical exposition in the famed six-part series *How An Aeroplane Flies* (1947).[81] As Michael Clarke put it, the company's films were 'informational', possibly 'entertaining' but were not 'entertainment'.[82]

Sir Arthur Elton

The pre-eminence of cold science at Shell can be attributed to the symbiosis of Wolcough's public relations outlook with the interests of his producer Elton. Elton was a scholar of science and technological history, and a collector of illustrated materials related to the industrial revolution.[83] He wrote that 'the media of mass communication – press, radio and film – themselves the products of scientific technology, have a special function

Ronald Tritton

in illuminating the problems of this age'.[84] The effect for Shell was to position the company as learned, professional, associated with the objectivity of science, and competent to understand and solve technical problems. 'You can be sure of Shell': the documentary films subconsciously reinforced this slogan used in the advertising of Shell products.

At BP, film-making was an almost entirely post-war development. Tritton was acutely conscious both that his employer was a late developer and that it was deeply conservative. Treading with due care, he focused initially on *Oil Review*: documentary cinemagazine films aimed, like Unilever's similar series, at schools. His first triumph with adult audiences was *Rig 20* (1952), a spectacular actuality record of the battle with a giant fire in an Iranian well. He had determined that his film programme mustn't compete with Wolcough and Elton's, and should instead take a very different tack, concentrating on the oil search film mixed in with 'people' films. One of his regular directors remembers Tritton advising him that BP sought films on subject matter that 'will give pleasure to audiences and show the world that BP are nice people'.[85]

Corporate strategies are never, of course, immutable. BP had suffered because the post-war nationalist feeling rising within Iran was fuelled by anger over the distribution of oil profits. In 1951 the Iranian government voted to nationalise the Anglo-Iranian Oil Company (AIOC), prompting the British government to intervene, unsuccessfully. Greenpark Productions' *Persian Story* (1952) was shot in the last few months before company staff left Abadan. A political coup in 1953 replaced the nationalist government of Mossadegh with a more favourable regime, allowing Anglo-Iranian to return to the country but under much less profitable terms. It was in 1954, reflecting these new political realities, that the entirety of AIOC became known as British Petroleum or BP. The episode caused the company to appreciate the necessity of expanding beyond the Middle East to find new reserves less prey to political instability. In June 1953, the company set about a worldwide review of oil prospects.[86] BP's expanded regional interests were to be increasingly represented in the films. *Station 307* (1955), directed by Louis Malle, no less, followed the famous diver, Jacques Yves Cousteau, abetting the search for undersea reserves in the Persian Gulf. BP's truly global vision was announced by the same year's *The New Explorers*, by James Hill, which begins in the familiar Middle East before moving on to Canada, Papua, Zanzibar, Trinidad and Italy. The same director's *Skyhook* (1958) and *A Walk in the Forest* (1958) concentrated on New Guinea.

A benign image for the company was painted on to the global canvas through human-interest stories such as three films from 1956: Greenpark's *Distant Neighbours*, Random's *Trawler Boy* and Jack

Howells Productions' *Journey from the East* in which brothers, an apprentice and an oilman's son respectively, all benefit from the use of oil products. The logical conclusion for Tritton's homespun approach was the semi-documentary light fiction film, whose high point came with James Hill's *Giuseppina* (1959), a tale of a rural Italian service station that received the Academy Award for Documentary Short Subject. Despite the award, the film was completely fictional, a PR success that lived on as a popular television item, and inspired the similarly charming *Mikhali* (1961) and *Cantagallo* (1969).

While the Shell Film Unit's output in the 1950s continued to favour scientific exposition it concurrently began an acclaimed sequence of high-minded social documentaries on international concerns. The first form was epitomised by *Schlieren* (1958), an explanation of Schlieren photography, which makes visible any phenomenon that changes the refractive index of transparent substances.[87] The second was announced by the smash hit *The Rival World* (1955), by Dutch film-maker Bert Haanstra, which depicts the struggle against hunger and sickness as brought by man's insect enemies. The newer form owed much to the allocation of Stuart Legg as producer within Film Centre, with Elton himself moving directly under Shell's employ. In many ways *The Rival World* was in fact a hybrid: while the film considers the work of the United Nations' health and food departments, it finds solutions to pestilence in technological fixes that match Shell's interests. Shell was broadening into chemicals and the types of science the SFU covered were broadening too. *The Rival World* tells us that Man has interfered with the balance of nature and now can only come to terms with his rivals by using organised scientific methods of control. A range of films made in cooperation with, or with the collaboration of, UNESCO and the World Health Organisation would follow, positioning Shell as concerned global citizen, a more grandiose version of BP's 'nice people'.

In line with Shell's international aims, *The Rival World* was produced in twenty-seven languages for global distribution and exhibition. Shell's internationalism was also exemplified by the creation of a family of Shell film units, such as those led by J. B. Holmes in Egypt in 1954, James Beveridge in India in 1955, Douglas Gordon in Nigeria in 1959 and Lionel Cole in South East Asia in 1960.[88] The increasing expansion of the oil industry brought rich benefits for both Shell and BP, and in the 1960s both opened new company headquarters in London, signature buildings that literally towered over the capital: Shell Centre and Britannic Tower. Both were lavishly appointed with facilities for exhibiting

'FOOD — OR FAMINE'

'FRONTIERS OF FRICTION'

'INTRODUCTION TO OIL'

Food—or Famine? Asks new Shell Film

Can we win? Today's pattern is one cultivated acre for everyone alive – and it's not enough.

An informative, sometimes frightening new colour film by Shell explores the possibilities of world food production keeping pace with world population, and offers some constructive thoughts.

Like all Shell films you can borrow FOOD – OR FAMINE free to show to societies or institutions throughout the country. And it is typical of Shell's responsible approach to world problems. For instance, in FRONTIERS OF FRICTION Shell show you how today's knowledge of the properties of oil is easing the world's transport load. And in INTRODUCTION TO OIL you are invited to a fascinating 16-minute summary of the oil industry itself.

Shell films are of the highest technical quality (they come in 35 or 16 mm). Many have won top awards. Yet to choose from the two hundred existing films, which are constantly being added to, is an art. You need the Shell film catalogue. Simply write to the address below for full particulars about how to borrow these wonderful films.

Write for the Catalogue 'SHELL FILMS'

SHELL INTERNATIONAL PETROLEUM COMPANY LTD. (TRS/213), SHELL CENTRE, LONDON, S.E.1

film.[89] At the start of the decade there were 200 staff in Shell's Public Relations Department.[90] By 1960 the company assessed the international audience of Shell films, exhibited in around thirty countries, had grown to 45 million.[91] Two years later, Shell claimed to be sending films to over seventy countries, with 4,500 prints being ordered annually for distribution by their operating companies.[92] In 1963 they claimed that an annual global non-theatrical audience of 70 million saw their films.[93] How exact such figures are is open to question, but the overriding scale and momentum are clear.

Until his retirement, Stuart Legg directed Shell's film programme onwards from Film Centre with documentaries of international responsibility. *Food or Famine* (1962) was the final film directed by the documentary veteran, and in many ways a descendant of Paul Rotha's *World of Plenty* (1943), produced by Shell in support of the Freedom from Hunger campaign of the Food and Agriculture Organisation of the United Nations. Its immediate parent was *The Rival World*, however, and the film is pro the original 'green revolution' of petrochemical intervention in agriculture.[94] Alan Pendry's *The River Must Live* (1966) introduced the concept of the oil-funded environmental film concerned not just with the problems of the world, but with the sponsor's own impact on (and responsibility for) that world. The decade's output wasn't all so worthy, however, and the exuberance of rising profits exploded onto the screen in *Shellarama* (1965), an extracurricular directorial effort by senior BBC documentarist Richard Cawston, which displays the confidence of expansionist technological capitalism. Shot in Technicolor's Super-Technirama and released on 70mm prints, *Shellarama* is a true 'documentary of attractions'. The future of Shell and of the Film Unit's output was better glimpsed in John Armstrong's film *The Underwater Search* (1965). The easily accessible oilfields were running out; areas under the oceans seemed to offer the best unexploited sources. This film's clear purpose was to demonstrate Shell's engineering expertise and experience in undersea oil production. It was shown, in specially edited local versions, to government ministers, engineers, technologists and economists in countries where Shell was touting for offshore drilling contracts.

At BP, where Tritton had originally run the films programme personally, as part of his wider brief, his success and the resulting growth of the programme caused him to appoint a fellow PR man, Dudley Knott, as a full-time films officer in 1960.

On Tritton's 1964 retirement, Knott moved elsewhere in BP, and Roly Stafford took over as head of film, recruiting Ian Brundle as his assistant. In 1977, Brundle succeeded Stafford, himself promoted to a more senior public affairs role. These were fascinating developments. While Tritton and Wolcough were PR men who had been drawn to film, Stafford had travelled in the other direction – he had been a junior at the Crown Film Unit, then a cameraman and director at Greenpark Productions. Initially, Tritton's policies were continued by Knott and Stafford, with the 'people and places' themes connecting titles as varied as *The Pitcairn People* (1962) showing the life of the Pitcairn islanders and their reaction to modern life; *The Cattle Carters* (1962) on men transporting cattle in Western Australia to the markets of Perth; and Geoffrey Jones's *Trinidad and Tobago* (1964), an impressionistic look at life on the islands. Hill's *The Home-Made Car* (1963) attempted to repeat the success of the same director's *Giuseppina*. BP continued to make oil-search films, too, following the company as it sought new fields in inhospitable regions such as Alaska, prompting a string of documentaries which, from the prospecting of *North Slope Alaska* (1964) to exportation of oil in *Pipeline Alaska* (1978), told the whole story of BP involvement. As this example illustrates, there was continuity from Knott's through Stafford's and then Brundle's periods. However, Stafford also broke new ground, especially with the cycle of environmental films starting with *The Shadow of Progress* (1970), putting the environmentalism of *The River Must Live* onto a bigger canvas than ever before, a risky move indeed.

Meanwhile, in 1970 the Shell Film Unit producers were placed on freelance contracts and budgets frozen. In 1973 Arthur Elton died, heralding the end of Film Centre, its long relationship with Shell and a direct connection to the British Documentary Movement that had lasted forty years. In fact, Shell had already reverted to a more standard industrial films arrangement with the appointment of the respected Dora Thomas as in-house films officer. Without the presence of Legg and faced with the new realities of Middle East oil embargoes and a harsher business climate, Shell films effected a gradual shift of emphasis from international socio-economics to ones closely associated with the oil business itself.

Films officer, Chairman, Director, Producer: Roly Stafford, Sir Eric Drake, Derek Williams and Humphrey Swingler at the premiere of *The Shadow of Progress*

In theory, the making of history in Britain's North Sea should have brought a grand finale for the British documentary tradition, for few subjects seem better suited to the documentary project as the Grierson of *Drifters* had conceived of it. Film-wise, the North Sea proved something of an anticlimax. There can be no contesting that the discovery of its oil occasioned tremendous engineering accomplishments, nor that much of Britain's security and affluence has since rested on its platforms. Indeed, huge numbers of films were made, including a new lease of life for films by Shell and BP's lower-rent competitors, as well as many by the two giants. As one of the earlier films had it: 'Now the North Sea is a chessboard of concessions – and these rigs and platforms are its kings and castles.'[95] The chessboard effect is one of the very defects of this composite documentary record: the vastness of the national venture itself, pursued by so many rival companies, can only be inferred from these fragments. Another shortcoming is that North Sea conditions militated against a stirring cinematic interpretation. Cramped, overcrowded platforms, peopled by impatient engineers concerned with practicality ahead of posterity, forced on directors a television repertoire of close and medium shots. In keeping with the gloomy weather under which these shots were typically taken, design and construction tended to be so similar from one platform to the next that monotony soon sets in. Individually, these films were useful to their sponsors for showing to City investors, but they did not have the inspirational effect on the public that they could, and arguably should, have done. The decline of the documentary industry had now cut too deep to reverse, even as oil's fortunes were again on the rise.

In 1983 the budgets of Shell's film and video units were cut again.[96] Although the Shell Film Library in the UK still had around 40,000 16mm film bookings a year, by 1986 the release of new material on 16mm film had almost ceased, replaced by videocassette.[97] The appointment of Maxwell Michie as Head of the Film and Video Unit in 1986 heralded the end of the distinction between the company's film and video arms. Under Michie the output further shifted from public affairs films aimed at an external audience towards more prosaic training, marketing and internal communications films, though the schoolroom audience still remained in his sights. In 1994 as Shell celebrated the sixty-year history of its internal film unit, it began divesting itself of internal production capability and of the large collections of film negatives and prints accumulated over the decades. Like those of British Transport and the NCB a few years earlier, and of BP a few years later, these now made their way to the vaults of the BFI.

THREE GRACES: ICI, UNILEVER, FORD

> The objective nature of the films has given them a much wider circulation than could otherwise have been achieved, and the ICI symbol has come to be regarded as the sign of a good documentary film.[98]

> Entertain first, inform second and sell third.[99]

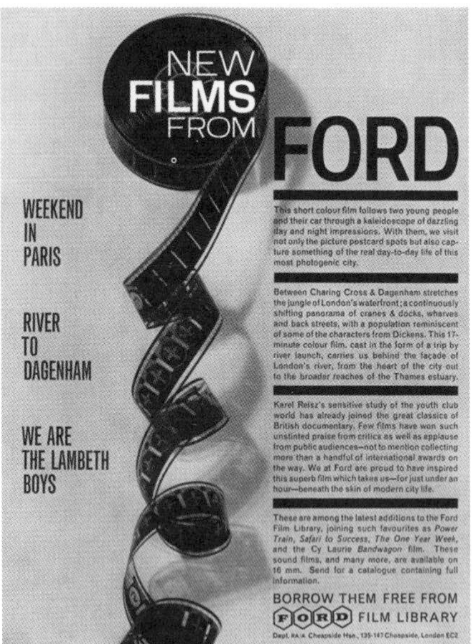

Chemicals ... consumer goods ... cars ... trades on the post-war rise, they account for the three remaining big sponsors of post-war documentary. They also make for instructive comparison. Ford confidently turned the cameras on its own commodities for the pleasure of adult audiences, while ICI and Unilever more often took the high road.[100] All three films programmes came under their parent companies' PR departments, each closely identified with their long-serving films officers. Gordon Begg at ICI, Laurence Mitchell at Unilever, Norman Vigars at Ford were all big fish in the small sea of sponsored film-making but relatively low down the pecking order of their own organisations. Indeed, Mitchell and Vigars fell victim to the 1970s slump, dextrously evaded by the entrepreneurial Begg.

By the end of the post-war period British chemicals giant Imperial Chemical Industries (ICI) had racked up some 300 films. ICI was unusual in embarking on systematic sponsorship during World War II. Early films, much like Shell's, used their sponsor's technical expertise as a springboard for documentaries of general or educational interest. Strand's *Colour* (1942), directed by Jack Ellitt and photographed by Jack Cardiff, was an early hit and remained popular for many years (it was eventually remade for the 1970s). Agriculture and medicine were much the most common early themes, and would remain well represented in the post-war output.

A structure crystallised in the late 1940s. A film library at London HQ was set up in 1948, loaning prints free of charge to both external and internal users. ICI's regional head offices provided a second channel for some titles and arranged local shows, particularly for farming and medical audiences. Abroad, overseas officers or company agents made local distribution arrangements, complemented by COI and British Council circulation of selected titles. For production, an ICI Film Unit was set up and headed by Begg but, much like his state counterparts, he balanced its schedule and capabilities with continued outsourcing. The internal unit tended, especially, to handle jobs requiring intimate company knowledge. Key personnel at different stages in its history included Peter Griffiths and David Evans. By the early 1950s, most outsourcing was to Film Producers Guild members.

The mix of productions bears comparison with that of BTF, NCB and Shell. Generalised PR objectives were interpreted on film with a degree of creative freedom: as at Shell, ideas often came from the film-makers. Simultaneously, sponsorship requests were taken from numerous internal divisions. Internally, film had a readymade managerial role: helping instil in ICI's hundred factories an appreciation that they were all interlocked in a meaningful pattern of national activity, through documentaries about particular divisions, and a staff cinemagazine, *Panorama* (1951–6). Two unusual cartoon films, made by Larkins, deserve special mention. *Enterprise* (1950) wrapped a boardroom-to-factory-floor elucidation of the company's structure in pro-enterprise rhetoric, while *Balance 1950* (1951) used animation to explain the previous year's company balance sheet. Both films, using animation, rhyming commentary and song, became non-theatrical favourites, and were oft-cited as boldly original experiments in industrial communication. Later, ICI was, with the NCB, one of the few firms to run a bespoke programme of work-study films (rather than relying on BPC titles).

For all this, ICI was an outward-looking sponsor, whose films for external audiences won general respect. Within set categories, laterally related to ICI's work, the sponsor's editorial stance was self-consciously enlightened, shades of Shell.

Elsewhere ICI made films to appeal both to export markets, like *Signs and Portents* (1962), and to interest British viewers *A Girl in a Pink Turban* (1967).[101] ICI's products inspired about half its film output. There were pictures about paints, plastics, fibres, pharmaceuticals, explosives, shotguns and zip fasteners. ICI was at pains to stress that these were 'not direct advertising films' and kept them in the public catalogue long after their original purposes passed, believing that general audiences might find them interesting.

Simultaneously, ICI remained a leader in agricultural and veterinary film-making, and it rapidly became the chief source of films, usually made in collaboration with teaching hospitals, for training doctors and nurses. Most propitious were films calculated to spread safety consciousness through ICI's own divisions, but which proved to be vivid little slices of cinema, of general application. *Black Monday* (1962), unfolding in a research lab, where carelessness causes disaster, was a particular hit, quickly becoming well known and widely used by safety trainers in many industries. Begg's team had found a forte that, much later, would prove their saving grace.

Last and definitely not least were the films designed for screening in secondary school science lessons. ICI flaunted a policy of attaching to every schools film (and many of its science films for adults) a scientist expert in its subject, to verify its accuracy and sometimes even to appear on screen. These steadily grew in volume until, by the 1960s, they accounted for a quarter of all items in the catalogue. At the end of that decade, ICI boasted that nearly 40,000 prints were reaching some 2 million pupils in 8,000 schools, and that many of its films were 'regarded by science teachers as the standard works'.[102] Practising the didactic method, many of ICI's classroom films are as monotonous as they sound. Yet a certain crusading, if calculated, idealism animates them all. Verity Films' *New Minds for a New World* (1960), perhaps inspired by C. P. Snow's 'two cultures' thesis, has Christopher Chataway discussing perceptions of science and industry with school pupils at some length.

Unilever was, like ICI and unlike Ford, an exceptionally varied industrial group, formed by a merger between British soap and Dutch margarine makers in 1930. The British half, Lever Brothers, had already furnished the screen with documentary footage of its African operations, as well as with entertaining adverts. The innumerable semi-autonomous companies sitting under the Unilever umbrella had day-to-day responsibility for manufacturing such products and for selling them, under their own brand names. So Unilever *per se* was never likely to look to the documentary film as a sales tool, nor, unlike ICI, as a central service at the call of its constituent bodies. Unilever's entry into the sponsored-film field was marked by a trio of prestige history films that commemorated its binary corporate heritage: *The Tree of Life* (1948) was a one-off made by Congolese-based Belgian film-maker Gérard de Boe that predated the main production programme that began in 1951,[103] then *A Story of Achievement* (1951) and *Portrait of a Man* (1952) remained permanently available. The first was a dramatised documentary of the nineteenth-century Dutch margarine industry, produced by World Wide Pictures but made in the Netherlands, a precedent which wasn't followed. Hereafter, film sponsorship mirrored corporate structure: like Royal Dutch Shell, Unilever was a dual-listed company, London and Rotterdam engaged in a joint venture but reporting to different shareholders. A handful of Unilever's later British films would be translated into Dutch, but apparently no Dutch production ever made it to Britain.

Editorial Film Productions, one of Soho's small production companies, produced *Portrait of a Man* and thence almost all of the sponsor's films up until the late 1950s. This period was dominated by straight documentaries of wide appeal. Their persona – pleasant, informative, unchallenging – could be likened to that of a middle-market Sunday supplement, produced to an easy-going public relations brief from Mitchell. Indeed, for five years, Editorial's main business was making *Unilever Magazine* (1951–6), which occasionally made it into cinemas. Many of the items, their subjects ranging from African textiles and UK ice-cream distribution to the life cycle of the oyster, were also released on 16mm as films in their own right. This series had the same documentary qualities as Editorial's longer Unilever films, and the same appeal across gender lines. For Unilever, unlike ICI, 'the housewife' was as pivotal a demographic as the farmer or the industrialist. A few *Drifters*-descended fishing films, culminating in the excellent *Bars of Silver* (1956), tell the story behind the food in an average shopping basket.[104] *The Purfleet Floods* (1954) reports the effects of 1953's notorious floods on Unilever's vast Essex margarine factory and the surrounding community.[105] The *Men of the Mersey* (1956) are the Wirral dockers unloading the incoming palm oil, uploading cargos for export, and personifying a business facing both ways. Indeed, several Unilever/Editorial documentaries, like *The Oil Rivers* (1956), *The Twilight Forest* (1957) and *The Surf Boats of Accra* (1958), were filmed overseas, and show the sponsor's continued presence in West Africa. These films were revised and reissued in the 1960s, as Africa assumed greater importance in Unilever's use of the medium.

In the second period, roughly 1959–71, Editorial's monopoly was replaced by a mixed roster of production units. Film-making was now dominated by overseas subjects. *Enterprise in Nigeria* (1961), *The New Traders* (1961), *African Awakening* (1962), *Towards the Highlife* (1965) and *Ghana – A Report* (1969) were neither travelogues nor (overt) self-promotions but documentary accounts of societies in industrial flux. They were also probably the most expensive films Unilever ever made, which suggests their perceived importance for the sponsor in cementing relations with emerging nations. Though made by London-based film-makers, Unilever in Britain effectively co-sponsored them with its subsidiary the United Africa Company (UAC). Their primary intended audience, for whom UAC organised road-show screenings, was African. Similarly, broadened corporate horizons came into view in *Asian Crescent* (1964), about Malaysia, and *Four Men in India* (1967), a co-production with Hindustan Lever.

The second drastic change in Unilever's film-making was that, overseas epics aside, Mitchell now turned the production programme over almost entirely to educational films. While some dealt directly with the science behind the oils, fats and detergents on which Unilever's own scientific research was concentrated, others introduced broader areas of science curricula like molecular chemistry, physiology and genetics, as well as domestic science, deploying a generally perkier style than ICI's. Like ICI, Unilever emphasised the veracity of its films for schools, assured by expert oversight. In Unilever's case, this was effected by attaching to every production both a relevant advisor in the company's own research department and a practising schoolteacher in the subject concerned. Unilever's own analysis of 1965 bookings claimed 3 million classroom viewers, adding 'two points which have received unanimous praise from teachers are the summary at the end of science films and the lack of self-emphasis in Unilever's educational films as a whole'.[106] Just as the overseas films were available in Britain, so Unilever's teaching films were distributed abroad. And again, they were put to slightly different ends in Africa than at home: 'dealt with at what in this country would be regarded as an O-Level standard ... in Africa they are shown to sixth forms and in universities, which perhaps shows the difference in educational achievement and the gap that has to be closed'.[107]

The full screen history of the Ford Motor Company Ltd (aka Ford of Britain) has been obscured by the very fame of its two best-known films: Lindsay Anderson's *Every Day Except Christmas* (1957) and Karel Reisz's *We Are the Lambeth Boys* (1959). Had it not been for Reisz's short tenure as Ford's films officer (acquired when he speculatively responded to the job advertisement), these films wouldn't have been made and that small canon of films known as Free Cinema would have had a different character. So far as Ford was considered, these 'Free Cinema' films, released under the heading of *Look at Britain*, were a form of prestige, if previously untried, public relations.

In fact, Henry Ford's depression-era decision to make Dagenham Britain's Detroit had led to several pre-war films. In the early post-war years, Ford often worked with Verity Films – for instance, to explain *How the Motor Car Engine Works* (1946). Still more deeply rooted in Ford's relationship with the British Isles was its range of agricultural vehicles, hence the *Fordson Newsreel* (1953–60), embedding gentle product placement into items of general, local and farming interest.

It wasn't until 1956, after twenty-seven years of sporadic film-making, that Ford employed Reisz as the company's first films officer. As well as the off-the-beaten-track *Look at Britain* series, Reisz directed more conventional fare such as *Three Graces* (1956), a story of two British couples holidaying across Europe. One couple drives a Consul, another a Zephyr convertible. Later a Ford agent takes them on an Alps tour in a Zodiac, the third 'Grace'. The point of making such a film in 1956 was that all three cars were restyled that year with a new family-orientated design. Look at Britain, indeed.

Former Fleet Street journalist Norman Vigars replaced Reisz in 1957. Housed with the Publications department of Ford's Public Affairs division, he ran a tiny film unit of four or five people meeting the company's day-to-day audiovisual needs and making some of its films, while others were produced by external contractors. Vigars liked to blend the two solutions, having in-house and bought-in film-makers working together on the same production. Unlike Unilever or ICI, Ford contracted out its distribution. By 1965, Ford was claiming over 4 million UK viewers per annum, and 750 prints were despatched around the nation every week – none of them to conscripted classroom audiences. In fact, 50 per cent of Ford's domestic bookings were said to be from motoring clubs, of whom post-war Britain had many. (We can assume that Ford, unlike a Unilever, expected its core audience to be male.)

Looks-at-Britain notwithstanding, many of Ford's films were unashamed celebrations of the motor vehicle, a subject deemed of intrinsic interest to viewers to an extent that coal, oil and chemicals were not. Stylistically, films ranged from slight travelogues, fair to excellent social documentaries (it was Vigars who commissioned Reisz's *We Are The Lambeth Boys*) and decent human interest to glossy, sexist jazz-hymns to conspicuous consumption, smooth driving and fine upholstery design. The importance of motor-racing events also began to colour Ford's filmic output. *Nine*

Days in Summer (1960) referred to Jim Clark and Graham Hill's nine formula races under the Lotus-Ford banner, while *Year of the Cortina* (1964) rammed home the Cortina's domination of international saloon-car racing. Ford was also part of the 1960s' trend for 'novelty' sponsored films. *A Child's Guide to Blowing Up a Motor Car* (1965) remained a popular non-theatrical booking for several years. While these films entertained audiences in Britain, from 1963 Ford began to see film as a tool to help it win export markets, as with a film like *Project D* (1965), concerned with the D-range of commercial vehicles designed with large-scale export to the continent as a key objective. Surely the 'anti-*Lambeth Boys*' among Ford's films, *Project D*, hailed as a great success within the company, was aimed at dealers, among whom prints were said to be in constant circulation.[108]

Henry Ford's plan for coordinated European operations had collapsed as early as the 1930s, leaving British Ford in competition with its continental counterparts. This situation was ended by the creation of Ford Europe in 1967. Integration found its way into the British films, as in *Prototype* (1970), showing coordinated UK-German R&D of a new range of cars. Vigars' last major release, however, was a wistful return to the patronage of subjects entirely unrelated to corporate interests. *The Bacchae* (1973) documents the mounting of Euripides' play by public schoolboys at Bradfield College.

While economic pressures caused Unilever (in 1971) and Ford (in 1974) abruptly to withdraw from film-making, the ICI Film Unit was renamed Millbank Films in 1966 and found a new lease of life. Although a wholly owned ICI subsidiary, encouraged to become self-financing Millbank began making films for outside agencies. Above all, Millbank started making generic training films, on cannily chosen subjects, on a speculative basis – anticipating, to some extent creating, a market for them across British industry, and asking high booking fees. The earned income at first cushioned the unit against the economic climate that was bringing others down, then took it into profit (eventually, Millbank would leave ICI altogether). The emergence of this type of film was part of the splitting apart of the documentary film and the industrial film, which heavily contributed to the demise of both (in their post-war forms).

Millbank's safety and general training films tended to be dramatic in form. Perhaps their biggest fascination today is as a fragmentary map of the lost working world of the 1970s. Sample titles include: *Man in the Middle* (1976), *When Fire Starts* (1977), *Something to do with Safety Reps* (1978), *Coping with Conflict* (1979). In July 1982, a school year ended and ICI's educational library closed, but Millbank, under Begg's successor David Evans, managed the transition to the video era. A 1988 merger with Rank Training was the first of several buy-ups with Millbank's name and catalogue currently sitting with Outtakes, a production company specialising in health and safety, currently exploring online and interactive training technology. The story of ICI itself ended in 2008, with its acquisition by the Dutch multinational AkzoNobel.

NOTES

1. John Roberts, 'The Aims of Films on Industry', *Guardian*, 20 April 1964, p. 27.
2. John Chittock, 'Who Wants a Films Officer?', *Financial Times*, 5 April 1966 p. 15. One of the latterday 'Griersons' of whom Chittock was writing (Norman Vigars at Ford) elaborated: 'The films officer must be schizophrenic ... the right hand can have a wonderful time in stimulating ideas and utilising the varied talents of the film-makers, the left must be aware that he owes not only a basic employee-loyalty to the people who pay his salary cheque, but he must also, to survive, go along with their business systems and be himself a man of finance, a planner and co-ordinator ... I don't think a

man would make a good films officer if, for instance, he had spent 15 years in cost accounting ... because he would be too close to budgetary control. But any brilliant producer ... with a flair for the avant-garde and inspirational, would be as likely to come unstuck.' Quoted in Gloria Tessler, 'Talking to Sponsors', *Film User*, November 1968, pp. 12–13.

3. Sir T. Fife Clark, director-general of the COI (1954–70) in Fife Clark, *The Central Office of Information* (London: George Allen & Unwin, 1970), p. 71.
4. Last line of the chapter on 'Film-Making by the Nation', in Derrick Knight, and Vincent Porter, *A Long Look At Short Films: An ACTT Report on the Short Entertainment and Factual Film* (Oxford: Pergamon Press, 1967), p. 131.
5. See, for example, Leo Enticknap, 'The Non-Fiction Film in Britain, 1945–51' (unpublished PhD thesis, 1999). Available online at <wwww.enticknap.net/leo/index.htm>. Also A. J. Harding, 'The Closure of the Crown Film Unit in 1952: Artistic Decline or Political Machinations?', *Contemporary British History* vol. 18 no. 4, Winter 2004, pp. 22–51.
6. Gerry Boarer, Films Officer of the GPO reported, 'all government departments had to go through the COI who acted as surrogate producers (with a mark-up of 40 per cent)', in Gerry Boarer, 'Mail and Movies – History of Post Office Film Making' (unpublished, c. 1986), p. 18, Royal Mail Archive POST 108/89. A reference to 30 per cent 'oncosts' for film is mentioned in D. J. Etheridge, 'Home Departments: Summary of Points from Replies to the Priestley Team on Repayment' (16 July 1979), in TNA INF 12/1421, *Funding of COI Services.*
7. TNA CAB 124/1025 Documentary Film Enquiry.
8. Sir Henry L. French (Chairman), *Report of the Committee on the Cost of Home Information Services* (Cmd. 7836), TNA CAB 124/74, p. 11.
9. Central Office of Information, *Relations between Sponsoring Departments, the Central Office of Information and Film Contractors in the Production of Films made for Theatrical and Non-Theatrical Distribution*, a paper produced after discussions with the ASFP and circulated to Ministerial departments in September 1958.
10. *Third Report from the Select Committee on Estimates together with the minutes of the evidence taken before Sub-Committee F and appendices. Session 1959–60. The Central Office of Information* (Paper 259) (London: HMSO, 1960).
11. Philip Mackie, 'Production History of a COI Film', in *Monthly Review; COI Films Division* no. 11, August 1947, pp. 7–9.
12. Marjorie Ogilvy-Webb, *The Government Explains: A Study of The Information Services* (London: George Allen and Unwin, 1965), p. 66.
13. Joseph Ball, Head of the Films Division, MOI in *Films Division General Plan of Operations* [September 1939], TNA INF1/194 MOI.
14. Enticknap, 'The Non-Fiction Film In Britain 1945–1951'.
15. French, *Report of the Committee on the Cost of Home Information Services.*
16. See John Taylor's BECTU History Project Interview (recorded 1988). Taylor was producer-in-charge at Crown Film Unit, 1947–52.
17. John Taylor is quoted to this effect in Knight and Porter, *A Long Look At Short Films*, p. 116.
18. French, *Report of the Committee on the Cost of Home Information Services.*
19. Anon., 'Cut!', *The Economist*, 16 February 1952, p. 386.
20. See, Cinematograph Film Production (Special Loans) Bill, *HC Deb 25 November 1953 vol 521, HC Deb 25 February 1957 Vol. 565*, also the *Third Report from the Select Committee on Estimates, Session*

1959–60 – the Central Office of Information (Stationary Office, 1960), 'COI Want New Government Film Unit Production Of Rapid News And Features Aimed At TV', *The Times*, 7 October 1960, p. 8.

21. *Summary of the Report of the Independent Committee of Enquiry into the Overseas Information Services* (the Drogheda Report) (Cmnd. 9138).
22. 'Big Changes at the COI', *Film User*, February 1961, p. 96.
23. See Emily Crosby and Linda Kaye (eds), *Projecting Britain: The Guide to British Cinemagazines* (London: British Universities Film and Video Council, 2008).
24. Clark, *The Central Office of Information*, p. 19.
25. *White Paper on Representational Services Overseas* (Cmnd. 2276).
26. Linda Kaye, 'Overseas Television 1954–64', in Crosby and Kaye, *Projecting Britain*, p. 85.
27. Clark, *The Central Office of Information*, p. 72. Movietone cameramen and sound teams were among the contractors used for this work. The COI did, however, retain editors and had production staff for overseas production, see Frances Cockburn BECTU History Project Interview (interviewed 15 March 1990 by Margaret Thomson). Cockburn had previously worked at Crown and at World Wide Pictures and rose to become a respected Head of Films Division in the 1970s; later she joined the board of Balfour Films.
28. See TNA FCO 26/619, *Review of Central Office of Information by Sir Gordon Newton*, and TNA FCO 26/623, *Future of Central Office of Information*.
29. See Frances Cockburn BECTU History Project Interview.
30. TNA INF 12/1550, a review by Sir Ronald Melville to investigate ways of streamlining the various activities of COI, paying special attention to overseas information work. The fall-out from Melville's report also makes up TNA INF 12/1173 and INF 12/1174, Sir Ronald Melville's review of COI redundancies including Association of Cinematograph Television and Allied Technicians members, and TNA INF 12/1183, Implementation of the recommendations of Sir Ronald Melville's report on the Association of Cinematograph Television and Allied Technicians: correspondence with Lord Privy Seal.
31. *The United Kingdom's Overseas Representation* (Cmnd. 7308) (London: HMSO, 1978) and TNA INF 12/1421 *Review of COI Expenditure and Practice in Relation to Central Government Policy: Allied Service and Repayment Steering Group*.
32. See COI fears expressed in a memo from D. J. Etheridge (COI Finance and Accounts) to the Director General (3 January 1979) in TNA INF 12/1421, *Funding of COI Services*.
33. See Etheridge, 'Home Departments', TNA INF 12/1421, *Funding of COI Services*.
34. 'Central Office of Information (Film Unit)', *HC Deb 30 October 1981 vol. 10 c473W*.
35. 'Central Office of Information (Film Unit)', *HC Deb 07 December 1981 vol. 14*.
36. See letter from John Langston, Director of the COI Films Division, in 'Appendix 8; Central Office of Information, Profits on Film Production Contracts. Letter from the COI to the Clerk to Sub-Committee F', in *Third Report from the Select Committee on Estimates together with the minutes of the evidence taken before Sub-Committee F and appendices. Session 1959–60. The Central Office of Information* (Paper 259) (London: HMSO, 1960), p. 279.
37. Paul Fletcher, 'To Raise Britain's Productivity', *Film User*, June 1955, p. 288.
38. Wording used in several editions of the Gas Council's film catalogue.
39. 'One of the main reasons why the Gas Council prefers to engage outside producers is just that indefinable stamp that every good director impresses on his work ... *Guilty Chimneys* [by Pathé] has a

sonorous poetic commentary over visuals of ugly industrial towns ... *Keep it Clean* [by Realist] ... has a crisp colloquial commentary over scenes of squalid domestic life. Each is admirably suited to its context and although both films are in the documentary tradition and intended to make people think, they are in complete contrast ... there is a risk of becoming stereotyped in confining production to one unit.' Stanley Irving, 'Audience of 600,000', *Film User*, May 1963, p. vii.

40. Fletcher's wife, Yvonne Fletcher, worked at Paul Rotha Productions (she was generally believed to be Rotha's mistress). She directed a number of interesting films in the 1940s, including the touching Save the Children wartime short *The Children See It Through* (1941).
41. *Visual Aids*, June 1956, p. 7, Ken Gay collection, Box 34.
42. Paul Fletcher, 'How We Use Films 11: To Raise Britain's Productivity', *Film User*, June 1955, p. 289
43. Quoted in 'Productivity: Better Ways on Film', *Film User*, May 1953, p. 179.
44. 'Old prejudices, hitherto dormant, sometimes become reactivated. And this is true of both shop-floor and management ... the British Productivity Council starts, of course, with the advantage that it reflects the interests of both sides ... over the years this dual viewpoint has become accepted and respected throughout industry.' Ronald Veltman (Head of Visual Aids and Education), 'Film and Productivity', *Imagery*, Autumn 1963.
45. Member countries were advised to give notice to the EPA of planned productions which may be of wider European use. If at least five out of the EPA's seventeen members gave the project their green light then 49 per cent of its budget would be paid by the EPA, on the expectation that translated prints would be distributed to those other countries. Their own national productivity centres were all entitled to have input into the film's treatment, but production itself would remain under the control of the national productivity centre which had initiated the film (a sign of the BPC's political weakness, though, was that the Board of Trade, not the BPC, was the UK's designated national centre). Around 50 per cent of the BPC's 1950s films, certainly including most of those about work study, benefited from this arrangement and so were, presumably, extensively distributed abroad, in translation. A senior visual aids officer at the EPA was Britain's Langton Gould-Marks, a former Films of Fact and Merton Park and a future DATA and NCB film-maker. Gould-Marks frankly stated that the EPA sought 'to act as a coordinator between the countries of Western Europe on the one hand and the United States on the other'.

    In addition, on acquisition of BPC prints for UK and overseas distribution (every film went into the Central Film Library), the COI was entitled to recoup all associated costs from the Board of Trade's US aid account. That so much BPC activity depended on American money is apposite: much of its work was about importing the 'scientific management' of workplaces rooted in nineteenth-century American theory and making them locally acceptable. (Heading a UK visit, which took in appointments with BP, the COI, British Transport, the NCB and the Film Producers Guild, Jean le Harivel, head of EPA technical aids and, incidentally, a former Guild employee, declared that the UK was 'ahead of Europe in this increasingly important field' [one EPA task was collating and publicising lists of its members' relevant productions; as at 1955, 159 of 178 were British].)
46. A. J. Speakman, quoted in 'Industry's Screens', *Film User*, April 1956, p. 165.
47. 'Sir Charles Norris, 'The Film and Productivity', *Film User*, April 1958, p. 150.
48. *3 New Films on Productivity*, Ken Gay collection, Box 34.
49. Quoted by Paul Smith in 'British Transport Films: The First Decade', on BTF fansite, <www.britishtransportfilms.co.uk>

50. Text of Beeching address to Institute of Public Relations, 19 April 1963, TNA AN 18/15.
51. Anstey's board memberships included the Children's Film Foundation, the Royal College of Art, the BFI and its Production Board, the Board of Trade's Cinematograph Films Council and the British Film Academy and its successors.
52. Edgar Anstey, 'How We Use Films', *Film User*, May 1955, pp. 213–15.
53. Lines from the scripts of *North to the Dales* (1962) and *Any Man's Kingdom* (1956).
54. Charles Potter, 'Reels on Rails', *The Veteran* no. 7, Winter 1993, p. 11.
55. *BTC Outline Plan: Public Relations*, 10 April 1962, TNA 111/144A. A memo in the same file notes 'a conflict between the Traffic Departments who wish hard-selling points and the Chief Officer (Films) who has to place his films with Cinema Circuits, Television and exhibit overseas'.
56. Anstey had argued: 'apart from the economic advantages of the internal unit for an organisation as large as the Transport Commission, there are great psychological benefits and benefits of "know-how" coming from a film unit which is part of the transport family and can both give and receive some of the good things of healthy family life'. Edgar Anstey, 'How Films Serve the World's Biggest Employer', *Industrial Screen* vol. 3 no. 2, May/June 1959, p. 93.
57. Sir Derek Ezra, 'Why the Coal Board uses Film and Video', *Video and Film Communication*, September 1984, p. 8.
58. Donald Alexander, 'NCB – the First Twelve Years', *Film User* vo1. 3 no. 150, April 1959, p. 176.
59. TNA COAL 32/16.
60. Ex-Crown Film Unit man, Elton was the brother of Arthur, with whom he shared the family mansion, Clevedon Court. It is said that Arthur powered his half using oil-fired central heating, while Ralph used coal. A perfect mixed-economy metaphor.
61. Six years earlier, Alexander had written: 'a long time ago, you as good as said that I was intent on building an Empire. If you only knew how wrong you were! You could say that to Edgar Anstey, who will grow venerable with a long white beard in his Estate, but not to me. My hero is Cincinnatus, who came out and did what had to be done, and then retired to his vineyards.' Alexander to Gee, undated (but probably 1957), SSA: 4/20/41.
62. Gysin had first encountered Robens, the NCB's first twentieth-century-born chairman, when assistant-directing Rotha's *A City Speaks* (1947) to which, as a then Manchester councillor, Robens contributed narration. *Mining Review 14th Year No. 6* (1961) is a fascinating portent. Most of the issue is taken up with the handover from Sir James Bowman to Robens. Bowman, a former mineworker, is touchingly awkward; Robens, until recently a right-wing Labour politician, projects an informed confidence in his own screen presence.
63. He and Budge Cooper also filmed a series of *Mining Review* profiles of the individual coalfields (such as 'North Star', about the Yorkshire coalfield, in *Mining Review 20th Year No. 9* [1967]).
64. Ken Gay, who worked for both Alexander and Gysin, remembered, 'Francis was notorious for his ability to run things from a bar stool ... Francis was decisive and efficient and ran the Film Unit with brio; he was greatly respected throughout the Board ... Working in a pub was just his style'. Ken Gay, *Hand in Hand with Time: A Memoir* (London: Honeysuckle, 2009), p. 202.
65. Lee Hall, 'Going Underground', *Sight & Sound* vol. 19 no. 10, October 2009, p. 26. Hall, the writer of *Billy Elliot* and *The Pitman Painters*, was spokesman for the BFI's *King Coal* project, which included the first DVD compilation of NCB films, *Portrait of a Miner*.
66. *Monthly Film Bulletin* vol. 31 no. 365, June 1964, p. 96.
67. *Listen to Steel* brochure, Ken Gay collection, Box 5.

68. Over two years later, claims for negligence against RT&B were settled, the firm admitting liability. Guild Holdings Ltd was also sued, for taking out insufficient insurance, and settled on a payment to Villiers' and Gill's estates without admitting liability.
69. BP, 'Why did the Oil-man Win an Oscar?', *The Times*, 13 September 1965, p. viii (*The Times Supplement on the Arts in the Commonwealth*).
70. John Cuff, 'Post Office Publicity', *Penrose Annual* 41 (1939), p. 22. Quoted in LeMahieu, *D. L. A Culture for Democracy: Mass Communication and the Cultivated Mind in Britain Between the Wars* (Oxford: Clarendon Press, 1988), p. 267.
71. The name Shell is used throughout to refer to the multinational company Royal Dutch Shell Group birthed by the merger of the Royal Dutch Petroleum Company and the Shell Transport and Trading Company in 1907. The name BP is used to refer to the company formed in 1908 as the Anglo-Persian Oil Company, renamed as the Anglo-Iranian Oil Company in 1934 before becoming the British Petroleum Company in 1954. The company had previously used BP as a brand name for its retail products.
72. Wolcough started at Shell in 1934 and remained there for three decades. Tritton had done PR for the Savoy Hotel pre-war and during World War II was in the War Office – where he rubbed shoulders with Wolcough's colleague Jack Beddington, and with Elton (then at MOI). He was then Director of the Films Division at the early COI before joining Anglo-Iranian in 1948.
73. Tritton, 'How We Use Film 1: At Anglo-Iranian', *Film User*, September 1953, pp. 464–5.
74. Elton, 'How We Use Films 17: In Shell', *Film User*, August 1956, pp. 344–8.
75. Douglas Gordon, *Shell Films: The First Sixty Years* (London: Shell Film and Video Unit, 1994), unpaginated.
76. Eynon Smart, 'BP makes Mark from Skilled Productions with Insight on People', *The Times*, 17 March 1975, p. 16. BP's budgets were on average appreciably lower than Shell's. However, as BP operated a travel company, budgets on international productions were able to stretch further than they otherwise would.
77. In 1957 the company National Benzole joined Shell-Mex and BP while continuing to trade separately. National Benzole also sponsored a number of films between 1957 and 1974, notably the *Our National Heritage* series (initially with John Betjeman), which mirrored Shell-Mex's *Discovering Britain* series. They favoured the director Peter Mills and his company Random Film Productions.
78. Geoffrey de Gruchy Barkas, 'How We Use Films: 10', *Film User*, October 1954, p. 468.
79. Mobil engaged lower-end Film Producers Guild companies like T&S at the same time BP was engaging higher ones. The sponsor's most memorable production was *Signorina! It's Important* (1962), directed at T&S by David Villiers, a jaunty counterpart to Shell and BP films that evoke oil's circulation throughout western society. Esso had a more ambitious programme, including many general-interest documentaries and some prestige items, more comparable to those of Shell and BP but shot on lower budgets.
80. Michael Clarke, 'Discovery and Invention', *British Universities Film & Video Council Newsletter*, May 1985. The alternative but comparable phrase 'the aesthetics of lucidity' appears in an article by the Head of Special Techniques in the Shell Film Unit, see Denis Segaller, 'Animation and Other Visual Techniques in Scientific Films', *Science and Film* vol. 7 no. 2, June 1958, pp. 12–24. Clarke also recalled: 'The growing success and rising esteem of the SFU were envied by many. Its austere codes and styles were widely resented. Lindsay Anderson and Karel Reisz had sponsorship from Ford which allowed them to make "human films", and in a memorable discussion meeting at the Crown Theatre in Wardour Street they openly challenged Elton, Legg and Film Centre colleagues to produce "human

films" about the oil business. They claimed that the aviation films dealt only with things and had hardly one shot of a living person in them. I remember trying to rebut this by suggesting that they were the work of a human (P. de Normanville) and that they were a tribute to human ingenuity, persistence and daring'. Clarke, 'Notes on the Shell Film Unit and Film Centre', January 1994 (unpublished), held by BFI National Library.

81. A series that would be used by air forces and flying schools around the world as an introduction to basic aeronautics and was so successful it was remade and updated in 1974 to take account of subsequent developments in jet-engine technology.
82. Michael Clarke interviewed by Colin Burgess (January 1994).
83. Elton's books include *Why Aeroplanes Fly* (London: Longmans, Green and Co., 1936), *How Motor Cars Run* (London: Longmans, Green & Co., 1939), *British Railways* (London: Collins, 1945), *The Book of the Jet; A Simple Account of the Gas Turbine* (London: Shell-Mex and BP Ltd, 1952), et al.
84. Arthur Elton and Sinclair Road, *The Popularization of Science Through Film* (Paris: United Nations Educational, Scientific and Cultural Organization, 1949), p. 2.
85. Ronald Tritton quoted from memory in a letter from Derek Williams to Patrick Russell (24 January 2010).
86. J. H. Bamberg, *British Petroleum and Global Oil, 1950–1975: The Challenge of Nationalism* (Cambridge: Cambridge University Press, 1994), p. 106.
87. Some later technological titles, like *Prospect for Plastics* (1962), directed by Ramsay Short, and *Cast in a New Mould* (1964), directed by Michael Heckford, have a less ascetic, more expansive and atmospheric style.
88. Global activity was not all plain sailing, however, and, among the valuable oilfields of the Middle East, countering the rising tide of nationalism drove oil company public relations, not least at the Iraq Petroleum Company – an international consortium of European and American oil interests including both Shell and BP. Between 1952 and 1958 those British interests sponsored films legitimating the company's presence in the country, with productions in both Arabic and English. In 1953 the company explicitly laid out their aim 'to use film for a ... serious purpose – to prevent Persian happenings repeating themselves in neighbouring Iraq, by showing the public there that the activities of an oil company benefit not only the shareholders but the country which owns the oil'. The Suez crisis in 1956 added further impetus to the PR drive. Film Centre was recruited to produce films through the 'Iraq Petroleum Company Film Unit', including John Armstrong's six-part *The Study of Oil* (1958) and an Arabic-language cinemagazine aimed at an Iraqi audience.
89. Anon., 'The Shell Centre Theatre: Function with Beauty', *Business Screen* vol. 29 no. 3, 1968, p. 36.
90. Kevin Moloney, *Rethinking Public Relations: The Spin and the Substance* (London: Routledge, 2000), p. 79.
91. John Drummond, 'Shell Film Operations' (16 December 1960), Shell Group Archive, PAC/21 B SFU 14, quoted in Rudmer Canjels, 'From Oil to Celluloid: A History of Shell Films', in Jan Luiten van Zanden, *A History of Royal Dutch Shell: Appendices, Figures and Explanations, Collective Bibliography, and Index* (Oxford: Oxford University Press, 2007), p. 18.
92. *Films* (SIPC, 1963), Shell Film and Video Unit Archive quoted in Canjels, 'From Oil to Celluloid', p. 22.
93. Robinson P. Rigg, 'Films Across the Frontiers', *Business Screen* vol. 24 no. 4, 1963, p. 25.

94. Many subsequent films would follow its model, for example, *The Land Must Provide* (1968), *Bandits in the Barley* (1970), *Time to Spray* (1973), *Pesticides in Focus* (1971). The film itself would be revised in 1974.
95. Commentary from *North Sea Quest* (1967), sponsored by BP and produced by World Wide Pictures.
96. 'Films and Television Meeting' (10–11 October 1983), Shell Film and Video Unit Archive, quoted in Canjels, 'From Oil to Celluloid', p. 24.
97. Ibid.
98. B. W. Galving Wright, (Deputy to Controller of Publicity, ICI), 'ICI Films', *Imagery*, no. 4, December 1949, p. 20.
99. Ford's films policy as summarised by Tessler, 'Talking to Sponsors', p. 12.
100. 'Fortunately, it is to everyone's advantage that young people should be encouraged to grow up not only accepting, but also understanding, their technological environment ... school-leavers are strongly influenced by the reputations of their local firms. A company may find, however, particularly if its name is not a brand name, that unless it disseminates information about itself and its activities it may be little known, and even less understood, outside the City and the financial pages of the national press ... As a means of communication, film has a unique ability to capture the interest and stimulate the imagination ... to show some of the company's major interests and also the varied fields in which [it] can be regarded as a source of authoritative information.' 'Film at Work 3: Three Million at School', *Film User*, May 66, pp. 214–15.
101. Verity Films' *Signs and Portents*, co-directed by Seafield Head, Peter Jessop and Bob Turk, is an impressionistic survey of ICI's varied exertions, and exemplifies the openly celebratory brand of corporate prestige: not only in its content but in its use. 'We decided that in each country in Europe we would use this film to create a pleasant occasion on which, in the presence of the British Ambassador and one of our own directors, we could entertain the leading commercial and financial personalities of the country.' (The film thereafter went into general distribution.)
102. 'ICI Films for Schools', press release, 21 January 1970, Ken Gay collection Box 21. Lawrence Hogben, 'An Experiment in Using Films to Aid Export Salesmen', *BIFA Bulletin*, July 1965, pp. 8–9.
103. As its unintentionally ironic title suggests, de Boe's film proffers a remorselessly sunny account of the brutal legacy of William Lever.
104. Ken Gay made use of this film to pursue his argument with Free Cinema: 'Lindsay Anderson says he has eschewed statistics and ... captures common people and local atmosphere. I ask myself how does this compare for example with Editorial's film about the fish market's *Bars of Silver*, which passed unnoticed without any press publicity at all, and find that real people (this time Billingsgate types) are just as much captured there.' Ken Gay, 'How Free Can We Be?', *Films & Filming*, September 1957, p. 33.
105. Stylistically a curious throwback, *Purfleet* was written by Stuart Legg, which suggests Film Centre might have had some hand in Unilever's film-making at this time.
106. 'Film at Work 3: Three Million at School', *Film User*, May 1966, pp. 214–15.
107. Kenneth Myer, 'Films and Africa', *Film User*, May 1971, pp. 18–19.
108. At the premiere: 'Two thousand dealers from all over Europe were flown into Copenhagen. We showed them the film and it is true to say that all we had to do was pour out the cocktails afterwards.' Walter Hayes, 'How Ford Tackles the Problem of Export Sales', *BIFA Bulletin*, July 1965, pp. 7–8. The company estimated that its overseas audience had quickly doubled the size of the domestic one. Nevertheless, these export films were available in Britain too, and not only to dealers. The balance between 'selling', 'informing' and 'entertaining' varied, depending on who was viewing the film at the time.

6 Themes in Post-War Documentary ...

> [T]he division between the documentary film and the industrial film ... exists only in the minds of the disciples and the cynics ... It is the world, rather than documentary films, which has changed ... Indeed, the range covered by the present day industrial film is so enormous that it is more truly representative of society than the pre-war documentary.
>
> John Chittock[1]

> Where in the thirties they made valuable films about life as it was lived in this country, and tried to lead public opinion towards enlightened legislation, today they make at best the (admittedly valuable) scientific film or, at worst, spend their time 'projecting Britain'. This means films about the Lake District, Stirling Moss, old trams and the beauties of spring.
>
> Karel Reisz[2]

Though the 'social' and the 'industrial' film represented different strands of the post-war documentary, they were intertwined. In numerical terms, industrial documentary predominated, in line with the plurality of industrial sponsorship. (It is worth emphasising that the 'social problem' film, epitomised by *Housing Problems* [1935], had only ever constituted a highly-visible-to-critics minority of pre-war Documentary Movement output.) However, most film-makers made their share of both (even if most tended to have greater aptitudes in one or the other). Many sponsors funded both. Industrial films often contained social elements and vice versa, and plenty of films – many of those dealing with science or culture, for example – did not fit straightforwardly into either category.

Cutting across this spectrum was a second. Social, industrial or other, most documentaries were related to either one of two sets of sponsoring motives: pursuit either of the prestigious, or of the practical. Again, the dividing lines are not rigid, though the concepts are easily distinguishable. 'Prestige documentary' was a term that already existed at the outset of the period but grew to ubiquity, especially after the first Harrogate festival. It did not have a single clear definition, but rather a cluster of related meanings. Simply put, a prestige film was one which existed at least in part because, *simply by sponsoring it*, its funder hoped for enhanced organisational prestige and often no other direct result. At its simplest, this could mean productions of above-average quality, budget or creative or distribution ambitions (*Song of Ceylon* is perhaps the best of pre-war Movement comparisons): the quality of the film implying something about its patron. At is purest, it meant films about subjects only tangentially, or not at all, related to their sponsor's main business (in Movement terms, think *Song of Ceylon* again, *Spare Time*, or, yes, *Housing Problems*). At its basest, it meant almost the opposite: films exalting their sponsor by covering the *whole* of their work, rather than just one aspect, and turning it into an artistic statement (think *Night Mail*!). Many film-makers judged the prestige film, especially the second of these three kinds, to be the most liberal of sponsored genres, and to offer them the greatest artistic rewards and possibilities for recognition. Although to an extent they were correct, the fact is that the 'nuts-and-bolts' film had its own real value, rooted in much of the best of post-war documentary's pre-history. To do its job well, the functional film demanded, and often received, the highest craftsmanship, often generating fewer opportunities for basic conceptual conflict between the sincerity of the film-maker and that of his sponsor. Among the categories into which these films fell were those directly to promote products or services; those intended for educational use, and those designed for a wide range of training purposes or for recruitment. The growth of the 'internal' film, still 'documentary' and not yet 'corporate video', was one of the most significant features of the epoch.

The thematic character of post-war documentary was a product, then, of social and industrial film-making, prestige and practical documentary, interacting with one other and with post-war social and political change. An incomplete list of some of the themes that emerged follows. In the social documentary, film-makers were to find few opportunities (had they even wanted them) either for partisanship or for political controversy and exposé, which TV found more room for. What they were able to do was to bring their talents to social subjects calling for a compassion which, if it lost political edge, was also happily shorn of much of the crude sociology of many Movement films. It is no wonder that the subject of childhood prompted many of the most engaging and poignant of post-war documentaries. This theme was universally resonant, in itself apolitical, and experiencing a progressive shift of meaning due to changes in the education system and the rise of more liberal parenting. Some film-makers – Margaret Thomson and Brian Smith early in the period, John Krish a few years later – became well known in the business for their expertise with directing children and covering childhood subjects. Films like Thomson's *Children Learning by Experience* (1948), Smith's delightful commentary-free *It's A Small World* (1950) and Krish's *I Want to Go to School* (1959) remain among the easiest of post-war documentaries to enjoy.

In the wider field of health and welfare, the setting-up of the NHS gave film-makers plenty of practical things to do. DATA's early *Here's Health* (1948), propagandising for the system's creation on behalf of the Ministry (in opposition to Richard Massingham's *Family Doctor* [1946], propagandising against, on behalf of the BMA) was not typical of the films which would follow, serving the innumerable facets of the new organisation in a more functional fashion. The most regular of these many streams of documentaries were those promoting the blood transfusion service, which needed a new campaign to recruit donors every few years. More interesting than the changing *structures* for health provision registered by post-war documentary are changing *conceptions* of good health itself. Public health films like *Enough to Eat?* (1936) or *Health for the Nation* (1939) fixed their gaze on the gross case, above all on the general state of health of the working classes, rather than on individual manifestations, let alone exceptions. For instance, it is striking how many more post-war films concern themselves with people with disabilities of some kind. Lindsay Anderson and Guy Brenton's *Thursday's Children* (1954), despite not being a conventionally sponsored film, exemplifies many of the strengths of the richly crafted, apolitical 'humanist' sponsored documentary. (It makes an interesting comparison with DATA's British Council-sponsored *Education of the Deaf* (1946), directed by Jack Ellitt.)

A parallel development was the greater attention paid to mental health and illness. This played to the post-war documentary's infinitely greater psychological insight in comparison with the much more *sociological* Movement documentary, less interested in inner lives than almost any other type of film-making (the story documentary began to break away from this and was often the brand of wartime documentary preferred by many post-war documentarists). At the same time, it registered – and aided – the growing respectability of psychology and psychiatry as specific themes. Taking its cue from a couple of restricted wartime films concerned with combatants' rehabilitation, from Philip Leacock's late Crown drama-doc *Out of True* (1951) onwards, a steady stream of 'psycho-documentaries' flowed. The documentary film sector's contributions, more often than not making heavy use of dramatised technique, provide for absorbing comparison with those of documentary television, and of the psychiatric community itself.[3] They also register their own internal changes. There is much to be gained from studying Thomson's trilogy of public-sponsored psycho-documentaries aimed at hospital nurses (*The Troubled Mind* [1954], *Continuous Observation* [1955] and *Understanding Aggression* [1960]) in comparison with Eric Marquis's trilogy of pharmaceutically sponsored ones aimed at GPs (*And Then There Was One ...* [1965], *Time Out of Mind* [1968] and *The Savage Voyage* [1970]). Marquis's more radically stylised techniques, and the move from therapeutic and physical to therapeutic and chemical intervention, are among the most vivid differences. Marquis's films are also a good example of films that are industrial and social documentaries simultaneously. Later sponsored films on the subject tend to adopt a lower-key TV technique, often betokening a more mature understanding of the subject, though bringing less excitement to it.

An ever-growing emphasis on physical safety and accident prevention is one of the features of post-war life strongly represented by the work of practical documentary, announced by a fleet of road safety films in the early post-war years, and sporadic successors into the 1970s. From the 1950s, health and safety at work emerged as a major subject for industrial documentary, with some of the most stylish examples (often coming from the Film Producers Guild) becoming *causes célèbres* on the specialised films scene. Consider Greenpark's *Criticality* (1957) for the UK Atomic Energy Authority and Interfilm's *Hazard* (1959), directed by Tom Stobart for the British Iron and Steel Federation. The former was much lauded on the international scientific film festival circuit. The latter (ingeniously set not in a steelworks but on the Alps) had the rare distinction, for a safety film, of wide cinema release. Meanwhile, the BTF and NCB units produced increasingly many films (and in the NCB's case some bizarrely imaginative ones) which aided the genuine humane triumph of the immense post-war reduction of employee death and injury in their sponsoring industries. The formation of the Health and Safety Executive in 1973 led to a new spate of films on safety at work through the COI, though the most imaginative, best-remembered and controversial productions of that decade were both films aimed at children: *The Finishing Line* (1977), directed by John Krish at British Transport Films and *Apaches* (1977), by John MacKenzie (of *Long Good Friday* fame) for the HSE. It is easy to dismiss films on such subjects as no more than sources for nostalgic amusement, and examples of how documentary, especially when working through the COI, had lost sight of the bigger picture on which the Grierson generation had fixated. The truth is that these films are directly descended from the Griersonian tradition, which could have no more serious subject than the saving of life, though increasingly far removed from that tradition in style and method.

Work was, of course, a dominant theme of 1930s and '40s documentary, and remains so in the post-war period. However, documentary's engagement with the times and with new sources and requirements of sponsorship meant a much greater focus than ever before on industrial relations as a topic, and 'internal' audiences as a target, especially from the late 1950s. On top of the British Productivity Council films, the introduction of work study was featured in such documentaries as Tony Thompson's BTF title *Work Study and Tom Howard* (1958) and over a dozen NCB titles; the

COI and, occasionally, corporate sponsors tackled industrial relations more broadly. Some films took a sober documentary approach, as in the BPC's *People, Productivity and Change* (1963), while a larger number, like the same sponsor's *A Company of Men* (1959), used drama – or even comedy. In both cases, the classic persuasion technique is one which incorporates more than one viewpoint into its narrative, in particular by strengthening a film's message through the superficially counterintuitive inclusion of viewpoints opposed to it. Perhaps the ultimate documentary *à clef* is the COI's *The Film That Never Was* (1957) which takes a case of documentary film sponsorship gone wrong as the serio-comic setting for its study of post-war industrial relations deeply deadlocked. Films on this subject well illustrate the post-war documentary's frequent role of both expressing (sometimes sourly), and suppressing (with mixed success) the tensions in the mixed economy which provided the documentary film with its funding and most of its themes. The Basic Films/COI production *Branch Meeting* (1961) promotes involvement in trade unions via a comedy-documentary story which makes bizarre viewing in the post-Thatcherite era. As with safety films, there is much to be learned by studying the industrial relations documentary for its range of different perspectives it instantiates on what balance to strike in order best to engage with viewer psychology. In drier vein, films intended to explain new techniques, such as work study, were painfully dull at worst, but at their best produced fascinating austere studies in highly analytical film-making mimicking the rigour of the work-study engineer in their very form and technique.

Films on workplace relations, though industrial by definition, had 'social' motives and content, and were a post-war departure for the documentary school. 'Pure' industrial documentary saw the growth and perfection of films about almost the oldest documentary subject of them all: how things are made and how things work. The 'industrial process' (or 'from farm to home') film which in Britain dates back at least as far as *A Visit to Peek Frean and Co's Biscuit Factory* (1906) now reached near-perfection of form and technique. It was an attractive genre for two distinct directorial personality types. On one hand, the film-maker fascinated by concrete mechanics, and the abstract logic hidden within them, was challenged to produce clear but stimulating works. On the other, the film-maker inclined to formalism and stylisation found here a splendid outlet, paralleling the humanist film-maker finding a home in social welfare subjects. From such divergent examples as Lindsay Anderson's *Three Installations* (1948) to Anthony Short's *Guinness for You* (1970), via Paul Dickson's amazing, almost balletic *Stone Into Steel* (1960), some of the most exciting examples of documentary style are to be found in this field. And, in the best pre-war tradition, even it was prone to blending the social with the industrial, as in such films as *From First to Last* (1962), directed by Anthony Simmons at Graphic Films, and *Self Portraits* (1968), made by Stephen Cross at Derrick Knight & Partners, which incorporate the thoughts or lives of workers into their depictions of process.

As well as perfecting the 'process' film, post-war industrial documentary saw the huge rise of the 'project' film: the 'coverage' production documenting a significant industrial enterprise. There are hundreds of examples, from the sinking of new collieries to construction of the Forth Bridge and from Derrick Knight's T&S film *The Moriston Project* (1958), about dam-building in the Scottish Highlands, to Peter Bradford's World Wide production *Rain from the Danube* (1973) about an irrigation project in Romania. The idea that film was an exceptional means of telescoping large-scale enterprises was an attractive one to post-war industry – and government, which sponsored few such films but distributed many, via the Central Film and overseas film libraries. Films like these were often felt to be of particular interest to predominantly male audiences with technical and engineering enthusiasms. The preponderance of arts graduates among documentary critics may partly account for their lack of interest in paying such films much regard. It is true that too many of these films sacrifice cinematic form to logistical detail (the project film is Aristotelian in character, recording an unrepeatable, actual set of events, which took place in the recent past, over a finite period, unlike the more Platonic process film usually dealing in general cases, a cycle of actions that took place innumerable times before shooting started, and that will take place again many times after editing is complete). However, the close student of post-war documentary is certain to expand their knowledge of the scale and range of British civil engineering and its economic contribution. Among other things, this body of work documents the increasing internationalising of economics – and of British documentary itself, so much more focused on the home front in the 1940s and before, so much more often now shooting abroad.

Industry eventually came to accept the necessity of addressing on film the negative as well as the positive effects of its ever-expanding activity. The Environment became a major documentary theme in the latter half of the post-war period. Earlier, in such films as the Gas Council's famous *Guilty Chimneys* (1954), or the NCB's widely distributed *The Air We Breathe* (1961), air quality was the predominant issue. As these examples indicate, the background question of where Britain should get the bulk of its energy is one that was fought out on the post-war documentary screen over a period of many years. In the 1970s, it took on added *frisson* when the threat of there not being *enough* energy begins to be impressed upon the population. Already, from the late 1960s a broader environmentalism was informing the documentary short, and this reached a new peak in 1970: European Conservation Year, for which many industrial sponsors made expensive and memorable, deeply sober films such as Millbank and ICI's *The Choice* and, most famously, BP's *The Shadow of Progress*. Here was a new blend of industrial and social. BTF and the NCB went on to make many conservation films, like *Railways Conserve the Environment* (1970). The theme was further inflected by state and NGO sponsorship of films scrutinsing the built urban environment, like World Wide Pictures' very successful *A Future for the Past* (1971) or James Garrett and Partners' haunting if slightly portentous *Habitat UK '76* (1976), directed towards architects and signalling the demise of post-war planning philosophy. This 1960s and '70s phase of environmentalism was ideally suited to the documentary school. It allowed for a serious, but largely non-politicised response to national and world problems. The highly *visible* nature of environmental damage at that time – unlike that debated today – allowed film-makers to express that response in cinematic terms. These films undoubtedly played their part in awakening the public to their subjects, and often speak to the bravery of those sponsoring them from within organisations which had some reason for fearing the rise of the green movement. For the organisations themselves funding these films represented the last highly strategic collective act of industrially sponsoring films of social concern, sometimes with practical functions but primarily designed to enhance or protect industrial prestige. Putting them in the best light, they sought to prove that the shadows cast upon the modern environment were not their own – or not theirs solely.

As important and revealing as post-war documentary's thematic strengths are its corresponding weaknesses. For instance, it is notable how few documentary films of this stripe had much to say about Britain's growing ethnic and cultural diversity. Ultimately, the post-war documentary film dealt in a diversity of themes, whose total scope was delimited by its sources of finance which, for the most part, did not allow its interpreters to step as far outside general consensus as some of them (by no means all) would have liked. Its greatest achievements and points of interest arise from what it did with the scope it had: not enough, by the end of the period, to save it from the cultural periphery. A minor facet of post-war history had been the change of meaning of the very words 'documentary' and 'sponsorship'. In 1979, a poignant exchange took place between Edgar Anstey and John Shearman in BISFA's journal (in 1945, they would have done such debating in *Documentary Film News*). The correspondence deserves quotation at length. Anstey's faith in past models is thrown into sharp relief by Shearman's recognition of reality.

Shearman:
'I believe that [liberal] public relations sponsorship has not vanished but has shifted its attention ... There are today many ... examples of patronage (in the Renaissance sense) in the arts, in sport, and in human endeavour. If the sponsored enterprise seems to demand a film, then the film gets made as part of the enterprise.
'... So it looks as if enlightened sponsorship has moved from "the creative treatment of actuality" (Documentary film) to the devised event – concert, contest, circumnavigation. The film has become a necessary product of the sponsorship, but is no longer its prime object.

'If we take a few examples the shift in emphasis may become clearer. The Eskimos did not evolve so that *Nanook of the North* could be filmed. Slums and malnutrition were not imposed so that *Housing Problems* and *Enough to Eat?* could be shot. 149 Squadron, Royal Air Force was not formed, equipped with Wellingtons and stationed at Mildenhall so that *Target for Tonight* could be created. Fires were not started ... need I go on? In those days it was the film that was being sponsored, not the subject that it depicted ...

'The social Documentary exemplified and pioneered by *Housing Problems* and *Enough to Eat?* has now (in this country) migrated to television and commands huge (though sometimes half-attentive) audiences. But neither the BBC nor the Independent Companies are "sponsors" in the sense that Anstey or I would use the word ...

'Enlightened sponsorship, fostered Documentary. Enlightened sponsorship fosters Opera, Cricket ... you name it. Good. I just think we've got to be a bit careful not to find ourselves making the film of the book of the TV programme of the camera rushes of the exploit that was sponsored by the House-That-Jack-Built Property and Construction Trust Ltd (JACKUP).

'Real life is still down the street.'

Anstey:
'I do appreciate his timely comment on the sponsorship of sport and the arts. This is in a good tradition and would be regrettable only if it were regarded by the sponsor as a convenient excuse for not telling public and staff what happened about the rest of the money. However – being that as it may – our society is in little danger of collapse from lack of art or sport. By contrast, hardly a day passes without news of some ominous new social consequence of haphazard (albeit competitive) economic activity. BISFA's experience has shown that the demanding effort to articulate and then to communicate industrial and commercial policies proves educational for the sponsor and therapeutic for staff and public. In the oil industry for example we have seen the value of the documentary film as an admission ticket to the side of the angels ...

'I am sure John Shearman agrees with me because he has himself contributed scientific precision – and wit – to industry's account of its stewardship in both Oil and Transport. Indeed television has not done it nearly as well. On present evidence I fear that television is too much the victim of the current fashion in instant sensation to develop on the screen ecologically viable solutions to current economic problems with the same zest it brings to reporting villainy and doom. Whether shown on the large or the small screen, I believe this is a production responsibility, for which industry itself is strongly motivated. For industry itself is at stake. If industry (including, however belatedly, the trade unions) cannot offer a means of peaceful transition into a socially acceptable planetary economy I am afraid it (and we) must face an explosive interruption before the survivors can crawl back to the drawing board.

'For both optimists and pessimists, required reading is Forsyth Hardy's *John Grierson, a Documentary Biography* (Faber & Faber, £7.95) and *Grierson on Documentary* (now reprinted in Faber Paperbacks). If enough BISFA members read them – including existing and potential sponsors – all may yet be well!'[4]

NOTES

1. John Chittock, 'Documentary – or Industrial?', *Financial Times*, 19 April 1966, p. 19.
2. Karel Reisz, 'A Use for Documentary', *Universities & Left Review*, Winter 1958, p. 24.
3. In Britain, the most sustained post-war commentator on psychology and film was Dr T. L. Pilkington, a senior medical director and sometime academic at several hospitals and universities respectively, and a very prolific writer. From the 1950s, Pilkington's byline was frequently to be found in film and clinical journals alike. He drew a distinction between two branches of psychology film, complementary but fundamentally different. Many films, such as those taken in the course of research, were extensions of clinical practice. They would usually be produced on 16mm and 8mm by medical officers, staff or students. Then there was what Pilkington termed 'psychiatric propaganda'. This, he argued, should normally be entrusted to professional film-makers, albeit suitably advised. In the years after *Out of True*, psychiatric propaganda for the masses largely transferred to television: the landmark was the BBC's *The Hurt Mind* (195700 in which reporter Christopher Mayhew enters a mental hospital. From this point onwards, the documentary film tended to be aimed more at professional audiences.
4. *BISFA* no. 81, March 1979, pp. 10–12.

PART TWO:
The New Explorers: Careers in Post-War Documentary

Introduction

Sixteen essays follow, about nineteen post-war documentary-makers.

Why *these* nineteen?

This isn't a definitive list of the important film-makers. For a start, the focus here is on directors, born mostly in the 1920s, who entered the industry in the 1940s or the early 1950s. As we've seen, many of their predecessors, the 'first' generation, remained active alongside the second. Among those who started before 1939 and were still directing in the 1960s or later, J. B. Holmes, Margaret Thomson and John Taylor are just some of the major names that stand out. Nor should a *third* generation of documentarists be overlooked – Rodney Giesler, Richard Need and Euan Pearson are three examples among the very many who found themselves working alongside both earlier generations of documentarists and subsequently moved into the corporate video era.

Even sticking with our loosely defined 'second generation', many more names have been left out than have been included. Michael Clarke, Joe Mendoza, John Armstrong and David Villers are four of the more obvious absences. The film-makers covered here were chosen to represent a suitable range of professional circumstances, and a range of possible responses to them. Here are film-makers devoted to documentary and others who escaped it as soon as they could, ones who fitted comfortably into the world of sponsored film-making and others who were round pegs in its square holes (sometimes pursuing other paths in parallel), film-makers who stuck with the same units and sponsors, and itinerants who moved around. In each of these cases, different relationships play out between the sponsored documentary and a range of other cultural forms (the earlier Documentary Movement; Free Cinema; documentary television; advertising; feature films; political film-making; and others). These stories should prompt others to be researched and told.

And why *any* nineteen?

As Erik Hedling notes in his piece on Lindsay Anderson (whose very presence is a reminder, by his early output of industrial films, that the boundaries between movements were not fixed), the wisdom of focusing any look at mainly sponsored films on their directors is open to reasonable question. As argued earlier, most of these films were a form of applied, rather than fine, art. Applying to this a moderate and commonsensical auteurism has plenty to recommend it. The career narratives of those who toiled in post-war documentary make for absorbing human stories. They are also revealing micro-studies in how the industry at large functioned and changed. Finally, as part of a collaborative process, the director undoubtedly did play an important role in mediating the sponsor's brief and the viewer's experience. The following chapters prove how often this was the case. Ultimately, these insights are less about Art than about Work. Reconciling our circumstances with our inner selves, applying our talents as best we can, while drawing an honest wage ... it's what most of us do in our jobs. If we're lucky.

7 People, Productivity and Change: *Peter Bradford*

TIMOTHY BOON

> I have been interested all my life in craftsmanship, particularly the craft of being a human being.
>
> Peter Bradford, 2008[1]

Sometimes the recent past can seem remarkably remote. Archive film's great potency is that it can bring this vividly to our attention. The shock is all the greater when the author of the films in question is alive as witness to all that has changed in his long lifetime; such is the case with Peter Bradford, who celebrated his 90th birthday in late 2009. His working life in films stretched from the end of World War II to the mid-1980s and produced in the region of a hundred documentaries. For virtually all that time he was making films under sponsorship, for government departments, quangos, charities and commercial companies. As is usually the case with documentaries, his were films made for their particular present, not for us or for posterity.[2] And, because of his skills as a film-maker, they were acutely attuned to the requirements of their time. Bradford's work over forty years is that of the craftsman; his films demonstrate precision and an attention to detail that ranges from the composition of shots to the care of their expository structure, and an awareness of the educational impact of each film's quality. As a second-generation documentarist starting work during the war, it is the technique of documentary, rather than its politics, that he stands for; by his own account 'I wasn't very politically motivated at all.'[3] His career as film director and producer spanned several distinct phases, which we may conveniently see as being marked out by his main employers: apprenticeship with Paul Rotha (1944–8); consolidation at Associated British Pathé (1948–57); director into producer at World Wide Pictures (1960–80); and late work for the Shell Film Unit and others (1980s).

APPRENTICESHIP WITH ROTHA

Bradford's recollections of documentary date to a 1937 visit by Basil Wright to his boarding school, Bryanston in Dorset, to show *Song of Ceylon* and *Night Mail*.[4] Bryanston followed aspects of the 'Dalton Plan', an offshoot of the Montessori approach – essentially a liberal and child-centred method in education, which aimed to focus on each pupil's interests and abilities, promoting their independence and sense of responsibility towards other people. Although he has said that he left school with 'little confidence in my ability to do anything at all', traces of this liberal education are visible in the essential decency of the attitudes revealed in his films. Bradford next attended the photography department of the Reimann School of Art in London, where Bauhaus influences were strong, between 1937 and 1939.[5] Here he developed an interest in the artistic potential of photography, as he studied life drawing, still photography, display layout and typography, poster design and cinematography. The outbreak of war prevented him from his planned course of action, which was to open an experimental photo studio for Everetts Advertising London. Following a serious illness that rendered him unsuitable for military service, followed by a short period working in a prep school, in 1941 he started, and ran for three years, the Photographic Department for the Admiralty Naval Intelligence Section, based in the geography department at Oxford University. To feed his interest in artistic photography, he began to give weekly evening classes in photography at Oxford's School of Art and Technology. Here he began making a 16mm film on photographic technique for his students. Via this work, he also encountered the architect Basil Ward, who effected an introduction to his old friend Paul Rotha.[6] Bradford had also met, via a fellow tutor Barbara Young, Otto Neurath, the Viennese expert on visual communication and inventor of the Isotype system of pictorial statistics, who had settled in Oxford after a spell of internment.[7] Neurath had at that time started providing diagrams that required animation to Rotha's production company, Films of Fact. Bradford initially advised on the details of the effective translation of Isotypes into the cinematic components that Rotha required; this was a new kind of work for Diagram Films, the subcontracted company. It was pernickety, partially because Neurath insisted on the following of a set of very specific rules in the use of Isotypes, and partially because the final sequences had to synchronise exactly with commentary. Neurath had a significant impact on Bradford; he recalls Neurath saying to him ' "Peter: why do you always look so worried?" I said, "So many people tell me things I don't understand." To which he replied: "It's their fault, not yours ... The speaker has the responsibility of seeing the person who is listening understands." ' 'That', Bradford recalled, 'really opened my eyes.'[8] This stress on the communicator's responsibility, joined with Neurath's exactitude, rubbed off on Bradford, leading him to emphasise clear sequential exposition in his film-making. It was also via the agency of Neurath and his second wife Marie, that Sylvia Crammer, a PPE graduate of Somerville College and mainstay of the university film society was proposed as a potential assistant to Bradford at Films of Fact after the war. Crammer joined Rotha's company, and shortly afterwards, she and Bradford married.[9]

By the time that production of Rotha's film *Land of Promise* was underway in 1944, Bradford had been taken on as a general assistant in Rotha's company. Many of the documentarists came from university backgrounds; the fact that both Rotha and Bradford attended art schools (Rotha went to the Slade) may have contributed to the success of the appointment.[10] At Films of Fact, Bradford worked as scriptwriter, animation supervisor, film cameraman and film director. Rotha also used him for his art school training, for example when he had him design the jacket and picture layout of the new edition of *The Film Till Now*, eventually published in 1949. One early film project in his time with Rotha was a film, now apparently lost, on the endocrinology of the menstrual

A garden party for Paul Rotha, 1975. Left to right: Sylvia Bradford, Peter Bradford, Michael Orrom, James Ritchie, Mary Beales, Rotha

cycle, which he made with the gynaecologist Alfred Loeser. The project had been stimulated by a particular case in which a young woman's periods had been affected by the trauma of an air-raid, giving an opportunity for Loeser to apply his research-driven preference for hormone therapy in place of the more usual surgery.[11] Bradford has emphasised the impact that Rotha's focus on quality had on him, recalling how his employer would only permit those directly involved in a production to view film rushes. On one occasion Rotha berated a director on the grounds that 'there is not one shot here that could not have been done by any other film company. Even if it is an experiment that doesn't work, you must push yourself to getting material which includes shots which are unusual and meaningful.'[12]

Bradford's resulting interest in the precision and craft of film-making is clear from early in his career. He has recalled the impact that close viewing of Riefenstahl's *Triumph of the Will* had on him in 1945, when Rotha asked him to select some sequences for use in the film *Total War in Britain*:

> Never had I seen such a juxtaposition of camera angles and movement, music, action and reaction, resulting in a fantastic glorification of Nazism. The building of relaxation balanced with periods of sound and visual tension was stunning. I was completely gripped. When I went out for lunch, Soho Square had shrunk. I was still buoyed when turning into Charing Cross Road I saw the current *Picture Post* clipped to a newsstand. It showed the first of those terrible photographs ... of the concentration camps. I turned back to sit in Soho Square sickened by the turmoil of emotion.

In retrospect he identified this as a turning point in his career:

> Up till that day I had been naive about the world I had grown up in, and had mostly been interested in the technical side of picture making. I had never thought what pictures could do to people. My admiration of Leni Riefenstahl's skill confirmed in me that I could want nothing more than a career in films, but from now on I realised that it's not only pictures that must be in focus, but ideas. Up to that moment I had been vague and groping about my future. What an exciting day! I saw my life stretching ahead, mastering the creative force of film to increase understanding and human sensitivity.[13]

He would seek to emulate Riefenstahl's technique, but press it into service of liberal democratic values.

During this time, Bradford – on loan from Films of Fact – made a film as director, under the auspices of the DATA cooperative. This short (also apparently lost) was for a regular DATA sponsor, the Cotton Board, an organisation set up in 1940 to promote the welfare of the cotton industry by reorganisation, exports, research and propaganda. DATA chairman Donald Alexander was their films advisor. Filmed at Clegg's Mill in Rochdale, Bradford's film was a technical description of the operation of cotton-carding machines, involving high-speed camerawork and diagrams.[14] When Bradford enquired of the Cotton Board some time later how the film had been received, he was alarmed to hear that 'it caused the next best thing to a riot I've seen; we only needed to show it once'. Bradford argues that because it opened up one of the closely guarded trade secrets of the rival mills that came under the auspices of the Board, it provoked discussion between the rival companies for the first time, and hastened the kinds of cooperation that the Board existed to promote.[15]

At Films of Fact from 1946, Bradford came to be centrally involved in an educational project on the history of writing, printing and papermaking, working with the archaeologist Jacquetta Hawkes, under the auspices of the Ministry of Education. He prepared the treatment for the visual units of *The History of Writing*, *The Story of Printing* and *The Story of Papermaking*, proposing the last of these to Hawkes as a necessary corollary of the printing film. These 'visual units' included films, film-strips, wall-charts, display material and handbooks.[16] Directing *The Story of Printing* and *Papermaking* (*Writing* was given to John Martin-Jones) provided the opportunity for Bradford to develop the careful expository style which became one of his trademarks. He has described the spirit of the project thus: 'I was launched into my new career, and was working with colleagues with the same principles. We were all idealists eager to build a better world out of the rubble.'[17] *The Story of Papermaking* is typical of the series, which uses mute acted sequences, Isotype diagrams and maps (animated by Unifilm Studios) and live-action shooting; sound is limited to the voice of an authoritative male commentator, which is used non-continuously, the eye being allowed to learn as much as the ear. The adviser on the film was Robert H. Clapperton, an authority and author of several books on the subject. The film's titles explain that the film is part of the 'printing and papermaking' visual unit. The film starts with an actor playing a Native American writing on hide, one of several sequences borrowed from the *Writing* film. Simultaneously, the commentary explains, 'for many centuries, long before paper was invented, men have wanted to draw or write. In North America, people made picture records on the skins of animals.' The next sequences show the Assyrian practice of marking characters on clay tablets; then Indian palm leaves; and finally papyrus. The origins of paper in China, in 105CE, where silk was previously used, are explained. Rags, bits of rope, old fishing nets were the raw ingredients. We see selection and pounding by foot, and the washing of the resulting short fibres. 'The paper is made in just the same way in India today' (shots illustrate this and the remainder of this sequence). 'Next the fibres are mixed with clean water'; a bamboo tray captures the fibres; drying and surface treatment are shown. The commentator explains, over an animated Isotype map, that for 600 years the Chinese kept paper an imperial secret. But from 750CE Arabs spread the technology, and manufacture spread to Egypt, Spain, France and, 'most important', Italy by 1276, and the factories of Fabriano. The 1450 invention of printing, shown in an acted sequence, greatly increased the demand for paper. Refugees and colonists took the craft to the New World. A summary animated Isotype map shows how, over 1,600 years, knowledge of papermaking spread across the world, using essentially the original Chinese technique (we see the frame dipping and shaking again). 'Then, about 1800, a machine was invented which would make paper in one continuous sheet.' Tracking and detail shots show the operation of such a machine, ending up on a reel of paper. 'Miles of paper could be made in a few hours', exacerbating the pre-existing shortage of rags. The next sequence enumerates alternative sources of fibres: potato tops, cabbage stalks, fir cones, straw and nettles (all shown); none was a good substitute for rags, given the increase of demand from printing. The introduction of Esparto grass took place in 1860 (we see a pounding mill). From 1880, wood was successfully used. We see felling of spruce trees and transport by train and river to the mills. The commentator explains the process of manufacture and film sequences illustrate. Larger versions of the 1800 machine produce more than 300 miles of paper every twenty-four hours, though a modern newspaper uses up two to three times that amount in a single night. High-quality paper – for legal, scientific and artistic purposes, for example – is still made by hand. 'And this hand process is exactly the same as the one invented in China nearly 2,000 years ago.' We see 1940s workers engaged in this.

Bradford was kept on at Films of Fact until the end of April 1948 to complete the majority of the work on the Board of Education project, despite bankruptcy forcing the closure of Rotha's company from the end of 1947.[18] The late 1940s were difficult times for documentarists, adjusting to the reduced volume of film-making required by the state in this 'age of austerity', but with commercial sponsorship not yet as commonplace as it would soon become. Bradford, finding himself briefly unemployed, pressed his art school training into service, envisaging an exhibition that could make the case for documentary. He published the idea in *Documentary Film News* and the exhibition, contrasting the documentary and the feature-film approach, was seen in schematic form at the Edinburgh Documentary Film Festival in 1948 (where Bradford's printing film was also shown).[19] In addition to specialised documentaries for 'teachers or probation officers or tomato growers', he argued many more films of general interest could be made 'if the public knew enough about them to realise their potential value. As long as there is no demand for this kind of film, producers will only rarely, and under special circumstances, be able to make them.' While he was knowingly restating an old problem, this sentiment showed foresight, at least as far as documentaries for projection were concerned. The focused and specialist audience for documentary films grew in importance, and general audiences increasingly looked to television to serve their needs. Indeed, Bradford, becoming more interested in the context of the showing of his films to their specialist groups, came to see this as the distinction between television and 'documentary'; for him, the former is mainly solitary, whereas the latter produces group interaction. He wanted his films to be seen by groups of people – in work situations, or in film societies, and in schools – where they could be discussed, in a way that echoes the views of Rotha in the early 1930s. He has said that he felt that everyone taking part would be bringing their own life experience and thoughts and would contribute to the discussion, and learn from it, and take away ideas to use afterwards. He was always interested to find out the reaction of the groups watching his films and getting their feedback. He became interested in the mediating role of the person who introduced a showing and he also provided notes that were designed to assist by providing background information. 'The people showing the films should know a little more than the audience so the film doesn't upstage them.'[20]

CONSOLIDATION AT ASSOCIATED BRITISH PATHÉ

After Films of Fact, Bradford gained brief employment at Gaumont-British Instructional, as the latter was slowing down. At this time, Arthur Elton had been approached by both the Banking Information Service and the Corporation of the City of London with potential film projects. Elton suggested to Howard Thomas, producer at Pathé, that they be made there, with Bradford directing. So Bradford moved to Pathé's documentary and newsfilm department, where he worked from 1948 to 1957.[21] The Pathé Documentary Unit, part of Thomas's project of raising the tone of Pathé's factual films, made its share of sponsored films, sometimes taking contracts via Elton's Film Centre. Bradford was, for several years, the only staff director within the team headed by Peter Baylis. Together this team made films which honoured their sponsors' needs and were well targeted to specialised audiences (though some had a theatrical life, because of Pathé's strong position in relation to distribution). That Peter Bradford should have moved from the documentary purism of Films of Fact to the commercial end of factual film production is a good illustration of how permeable were their borders. Within this commercial documentary context, Bradford, unencumbered by his first boss's hard Left politics and formalist film-making concerns, was able further to develop his film-making craft. He even directed at Pathé a story film for the Children's Film Foundation, *Heights of Danger* (1953), an efficient children's feature from a more innocent age, featuring a motor race and rapacious baddies trying to purchase the garage run by the hero children's penurious father.[22]

Peter Bradford, second from left, directs a Pathé shoot

Banking and the Farmer, directed by Bradford in 1950, was one of the films that had come in via Elton. It was sponsored by the Banking Information Service, which represented the 'big five' banks, an organisation that had previously employed Gryphon Films (a lesser-known member of the Film Producers Guild) to make *Overseas Trade* (1948). The sponsors intended the film to promote the role of banks in rural areas, and especially to encourage farmers to open bank accounts and to borrow money. In the research phase, Bradford soon discovered that farmers almost universally had bank accounts (which had been necessary to administer wartime subsidies); he began to see the purpose of the film as being to educate the *banks about farmers* as much as its intended reverse purpose. His film builds its story round an individual (unnamed) bank manager in a small market town. It stresses his importance as a professional immersed in the local community able to make sagacious lending judgments on the basis of a deep understanding of farming, farms and his clientele. The argument is not unlike the anti-NHS film *Family Doctor* (made for the BMA by Richard Massingham in 1946).

Bradford was employed on two projects in connection with the Festival of Britain. He scripted and directed a stereoscopic film *A Solid Explanation* (1951) and, more substantially, with Baylis scripted, produced and directed the other film that had come via Elton, *The City of London* (1951), which was the Festival Film of the Corporation of the City of London. This conspicuously well-made documentary is at the same time a rather backward-looking film for a conservative client, an observational 'day in the life' feature somewhat in the spirit of the earlier 'city symphonies', though containing more explanatory commentary. It has footage of many London landmarks, starting with shots of the City from the River Thames in the early morning and a sequence of tourist landmarks; St Paul's Cathedral, narrow streets, a churchyard, Samuel Johnson's house and the Monument. As the morning progresses, we see market traders, children arriving for school, City workers arriving at Bank, the Bank of England and other banks, businessmen inside the Stock Exchange and other City institutions. There follow aerial views of Bank, Tower Bridge and River Thames, unloading cargo at the Pool of London and a sequence of the specialist goods traded in London, including wine, tea and spices. A lunchtime sequence starts with an organ recital – from Handel's *Water Music* – at St Bartholomew the Great, the oldest surviving City church. First there are pans around the church revealing details of monuments, then increasing cuts to external details of people eating sandwiches in the sunshine. A segue takes the viewer from a plaque commemorating Dick Whittington, via a cat eating from a saucer to the Lord Mayor and Aldermen eating lunch. Then we return to sightseeing: Guildhall Library, Court of Common Council, the Old Bailey and the Scales of Justice and Smithfield Market. A sequence shows the Lord Mayor presiding over the Court of Common Council – 'a parliament older than Westminster'. Then another return to sightseeing, but now the institutions are explained as governed by the Common Council: the Old Bailey and the Scales of Justice; the City Constable guiding traffic; Smithfield Market; the Corporation Cleansing Department. The commentary explains that the most important part of the Council's purpose is 'the perpetuation of all that is best about the City's past'. We see a signboard marking the site where the first bomb of World War II fell on London. A series of street signs introduces City Livery Companies and traditional trades: Clothier Street, Cutler Street, Goldsmiths Street; we see silversmiths at work. In summary, the commentary argues, the City stands for excellence in traditional craftsmanship. We see a secret ballot electing a new member of the Baltic Exchange; the commentary hymns the integrity of the City traders and institutions: 'so, on the floors of the exchanges, business flows freely, for there each knows the other's integrity, for it has been measured and matched to his own'. Early evening scenes follow; we see people in the streets leaving work, sunset on the Thames, then St Bartholomew the Great in darkness, silversmith's tools left idle and darkened streets. In this film, we see Bradford achieving something that Rotha would have found very difficult; where Bradford could produce the celebration of institutions that the client required, his erstwhile employer would surely have insisted on finding some way to bite the hand of the sponsor, as he often chose to do when required to represent privilege – see, for example, *Roadwards* (1934) or *The Times Film* (1940).[23]

The Pathé Documentary Unit also made *Wealth of the World*, a short-lived newsfilm series, whose theme was 'the development of natural resources and productivity in the service of man'.[24] Peter Bradford was involved in directing two of these in 1950; those on transport (sponsored by the British Transport Commission as one of the first four films to be made under the auspices of Edgar Anstey's new British Transport Films) and oil (sponsored, on the other side of the mixed economy, by the Petroleum Films Bureau).[25] *Wealth of the World: Transport* has conspicuously high-quality cinematography, animated diagrams (though not from the Isotype Institute) and a magisterial score by Thomas Henderson. A contemporary review argued that the film 'avoids the impersonal statistics and exhortations that make one so apathetic towards commentators, by employing a variety of voices on the soundtrack'. Bradford was developing his own style using contrasting commentary voices for the different sections, in place of Rotha's approach of closely textured dynamic interplay of several voices in dialectical conversation. And it should be acknowledged that, although the different voices may connote different views, in *Transport* the workers' voices remain firmly linked to the authoritative voice of the film; these are not competing with, but endorsing, the policies of Attlee's government.

In sum, *Transport* is an argument for nationalisation under the 1948 Transport Act, not just of railways but of road freight and waterways as well. The film begins with a potted history, typically for the time stressing the industrial revolution and its transport needs: better roads, canals, railways.[26] Just when the commentator is becoming triumphalist about the wonders of the nineteenth-century railway revolution, a Leicester voice with an animated map demonstrates the wastefulness of commercial competition. The lesson is repeated again with road versus rail in the interwar period. The film builds to the 1948 Act, then argues for its rationality, despite the significant difficulties it presents. *Transport* is credited to Peter Bradford as director, although he has stated that his job was limited to directing sequences that would fit in between footage already held in British Transport Films' library.[27] *Wealth of the World: Oil*, the story of the Anglo-Iranian Oil Company, is similar in style, structure and tone.

Majesty in the Air (1955), covering similar ground to Bradford's *Travel Royal* (1952), provides another example of a film from later in his period at Pathé that serves its brief well. This is a 'new Elizabethan' fantasy in Technicolor, combining scenes of royal pageantry with a travelogue on British traditions, repeatedly intercut with references to BOAC (the film's sponsor) and its engineering base. With its warm 'voice of god' narration, it is the quintessence of the commercial sponsored documentary.

When Independent Television first opened in 1955, Pathé was in the forefront of making its advertisements. Accordingly, towards the end of his time at the company, as other staff moved on to work in commercials, Bradford was asked to run the production of *Pathé Pictorial*, the cinemagazine familiar to audiences since 1918. He says that 'I had doubts about my ability to orchestrate suitable subjects, but I was told that all I should think was whether the audience reaction would be "Fancy that!"'[28] The world had moved on from Rotha's technocratic 'win the peace' newsreels, and the commercial context he was working in required that a format be followed and an audience be entertained.

Creative treatment of actuality? A colleague's caricature of Bradford directing a commercial

During 1956–7, Bradford, too, moved to work in the advertising department, based in the top floor studio of Pathé's Wardour Street offices. In that year, he estimates that he worked on nearly 300 advertisements, for a rate of pay nearly three times that for writing and directing documentaries. Between late 1956 and early 1958 he was on the staff of the agency Mather & Crowther as a senior television producer, where he was responsible for television advertising campaigns for products including Encyclopaedia Britannica, Sanatogen tonic wine, Pascall's sweet assortment, Max

Factor, Hovis and the Co-op, and for live TV shopping magazine programmes.[29] He records that he valued the experience, but the commercial world quickly turned out not to suit him: 'a large London agency was a wonderful forcing house for creativity but for simple honesty and reality ...? I returned to documentary and a more modest lifestyle.'[30]

DIRECTOR INTO PRODUCER AT WORLD WIDE

After his spell in advertising, Peter Bradford moved to Rayant Pictures, an unhappy interlude which ended with him successfully applying to World Wide Pictures. In his twenty years at World Wide (up to 1980), Bradford mainly worked as a producer, directing only around 10 per cent of the eighty-two World Wide films recorded as made with his involvement.[31] He later recalled with satisfaction that he enjoyed his 'position of being able to nurture others in cinematic and TV skills, and offer opportunities to directors, writers and musicians'.[32] Some of these productions represent the best of the changing craft of documentary across the decades of the 1960s and '70s. *People, Productivity and Change*, released in 1963, one of the most striking of the films directed by Bradford himself, saw him working as both producer and director. This was the year that Harold Wilson famously espoused a restatement of 'socialism in terms of the scientific revolution' and promised that 'the Britain that is going to be forged in the white heat of this revolution will be no place for restrictive practices or for outdated methods on either side of industry'.[33] The film, sponsored by the British Productivity Council in what it had designated National Productivity Year (November 1962–November 1963),[34] provides eloquent evidence of this spirit in action. The film's title appears against a grid of faces, the people whose testimony makes up the substance of the film. The opening comprises five of these expressing sceptical views of time and motion study. The first is later identified as Peter Fawkes of the Amalgamated Union of Building Trade Workers working for Wallsend Council. His is the most disarmingly negative view expressed in the film; he says 'I'm all against timing a man's work. I'd rather have the old-fashioned foreman with an old-fashioned bowler hat on coming up to you and saying "get on with it" rather than a man with a stopwatch. I think there's something un-English about it.'

People, Productivity and Change: opening title and accompanying discussion notes

The film moves on quickly to a selection of workers; the next two voice concerns about redundancy; a shipbuilder recognises that new technology must be accepted, even if it means job losses. Ted Hill (the first to receive a caption), General Secretary of the Boilermakers' Union (and erstwhile Chairman of the TUC)[35] in a screen-filling close-up, is sceptical: 'you can't measure productivity with a slide rule what increased productivity you're going to get. It'll all be determined by the conduct in the workshop by both sides of industry. If there is that necessary goodwill and understanding between the two sides, increasing productivity is automatic.' Then after a vision cut, as if encouraged to be more emollient: 'I think there is a need for increased productivity. I think there is scope for it.'

Next comes a linking commentary typical in its balance of Bradford himself, spoken over scenes of workers leaving a workplace:

> Many people. Many opinions. All depending on our managements, on our unions and on one another. Each with our own problems, but all with a shared problem – our future. We all have views of the best way to do our work and on the hours we should spend doing it. And these are some of the things which are some of the concerns of the department of Industrial Administration here in Birmingham.

Dr Tom Lupton is then introduced, first via a wide shot of his department, then a shot of his office door, which opens to reveal him in conversation. Lupton, head of the Industrial Administration Department of Birmingham's College of Advanced Technology (later Aston University), specialised in 'industrial behaviour and personnel management'.[36] Over a shot of Lupton at his desk, flanked by three colleagues, a commentator explains:

> The people here are from industry and all are deeply concerned about our industrial future. They value the opinions of both management and unions. But, to understand what lies behind our national problem, they need to know about people who've already been affected by productivity ideas. And so, Dr Lupton spoke to many men and women who've been involved in recent changes.

The remainder of the film is carried by Lupton as interviewer and commentator. Each of the featured organisations, which range from a Co-operative wholesale packing plant in Cardiff to the London Computing Centre for Barclays Bank, via the maintenance department of Wallsend Council and Tyneside shipbuilders, had recently undergone a productivity analysis via work study. In general, the interviewees are significantly more positive about the improvements introduced by the men with the stopwatches than the opening montage might lead the viewer to expect.

In the end credits, the BPC 'thanks the ... organisations and trades unions who have given facilities and encouraged their members to express their own ideas freely'. This free expression of ideas gives the texture of the film, and reveals the influence of televisual modes – especially the BBC's Talks Department tradition – on documentary. The participants speak in response to prompts; the closely scripted commentaries of documentary's first generation are (temporarily) forgotten.[37] The soundtrack is dominated by the voices of the interviewees, and there is little location sound, other than a stylised space-echoed industrial noise over the titles. Most of the participants are filmed in synch and close-up, with longeurs and fluffs edited out and covered by cutaways and the occasional 'noddy'. Lupton provides occasional narrator's links. The participants are permitted to speak at length about their perceptions of their working lives and the attempts at rationalisation imposed upon them. It is difficult to identify the precise genealogy of the film's style, with its visual focus on well-lit and lived-in faces, but it may be thought of as a kinder version of the famous BBC *Face to Face* series, which ran between 1959 and 1962. Inevitably, the participants vary in the articulacy with which they express their position. But the men (and one woman) interviewed give striking testimony to today's viewer of the pre-Thatcherite world of industrial relations, in which it had become natural for working people to be heard talking about work. Eddie Thomas, Vice Chairman of the T&GWU branch at the British Aluminium Company factory in South Wales, is given the closing words. Of all the interviewees during the main substance of the film, he has been the most reflective. In this closing section over shots of him overseeing metal panels coming out of a flash-annealing furnace, he states that,

> If workmen are to be won over to the new ideas, managers too are to be won over to the new ideas. I do find it a little, er, a little one-sided. I do find it a one-way business ... very often. I find that managers like the idea of change but, er, only change of method, not change of general set-up, not change of attitude so much.

In this way, Thomas provides the synthesis to a film which starts by expressing criticisms of work study and then spends most of its length giving a more nuanced and positive account via its case studies. These last cadences of testimony imply that workers have upheld their side of the bargain and pose a question about the management side's responsibilities. Bradford, as curious as ever about the impact of his films, asked to attend a viewing of the film at the TUC incognito. He was alarmed that the fifteen or so shop stewards attending slated the film, describing it as insensitive and a waste of their time. The TUC official explained to him that this was the beginning of a ten-day course, and they would be shown the film again at the end. This response was normal at the beginning, he explained; on previous occasions delegates seeing it at the conclusion had even denied it was the same film. In between, it was a most valuable stimulus to discussion: the differing responses at beginning and end were an index of the success of the course.[38]

The construction company George Wimpey was a very important client for World Wide, commissioning films from the production company for more than a quarter of a century from 1955, including a regular newsreel in the 1970s. *Riverside 2000* (1966),[39] one of the films that Bradford directed for Wimpey, sets out, unlike World Wide's more specific films for the sponsor, to show the breadth of the company's activities constructing factories, chemical plants, offices, housing, airports, roads, railways and ports across the world. It belongs to the sub-category of prestige films that present a collage portrait of their corporate sponsor. Accompanied by a light orchestral score by John Scott, as made by Bradford it also had a rhyming commentary by the well-known writer of light verse Paul Jennings. However, on being acquired by the COI for government distribution, the government agency explained that it needed to be translatable for foreign distribution by the Overseas Film Library. At the COI's behest, it was released with a prose commentary. With this example, we can see how the COI, a government agency, could still have an impact on the commercial trade via its distribution arm. So we find that the original, for example, has:

> Oil from fantastic refineries all futuristic,
> Towers distilling the fractions of polysyllabic confections
> Grangemouth, Altona, Trinidad, Aden or Hythe,
> Miracle marvellous polymers, yields like a tax or a tithe,
> More and more molecules magicked from oil.

This is translated into prose as: 'At one refinery it [Wimpey] has been on site for seventeen years, continually developing the plant and helping to expand the output.' At another point, 'And all the time, building goes on. A complete new National Road Research Station' replaces 'Building Road Research Laboratory where boffins/try to stop cars from filling coffins'. This film shows Bradford as producer and director setting out once more to serve the sponsor's brief, but on this occasion not managing to please. If the original may sound a little smug in places its replacement is much less distinctive and, well, prosaic. But Bradford had the last laugh when it was revealed to him by Wimpey that the verse version was proving much more popular with users, despite the preference of some at the head office for its plainer replacement. *Fine Timing* (1981), a late film for Wimpey, is more typical of the scope of the films he produced for the sponsor. Directed by Charles Davies, previously an editor at World Wide, and narrated by Brian Redhead, it clearly shows the timing and technique for resurfacing the runway at Manchester International Airport, a process undertaken at night so as not to disturb the daytime schedule of arrivals and departures. The opening sequences intercut a slight story of a mother separated from a child before the final flight of the day to emphasise the pressure of time on the work depicted. The film was intended for airport authorities, government departments in the UK and overseas and consulting engineers.

Of all Bradford's films from the World Wide period, the most lauded by far was *A Future for the Past* (1971), which he produced and directed for the Civic Trust, a conservation organisation which, between 1957 and 2009, espoused improvements to the quality of buildings and public spaces and the quality of urban life.[40] The film was scripted by Michael Middleton, the Trust's director, who had previously written the commentary for *Moving Big Trees* (1963), the Trust's previous film with Bradford and World Wide. *A Future for the Past* describes conservation areas established under the 1967 Civic Amenities Act. The film uses a question and answer technique, in which the commentator Phil Harland responds to points and questions raised by words 'typed' onto the screen (accompanied by a typing sound). This highly effective echo of Rotha's multi-voice technique allows sceptical questions to be raised without endangering the essentially liberal pro-conservation line of the film. *The Times*'s obituary of Middleton argues that the 'the Civic Trust under Middleton's tutelage was pivotal in curbing the worst excesses of the postwar development boom',[41] which places the work of the Trust within the backlash against *laissez faire* modernisation, as a form of modernistic preservationism in which planning is highly valued.[42] Once again, it is worth reflecting on the state of the nation that this film was made for; while to the modern eye it may look conservative as well as conservationist, at the time conservationism was in some senses a radical challenge to widespread assumptions about the form that urban change should be expected to take.

The film starts with one of the typed stimuli, stating that 'this is not an entertainment./it is a call to action./it is about places/and buildings.' Over an archive print of a village the commentary picks up, 'it's about people too – you and me – and whether the sorts of towns we live and work in matter to us'. A quick resumé of the history of urbanisation using rostrum-shot pictures and sound effects follows. Then another typed provocation: 'and such is the pace of/development that over/the next thirty years/we shall build as much again/as everything now standing'. A montage of several different British towns follows, a mixture of aerial shots and street scenes; the commentary observes that the towns 'reflect the values of those that built them ... every town has its own relationships between spaces and buildings', so that every town is 'a living museum on free show'. The warm encomium of heritage is interrupted with shots of workmen wielding sledge hammers on a building; the commentary observes that 'assets, values, built up over centuries can be destroyed in weeks'. Type: 'but you can't stop progress!' Commentary: 'Progress and preservation. Somehow we have to hold a balance between them.' There follows a sequence of photographs of demolished buildings ringed with flames and interspersed with the sound of pneumatic drills.

Stamford in Lincolnshire, which had the first designated conservation area, is taken as an example: 'Everything is individual, yet all of a piece. The town itself – not just the separate items that make it up – becomes a work of art, unique and unrepeatable.' The 1967 Act is introduced and explained. A montage of different towns' conservation plans follows: 'Now we know what needs to be done and can move to positive action.' Type: 'like restoring old buildings?' Commentary: 'Not yet – let's take things in the correct order.' The film explains that change comes to towns either because of loss or gain of population; it catalogues the problems that emerge under both scenarios, taking concrete examples of towns that exemplify each. The typed voice then intervenes 'now surely the buildings must come next'. The unruly development of Chippenham High Street is taken as an example, with archive photographs from 1929, 1934, 1955 and 1967 and, in an echo of sequences in Rotha's *Land of Promise*, animated superimposed lines make the point about uncontrolled demolition and replacement. The film is quick to argue that it is in favour of modern buildings that are designed to be in sympathy with the existing buildings and streetscape. The typed voice adds the necessary sceptical counterpoint: 'brave words'.

The film then takes a series of what it presents as sympathetic developments; a shopping centre inserted behind old preserved buildings in Salisbury; the Lanes area in Brighton regenerated with shops and new flats; new houses in sympathy with neighbours in Cirencester. The final section stresses the need for maintenance once works have been completed, and attention to details of street furniture. Examples are given of towns that have had television aerials, and overhead power and telephone cables removed. The canals of Birmingham are given as an example of how a derelict industrial problem may become a regeneration asset. Finally there is an appeal to action: Type: 'so who actually starts?/who makes the first move?' Commentary: 'Even as individual householders we can influence things. In a group – a civic society, a chamber of trade – we can do more.' A final example – of the Edinburgh Georgian New Town – is given. The opening type is repeated: 'this is not an entertainment./it is a call to action ... BUT TIME IS RUNNING OUT. How much do you care?' The type is magnified in steps until the word 'you' fills the screen. There is nowhere to turn; the viewer must be a preservationist or a sceptic. The film won many accolades, including the first Grierson Award (at that stage known as the Film Society Short Film Award); a silver award at the seventh Berlin International Film Competition in 1972; and the premier award in BISFA's construction films competition. It was broadcast on BBC2 in February 1974. Its success led to a Europe-wide follow-up, *Europa Nostra* (1973), which has many of the same virtues.

Bradford also produced *Not So Much a Facelift* ... (1976), another film on urban improvement on behalf of the Department of the Environment and directed by Philip Harland, commentator on the previous film. Here, a young couple looking for a home discover the attractions of an older house in a General Improvement Area. Norwich's Chief Improvement Officer, architects and planners from Blackburn and Norwich, and a community physician from Oxford all discuss the social, environmental and aesthetic implications of General Improvement Areas. Bradford opted to enliven the film by employing the folksinger Frank Sutton to provide interludes of sung narrative for the film, repeating an experiment previously trialled in his film on heart disease, *The Illness of our Time*, released two years earlier.

Cough and You'll Deafen Thousands: A History of British Broadcast Engineering 1922–1953 (1972) is a reminiscence-based engineers' view of the history of British broadcasting. The emphasis is on BBC radio, then television. A workmanlike job, it uses footage from *BBC – The Voice of Britain* and *Listen To Britain* to add period colour to the collage of stills and oral history interviews with participants. Directed by Michael Currer-Briggs, with a commentary written by Richard Wade, it was sponsored by Mullard. Its style is very much that of the television programme, and indeed it was broadcast in November 1972.[43]

Bradford's film *Rain from the Danube* (1973) shows the construction of the World Bank-financed Sadova Corabia irrigation project in Romania. It was made for another construction firm, Taylor Woodrow, which had previously had films made by Orion Films and the Film Producers Guild; they turned to World Wide because they were impressed by the quality and success of the Wimpey films. Having checked that Wimpey didn't object, Bradford took on the project, on which he became director as well as producer. The film's commentary was scripted by Patrick O'Donovan, the *Observer* journalist whose previous film and television work included the commentaries on *Brief City* (1952), by Richard Massingham's company, and the *World Without* series (1971), by Derrick Knight's. According to the titles, it was made with Sahia Film, Bucharest, on behalf of the Romanian Ministries of Agriculture and Land Reclamation. GEC Electrical Projects Ltd, SPP Group Ltd and Vickers Ltd are also listed here. *Rain from the Danube* was an important film for Taylor Woodrow, which was looking for more business beyond the Iron Curtain, and so wanted a film that would show that it could work with a communist government. The project proved to be something of a diplomatic adventure for Bradford. On an early research visit, he was so incensed by the uncooperative and selfish behaviour of his Romanian hosts, who were not offering refreshments to a five-hour meeting, and were being negative about his proposals for the film, that he lost his temper, 'something I'd never done before'.[44] This turned out to be the necessary step in getting the collaboration he needed. The project tested Bradford's essential decency, as he expected the local film crews to have the same commitment to making an effective film as he himself had. He had not reckoned on the corrosive effect of the Romanian communist regime. Only state film crews were available, which surprised Bradford, who had been disappointed by the quality of their films and had hoped he would be able to employ freelance cameramen. As he has said, 'it shows how politically naive I was'. On the first day, an 'assistant cameraman' not pulling his weight turned out to be the party member overseeing the production. After the second day, the unit insisted on Bradford going for a drink once the party member was off duty. Although he protested that he was very tired, given the improvisation with unsuitable equipment that had been necessary, he eventually conceded. Over a drink they explained 'the party system is such that everybody gets paid the same whether they turn up late, early; whether they do one job or another. And we all feel we want the film to be a success. And we haven't felt this way for years.'[45]

Rain from the Danube is an impressionistic documentary in the late style, not unlike Atma Ram's *Peaceful Revolution* (1961) or Stuart Legg's *Food – Or Famine* (1962), representing the modernising spirit of technology in transforming the fortunes and economy of underprivileged areas.[46] This similarity extends to the gentle iterative dialectic of traditional ways of life in the Romanian countryside compared with transformative expertise, heavy machinery and high technology brought from Britain. An animated map introduces the 16,000 square miles of Romania that would benefit from irrigation. It zooms in on Oltenia, a 300-square-mile area, then uses an animated illustration to explain the irrigation canals and two pumping stations needed to overcome the geology in the featured project. It is explained that the ancient farm boundaries had to be replaced by new land blocks. Technical details and quantities are enumerated by the commentator, assisted by pictures. A local labour force of 3,000 was supervised by 250 Romanian experts and a hundred British engineers and planners. A montage showing construction work with heavy machinery is accompanied by a slightly discordant jazzy score and details of the scheme described by the commentator. British experts, it is explained, teach the locals how to use the equipment, which will also be used for future projects. 'Tools of precision, made in Britain, cross the frontier of politics and nationality to change and enrich this land.' We see a meeting of engineers; given the difficulties that Bradford experienced in making the film, the commentary sometimes sounds optimistic, even facile: 'There were almost daily meetings between the British and Romanian engineers, for this was a joint effort. The Romanians asked for British engineers ... because they wanted the advice of experts and friendly strangers.' An expository sequence accompanied by music (often using Romanian folk modes) and intermittent brief commentary sketches the surveying and building process. The engineers' problem of weather extremes, especially the cold of winter, is discussed. We see the selection of the new plant types that will thrive in the new conditions. The traditional culture of the Oltenians is described – we see folk music played – so that ancient and modern can be contrasted; traditional embroidering is intercut with modern construction techniques. 'It all means a revolution in a way of life; upheaval on an almost wartime scale, but with fruitfulness rather than death as the product.' The electrical control gear is emphasised (not surprising, given the involvement of GEC and Vickers) and the commentary outlines the system. The first flow of water under computer control into the canals is shown. Aerial shots follow the course of the canals that we have seen in pictorial form at the start. The commentator emphasises that 'this is one of the most sophisticated irrigation projects in the world'. A series of split-screen shots visually link the use of water by farmers to the mechanisms of supply and control. New crops are shown being harvested, especially grapes, leading to wine. The film concludes with the agricultural products of the new scheme being exported to Britain.

In the midst of this work for World Wide, Bradford was invited to direct a single, slightly uncharacteristic, but very effective television programme – the hour-long *The General Strike* (1971) produced for Granada Television by Jeremy Isaacs. This was at the suggestion of Denis Forman, long before an employer of documentary units at the early COI, later head of Granada. This programme, written by the political journalist Henry Fairlie, differs from the rest of Bradford's output by the fact that its visual material is almost entirely made up of archive film and rostrum-shot photographs given immediacy by careful addition of sound effects and a brass-band score by Richard Arnell. In a throwback to earlier experiments with multiple narrators, the programme uses one voice (the actor Brian Cobby) for the anti-strike narrative and another (Robert Reid, the veteran presenter of the BBC's breakthrough current affairs series, *Special Enquiry*) for the strikers.[47] This richly textured programme follows the strike day by day, including incidental social historical detail. Like so many of the films that Bradford was involved with, it is a fair-minded, balanced account where it might have been more conventional to come down on one side or the other. Bradford's style had translated effectively from the large screen to the small.

EDUCATIONAL FILMS

In parallel with these many films with direct commercial purposes, Peter Bradford also produced a series of educational films for school use. One of his early projects at World Wide was *History of Modern Science: Girdle Round the Earth* (1961), directed by John Rowdon and Bruce Sharman from a script by Glyn Jones and Malcolm Stewart, with W. Ashhurst advising and sponsored by Mullard, the Educational Foundation for Visual Aids, and the GPO. This was a late addition to the Mullard-sponsored *History of Modern Science* series made 'on behalf of the countries of the Western European Union'. This had included two films made by Alex Strasser at the Realist Film Unit, *Mirror in the Sky* (1956), which explains the role of the ionosphere in the transmission of radio waves, and *Conquest of the Atom* (1958). *Girdle Round the Earth* is a film on the history and science of telecommunications: telephones, telegraph and wireless transmission. Like the earlier educational films Bradford had directed back at Films of Fact, this one relies on live-action shots and Isotype-style diagrams by Bill Palmer and Reg Lodge illustrating points made by the authoritative male commentary voice. The sonic palette is wider than the Ministry of Education films, however, featuring the sounds of machines, and (uncredited) electronic music in opening and closing sequences. The tone is educational and unafraid of technical detail, the pace is efficient and measured, and the structure carefully sequenced. The opening explains the title; in *A Midsummer Night's Dream*, Shakespeare's Puck promised to place a girdle round the earth in forty minutes, but modern telecommunications are instantaneous; we are shown a montage of a cable ship, telephones, telegrams and emergency services scrambled by police phones. The commentary makes a link from the present to the past: 'telecommunications today are intricate and complex, but their world of advanced technology rests on some simple, basic, principles of electricity'. This introduces a series of dramatised reconstructions, starting with the discovery of the electromagnet by Oersted in 1820. Here, as in the *Papermaking* film, we have a mute historical reconstruction followed by an animated diagram explaining the science, a pattern repeated throughout the film. Next we see sequences of the application of the electromagnet to communication by Ampère, and especially Cooke and Wheatstone (we see the five-, four- and two-needle telegraphs from the Science Museum's collection). The need for 'repeaters' to maintain signal strength is introduced using animated diagrams. This features as an explanatory trope at several points in the film. The American Morse code approach to telegraphy is briefly presented via another dramatic reconstruction. The film describes the laying of a telegraph cable beneath the English Channel, and the much more challenging Atlantic cables. Sound effects, commentary and rostrum-shot contemporary illustrations convey the story. We see a reconstruction of Lord Kelvin, brought in to deal with the problem of signal loss over the length of the submarine cable by inventing the spot galvanometer. Next the film explains, using animated diagrams, the physics of signal loss and cable capacitance. The film continues by describing the development of the telephone by Alexander Graham Bell and Edison and its means of operation. A section covers wireless communication following Marconi's successful transatlantic radio transmission. 'Within a few years, wireless telegraphy put a new girdle round the earth.' The development of electronic valves and their application to worldwide speech communication by telephone is described, using clips from some 1930s GPO Film Unit films. The development of radio and television is mentioned. The commentary explains that because reliable transmission of radio waves can be affected by changes in the ionosphere, cables continued to have a use. With the invention of the new insulator polythene, a new transatlantic cable capable of carrying speech could be made. This was installed from 1955, capable of carrying thirty-six modulated audio channels, or even – slowly – of sending moving pictures. The commentary summarises and looks forward: 'this cable is but one aspect of the wealth of modern communications, a far cry in their complexity and wide ranging uses from Oersted's simple experiments. But what lies ahead?' The film describes a new Commonwealth telephone cable. Increasing demands drive the need for new valves (core business for the sponsor, Mullard) and other devices so that the capacity of cable links can be improved. The new satellites are mentioned, along with the earth station at Goonhilly. The film concludes by referring back to its start: 'today we are continually adding to the history of telecommunications started by Oersted's discoveries over 150 years ago'.

But Bradford's longest association with classroom films came under the sponsorship of Unilever, who had already made films with World Wide, such as *Your Hair and Scalp* (1963) and *Your Feet* (1965). Bradford's involvement started with the multi-award-winning *The Physics and Chemistry of Water* (1965), directed by Sarah Erulkar, which uses live action and animation, accompanied by a remarkable commissioned score recorded in Paris, composed by Jacques Lasry and played on the sound sculptures of François and Bernard Baschet.[48] The film starts with the physical and chemical characteristics of water, and how hydrogen and oxygen combine to form it. The atomic structure of the water molecule, its three states – liquid, solid and gas – and its unique properties are explained. Following the pattern of Bradford's earlier educational films, it pauses in the final sections for recapitulation of all that has been conveyed to that point. *Water in Biology* (1965), directed by David Morphet, demonstrates the vital role played by water in the plant and animal worlds. It examines the processes of diffusion and osmosis by which water enters living cells, the means by which it carries nutrients to and fro, and it explains the role of water in photosynthesis. Bradford explained how the sponsorship process worked using this case:

> A film brief from the sponsor tells the production company something about the intended audience, outlines their feelings about the subject, presents leads from which further information may be sought, and lists possible items or ideas for inclusion. From then on it is the responsibility of the filmmaker to forge the shape of the film. Form and shape must be determined by function, and the particular function we had in mind was to excite the imagination of both pupil and teacher by pictures and sound, by bringing them into contact with basic concepts of modern scientific thinking in such a way as to make them feel the inevitable pattern in science and nature. The thought process behind making films of this kind entails in the first place simplification. When this is achieved, it is possible to decide what are the minimum of relevant additions – decorations – to stimulate even an apathetic viewer.[49]

These films, supervised by Professor J. D. Bernal of Birkbeck College, London, are models of calm and careful exposition, principally using animation, to convey their sets of scientific principles. *Genetics and Plant Breeding* (1968), directed by David Morphet,[50] and *Your Mouth* (1969), directed by Charles Smith,[51] share the mixture of techniques, style and pacing of the earlier films. All the films in the cycle are highly informative and well structured; many won awards. To today's viewer, these films may seem to have a leisurely pace. In fact, this was the deliberate application of educational technique; as K. Lockhart-Smith, stated in his capacity as President of the Federation of Specialised Film Associations:

> Tempo ... is a very important factor in the successful use of films for communication. Not only must the degree of knowledge possessed by the desired audiences be taken into consideration, but also the speed and the degree of ability to assimilate and understand ... As an example, it is usually accepted that in an elementary classroom film for children, the tempo at which the information is given should be slower than for instance a sales film designed for engineers or scientists. The matter of using the right tempo can be the difference between success and failure.[52]

Here, once again, we see Bradford's concern for the effectiveness of the film with its intended group audience. His sequence of educational films concluded with the production of a new generation of sex education films, using the new technology of U-Matic video recording in place of film. These simple discussion-stimulus films adopted some of the style of television soap opera, and used semi-improvised dialogue. *If Only We'd Known* from 1971, sponsored by the Health Education Council and the Spastics Society (since 1994 called Scope) is a film in three parts written and directed by Michael Bakewell and produced by Bradford. *Debbie and Linda* starts with a framing (male) voiceover explaining that Debbie is sixteen years old and pregnant. She goes to seek advice from her worldlier friend who is in the same position. Linda tries to dissuade Debbie from seeking medical help. After the conversation, the film changes mode, using black-and-white stills of the protagonists, with discussion-stimulating voiceovers from them both. For example, Linda asks, 'So, what do you think about the advice I gave Debbie? Should a girl be worried if she misses two periods?' Debbie asks, 'And what would have happened to me if I'd done like she said?' The second section, *Clinic Talk*, starts with a conversation in the GP's waiting room between Debbie, now used to her status and seeing the doctor, and a Sarah, a young woman pregnant for a second time, visiting her GP before being collected by her partner Eric. In the third, *Sarah and Eric*, the couple learn that their lives will have to change if they are to live up to their responsibilities as parents. Once again, there are conversation-stimulating voiceovers at the conclusion. Because of the deliberate use of trigger questions, this late project, part of a larger set of sex education films, sees some of the most explicit expression of Bradford's concern with how his films could be made to work in group settings.

LATE WORK FOR SHELL FILM UNIT

In 1980, at the age of sixty, Bradford found himself somewhat abruptly required to retire from World Wide. He was given leave to finish the films he had under way, and promised freelance work. On the day he formally finished with his old employers, he was called by Dora Thomas at Shell, who offered him some work. Accordingly, in 1984–5, Bradford made two films for the Shell Film Unit; taking advantage of the several global locations for *Malaria* (released 1985), he and a very similar production team also made *Search for Oil* (1984). In this way, this late commission for Bradford

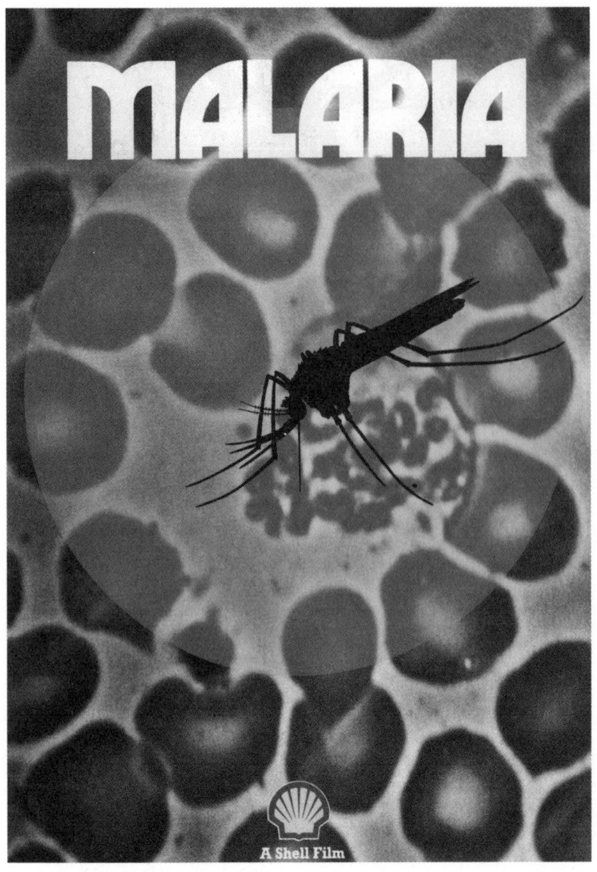

exemplified two different sides of Shell's film-making practice: its broad humanitarian subjects and its technical expositions of oil-industry functioning. Clive Mitchell directed; Bradford both produced and scripted; Nobby Smith and Tim Chad (Rafi Rafaeli on the oil film) shared cinematography, and the editors were Ken Morgan, on the malaria, and Peter Day on the oil, film. Shell had been behind several generations of film-making on the subject of malaria, starting with the Film Unit's 1941 film with that title, directed by Grahame Tharp with micro-cinematography by Percy Smith. This was updated in 1959.[53] They also made *Venezuela Fights Malaria* in 1953. Bradford's film was also, at his suggestion, made on behalf of the World Health Organisation (WHO). It is a fine late example of the ostensibly disinterested oil company-financed humanitarian film. Shell, with its many international interests and a globally distributed workforce, was well placed to make such a documentary. It updates the 1959 film, covering much of the same territory, but in a contemporary style that would have been familiar to viewers of science television at the time. Like some other examples discussed earlier, it seems to have learned from television, but in this case from the 'high' end of BBC2 documentary: it is not just the use of the uncredited Paul Vaughan to deliver the commentary, but also the combination of instruction in scientific principles with a selection of global case studies, that makes it reminiscent of the BBC's *Horizon*.

The first section of the film, after some quite shocking clinical footage of patients suffering from the disease, explains the interconnected life cycles of the malaria parasite and the species of mosquito that carry it. Animations are skilfully combined with live-action sequences, both macro- and micro-cinematography – for example, cutting from footage of a female mosquito taking a blood feed from an arm to a cross-section animation of the process. A stylised animation sequence shows how the mosquitoes, not carriers until they encounter someone with malaria in their bloodstream, become carriers and cause the spread of the disease. A world map shows how malaria-infected areas have shrunk, but the commentary explains that mosquitoes are becoming resistant to the DDT that has been used as a control. The remainder of the film is made up of detailed studies of the management of the disease in Sudan, India and Thailand; the differences are instructive. In the Blue Nile Health Project, the prevalence of the disease in areas turned from desert to agricultural land by the introduction of irrigation is discussed; we see the public health officials promoting self-help via lectures and education; the taking of simple blood samples and their examination under microscopes are shown. In Bombay, the measures taken to ensure that water supplies and standing water do not provide breeding grounds for mosquitoes are shown; the organisation of the public health service to ensure this surveillance is explained, and the preventive measures, including the introduction of fish to eat mosquito larvae, is shown. In Thailand, the malaria problem is represented as the product of a society in transition, in which the building of roads and the clearance of jungles provides more opportunities for the human vector to carry the disease to previously untainted populations of mosquitoes. We see more self-help; volunteers in more remote areas are taught to take blood samples on microscope slides; these are collected by a house visitor on a motor scooter partly paid for by the Thai state. One particular outbreak is traced to gemstone hunters travelling on a particular bus route. A concluding commentary knits together the three examples as typical of the way that the WHO uses local knowledge in its global fight against malaria. The film won the Gold Award of the British Medical Association Film and Video Competition in 1985.

CONCLUSIONS

Peter Bradford's film career over four decades spans different eras; from post-war planning and promotion of the newly nationalised industries, via promoting the interests of global construction companies, to sex education that embraced the liberated attitudes of the post-'68 scene. The social worlds that his films open up to our scrutiny and interest are compellingly conveyed. That a significant proportion were either specifically or effectively conceived as stimulus films to promote interaction in groups must also contribute to the directness with which they speak of particular moments in post-war history. But they are not all of a kind; the compelling informality of the participants in *People, Productivity and Change* is remote from the commercial platitudes of the prose version of *Riverside 2000*. The sure-footed but conservative authority of *The City* differs hugely from the improvised soap opera of *If Only We'd Known*. But there are also continuities and growths in technique; the development of alternatives to Rotha's multi-voiced dialectic, in the less combative sequential voices of *Transport*, or the spiky typed interjections in *A Future for the Past*. Most of all, it is his concern with effectiveness and clarity of exposition in educational film-making, first learned in the *Printing* and *Paper Making* project, that denotes Bradford's style. That, and a fundamental belief in decent liberal values, rather than the committed Left politics of his mentor, Paul Rotha. For Bradford, a late diagnosis of dyslexia at the age of seventy-two has provided an explanation of his difficulties at school and his drive to simplify the complex subjects presented by the subject advisers to his films.[54] It may be tempting to take this cue to psychologise Bradford's oeuvre as the by-product of his own processes of coming to an understanding of his films' subjects. But this would be to underplay the particular historical circumstances that also strongly influenced what he would represent, and much of how he would do so. There is explanation enough in his own history – especially the early encounters with Neurath and Rotha – for us grasp the origins of his style. However deep the roots of his approach, surely it is these characteristics – not strongly political, espousing decent liberal values, wanting to do a good job – that guaranteed Peter Bradford almost continuous employment and enormous productivity across the troubled and rapidly changing years of post-war documentary that this book describes.

NOTES

1. Peter Bradford interviewed for *Land of Promise* DVD, modified by Bradford in interview with the author, 26 March 2010.

2. The general point made in Tim Boon, *Films of Fact: A History of Science in Documentary Films and Television* (London: Wallflower Press: 2008), pp. x–xi.
3. Bradford interviewed for *Land of Promise*.
4. Peter Bradford, 'Peter Bradford', *Old Bryanstonian Yearbook* 66, 2002, pp. 126–8. Hereafter *Old Bryanstonian*.
5. See Yasuko Suga, 'Modernism, Commercialism and Display Design in Britain: The Reimann School and Studios of Industrial and Commercial Art', *Journal of Design History* vol. 19 no. 2, pp. 137–54.
6. Peter Bradford, CV and Biographical Statement, August 2007. BECTU History Project interview with Bradford conducted by Rodney Giesler. Ward was doing war work for Naval Intelligence, based at Oxford Manchester College, where he was involved in producing the Naval Intelligence Handbooks, which were intended for use by Allied Armed Forces, and covered not just the coastal regions but also whole countries. (See Hugh Clout, and Cyril Gosme, 'The Naval Intelligence Handbooks: A Monument in Geographical Writing', *Progress in Human Geography* no. 27, pp. 153–73, 2003.) Manchester College was across the road from the Geography Department, and Bradford was adapting photographs for the Handbooks. Bradford, interview with the author.
7. Bradford, interview with the author; Boon, *Films of Fact*, pp. 127–8.
8. Bradford, interview with the author.
9. Sylvia Bradford stopped work to raise their family, but continued in close support to her husband throughout his career.
10. Bradford, interview with the author. The art school connection was taken up again later in Bradford's career when he was invited to become an independent governor of the Bath Academy of Art, a position that he fulfilled for a decade in the 1970s.
11. Bradford, interview with the author. Loeser obituary, *British Medical Journal*, 22 December 1962.
12. Bradford, interview with the author.
13. Peter Bradford, 'Film in My Life', undated, unpublished typescript.
14. Bradford, interview with the author.
15. BECTU interview; Bradford, interview with the author.
16. Bradford, CV and Biographical Statement. See Christine Finn, 'Ways of Telling: Jacquetta Hawkes as Film-maker', *Antiquity* vol. 74, March 2000.
17. Bradford, CV and Biographical Statement.
18. John Wales to Bradford, 18 December 1947; Rotha to Bradford, 16 April 1948 (letters in Bradford's possession). The films were finished by April 1948; Bradford was given a separate contract for the educational materials.
19. Peter Bradford, 'An Exhibition about Documentary Films', *Documentary Film News*, September–October 1948, pp. 99, 108. BECTU interview.
20. Bradford, interview with the author; Sally Juniper, emails to the author reporting conversations with Bradford, 20 and 27 February 2010.
21. BECTU interview; *Old Bryanstonian*.
22. 'Before negative cutting, it had to be approved by Mary Field. She wanted to watch the film, without sound, because she felt that it was important that the films should be completely clear in every way if the dialogue was not heard – particularly for an audience of children. And it was.' Sally Juniper, email to the author 6 May 2010, quote conversation with Bradford.
23. Paul Rotha, *Documentary Diary: An Informal History of the British Documentary Film, 1928–1939* (London: Secker and Warburg, 1973, ch. 11); T. Boon, '"The Shell of a Prosperous Age": History,

Landscape and the Modern in Paul Rotha's *The Face of Britain* (1935)', in C. Lawrence and A. Mayer (eds), *Regenerating England: Science, Medicine and Culture in the Interwar Years* (Amsterdam: Rodopi, 2000), pp. 107–48, especially p. 112.

24. Peter Baechlin, Maurice Muller-Strauss and James Beveridge, *Newsreels across the World* (Paris: Unesco: 1952), p. 69; Emily Crosby and Linda Kaye (eds), *Projecting Britain: The Guide to British Cinemagazines* (London: British Universities Film & Video Council, 2008).
25. Another, *Congo Harvest*, covered cultivation of nut trees for vegetable oil in the Belgian Congo.
26. On documentarists' representations of industrialisation, see: Tim Boon, 'Industrialisation and Catastrophe: The Victorian Economy in British Film Documentary, 1930–1950', in M. Taylor and M. Wolff (eds), *The Victorians Since 1901: Histories, Representations and Revisions* (Manchester: Manchester University Press, 2004), pp. 107–20.
27. Bradford interviewed for *Land of Promise*.
28. Bradford, CV and Biographical Statement.
29. Bradford, CV and Biographical Statement.
30. *Old Bryanstonian*. In this period, he also wrote a report for UNESCO advising on the use of audiovisual material to implement the work of their second decade and worked with Dr Alma Wittlin, author of *The Museum: Its History and Tasks in Education* (Routledge and Kegan Paul, 1949) on experimental teaching at the Victoria and Albert Museum. See Bradford, CV and Biographical Statement.
31. *Old Bryanstonian*.
32. BECTU interview.
33. Speech at Labour Party conference, 1 October 1963. Labour Party Annual Conference Report, 1963, pp. 139–40.
34. J. Tomlinson, 'The British "Productivity Problem" in the 1960s', *Past and Present* 2002 no. 175, pp. 188–210, 193.
35. 'The TUC participated wholeheartedly in this work: its senior officers served as members of the BPC, trades councils were pressured into joining local productivity associations, and one General Council member, Ted Hill, was disciplined by the TUC for his public criticism of the productivity campaign.' Anthony Carew, 'The Anglo-American Council on Productivity (1948–52): The Ideological Roots of the Post-War Debate on Productivity in Britain', *Journal of Contemporary History* no. 26, 1991, pp. 49–69, 66.
36. The title of one of his books, published the following year.
37. See Boon, *Films of Fact*, pp. 195–9, 209–14.
38. Bradford, interview with the author.
39. The title alludes to the company's telephone number RIVerside 2000.
40. The Pilgrim Trust and the government's Department of the Environment were co-sponsors.
41. <www.timesonline.co.uk/tol/comment/obituaries/article6793780>, accessed 30 December 2009.
42. See D. Matless, *Landscape and Englishness* (London, Reaktion: 1998), pp. 50–61.
43. 12 November 1972.
44. Bradford, interview with the author.
45. BECTU interview.
46. See Boon, *Films of Fact*, pp. 177–82.
47. For Reid, see Norman Swallow, *Factual Television* (London: Focal Press, 1966), p. 73.
48. See François Baschet, *Les Sculptures Sonores-the Sound Sculptures of Bernard and François Baschet* (Chelmsford: Soundworld, 1999).

49. P. Bradford, 'What is the Value of a Film Prize?', *BIFA Bulletin*, July 1966, pp. 6–7.
50. Mendel's laws of inheritance, and how the passage of dominant and recessive characteristics from one generation to another depends on discrete particles of matter, particles which are now known to be the genes on the chromosomes in the cell nucleus. The use of genetics to produce new varieties of plants is seen.
51. The human mouth from babyhood to maturity: growth of temporary and permanent teeth; function of gums, tongue, kops, muscles, nerves, saliva as a protector etc. With the help of x-ray photography this film examines many aspects of the mouth's development from babyhood to maturity. In addition, the film covers the part played by the mouth in more complex activities, such as the exercise of taste and smell, and, above all, the uniquely human accomplishment of intelligent speech.
52. At the BIFA Conference in June 1965 (Text of Lockhart-Smith's address held in Ken Gay collection, Box 12).
53. Bradford, in his BECTU interview, says that Michael Clarke made a version '15 years before', but the identity of this film is not clear.
54. Bradford, interview with the author.

8 The World Still Sings: *Jack Howells*

DAVE BERRY

There was a tantalising, elusive quality in the pronouncements – and achievements – of documentary writer/director Jack Howells (1913–1990). He treated his reputation as a 'wordsmith' or 'lyricist' with a hint of irony or self-deprecation, yet it seemed singularly apposite that Howells, a prolific and, at times, genuinely poetic writer, should win a 1963 Academy Award for *Dylan Thomas*.[1]

For Howells, still the only Welsh film-maker to win an Oscar, the movie marked both a career turning point and the summation of twenty years' work in the film industry. Although Howells considered himself a descendent of John Grierson, Paul Rotha and Robert Flaherty, from the Thomas film onwards he began to work more often in television. The smaller screen, as it turned out, gave him greater leeway to develop his own ideas than the world of sponsored film-making.[2] That Howells straddled both worlds makes him an interesting case study for anyone interested in comparing the strengths and weaknesses of the two forms.

From Abertysswg in the Rhymney valley, in industrial South Wales, Howells had what many might consider the best possible grounding in films for a coalminer's son with a literary bent, for his first screen work was on socially conscious shorts with the DATA collective, under the guidance of ex-Rotha man Donald Alexander. But, in fact, it was Howells's next working period, in an environment far from any socialist strictures, that was among the happiest of his life. At the Pathé Documentary Unit, he worked on three compilation featurettes about the changing face of twentieth-century Britain, films aimed, via Pathé's exhibition and distribution set-up, at mainstream cinemas around the UK – *The Peaceful Years* (1948), *Scrapbook for 1933* (1950) and *Here's To The Memory* (1952). While making these films Howells learned the skills and value of montage from his cutting-room collaborator Peter Baylis. He also absorbed the gifts of rhythm and

Jack Howells celebrating the Oscar win for *Dylan Thomas* (courtesy of the National Screen and Sound Archive of Wales)

pacing, and the nuances of switching mood – by moving, for instance, from grim scenes from the two world wars to beguiling images of the British at their most eccentric. Much of this work involved trawling the voluminous Pathé library at Pinewood, foraging fruitfully for telling outtakes. However, even with Pathé, from early on Howells strained at the leash for greater latitude, and gambled on going freelance, earlier than many, in the early 1950s. If some of his later sponsored documentaries were unremarkable, they bore his stamp often enough, and were shot through with dry humour. During the late 1950s and early '60s his production company, Jack Howells Productions, gave him the components he needed to become a rounded documentary film-maker and an appreciation of teamwork. In particular, he valued the contributions of his cameramen (such as Hone Glendinning, Harry Orchard and Arthur Wooster) and his frequent musical collaborator Edward Williams.

During the course of his career Howells wrote around thirty documentaries and produced or directed the same number of non-TV films. From the 1960s onwards he turned out sporadically impressive television work for HTV (Harlech Television): beguiling personal and impressive shorts such as *Return to Rhymney* (1972) and *Penclawdd Wedding* (1974). Arguably for the first time in his films, ordinary men and women featured as personalities in their own right rather than symbols of their social class or representatives of work processes.

It was with *Dylan Thomas*, however, that all the director's talents and skills were assimilated. The poet held a lifelong fascination for Howells, and he was developing a version of Thomas's short story *The Outing*, when he died. *Dylan Thomas* itself merits detailed examination. The film is compelling on several counts, not least for what Howells reveals of his own romanticism, his penchant for rhetoric and his essential pride in his Welshness. It is also Howells's best-known and appreciated work, though it is an unashamedly impressionistic, uncritical paean to the poet's talent. It carries a sense of both mortality and transience, capturing what Howells probably regarded as the poet's fascinatingly ambivalent attitude to his life. The director makes great play of Dylan's poem 'And Death Shall Have No Dominion' and the influence of *Under Milk Wood*.[3] The film *is* elegiac, but for lost childhood rather than loss of life itself: specifically, Thomas's early stamping grounds, Swansea's Cwmdonkin Park.

No one watching this film could suppose that Howells was solely a scriptwriter, or 'wordsmith' – though surviving collaborators including Edward Williams talk affectionately of his tendency to declaim his own lines repeatedly to them during production! The 'poetic lyricism' in the Thomas film is pervasive, not least in the imagery, with deft use of superimpositions and lap dissolves conveying an ethereal quality. *Dylan Thomas* is an intensely felt film, conveying the director's own love of the Welsh landscape. A tracking shot through 5 Cwmdonkin Drive, the former Thomas family home in Swansea, carries a special charge, and a profound sense of the poet (and perhaps the director) both experiencing feelings of *belonging* in Wales – and *longing* (the Welsh 'hiraeth') for his native country when away. Swansea, in the aftermath of the 1941 German bombing blitz, is captured with artfully assembled stills. Over these once-traumatic images of devastation Howells, in a moment of engaging self-indulgence, can be heard on the soundtrack delivering amusingly droll lines from the poet's essay *Return Journey*.[4]

The film features Richard Burton as narrator, on screen as well as off, a sort of surrogate Thomas. Shots of Dylan's west Wales retreat, Laugharne, have rare beauty and Burton speaks the poet's lines (and Howells's linking narrative) with weight and humour. Near the finale Howells unexpectedly introduces Thomas's own lugubrious voice, redolent of the pulpit. By the early 1960s,

Dylan Thomas: Richard Burton in country and in city (courtesy of the National Screen and Sound Archive of Wales)

Burton himself carried much emotional baggage and Howells's film at times intimates a conflation of performer and subject. The film's sequences in London, where incidentally Thomas wrote or co-wrote fourteen documentaries for the Strand Film Company in the 1940s, are less involving, except when the camera tracks in to Burton leaning on a pub bar. His intense glance at camera pulls us in, as he reads the famous self-denigratory lines of Thomas on his own character, then Howells pans from Burton to the Augustus John painting of the poet which suggests not merely cherubic innocence, but incipient fleshy dissipation. The quality of the film is that it always hints at more than is readily apparent.[5]

Elements of *Dylan Thomas*'s style are pivotal to much of Howells's work, and link him to the wider documentary tradition. He had absorbed basic early ideas from Grierson, while appreciating the need for flexibility. On *Dylan Thomas* he took painstaking care to encourage and draw the best from cameramen Glendinning and Orchard, especially with what he termed the 'overcorrected' black-and-white 'mood' photography of, for example, the darkening-cloud effects on the Laugharne estuary. More significantly, the film typifies Howells's career-long penchant for assembling library footage to help drive narrative.

This all said, a seductive argument might be made that, for all his emphasis on technique and style in later years, Howells might have been a more creative force had his work been more consistently concerned with social purpose or propaganda. He clung to elements of Grierson's early film precepts and practice for much of his career – while 'Labour' he tended to distance himself from the generally anonymous working-class subjects who peopled many of his films. He adhered to Grierson's advice that the pragmatic film-maker should 'do his utmost within the limitations set'.[6] However, Howells's work away from DATA suggests a conscientious craftsman who lacked the 'reforming' motivation that energised the early Movement documentarists. Of course, he was still capable of making impressive, occasionally inspired documentaries, especially when emotionally engaged with the subject.

Admittedly, his scripts occasionally had a discernible Paul Rotha agitprop influence, perhaps a legacy of Howells's writing for DATA. *Guilty Chimneys* (1954), made for the Gas Council by the Pathé Documentary Unit (directed by Gerard Bryant but scripted by Howells), was a stark reminder of the perils of smoke pollution that recalled Rotha's *The Face of Britain* (1935). Howells never followed through, either as writer or director, with any similarly trenchant reflections on the state of Britain. He was more interested in documentary film form and the ordering of expressive images and commentary than radical, or even 'socially purposive', subject matter. Howells also had a predilection (or weakness) for teasing wit and banter in his films, and that may have led him further away from Alexander and DATA.

As a film-maker, the Welshman rarely ever left the editing bench in post-production – and for all his references to others' description of him as a 'wordsmith' he thought 'the cutting room is where the real art of cinema resides (and) ultimately where my kind of film is made'. His admiration of Britain's wartime Movement film-makers and, particularly, their montage and construction skills is evident in the 1930s and '40s passages of the Pathé compilations. Howells was particularly inspired by the Carol Reed/Garson Kanin feature *The True Glory* (1945), as well as by Crown's *Target for Tonight* (1941) and *Fires Were Started* (1943).[7] Edward Williams said of Howells's work in the cutting-room:

> He had a great enthusiasm for music. He also knew I respected his words and he was always reciting and repeating parts of his script to me – he thought it important for me to get the rhythm of the lines. He knew the craft involved setting off a word against a group of notes and the image so that all these three elements could be enriched.[8]

Howells was an undoubted romantic who sometimes needed to rein in a florid narrative style, and resist the temptation to pad the most unpromising of his sponsored material with narration, but he had a fine, filmic grasp of speech and cadence. Howells was also *too much* of an aesthete, by inclination at least, to allow a film to be subjugated to commentary or the flip one liner. By the mid-1970s, Howells had achieved enough to be acknowledged, alongside Paul Dickson and John Ormond, as one of a formidable trio of post-war Welsh documentarists.[9]

AT DATA

In retrospect, Howells's immediate post-war relationship with DATA in Soho Square seems curiously uneasy and ambivalent, especially as he almost certainly gained invaluable editing experience there.[10] Lessons in economy, montage and basic theoretical principles would have served Howells well enough as a technician. Equally, Howells had similar left-wing credentials to Alexander, having been an active president of the Students' Union at university in Cardiff in the early 1940s. Later, in the 1960s, a treatment he wrote for a Labour Party campaigning film would apparently be deemed too hot to handle. Howells claimed he was recommended for the task by staunch ACT stalwart Ralph Bond, but Labour Party Secretary Morgan Phillips apparently rejected the treatment, saying the writer, a fellow Welshman, had 'too much fire in the belly'.[11] However, post-DATA, Howells's 1950s and '60s work was funded by private-industry backers and is devoid of the wider industrial and social contexts we associate with Rotha in the 1930s. Howells in his late career took a kind of grudging pride in his links to DATA. DATA was, he regularly reminded people, 'spun off from Paul Rotha and in the tradition of Grierson and you couldn't get more purist than that'.[12]

Alexander persuaded Howells to join in 1946. He resigned nearly three years later, after spells of ill health, claiming the film-makers there were 'too earnest for me'. The break with DATA may offer a clue to his later thinking and career pattern. DATA had clearly been savouring the implications of the 1945 Labour election victory. It's easy to infer from Howells's own surviving documentation, however, that he felt ill at ease with the collective and probably with Alexander in particular: a slightly taciturn former Shrewsbury public schoolboy. As the offspring of a South Wales pitman, Howells felt alienated by what he perceived as their 'condescension and romanticising of the miners'. While at Soho Square, Howells sparked disagreement over a dialogue exchange in one DATA film – 'Have we got plenty of food?' 'Oh, lashings and lashings.' Howells claimed the reply was 'too schooly and middle class. People don't talk like that. Well, *your kind* might, but not mine. You wouldn't last two minutes without sponsorship,' he claimed to have told Alexander. After joining Pathé, Howells sniped at DATA, referring to the 'academic purlieus of Soho Square' and implied people there were divorced from the 'real film industry', from Wardour Street, home of British Pathé two minutes away.

Howells may have found the unit staffers' emphasis on political theorising oppressive and may have also been bemused by a certain antipathy towards Grierson. The feelings of many documentary tyros in those days are reflected in a review of *Grierson on Documentary* by Margaret Thomson (then of the Realist Film Unit) in 1946. She had approached the book with 'a certain amount of scepticism' but found it 'something of a revelation' and added:

> He makes one feel the sky's the limit. That surely must be the secret of his leadership of the documentary movement. The younger generation of documentary workers have been fed on Grierson by remote control for so long. We have seen a perpetual harping back to what Grierson once said or thought. We witnessed from time to time the spectacle of our elders being hypnotised by what seemed to us a legend; so that many of us had begun to doubt whether the Grierson myth had any truth in it at all by now.[13]

Ironically, Howells, despite giving up on DATA as 'too earnest', retained a strain of the tetchy pedagogue in later years. In the early 1970s when he revisited his native Rhymney valley in Glamorgan, Howells declared, 'I'm still a teacher at heart.' In the 1940s, he taught at holiday camps for the unemployed, as Alexander had done in the previous decade.[14] Yet Howells, as a London-based professional in the 1950s, soon confirmed a cutting-room propensity for leavening more intense sequences with levity. What other documentarist would describe himself as a showman and reconcile his rift with DATA by claiming he was 'more showbiz'? Rather than seeking to express political or socially conscious inclinations in his work he was prone to cleave, almost as a mantra, to a comment from Ted Kavanagh, writer/creator of the hugely popular BBC radio wartime revue *It's That Man Again*. Kavanagh considered that any good broadcaster, and by implication, documentary film-maker, needed to be a 'teacher, preacher and wit'.[15] Howells saw himself as a little of all three, but in his work sought to restrain any proselytising tendencies and remained, at bottom, an individualist. He regarded himself (certainly after his Pathé stint) as a film-maker who had to engage an audience through the emotions and the funny bone.

Whatever Howells felt about DATA's intensity, he had been deeply impressed by Alexander at one level: 'He had a mind like a cathedral and in those days I lived for a smile from Donald – and flinched at his Scottish flintiness.' When criticism came it was blunt and chastening. After Howells had written what he thought was a fine treatment for *Scottish Universities* (finally released in 1949): 'Donald told me I'd written a cheaply fictional script, and to be true to the poetry within me and to learn to sculpt from the inside. Good advice.' Howells also agreed with DATA's general principle that 'the camera should be used to show how the ordinary man lives and what he does'.

We know that Howells scripted DATA's *Dover, Spring 1947* (1947), a film, directed by Mary Beales, about the rebuilding of the Dover port – after the bombing – as seen through the eyes of an American visitor, and one which allowed scope for humour. Around late 1947 Howells's health failed. He had been incapacitated with tuberculosis just before joining DATA and it apparently returned in the second half of his spell there. There might also have been tensions over some of his scripts. 'DATA had qualities I don't have and I had qualities they didn't and I could write dialogue – I could make people laugh and cry and this was too emotional (for them), I suppose, but to me it was just showbiz.'

Faced with Howells's disparaging 'your kind' comments Alexander might have argued that he was closer to the working man, even the *Welsh* working man, than Howells had been in his career. Howells, for all the pit references in his later films, showed comparatively little inclination to match on screen Alexander's commitment to the idea of better conditions and a better image for miners.

AT PATHÉ

The Welshman's move to Pathé in 1948 proved timely. The company's producer-in-chief, Howard Thomas, soon recognised that Howells was too much of an individualist to relish the constraints of working on commentaries for *Pathé News*. Howells, by his own later admission, had, before his company features, written links for *Pathé Pictorial* – 'generally flippantly, lightly. I enjoyed it but couldn't take it seriously, apart from the craftsman's challenge of making the words fit when recorded on a live dub or at rehearsal.'

Howells was assigned to join Peter Baylis in the newly formed Pathé Documentary Unit just as Baylis, following his *Scrapbook for 1922* (1947), embarked on *The Peaceful Years*, an impressionistic film of Britain in the 1918–39 period, heavily dependent on the selection of images culled from the company's *Pathé News* and *Pathé Pictorial* archives.[16] By the early 1950s the Welshman had gained sound cutting-room training as a virtual founder member of the Documentary Unit. He had also helped create engaging compilation features for mainstream cinemas, pleasing audiences and critics.

The Peaceful Years and *Scrapbook for 1933* flow seamlessly while touching on an impressive span of British twentieth-century life. *The Peaceful Years*' footage contains stark images of the 1914–18 war and of foreboding through the 1930s, where, for the most part, the right cautionary note is struck. In the immediate aftermath of the Great War, says narrator Emlyn Williams, 'the great thing was to be back in one piece'. Then large film titles remind us of unpalatable realities (in the strident shock-effect style of Dziga Vertov) – '18 million dead, 21 million maimed.' The scale of unemployment is also noted. However, the treatment is schematic, though the sequences are skilfully blended. Howells relished writing what he rather optimistically called the 'philosophy part of the script rather than the history', losing no opportunity for genial observation or acerbic wit.[17] The compilation mode suited his style and temperament and there are felicitous scenes in which narration and imagery gel, especially when hazy images seen obliquely through glass in the Palace of Versailles prompt the words: 'Peacemakers in the hall of mirrors saw but reflections of a Europe that had gone forever.' Howells and Baylis had been influenced by the multi-voiced commentary on *The True Glory* and the Pathé pair introduced voices from different social classes to observe from their contrasting perspectives, with Howells relishing writing 'colloquially characterised language'. (Multiple voices had also been central to Rotha's most memorable work.)

The selection of salient images regularly varying the mood and tone – light and shade – ensured *The Peaceful Years'* appeal. This feature bombards us with information but the film-makers, aiming to hit the audience consensus, vacillate by showing us events rather than their underlying causes. Despite its shortcomings, the film was an encouraging primer for Howells, anxious to learn the tricks of orchestrating audience response. Even a reviewer for *Documentary News Letter*, with its often-astringent purist standards, thought *The Peaceful Years*,

> serious enough to make people look into their daily news and wonder if we haven't already started another 20-year march to some bigger catastrophe. To set people thinking is unusual enough for a film in an ordinary cinema programme. To do so without grinding an axe and with real humour and wit is an even rarer achievement.[18]

Howells later expressed unqualified admiration for Baylis who had a 'mind like a razor'. Baylis and he had 'collaborated to a degree that I've never found before or since'. Yet after that first feature Howells resigned to freelance – though was shrewd enough to negotiate an annual retainer at Pathé. He was pleased with an arrangement that meant 'being part of a large organisation without being trapped in it'. He was undoubtedly sustained by this Pathé link in the next few years. This deal meant he teamed up again with Baylis for *Scrapbook for 1933* – a year selected because of the Reichstag Fire footage and other foreign material recently acquired by Pathé.[19] The film attempted to show three distinct Germanys – the nation of tourism and the travel poster, the workaday country and its people and the elements which 'could bring the world to blood and fire' – the last phase sketching the rise of Hitler and the Nazis. The feature's shadow and light alternation was again skilfully maintained. Howells wanted the film to start in sunshine and end with the Burning of the Books. In fact, he and Baylis used an intriguing opening device of the kind seen many times since – a prowling camera in a cluttered room alights on bric-a-brac, each item symbolic of themes and events to be explored later.

Howard Thomas then invited Howells to submit ideas for *The Half Century*, a film he could direct. It would embrace the end of Victoria's reign and enable Pathé to use images from the early years of cinema. Baylis left the company's direct employ during 1951 and Howells, directing his first feature, faced a difficult task alone. The film, emerging as *Here's To The Memory* (1952), suffered from the decision not merely to abandon the multiple-voice approach (which needn't necessarily have affected the film's rhythm), but, furthermore, to announce each discrete theme with a studio discussion led by actor Norman Wooland. The initiative led only to stasis and self-conscious rote responses. To many, the Pathé compilation formula seemed rather shop-worn by now, but before Baylis left he had also linked up with Howells for several noteworthy sponsored documentaries.[20]

SPONSORED DOCUMENTARY

Howells formed his own company, Jack Howells Productions, in the mid-1950s. It was often reliant on industrial sponsors. He later bemoaned the way commercial TV advertising had squeezed out much of the best sponsorship work, and how, from the 1970s, video had similarly affected non-theatrical opportunities. Howells, reconciled to working with the more 'enlightened sponsor', argued for promotional films that kept a firm distance from overt propaganda. It was fortunate for him that

Ronald Tritton should have implemented exactly such a films policy at BP. When a senior Kent Oil Refinery man expressed misgivings about a particular dialogue scene scripted by Howells for his production *Journey From The East* (1958), Tritton replied:

> As Howells has written, 'the underlying purpose of the film is to convey the thought that the whole complex business is concerned with people – and for people. The film will enhance our reputation as enlightened and intelligent sponsors. People and their problems are not to be regarded as a necessary evil but as a vital ... part of our undertaking.' There's nothing derogatory to your refinery in portraying those who work in it as ordinary human beings with ordinary human foibles.[21]

Howells did not encounter undue censorship problems from sponsors but was to make only one short in which (credits aside) they virtually effaced themselves – *The World Still Sings* (1965), his film on the Llangollen International Music Festival. Howells was entrusted by his sponsor, Esso, with 25,000 feet of stock for shooting, before, after and during the Festival. *The World Still Sings* is a late example of 'pure' prestige film financing, in which the very act of sponsoring a film with no obvious connection to its funder was deemed to be good public relations. Howells told the ACT journal's readership:

> Last year, a kind of little miracle happened to me. As an independent film-maker (and, I suppose, a Welshman) I was asked to make a film about it all; a personal miracle because I had always wished to do it and now Esso asked me to make it as a tribute to Wales. How were we to do it? The Eisteddfod, after all, has been covered each year on television – much on the lines of an outside broadcast, say, or a Test Match. Were we then to mount our cameras and merely turn hour after hour, eating up, not mere electricity with TV, but precious Eastmancolor film stock ... Commonsense, economics and the nature of film technique, of course, said no.[22]

Earlier, Howells had been involved in writing and helping edit one particularly rewarding sponsored short, made by his former employer the Pathé Documentary Unit, and notable for its clarity and dramatic impact. The Gas Council's *Guilty Chimneys*, unlike other smoke-pollution films or segments from the 1930s onwards, had an immediate *raison d'être*. It championed the creation of smokeless zones after perhaps the greatest British environmental tragedy of its decade – the great London smog of December 1952, estimated by some experts to have caused 4,000 deaths in the ensuing weeks and months. The film opens with a brief rustic scene as a countryman returns home in sunlight to his cottage. Suddenly, in a pacey montage, we're among terraced houses and chimneys spewing smoke in the film 'present' – a not unfamiliar narrative trope from Strand Film Company agitprop of the 1930s. *Guilty Chimneys* then plunges us into a pea-souper – and an ambulance with a patient is guided by officials through the fog and enters hospital grounds. A Medical Officer of Health helper tells us, in voiceover: 'This is not a road-crash victim. Let's be kind and call it manslaughter, or if you like murder. The culprit is known – we created this and the victim will be dead within a week.'

The film seems initially to blame all its viewers for the disaster, but we're then told 'records show' that 4,000 people will die soon in prevailing conditions in Britain, allowing the audience to distance itself a little.[23] The domestic chimney is then identified as 'the villain of the piece'. We learn that much of coal 'goes up in smoke' (or wastage) and admirably choreographed scenes show the effects on health, crops and buildings. The documentary advocates prevention – using flexible smokeless fuels such as gas, coke and nuclear power. The familiar Rotha-inspired dialectic of thesis, antithesis and synthesis is retained – clean air gives way to the poisonous fumes of house chimneys but resolution is achieved in shots presenting the alternative smokeless fuels. The ending is less comforting than it might be. Children are seen playing in sunshine but with the old buildings still towering over them, albeit now smoke-free. We are told all of us must cooperate to make prevention of deaths possible. Purcell's *Nymphs and Shepherds Come Away* was a resourceful choice by Howells and Edward Williams over the children shots and the music runs (at least *partially*) counter to the shadowed final images and the film's cautionary rider.[24]

The health and economic costs of pollution – so relevant to us today – became a recurring theme in Howells's work. The subject was explored again in *District Heating* made by the National Coal Board Film Unit in 1971 during Francis Gysin's period running the NCB's films programme. Howells, working freelance for Gysin's unit and credited as 'director and reporter', travelled through Britain interviewing specialists from institutions and councils pioneering district schemes for community housing and flats to prevent fuel and coal waste, in particular, by providing heating from central points and boilers. These projects, we're told, provided constant warmth, eliminating condensation and pollution from dozens of individual house chimneys, and included projects combining heating with incineration. Howells, noted for rigorous research, conducted the interviews on camera. He always considered the viewer felt more reassured watching sponsored films if facts came directly from experts or department chiefs able to speak with genuine conviction in their natural milieu.

Howells occasionally ensured that interviewees were questioned on photogenic and pertinent vantage points, such as exteriors in the shadow of Nottingham castle and on a tower there, the better to reveal striking vistas and the contours of a new scheme for the city. The film wasn't particularly cinematic or controversial overall, but Howells's questioning about the much more advanced district schemes in Denmark, Sweden and Finland gave it a rewarding edge. With another NCB district heating film, *Penrhys* (1970), Howells, unfortunately, was to fall prey to the frequent kind of retrospective pitfall awaiting those making largely uncritical documentaries on social subjects. The film extolled the virtues of a new housing development in the Rhondda which led, before too long, to the area gaining national notoriety. The scheme proved hugely expensive and prompted a worrying exodus of people in the 1970s. As impoverished residents from less advantaged areas arrived to plug the gaps and various amenities could not be sustained economically, the estate acquired a reputation for violence and by the 1990s its population, once of 900 residents, had slumped to around 300.

In the almost perversely cosy *New Neighbours* (1967), made for the Central Electricity Generating Board, Howells also endorsed a project which proved highly controversial – skirting around the fears and problems created by the then-new nuclear power station at Wylfa, Anglesey. Of course, time and changed values systems can easily produce embarrassments in hindsight, as Howells probably learned much earlier on with the *Wealth of the World* series (1950–1), produced by Baylis for British Pathé. The films' obvious limitations are symptomatic of British 'national' propaganda shorts from the 1930s to the 1950s. They sought to create a comforting sense of global unity and homogeneous communities ripe for expansion and primed for education. In *Oil* (1950), the first of the series and most visually impressive of the three Howells, sought to establish the primacy of that fuel's role. His script stressed the rise in oil consumption from 280 million to 480 million tons in ten years. Low-angle vistas of steel and pipes thrusting into arid landscapes create an extraordinary feeling, almost of a post-Apocalyptic world, while Howells's words emphasise the enormity of industry's feat in wresting the commodity from beneath the sea and transporting it over intractable land surfaces to the Persian Gulf. The film is impressive visually but there is little *intimate* sense of the workforce's daily struggles. The second in the series, *Transport*, directed by Peter Bradford, was lively and engaging, creating a bracing feeling of modernist dynamism, with its theme of the need for unifying Britain through an integrated transport system. Much more dubious from the twenty-first-century perspective, at least, was *Congo Harvest* (1951), with Howells's commentary permeated by both a patronising outlook and casual racism, as we learn how conditions have improved since Lord Leverhulme gained a concession from the Belgian government to develop large-scale production of palm oil from fruit trees. Colonial 'authority figures' insist that the natives are 'a simple people and when they receive an advance in pay we have to make sure they put their mark to a decent contract' (we see a thumb placed over a name). We never see progress from the perspective of the natives and there is no mention of the appalling exploitation of the Congo by the Belgians under Leopold.

More successful on their own terms were the Howells films centring on the building or launch of ships – *SS British Sovereign* (1950), which followed in Rotha's *Shipyard* footsteps in filming at the Vickers' shipyard, Barrow-in-Furness, and *The Sea Shall Test Her* (1954). These were made at British Films. Though none of Howells's sponsored films bring ordinary men into focus as individuals, he was here involved with a small group of industry films of undoubted merit. They present, and respect, the dignity of the labour force through close observation of working practices. *The Sea Shall Test Her* is extremely assured, suggesting an emotional investment of the film crew and shipyard employees and officials. Activities at the Harland and Wolff shipyard, Belfast, are offset with tactile close-ups of workmen wedded to a common purpose. In shots aboard the SS *Bloemfontein*, isolated machine parts suddenly complement each other as if by osmosis and the editing rhythm matches machinery movement.

Across Great Waters (1956) also promised to be one of Howells's most ambitious works, filmed on a lengthy journey aboard the British liner SS *Southern Cross* as it made its way around the world. Yet the short showed little originality even in its selection of 'local colour' (Tahiti native girls, a Trinidadian steel band). The lack of much synch sound stifled the film-maker's attempts to convey the personality of anyone aboard. Yet the film had its atmospheric moments at the start of the voyage with the ship seen against lowering skies and Edward Williams's solemn music welling up, suggesting anticipation and apprehension. The journey is dubbed 'a second baptism' for the *Southern Cross* as Howells inserts flashback footage of the Queen launching the ship in Belfast. Howells's script invokes 'the miracle' of the Panama Canal and the thousands of labourers who died of dysentery and yellow fever working on it. The camerawork is impressive and we enjoy Howells's attempts to convey the passing of seasons as the odyssey embraces a 'spring, winter, autumn and two summers'. Howells, with typical wry humour, occasionally undercuts eloquent seascape images with shots of florid-faced old buffers who, we're told, 'have seen it all before' and while the hours away in the bar, oblivious to the intense excitement gripping some passengers starting out for (or returning home to) Australia and New Zealand. Problems on the film are illustrative of those besetting film-makers doing the more cheaply sponsored work in the 1950s. With only 5,000 feet of stock, Howells worried about conserving film and found the entire business a 'sombre, chastening, and misery-making experience'. The film, expected to be 2,000 feet long, was finally extended to almost 3,000 feet. In Howells's view 20,000 feet would 'barely have been enough' to convey sufficiently elements of the ship's journey.[25]

Jack Howells Productions' *Mine Shaft Sinking* (1964), directed by Howells, and British Transport Films' *The Site in the Sea* (1971), scripted by and associate-produced by Howells but directed by Gloria Sachs, are respectable examples of the men-at-work documentary mode, though processes are paramount and the first film, in particular, suffers a surfeit of mechanical detail. It centres on the creation of a fourth shaft at Cynheidre Colliery, near Llanelli, west Wales. The film has a hermetic feel and slightly outstays its welcome, yet a certain abstract beauty resides in some of the Eastmancolor images. Howells's script for *A Site in the Sea*, a British Transport film on the £20-million building of a Port Talbot tidal harbour by Thyssen (Britain), is meticulous in expressing the enormity of the scheme, involving building breakwaters across 400 acres of Swansea Bay, and there are effective point-of-view shots from trucks, cars and aircraft. The editing and music bespeak consummate teamwork. Early shots of harbour cranes against leaden skies whet the appetite and we're never disappointed thereafter.

The revolution that the discovery of natural gas has brought about in the gas industry. It's called 'Flame of the Future', and anyone interested in the future of Britain should see it. Because natural gas is probably the biggest stroke of luck this country has had in a hundred years.

Fill in the coupon below and we'll send you a crammed catalogue giving all the facts about this and many other exciting films in our library. Films that will keep your audiences entertained and educated for as long as you like. They're all colour, 16 mm, sound and FREE.

To: The Gas Council Film Library,
6/7 Great Chapel Street, London, W.1.
Please send me your illustrated catalogue and order form for rent-free 16mm sound and colour films.

Name_____

School/Organisation_____

FU

Most ambitious was the Gas Council production *Flame of the Future* (1970), photographed by ex-Pathe cameraman Billie Jordan, a portrait of contemporary gas control and communication, distribution and supply, research and conversion. Ken Gay commented that Howells's film 'works in a straight British documentary tradition'. Kenneth Myer wrote in the *Guardian* that:

> Environment is to be the vogue word of the next decade. Businessmen and scientists, politicians, and preservationists, all now profess themselves concerned with the bettering of our environment, indoors and out. It is estimated that more than 20 films are planned to appear this year which one way or another deal with improving our surroundings and our way of life ... The Gas Council ... has a new film, *Flame of the Future*, a survey of the whole gas industry and the 120,000 people who work in it. Many a survey has collapsed half way through under the weight of the material, but this film preserves its balance, is informative and has many touches of humour. Unfortunately, some of this is unconscious: 'The word gas,' intones the commentator, 'comes from the Greek word chaos.' We might have guessed!

Overall, the standard of Howells's sponsored work is predictably variable but the positive disciplines it imposed upon him were to find their finest expression in his best TV work. In the most striking of these films he was able at last to convey his true affinities for individuals and communities.

Dylan Thomas, for all its merits, attracted surprisingly mixed notices from reviewers. Dilys Powell, in the *Sunday Times*, said she was moved to tears at times and praised the 'beautifully evocative seascapes', but Philip Oakes of the *Sunday Telegraph* castigated Howells's film as a 'woozy essay in hagiography' and 'documentary crying in its beer'. In the wake of the highly motivated British documentary films of the 1940s and loosely linked but 'socially realistic' films among the Free Cinema presentations of the 1950s, certain critics clearly found Howells's type of impressionistic essay outmoded.[26] Yet *Dylan Thomas*, beset by production financing problems, and three years in the making as a TV film, was picked up by British Lion for British cinema release, and also gained US theatrical screenings, making it eligible for the Oscar.

TELEVISION

Nye (1965) might just have been Howells's urbane response to the 'hagiography' jibe. The film was entirely composed of stills, with colourful alternate soundtrack contributions from the Welsh politician's opponents and champions. The film, predicated on the notion that 'Bevan was reviled and venerated equally' is surprisingly well balanced, given Howells's professed admiration for the Tredegar politician.

At the film's core, it transpired, were statements scrutinising the wisdom or otherwise of Bevan's politically fatal (but maybe misunderstood) remark at the 1957 Labour annual conference that no Foreign Secretary should go naked into the conference chamber, which most British politicians and pundits interpreted as a plea to retain nuclear weapons. The film, while not stinting on Bevan's singular achievements (in winning doctors over to voting for the National Health Service, for instance) produces stimulating arguments on the politician's failures, and personality.[27]

In *Let Us Sleep Now* (1980) Howells once more employed stills, to evoke World War I through the eyes of its poets and artists. The tone was exemplary, with Edward Williams's music unobtrusively matching the different moods. Howells used some familiar material (Sassoon and Owen featuring large), but other work (such as poetry by Wilfred Gibson and artwork by Paul Nash) was powerful enough to stir all but the most blasé. Howells had gained much from his battlefields visit while scripting Stephen Weeks's *Scars* (1974), another Great War subject. The film-makers visited Verdun and made sharply sardonic visual and scripting observations on notions of heroism, and the contrast of 1914–18 trench realities with the present, when mercenary traders fed on visitors' ravenous appetites for souvenirs.

Two 1970s Howells films mark a significant style change, though montage is a significant aspect of the first of them. *Return to Rhymney* was inspired by Howells's feelings for his own childhood (spent in Rhymney, a mile from his birthplace) and memories of the impact of the General Strike on the South Wales coalfield. He employs stanzas from 'Do you Remember 1926?' by local poet Idris Davies, with its empathy and righteous anger. The vivid sense of regret for a Rhymney in decline but once at the forefront of nineteenth-century Welsh industry was complemented by the song 'The Bells of Rhymney', inspired by the Davies poem of that title and performed by Pete Seeger. A sense of wistfulness for what has gone pervades the film and there's a neat moment when Tony Impey's camera moves up the empty galleries of a chapel and slides up organ pipes as music mounts, and a building is glimpsed through windows. It seems like another chapel, but is soon revealed as a ruined (pit) engine house. This moment suggests, implicitly, the paradoxical, enduring spirit of a mining community and tragedy of a village, which Howells described in notes as 'dead, except for its people'. The film's most individual features, given Howells's contrasting recent past work, are the sympathetic interviews with local inhabitants, their memories crystallising the images.

Penclawdd Wedding was set in a West Wales seashore village, renowned for its cockle pickers and with a certain fierce reputation for insularity. Howells found a couple likeable enough to sustain audience interest in their marriage preparations. The director, at his most avuncular, mixed with convivial locals on screen, but more memorable shots were of women picking cockles at dawn, then taking them to the nearest railway station by cart for sale at Swansea market. These scenes, with slow takes and long shots, conveyed not a quaint, anachronistic flavour, but a comforting immutability.

Penclawdd Wedding and *Return to Rhymney* demonstrated that, as a director, Howells was most comfortable on his own terrain and thrived on relating directly to his subjects. Both these documentaries are disarming and well crafted, with locals expressing their opinions with bracing candour. Howells had proved himself from Pathé days to be a meticulous technician but suspicion remains that until his last works he had perhaps lost his way, as other documentarists did after World War II. He never slotted comfortably into any school of documentary post-Grierson and his more personal work tended to look back not forward. It seems regrettable that for the most part he either shunned, or was never given, the opportunity to make social or politically conscious films in the 1950s and '60s. Could the earlier experiences at DATA have deterred him? It's interesting also to speculate what he might have achieved, given his proven editing skills, had his films possessed a greater intrinsic drama of the kind seen in the wartime propaganda documentaries.

The two 1970s Welsh TV films I've mentioned at least confirm that Howells was not merely a professional fired by the challenges of the cutting bench, but a director with an appealing empathy with South Wales' people, history and landscape. *Penclawdd Wedding* and *Return to Rhymney*, lacking hard edges but replete with rewarding character observation, seem more human, more personal than his previous films – *building* on his editing flair to celebrate individuals who have left their own local legacy. It's tantalising to speculate whether, in more propitious circumstances, close up, observational social film documents such as these might have proved his true *metier*.

NOTES

1. Material on *Dylan Thomas* is in Archive Collections No. 493 Box 1 of Howells collection at the National Screen and Sound Archive of Wales, National Library of Wales, Aberystwyth.
2. In the ACT's journal, Howells wrote a review of Arthur Calder-Marshall's 1963 monograph on Flaherty: 'The trouble with the Flahertys (and their kind are sprinkled thinly in the world's history) is that they are born to do what it is they have to do, they do it in their own way, in their own time, usually on other people's money, and in the process infuriate more logical, analytical, orthodox, "respectable" people, who find out with a great shock of surprise that the object of their temporary "hate" is universally loved ... Maybe the question we should ask ourselves is where would he shine today? In the world of commercial films? Working for that enlightened, dedicated, enthusiastic patron of the film artist, the COI? Allowed to do a little "journalism in depth" ... I don't know what it means, except to suggest that the rest is shallow. It is a phrase that has the echoes of all that jazz you hear coming from big buildings. It seems to me that if by journalism we mean an attempt to report upon the human situation, then poets are the greatest, certainly the deepest journalists of all.' Jack Howells, 'Robert Flaherty. "The Innocent Eye" of a Great Documentarian', *Film & Television Technician*, June 1963, p. 181.
3. *Under Milk Wood* first broadcast 25 January 1954, BBC Home Service, with Burton as First Voice. He later starred in Andrew Sinclair's 1971 feature-film version.
4. *Return Journey*, Thomas's essay, can be found in the collection of his radio pieces *Quite Early One Morning* (London: Aldine/J. M. Dent, 1975). The Thomas film contains Howells's most overt use of the Welsh landscape, but back in 1959 Howells had scripted Kenneth Talbot's *Mountain Rescue*, an

impressively shot and constructed short from President Pictures set in Snowdonia, containing both a courageous rescue of a sheep in hostile terrain and a muted but telling plea to support the future of Welsh hill farmers.

5. Thomas wrote most of his Strand scripts from 1942 to 1945 – his finest efforts were probably *Our Country* (1943) and *Wales, Green Mountain, Black Mountain* (1944), both directed by John Eldridge. Also see John Ackerman (ed.) *Dylan Thomas: The Film Scripts* (London: J. M. Dent, 1995).
6. See Alan Road, 'Howells The Oscar', *Guardian*, 29 April 1963. Box 1, Howells collection, as above.
7. Howells quotes in documents in Box 3 of Howells collection. 'He was glad he learned his editing skills in London.' Carwyn James, 'Jack Howells, Welshman and Filmmaker Extraordinary', *Western Mail* (Wales's national newspaper), 1 July 1975; and also see Road, *Guardian*, as above. Also see David Berry, *Jack Howells: Cutting for Effect*, booklet issued by HTV Wales for a retrospective of his television films, 1991.
8. Interviews with Edward Williams, Bristol, April 2002 and February 2009.
9. John Ormond's *Borrowed Pasture* (1960) and *Once There Was A Time* (1961) are cited approvingly by Grierson in *Grierson on Documentary*, as above, p. 370, and praised by Norman Swallow in his book *Factual Television* (London/New York: Focal Press, pp. 176/177, 184, 188). Paul Dickson's *The Undefeated* and *David*, in particular, had earlier earned wide praise. For an appraisal of the three Welsh directors see David Berry, *Wales and Cinema: The First 100 Years* (Cardiff: University of Wales Press, 1994), chs 14 and 15. See also Leo Enticknap's chapter on Dickson in this book. Almost the same age as one another, Dickson is an example of the film-maker whose documentaries remained sponsored, for the large screen, Ormond of one who developed the television documentary form, at BBC Wales. Howells, older than both, straddled the two.
10. Notes on Howells's experiences at DATA are in Box 2, Howells Collection.
11. Paul Rotha, *The Film Till Now* (London: Vision Press, 1949 edn) footnote 1, p. 229. A treatment headed 'First Thinking on a Projected Film on the History of the Labour Party' is in Box 2, Howells Collection. Howells's 'fire in the belly' anecdote is in Box 3, Howells Collection.
12. Howells in a documentary film discussion in *Late Night Line Up* (BBC Wales, 28 October 1966) lost no opportunity to remind viewers of John Grierson's crucial influence on early documentary. Howells also took part in an important discussion, *A National Film School for Wales?*, televised by BBC Wales (recorded 8 May 1966). From 1957 to 1967 Grierson edited material, in Cardiff, for his popular compilation programme *This Wonderful World* (Scottish Television) and he was patron and part-time lecturer, in the 1960s, of the Newport, Monmouthshire College of Art Film department (later known as the Newport Film School).
13. Review by Margaret Thomson, in *The Federation of Documentary Film Units Newsletter No 2*, October 1946, circulated at a DATA meeting. In 1963, Howells wrote and produced at his own company *The Most Precious Gift* (1963), directed by Thomson: an admirably pithy Gas Council film warning of food and other health dangers for the ordinary family.
14. Article by John Hughes, *Rhymney Advertiser* (undated but c. 1972).
15. Box 3, Howells Collection. *ITMA* ran from 1939 to 1949.
16. 'He [Baylis] taught me much about discipline, film economy and the compression of ideas, visually and verbally. I gave our films some Celtic depth, poetry and humour'. Howells document 'Personal Views', file 4.10 in Box 3, Howells Collection.
17. Cutting from Jack Howells's personal scrapbook, loaned to the present author in the 1980s.
18. Files 2.2 and 2.3, Box 1, Howells Collection.

19. Letter from Pathé Documentary Unit to Jack Howells, during another period of illness, 16 July 1951.
20. *Cricket* (1951), for instance, is a pleasing miniature – a reflective, impressionistic look at cricket history through the caricatures of past players and paintings in the Lord's Cricket Ground Museum London – intercut with shots from the 1948 England-Australia Test series, and early film of batsmen W. G. Grace and Ranjitsinghi. Howells wrote an original treatment and elements of the final script.
21. R.E. Tritton to C.S. Cleverly, Kent Oil Refinery, 7 February 1956. Tritton to Howells, 14 March 1957. Both in Howells Collection, Box 2, file. 2.5. Howells noted in file 4.18, Box 3, that BP, Shell and Unilever had 'allowed documentary film-makers to work on social and allied subjects, well away from the crudities of direct advertising'. Howells's introduction to Tritton had presumably been on Pathe's *Oil*. He also scripted, under contract with Greenpark productions, the Aden refinery film *They Saw a Valley* (1954), directed by Humphrey Swingler.
22. Howells's account in *Film & TV Technician*, March 1965, pp. 50–2.
23. *Guilty Chimneys* script, Box 1, file 2.4, Howells Collection.
24. Interview Bristol, February 2009. See Brian Winston, *Claiming the Real* (London: BFI, 1995), p. 55. Winston argues that poetry conditioned even the most supposedly engaged of the social purpose films of the Documentary Movement – Howells's choice of this music was the kind of poetic intervention Winston might have cited. A review of *Guilty Chimneys* appeared in the journal *Smokeless Air* vol. xxiv no. 90, September 1954.
25. Detailed report from Howells after the voyage and his letter to Shaw Savill, 14 July 1955, suggesting they write to British Films requesting a supplementary budget, both in file 4.16, Box 3, Howells Collection.
26. Reviews, undated, in Howells Collection.
27. See Michael Foot's *Aneurin Bevan: Vol 2 1945–1960* (London: Granada, 1975), pp. 561–75. Jennie Lee, shown the film before transmission, objected to the documentary's representations of Bevan's nuclear war speech and Bryan Michie, TWW programme head, apparently ordered alterations, to Howells's disgust. Howells brought in to help re-edit the film a non-staffer, Harley Jones, first head of the Newport College Film department, but then working with Grierson on *This Wonderful World*. Jones was credited as associate producer.

9 'I don't think he did anything after that': *Paul Dickson*

LEO ENTICKNAP

At first sight, the career of Paul Dickson (b. 1920) appears to be just another manifestation of the 'decline and fall' narrative through which the Documentary Movement is typically characterised. He received his initial training as a cameraman in the Army Kinematograph Corps and as a scriptwriter working for Basil Wright at the Crown Film Unit towards the end of the war.[1] He then worked briefly for Paul Rotha's company Films of Fact before joining World Wide Pictures in 1948, a company with which he would intermittently be associated with throughout the rest of his working life. Shortly after being taken on at World Wide, Dickson directed two state-sponsored feature documentaries which established his professional reputation: *The Undefeated* (1950), promoting state support and welfare for soldiers who had been disabled in combat during the war, and *David* (1951), a biographical portrait of a school caretaker and amateur poet in South Wales, commissioned by the Welsh Committee for the Festival of Britain. Both were critically celebrated and *The Undefeated* won two major awards. Thereafter, the bulk of Dickson's output consisted of commercially sponsored promotional shorts, advertisements and television drama, a body of work which, unlike these two earlier films, has been almost entirely ignored by critics and historians. This essay will argue that by identifying stylistic and ideological links between Dickson's output pre- and post-*David*, it is possible to discern stylistic and thematic similarities between work made during and after the Documentary Movement's period of cultural prominence, thereby illustrating some of the ways in which its legacy influenced film and television thereafter. *David* makes a useful transition point, for it and *Life in Her Hands* (UK, 1951, directed by Philip Leacock) were arguably the last ideologically motivated cinema feature documentaries to be commissioned by the British taxpayer as the incoming Conservative administration of 1951 drastically reduced the scale of official film-making. This reduction included the closure of the Crown Film Unit in April 1952, the event often cited as marking the end of the Documentary Movement as a cohesive cultural force in British cinema.

The establishment of Dickson's career embodied all the elements that would characterise the main period of his working life. Drawn to the cinema as a child, he was conscripted at the outbreak of the war, and towards the end of it applied successfully to transfer from the artillery to the Army Kinematograph Unit. Through family connections he also secured part-time work as a scriptwriter with an advertising agency, before being taken on by Paul Rotha's company Films of Fact in 1945, where he progressed to his first directing assignment.[2] In the four years or so between his first paid work in the film industry and his full-scale directorial debut, Dickson was exposed to three genres and production contexts that would shape the remainder of his career: the state (as a military cameraman), the Documentary Movement (working for Rotha) and the commercially sponsored film (advertising). This formative period would also embed the three principal characteristics which can be found to varying degrees in the bulk of his subsequent output, and to which he makes extensive reference in later interviews: the use of carefully scripted and often fictional narratives to illustrate real-world issues and debates, an emphasis on the resolution of problems or disputes (a cause-and-effect approach that would prove particularly suited to episodes of television drama series) and the use of these techniques across both public-sector and commercial projects.

Writing at about the time Dickson started working for Films of Fact, the commentator and director of religious and instructional films Andrew Buchanan opined that the documentary was already in decline:

> In time, this paradox [between the perceived public enthusiasm for documentaries during World War II and the decline in production thereafter] created one of the most extraordinary situations in filmdom's history – documentary technique advanced rapidly, became increasingly popular, demand and supply were present – yet showings dwindled away.[3]

It is certainly the case that Dickson entered the sector at the peak of its ideological influence and institutional viability. The 'documentary-realist' tradition had been heavily promoted by commentators and press critics as an expression of indigenous cultural values in a propaganda context, both in the promotion of non-fiction films themselves and the incorporation of themes and styles deemed to be more 'real' than the alternative of Hollywood escapism. According to John Ellis, these writers were as influential as their subjects (or at least, they aspired to be), claiming that 'they hoped to change the nature of mass cinema in Britain' to encompass the discursive and public-service ideals originally espoused by Grierson and his associates.[4] Dickson would only spend five years or so of a thirty-year career as an active film-maker working directly within the organisations most synonymous with the Documentary Movement, but it is clear both from his later work and his recollections in retirement that they were influentially formative ones.

His earliest work having been in screenwriting, Dickson's first pieces as director were items in Rotha's MOI-commissioned cinemagazine *Britain Can Make It*, on the manufacture of bricks[5] and drilling for oil in Nottinghamshire.[6] There then followed the film that bore his first on-screen credit as director, *Country Homes* (1947), produced by Films of Fact to a commission from the Ministry of Health. This eleven-minute short promotes the use of a prefabricated residential dwelling, the Airey house, as a solution to the acute shortage of rural housing stock that resulted from focusing the post-war reconstruction effort on heavily bombed cities. *Country Homes* represents the post-war so-called 'age of austerity' in which it was inspired: the eleven minutes of mute footage, unaccompanied by music, has a bare commentary script filling in information that cannot be conveyed in silent images alone. Emphasising that the components of the house can easily be transported over long distances by road and then assembled by two labourers in under a week, *Country Homes* offers a miniature, utilitarian take on the 'why we fought' agenda addressed more prominently in a series of feature documentaries promoting the town planning movement during and immediately after the war, notably Rotha's own *Land of Promise* (1945). Dickson's final film for Rotha, *Shipshape* (1947), was a three-minute fundraiser commissioned by the Royal National Lifeboat Institution. It was also his first to include scripted and rehearsed dialogue scenes, in this case with a non-professional cast of lifeboatmen playing themselves. Dickson would later claim that this was fundamental to his directing technique in both film and television ('Directing is essentially about asking two questions: where do you put the camera and what do you do with the actors?'[7]), though in his BECTU History

Project interview he attributes the origins of this belief to his work as a rehearsal director and dialogue coach in feature films in the 1950s and '60s. He doesn't mention *Shipshape* at all, either in the BECTU interview or in an extensive videotaped interview carried out by the BFI in 2007. Films of Fact went into voluntary liquidation in November 1947, primarily as the result of significant losses sustained on Rotha's last feature documentaries *The World is Rich* and *A City Speaks*. Dickson was then looking for work.

After a final project for the Army (a training film, *Personal Hygiene*, made in 1948 with Richard Massingham), Dickson made the decision that would arguably have the greatest impact on the remainder of his career: joining World Wide Pictures as a director, in the autumn of 1948. His first project was the first of the two feature documentaries on which his critical reputation largely rests to this day: *The Undefeated*. These two films can be regarded as transitional work, midway between the state-commissioned, 'information with a purpose' approach celebrated by Grierson, and the commercially sponsored film that would become one of the mainstays of Dickson's work from the 1950s to the 1970s (advertisements, television drama and dialogue direction on features being the others). They were commissioned by government departments rather than by the private sector (the Ministry of Pensions and the Welsh Committee of the Festival of Britain respectively), but from an independent production company that was given more or less a free hand in its treatment of the subject matter and approach to the propaganda objective.

The approach that Dickson took was essentially that of a fictional treatment, developing a small-scale, self-contained drama in order to publicise the role of the Ministry of Pensions in rehabilitating ex-servicemen who had sustained serious and permanent disabilities during the war. The result is that *The Undefeated* is very clearly a descendent of the wartime story documentary, built around a hypothetical case-study narrative into which certain fictitious aspects were inserted, either for dramatic effect or to convey information required by the film's commissioners. The principal character, named Joe Anderson, was played by an actual disabled ex-serviceman, Gerald Pearson, 'picked by chance from hundreds' of Ministry of Pensions files.[8] He is a former RAF glider pilot who lost both his legs in action and lost his voice as the result of what would now be called post-traumatic stress disorder. The former reflects Pearson's actual experience, whereas the latter was invented for dramatic effect 'to make sure that the audience would be hooked on Joe's story'.[9] The film follows Anderson's progress from initial medical treatment, through fitting and training with artificial limbs, his reintegration into the home and workplace and, eventually, the restoration of his voice. The role of the Ministry of Pensions and their welfare officers in coordinating this is emphasised in strategic sequences along the way, most of which take the form of extended dialogue scenes detailing the interview process. This presumably was an attempt to fulfil the Ministry of Pensions's stipulation that one of the objectives of the film was to demystify and destigmatise the process of seeking state support for dealing with the consequences of serious injuries.

Unusually for a documentary with such a specialist objective, *The Undefeated* secured a commercial, theatrical release after test screenings organised by the COI. Following a screening at the Edinburgh Film Festival on 10 September 1950, it opened at the Elite Cinema in Middlesbrough on 23 October,[10] in a bill with *The Dancing Years* (UK, 1950, directed by Harold French), an adaptation of a 1939 stage musical starring Dennis Price, and *Holy Year* (UK, 1950), a sixteen-minute religious film featuring the Pope. There then followed an eight-month hiatus until a small-scale and low-key general release by Associated British-Pathé on 7 May 1951.[11] This led to accusations by some critics that the government had got cold feet over the film; possibly as the result of negative audience reactions, or the belief that a film highlighting the impact of military injuries might undermine a recruiting drive then under way for the Korean War.[12] Interestingly, this echoed a similar controversy four years earlier when J. Arthur Rank was accused of trying to bury Jill Craigie's film *The Way We Live* (UK, 1946), because, it is speculated, he opposed the film's strong espousal of the Attlee government's centralised urban-planning initiatives.[13]

The Undefeated received extensive press coverage, generally positive and in accordance with Ellis's account of the critical celebration of the documentary-realist tradition during and immediately after the war. *The Times*'s anonymous reviewer, for example, praises Pearson's performance as 'admirably free from self-pity and exaggeration', which elevates the film to 'much more than just an advertisement for the Ministry of Pensions'.[14] The following year, a report from the Edinburgh Film Festival claimed that it was 'widely acknowledged as a work of considerable distinction'.[15] *The Undefeated* also received the award for best documentary both from the British Film Academy and at the Berlin Film Festival in 1951.

Dickson's recollection of the production process suggests that he was consciously influenced by some aspects of the Documentary Movement's ideological motivation and production practices, but was either unaware of or rejected the others. In the two extensive recorded interviews Dickson gave in 2004 and 2007, he repeatedly emphasises the importance of screenplay, performance, dialogue and story structure in producing an effective result, whether for a general or a specialist audience. Recalling the production of *The Undefeated*, he justified the introduction of fictional elements with this in mind:

> There were still a lot of very interesting documentaries being made, but often for specialist audiences who were interested in the subject. But for the general audience I think they are interested in what they see on the screen, and so they will respond and give themselves to the stories, to the characters, providing the characters are worth being given to.[16]

This approach was not unique to Dickson, but rather one he inherited and adapted from a process of evolution that had taken place since a group of directors (principally Watt, Jackson and Holmes) had rejected the more didactic formulae favoured by Grierson and Rotha in favour of the story documentary. As Pat Jackson had recalled in respect of an aborted project about the work of cable ships, 'I repeated what my master, John Grierson, had done years before ... We had both produced several cans of unusable film, and for the same reason – no shape.'[17] Furthermore, and most significantly in the context of this discussion, the attempt to find that shape by using narrative, staging and performance to structure information and argument was not confined to the Movement's leading figures and most prestigious productions. The precedent they set was gradually adopted in a wider range of applications, and within a couple of decades would become a staple technique of the industrial and sponsored film. During Dickson's formative years, for example, Max Anderson deployed it to striking effect in *The Harvest Shall Come* (1942), a biographical story about a Suffolk farm labourer made to highlight the low standard of living of the rural working classes, and again in *Four Men in Prison* (1949), emphasising the rehabilitation of offenders by the penal system.

Within a generation of the flagship propaganda films that had pioneered the genre, the story documentary formula became a widespread technique both in television drama and in promotional, educational and industrial film. In stylistic terms, *The Undefeated* and *David* can usefully be seen as milestones along that road. Dickson did not, however, consciously regard the two films as being a

Faces of story documentary: *The Undefeated*, *David*, *The Film That Never Was*

part of this process of evolution. He was not aware of the collection of London-based state and sponsored film 'units' being part of any collective movement, recalling that 'there were these little units in and around Soho, making films: I knew them, I was in touch with them, but I wasn't aware of any particular sort of movement. I don't think it really existed until afterwards, with people writing about it.'[18] He also recalls not having been aware of the phrase 'the creative treatment of actuality',[19] or having seen *Housing Problems* (1935) or *Song of Ceylon* (1934).[20] Yet his first (albeit ultimately aborted) scriptwriting project was commissioned by Wright and his first full-time job in the industry was working for Rotha and Films of Fact. This would suggest that he must have absorbed some of the Movement's practices and objectives, even if he rejected many of its ideological positions, notably Grierson's and Rotha's almost Brechtian opposition to subjective characterisation and the idea of commercially motivated entertainment.

David was one of five productions (not including the three-dimensional experimental films commissioned for the Telekinema) directly commissioned for the 1951 Festival of Britain, in this case through the COI, which asked World Wide to provide a film to 'show Wales to the world', on behalf of the Festival's Welsh Committee.[21] (Dickson himself is Welsh, born in Cardiff.) That two of the others were effectively the swan songs of Documentary Movement heavyweights (*Waters of Time*, the last film Wright made that attracted significant critical attention, and *A Family Portrait*, Jennings's last completed work) underscores Dickson's role as a transitional figure from its period of cultural prominence to one in which the ideas and techniques it pioneered fragmented and diversified into other settings. The film is a thirty-five-minute autobiographical drama about a school caretaker and former miner in the South Wales valleys, who comes to terms with the death of his son from tuberculosis by taking up poetry and entering an Eisteddfod. The main protagonist, D. R. Griffiths (brother of the politician Jim Griffiths, Secretary of State for Wales in Harold Wilson's first government, from 1964–6) plays himself, while the rest of the cast are professional actors. Griffiths's life is seen largely in flashback through the first-person narration of one of the pupils at his school. *David*'s release and critical reception effectively mirrored that of *The Undefeated*. Apart from theatrical screenings in conjunction with the festival itself,[22] *David* secured what was, this time, a relatively extensive commercial release, distributed in a (somewhat incongruous) double-bill package with *The Tales of Hoffman* (UK, 1951, directed by Michael Powell and Emeric Pressburger).[23] It was also distributed by the COI on 16mm 'to people in Government service and film societies'.[24] The film was almost universally praised for its integration of a political and ideological objective (in this case, the celebration of Welsh national identity within a UK context) with a sensitively handled human-interest story, by journalists at the time, by the documentarists and in the comparatively little that has been written about it by film scholars since. Writing nearly half a century later, David Berry described it as 'one of the finest films ever made in Wales'.[25] Interestingly, the one dissenting voice was that of Dickson's former employer Paul Rotha:

> But for all Dickson's skill as a director, and it is considerable, a superficiality of handling prevents me from being as deeply moved as I should be by such a theme. The technique is facile. Is Dickson really affected by his characters and their struggles? The continuity structure is ill knit. Sequences end awkwardly and are too episodic for the film to have a unity. [In his next film] ... he must avoid the pit into which so many feature directors fall, where technique becomes an aim in itself.[26]

From these two films it is clear that Dickson had successfully integrated his belief in the importance of script and performance as the principal vehicles through which his films would engage an audience with the need to address the political and informational agendas set by his sponsors. Both are built around the interaction between two principal characters, one of whom tells the story of the other in the first person. In *The Undefeated* they are, in fact, the same person, alternating between the perfect and present tense: *David* employs the same distinction between flashback and the present, only this time using two separate characters. The scripts are also structured around the idea of solving a problem: the rehabilitation process in *The Undefeated* and coming to terms with the loss of a child in *David*. In fictional feature films and television drama this is effectively the same thing as Robert McKee's 'three-act structure', in which an equilibrium is established, broken and then the audience is engaged through the process of resolving or re-establishing it.[27] Given the prominence of this structure in television serial drama it is hardly surprising that it is that field of film-making that accounts for the bulk of Dickson's later directorial output, yet it is also a recurring device in a number of Dickson's later sponsored films. It also provides the context for Rotha's objection, he believing in the didactic, 'filmed debate' model of documentary rather than expressing the debate's arguments through human terms of reference. This schism having opened up in the Documentary Movement as far back as the late 1930s, Rotha positioned himself on one side of it, and Dickson the other. Margaret Thomson, who worked with Dickson at World Wide, recalls that shortly after *David*:

> I think he was lured away into making commercials, or involved with something in Hollywood. I can't remember now, but the thing was that it seemed to me that Paul was going away from a region in which he could really be supreme into something where he would be just another man, just another director. And this is what seemed to me to happen, because I don't think he ever did anything after that. And if he'd stayed in documentary he would have been remembered as Humphrey Jennings is remembered.[28]

This view is echoed by David Robinson, who, writing in 1957, described Dickson as having been 'the one true hope of British documentary' a decade earlier, but whose career had been in steady decline after *David*;[29] and by David Berry, who concludes that Dickson's career 'began to stutter badly' after *David*, and that the film remains his 'finest legacy'.[30] Dickson himself claims to be content that *The Undefeated* and *David* remain the two films on which his reputation rests.[31] I would argue that this reputation exists largely as a result of the critical canonisation of the Documentary Movement in the decade preceding them, and that the only reason many of his later sponsored films are not generally considered part of the mainstream of the British non-fiction cinema is that when the Documentary Movement itself fragmented, so did the cultural kudos its leading protagonists successfully sought for themselves. Although Dickson's suggestion that the movement itself was purely a critical construction that emerged decades after the event is obviously problematic – they clearly did see themselves as a politically and ideologically cohesive group, as evidenced through periodicals such as *World Film News* and *Documentary News Letter* – he has a point in that the first generation of historical writing about the work of Grierson and his associates was written by Documentary Movement acolytes and supporters (e.g., H. Forsyth Hardy and Elizabeth Sussex) and tends to dismiss the period after the late 1940s as one of a decline and fall. This is exacerbated by the fact that there has been almost no substantive research into the sponsored film in Britain except in the context of its relationship to the Documentary Movement. The bulk of Dickson's contribution to non-fiction cinema after *David* is within this field, and it is here that we must look in order to identify some of the ways in which the documentary-realist tradition metamorphosed and was absorbed into other forms of film-making.

The American archivist and ephemeral film expert Rick Prelinger argues that 'the late 1940s and 1950s were the golden age of the sponsored film',[32] though in Britain at least, its origins go back significantly further. The sponsored film (as distinct from the documentary made directly by the state, e.g., the Crown or armed services film units) had been entwined with the Documentary Movement from the early 1930s, and promotional films go back almost as far as the cinema itself. In the period before the Documentary Movement began to exercise any cultural influence, the boundary between straightforward advertising films and the idea of a sponsored film as we now understand the phrase (in crude terms, a film that is intended to integrate a public-service and/or entertainment function with the promotion of a sponsor's products and services) was fluid and changing. The cinema pioneer Charles Urban is described by his biographer is a 'keen advocate of sponsored film-making',[33] spending much of the period before World War I producing actuality shorts for such companies as the Harland and Wolff shipyard as early as 1897, and travelogues for various railway companies worldwide throughout the following decade. The sponsored film continued to develop before the onset of the Movement, and in parallel with it while outside its sphere of influence.

However, the Documentary Movement did attempt to exert a significant emphasis on the role, context and audience of the sponsored film, promoting it as more philanthropy than straightforward advertising and encouraging overlap between its film-makers and those employed in the public sector. In truth, many of the films that resulted from this interaction differ from their predecessors and those made at around the same time, but without the involvement of people like Grierson and Rotha, only in the emphasis in their social message: hence, in *Port Sunlight* (1919) the benevolent capitalism of Lever in providing a high standard of living for their employees is the message being sold; whereas in *Housing Problems* (made for the Gas, Light and Coke Company) it is the benevolent socialism of the local authority in tearing down slums, not the fact that their replacements will be heated by gas. As Brian Winston cynically but elegantly surmised it, the Documentary Movement hijacked sponsored film-making and tried to turn it into a mixture of 'left wing kudos, right wing money and films of dubious social worth in the middle'.[34]

It was just over a decade after this interaction started that Dickson began his career as a director of sponsored films, with *The Undefeated* and *David*, the sponsor in these cases being the taxpayer. As the post-war period wore on, the documentary units, if they survived, increasingly made films to commission from the private sector. Dickson and World Wide offer archetypal examples of how sponsored documentary film-making gradually shifted from the public to the private sector, taking some of the Movement's beliefs and methodologies with it, but incorporating them with others as the 1950s and '60s progressed.

A 1959 manual, *Business Films: How to Make and Use Them*, sets out the rationale behind the sponsored film from the prospective sponsor's perspective. A common thread running throughout the text is that 'every industrial film should be made for a specific purpose and for a specific audience',[35] the argument being that what distinguishes a sponsored film from a straightforward advertisement is that it should be a more precise and technocratic form of communication, designed to convey detailed information and/or ideas to a carefully selected audience, rather than deliver a generally positive message to a mass audience. This overlaps significantly with one aspect of mainstream Documentary Movement thinking. In a trade press article written in 1946, Rotha had called for what was effectively a move away from Grierson's creative treatment of actuality, to repositioning the movement as 'a body of technicians, skilled in dramatising facts and information and argument'.[36] *Country Homes* can perhaps be seen as an embodiment of this belief. The influence of the 'creative' types that Grierson employed and nurtured, such as Auden, Britten, Lye, Milhaud etc., is nowhere to be seen: what we get is a straightforward, no-frills exposition of why a rural house-building programme is needed and how the proposed solution will do the job.

Marsha Bryant argues that the 'creative' aspect of Grierson's original project was an inherent contradiction, one that 'became insurmountable by the end of the thirties'[37] (Jennings, presumably, being the exception to that rule). The context is her accusation that Grierson was promoting the social injustice of British imperialism through the use of films celebrating the Empire, fingering *Song of Ceylon* as the prime culprit. But it can also be applied to the interaction between the Movement's treatment of domestic issues and their audience, and by doing so we can begin to understand why, after the Rotha/Wright/Taylor tendency had shorn the documentary of its overt ideological and cultural baggage, there was a lot of overlap in the methodology, ideology and technology of the final phase of the Documentary Movement (elegantly characterised by Patrick Russell as 'micro-managing change'[38]) and the commercial sponsored film in the second half of the twentieth century.

Business Films proposes four categories of audience and five methods of distribution for the sponsored film. The former are 1) VIPs, that is, strategic decision-makers; 2) 'People who need to be instructed in the use of the sponsor's products or services', 3) 'Sections of the public with a clearly identified interest in the sponsor's products or services' and 4), 'General audiences in national or regional groups'. The latter are 1) shows to specially invited audiences, 2) 'Roadshows, on a contractual basis', 3) 'the loan of prints to suitable organisations', 4) 'small screen shows at trade exhibitions, etc.' and 5) theatrical or television distribution at commercial advertising rates.[39] As far as the author is concerned, the latter was such a small market for most sponsored-film production as to be an effective irrelevance. The common characteristic of the four remaining categories of audience and distribution method is that none of them involved a straightforward commercial transaction in the way that mainstream cinema did. Put crudely, commercial cinema (and less directly but still in principle, television) audiences bought a product, whereas the audience for sponsored films were sold one. Ironically, the distribution infrastructure for the sponsored film that had developed by the 1950s was very similar in conception to the one Grierson imagined and campaigned for in the 1930s as a means of bypassing the mercenary capitalism (and American cultural imperialism) of the mainstream distribution and exhibition sectors, being based on 16mm projection and in venues other than cinemas. The irony comes in that this alternative infrastructure came to serve the private sector as much if not more than the public. In her discussion of sponsored cinemagazines, Emily Crosby quotes the president of the Federation of British Industry in 1954, claiming that 'some 23,000' 16mm projectors were in use in non-theatrical venues across the UK, including 'schools, social clubs, churches and unions'.[40]

The other primary source of information we have is *Film User*. In relation to theatrically distributed fiction films, the trade press (represented mainly by *Today's Cinema* and *Kinematograph Weekly*) has been used extensively by historians as a primary source of industrial, institutional and economic context for their distribution and exhibition. Many who have done so were later criticised for relying too heavily on trade papers, accepting the viewpoints expressed therein uncritically and not always corroborating information through other sources.[41] This historiographical health warning also applies to the use of trade periodicals as a source of primary evidence in researching the thus far largely ignored area of British industrial and sponsored films. Nevertheless, *Film User* does at least provide some indication of the extent of the sponsored-film sector, the range of films that were made, the motivations of public- and private-sector sponsoring organisations and the ways in which these films reached their constituent audiences. What it doesn't do is to identify explicitly links between sponsored films and British film culture in a broader sense, which I argue is probably the most important aspect of Paul Dickson's career, especially in relation to the Documentary Movement and the realist tradition. But it does give us some of the raw material.

The remainder of this chapter will discuss a representative selection of Dickson's sponsored industrial films from his post-war career. His work as a dialogue director on feature films, as a director of advertisements, television drama and, during the final decade of his career, as a teacher at the National Film and Television School, falls outside the scope of this book; though reference will be made to points in common between the techniques and approaches in these genres and his sponsored films. These are *A Story of Achievement* (*Opkomst van een industrie*) (1952), *The Film That Never Was* (1957), *Enquiry Into General Practice* (1959) and a series of promotional films made for the British steel industry: *Stone Into Steel* (1960), *Character of Steel: An Autobiography* (1978) and *Steel: The Secret* (1981).

Dickson's first commercially sponsored film, *A Story of Achievement*, was commissioned by Unilever in 1951 and completed the following year. Both branches of the Anglo-Dutch Unilever were keen from the outset to stress their ethical credentials. Lever Brothers had made or sponsored promotional films and advertisements since at least 1910, and a snapshot survey of Lever Brothers' earlier output reveals clear precedents for the tone and approach of Dickson's film. The company's first major production was *Port Sunlight*, a forty-eight-minute travelogue promoting the model village built next to Lever's soap factory on the Wirral Peninsula as his attempt 'to socialise and Christianise business'. The second part of the film describes the soap manufacture process, once again emphasising the product's role in improving public health. *Congo* (1923) seeks to convince viewers of the humane and enlightened treatment of the native workforce in Lever's palm oil operations in what is now the Democratic Republic of Congo, and the town built to house them, Leverville (since renamed Lusanga). *Grime Doesn't Pay* (1935) stresses the public health advantages of regular washing, especially with Lever's soap products. By the mid-1950s, Unilever's Information Division were claiming that their documentary film-making programme existed to 'fill a social need', and that the majority of the audience were schoolchildren in classroom screenings.[42]

Margarine Unie also stressed its contribution both to the Dutch economy and British public health in its promotional activity, by exporting large quantities of the food to British factory workers at a time of industrial expansion and a shortage of dairy produce in the face of agricultural contraction. *A Story of Achievement*, commissioned as Unilever's Dutch operations were recovering from the wartime occupation and being re-established as a major export industry, is a fictionalised account of the invention of margarine through the eyes of the rival industrialists Samuel van den Bergh and Antonius Jurgens (whose companies merged to form Margarine Unie in 1927) in the late nineteenth century. In a throwback to a practice that briefly flourished for a few years during the conversion to sound, the film was produced in multiple-language versions (MLVs).[43] The mainly Dutch cast performed in successive takes with Dutch and English dialogue, resulting in two films that are substantively identical apart from slight variations in the commentary script to emphasise the Dutch or British contributions to Unilever's origins for their respective audiences.[44] The location recording was done on magnetic tape, chosen largely to enable easier editing of the multiple sound mixes, making A *Story of Achievement* probably one of the earliest British productions of any significant scale to do so.[45] Given that Dickson claims never to have spoken a second language,[46] the continuity and dialogue direction in the Dutch version is remarkably fluent and assured; though an additional credit not present in the English version states that the 'production, commentary and editing were completely revised [i.e., from the original English screenplay written by Ted Willis] by' Johan Raab van Canstein,[47] a minor figure in Dutch cinema history remembered today mainly for his quasi-surrealist documentary *Als de halmen buigen* (*When the Corn Bends in the Wind*) (1929), made with Jean Dréville.[48] *A Story of Achievement* is instantly recognisable as the work of the director of *The Undefeated* and *David*. Once again it is structured around the premise of solving a problem: in this case, malnutrition caused by the shift from an agrarian to an industrial economy and the consequent need to synthesise and mass-produce foodstuffs as an industrial process. As with the government agency in *The Undefeated*, big business, in the form of Unilever, is portrayed as having retained the ethical values of the small family firms it was formed from, while using major industrial muscle as a progressive force for social improvement. The early scenes portray Jurgens and van den Burgh undertaking the initial research and development work, and then expanding the scope and scale of their manufacturing and distribution operations. Towards the end of the film Unilever research scientists are seen experimenting with ways to add vitamins to margarine in order to protect public health in wartime. As with Dickson's two previous feature documentaries, the principal storytelling technique is that of dramatic reconstruction, this being his first film in which almost the entire cast were professional actors.

In essence *A Story of Achievement* can be seen as an example of the sponsored film in transition, and of the legacy of Movement ideology starting to metamorphose into a more utilitarian genre. Interestingly, it is likely that the English-language version of the film did have some sort of a theatrical release, even if only a limited one ('it is intended for staff education, but has turned out so well that it will have a general release'[49]), as it was examined by the British Board of Film Censors and given a 'U' certificate on 2 April 1952.[50] As with *David*, a live political issue may have provided some of the context: a Unilever representative 'reluctantly pointed out that its appearance at this time in no way foreshadows the end of margarine rationing'.[51] On the non-theatrical front, *Film User* pronounced *A Story of Achievement* to be 'a most inspiring film for those inside the industry today, and for those outside it something of a revelation. Successful booking for any audience: of value in the schools for children of 14-plus.'[52]

In stark contrast to the Movement's earlier faith in the benevolent capitalism of sponsored-documentary production, Spooner's *Business Films* manual expresses the transition as follows:

> In the 'thirties, film sponsorship was often a form of art patronage. Big organisations like the Post Office and the Tea Marketing Board led the field, and their best efforts achieved recognition and fame (at least, they are still going the rounds of film appreciation societies). After the war the pendulum swung in the other direction: a good thing from the standpoint of this book, but regrettable to people whose interest in films is mostly aesthetic.[53]

Writing five years earlier, a columnist in *Film User* also agreed that the 'arty' sponsored film engendered by the Documentary Movement had become a cultural anachronism, one which was no longer compatible with the very specific public relations needs of industrial sponsors:

> 'How to sponsor a fiasco' ... what a glorious theme for a film! All the mistakes demonstrated, and ridiculed, in one lovely reel! The script should be written by the film critics and the sponsorship done by some of the documentary film producers. Such a film in 15 minutes could clear away those many misconceptions that so often require dozens of sponsor-producer conferences.[54]

Dickson's career for the remainder of the 1950s concentrated mainly on television drama, B-features, advertising and dialogue directing on the growing number of Hollywood features that were being shot on location in European studios following the collapse of vertical integration in the American film industry. Following the Television Act 1954, which enabled the introduction of commercial broadcasting (the first advertisements were broadcast in Britain on 22 September 1955), World Wide diversified into television and Dickson recalls that 'I made some of the first commercials that went on the air.'[55]

His next major sponsored film, *The Film That Never Was*, was commissioned from World Wide by the COI on behalf of the Ministry of Labour and National Service, and financed through the Marshall Plan's Conditional Aid Scheme.[56] Its aim was to promote the use of works councils as a means of defusing industrial disputes. Industrial relations in the UK had steadily worsened throughout the early to mid-1950s: during the economic crisis that immediately followed World War II, the nationalisation of major industries and a popular consensus that an austerity economy was necessary to balance the books resulted in a steady decline in strike action between 1946 and 1953: but as the 1950s wore on there was an increasing expectation of higher living standards and a strong trade union movement that effectively become part of the apparatus of government while Attlee was in office. Between 1956 and 1957 alone the number of working days lost to strike action in the UK jumped from 2,083 to 8,412.[57] Strikes and trade union militancy became a deeply ingrained aspect of British popular culture in the 1950s, from the Boulting brothers' satirical feature film *I'm All Right, Jack!* (UK, 1959, directed by Roy Boulting), to which *The Film That Never Was* makes an intriguing counterpoint, to the BBC television sitcom *The Rag Trade* (1961–3), starring a militant factory shop steward who routinely calls all-out strikes at the slightest provocation. The economic damage being caused by worsening industrial relations was almost certainly the principal reason for commissioning *The Film That Never Was*, and a leaflet circulated with each print confirms the politically charged atmosphere it was intended to defuse: under the heading 'Discussion after screening', it is suggested that 'the chairman might usefully try to guide the discussion away from considering whether the balance between management and workpeople is fairly upheld, to the basic factors making or marring Joint Consultation which the film suggests'.[58]

In many ways the film is precisely what the 1952 *Film User* editorial called for: mistakes are demonstrated and ridiculed, and misunderstandings perpetuated at endless sponsor-producer conferences. Indeed, David Robinson pronounced it to be 'more a documentary on film sponsorship than on joint consultation'.[59] The scene opens in a Ministry of Labour office, in which a mythical documentary director attends an initial meeting to discuss a film about works councils. A caricature employers' representative and trade unionist call for a film that involves equally two-dimensional caricatures, in order to represent their interests in the best possible light. They are not receptive to the idea that 'everyone is not perfect' and that the film should promote the idea of compromise. The film-maker proposes a treatment set in a factory, in which the works council is portrayed as dysfunctional and ineffective because neither the autocratic manager (who believes in 'factory efficiency through practical means') nor the union leader believe in its ability to deliver real change. When the firm receives a lucrative contract, this proves the catalyst needed for the two sides to bury their differences. 'What are you writing – a fairy story?', responds the sceptical union boss. Neither side can accept the treatment on the grounds that it shows their perspective in a negative light. The union leader declares that he wants to see a 'typical worker'.

The Film That Never Was

We then cut to the film-maker's office (clearly inspired by the cheap, rented accommodation used by the documentary units of Soho, with film cans on the desk and an award certificate on the wall), where he ponders what is meant by the term 'typical worker'. Another scenario is imagined, in which the mutual mistrust between the management and workforce escalates into an all-out strike. In a fantasy scene a lazy factory worker is contrasted with a Dickensian, top-hatted manager ('the stock figure of a capitalist, wearing striped trousers, a top hat and spats, but in his shirtsleeves. He chews a cigar, carries a tommy gun under one arm and cracks a whip with his other hand'[60]). Once again this scenario is rejected by the sponsors, who suggest an approach based on actuality footage and interviews. In what is possibly the clearest statement of Dickson's approach to documentary film-making, the producer replies that 'People aren't typical in themselves: they're typical in relation to each other. Live interviews would be useless.' Eventually the disagreements between the sponsors prove insuperable, the Ministry official stating that 'we don't want to spend government money fomenting industrial strife', and the project is abandoned; hence the film's title.

The use of professionally acted, tightly scripted and carefully rehearsed and staged dramatic reconstruction was becoming a Dickson hallmark, doubtless honed by the experience he gained in television drama during the early part of the 1950s. Dickson summed up his motivation to become a film-maker by recalling that, 'I suppose, in a way, I was interested in storytelling,' but the environment in which he spent the early part of his career prevented that interest from manifesting itself as conventional, fiction-film storytelling.[61] But neither were *A Story of Achievement* and *The Film That Never Was* story documentaries in the World War II sense of the term: they used a professional cast and stories inspired by historical events (*A Story of Achievement*) or hypothetical ones (*The Film That Never Was*) in order to achieve very specific promotional objectives. Interestingly, *The Film That Never Was* received a national television broadcast, on 13 March 1957 at 10.15pm, which was introduced by a public relations officer at the Ministry of Labour. The press coverage it elicited was largely negative: typical is the *Punch* review, which opined that 'botched work of this kind makes the task of serious industrial commentators infinitely harder'.[62]

Enquiry Into General Practice refined the approach of *The Film That Never Was*. Sponsored by the medical equipment supplier Medical World and produced by World Wide, it sought to persuade an audience of doctors of the importance of the general practitioner as a gatekeeper to more specialist treatment in an increasingly technocratic National Health Service. As with *The Film That Never Was*, there is a political back-story to the film's agenda. The establishment of the NHS in 1948 had met with intense opposition from the political right and, in particular, doctors' representatives in the form of the British Medical Association. In broad terms, hospital specialists supported the establishment of the NHS, as they anticipated a more stable source of income as the result of being employed directly by the new state agency rather than working on a self-employed basis. General practitioners, however, opposed it, as they feared that the effective end of private general practice would have an adverse effect on their income and working conditions.[63] The GPs' fears turned out to be largely justified: in the first decade of the NHS's existence, the bulk of the new investment was concentrated in hospitals and specialist treatment centres at the expense of general practice. Characterising the 1948–60 period as one of stagnation in general practice, a medical historian writes:

> The dominance of the hospital service added to the disadvantage already experienced within the field of general practice. Not only were general practitioners pushed out of hospitals by the new generation of salaried

> specialists and consultants, but increasingly the dominant hospital medical profession looked upon general practitioners as minor functionaries, suitable for little more than sorting out patients for referral. The positive strengths of the early NHS therefore exacerbated the already serious problems of low morale in general practice.[64]

By the late 1950s this approach was widely acknowledged to be highly problematic, with negative implications both for patient care and the overall efficiency of the service, largely because many patients who could be treated at local level were being referred unnecessarily for hospital treatment. A process began of attempting to enhance the role of the GP into a more autonomous decision-maker who uses local knowledge that the hospital specialist cannot, one which is promoted by the 'discussion film' (as *Enquiry Into General Practice* is subtitled) commissioned from Dickson. Opening with a declaration that modern medicine is an 'age of specialisation', the film argues that the development of medicine into specialist fields has inherently undermined the role of the GP, suggesting that 'the less the scientific knowledge, the stronger the doctor–patient relationship'. In the absence of such knowledge, the perceived wisdom of local doctors and the importance of the service they provided gave them significant political and cultural authority in their communities. But scientific developments 'reduced the priest and the doctor to the level of ordinary men'. The second part of the film, headlined 'The Desire for Action', argues for the GP to become a conduit through which specialist medical expertise is cascaded down to and applied at local surgery level; a purveyor of 'organised medicine for organised illness'. 'We're trying to make the GP into a sort of scout master, social worker or parish priest,' the commentator explains, giving as an example of how these functions can be integrated effectively when a doctor is faced with trying to diagnose an unmarried mother who had been trying to conceal her pregnancy. As a final emphasis of the medical establishment recognising the importance of general practice, the film ends with a short speech delivered direct to camera by Sir Russell Brain, a prominent neurologist and government health advisor, stressing the importance of integrating the GPs' and hospital consultants' work. Unlike Dickson's previous documentaries for World Wide, *Enquiry Into General Practice* is not built around a single structuring narrative, but instead on a series of tableau scenes. But as with his earlier work, professional actors and a crew offering significantfeature-film experience were used (including the later-to-become prominent cinematographer Walter Lassally) and the moral of the story is one of human reaction and interaction dictating the outcome of scientific, technological or political processes.

Dickson's other significant body of sponsored film-making was a series of productions for the steel industry. Between them they cover the period immediately before and after the industry's renationalisation in 1967. These were *Stone Into Steel*, *Steel Bars for the '80s* (1976), *Character of Steel: An Autobiography* (1978), *The Man Who Finished With Steel* (1979), *Framed in Steel* (1980) and *Steel: The Secret*. The iron and steel industry had embraced promotional and sponsored film-making since at least the 1920s. By the mid-1950s the industry had become a major sponsor of promotional films: nationalisation had been on the political agenda since 1945, and had partially taken place in 1951. The Conservatives, largely on ideological grounds, reprivatised the industry in stages during the mid-1950s, and the major companies fought a continuous PR battle to avert renationalisation between then and eventual creation of the British Steel Corporation by the first Wilson government in 1967.[65]

Dickson's first steel film, *Stone Into Steel*, was both the most striking and also the most controversial. It uses no dialogue or commentary, its images shot by Wolfgang Suschitzky showing the production process from ironstone mining to slab rolling against a specially commissioned music score (written by Edward Williams). Towards the end of the film, the steelmaking scenes are intercut with brief snapshots of the private lives of the factory workers: once again, the 'human face of industry' motif that can be found in most of Dickson's other sponsored films, but this time appearing late in the film. In Dickson's words, he 'intercut the process with the human experience ... out of their heads they were coming up with ways of treating it [ironstone], until finally they ended up with steel'.[66] The film was marketed effectively as an artistic experiment, being described by its sponsor, United Steel, as 'a dramatic and colourful film which conveys the size and scope of a vast steelworks'.[67] *Stone Into Steel* was awarded the first prize in the documentary category in the following year's Venice Film Festival, but did not in the long run prove popular with its sponsoring industry. Dickson recalled that at the outset of every subsequent project he worked on for the steel industry, he would be asked for a more conventional approach and told in no uncertain terms that 'we don't want another *Stone Into Steel*'.[68] The *Film User* review gives some idea of why:

> In a shorter film, confined to meaningful shots of essentials, this reliance on visuals alone might have succeeded. Here it does not, partly because the camera is too often used to capture striking pictorial effects that convey little or no information, partly because the story of steel is interrupted by character sketches – two of them startling and one incomprehensible – of a few of the men who make it.[69]

The style of this film is so atypical of Dickson's other output, both before and after it, that its significance, both in terms of the genre and his career, are hard to assess. If the brief he had been given was to illustrate the industrial process of steelmaking in factual detail, he may well have concluded that this had been done many times before (e.g., in Dorman Long's *From Raw Material to Finished Product* as early as 1932), that the technical minutiae were unlikely to engage a mainstream audience and that making what was in effect a silent film with an emphasis on aesthetic impact was the best way to integrate his approach of equating commercial activity with human activity. It seems, however, that the result pushed his sponsor too far.

Nevertheless, some of Dickson's later steel films still retain an unorthodox streak which is seldom to be found in the majority of sponsored industrial films from the period. *Character of Steel* is narrated in the first person (by James Bolam) as a rolled-steel joist being transported from a steelworks to a building site: the audience is encouraged to speculate as to its final destination and purpose. *Steel: The Secret* features an architect whose marriage is under pressure from overwork but who is able to restore his work/life balance through the use of prefabricated steel sections in his buildings. As with his sponsored film-making from *The Undefeated* onwards, *Stone Into Steel* excepted, Dickson's approach is to portray a technology, process or political issue as a solution to a human problem.

The final decade of Dickson's career was spent as a tutor at what was then called the National Film School (NFS). He recalls having been head-hunted in the mid-1970s by Colin Young,[70] the school's inaugural director, who had formerly taught on one of the first formal training programmes to be established for film-makers, at the University of California at Los Angeles. The first generation of film-production degree programmes in American universities are generally credited with having nurtured the 'Movie Brats' – the group of directors such as Martin Scorsese and Steven Spielberg who emerged in the late 1960s and who are often credited with having reinvented the style and technique of mainstream cinema away from the conventions of the classical period. Dickson recalled that the emphasis of his teaching at the NFS was on dialogue direction and rehearsing actors. The School's website describes its early curriculum as 'a loosely structured affair; sporadic seminars and workshops were secondary to production, with students spending most of their time doing exactly what they had come to the School to do – making films'.[71] This would seem to be in keeping with the techniques that Dickson emphasised throughout his working career, most notably writing, dialogue and performance. Not that this was incompatible with non-fiction subjects, as Dickson explained: 'Documentary should try to engage audiences more by getting them interested in the problems and predicaments of their subjects.'[72]

In the same way that the advent of formal film education and production training marked the start of a shift away from the 'on the job' learning process through which the writers and directors of Dickson's generation began their careers, so Dickson's own career spanned a process of change, from 'documentary' being a term that carried a lot of cultural and ideological baggage (as Grierson, Rotha and their ilk always intended it to) to a routine tool in the box for film-makers working in a diverse range of genres and contexts. From both an examination of his output and his recollections in the two oral-history interviews, it is clear that Dickson did not perceive an ideological divide between an episode of *The Avengers*, a toothpaste commercial and a sponsored documentary about the production of steel bars: all were stories of human interaction and dynamics, to be portrayed through similar styles, techniques and emphases.

So why does the comparatively little that has been written about Dickson thus far praise him to the heavens for *The Undefeated* and *David* and then assume that he disappeared off the face of the planet? This question brings us back to that inevitable old chestnut, the Documentary Movement, whose unmatched powers of self-promotion and attractiveness to left-wing academics since set an agenda for what British non-fiction cinema should and shouldn't be that still retains a lot of its cultural influence, almost three-quarters of a century after the peak of its activity. In an American context, one of the few serious historians to address the subject concludes that 'numerous questions need to be asked about the sponsored film'.[73] This is equally true of the genre in Britain. It existed as a significant sector of the film industry in its own right for decades before and after the Documentary Movement, and it was in that sector that the bulk of Dickson's contribution to non-fiction (in a very loose sense) cinema lies. From a brief discussion of Dickson's output alone, it is clear that sponsored film-making offers a wealth of primary-source material relating to the post-war industrial recovery, the role of the public sector in the economy and society, social norms and attitudes, consumer behaviour and much else besides.

Dickson summed up his working life as 'not particularly creative in the sense of becoming an outstanding figure, but as a journeyman director'.[74] It is precisely this attractively self-effacing assessment that makes him such an illuminating figure for understanding the British film and television industries and cultures during the second half of the twentieth century, and why critics and historians of authorship in the cinema must temper their natural desire to concentrate on exceptions that prove rules. You will not understand what cinema meant for the average American in the 1940s purely through the textual analysis of *Citizen Kane*, and neither will you understand how films dealing with real-life subjects were made and communicated with their audiences through the textual analysis of *Night Mail* or *Land of Promise*. You might make more progress, however, by trying to understand how the ideas and innovations in these films were absorbed into the work of the numerous journeymen that came after them. Assumptions such as 'I don't think he did anything after that' make a useful starting point.

NOTES

1. Dickson describes this period in his career in a biographical interview by Rodney Giesler, recorded for the BECTU History Project on 25 August 2004 (hereafter 'BECTU interview').
2. In the BECTU interview, Dickson recalls the agency as having been Pearl and Dean and that he worked for Gavin Lambert, describing him as Pearl and Dean's 'literary editor'. However, the agency can't have been Pearl and Dean, as it was not founded until 1953. Second, Lambert (1924–2005) would only have been aged twenty or twenty-one at the time Dickson describes, and therefore presumably conscripted himself, so it's unlikely that he reported to Lambert at this time. Dickson's interviewer (Rodney Giesler) also found this recollection surprising, commenting, 'I'd no idea that Gavin worked in advertising ... I only knew him when he was at *Sight & Sound*'. At several other points during the interview Dickson himself emphasises that his memory of certain events is unclear, and gives factual information that isn't consistent with other primary sources. Just as with most oral history recorded many decades after the events being discussed, the factual recollections on this tape should not be presumed to be correct in every detail without additional verification.
3. Andrew Buchanan, *Film and the Future* (London: George Allen & Unwin, 1945), p. 29. Buchanan (1897–1952) was a minor figure in the Documentary Movement, who began his career writing commentary scripts for the Empire Marketing Board before working for Gaumont-British Instructional.
4. John Ellis, 'Art, Culture, Quality', *Screen* vol. 19 no. 3 (1978), p. 11.
5. *Britain Can Make It*, no. 11 (1946).
6. *Britain Can Make It*, no. 14 (1946).
7. BECTU interview.
8. *Manchester Daily Dispatch*, 13 October 1950. Some of the references to press coverage hereafter lack page numbers, as they were taken from books of press cuttings compiled by World Wide which were on loan to the BFI at the time of writing.
9. Dickson, BFI Video Interview, 16 November 2007. This was conducted for the *Land of Promise* DVD set, and extracts are included on the disc.
10. Advertisement in the *North Eastern Evening Gazette*, 17 October 1950.
11. *The Cinema*, 6 April 1951.
12. Richard Winnington, *News Chronicle*, 13 October 1950.
13. For an account of this controversy, see Leo Enticknap, 'Postwar Urban Redevelopment, the British Film Industry and *The Way We Live* (1946)', in Mark Shiel and Tony Fitzmaurice (eds), *Cinema and the City: Film and Urban Societies in a Global Context* (Oxford: Blackwell, 2001), pp. 233–43.
14. *The Times*, 29 December 1950, p. 4.
15. *The Times*, 9 August 1951, p. 51.
16. Dickson, BFI Video Interview.
17. Pat Jackson, *A Retake, Please!* Night Mail *to* Western Approaches (Liverpool: Liverpool University Press, 1999), p. 64.
18. Dickson, BFI Video Interview.
19. Ibid.
20. Ibid.
21. The others were *The Magic Box* (UK, 1952, directed by John Boulting), *Waters of Time* (UK, 1951, directed by Basil Wright), *A Family Portrait* (UK, 1951, directed by Humphrey Jennings) and a series of four experimental short films, *Painter and Poet* (UK, 1951, produced by John Halas and Joy Batchelor).

22. The inaugural screening at the Festival included 'an interview [with Compton Mackenzie] televised in the foyer and straightaway flashed on the screen, three of the new three-dimensional films and a documentary called *David* (no glasses needed)'. *Morning Advertiser*, 1 May 1951.
23. *Cambridge Daily News*, 9 October 1951, and *Today's Cinema*, 2 November 1951.
24. *Film User*, July 1951, p. 368.
25. David Berry, *Cinema and Wales: The First Hundred Years* (Cardiff: University of Wales Press, 1993), p. 246.
26. *Public Opinion*, 25 May 1951.
27. Robert McKee, *Story, Substance, Structure: Style and the Principles of Screenwriting* (London: Methuen, 1999), passim.
28. Margaret Thomson, BECTU History Project interview.
29. David Robinson, 'Looking for Documentary: The Ones that Got Away', *Sight & Sound* vol. 27 no. 2 (Autumn 1957), p. 74.
30. Berry, *Cinema and Wales*, p. 249.
31. Dickson, BFI Video Interview.
32. Rick Prelinger, *The Field Guide to Sponsored Films* (San Francisco: National Film Preservation Foundation, 2006), p. vii.
33. Luke McKernan (ed.), *A Yank in Britain: The Lost Memoirs of Charles Urban* (Hastings: The Projection Box, 1999), p. 77.
34. Brian Winston, *Claiming the Real* (London: BFI, 1995), p. 67.
35. Peter Spooner, *Business Films: How to Make and Use Them* (London: Business Publications, 1959), p. 27.
36. *Today's Cinema*, 2 January 1946, p. 39.
37. Marsha Bryant, *Auden and Documentary in the 1930s* (Charlottesville: University Press of Virginia, 1997), p. 170.
38. See p. 50 of the booklet accompanying the BFI DVD *Land of Promise: The British Documentary Movement, 1930–1950* (2008).
39. Spooner, *Business Films*, pp. 270–1.
40. Emily Crosby, 'The Sponsored Cinemagazine', in Emily Crosby and Linda Kaye (eds), *Projecting Britain: The Guide to British Cinemagazines* (London: British Universities' Film & Video Council, 2008), p. 48.
41. Jon Burrows issues an even stronger health warning, claiming that '[Rachael] Low's work can be a problematic and even misleading source of information.' Andrew Higson (ed.), *Young and Innocent: The Cinema in Britain, 1896–1930* (Exeter: University of Exeter Press, 2002), p. 357.
42. 'How We Use Films – Unilever', *Film User*, December 1955, pp. 602–5.
43. For more on MLVs, see Ginette Vincendeau, 'Hollywood Babel: The Coming of Sound and the Multiple Language Version', in Andrew Higson, and Richard Maltby (eds), *Film Europe and Film America: Cinema, Commerce and Cultural Exchange, 1920–1939* (Exeter: University of Exeter Press, 1999), pp. 207–24.
44. Despite the different titles – the Dutch title translates literally as *The Growth of an Industry*.
45. Reported in *The Cinema*, 23 April 1952.
46. Dickson, BECTU interview.
47. Original credit text: 'Productie, Commentaar en Montage geheel herzien door Johan van Canstein'.
48. Richard Abel, *French Film Theory and Criticism: A History/Anthology* (Princeton, NJ: Princeton University Press, 1988), p. 45. See also <www.geheugenvannederland.nl/?/en/items/FILM01:30/>,

and Karel Dibbets, 'Een landschap tussen hemel en hel' ('A Landscape Between Heaven and Hell'), <www.geheugenvannederland.nl/hgvn/webroot/files/File/PDF/Dibbets-Landschap.pdf>. Of the film, Dibbets writes (my translation): ' A decade later [i.e., by the 1930s], the Netherlands finally had a flourishing film culture. Film-makers were imagining an ideal of Dutch national identity. *Als deb halmen buigen* [When the Corn Bends in the Wind] (directed by Johan Raab van Canstein and photographed by Jean Dréville in 1930) was a celebration of rural life as perceived by some holidaymakers from Paris. But it's not just Paradise – it's a *working* paradise, untiring and beautiful to see. These films promote the idea of Holland not just as a holiday destination, but as an Arcadian symbol of Dutch national identity. This isn't just an ideology, but also a practical means of support and cohesion. It is above parties and factions, defeating sectarianism to promote unity. It's also a marketing concept – the highest common denominator.'

49. *Birmingham Post*, 22 April 1952.
50. British Board of Film Censors (BBFC) reference no. AFF035878; <www.bbfc.co.uk/website/Classified.nsf/0/2BCE6D31173E93BF802566C80030E353?OpenDocument>. BBFC examination was only a requirement for theatrically distributed films: it was not necessary for films that were never intended to be shown in public cinemas, and as the examination fees were significant the majority of industrially sponsored films were never certificated by the BBFC.
51. Quoted in the *Sussex Daily News*, 22 April 1952.
52. *Film User*, June 1952, p. 298.
53. Spooner, *Business Films*, p. 39.
54. *Film User*, August 1952, p. 386.
55. Dickson, BFI Video Interview.
56. For more on the Conditional Aid Scheme for the use of counterpart funds derived from US economic aid, see N. F .R. Crafts, 'You've Never Had it So Good: British Economic Policy and Performance, 1945–1960', in Barry Eichengreen (ed.), *Britain's Post-War Recovery* (Cambridge: Cambridge University Press, 1996), pp. 246–70. *Just an Idea* (UK, 1957, directed by Guy Blanchard), promoting the professionalisation of public relations in industry, was also financed under this scheme.
57. Colin Crouch, *The Politics of Industrial Relations* (Manchester: Manchester University Press, 1979), p. 209.
58. 'How to use *The Film That Never Was*', National Archives, London, INF 8/611.
59. David Robinson, 'Looking for Documentary: The Background to Production', *Sight & Sound* vol. 27 no. 1 (Summer 1957), p. 10.
60. *The Film That Never Was*, shooting script, p. 13, National Archives, INF 8/611.
61. Dickson, BFI Video Interview.
62. Bernard Hollowood, *Punch*, 27 March 1957.
63. Peter Jenkins, 'Bevan's Fight with the BMA', in Michael Sissons and Philip French (eds), *Age of Austerity, 1945–51* (Oxford: Oxford University Press, 1986), p. 228.
64. Charles Webster, 'The Politics of General Practice', in Irvine Loudon, John Horder and Charles Webster (eds), *General Practice Under the National Health Service, 1948–1997* (Oxford: Oxford University Press, 1998), p. 22.
65. Colin Bodsworth, *British Iron and Steel: AD1800–2000 and Beyond* (London: Institute of Materials, 2001), pp. 394ff.
66. Dickson, BECTU interview
67. *Film User*, September 1961, p. 470.

68. Dickson, BECTU interview
69. *Film User*, September 1960, p. 520.
70. Dickson, BECTU interview. Dickson does not recall the precise year in which he began working at the NFS.
71. <www.nftsfilm-tv.ac.uk/index.php?module=Content&template=history>.
72. Dickson, BFI Video Interview.
73. David J. Perkins, 'The Sponsored Film: A New Dimension in American Film Research?', *Historical Journal of Film, Radio and Television* vol 2 no. 2 (1982), p. 138.
74. Dickson, BECTU interview.

10 Conflict and Confluence: *Michael Orrom*

KATY McGAHAN

In 1941 Michael Orrom (1920–1999) graduated from Trinity College, Cambridge, with a degree in physics and a burning ambition to 'wangle it into documentary'.[1] Through the actor Bernard Miles, the newly graduated Orrom was fortunate enough to gain an audience with Paul Rotha. At their first encounter, over lunch at a Soho restaurant near Rotha's d'Arblay Street office, Orrom later recalled, 'Rotha didn't take the slightest bit of notice of me for the whole meal.' If outwardly uncongenial, Rotha must have been sufficiently impressed by the young aspirant's science credentials to offer him a job as researcher/scriptwriter on *Science and War* (1941), a two-reeler illustrating how science was being deployed for the war effort. As it happened, the project had to be shelved because the subject matter was so heavily restricted by wartime security conditions, but the ill-fated commission marked the beginning of a substantial career that spanned five decades.

Fast forward to August 1979: Michael Orrom, by now an established stalwart of British documentary himself, was invited to introduce a retrospective of the work of his old mentor Rotha at the National Film Theatre in London. Rotha's own post-war career had been a sadder one. The rhetorical address Orrom delivered to the audience demonstrated that the youthful wide-eyed deference he must have displayed at the Soho restaurant all those years before had matured into what might best be described as enduring affection tinged with a hint of acrimony: 'Why the hell did I ever meet that bastard, Rotha? Nothing but trouble ever since!'[2]

In the decades after leaving Rotha, Orrom had become a director. Thanks to his old employer, he had spent a short time at the BBC and his final films were for Channel 4. Otherwise, his career unfolded largely in the sphere of the sponsored documentary. Orrom made films for four of its biggest commissioners: the COI, the National Coal Board, Shell and British Transport, as well as ones for less prolific sponsors such as Cable & Wireless, with whom Orrom would work for more than twenty years.

In an interview for *Zodiac*, the Cable & Wireless group's quarterly magazine, Orrom discussed the conjunction of science and art, recalling the rather romantic notion he had nurtured as a student at Cambridge, that 'at some point in my life, life and art would become one; that it would somehow miraculously have an artistic shape to it'. As he acknowledged, what had actualised was something rather more arduous and complex.

> It is only slowly and with great difficulty that I came to realise that this would not be so; that almost everybody's life is a dreadful muddle and the only shape you get out of anything is the one you make for yourself. The shape is in the work you do and this is what most creative workers are doing – trying to create an order out of the random life around them. You can see shapes and patterns in a particular area, but not in the whole

> of life. In documentary for instance, you go into a subject usually knowing very little about it. You burrow through one layer after another, then try to re-create the subject in a way that satisfies yourself in order to present it in its most dramatic and telling form to other people.[3]

The quest for pattern and the need to make sense out of what he perceived as a confused world evidently preoccupied Orrom and is discernible in much of his work. As a post-war documentary director his career varied in terms of genre, subject matter and the locations to which he was dispatched by the disparate bodies for which he worked. His career might have been even more wide-ranging had his numerous experimental art films advanced any further than the pre-production stage – for in tandem with sponsored commissions Orrom persistently tried to raise funding for personal projects. The director had further been inspired and motivated by the political convictions and the clarity of purpose that governed forebears such as Rotha, people who thought of themselves as social servants. However, the post-war world was a more uncertain place than the more polarised 1930s, and Orrom's attempts to impose a 'pattern' on his career would not always be successful. He belonged in that category of post-war documentarists who regarded sponsored work as a potential stepping-stone to other genres of film-making (as opposed to, for example, Peter de Normanville, who found his specialism early on in his career and made a decision to remain with sponsored documentary). In Orrom's case, however, this rarely transpired. Given his tendency towards experimental film and abiding reverence for the work of early Soviet and German exponents such as Eisenstein, Pudovkin and Wiene, it is tempting to speculate whether he might have had more opportunities to apply these approaches had he been of Rotha's own generation – that is, working in the 1930s, a period that afforded more room for, in Rotha's words, the 'aesthetics of experimental sound images' before the wartime remit of 'national interest' took hold.[4] One imagines he would have felt comfortable alongside Cavalcanti, applying avant-garde influences to documentary requirements. What happened instead was a career of distinctly fragmentary appearance, though Orrom's divergent interests in science, politics, adventure and formal experimentation can often be sensed at work behind the scenes.

One of the most personal films Orrom made was near the end of that career. *A Fragment of Memory* (1984) reflects on the 1930s, a time when he was a student at Cambridge and Rotha and others were running their Documentary Movement. Disparate 9.5mm film footage and photographs that Orrom took as a student are deftly woven with interviews of some of his peers to give a lyrical impression of what it was like to be an undergraduate during a time of extraordinary political upheaval. Images of fresh-faced students frolicking in the sun run in counterpoint to the gravity of the events described by Orrom in his commentary but the May Day marches betray the political commotion to which Orrom and his peers were exposed. Orrom's commentary offers plentiful historical context and imparts something of the sentiments of a generation living under the shadows of war and conscription. Collectively united against the easily identifiable evil that was Nazism, Orrom and his peers (including John Maynard Smith, Arnold Kettle and W. H. Auden) enjoyed 'beautiful political simplicity'.

Born in 1920 in Wolverhampton, Michael Orrom had demonstrated scientific interests and technological aptitudes from an early age. As a teenager he nurtured a fascination with electrical kits, astronomy and radio-set building. It was the acquisition of a 9.5mm cine-camera at the age of fourteen that spurred a new interest and set in motion his later career. He excelled in science as a student at Bristol Grammar School, but by the time he embarked on a physics degree at Cambridge at the behest of his father, he was already steadfast in his commitment to making a career out of film. In

Orrom's own words, 'There was a contradiction between the educational path I was pushed on and my desires.' As it turned out, his twin boyhood pursuits symbiotically informed his future career. It was his background in science that secured the commission from Rotha on *Science and War*, and approximately half of the productions he subsequently worked on had scientific subject matter. At university Orrom read mathematics for the first year, physics for the latter two years. He developed a particular fascination for atomic physics and spoke of the 'romance and beauty' of the structure of matter.

Ever since John Grierson surrounded himself with promising young talents at the Empire Marketing Board, the notion of 'apprenticeship' has exerted a strong influence over British documentary. Orrom had been 'thrown in at the deep end' on arrival at Rotha's company, Films of Fact: 'It was excellent training – you did a bit of editing, a bit of writing, a bit of cutting, in fact a bit of everything – from direction to sweeping the cutting room floor.' 'A bit of everything' quickly translated into 'production assistant' for his contribution to *Total War in Britain* (1945), Orrom's first on-screen credit. In his neophyte capacity he was able to hone his research, scriptwriting and editing skills. His cutting expertise was further sharpened by close acquaintance with the sacred texts: Pudovkin's *On Film Editing* and Nilsen's *Cinema as Graphic Art*. Orrom later stated that he was also greatly indebted to a series of four lectures at Bristol University that he had, at the recommendation of his maths teacher, attended as a film-obsessed schoolboy in the late 1930s: lectures given by the first generation of documentary film-makers. He later referred to John Grierson's lecture on 'the cut' as 'a piece of theology'.[5]

In his first professional assignments on Rotha's epic compilation documentaries, *Total War in Britain*, *A City Speaks* (1947) and *The World is Rich* (1947), Orrom was challenged with sourcing and assembling actuality footage, interviews and diagrams to present a coherent analysis of a social problem and prescribe a solution: in other words, to engineer shape and meaning from the synthesis of disparate elements. Future projects afforded much scope for exploring this procedure, consummated in *A Fragment of Memory*.

Following his abortive debut into professional documentary with the ill-fated *Science and War*, Orrom worked (uncredited) as production assistant on his second project, *A City Speaks*, which was already in development when Orrom joined Films of Fact. For *Total War in Britain*, made to convey the main points of the government's White Paper on Britain's economic war effort, it was Orrom's job to source visuals to fit Ritchie-Calder's script. The film was well received on its release, which must have heartened the relatively inexperienced young man. *Documentary Newsletter*'s review applauds the film's 'successful fulfillment of an important function of documentary – the interpretation in simple human terms of official documents and statistics'.[6] Grappling with the constraints imposed by sponsors (customarily tight production schedules and budgets) for most of his career, Orrom strove to bring vitality and shape to government policies or sober facts pertaining to industrial institutions.

On his next film, Orrom took another significant step up, becoming 'associate director' (Michael Clarke, himself later a major director in post-war documentary, took the production assistant role). This film was *The World is Rich*, one of Rotha's last major works as a documentary director. Orrom had struck up a friendship with *The World is Rich*'s scriptwriter, Arthur Calder-Marshall, while working on *A City Speaks* and the pair, Orrom later recounted, spent long winter nights matching footage to script in a cutting-room devoid of a heater. As well as a belief in what they were doing, the two shared a mutual dislike of the Isotypes so beloved of Rotha and tried to minimise diagrammatic explanation in favour of more 'human' filmic devices where possible. The *Documentary Film News* review commended the film's punchy narrative, harrowing imagery and the sparse usage of the Isotype.[7]

According to Orrom, he would have omitted Isotypes altogether had Rotha not insisted on their inclusion. Otherwise, Rotha left Orrom's final cut almost untouched apart from the removal of a scene depicting a German government food-drop to starving people in war-torn Holland. Orrom strongly disagreed with Rotha's 'ripping' of the scene and at the time felt that the omission 'ruined' his carefully composed sequence. The *Documentary Film News* review accords just praise for Orrom's well-judged contribution to the project: 'Again and again one is struck by the skill and meticulous care with which shots from innumerable sources have been collected and compiled.'[8]

Despite its warm reception, the production was fraught with problems amid which Orrom gained his first insight into what he considered Rotha's formidable 'power of persuasion with sponsors' – in this case, battling with COI officials for the film's completion. Orrom would have to learn the art of sponsor management in his own career and perhaps he discovered that it could be counterproductive to be as confrontational as Rotha often was.[9] The film was indeed finished, however, and went on to win a British Film Academy Award for Best Documentary of 1947 – securing it limited theatrical distribution.

The liquidation of Films of Fact marked the end of Orrom's illustrious apprenticeship. He was rescued from unemployment by Donald Alexander, who offered him work at DATA, and his first directing role: *Report on Steel* (1948), a pro-nationalisation account of the processes of steel manufacturing for the Ministry of Supply via the COI. Orrom also scripted and edited the film and later described the production as a 'one-man movie'. As a directorial debut it prefigures his later accomplishments in the industrial genre and also has many of the hallmarks of the pithy industry-themed *Mining Reviews* that were becoming the mainstay of DATA's output. A feat of editing, the film works concise animated explanations of how steel is manufactured in between iconic shots of monumental steel mills and raging blast furnaces. Orrom recalled how much he enjoyed collaborating with Malcom Arnold, who assembled some arresting rhythmic passages for the film score. Succinct and compelling commentary – 'steel is wanted everywhere' – over syncopated sound and punchy visuals successfully position *Report on Steel* to appeal to national sentiment and to service the post-war production drive. Orrom remained with DATA for just over a year, during which time he further broadened his experience directing various items for the NCB cinemagazine. 'A Dim View', from *Mining Review 2nd Year No 5* (1949), for example, addresses the problem of smoke pollution with an emphasis on the economic cost rather than the environmental damage. Before leaving DATA, Orrom was recruited to edit J. B. Holmes's *Probation Officer* (1949), while after departing the cooperative he turned his talents to shorter forms of public information via a six-month diversion into the eccentric world of Richard Massingham.

An unexpected reunion with Paul Rotha followed. The offer was to script a feature film based on *The Phantom Lobster* by Leo Walmsley, an autobiographical story set in Robin Hood Bay on the North Yorkshire Coast in the 1930s. Orrom enjoyed the book for its 'human interest' and good 'documentary background' and travelled up to Yorkshire, where he tracked down one of the main characters in the book, a local fisherman whom he interviewed at length. Rotha had earmarked a young unknown Welsh actor whom he had spotted around his Hampstead neighbourhood to play the lead. His name was Richard Burton. They presented Orrom's script to Ealing Studios, who promptly rejected it on the grounds that it 'lacked an X-factor'. Sadly, the project was shelved but another call from Rotha brought a second feature film offer, this time to adapt Ian Niall's 1948 novel, *No Resting Place*, which concerned the plight of itinerant workmen in Cumbria. The accidental killing of a game warden by the lead character (played by Michael Gough) in retaliation for his having shot his son provides the impetus for a sorry tale of hatred and vengeance. Orrom transposed the grim tale to rural Ireland and the completed film was eventually greeted with mixed reviews. It enjoyed a small theatrical distribution and competed in Edinburgh and Venice in 1951. At the Venice Festival it was shown alongside former documentary director Pat Jackson's *White Corridors* (1951), and both films were reviewed together by Gavin Lambert in a 1952 issue of *Sight & Sound*.[10] Although he is not name-checked, Orrom's contribution is applauded in a *Films in Review* article in the same year: 'The direction, cutting and editing show some of the good effects of Rotha's documentary training.'[11]

Unfortunately, what had begun as a potentially fruitful episode ended on a bitter note. The production was fraught with setbacks which Orrom largely attributed to the poor editing facilities that were made available to him in Ireland (he had to keep returning to England to edit at Clapham Studios) and Rotha's excessive drinking, which set back the production schedule. Mid-production, while cutting in London, Orrom was urgently summoned to Ireland by Lesslie, who pleaded with him to take over the direction of the film because Rotha had collapsed, 'seemingly from drink'. By the time Orrom arrived in Ireland Rotha had resumed control and Orrom's emergency sea crossing was rendered futile. Problems of a different nature ensued when, to use Orrom's own words, the director 'shafted' him for his fee. Rotha had promised Orrom an associate director credit and they had agreed on a sum for his contribution to the film. Later Orrom realised that Rotha had misled him and neither the credit nor the fee was actually going to materialise. He left the production somewhat embittered. It was Colin Lesslie (described by Orrom as 'a really decent chap') who, sensing something was amiss, had taken Orrom to one side before a production meeting to clarify matters and relay the news that Orrom's fee had not been accounted for in the production budget.[12] Rotha had not informed Lesslie about Orrom's promotion to associate director. Orrom received credits as co-scriptwriter and editor for *No Resting Place* – a film he described somewhat flatly as 'not bad'. With the money that he did receive for his work on the feature, Orrom travelled to Stockholm, where he exchanged £250 for the option rights to August Strindberg's play *Lucky Peter's Travels*, a story he had been carrying 'very close to his heart' and the basis for his next personal film project.

Dramatic camerawork in *Dodging the Column*

In 1952, without yet the means to make *Lucky Peter's Travels*, Orrom accepted work from Edgar Anstey editing and directing an altogether more conventional pair of travelogues: *Scottish Highlands* (1952) and *Channel Islands* (1952), for

British Transport Films. Not a signed-up aficionado of the genre, Orrom later admitted that he worked on these two mainly because he needed the money. *Channel Islands* is a less-than-outstanding BTF exploration of the attractions of the eponymous isles with some insight into their history, although it saw another successful collaboration with Malcolm Arnold. Orrom was more enthused by the directorial challenges promised by a third BTF project, *Dodging the Column* (1952), which charts the hazardous journey of a 130-foot long distillation column by road from Greenwich to the new refinery at Grangemouth. Orrom's recollection that the production was only loosely planned in advance and that the crew 'shot it off the cuff really', evinces a penchant on his part for adventure and for challenge – a taste that some of his later assignments, especially for Shell and Cable & Wireless, must have sated. *Monthly Film Bulletin*'s review gives an idea of the obstacles encountered on this industrial odyssey and something of the film-makers' gung ho approach to their brief:

> Bus stops signs have to be unscrewed, trees bent back, even garden fences dug up, and crowds collect from nowhere to just stand and stare. A humorous commentary spoken by members of the lorry and tractor crews describes how the various obstacles are tackled and the camera has caught some amusing aspects of the monster's progress. An entertaining short.[13]

Orrom attributed much of the film's success to camerawork by Reg Hughes (nicknamed 'Red Shoes' by the production crew). As previously with DATA, Orrom enjoyed the camaraderie at BTF. The collegial ethos extended through much post-war documentary practice and in 1958 Orrom attempted to formalise the situation by submitting a proposal for discussion at the British Film Academy: Needed – A Technicians' Workshop.[14] The establishment of an institutionalised forum for collaboration, he hoped, would open up new opportunities for the funding and the production of genuinely experimental film. Its aim was to bring together:

> Professional technicians interested in making experiments in film technique and expression – the kind of experiment for which opportunity rarely, if ever, occurs in the normal course of commercial film-making, but which, if successful, could well have a bearing on the making and development of the ordinary feature film. ... The whole idea of the Studio would be voluntary co-operation. ... I think it would be enthusiastically welcomed by many technicians who rarely, in the course of the work they have to do, get a chance to exercise their talents in a really creative way.

Though tabled at a meeting between the British Film Academy and the British Film Institute, chaired by Michael Balcon, the proposal was not taken up by the film establishment, despite strong moral backing from James Lawrie of the National Film Finance Corporation.[15]

Not long after work dried up at BTF a bittersweet chance reunion with Paul Rotha at Foyles bookshop on Charing Cross Road pivoted Orrom's career in an unanticipated direction. Rotha had recently been appointed Head of Documentaries at the BBC and was therefore in a position to offer Orrom work in television. After the *No Resting Place* debacle, Orrom accepted the offer more out of financial prudence than any burning enthusiasm to work for his mentor again, or to work in TV. Of the former, in a letter to an unknown recipient Orrom wrote: 'Of all the people Rotha has just phoned out of the blue more or less offering me a job. This is presumably in lieu of the money he owes me. He'll get the BBC to pay instead.' Of the latter, in a personal critique of the television medium, Orrom bemoaned its inability to match the 'visual sophistication' of film.[16] Orrom remained on the BBC payroll for three years, however. *The Waiting People* (8 October 1954), made for *The World is Ours* series (1954–6) was his television debut, the first of six BBC documentaries he worked on between 1954 and 1957. Thematically, these TV commissions meant a return to the human social problems that had been the concern of his earlier Rotha film commissions.

The Waiting People, scripted by Orrom and directed by Norman Swallow, outlines some of the measures adopted by the United Nations in addressing the plight of Europe's 10 million displaced people. At the time the film was made the British government had been holding back on its contribution to the UN fund to assist refugees still residing in camps some twelve years after World War II had ended. Very soon after *The Waiting People* was broadcast the government reinstated its contribution to the United Nations High Commission for Refugees. Such a direct correlation between television and government policy demonstrated to Orrom 'the medium's phenomenal power to influence and educate'. This successful convergence of politics and creativity, he later effused, gave him 'more pleasure than anything I've known'. During this period speculation and apprehension about the impact that television was having on cinema and non-theatrical distribution was beginning to reach documentary circles.

Orrom articulates his approach to television directing in a working treatment for the TV proposal, *Cinema in Transition*: 'one must try above all things to preserve what creative standards the cinema has achieved and extend them'.[17] Although Orrom acquiesced in the loss of picture quality on the small screen, he took pride in the fact that *The Waiting People* was one of the first BBC documentaries produced entirely on film, that is that it did not include the then standard live-studio footage. Orrom scripted or directed four of the eight programmes in *The World is Ours* series, all of which highlight some aspect of the UN's work.

Another noteworthy BBC commission *They Cry for Love* (16 January 1957), which Orrom directed and scripted for the groundbreaking *Special Enquiry* current affairs series, was an incisive investigation of the plight of Britain's homeless children. Orrom quickly came to appreciate that television programmes could be extremely powerful conduits for focusing public attention on social problems, and that in this sense they revived a part of the spirit of the pre-television Griersonian tradition. All the same, cinema people like Orrom and Rotha continued to decry the small screen's creative limitations and the boundaries between the two media were always (if not always clearly) demarcated. Rotha wrote in *The Quarterly of Film, Radio and Television*, about the broadcasting of his and Basil Wright's *The World Without End*:

> The makers of *World Without End*, especially the two cameramen, whose work is so fine, had perforce to accept the loss of picture quality on the small home screens and content themselves with the knowledge that the social message of their film – in fact their very impulse for making it at all – would reach a wider and more sympathetic knowledge by way of more than 4,000,000 TV receivers. If however the aim of UNESCO had been to recoup substantial financial returns, this TV distribution by the BBC would obviously not have been considered. Instead UNESCO would have secured the best deal possible from the best commercial renter.[18]

With reference to his own appointment at the BBC, Rotha confided to Orrom: 'I don't know how long I'll last Michael. Their methods are so different from ours.'[19]

Orrom was mindful that television was rooted in radio (the ubiquitous TV-studio presenter being borne out of the tradition of the radio announcer). Cinema, in his view, traced its derivation to theatre. 'After all, right up until the 1960s, the department producing all current affairs and factual programmes was called the "Talks Department".' The following anecdote, based on Orrom's experiences working on *Special Enquiry*, which was fronted by presenter Robert Reid (whom Orrom refers to as 'a worthy and earnest Scotsman'), suggests that one of Orrom's goals while working in television was to advance the medium further away from these perceived roots:

> The format was for him to introduce the subject by a piece to camera, then we would have the first story illustrating his thesis. He would then come on again and introduce the next filmed report, and so on. In other words it became rather like an illustrated magazine with a personality writer and picture captions. Having grown up in documentary films, I felt very much that the film should speak for itself, should carry the spectator along with it, but essentially let the spectator reach his own conclusions through logical and emotional involvement. I persuaded the producer to let me do this in the next one I was writing, on homeless children, and we shunted off Robert Reid simply to an introduction.[20]

Orrom was satisfied with *They Cry for Love*, primarily because, like *The Waiting People*, it served to enrich people's thinking about a particular human problem, but he also regarded dispensing with standard studio scenes as an artistic breakthrough. He even managed to incorporate a ballet sequence at the start of the programme that gave effect (albeit on a small scale) to his credo for film technique as promulgated in the publication *Preface to Film* that Orrom co-authored with Raymond Williams, of which more later: 'In some ways I can say it's my only piece of stylised action that carried through from what we were trying to do years earlier.'[21] Here he is referring to the experimental projects that he and Williams (as scriptwriter) had tried to get off the ground, of which, again, more later.

In the midst of a fallow period for his TV work, an auspicious phone call from the Shell Film Unit steered Orrom back into the realm of sponsored documentary. He seized the opportunity to work at Shell, whose output he rated as 'really glossy stuff'. Adaptability was a key requisite for the jobbing documentarist and given the diversity of Orrom's work (personal and commissioned) he was more than qualified in this respect. His ability, for example, to leaven highly technical subject matter with a judicious sprinkling of humour (first demonstrated in *Dodging the Column*) won him accolades for his first Shell commission, *The Carburettor* (1957), made as part of the *How the Motor Car Works* series. Dramatic handling of potentially arid raw material, in this case the function of the carburettor in supplying petrol to the internal combustion engine, characterised Orrom's punchy style and was acknowledged in a *Film User* review: 'The accelerator pump [has] a polished dramatic sequence to emphasise its usefulness ... This is a well made instructional film, lightened with humour.'

Orrom enjoyed the generous production budgets and travel opportunities at Shell. *The Two Stroke Engine* (1959), a beautifully crafted explanation of the technological aspects of the two-stroke and diesel engines, was filmed in Germany and Switzerland. Around this time Shell was preparing a film on the tercentenary of the Royal Society and wanted a prestige production that would present the society as the aegis under which science had been able to develop in various fields. With his science degree, Orrom was thought to be the right person. While scripting and shooting the American sequences for the film in the USA with a Hollywood crew, Orrom linked up with Philip Leacock and Ivan Moffatt, old documentary acquaintances who had traversed into feature film and were now residing in Los Angeles. While lunching at a 20th Century-Fox Studios restaurant with Moffatt, Orrom took the opportunity to show him the treatment for *Lucky Peter's Travels*. Although Moffatt apparently liked it very much he did not think there was enough time to get it off the ground before Orrom's return to the UK.

Had either of Orrom's final two commissions for Shell not been foiled, they might have provided opportunity for exploration of some of the creative techniques for which the director had so ardently been searching a means of expression. The task of the first was to direct and script a recruitment film designed to attract science graduates to the industry. The fact that Shell had to create international versions of its films was of interest to Orrom because it precluded the usage of synched dialogue, thereby better furnishing the application of his theories on sound.[22] Unfortunately, a dispute between Orrom and an executive producer at Shell over Orrom's script brought the project to a premature close. When the other Shell project was offered to Orrom, Stuart Legg told him: 'I want you to regard this as your own film. Do what you want with it.' As the writer, Orrom was naturally happy to comply but when he presented the treatment to Legg and executives at Shell the consensus was that Orrom's personalised approach – a focus on four peasant families – was not acceptable. An impasse was reached when Orrom failed to fathom the incomprehensible proclamation of the top exec: 'What we need is chemicals!'; and Legg did not support Orrom's take on the project. Orrom resigned from Shell and Legg went on to direct the film, eventually titled *Food or Famine* (1962), an investigation into methods of increasing food production which was highly rated, though Orrom's own reaction when awarded a 'Based on a Treatment by' credit was one of indifference. Much later, with reference to *Food or Famine*, fellow film-maker Sarah Erulkar asked Orrom 'Why did you make such a dreadful film?' This confirmed to Orrom that he had made the right decision in walking out of the project.

If Orrom's appetite for travel, adventure and 'glossy' film-making had been whetted at Shell, Cable & Wireless brought unanticipated cinematic challenges in some of the furthermost corners of the globe. Cable & Wireless was established in 1928 when, in the face of international competition, Britain's cable companies were merged. After the company was nationalised in 1947 it became the international communications arm of the GPO. At the time Orrom was taken on Cable &Wireless was still extant as a company, albeit state owned, that independently operated its overseas interests. Given its strong international ties, Cable & Wireless's films provided a useful means by which to promote the company's disparate operations to audiences at home and abroad. Concerned that the firm was increasingly regarded as a relic of Empire, its public relations department stepped its films programme up a gear in the 1960s.

Orrom's initiation into the world of telecommunications was a film dramatising the laying of the first 2,000 miles of the Commonwealth Cable across the North Atlantic from the Scottish fishing port of Oban to the shore at Newfoundland. This was made at a production company called Eyeline Films.[23] Directed and produced by Orrom, *Call the World* (1962) does more than meet its remit as a document of Cable & Wireless's technological prowess. The combined efforts of ship crew and engineers working day and night in hostile weather conditions are conveyed in an authentically moving way, and aptly culminate in the symbolic final cable slice at Newfoundland that links the Old World with the New. *Call the World* was chosen as an official British entry to the Venice Film Festival and the Vancouver Film Festival in June and July 1962. *Ring Around the Earth* (1964), produced by Orrom but with Peter Hennessy and Stanley Willis jointly directing, extends the theme of telephone cable-laying, in this case across the Tasman Sea and the Pacific. Its 'unusually ingenious script' was complimented by *Film User*.[24] Good use of location and the episodic handling of the laying of each section of the cable ensures the film's accessibility for general as well as technical audiences. Striking the right balance between exposition of the functions of industry or science and the inclusion of elements of contemporary life on which they impact is the key to Orrom's Cable & Wireless titles and it sets his enjoyable work for this sponsor apart from more schematic films for technological industries.

Orrom resumed a directorial role in subsequent commissions: several films for the COI's *Frontier* series, a notable example being *Frontier – Radio Astronomy* (1965), and *East West Island* (1966) for Cable & Wireless. By this point, Orrom's reputation was increasingly becoming that of a scientific film-maker. The former film, a description of some recondite research undertaken in radio astronomy across the globe, traverses Jodrell Bank, Cambridge, Sydney and Russia; its parent series, *Frontier*, consisted of fourteen short films dealing with various aspects of British research designed mainly for English-speaking audiences abroad (though also translated into Arabic, Persian and Asian English).[25] *East West Island*, Shell-esque in its freer interpretation of its sponsor's brief, fuses travelogue elements with scientific exposition in its account of technological progress (courtesy of Cable & Wireless) in Hong Kong. Only towards the end of the film, with an allusion to telecommunications, does the underlying remit fully surface. Hong Kong's energy and vibrancy is evocatively captured with the help of Manny Wynn's splendid photography, which gives an impression (rather than an explanation) of the place, its people and culture – an aspect underscored by Joss Ackland's commendably unobtrusive commentary. Judiciously foregrounding Hong Kong's Chinese elements over Western influences, Orrom's direction is astute. *East West Island* was distributed theatrically by British Lion, premiering alongside *The Spy Who Came in From the Cold* (1965), starring Richard Burton. Orrom's next Cable & Wireless assignment, *The New Caribbean* (1969), took the director to the outer reaches of the North Caribbean and down via Trinidad to Guyana on mainland South America. Again, the film eschews a basic analytic form in favour of a more sophisticated visual structure and an inventive use of multiple voiceover. Strong historical context provided by the commentary is balanced by a striking sense of immediacy brought by the final carnival sequences. This was attained through the utilisation of two hand-held cameras that weave the viewer through the Port of Spain crowds to the pulsating tunes of Ron Berridge and the Blue Rhythm Combo. Orrom was extremely satisfied with this sequence for again affording him the opportunity to apply some of his theoretical principles. It seems clear that, given the course his career took, Orrom was ultimately able successfully to incorporate his aesthetic doctrine only to sections of films rather than to whole films. As with *East West Island*, the vibrant *The New Caribbean* enjoyed a wide distribution in cinemas. From swathes of Atlantic Ocean to the midst of lavish street carnival, to the glamour of a glittering Hong Kong skyline, the residing message is that Cable & Wireless is meeting the growing telecommunications needs of the Commonwealth.

'Drab endless vistas of scree' was Orrom's first impression of Ascension Island, a bleak outpost in the South Atlantic Ocean, when he arrived there for the filming of *Apollo in Ascension* (1967). An impression possibly not a trillion miles from what Armstrong, Aldrin and Collins thought of their Apollo 11's lunar destination. It is unlikely that Orrom would have expected the first commission for his own new production company, Film Drama, to have been connected to such an iconic event as man's first landing on the moon. With his well-established links with Cable & Wireless and having had enough of being under Eyeline's wing and bringing projects to them, Orrom decided to produce his next project for the telecoms firm independently. He had already established Film Drama when applying for funding for his experimental projects but lack of cashflow had prevented it being more than a name. A hugely prestigious undertaking for a brand new production company,

Apollo in Ascension tells the dramatic story of the installation of an earth station for satellite communications to support the US NASA Apollo moon-shot (famously accomplished on 16 July 1969 with the Apollo 11 launch). The film was produced, scripted and part-directed by Orrom and was hounded by misadventure from the outset. Harold Orton, a producer at Eyeline with whom Orrom had collaborated on *East West Island*, tried to dissuade Orrom from 'going it alone' on *Apollo in Ascension*. When Orrom proceeded with his plans, Orton publicly questioned Orrom's capabilities regarding film finance. Orrom wrote to Orton threatening him with a libel suit, an action that seemed to curb Orton's diatribes. In the wake of this unfortunate besmirching, however, Cable & Wireless took the precaution of withholding production funds until Film Drama had delivered the first batch of rushes. If Arthur Elton had not stepped in and raised the initial finance through Film Centre, *Apollo in Ascension* might never have materialised. As it happened, the resultant film was widely acclaimed and ran throughout Expo '67 at the British Pavilion, as well as representing Britain at the Scientific Film Festival in Belgrade in 1968.

Given what lay ahead, the decision to entrust the business side of the production entirely to Film Centre proved a fortunate move on Orrom's part in that it allowed him to focus on the practical aspects of film-making. A dauntingly tight schedule imposed by Cable & Wireless, who ordered that the station be fully operational by September 1966 (Orrom and the Film Drama crew having only arrived on Ascension Island on 5 August) coupled with the remoteness of the location, caused formidable logistical difficulties for the Film Drama crew. Orrom later paid tribute to the cooperative spirit of the production team while suggesting the challenges of the location and subject matter:

> Everyone was most cooperative, and when I wanted some high-angle shots of the aerial construction a great galvanised tank (used apparently for bringing stretcher cases ashore) was brought up from Georgetown; and we spent a somewhat hair-raising morning in it suspended from the 100-foot jib.

Furthermore, the volcanic island with its all-pervading lava dust rendered cameraman David Muir's task interminably arduous in that he was forced to spend hours each evening stripping cameras and magazines completely to avoid the risk of scratched negatives. The Herculean unit managed to shoot almost half of the film (on 16mm, later blown up to 35mm for showprint purposes) in just over a week. Progress was most severely hampered when, while climbing out of a satellite dish onto 100-foot-high scaffolding, Orrom sustained a serious back injury and was incapacitated at the Georgetown Hospital for the remainder of the production. David Muir continued to shoot the crucial stages of the construction to be joined later by Orrom's stand-in, John Crome, who had edited *Ring Around the Earth*. Crome, who was flown in on an RAF training flight, did a sterling job as replacement director and received a co-direction credit for his efforts. Having miraculously completed the film on schedule, the crew returned to the UK to face the major task of editing 20,000 feet of 16mm footage. Orrom, who was somewhat revived by now, appointed, in his own words, 'the best editor around', R. Q. McNaughton of *Night Mail* fame. Some reconstructed sequences, of progress engineering conferences and contract signing, were shot at Mercury House to complete the story. Also interwoven was some NASA background film material of the space effort that Orrom sourced on a whirlwind trip to Washington.

The sense of urgency of the construction crew and scientists racing to meet the tight deadline and the uniqueness of the architectural marvel set against the eerie lunaresque backdrop gives *Apollo in Ascension* a distinctive tone. The film is further enriched by the incorporation of aspects of the

Portrait of Queenie

island's history – from the time when it was used as a dumping ground for victims of yellow fever to its contemporary hosting of space satellite systems. Another vital component is strong human interest. The viewer really senses the camaraderie of the workers and scientists (paralleling that of the film crew), unified in their fight against the clock. In Orrom's words: 'We selected and filmed the key parts of the operations, always trying to relate them to the people involved.' In whatever genre he happened to have been assigned to, Orrom sought to apply his longstanding precept that documentary should relate its subject to a wider social milieu. As he put it with particular reference to his Cable & Wireless work: 'I have tried in the films to bring out something of the social implications of communications to the setting in which they belong.'

In this period, a salient diversion from the vagaries of telecommunications had been *Portrait of Queenie* (1964), a musical documentary featuring Queenie Watts, the big-hearted, big-voiced East End jazz-blues singer and publican. The project was the brainchild of composer James Stevens with whom Orrom had worked on *Call the World* and *Ring Around the Earth*. Stevens had become acquainted with Queenie Watts on Joan Littlewood's recently released *Sparrers Can't Sing* (1962) (aka *Sparrows Can't Sing*), a feature film also set in London's East End docklands starring Queenie as herself. Produced by Eyeline and backed by British Lion to the tune of £12,000, *Portrait* was a forty-five-minute cinematic hymn to the Isle of Dogs that afforded Orrom ample scope for the creative expression and experimentation he had been hankering after. Jointly fired by its potential, and seemingly unhindered in any way by producer Orton (this was before their falling-out), Orrom and Stevens set about researching the project. In doing so Orrom became, as Stevens already had on *Sparrers Can't Sing*, a huge admirer of the dynamic pint-pulling songstress.

In the film, Orrom allows Queenie's larger-than-life personality and the convivial world of the pub over which she presides to speak for themselves. To achieve the naturalism they wanted, covert cameras were strategically placed around the pub for the duration of the three-week shoot, and soundman Bob Allen's on-the-spot recording was unobtrusive (only Queenie and her husband Slim were privy to the filming). The love, hardship and hopes of the people of the Ironbridge Tavern is captured through song, witty Cockneyisms and tales of the past. Beyond the congenial atmosphere of the pub, Peter Hennessy's long shots and tracking shots guide us through this post-war London outpost, at once ennobled by vestiges of industrial importance, and visibly bearing the scars of the blitz and more recent housing demolition. Over iconic external dockland shots and more intimate moments shared with us (such as Queenie putting on make-up), the couple talk openly about how they met and married; about the good times and the bad times (some of Slim's disclosures remind us that this was the stomping ground of the likes of the Kray brothers). As the film progresses the restorative role of the pub becomes ever-more clear, and the words of the numbers that Queenie belts out over of the din of Cockney chatter, ever-more resonant:

> Open up my heart you'll find a bitter sea
> And there a lonely seagull cries, 'But did he care for me?'

To do justice to Queenie's talent some of her songs were recorded in a studio and post-synched. The images cross time and space, with, on one side of the pub, old-timers cavorting around a piano, while, on the other side, beat boys and girls sway to the ultra-modern Stan Tracey group. No professional actors were used and most of the people featured were regular patrons. Once the setting and Queenie's personality and talent as a singer had been established naturalistically, Orrom sought to break a few conventions. Queenie's talking-to-camera has a jarring effect but at the same time exudes her characteristic East End warmth. More successful are the carefully considered counterpoint visuals and use of natural dialogue, often reduced to mere murmurings. The music label Eastside distributed a long-playing record featuring the film's songs on the film's release. Guest performers at the pub include Mike McKenzie, dynamic singer-composer pianist, and singer Beverley Mills. Queenie's unwavering attachment to her pub and the Isle of Dogs was certified when she turned down offers to sing in the USA and Germany following the film's release.

The use of the locals' natural dialogue did not go down well with Roy Boulting at British Lion. Orrom recalled that Boulting rather snootily remarked that 'he couldn't understand half the dialogue and if people paid to see a film they were entitled to hear the dialogue'. In the interests of the film, his demands for the characters' lines to be revoiced were quietly ignored by Orrom and Stevens. For Queenie, who had worked in theatre in the past, Orrom's award-winning film led to a media career that included *Romany Jones* (1973), *Yus My Dear* (1976), three BBC *Play for Today* stories and appearances in sitcoms such as *Dad's Army* and *On the Buses*.

After this brief excursion, Orrom resumed work in science and industrial films, remaining with Cable & Wireless until the late 1970s, where he helmed such prestige titles as *Arabia the Fortunate* (1974). *Arabia the Fortunate* charts social change in the Middle Eastern countries following the discovery and exploitation of oil. After a brief history lesson of the region, we are invited on a stunning tour of Bahrain, Abu Dhabi and Oman, taking in some beautiful panoramas of the landscape, people and their culture. Cable & Wireless is implicitly associated with the region's industrial growth, transport routes and the burgeoning tourist industry.

While pursuing such exotica, Orrom also responded to offers from provincial quarters including the Monmouthshire Education Committee Schools Council: *En Avant in Ebbw Vale* (1967) and

Michael Orrom directing *Arabia the Fortunate*

French From Eight (1967) both concern the teaching of French in primary schools. Film Drama also took a side-step into the industrial-training genre with the Tube Investments commission, *Talking of Industry* (1968) and subsequently *A Study in Change* (1970), a co-production by the Anvil Film and Recording Group and Film Drama on behalf of the British Productivity Council. The former, aimed at graduates and management trainees, uses the building of Tube Investments' new £10 million steel tube-rolling mill to illustrate in detail the potential logistical problems faced by management in a large and diverse industrial engineering group. (Tube Investments had undergone massive growth over the previous decade in which its assets increased from £44 million in the 1950s to £178 million in the 1960s.[26]) Both films provide insight into the different managerial problems affecting British industry at the time, with their respective emphases on logistical aspects of production and on strained industrial relations. Through its commentary, *A Study in Change* is introduced as 'a true re-enactment of the way the management and the work people in one particular firm tackle the problems change brought for them'. A truly fascinating feat of docu-drama, *A Study in Change* looks at how a firm and its employees faced inevitable changes caused by automation and was nominated for a 1971 Society of Film & Television Arts award for Best Specialised Film. The script is based on the minutes of meetings between management and workers at the Weldless Steel Tube Company in Wednesfield, West Midlands, and the naturalism of their non-professional performances is seamless. At a time of ever-increasing mechanisation in British industry *A Study in Change* captures the insecurity that permeated workforces in the 1960s, about to escalate to new heights in the new decade. Industrial processes are rhythmically captured by Norman Langley's camerawork and deftly intercut by editor Roy Ayton with various footage of men and their machines. Orrom's film gives us valuable snapshots, too, of contemporary factory life, capturing workers enjoying canteen camaraderie as well as in the throes of tough boardroom negotiations with management. The visceral determination of the workers struggling to maintain their livelihoods emotionally underpins some of the protracted meeting scenes.

Through his contacts and reputation, projects came Orrom's way without him having to advertise the services of Film Drama. The opportunistic approach resulted in a wide-ranging output: from *Face Value* (1973), demonstrating the advantages and disadvantages of toughened and laminated windscreens for the Triplex Safety Glass Company, to *Sickle Cell Disease – The Unkind Inheritance* (1977), a medical teaching film dealing with the striking variation in the natural history of the disease between different populations of the world, sponsored by the Arabian/American Oil Company.

In between commissions from sponsors Orrom managed to initiate some of his own projects. With his wife, Mary Beales (who, like Orrom, had directed a spate of *Mining Reviews*), Orrom produced a children's film, *The Secret Pony* (1970), a charming made-for-television documentary concerning the experiences of a ten-year-old girl who lives in the country and longs for her own pony. Other than this family film (for which Film Drama did not receive any payment from the transmission company), Orrom's attempts to break into television as an independent producer met with no success until the final two films of his career. As well as *A Fragment of Memory*, there was *Not Just Another University* (1987), also on the subject of university life. *A Fragment of Memory*, made for Channel 4, as mentioned earlier, is the more personal of the two. As a reminiscence of life at the Cambridge University of the late 1930s, it provides reflective closure on Orrom's career.

Following in the footsteps of Grierson, Rotha and other pioneers who gained wider currency for their socio-cinematic missions by also being theoreticians, Orrom intermittently engaged with intellectual film discourse throughout his career. In this respect, Orrom was something of an exception among his post-war documentary peers, many of whom preferred making films to writing about them. Orrom never wholly embraced the emergent naturalism of the mid-twentieth-century British feature film: instead, his tastes tended towards the stylisation and experimentation of early Soviet cinema and German expressionism. Raymond Williams, with whom Orrom had run the Cambridge University film club, and who went on to pursue a much celebrated career as a literary critic, subscribed to a doctrine similar to Orrom's, criticising contemporary modes of theatre for their failure to embrace experimentation. Orrom and Williams jointly promulgated their views in their publication *Preface to Film*. Described by Orrom as a 'film manifesto', it comprises two essays, by Williams and Orrom, on theatre and film respectively, and was self-published in 1954 by Film Drama, Orrom's yet to be activated production company. Orrom's contribution is an objective analysis of contemporary film methods followed by some guiding principles of film-making practice, but he carefully avoids mechanical diktats in concordance with a statement he makes in the book that 'there are no formulas in art'. In a *Sight & Sound* review, Liam O'Laoghaire commended *Preface to Film*'s 'plea for greater freedom of style and expression in film-making', but recognised, as did Orrom himself, that the task of proposing reforms to the creative process was fallible:

> The subconscious processes of the creative act are not always readily accessible to rational analysis, either on the part of the artist himself or of his critics ... in their post-script, the authors regret the lack of opportunity for experiment within the commercial structure of the industry, and rightly claim that art cannot stand still. This is always a defect worth calling attention to, and anyone who now investigates the 1916–26 film period will realize how courage and enterprise made it a truly golden age. The values which made that age will have to be rediscovered by modern film-makers, and this means not the imitation of remote styles but, rather, the creation of new manifestations of the human spirit.[27]

O'Laoghaire's suggestion that, given its inherent limitations, the 'proper substitute for this book is a film displaying the creative processes in which the authors believe', might have been the cue for Orrom and Williams to attempt to put their ideas into practice. The project they chose was a short fictional film, based on a traditional Welsh folktale, entitled *Legend* – a rites of passage story which chronicles the adventures a young boy who leaves his family and goes up into the hills where he has a 'formative' experience, the implication being that he undergoes some sort of sexual awakening. Orrom was particularly eager to explore Pudovkin's theory on the creative possibilities of non-synch sound, which he discusses in his essay in *Preface to Film*:

> The sound track offers many rich possibilities for combining voice with music. As in other dramatic forms, the words can be spoken, sung or 'sprechgesungen'. When the music is composed to a recitative (synchronized or non-synchronized) the result can be highly effective. Not many examples come to mind, but this method was used well by Walton in some speeches in *Henry V*; and it was done more or less continuously by Prokoviev in Eisenstein's *Ivan the Terrible* ... It is perhaps worthy of note, at this point, that some of the most highly conventionalized sound tracks have been in documentary films, where various forms of non-synchronized speech have been successfully combined with music ... It is a dismal thought that today, for the most part, it consists simply of synchronized naturalist dialogue, background music and effects.

Orrom hired art director Michael Stringer, who had recently worked on Philip Leacock's realist feature *The Brave Don't Cry* (1953), to do a set of colour continuities for the *Legend* proposal, and Raymond Williams wrote some sample poetic commentary. When Orrom discussed the project with Basil Wright, who was on the BFI Experimental Film Fund Committee at the time, Wright encouraged him to submit the project to the Committee together with their publication. Orrom bemoaned the fact that in those days the BFI was the only place one could go for backing for a project of this kind. Contrary to Orrom's expectations, the BFI turned the project down. Deflated, he went to see Stanley Reed who was then in charge of the Fund. In his feedback, Reed relayed to Orrom that the general feeling of the Committee had been that the project 'was just too expensive'. Orrom construed that the real reason was that 'people didn't like the project because they were all documentary people'. In his attempts to convince Reed of *Legend*'s potential Orrom pleaded: 'I'm convinced it would get a good distribution. It would be colourful and different and musical.' To which Reed made what Orrom considered to be a classic remark: 'Oh, a return in the cinema? That would be dead against the purpose of the experimental fund.' And so *Legend* remained a legend ...

Following the failure of *Legend*, Orrom and Williams collaborated on an adaptation of *The Secret Sharer*, Joseph Conrad's seafaring doppelganger short story. They considered it a good basis for the production of a more orthodox feature film, which, it was hoped, might have better prospects of funding – but, cleaving to their original remit, in its execution they would endeavour to break fresh ground in one way or another. To Orrom's frustration, three weeks into co-writing of the project Williams quit without any warning. He wrote Orrom a short rueful note: 'I can't go on. It doesn't convince any more.' Orrom recounted in his BECTU interview with Norman Swallow how his good friend, with whom he had studied and worked together for over a decade, 'just walked out' and he never saw him again.

Looking back on his career, Orrom regretted not having managed to get some experimental projects such as *The Secret Sharer*, *Legend* and *Lucky Peter's Travels* off the ground.

> I wouldn't do anything different. I wanted to make films and I made films. I wish I could have got past blocks in certain directions. If I were coming along now, there wouldn't be the blocks because the money available for so-called experimental films, which is what I wanted to do, is so much vaster than it was when I wanted to do it. To that extent it would have been good to be beginning now.

As stated earlier, only rarely and in sections of films rather than in whole films was the gap between Orrom's theoretical position and the circumstances in which he worked meaningfully bridged. The independently produced *Portrait of Queenie* benefits from the convergence of documentary virtuosity with experimentation. So does his deeply personal television documentary *A Fragment of Memory*. Orrom also found an outlet in certain sequences of films like *The New Caribbean* and *They Cry for Love*. Had his career progressed further in the direction of experimental film-making, the following quote taken from *Preface to Film* might have made more sense in relation to what transpired in practice: 'No art can ever stand still; nor will the attempted repetition of former successes make for real quality. That the film should develop as an art form is a strictly practical necessity.'[28] Through fluke, fate or mere practical necessity, the application of Michael Orrom's vision was largely to the sphere of sponsored documentary, which was notably better off for his contributions.

NOTES

1. BECTU History Project interview with Michael Orrom by Norman Swallow, 3 March 1992. Other biographical details included in this piece are indebted to this source. Swallow, one of the great television documentarists, had also worked under Rotha at the BBC. Unlike Orrom, he remained, and became acclaimed, in the medium.
2. Note, written by Paul Rotha, quoting Orrom, on reverse of a photograph of Michael Orrom taken at National Film Theatre, August 1979. Michael Orrom collection, BFI Special Collections.
3. *Zodiac: The Magazine of the Cable and Wireless Group* no. 9, 1975.
4. Paul Rotha, *Documentary Diary: An Informal History of the British Documentary Film 1928–1939* (New York: Hill and Wang, 1973).
5. BECTU interview. Orrom only recalled three of the four Documentary Movement lecturers: Grierson, Wright and Legg.
6. *Documentary Newsletter* vol. 6 no. 52, March/April 1946, p. 245
7. 'Animated diagrams make a rare and effective appearance on the screen. In summary here is a film which through its bold treatment of a brutal subject, can hardly be classified as entertainment, but which is an outstanding powerful and lucid document on a problem of vital concern to all.' *Documentary Film News* vol. 7 no. 61, January 1948, p. 5.
8. *Documentary Film News* vol. 7 no. 61, January 1948, p. 5.
9. *The World is Rich* (1947) was one of a triptych of films earmarked by the COI in 1946 to address a set of pressing post-war publicity problems. The other two, had they not been abandoned before completion due to financial problems, would have looked at world trade and the post-war production drive and were developed by the Realist Film Unit and the Crown Film Unit respectively.
10. *Sight&Sound* vol. 21 no. 1, August/September 1951, p. 20
11. *Films in Review* vol. 3 no. 5, May 1952, p. 244.
12. The younger sponsored film-maker Euan Pearson later complained of being treated in a similar manner by Orrom himself in terms of non-payment of fees, when freelance directing for Michael Orrom's company Film Drama.
13. *Monthly Film Bulletin* vol. 19 no. 226, November 1952, p. 160.
14. Michael Orrom, 'Needed – A Technician's Workshop', *British Film Academy Journal* no. 16, Autumn 1958.
15. Michael Orrom's unclassified notes on the development of the project *The Secret Sharer* with writer Raymond Williams, p. 24, Orrom collection.

16. Michael Orrom's unclassified draft letter and other notes outlining his views on television. Orrom collection.
17. Notes for proposal for BBC documentary: *Cinema in Transition*, Orrom collection.
18. Paul Rotha, 'Television and the Future of Documentary', *The Quarterly of Film Radio and Television* vol. 9 no. 4, Summer 1955, p. 366.
19. Rotha didn't last long. An account of his ill-fated BBC career can be found in Tim Boon, *Films of Fact: A History of Science in Documentary Films and Television* (London: Wallflower Press, 2008).
20. Unclassified notes, Orrom collection.
21. Michael Orrom and Raymond Willams, *Preface to Film* (London: Film Drama, 1954).
22. See Orrom and Williams, *Preface to Film*, pp. 102–13.
23. Eyeline was founded in the early 1960s by a group of feature-film directors to make commercials, documentaries and short features.
24. *Film User* vol. 19 no. 223, May 1965, p. 266.
25. British Universities Film & Video Council website, *News On Screen*, <bufvc.ac.uk/newsonscreen>
26. Anon., 'Training for a Particular Environment', *The Times*, 9 December 1968, p. 26.
27. Liam O'Laoghaire, 'Books and Magazines', *Sight & Sound* vol. 24 no. 3, January–March 1955, p. 160.
28. Orrom and Williams, *Preface to Film*, p. 121.

11 Documentary on the Move: *Tony Thompson, Bill Mason, Geoffrey Jones*

STEVEN FOXON

It is often written in the libraries and minds of documentary students that, in the pioneering days of the British Documentary Movement, John Grierson defined his own team's talents against the skills of differing professions. He described Arthur Elton as a film-maker with the mind of an engineer; Edgar Anstey took great pride in being referred to as the only trained scientist on Grierson's team. Basil Wright had been regarded by Grierson as a poet and Humphrey Jennings was without question the artist. Tony Thompson (poet), Bill Mason (engineer) and Geoffrey Jones (artist) are three post-war directors whom we can define similarly – unsung directors who travelled similar roads, crossed similar paths (notably at British Transport Films) but made very different marks on British documentary.[1]

In the post-war years when the end of depression and war had deflated the purpose and drive of some documentary practitioners, Elton and Anstey believed passionately that there was a strong need for the documentary in the field of industry and, while at the helm of Film Centre, they joined forces to establish the Scientific Film Association. It had long been the belief of both of them that the scientist, artist and technologist all shared a singular desire to impart information and that their form of expression was unparalleled in its abilities to meet the need to comprehend and represent the world around us. For viewers inside an industry, the screen documentary allows processes to be explained, machinery to be demonstrated in action, dangerous practices to be vividly exposed and management policies to be clarified. For audiences outside it, products can be advertised, users instructed and the prestige of a business enhanced.

It is not unfair to say that the documentary film, even to this day in its electronic manifestation on video and television, possesses all these characteristics in more abundance than any other medium because, unlike a written text, a photograph or a painting, it captures movement. Moreover, it conveniently destroys the concept of space and time. It does not matter that the scene enacted is a thousand miles away, at the bottom of the sea, or under a scientist's microscope. It does not matter that it happens at night or some other awkward hour, or even that it may never occur again. The audience is visually present for an experience that is unique. This, of course, was the lure that attracted many to the field of documentary in the first place.

With Grierson now elevated to the role of grandfather of the genre, and his closest of disciples having moved up to head their own units they – Elton and Anstey, exactly like Grierson before them – surrounded themselves with their own teams of artists, poets, engineers and scientists. The documentary field had grown throughout the 1930s and '40s and so had the number of people intent on working within it. With industry's appetite for films never greater, and such organisations as the Film Producers Guild, DATA and Film Centre acting as convenient sanctuary for freelancers, there was ample opportunity for the best of them to shine. For his newly formed film unit at the British Transport Commission, Anstey (who, like Elton at Shell, still held a place on the board of Film Centre) set about building a strong foundation of permanent staff that would ensure the success of his new unit. While Anstey sought the ongoing services of reliable veterans to head the technical and administrative sides of British Transport Films' work, he adopted a policy of keeping talent fresh when it came to directors. The freelance basis on which much of the 1950s talent pool operated allowed both for established and newer names to pass through. It wasn't long before Anstey noticed a young film-maker on DATA's books who was looking to better himself.

In 1940, Antony Fraser Thompson had begun working as assistant projectionist at the Carlton Cinema in Orrell Park, Liverpool. By 1942 he had become an assistant at the Soviet Film Agency where he had his first taste of editing. Unlike the many who had benefited from the expanding film services of the British government and the forces, Thompson joined, in 1944, the Czechoslovakian Film Unit, where he became an editor on informational films. He became a full-time editor at Gaumont-British Instructional the following year and by 1946 he had joined DATA – first as an editor, but quickly gaining the opportunity to direct. He made the transition with ease, directing many *Mining Review* stories. Analytical stories examining the work of the coal industry often required the patience of a saint and this was a training that would serve Thompson well in future years. His left-wing political sympathies and interest in workers' welfare also gelled well with those of DATA's founders. In addition to directing, Thompson was deployed to script many DATA films: the British Nylon Spinners and the British Iron and Steel Federation both benefited from his efforts. DATA's curious partnership with the Children's Film Foundation also saw him scripting and directing a children's short story in Dittisham, Devon. *Swift Water* (1952) is the tale of a small boy who, while on holiday in Devon, disobeys his aunt and goes sailing with two birdwatchers of similar age. He makes amends by rescuing her dog who has got caught in an outward-bound current. The well-known and charismatic yachtsman, Uffa Fox, aided Thompson's 'on yacht' location filming. Opportunities for fictional film-making didn't land that often in the hands of documentary practitioners and the documentary companies' contributions to the Children's Film Foundation were one of the few channels for those harbouring feature ambitions. As in this case, the stories were typically low-budgeted, and often very simple. Making the best of very little was a skill the factual film-maker knew all about.

Still in its infancy and keen to build a library of films quickly, British Transport Films often contracted productions out to other units when the internal crews were busy with other projects. The locomotive maintenance department of British Railways felt the need for a film highlighting the importance of a thorough internal cleaning of locomotives during turn-around times; it was wanted quite urgently and as no BTF crew could be made available the project was assigned to DATA and Thompson was given the task of directing. Never had the turn-around of a steam locomotive between duties been so closely observed. *Wash and Brush Up* (1953) was a hit with the department staff and the unit's head. Thompson's analytic skills had impressed themselves upon Anstey and after completion he invited the young director to join his unit.

With the reassurance of a permanent place at British Transport Films, Thompson's creative skills were encouraged to flourish and, partnered with BTF's house writer Paul le Saux, Thompson directed what is still possibly British Transport's single most famous film production, *Elizabethan Express* (1954). This was the story of the non-stop journey from Kings Cross to Edinburgh in six and a half hours behind British Railways' streamlined A4 class locomotive 'Silver Fox'. 1954 was too early for the film to be considered for awards, which did not become fashionable in the documentary world

Elizabethan Express: 'Silver Fox'

until some years later; however it quickly became, and has remained ever since, the unit's best-loved film among railway enthusiasts. It remained in constant demand from the BTF library right up until its closure. However, when new, the script did attract some critical comments on account of its rhyming couplets, which, it is true, wandered a little off topic for the convenience of rhyme. Nonetheless, the footplate photography is spectacular, the editing fast-paced and the musical score beautifully composed by Clifton Parker. *Elizabethan Express* provided Thompson with all the ingredients he needed to pull a masterful first film out of the bag, an auspicious start to his BTF canon.

Back at Film Centre, Arthur Elton was keeping a watchful eye on the welfare of his own staff. Managing both Film Centre and the demands of Shell, its biggest client, was no straightforward feat. Throughout the early part of the 1950s Shell had increased its film-making productivity not just in the UK but right across the Far East, where local film units had been established under the guidance of Film Centre representatives. This provided the opportunity for many British practitioners to travel and demonstrate their skills in parts of the world where the documentary tradition was a novel concept. It was a massive operation entirely managed from Film Centre, with all rushes and laboratory work passing through London's West End. The scale being so large, it was important to Elton that he should remain surrounded by capable staff. One day, a talented director came to see him to raise concerns about a project he had been working on in Trinidad.

Left to right: Tony Thompson, Ron Craigen, Billy Willams with 'Golden Fleece' (the 'Silver Fox''s stand-in for footplate scenes)

Bill Mason had been directing at Shell since the war. He was born Rowland Hill Berkeley Mason, a descendant of Rowland Hill the founder of the penny post. He had attended the same school as W. H. Auden and was a contemporary of Benjamin Britten. His school friends couldn't master the name Rowland Hill Berkeley so very quickly he became 'Bill'. As a schoolboy, Mason had had an encounter with Grierson as early as Empire Marketing Board days when, following a letter to see if he could visit the unit, Grierson invited him to witness the rushes of Elton's *Aero Engine* (1934). In typical Grierson 'off the cuff' fashion he invited Mason to tell him what he thought of Elton's work – with Arthur Elton and Basil Wright still in the room!

On Grierson's advice, Mason spent six months as a stockbroker before gong to Cambridge to study English. It was at Cambridge that Mason had his first taste of film-making, where he joined the Cambridge University Film Society and helped to make the rather haphazard but, for the time, unusually themed, *Psychology Today* (1937) on a shoestring budget. The film had a screening at the Arts Theatre Cambridge (where *Night Mail* had been premiered just a year earlier), but was withdrawn from circulation shortly afterwards as the crew was threatened with legal action for not paying the fee for recording the commentary. Mason left university in 1938 and, although he wanted to get into films, he joined the family engineering business.

Unfit for war service due to his asthma, he was interviewed in 1942 at the Ministry of Information but Elton, who was positioned there at the time, could not offer him any work. A chance meeting with Geoffrey Bell, who had also worked on *Psychology Today*, brought him into contact with Basil Wright and Edgar Anstey in Film Centre, Soho Square, where Anstey (at this time in charge of Shell's film work) put him to work as an assistant director on Shell Film Unit productions for the War Office and Army Kinematograph Service.

Mason recalled that life in wartime Shell was very good: 'We weren't paid an awful lot but we were looked after very well.' Production budgets, at this point, were low, and it was not uncommon to make a thirty-minute black-and-white sound film such as Mason's *Approach to Science* (1946) for as little as £1,500. After the war, Mason teamed up with John Shearman to work on the *How an Aeroplane Flies* (1947) series, allowing his scientific and engineering enthusiasms to come to the forefront. Stints on stories for *Shell Cinemagazine* gave him the opportunity to blossom further and with Anstey away in South America looking after overseas Film Centre business, Elton (now in charge at Shell again) invited Mason to share one of his own passions – for the Industrial Revolution and the steam engine. *The Cornish Engine* (1948) was a record of Britain's fast-fading industrial heritage. The steam-powered beam engines that had kept Cornish mines pumped dry for near on a hundred years were slowly and without notice being replaced by petrol and diesel pumps. Elton was so fervently convinced that these historic machines should not disappear without first being recorded that he decided to persuade the powers at Shell that a film should be made. Such was Elton's contagious enthusiasm for Shell films being educational as well as entertaining that they immediately agreed and allowed the film to be made, together with a further series of record films to be shot as an appreciation of the world around us. *The Cornish Engine* was one of Mason's first major 'on location' affairs and he spent many hours visiting sites in advance, writing shooting scripts and planning locations. The project also brought Mason into brief contact with Robert Flaherty. With no budget for music or any frills, Shell had left Elton and Mason no alternative but to record a very simple commentary, which ultimately came across as rather dry and dull. Anstey and Elton brought Flaherty into the viewing room as he was in London at the time and asked him to have a look. Flaherty's mind must have drifted elsewhere and he actually fell asleep throughout the screening. At the end when asked of his opinion Flaherty responded, 'Wonderful Arthur, but I'll have to see it again before I give it a fuller opinion.' Mason never forgot this encounter and he never forgave Flaherty.

Grand Prix

Motor-sport was Mason's real extracurricular passion (a passion that also passed to his son Nick Mason, who became the drummer in Pink Floyd). In 1949 Shell had decided that they wanted a record of the British Grand Prix, but they had been unimpressed by the standard of the motor-racing films that had gone before. Guided by Elton's wisdom, Mason proceeded to plan out the day's shoot with as many locations around the circuit to be covered as was possible. The film, *Grand Prix* (1949), was an instant hit, and although they were not to know it at the time, Mason's technique of multiple cameras at multiple locations with blanket coverage set the benchmark for all future motor-sport films to follow and is continued in the television coverage of racing today. It was clear to Elton that Mason excelled in the art of motor-sport coverage and several great motoring films followed. *Le Mans* (1952) proved to be the most comprehensive coverage to date of the twenty-four-hour race. Twenty-seven cameramen were strategically placed around the circuit, meticulously planned by Mason on his visit the previous year. When Mason wasn't covering races for Shell he was competing at Silverstone and elsewhere in his own 1930 4.5-litre Bentley.

In 1953, while planning to cover the famous Mille Miglia, he struck up a rare friendship with Enzo Ferrari who, on race eve, arranged for him to co-drive with Alberico Cacciari in his V12-engined Ferrari. Riding shotgun, Mason took a 16mm cine-camera with him and shot in-car footage that he used in the finished film. In addition to the unit's own cameramen, many local Italian film technicians were engaged and stationed around the 1,000-mile circuit: Mason was somewhat taken aback when he saw some of the home-made cameras with which many of them covered the race.

Anti-German feeling was rife in Italy, and on a fast section Cacciari made a point of shouldering aside two German Porsches as he overtook them. Soon after, on a twisty section of road, the Porsches regained and overtook; Mason recalled being immediately 'showered with paper bags, gnawed chicken legs and other foods' that the German drivers had devoured in transit.

Mason covered many other races for Shell including the Dutch TT and a series entitled *How the Motor Car Works* (1955) but he had become weary of the politics and red tape that were becoming rife at head office.[2] While working on Shell's global film with the working title *Look at Your World*, Mason had travelled to Trinidad to shoot the famous carnival. Having sent the negative back to London for processing, he received a telegram from HQ: 'Carnival fine STOP Essential film should be oil drilling!' Disheartened, the director questioned why he had been sent in the first place and knowing that there was no oil drill within a hundred-mile radius of Trinidad he replied, 'Delighted film oil drilling, Please send oil drill earliest!' To those in the know, this was highly amusing but on his return Mason made a beeline for Elton's office.

Elton's suggestion was that Mason should not leave Shell entirely but move over as a freelance to work under Film Centre. This way, he could still make films for the oil company but would escape the politics of Shell as an employee. Elton offered him the opportunity to cover the Olympic Games in Australia in 1956 and, eager to travel, Mason accepted. As an added bonus two notable racing drivers and friends of Mason's were on the same flight out; Peter Whitehead and Reg Parnell. Sadly for Mason, the Olympic Games was not a successful project to work on and he found himself operating to such tight turn-arounds that he and his colleagues felt themselves becoming newsreel crews instead of documentary teams; this wasn't the way to make films properly and with Elton's support Mason took a back seat and enjoyed the Games from the Grandstand. Instead, Shell asked him to fill the Australian aspects of various stories being putting together and a three-week project turned into about four months' work. On top of that, Mason managed to direct another film for the World Health Organisation on the subject of Argentine ants while stranded in Perth with a broken-down crew car. On his arrival back in the UK a brief editing stint completed his work and he began to investigate newer projects.

1957 had been an excellent year at British Transport Films and Tony Thompson added new spice to the unit for 1958 by directing the glossy, high-budget, three-reel Technicolor travelogue *The Travel Game* (1958), in which a passenger on the Hook Continental Express from London Liverpool Street imagines the destinations to which his fellow passengers are headed. The calming, softly spoken film that instilled in its viewers an appetite for travel was something that Thompson had, since joining BTF, now perfected: *Yorkshire Sands* (1955), *Any Man's Kingdom* (1956) and *Round the Island* (1956) were all notable travelogues made under his direction. Now it was Bill Mason's turn to try his hand with BTF as Anstey had called on him to direct a film for the railway civil engineers, to cover the laying of railway lines, and the testing of track and of infrastructure such as bridges and crossings. *Groundwork for Progress* (1958) was written and directed by Bill Mason and edited by Stewart McAllister. It was a happy but all too brief time for Mason at British Transport and it was the lure of motoring subjects that swept him away again, to the sponsorship of Shell-Mex and BP.

In the Shell cutting-rooms, BTF's Anstey had recently spotted another young talent, based in the animation department. Geoffrey Jones had been a student at the Central School of Art in the early 1950s, where he had developed an interest in photography and experimented with many different techniques and processes. He also took a keen interest in the school's film society, where he screened

Geoffrey Jones at Picton Place Studio (S. Foxon Collection)

the innovative work of Len Lye, Norman McLaren and Luciano Emmer. The influence of these films convinced Jones of the attraction of films produced with no commentary. Getting into the film industry, he took a circuitous route. A series of illustrations that he had produced satirising the bowler-hatted City commuter came to nothing as a film, but the drawings gained him a job at an advertising agency. By Jones's own admission he had no love for the advertising world, but it did prove useful in creating opportunities to develop ideas. Having at that time no cine-camera of his own, he followed the examples of Lye and McLaren, painting and scratching on clear and exposed 35mm film, making strips that could be rhythmically projected to music. These were shown to the advertising executives, who, to Jones's amusement, thought that the agency had acquired a movie camera! He then borrowed a 16mm Bolex camera for a study of the fairground ride 'the chair-a-plane'. In his mind this attraction held everything he needed for a film. All the dynamics were there: the vibrata of the chains crossing, the people coming towards one, going away from one, every possible camera position accessible and everything in motion. He submitted this material, to be screened with a recording of a Domenico Scarlatti Harpsichord Sonata, to the British Film Institute's Experimental Film Fund Committee, in the hope of getting funds for editing. He was offered the grant but, better still, all three members of the committee offered him a job. It didn't take him long to choose the offer from none other than Arthur Elton to be supervisory director of animation at the Shell Film Unit.

Jones's first documentary at Shell was a 'rescue' job from another film-maker who had himself been called away to 'fix' a film in Teheran. A three-hour speech on the subject of economics within the oil industry was originally to yield a forty-five-minute production; Jones shuddered at the thought and condensed the speech into seven minutes of sentences he could visualise on film. *Shell Panorama* (1958) was to be Jones's only film with a recorded commentary, but a positive review in *The Times* convinced Shell to give him free rein to experiment with his own ideas.

The animation department at Shell closed in 1961 in favour of using freelance animators but not before Jones had mastered all there was to learn from within. Persuaded by his producer Stuart Legg to form his own company, Geoffrey Jones (Films) was established the same year and won a contract with the Shell Transport and Trading subsidiary to make a series of advertisements that would be screened in cinemas. Of these, *Shell Spirit* (1962) caught the attention of the Designers and Art Directors association, who awarded it its Golden Award. It was this film that secured the attention of Edgar Anstey.

At Anstey's invitation in September of 1962 Jones began research for a film on the subject of design for the new British Railways Board. This project enabled him to travel all over the British

Isles, shooting 16mm notes on anything that he found suitably interesting or relevant. The material included a number of shots of trains in the snow, and sparked off an idea to make a film contrasting the comparative comfort of passengers with the cold, hard work that had to be done to keep the lines clear and the trains moving. At the end of January 1963 Anstey visited him to view the notes for the design film, and Jones outlined his idea for the film that was to become *Snow* (1963). Anstey listened with enthusiasm and promised a decision by 10am the next morning. As they parted company that night the snow was heavy and thick on the ground – it was obvious to both that this would probably be the last really heavy snowfall of that infamous winter and clear to all that the film had to be made immediately or put on hold until the next year. True to his word, Anstey called the very next day at 10am and by 12.30 the same day shooting had begun in the West Country; no treatment, no long contract between companies and no committees. With thirty years in the business Anstey knew how to spot a film and he saw the potential of this one. When completed, *Snow* was put into the BTF library and was seen by millions throughout the world; it received over fourteen major awards at film festivals and gained a Hollywood Oscar nomination in 1965. It differs enormously from the normal BTF documentary output, having a style that was all Jones's own. *Snow* is an impressionistic look at the railway system battling with the heavy snowfall of 1962–3. The rapid, abstract editing between individual images is choreographed to an energetic score, which has itself been electronically edited and arranged: it is a lively and constantly evolving montage of sound and image which amounts to a dynamic and striking treatment of the subject.

Jones's design film was put on hold until there was sufficient new technology apparent on the railways to be worth filming and after a stint working under BP's sponsorship in Trinidad and Tobago (shooting, among other things, the Trinidad carnival!) it later emerged under the short title *Rail* (1966). Building on his success with *Snow*, *Rail* cleaned up at international festivals the world over and gained a tour of duty on the cinema circuit with Rank. To Jones's disappointment and dismay, and for some inexplicable reason that can only be put down to opportunistic commercialism, Rank had requested the film be shortened and renamed 'Journey to Tomorrow' – a move that Jones described in a telegram to Anstey as 'Rank Stupidity!'. *Rail*, although technically in a similar style to *Snow*, is a rather more playful, thoughtful and adventurous film in two parts. To the majestic music of Wilfred Josephs, Jones essays a reflective study of the engineering and architecture of our ancestors, the demise of the steam age and its eventual wind down to the last puff of steam. Suddenly, the audience is then awoken to the fast-paced explosion of the electric age soon to come. The film is Jones's masterpiece.

The nature of freelance film-making never allowed any person to stand still for too long and it wasn't until 1974 that Geoffrey Jones partnered British Transport Films again. In fact, it was Anstey's final act before retirement to contract Jones to produce a film for the 1975 celebrations marking the 150th anniversary of railways. Anstey requested three treatments of differing durations and it was decided to go with a fifteen-minute proposal, this being the maximum amount of time it was thought anybody would wish to be seated when viewing a film as part of a larger exhibition. *Locomotion* (1975) features over 400 separate still images woven together with archive material and a strong accelerando arranged by Donald Frasier and performed by Steeleye Span. It combines traditional instrumental and compositional techniques with state-of-the-art, electronic synthesis. It did not, to Jones's disappointment, feature Edgar Anstey's name on the credits, but instead contained the name of the new producer in charge, John Shepherd.

Sadly, Sir Arthur Elton passed away during 1973, denied the retirement he had long deserved. Edgar Anstey chose to retire from BTF the following year after completing twenty-five years' service with British Transport. Between them and throughout their careers they had surrounded themselves with painters, poets, engineers, artists, architects, historians, scientists – all talented film-makers in their own right and all combining their skills, sharing their imaginations and stimulating their minds and ours with industrial documentary. For Anstey and Elton their journey was complete, their skill had become that of Grierson's – they used to joke that Grierson's real talent was not that of directing films, but of directing other people's lives. For the duration of the war and the thirty years that followed, Elton and Anstey had been doing the same, at the forefront of their own 'industrial documentary movement'.

But what of our three unsung film-makers: Geoffrey Jones, Bill Mason and Tony Thompson?

Geoffrey Jones, after *Locomotion*, applied to run the film unit of the Royal Society for the Protection of Birds: a post he was sadly denied in favour of Ian Ferguson, who had long worked closely with Anstey at BTF. This was a decision in which Anstey had actually played a part; he later revealed, through his personal jottings, that in hindsight he regretted not favouring the more dynamic Jones. Instead, Jones eventually found work with Thorn/EMI Video Productions and, remarkably, directed and produced many pop-music videos of the early 1980s. His style served him well in the music business and, although he is never credited, it isn't too difficult to spot his unique editing – a particularly obvious example being the video for Aztec Camera's 1984 hit 'All I Need is Everything'.

The British press sometimes claimed Jones's work as a forerunner to the music video but this was a comparison he had heard before, didn't agree with and often chose to hide away from. Jones wasn't very proud of his music-video work, considering it a lesser art form, if indeed he considered it to be an art form at all. Instead he preferred the respectability of the documentary field where his earlier work had been so warmly welcomed; so much so, in fact, that he often denied any involvement in shooting music videos whatsoever. In 2004, the BFI commissioned a short biographical film about Geoffrey's life and work and, along with his films, it was released in August 2005 as a compilation DVD. Unfortunately, Geoffrey Jones passed away the very same month but not before seeing his screen biography. 'I'd have made it differently!' he declared.

Bill Mason continued directing for another thirty years after his 1958 film with BTF. Several projects made, under freelance contracts, at Wallace Productions found him studying the operations of United Steel and one film, *Project Spear* (1965), became an epic documentary in the study of the management of staff relations (including a redundancy programme) within the industry at a time when traditional roles were being replaced by the great technological strides that the steel industry was so keen to proclaim. Running thirty-one minutes, the film took over five years to produce. This kept Mason's enthusiasm for engineering sated but his passion for motoring never wandered far and a film on automatic gearboxes for Ford entitled *Your Automatic Choice* (1958), made freelancing at Graphic Films, was followed by the legendary *History of the Motor Car* series for BP (begun at the Film Producers Guild, completed at the new Cygnet Guild Communications). In 1978, Mason returned to British Transport to make two more railway films under Shepherd, *The Power to Stop* (1979), an internal staff film about high-performance railway brakes, and *Maglev* (1979), a short introduction to the new method of passenger conveyance, the magnetic levitation railway, which was soon to be installed at Birmingham International Airport. Mason then moved into BTF video production and continued into the 1980s, returning to his first love of motor-sport for an unrealised epic video production with Daimler-Benz. Bill Mason passed away in January 2002; he is remembered today largely by the fans of the sport he loved so much, as a figure who knew nearly all the racing legends and did the day job they only dreamed about.

The saddest tale is that of Tony Thompson's, for his career was cut short while he was still in active service. For two years from 1960, Thompson's output at BTF was hampered by a rare, recurring illness that prevented him from working at the pace with which he had been turning films round previously. As soon as he was able, he jumped back in the saddle with a keen appetite to make films again; and in 1960 he directed the beautiful *Letter for Wales* (1960), starring Donald Houston as a man recalling the principality of his youth. *Letter for Wales* is an extremely pleasing travel-promotional film using smooth transitions to show the grim London termini of Paddington in black and white, against our Welsh destination portrayed in glorious colour. In 1961 Thompson directed a film to generate freight revenue, *Speaking of Freight*, and in 1962 he embarked upon a project that was never to be completed by his own hand. 1962 was to be one of BTF's busiest years and among some great triumphs the smiles were turned to sadness as news travelled throughout the unit's Melbury House headquarters that their friend and colleague had died. Thompson's illness had been progressively getting worse; he left behind him an incomplete travelogue but greater still he had left a very large hole in the movement which could not be filled.

Sing of the Border (1964) uses as its framework the songs of the Scottish Border country which relate the history and traditions of the region, blended with scenes of contemporary landscape. The people and dramatic landscape north of the Border had originally inspired Thompson when he was working on the earlier BTF production, *Any Man's Kingdom*, which dealt with the adjacent county of Northumberland. Echoes of that film, with its sharp emphasis on stark and tragic history set against a tranquil and pleasant present, are there in *Sing of the Border* but it was to be the last of Tony Thompson's efforts. Former colleagues at BTF were encouraged by Muir Mathieson to complete the film in accordance with Thompson's original conception. Kenneth Fairbairn and Mathieson eventually completed the film using Thompson's original script with the commentary spoken by Mathieson. It was not released until two years later. *Sing of the Border* had its world premiere at the ABC Regal Cinema, Edinburgh, on 23 August 1964 as part of the Films of Scotland, 'Scotland on the Screen' Festival; the screening was dedicated to his memory. No travelogue has been produced since that has contained the calm poetic trance that inspires one to travel like Thompson's films did. Upon Thompson's death, Anstey wrote his own goodbye:

> Many of his friends will feel the need to write a personal tribute to Tony Thompson. It was part of his quality that without self-consciousness and quite certainly without self-seeking he impressed upon us a source of reliable and tested judgments. He was in short a very wise man. It was wisdom as well as art that gave us films ranging as widely as *The Travel Game*, and *Work Study and Tom Howard*, *Any Man's Kingdom* and *Speaking of Freight*, three of them award winners. He rarely reflected an ephemeral taste but brought to his work the conviction that films could provide honest and permanent interpretations of human experiences, whether large or small. Truth was always the test.[3]

NOTES

1. This essay uses material drawn from personal interviews with the late Geoffrey Jones, John Legard, the late Bill Mason and Alan Willmott, as well as the unpublished notes of Edgar Anstey (S. Foxon Collection).
2. In *Films & Filming* (January 1955, p. 29), Ken Gay reported on a programme of Shell films introduced by Elton at which Elton had said, 'I was taught that when making a documentary you kept the camera still, you used a tripod and you never let people look at the camera. But in *The Dutch TT* Bill Mason, the director, does all those things and it comes off.'
3. Tony Thompson obituary, quoted from *Film and Television Technician*, September 1962, p. 162.

12 Pictures Should Be Steady: *James Hill*

JAMES PIERS TAYLOR

The careers of the post-war documentary film-makers were often not limited to documentary film alone, but the path of James Hill stands out as being especially diverse. There is simply no obvious defining feature one can identify in his films. Considering Hill as a documentary film-maker is to view his career from one vantage point, when from other perspectives this is a minor element of his work. Authors writing about his feature work often note that he began his career in documentary, but as an aside: a literal footnote in many cases.

There is the pilot war hero making documentaries about aircraft, but there is also the man who walked away from filming on an airfield when he learned that nuclear bombers flew from there. There is the man who makes films for big industrial sponsors like BP and Esso and then there is the man who makes the first ACT feature film with a kitchen sink drama, and who travels into communist territory to make the controversial *¡Cuba Sí!* (1961). There is the feature film director of cult films *A Study in Terror* (1965) and *Captain Nemo and the Underwater City* (1969) and there is the gentle touch of a director of children's films, one who finishes his career making the television series *Worzel Gummidge* (1979–89).

Born in 1919 into a prominent wool-industry family in Yorkshire, James Hill, familiarly known as Jimmy, had other plans for a career. Already acting as a teenager with the Bradford Civic Playhouse, in 1935, aged sixteen, he moved south and gained employment at Walton Studios. He worked his way up from tea boy to assistant at the GPO Film Unit and by 1937 he was working as an assistant to Paul Rotha. He appears briefly on screen acting in *New Worlds for Old* (1938), directed by Frank Sainsbury at Strand, with Rotha producing.[1]

Like many of his contemporaries (such as Paul Dickson, Peter Hopkinson and John Krish), World War II brought an early interruption to a novice career in film-making (or at least aspirations towards one) but provided an intense apprenticeship of its own within a forces film unit. While the previous generation carried on the documentary tradition into the Crown Film Unit and MOI-sponsored independents, younger men in the business were not protected by their age nor by a proscribed trade. They were conscripted like anyone else. The new forces film units that were born in 1940 needed the kick-start of people with film skills, however, and Hill was one of those new recruits who found themselves drawn away from combat and towards documentary in the RAF Film Unit.

Not that movement from a combat role took the young man out of wartime danger. The war proved an eventful chapter of James Hill's life. He piloted a captured German plane for David Lean and Noel Coward's *In Which We Serve*,[2] accompanied bombing missions over Europe, got shot down over Germany and was badly wounded. He made a thwarted escape from a German prisoner-of-war hospital and was interned in the infamous Stalag Luft III, where he assisted in digging the tunnel immortalised in *The Great Escape* (1963), but a camp transfer absented him from the escape itself and hence saved his life. Anecdotal evidence suggests that the character of Lt Col. Blythe, played by Donald Pleasence in the film version of the story, is based in part on Hill. Liberated in 1945 by out-of-control and piratical Soviet forces, Hill eventually returned to the UK and was awarded the Distinguished Flying Cross. Later publicity material issued by a film studio stated that he accompanied a Russian film unit that filmed the liberation of Berlin,[3] but this doesn't match with Hill's own recorded account[4] and must be industry hyperbole. In his subsequent career an adventurous streak, ease among the uniformed classes, familiarity with aircraft and a can-do attitude are all things bearing witness to James Hill's wartime experience.

The opportunities offered by war took Hill from lowly assistant to director: before being shot down he directed the short *Fly Away Peter* (1942) and the incomplete film *Mosquito Day Raid* (1942). Most of his wartime work was as a cameraman, however, and as a pilot officer (Flight-Lieutenant Hill) he accompanied several Bomber Command missions over Europe in 1941 and 1942. His dope sheets from the operations trace a progressively deepening passage into the continent, including two bombing raids over Berlin shortly before he was shot down in the November of 1943. Hill's notes speak of the conditions faced by all airmen – the cold, enemy fighters and flak – but also reveal something of the man, both as an individual and as a film-maker. In his notes on a mission over Europe, Hill remarks: 'pictures should be steady, and incendiaries filmed leaving aircraft. A James Hill Special'.[5]

After the war, in 1945, Hill briefly became a production manager at Grand National, a small British feature-film company that was resuming production after wartime hiatus. It was a short tenure, however, and in 1946 he reconnected with documentary through the association he had made with Paul Rotha pre-war.[6] For the next few years he moved between various of the independent production companies learning his craft.

The skills he had learned and the experience he had gained within the RAF Film Unit were already serving him well. At Films of Fact, Rotha's new documentary company, he went straight in as a director making *Britain Can Make It No7* (1946), sponsored by the COI. It was a magazine film with items on three subjects: Mablethorpe sea front, aero-engine design and Swindon Public Library. The same year Hill was also directing for Donald Alexander at DATA, another stalwart of the Federation of Documentary Film Units. The film *Science Joins an Industry* (1946), sponsored by the Cotton Board, used another familiar film format, the presentation of industrial process. Along the way it attempts to deal with the economic issues facing the cotton industry, but these were considered to be its weakest elements.[7] Hill's ease around aeroplanes got him some work doing photography for the Shell Film Unit on *Aircraft Today and Tomorrow* (1947). He was becoming an increasingly assured practitioner and he travelled back to his hometown of Bradford to speak to the local film society on the topic of the documentary medium.

In 1948 Hill became a member of British Documentary, the fledgling national section of the World Union of Documentary. At this point, then, he seems to be part of the resurgent Documentary Movement, directing solid, worthy documentary product and is associating with the organisations and individuals continuing to pursue a focused aesthetic and political view of the form. But in the same period he turns to an established part of the more commercial sector, joining Gaumont-British Instructional (GBI) in 1946.[8]

GBI was still involved in documentary, specialising in films for the educational market, but being related to the wider entertainment interests of its parent company, it was at a remove from the supposed purity of intention of the Movement. The move was just right for Hill, though: through his GBI engagement he got the opportunity to write as well as direct and to pursue what was obviously a personal attraction to the use of drama.

Initially, Hill continued the path he had been on at DATA and Films of Fact, with another sturdy industrial. *Behind the Flame* (1948), for the North Thames Gas Board, was a remake of the pre-war film *Making the Most of Our Coal* (1938) and followed the process of gas manufacture and distribution.[9] *Paper Chain* (1949), for Wiggins-Teape papermakers, was potentially another industrial in the same vein. The film presents the means by which its sponsor produces different types of paper in its mills across the country. It shows how both waste and raw materials are turned into quality paper at its plants; not all that different from *Science Joins an Industry* – but all of this is prefaced with an introductory sequence of a different stripe. The film begins with a depiction of a 1940s household and how it would fare in a world without paper. The man of the house reads the morning news from a block of stone: letters written on animal skin and stone drop through the letterbox, telephone numbers and addresses have to be written on the wall. A trip to the bank involves money being carried in a wheelbarrow. At a fish-and-chip shop a customer has nothing to wrap his purchase in, so it's put into his hat and liberally coated with salt and vinegar. The sequence gives a hint of the direction of Hill's future career, a path reinforced by his next two films for GBI.

Friend of the Family (1949), for the Queen's Nursing Institute, was James Hill's first film as writer-director, and also his first collaboration with the cameraman James Allen with whom he would work repeatedly thereafter. The film is a curiously dark tale of a career in nursing that seems, as an attempt at recruitment, rather odd. There's something of the preceding war hanging over the film's sensibility and Hill over-eggs the drama. Not content with attempted suicides, rural childbirth, bitter hermits and hastily executed surgery on the dining-room table, he decides to kill off one of the main protagonists and make her available only in flashback. This is drama-documentary – real nurses play the main characters (Hill's decision[10]) – but the emphasis is heavily on the drama. A lighter touch is evident in *Journey for Jeremy* (1949), the first of Hill's films for children. It's the story of a small boy's ambition to become an engine driver. One night he dreams he drives the Scots Express from Glasgow to Euston. While pure drama, the first completely fictional film in Hill's career, *Journey for Jeremy*'s attention to real locations and actual trains maintains a certain commitment to the real.

The director's next film, *This Way Please* (1950), which sadly appears to be lost, was made for the Cinema Managers Association. It presented the operations involved in running a modern cinema, from the duties of the manager to those of the usherette. One review described it as 'technically excellent' and as being in the 'straightforward documentary style', but it clearly uses the dramatised version of 'documentary style' as the film's 'story' is also described and the review relays that 'only a few professional actors took part; for the rest, the cast comprises the CMA's own personnel'.[11] *This Way Please* was designed for screening to CMA employees around the country. Hill's longest film to date, it clocks in at a whopping sixty-three minutes.

James Hill's run at GBI was interrupted by an opportunity offered up by the Economic Cooperation Association (ECA), the US government agency administering Marshall Plan aid to Europe. The ECA made a point of employing European film-makers[12] and had recruited Britain's Editorial Film Productions (better known later for its work with Unilever). Hill came on board as a director and made twelve issues of *The Marshall Plan At Work* (1950), a newsreel-type production that presented post-war reconstruction in the western European countries.

When he returned he was quick to seize the opportunity for fiction work that was offered by the formation of the Children's Film Foundation (like GBI, a part of the Rank film empire). He wrote and directed *The Stolen Plans* (1952), the Foundation's first ever production, *Journey for Jeremy* having proved his suitability. The new film was the story of a young boy and girl who help an aircraft designer to outwit a gang of spies trying to steal secret plans. The story reflected something of Hill's aviation past but it was his sensitive approach to film-making for children that pointed towards his future. *The Stolen Plans* won a Silver Gondola for best children's film of the year at the Venice Film Festival.[13] He followed it up with *The Clue of the Missing Ape* (1953), filmed on location: the story of how two youngsters round up crooks planning to blow up the British fleet off Gibraltar.[14]

Hill's aviation experience was put to use again with *Britain's Comet* (1952), which showed how the eponymous aircraft was designed and put into production. This was another straight documentary that reviews found to be a 'well produced and thoroughly workmanlike job'[15] and to be 'non-technical and inspiring'.[16] The director's aviation background was called upon again when he got the opportunity to work on a major feature, as the 2nd Unit director on *Reach for the Sky* (1956), Lewis Gilbert's feature film about pilot Douglas Bader.[17]

Somewhat less inspiring, no doubt, were *Tips* (1952), a series of four-minute shorts for the cinema, produced by Gerard Holdsworth Productions, that gave hints on solutions to everyday problems. Work more amenable to Hill's talents came with the *Gasmanship* series for the Gas Council produced by Harold Goodwin Productions of the Film Producers Guild. Hill had worked with Goodwin as his producer at GBI in the 1940s. The three parts of the series, *Demonstrational Selling*, *Lost Sales* and *Showmanship* (all 1956), were training films for salesman using dramatised comedy set-ups. They were designed for Gas Board sales staff but they were distributed widely for more general sales-training use.[18] *Demonstrational Selling* was later shortened and revised as *Burning to Serve You* (1958).

The next important move of Hill's career came through recruitment to World Wide Pictures and a commission from BP for a film covering their global attempts to find new oil reserves. *The New Explorers* (1955) was part of a loose series of separate films promoted to film bookers as *Oil on Screen* that followed the stages of oil formation, exploration and exploitation. Shot in colour in five different countries across the world, it was Hill's most ambitious film to date. The filming schedule alone was epic in scale, taking in location shooting in Abu Dhabi, Canada, Zanzibar, Papua, Trinidad and Sicily. Four different cameramen were used across the six locations. Hill wrote that during production he 'travelled nearly 100,000 miles by car, jeep, train, liner, launch,

James Hill (seated) directs *The New Explorers*

dhow, canoe, catamaran, bicycle, aircraft, flying-boat, camel, helicopter, horseback and foot'.[19] The production's expense and the inaccessibility of several locations led to the use of the cheaper and more portable 16mm film gauge rather than the higher-quality 35mm generally favoured by companies like World Wide and sponsors like BP. But the film still packed a visual punch with its exotic shots of tundra, desert and jungle. Hill shot the aerial sequences himself from a BP helicopter. In Papua, he and cameramen Allen found that one journey involved hanging on to a log and swimming several miles down a 'crocodile-infested' river. Such *Boys Own* adventuring was tempered by the death from fever of one of the crew. Hill kept a photograph of this man on his desk for years to come.[20]

Another film for the Children's Film Foundation followed at World Wide: *Peril for the Guy* (1956), the story of a group of children's efforts to prevent a gang of evil oilmen from stealing an invention for detecting the presence of oil. Hill's script obviously benefited from his recent BP excursion, its subject matter ironically reflecting the fact that no oil was found in *The New Explorers*. *First Aid for Soldiers* (1957), for the Army Kinema Corporation, also made at World Wide, told a different kind of story and used drama to indicate the correct procedure for dealing with four injured soldiers, each suffering from a different cause.

The same year, Hill made *Cold Comfort* (1957) for C. M. George Film Productions, a comedy short with Peter Sellers on 'how to catch a cold and keep it'. The film parodies the kind of government-information filler that had been the bread and butter of many documentary filmmakers' early careers. Sellers is in silent movie pratfall mode and provides an ironic voiceover.

The New Explorers was a great success for BP who considered approaching Hill directly to offer him more work. He was initially considered as director for the film *Journey from the East* (1956)[21] but Ronald Tritton wrote in an internal memo that 'James Hill, although a suitable director artistically and because of his oil knowledge, was not suitable due to an embarrassing situation which would arise with World Wide'.[22] In 1957, Hill formed James Hill Productions as a mark of his independence and BP's earlier qualms evidently evaporated as they promptly offered him a three-month commission to return to the Papua leg of *The New Explorers* and make two new films. The fruits of that commission were *Skyhook* (1958), about an oil rig airlifted by helicopter into the island's wild interior, and *A Walk in the Forest* (1958) about the work of a survey team.[23] Like *The New Explorers* before them, these films have something of a neo-colonial air, British Petroleum walking as the British Empire walked before it.

1959 saw a number of Hill-directed films released. *Pharmacy For You* (made for Greenpark Productions with sponsorship from Boots) was a recruitment short for pharmacists aimed at school leavers, which followed a young man as he trained for the job. It was shot in a chemist's shop in south-west London and used the shop's manager and staff as its cast, even roping in some customers. The same year, the Children's Film Foundation released another Hill-directed project, *Mystery in the Mine*, an eight-part serial about kids foiling the dastardly plans of a pair of villains. The year's most significant release, however, was another film for BP.

Giuseppina, produced by James Hill Productions, was the director's breakthrough success. Rather than write a treatment and get approval from the sponsor, Hill presented BP with a completed script including Italian dialogue (allegedly provided by an Italian girlfriend). It's another story film, about the daughter of an Italian filling-station proprietor and the customers that pass through in one day. *Giuseppina* won the 1960 Academy Award for Documentary Short Subject and became Hill's calling card. The film's status as documentary seems strange to most contemporary viewers:

the characters, location and story are all entirely fictional and apparently concocted for the purposes of light entertainment.

In fact, *Giuseppina* was also a powerful public relations tool with clear objectives. BP were entering the retail petrol market in Italy for the first time: their brand name was unknown and the Italian public had a reputation for being wary of and indisposed to foreign oil companies. This film sought to avoid the impression that BP was a distant, giant corporation, by presenting it on a human scale. It was designed primarily for the Italian market and released to coincide with the sales launch of BP-branded petrol in the country.[24] However, by using minimal amounts of dialogue and depending on visual storytelling Hill created a film that could play easily around the world.

BP had provided a range of opportunities for film-making that gave James Hill a pretty free range and had finally led, unexpectedly, to Oscar success. Hill's documentary output from this period is some of his best known and most viewed (though few viewers could put a name to its director) as, in addition to its international distribution and UK non-theatrical exhibition, it later formed part of the backbone of trade-test films broadcast repeatedly on the BBC to check and promote the new colour service.

The Oscar raised Hill's profile but at the height of his documentary success he began to leave the genre behind. The profile-raising afforded him greater ease in pursuing his feature-film ambitions and new opportunities arose, too, in television. The director's first feature film for adults was made for ACT Films, a new venture by the film technicians' trade union. This was an adaptation of Arnold Wesker's play *The Kitchen* (1961). Hill makes the best of some clichéd characters and stagey dialogue, but the film is ultimately a curio period piece that compares poorly to the kitchen sink features of Karel Reisz and Tony Richardson. Its tight focus on the workings of a restaurant kitchen did at least allow Hill's documentary eye some action, with an interesting emphasis on the tools, practices and behaviours of the chefs and their underlings. Many of these were details added by Hill as the original play mimed both location and props. His next feature, *Lunch Hour* (1962), was a more successful work, the conceit of its John Mortimer story much more suited to cinematic exploration and its story and dialogue writing simply better. Hill adds his own conceit with the film crafted into the duration of its subject matter with an almost *nouvelle vague* aplomb. The shooting was mostly on location, affording interesting views of both central London and factory interiors. Hill's own trade reputation as a lothario gives an added piquancy to the tale of a married man's affair.

Lunch Hour was followed by *The Dock Brief* (1962), another Mortimer adaptation that reunited Hill with Peter Sellers. In 1963, Hill began filming the third Cinerama film – *Milly Goes to Budapest*, starring Hayley Mills. But the producers lost faith in both Hill and the three-camera Cinerama system. He was replaced by Richard Thorpe, Mills left and the film became *The Golden Head*.[25] *Every Day's a Holiday* (1964) was a third-division comedy musical with British pop acts, that drew *The Times* film critic to note that Hill was no Jean-Luc Godard.[26] Hill was brought in as director on *Born Free* (1965), a few months into filming, due to the ill health of original director Tom McGowan.[27] This was, perhaps, a mark of a reputation as someone who could get the job done and deal with the exotic location (Africa) and the danger (real lions!). It was a mark of his steadiness of approach. He was a safe pair of hands with his experience of location work around the world, of getting performances from actors and non-actors alike and of operating within the generally tight budgets of sponsored work.

Similarly, *A Study in Terror* a moody Sherlock Holmes piece, was handed over to Hill at the last minute, after initially being associated with another director, Jim O'Connolly. Hill's other features ranged across genres indicating an opportunistic pattern of taking work where he could find it rather than any auteurish sense of personal vision. *The Peking Medallion* (1966) was a crime thriller, *The Specialist* (1966) a comedy short, *Captain Nemo and the Underwater City* a science-fiction film based on Jules Verne's character, *Black Beauty* (1971) an adaptation of Anna Sewell's novel, while *The Belstone Fox* (1973) adapted David Rook's book *The Ballad of the Belstone Fox. London Conspiracy* (1976) included an episode of television series *The Persuaders* directed by Hill. *The Man from Nowhere* (1976), produced by Charles Barker Films, was Hill's final feature film for cinemas and made, like his first, for the Children's Film Foundation.[28] For a while in 1979 Hill was associated with a proposed adaptation of *The Marvellous Mongolian*, a children's novel by James Aldridge, which the producer Sidney Glazier was pushing as the first Sino-American co-production, with a screenplay written by Han Suyin. The story concerned a child and a horse and Hill's *Black Beauty* adaptation evidently brought his name round the Rolodex, but the project came to nought.

The 1960s had also seen Hill moving into TV drama, and television work would continue until the end of his career. He directed episodes of several series: *The Human Jungle* (1963), *The Saint* (1963–4), *Gideon's Way* (1964), *Journey to the Unknown* (1968), *The Avengers* (1965–8), *The Persuaders* (1971), *Moses* (1974), *The New Avengers* (1976), *Search and Rescue* (1978), *Worzel Gummidge, Dick Barton* (1979), *CATS Eyes* (1985), *Prospects* (1986), *Worzel Gummidge Down Under* (1987–9). He also made a couple of longer television films, *Owain Glyndwr, Prince of Wales* (1 March 1983) and *The Young Visitors* (25 December 1984), more in line with his features work. Hill wasn't alone in turning to this type of jobbing on television serials for income, but he had more of a flair for it than some other documentary film-makers.

The early 1960s had also marked a move into hard-hitting broadcast documentary with a handful of programmes made for Granada and the incipient *World in Action* team.[29] *A Sunday in September* (18 September 1961) covered the sit-down protest by the Council of 100, the radical offshoot of CND. The film was unscheduled, planned and executed at speed and broadcast the day after the events it recorded.[30] Hill directed several camera crews spread across Trafalgar Square. Shortly after it was shown, the director's four-part series *¡Cuba Sí!*, about post-revolutionary Cuba, followed it to television screens. The first episode, *The Past* (29 September 1961), told the history of Cuba from Columbus to Castro and included footage of the revolution previously unseen in the UK. *The Alphabetisers* (6 October 1961) told the story of the post-revolutionary literacy campaign.

James Hill (standing on desk) directs *A Sunday in September*

Havana (13 October 1961) focused on the capital city in its pre- and post-revolutionary incarnations. The final part, *The Future* (20 October 1961), asked what impact the Cuban revolution would go on to have on the rest of the world. Hill and his producer, *World in Action* supremo Tim Hewat, faced difficulties from all sides with these films. The Cuban authorities were suspicious of foreign propagandists and the series had to be filmed secretly. Once home and broadcast, the documentaries faced accusations that they were partial and riddled with anti-American bias.[31] This only seems to have encouraged Hewat and Hill. A subsequent collaboration, *Paris: The Cancer Within* (13 December 1961), covered Franco-Algerian tensions in the French capital at the height of the Algerian crisis (and allegedly got Hill banned from France).

There seems to be an exciting opportunity here for Hill – a career in television documentary. Yet despite the fact that he would return to Granada to make *The Undertaking Business* (aka *The British Way of Death* [17 December 1963]), he was shortly off again following other openings. The prospect of making feature films seems to have been his main driver.

Inevitably, then, Hill's career as a documentary film-maker was in decline, but despite the features and the TV work, the director kept his hand in the industrially sponsored field, sticking to the drama-documentary or the entirely fictional promotional film. *David and Golightly*, made by James Hill Productions for Esso in 1961, was a study of the work of a small coastal tramp steamer and of crew life, as seen through the eyes of David the new galley boy. *The Home-Made Car* (1963), produced by James Hill Productions for BP, was an attempt to recreate the success of *Giuseppina* with a wordless light comedy featuring a young girl and a man restoring a vintage car; although not so successful, again it became a cult hit through its many later trade-test broadcasts. Hill's last film for BP, *Dial Double-One* (1965), enjoyed a more adult theme and followed the work of the Air Rescue Guard of Switzerland. It remained in the drama-documentary genre, though, with its stories of two emergency rescues: one of a holiday skier who breaks his leg, and the other of a group of Swiss woodmen who are overwhelmed by an avalanche.

Focus on Sight (1967), produced by James Hill Productions with sponsorship from the Royal Commonwealth Society for the Blind and the World Health Organisation, was a now-rare for Hill straight documentary, showing the effect throughout the developing world of four major causes of blindness: trachoma, river blindness, cataracts and malnutrition. The requirements of a charity sponsor apparently demanded a different approach from Hill's default mode. *'Pru'* (1977), produced at Charles Barker Films for sponsor the Prudential Assurance Company, saw Hill back on familiar ground and explored the historical and present working conditions and concerns of the client and its staff. It utilised current staff members playing both themselves and their costumed forebears.[32] *Challenge of Choice* (1979) reunited Hill with World Wide Pictures in a film for Standard Telephones and Cables that again used dramatised reconstructions to show the importance of communication. The director's last industrial film was *You Know What I Mean*? (1983), made not for a corporate sponsor but for Hawkshead Communications/Dunchurch College of Management, one of that newer breed of organisations making generic training films. This one was on how to deal with the problems of speaking English to potential foreign customers and used actors James Bolam and Derek Fowlds. It seems likely that Hill would have excelled at films of this type, popularised by the likes of Video Arts, had he not effectively left the industrial film-making field just as they were really taking off.

Hill's feature-film success meant that his documentary output was not limited to industrially sponsored work. The fondly remembered *Born Free*, a biopic shot at the real location with real lions, was practically a drama-documentary itself, certainly by Hill's standards. It led to a series of non-fiction films on wildlife largely initiated in partnership with *Born Free*'s stars Virginia McKenna and Bill Travers and through Travers's company Swan Productions.[33] In his teen years, Hill had considered a career as a veterinarian and natural history subjects cross over his feature and documentary work. *The Lions are Free* (1967) was a documentary return to Africa to find out what had happened to the lions that took part in *Born Free*. *An Elephant Called Slowly* (1969) was an adventure comedy featuring McKenna, Travers and George Adamson playing themselves alongside a real elephant. Hill did some initial scripting for the *Born Free* sequel *Living Free* (1971), but that film, directed by Jack Couffer, featured none of the original cast and crew.

The Lion at World's End (1971) was a documentary on the transportation of a lion that had been kept as a pet to Africa and of George Adamson, the man Travers had played in *Born Free*, who supervises its release into the wild. *Christian the Lion* (1976) similarly followed Travers and McKenna as they become involved with the problem of returning a young lion born in a London zoo to his native environment. Hill and Travers acted as producers for *The Wild Dogs of Africa* (1973), a documentary, directed by Hugo Van Lawick, following the 'genghis pack' of wild dogs in Africa. *Death Trap* (1975), co-directed by Hill and Travers, was a documentary on carnivorous plants. The director's final film in this genre was a solo effort from Hill with *The Wild and the Free* (1980), a programme about chimpanzees made for American television.

Not all Hill's non-sponsored documentary work was concerned with wild animals. *The Great Pram Race* (1977), a self-funded effort made through James Hill Productions, was a late collaboration with cameraman Allen and covered the highlights of the Annual Pram Race at Hertford Heath over a 'gruelling' two-mile course, including six public house 'pit stops'. *The Queen's Garden* (1977), Hill's last film made in association with Bill Travers, replaced the wilds of Africa with more sedate flora and was a documentary about a year in the life of Buckingham Palace's garden.

One of the most successful of his generation of film-makers in terms of number of films made, number of features films directed and number of major awards received[34] – there remains a sense of underachievement about James Hill's oeuvre, or at least of routes untaken, of work unmade. When his career is taken in total, the features seem a distraction, the TV episodes minor works that filled too many years, much of the sponsored work makeweights. From the perspective of 1948, it must have looked like Hill could have played a significant part in the post-war British Documentary Movement that, as things turned out, never really materialised in its intended form. In the early 1960s he might have begun a career in TV documentary and performed a valuable service by applying the film documentary sensibility to the new journalistic form. But it was movies that had lured him from Bradford to London in 1935 and the movies that captured him anew in 1961. Perhaps he was really a children's film-maker all along. From *Journey for Jeremy*, through *Giuseppina* to *Worzel Gummidge*, James Hill was most successful when he saw the world through children's eyes. Ultimately the career, like the pictures, was steady – reliable, unremarkable perhaps. James Hill died on 7 October 1994.

NOTES

1. Paul Rotha, *Documentary Diary: An Informal History of the British Documentary Film, 1928–1939* (New York: Hill and Wang, 1973), p. 227.
2. Kevin Brownlow, *David Lean: A Biography* (London: Richard Cohen, 1996), p. 163 (information is from 1993 letter from Hill to Brownlow).
3. Micro jacket of press information on James Hill held by the BFI National Library.
4. Audio interview with James Hill recorded 17 December 1986, held at the Imperial War Museum Sound Archive (Item: 9541).
5. Dope sheet OSX 128 regarding mission over Mannheim Germany (5–6/9/1943), held by Imperial War Museum Film and Video Archive. Written a couple of months before Hill was shot down.
6. Peter Noble (ed.), *The British Film Yearbook 1949–50* (London: Skelton Robinson, 1949), p. 572.
7. See review in *Documentary News Letter* vol. 6 no. 53, 1946, p. 39. Also *Sight & Sound* vol.15, 1946, p. 39.
8. Darrel Catling, 'Life and Death of GBI', *Cine Technician*, February 1955, p. 22.
9. Reviewed in *Film User*, October 1950, p. 588.
10. See E. J. Merry, 'The District Nursing Film', *Queen's Nurses' Magazine* vol. xxxvii no. 7, July 1949, p. 81.
11. *Today's Cinema* vol. 77 no. 6332, 7 September 1951, pp. 3, 10.
12. Barry Machado, *In Search of a Useable Past: The Marshall Plan and Post War Reconstruction Today* (Lexington: George C. Marshall Foundation, 2007), pp. 27–8.
13. Eric Gillett, 'Flying Start for Children's Film Foundation', *The Children's Newspaper*, 22 November 1952, p. 7.
14. Anon. [Pinewood correspondent], 'Round the Film World', *The Cine-Technician* vol. 19 no. 104, August 1953, p. 94.
15. *Monthly Film Bulletin* vol. 19 no. 222, July 1952, p. 99.
16. *Film User* vol. 7 no. 79 , May 1953, p. 258.

17. The film was written by Paul Brickhill who, like Hill, had been imprisoned in Stalag Luft III.
18. Anon., 'Factual Films', *Film User*, August 1956, p. 360.
19. James Hill, 'All for One Film', *Film User*, February 1958, p. 80.
20. A recollection of the director Derek Williams, whose time at World Wide Pictures overlapped with Hill's.
21. The film was later directed by George Sturt for Jack Howells Productions.
22. A file note written by Ronald Tritton (dated 7 January 1954) in a Historical Miscellaneous file including items related to *Journey from the East* held by BP Video Library.
23. Anon., 'In the Wilds', *Film User*, March 1957, p. 107.
24. Anon., 'More Industry Films: Public Relations Medium', *The Times*, 25 January 1960, p. 17.
25. Robert E. Carr and R. M. Hayes, *Wide Screen Movies: A History and Filmography of Wide Gauge Filmmaking* (North Carolina: McFarland, 1988), p. 31.
26. Anon., 'Film with Unpredictable Plot', *The Times*, 26 November 1964, p. 7.
27. John Mark Jay, *Any Old Lion* (London: Leslie Frewin, 1966).
28. The following year saw the release of *Mr Selkie* (1977, directed by Anthony Squire), a Children's Film Foundation production with a script by Hill.
29. Peter Godard, John Corner and Kay Richardson, *Public Issue Television: World in Action, 1963–98* (Manchester: Manchester University Press, 2007).
30. Bernard Lewis, 'A Sunday in September', *Film & Television Technician*, October 1961, pp. 184, 186.
31. Goddard, Corner and Richardson, *Public Issue Television*, p. 19.
32. Anon., 'Careers: Serious Sponsored Films', *Education* vol. 149 no. 20, 20 May 1977, p. 347.
33. Bill Travers, interviewed in February 1991, in Brian McFarlane, *An Autobiography of British Cinema* (London: Methuen, 1997), p. 568.
34. His documentaries garnered success not only at the many industrial film festivals, but also at Berlin, Vienna and, of course, the Oscar for *Giuseppina*.

13 Less Film Society – More Fleet Street: *Peter Hopkinson*

JAMES PIERS TAYLOR

Peter Hopkinson was a documentary and instructional film producer, director, writer and cameraman who, across his working life, made films on every populated continent. He was also a cinephile from the start, drawn into film-making by the allure of fantasy and adventure in the films of the 1920s and '30s, enthralled by the thrills of *Metropolis* (1927) and *Things to Come* (1936). An obsessive film fan, he acquired a 35mm silent-film projector discarded by the Harrow Coliseum when it converted to sound, erected the monster in his bedroom and ran inflammable reels of nitrate on any subject he could obtain, discovering the travelogues and interest films that were documentary precursors of the work he would later complete.[1]

What began as a form of entertainment became a medium of expression of conviction. Hopkinson's second volume of autobiography was titled *Screen of Change*. He believed passionately that the film medium could act for a higher cause, that film was an agent for transformation. It was a belief that placed Hopkinson in common cause both with his forebears in the British Documentary Movement and with Marx's thesis against interpretation. His parting recommendation to young film-makers was that they should use their films in 'the service of revolution'.[2] By his own description he was a 'politically committed animal', he was left-leaning but with a better understanding of geopolitics than many of his peers and no slave to ideology: his career reflects the progressive internationalism of the post-war era.

Hopkinson was born in Ealing in 1920. He left school aged sixteen and rushed to join Ealing Studios, taking up an unpaid position in the camera department as loader boy. His enthusiasm and eagerness to learn were impressive enough for him to be taken on as a salaried clapper/loader after four weeks of voluntary graft. His first paid job was working on *My Partner Mr Davis* (1936, directed by Claude Autant-Lara). For the remainder of the 1930s he learned his craft working on features in the British studios. In 1937 he moved over to Denham where he worked on *Yank at Oxford* (1937, directed by Jack Conway), *The Citadel* (1938, directed by the great visiting American film-maker King Vidor), Michael Powell's *The Spy in Black* (1939) and *The Thief of Baghdad* (1940, directed by Ludwig Berger *et al.*), rising in the ranks to the role of 'camera assistant'. Among the other studio employees with whom he became friends were Rod Neilson-Baxter and Kay Mander. Desirous of a career as a director, outside his lowly weekday position he took up a 9.5mm camera and shot actuality film on subjects like 1939's May Day. A career in the movies appeared to beckon, but as with the plans of so many others a war in Europe intervened.

Hopkinson had joined the Territorial Army in the late 1930s as a way of avoiding the tighter restrictions of peacetime conscription, which seemed likely to be introduced imminently. When war was declared the strategy backfired and he was at the front of the queue for service; in September

1939 he was placed in a machine-gun troop in the British Army. It was the period of phoney war, though, and Hopkinson had little to do. He wrote repeatedly to David MacDonald, who was organising film-making for the Army: Hopkinson had known him in the studios and tried to work the contact for all it was worth. In the summer of 1941 the Army Film and Photographic Unit was formed and was looking for people in the military with prior film experience. Hopkinson joined and would spend the next five years in the AFPU's employ.

Initially, Hopkinson was sent to the Middle East. A couple of years earlier he had loaded film in a London studio dressed as Iraq: now he sweated it out in the real thing. Hand-held Debrie cameras replaced the large studio models and a single Newman Sinclair, the newsreel and documentary camera of choice, was shared between the unit. The set-up was more journalistic than documentary and the stills photographers Hopkinson met were largely drawn from the staff of newspapers. Most of the footage the unit shot was immediately despatched and edited elsewhere for purposes such as the *War Pictorial News*. But it was here that Hopkinson gained his first directorial credit with the film *Via Persia* (1942), an item that followed supply routes for Russia, from the Persian Gulf to the Caspian Sea. In the autumn of 1942 he was in Africa and saw action as a combat cameraman with the British Eighth Army at the Battle of El Alamein shooting footage used in Roy Boulting's *Desert Victory*. Then he was on the move again, first to Italy (where he worked alongside Alan Whicker[3]) and then to Greece where he witnessed the liberation of Athens.

When the conflict in Europe ended, Hopkinson filmed all the way back to Britain, following repatriated Eighth Army soldiers on their journey home. Once back in London he received his next assignment to the Asian theatre and headed off to Singapore, before filming across South-east Asia. Victory in Japan followed shortly after and the war was over. Sat awaiting his repatriation in Thailand, Hopkinson received a copy of the *ACT Journal* and filled in an enclosed questionnaire asking members what they were going to do when the war had ended and they got out of the military. He realised then how much he enjoyed the high of being involved in historical events as they happened; the feature business had lost its earlier appeal.[4]

Nevertheless Hopkinson found himself back at a London studio, in Elstree, guarding equipment while he waited to be demobbed. Despite his doubts, he fully expected to return to loading film for the movies. The excitement about being out in the real world with a hand-held camera remained, though, and before he was released from military service a new avenue opened up. In May of 1946 he leapt at the chance to join the recently formed United Nations Relief and Rehabilitation Association (UNRRA) filming their activities in war-devastated Europe.

Before the year was out, Hopkinson was shooting material for an unrealised film *Droga do Kraju* (aka *The Way to the Homeland*) about the repatriation of Polish people held as slave labour in Germany during the war. Again he was shooting hand-held, using a clockwork Eyemo camera fitted with 100-foot rolls of 35mm film. This camera allowed a journalistic style that incorporated fast movement and proximity to the action. Soon Hopkinson was travelling further east, going on to film material on the terrible conditions in Minsk, Kiev and Odessa during the winter of 1946–7 and UNRRA's relief measures.[5] But by the time he had finished shooting, UNRRA had ceased operations in Europe, under pressure from the increasing Cold War tensions. Hopkinson returned to London unemployed, with the unprocessed film he had shot.

A negative and a print were made and sent to UNRRA offices in London, but a second print remained with Hopkinson. The UNRRA films officer in London, Olwen Vaughan, arranged a screening of this print for Documentary Movement luminaries, including Paul Rotha and Edgar Anstey. Uncensored footage of life in the Soviet Union was nearly impossible to obtain and received a ready audience. From Anstey, there was talk about re-presenting Hopkinson's footage in *This Modern Age*. There was also strong interest from across the Atlantic, though, and as the UN wanted the widest possible screening in the USA the material was offered to *March of Time* who issued it within a special release under the title *The Russians Nobody Knows* (1947). The film was widely acclaimed across the political spectrum, the *Daily Worker* at one end finding it an 'extremely stimulating picture' despite its 'innuendos' and 'wilful misrepresentation'[6] and the *Daily Mail* at the other enjoying its depiction of 'the rich red life'.[7]

It was the appreciation of his work among the film-makers that was more important to Hopkinson. His camerawork was commended and the COI quickly sent him out to the Ruhr to film German sequences for Rotha's *The World is Rich* (1947), a film being made by Films of Fact for another UN agency: the Food and Agriculture Organisation. Hopkinson's contact in the country was Arthur Elton: another useful person to know. Hopkinson later wrote that 'an obvious move on my part would have been into the then booming and confident world of the British Documentary film', but his aspirations were different. The British documentary scene seemed to him a little bit too safe, too 'English middle class' and he wanted to do something more abrasive 'journalistic rather than aesthetic. Less Film Society – more Fleet Street'.[8]

March of Time, concerned that simply presenting the footage as it was would make it look like Soviet propaganda, had decided to film new sequences of Hopkinson himself and build into *The Russians Nobody Knows* the story of the man who shot the material. A review in the serial's parent magazine *Time*, reinforced the objective: 'the Soviet bureaucracy, whatever its sins and shortcomings, appears to have a strong sense of responsibility toward the masses – if none toward individuals'.[9] It was Hopkinson's first service to Cold War propagandists but not the last.

In April of 1947 Hopkinson was offered the opportunity to join the *March of Time* team as a cameraman. While a respecter of *March of Time*'s crusading 1930s output, Hopkinson felt less comfortable with its current approach. However, it was an offer too good to turn down. Jimmy Hobson of *March of Time*'s London office gave him some advice on filming for the serial and warned him off the experimental trappings of GPO Film Unit-style documentary, advising him not to move the camera and only to shoot at eye level: 'we don't have any of them post office angles'.[10] This was journalism under strict editorial control.

Hopkinson's first assignment was to cover the run-up to Indian independence, material subsequently released as *Asia's New Voice* (1949), with other footage making its way into *New India's People* (1949). En route he was dispatched to gather material in Greece for a report on the civil war between communists and royalists: *Battle for Greece* (1948). After India he was sent to film *MacArthur's Japan* (1949), about the social changes occurring during the American occupation. Hopkinson's employers also made films for sponsors and thus he contributed to *Battle for Bread* (1950), a review of the work being done by, again, the UN Food and Agriculture Organisation to increase the world's supply of food. In 1950 he followed Eleanor Roosevelt around Europe for *My Trip Aboard* (1952) sponsored by the Economic Cooperation Administration (ECA), the US government agency managing the Marshall Plan. Straight work for *March of Time* continued with *The Promise of Pakistan* (1950) on the forming of that country and *Flight Plan for Freedom* (1951), a report on the UK-based operations of the Strategic Air Command of the US Air Force. He was back in Asia for *Formosa – Island of Promise* (1951) on the Nationalist Chinese government stronghold of Formosa (modern day

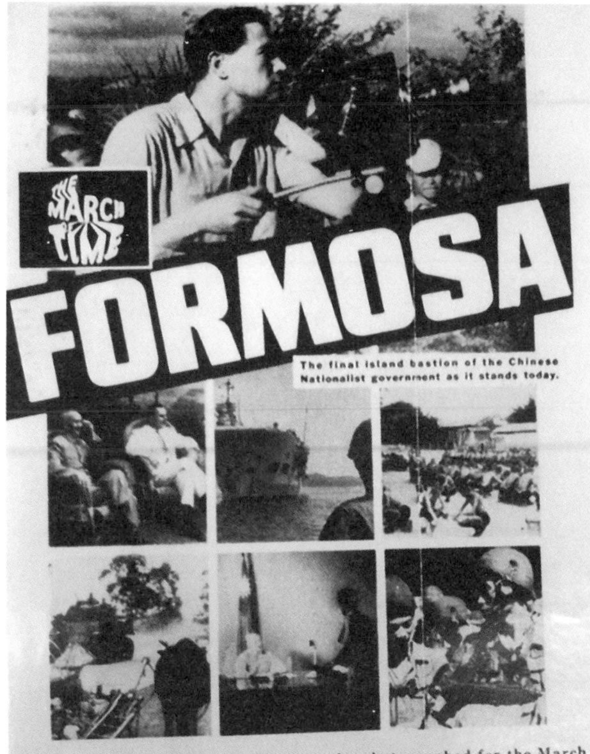

Shown at the top is Peter Hopkinson as he photographed for the March of Time — "Formosa". Produced by Richard de Rochemont this im- portant short subject reveals little known conditions existing on this Nationalist Chinese stronghold. The center scenes, taken from the film, show Governor Thomas E. Dewey of New York talking to Chiang Kai-shek, a U. S. aircraft carrier, Chinese Nationalist troops in various stages of training and K. C. Wu, governor of Formosa as he is talking to an assistant.

Mat No. M.T. 6-2A

Taiwan), while simultaneously shooting background footage for the ECA. It was an exciting spin about the globe, getting close to major world figures and recording the emergence of the post-war world.

The pattern on all these films generally remained the same. Hopkinson would be sent out to gather footage in support of a provided *March of Time* script. The footage would come back to *March of Time* offices in the USA, be edited and the script then tweaked to fit the film. While he was independent in the field, Hopkinson's editorial influence was minimal and, despite the fantastic opportunities, he was becoming frustrated with how the footage he was shooting ended up being used, and often felt little more then a hired mercenary.[11] Opportunities to make projects about the British in Korea and a feature-length film on India were promised to him but were never realised.

As his own doubts increased, the rise of television in the USA was diminishing the market for the cinema shorts he was photographing and *Formosa – Island of Promise* proved to be the last theatrically released *March of Time*. Hopkinson was unemployed again; he decided to seek work with the Crown Film Unit. But Crown was in its final days as government resources were being pulled away from the COI. James Carr offered him a job at World Wide Pictures but the move didn't seem quite right and Hopkinson turned him down.

As it was to prove so often in his professional life, it was Hopkinson's contacts that were to provide the next career move. The ECA, for whom he had worked through *March of Time*, had money available for documentary films in promotion of the Marshall Plan: propaganda supporting the 'anti-communist crusade'. The Marshall Plan's films officer was Lothar Wolf, a former chief film editor at *March of Time*. Introductions were easy and Hopkinson was employed to make films on the general theme of economic recovery in Europe. They were for broadcast on American TV screens via the ABC network, in a series called *Strength for the Free World*. Hopkinson set himself up in Cinetone Film Studios in Amsterdam accompanied by producer Philip Mackie, a former COI production control officer, with a single-system 35mm Mitchell and two Arriflex 16mm cameras.

It was in 1952 that Hopkinson directed and photographed a number of films for the series. Subjects took him across the continent: *North Sea Harbor* saw him in Hamburg, *The Ruhr* back into Germany's industrial heartland, *Keep 'Em Flying* was at Chateauroux in central France, *The Other Paris* in that nation's capital. He returned home for *The Smiths of London*. For someone of left-wing politics, Hopkinson seems to have adapted very easily to promoting the Cold War needs of the USA. These films were more ideological than the *March of Times* he had made. Yet the Marshall Plan was composed of strange bedfellows – while the plan constituted propaganda for the capitalist democracies, it also furnished state support for rebuilding housing, schools and hospitals. Many of the problems facing war-ravaged Europe matched those faced by Britain's pre-war working classes: cramped living conditions, inferior food quality, the need for universal education: all issues feature in *North Sea Harbor*. The cause of European unity was a bulwark against further war, and freedom was being protected from fascism as much as from Soviet communism. Nevertheless, *The Other Paris* was a clear attack on France's popular Communist Party and *The Smiths of London* (and its re-edit *The Smiths and the Robinsons*) were products of the Korean War and in support of NATO. But Hopkinson saw an opportunity in these films. A few years later he would write that the Marshall Plan offered the 'one great opportunity of vast and almost unlimited financial and thematic freedom ... offered to the European documentary film movement and the fact that it failed to rise to the occasion is very significant'.[12] While his politics fell to the left, Hopkinson was not a fellow traveller of the Soviet Union and for him the cause of establishing a civilised unity among the European states appears to have been a higher concern than East–West rivalries.

The film-maker came in at the tail end of Marshall Plan beneficence and by the time he was making these films concerns were being raised in the USA about the use of American taxpayers' money on propaganda appearing back on their own television screens. *Strength for the Free World* was cancelled and Hopkinson was out of work again. A timely telegram from England informed him that *March of Time* was moving into television and that there would be work for him if he wanted it – leading the direction of international subjects. Despite his previous reservations, economic concerns prevailed and he decided that the opportunities for assignments all over the world were appealing again. Prior to beginning shooting, Hopkinson spent several weeks testing the 16mm camera and sound equipment that would go out around the globe.

He had three films shown in the television series. *Germany Today* (8 October 1952) was about life in West Germany, its post-war reconstruction, relations with the East and how it dealt with East German refugees. *Vienna Today* (19 November 1952) covered life in that city under the Four-Power Commission and examined the political, military, social and cultural aspects of Viennese existence. *The Middle East: Powderkeg on the Rim of the Communist World* (10 December 1952), meanwhile, was about events and trends in Egypt, Iran, Kuwait and Israel. As the tensions of the Cold War increased, Hopkinson felt the editorial line was increasingly presenting unappealing (to him) right-wing attitudes.[13] The company presented him with another five subjects to film, but he resigned, seeking more autonomy.

A new opportunity arose in the form of Louis de Rochemont, pioneer of the 1930s *March of Time* that Hopkinson favoured over its later, more conservative incarnation. In February of 1953 Hopkinson was contracted to de Rochement, working as the European Director of *Our Times*, a proposed new documentary television series that would cover 'topical subjects bearing the fire and controversial aspects of the early *March of Time* issues'. The films were to be in colour and be about the 'men, ideas and events which distinguish today from yesterday and tomorrow'. Hopkinson was tasked with putting together a film crew in England.[14] He got to work writing scripts about Hong Kong, GIs and the origin of the opera *Carmen*. He was finally in an editorial position and able to shape the material, yet was to be thwarted by circumstance. The series was never made, partly because Hopkinson and de Rochement fell out when a film was suggested on the recent treatment of Charlie

Chaplin by McCarthyite America, and partly because de Rochmenont's fickle interests had moved to the Cinerama process. The situation was frustrating, but despite the end of *Our Times* Hopkinson remained under contract to de Rochemont. He unenthusiastically became involved in shooting footage in Switzerland for *Cinerama Holiday* (1955, directed by Robert L. Bendick and Phillipe De Lacy). Before the contract expired he found more enthusiasm working for Louis de Rochemont Associates on a final film project made in collaboration with John Halas, *To Open the World to the Nations: Suez* (1955), about the history and importance of the Suez Canal, which took him back out into the developing world.

Leaving de Rochemont, Hopkinson found all his useful contacts to be in the USA. In 1955 he joined the American broadcaster NBC, making programmes on international subjects for their news documentary series *Background. Duel for Germany* (1954) considered the struggle to reunify that country. *Italy on the Brink* (1954) was another red-scare film reporting on Europe's largest Communist Party. *Escape* (1955) was about the exodus of people from the Eastern bloc countries into the freedom of Austria and followed one Hungarian refugee as she tried to obtain an American visa. *British General Election* (May 1955) looked at political activity in a range of constituencies running up to the 1955 election and featured an exclusive interview with Aneurin Bevan on his political philosophy. *Meeting at the Summit* (17 July 1955) gave the background to the Geneva conference between Eisenhower, Kruschev, Eden and Faure. NBC presented other opportunities for Hopkinson and he directed two episodes of their series *Youth Wants to Know* at the International Conference on the Peaceful Use of Atomic Energy. The series featured high-school and college students asking major industrial and government officials questions relating to major issues of the day: in these two they questioned Admiral Lewis Strauss and Homi J. Bhabha. Hopkinson's greatest opportunity came with the series *Project 20* for which he directed and photographed *Call to Freedom* (7 January 1957), a feature-length production on the reopening of the Vienna State Opera and its opening production of Beethoven's 'Fidelio'. When he had finished shooting, in 1955, Hopkinson left the employ of NBC and returned to England.

Back in London as commercial television was beginning in the UK, Peter Hopkinson's experience working for a major American network would seem to have put him ahead of the pack. In 1958 he wrote that 'television can be an adult crusading medium with a power and significance that is the natural successor to the documentary film movement of the 'thirties'.[15] But he couldn't find a way into the British industry: despite repeated attempts during his career he made no more TV films until the 1980s. By his own analysis he was too young to be part of the original British documentary scene yet too old to join those emerging in the new television documentary of the 1950s.

It was a figure from that original documentary scene who offered him a way forward. In 1956 he met Arthur Elton again and was invited in to Film Centre. There he was also reacquainted with Sinclair Road whom he had met working for the ECA. Film Centre were working for the oil consortium known as the Iraq Petroleum Company, and through Shell had set up a local film unit making magazine programmes for local consumption. Each year they also made a prestige documentary, and Hopkinson was invited to make the next one on the development of Iraq.[16] Nationalist tensions in the Middle East were building, Mossadegh's election in Iran had worked out badly for Anglo-Iranian and the oil companies wanted a film that would communicate to Iraqis where the oil revenue was going, by highlighting infrastructural developments.

Between May and December of 1956 Hopkinson made two films for the Iraq Petroleum Company: *The Great Question* (1956), about the impact of oil on Iraq and the industrial development of the country, showing Iraqi government schemes for housing, hospitals and the control of diseases; and *Rivers of Time* (1957) which recreated the story of Sumeria and the later expansion of the Arabic culture in this area. These were the last films that Hopkinson photographed himself as cameraman/director. The instability of the region confounded this work: the Suez crisis interrupted filming and between completion and release came revolution in Iraq. The films were never shown in that country.

On returning to the UK, George Seager at Film Centre suggested that Hopkinson contact James Carr at World Wide Pictures. Hopkinson was reticent, having turned down Carr's earlier offer, but in September of 1957 he wrote to World Wide seeking employment. Carr wrote back inviting him to the offices for a meeting but added 'in the immediate future there is little I could offer you'.[17] In fact, Hopkinson was recruited almost immediately and dispatched to Wales to shoot material for the COI.[18]

Modern Wales (1958) was a prestige film for the Foreign Office, designed for overseas distribution. It told how the principality had recovered from the depression of the interwar years and was moving in to the future. It was the first film Hopkinson had made in the UK with a full crew. Carr also encouraged him to script the film's commentary and it became his first writing job. Hopkinson was dubious about the sort of sponsored film that had become World Wide's stock-in trade – but he got to work making a number of films for Ford. *Band Wagon* (1958), based on a script by John Krish, introduced a new Ford van using the music of Cy Laurie's Jazz Band and featured no spoken words. It was a critical success and the same model was followed for *Star Performer* (1961) in which a commentary-free circus fantasy set to music espouses the virtues of the Ford Thames 5/7 van. *The One Year Week* (1960), also for Ford, is lost and its contents unrecorded.

In 1959 Hopkinson did some photography for *Small Town Holiday* (1960), a film directed by Harry Watt for the COI following football fans on Norwich City's FA Cup run to the semi-finals. The same year he began his first large-scale sponsored film: *Kerosene* (1962); despite its basic title it was a prestige documentary for Shell. The film was made to communicate the importance of kerosene and its uses throughout the world. The commission was the product of internal manoeuvrings at Shell. Some inside the company were beginning to suspect that the Shell Film Unit was an extravagance and that Arthur Elton was profligate in his spending.[19] John Heyer of the Shell Film Unit Australia had been brought to London to examine the issue and he reckoned a top-quality film could be made for Shell externally for a lower cost than by the Shell Film Unit. Heyer asked World Wide to make a 'romantic *March of Time*-style thing on Kerosene'. Hopkinson wrote a script that showed the uses of kerosene in a range of settings from third to first world, to be filmed in the Sudan, Singapore and Australia. The completed film was never shown, however, Shell internal politics apparently having shifted during its production. Nonetheless, the film had shown what Hopkinson was capable of and that his previous newsfilm experience could be put to use in the longer-form sponsored documentary.

Hopkinson's next film, for the United Africa Company (i.e., Unilever's huge African subsidiary), would be a high point of his career. He began making this film, *African Awakening* (1962), about developments taking place in the newly independent West African nations of Ghana, Nigeria and Sierra Leone, in 1961. The topic of international development was close to Hopkinson's heart and he was given free rein to interpret the theme and a blank cheque to complete it. It was the first opportunity he had to realise his creative vision on screen, and he wanted to combine spontaneous, journalistic, footage of Africans speaking to camera, with a creatively conceived framework that would structure the film: to combine the schools of television and Griersonian documentary, or, as he later described it, the styles of Vertov and Eisenstein.[20] The interests of the sponsor were clear to Hopkinson: they wanted to show the new generation of post-colonial African leaders that the United Africa Company was a good thing and that 'private enterprise such as our own' should have a role in shaping the minds of West Africans.[21] As he visited Africa and developed his script, Hopkinson became convinced that the film should speak with an African voice and feature no externally written and spoken commentary. In Nigeria he met the writer Wole Soyinka, the perfect vehicle for expressing the new mood of African aspiration. Structurally the film contains some allusions to Humphrey Jennings's *A Diary for Timothy* (1945), the documentary that Hopkinson considered the most evocative and poetic of World War II.[22] In his own film a newborn African child plays surrogate for Timothy and it is a continent looking forward rather than a single nation. The film was widely praised and submitted by the British government as the UK's entry for the UNESCO Kalinga Prize.

African Awakening was to be the first of a global series in which the United Africa Company's parent corporation, Unilever, would show developments around the world, with other editions featuring India, Pakistan, Indonesia, the Philippines and Malaya. The public relations department of Unilever quickly cancelled the Indonesian and Philippines editions after finding corruption in those countries. Paul Dickson was to direct the Pakistan edition but couldn't get approval of his script. James Carr approached Satayit Ray to direct the Indian edition but he declined, and Hopkinson wrote a script that harked back to his *March of Time* film *New India's People*, which was eventually made by Caryl Doncaster as *Four Men of India* (1967).[23] In the film four employees of the

African Awakening

Hindustan Lever company are seen living and working in the Rajasthan desert, tropical Kerala, the Kulu valley and Calcutta. The country's traditional customs are shown against the background of a slowly advancing industry. Hopkinson also wrote and himself directed the Malyan edition. Shot in 1962, *Asian Crescent* (1964) was almost an *Asian* awakening, focusing on the formation of a new unified state: the Federation of Malayasia. It was about the efforts to create a multiracial society that was inclusive of Malayan, Chinese and Tamil peoples as well as the populations of Sarawak and Borneo. It looked at rural development, new industries, the use of education and how Malay was used as a common language. The film was made with the assistance of the Malaysian Film Unit and had some impact on Hopkinson, who would return repeatedly to this part of the world.

Work in the service of corporate prestige led to work in the service of national prestige, when the COI approached World Wide Pictures to make a film promoting Britain for the Colonial and Commonwealth offices. The project was presented to Hopkinson and the COI offered him 'an absolutely free hand' and promised to keep the commissioning department off his back until he had finished the film. He set to work almost immediately, planning the look and feel of the film. He amassed a dossier of images and his written impressions of different facets of British life. His vision was for a commentary-free fifty-minute epic. Where *African Awakening* had spoken with the voice of the African, this film would speak through the images and sounds of the British nation. When he submitted his treatment he faced instant attrition of his ideas: his hand was not free after all, as COI budget restrictions forced several planned scenes to be cut, others to be reworked in cheaper form. A commentary was desired and requested. It was a morale-sapping experience. The film eventually produced, *Today in Britain* (1964), was a shadow of the one Hopkinson had planned but its scope remains wide-ranging, showing recent developments in industry, atomic power, sport and education. It celebrates the achievements of Britain's past, while looking forward to the post-imperial nation contributing to world development through UNESCO and the multiracial Commonwealth. The influence of Jennings is there again: this is, in some ways, a nation symphony like *Listen to Britain* with the addition of glorious colour. It actually feels a little too long at twenty-six minutes, half the length of Hopkinson's proposed *Profile of Britain*, a film that cannot be judged. The commentary was a reasonably happy collaboration with legendary journalist James Cameron, but the soundtrack was a very different result than the one he had planned with no commentary at all. *Today in Britain* was translated into twenty-three different language versions for the widest international distribution and was considered a success by its sponsor and by critics. Hopkinson considered it his greatest disappointment.

Today in Britain

It was also the beginning of the end of the sort of prestige film-making that could bring creative satisfaction, although less interesting sponsored work continued. The director's Unilever experience in Malaysia made him a candidate for *Naturally its Rubber* (1964) and *Standard Malaysian Rubber* (1969), both for the Malaysian Rubber Fund Board. The first trod the familiar path of showing how industrialisation and western-style economics were raising the national standard of living, while the second was a record of industrial process. Hopkinson's reputation for the nation-building film also brought him *Flame in the Desert* (1968), the story of the rise of Qatar from Bedouins to oil barons, filmed in 1967.

There were also more films for government, but these too became progressively less interesting. The Armed Forces took the lion's share of COI publicity resources and Hopkinson's military background made him a suitable choice for a variety of films for the MOD and the Army. *School is Everywhere* (1965) was about the educational systems for servicemen's children overseas and intended for Army teaching staff and service families. *Three Hundred Years On* (1965) was a film for the Army Kinema Corporation giving an overview of British military history. The same sponsor commissioned the less celebratory *Home is the Soldier* (1967), which looked at the problems of a young soldier and his family when they look for a home and was intended to encourage servicemen to put money aside for house purchase when they become civilians. *Rock Climbing* (1969), meanwhile, was a prosaic training film for the Navy, teaching the principles of safe climbing.

The tendency towards the prosaic was becoming inescapable; *A Crop for All Seasons* (1964) for the Potato Marketing Board was the sort of sponsored film that made the genre so unappealing to sophisticates. It was a description of some of the research and experimental procedures being undertaken to produce the perfect potato to satisfy both the housewife and the farmer. Hopkinson also wrote scripts for two World Wide films he didn't direct, on steel manufacture and decimalisation: the widely distributed *Study in Steel* (1968), directed by Alan Pendry, and *All Change* (1969), realised by Stephen Clarkson. In 1966 Hopkinson directed a TV message by the Duke of Edinburgh on behalf of the Royal Society for the Prevention of Accidents.

The sponsored work was becoming less and less appealing and in 1969 Hopkinson left salaried employment at World Wide, realising that there were to be no more *African Awakenings* as the commissioning companies were becoming increasingly disinterested in prestige film-making and only wanted to fund films that 'stuff the product in your face'.[24] Ten years earlier he had noted that value for money was the objective of the post-war film sponsor: 'no longer do we have the amiable pre-war climate in which enlightened sponsors would give a virtually free hand to film makers to practise their own techniques and social criticism'.[25]

He had spent a lot of time considering the state of documentary, as for months his weekends had been occupied with writing a volume of autobiography, published in 1969 as *Split-Focus*. Olwen Vaughan, who had arranged the exhibition of his UNRRA footage to the British documentary luminaries, intervened again and sent proofs of the book to John Grierson and Basil Wright. Grierson responded with praise and Wright wrote to the author inviting him to lunch. Another British documentary veteran, Alexander Shaw, was now at UNESCO and had recruited Wright to provide film education in the developing world. At that lunchtime meeting Wright asked Hopkinson to accompany him to the National Film Institute of India 'to run a crash course on documentary for young *film*-makers from Indonesia, Malaysia, Singapore and Nepal as well as from India'.[26]

For six weeks Hopkinson and Wright trained these Asian film-makers. The emphasis was on how film can be used as part of the development process and all the students made final films on development subjects. They were split into two groups: one made a film on population under the supervision of Wright, the other on the subject of water supervised by Hopkinson. It was a shot in the arm for Hopkinson's flagging enthusiasm and from this point on his career essentially followed two separate but parallel paths. He worked on the use of the moving image in international development work and he continued with the corporately financed work that paid the grocery bills. In 1971 he published *The Role of Film in Development* for UNESCO. It was a manual addressed to those connected with film-making in the developing countries and built on his experiences working with Wright and the students in India. One of Hopkinson's key messages was that appropriate media should be used to achieve communication aims: that, *pace* McLuhan, the message was more important than the medium.

That book led to more employment with the United Nations and UNESCO invited Hopkinson to make family-planning films for the third world. UNESCO wanted to use the film medium to find a way of presenting the challenge of population control sensitively. He applied his own dictum and made a series of films about different methods of communicating the family-planning message. The film series *Family Planning Communication* moved across the globe to show appropriate methods being used in different contexts: the use of *Folk Media* was recorded in India, of *Low Cost Media* in Kenya and of *Mass Media* in Iran. All of these 1974 films were produced under the auspices of Peter Hopkinson Associates. They were subsequently compiled at World Wide Pictures into a single film, *A Matter of Families* (1974), including a record of research and evaluation of the results of using the various media made in Venezuela.

The same year, Hopkinson took up a post through UNESCO as the Chief Training Adviser to a television documentary production unit in Costa Rica. Funded by the United Nations Development Programme, Hopkinson trained local people to make monthly broadcast TV programmes. In the year he was there, the themes covered included: deforestation, rainforest conservation, rural cooperatives, prison reform, alcoholism, black plantation workers and breast-feeding.

In 1976 the director made another film for UNESCO on the *Coin Collections* (1977) of the British Museum as a freelancer for his old employer World Wide Pictures. In fact, despite leaving a salaried position at World Wide, Hopkinson maintained a relationship as a World Wide freelancer into the 1980s, making films for a range of corporate clients. For the Rio Tinto Zinc Corporation: *Ore Sorters* (1971), an industrial process film, *Partnership for Prosperity* (1971), about an aluminium smelting works, and *Better Than The South* (1971), about copper mining. For British Steel: *Electric Arc Steel Making* (1971). For the construction company Wimpey: *Focus on Training* (1976) and *Joint Venture in Housing* (1977), thrillingly followed by *Joint Venture Confirmed* (1979), on building public housing, *It All Starts Here* (1981), on mechanical engineering, *Magnus* (1982), on oil rig construction, and *The Dead Sea Lives* (1983), on potash recovery. *Multiply and Divide* (1979), for Post Office Telecommunications, was about the sponsor's area telephone directories being restructured into two or more volumes. Needless to say the topic didn't provide many opportunities for 'post office angles'.

Hopkinson also freelanced for other companies. *Ghana – A Report* (1969), made at Birch-Hill Film Productions for Unilever, returned to one of the awakened African nations.[27] But the story in West Africa was not such a happy one now: Sierra Leone lurched from one military government to another, Wole Soyinka was imprisoned by the Nigerian regime while the country descended into civil war and Ghanian president Kwame Nkrumah had been deposed in a military coup in 1966. The country was bankrupt. *Ghana – A Report* was about the steps being taken to restore national stability through investment from overseas and it offered up the riches of Ghana to the foreign investor – timber, bauxite, manganese and industrial diamonds. .

It was a more interesting film than most of those produced by Hopkinson in the 1970s. Work for several other production companies resulted in more films for the COI. *Grey and Scarlet* (1970) was a recruitment film for the Queen Alexandra Royal Army Nursing Corps aimed at young women. *Physics and Engineering* (1971) was about how the study of physics relates to modern technology. *Metrication and Agriculture* (1971) was for the Metrication Board, *Work with Water* (1973) for the Department of the Environment, *Method Study in Agriculture* (1971) for the Ministry of Agriculture, Fisheries and Food.

Hopkinson was an amazing archivist and chronicler of his own career, with two published autobiographies, a more than usually extensive interview given to the BECTU History Project and a personal collection of notes and ephemera donated to the BFI. Throughout, though, there is a notable absence of record or information on this sponsored work. The director's filmography becomes patchy where these films are concerned, many titles are lost and information on them, even synopses for a few, are entirely absent. Although the industrial-films field contains its share of forgettable productions, this is an oddity in Hopkinson's otherwise thorough record. There's a real sense that much of this part of his career he simply didn't regard as part of his creative oeuvre: it was just work.

This is most noticeable when it comes to his company Peter Hopkinson Associates, which receives no mention in his autobiography. The firm was incorporated in 1954, the year Hopkinson's contract with Louis de Rochement expired and he joined NBC. Correspondence in his personal files indicates that in 1956 the company made two films, *Planned Presentation* and *Recipe for Reliability* for the sponsor ITD, and that in the same year he was approached by the Mayflower Project to make a film on Anglo-American relations. While in Iraq for Film Centre he also made under the Peter Hopkinson Associates name *Under the Sun* (aka *Daughter of Babylon*) (1957), a film of dancers in a variety of locations, including Samarra, Chosroes' Arch and Babylon, using a soundtrack of classical music and quotations from the Old Testament. Then the company name disappears from the record until the 1970s, but whether this reflects its being in abeyance during Hopkinson's tenure at World Wide or simply that no record remains of activity in the intervening period is unclear. In 1973 the company made two films for the Malaysian Tin Industry Research and Development Board about their work: *Time for Tin*, a short film made for an international audience, and *Timah*, a longer documentary made for domestic screening in Malaysian schools. The same year saw another film on a Malaysian export product: *Rubber – The Natural Way* (1974) made for Rank Audio Visual. Hopkinson's Malaysian connection, which dated all the way back to a wartime stay in Singapore and was ignited by *Asian Crescent*, continued to provide a rich source of inspiration. In 1979 he formed another business, a joint-venture company in Kuala Lumpur, to develop and produce Malaysian-based factual and drama TV series. This company, Perkhidmatan Pengurusan Perfileman, drew on his UNESCO experiences in Costa Rica. Hopkinson directed two films, entitled *Settling the Future* and *Malaysia Outward Bound* (both 1979).

Reaching state retirement age in 1985 didn't put a stop to Peter Hopkinson's career and, while his output decreased, he still found time to produce a few films that looked back across the span of his life and career. There were two late prestige films produced at World Wide. *Power to the People* (1985) for the Central Electricity Generating Board considered the development of the National Grid from the time it came into full commercial operation in 1935 until the present day, detailing the social and economic benefits it had brought. *A Quality of Life* (1985) for Shell UK compiled archive film to tell a three-part history of Britain from the 1930s to the 1960s: *Transport and Communication*, *Industry*

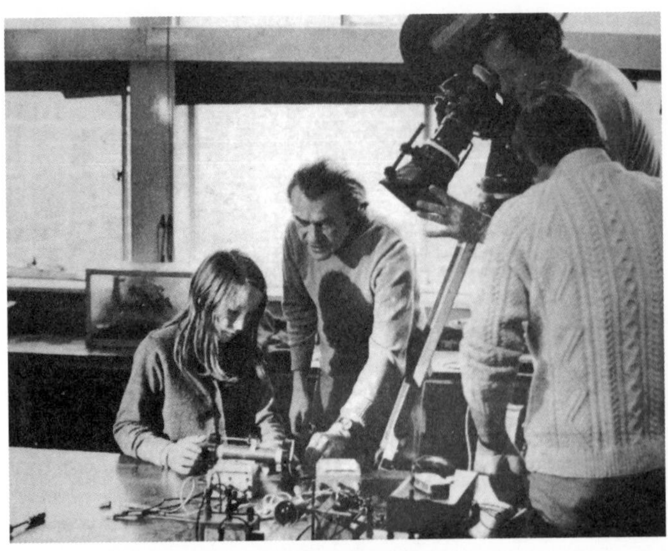

Peter Hopkinson directs *Physics and Engineering*

and Technology and *Social Developments*. The film won an award from the British Film Institute in 1986 for archival achievement. In 1990, Channel 4 broadcast *Orphans of Minsk* (1990), credited to the production company Hopkinson Partnership, in which Hopkinson returned to the scene of the UNRRA film that had kicked off his career.

In 1995 the director gave the BFI's Ernest Lindgren Memorial Lecture on the 'Uses and Abuses of Archive Film' and directed the accompanying film for the BBC's *Centenary of Cinema* season: *Power Behind the Image* (1995) was a look at the development of the moving image in parallel with that of electricity, with the latter making the former possible. The film summarises the early development of film and electrification, going on to look at the arrival of sound and the depression of the 1930s. It was a conceit encouraged by the involvement of the National Grid Company: a surprising late twist in the history of sponsored film-making.

This was to be Peter Hopkinson's final directorial credit and a fitting end to a career that had explored the power *of* the image. Through his international work, Hopkinson had successfully maintained a career in social documentary – the problems of the world replacing the problems of the nation espoused by the 1930s' documentary pioneers. The work for UNESCO training film-makers in the developing world is probably Hopkinson's greatest legacy, his work for UNRRA, *March of Time*, the ECA and NBC the most interesting part of his career, and *African Awakening* his most complete artistic statement. In his engagement with both film and television documentary, Hopkinson provides an opportunity for considering the relationship of those forms, of how Film Society met Fleet Street, of where and how documentary meets journalism. He also offers us another story, about how the industrially sponsored film related to documentary, as he sometimes used sponsorship to support his own artistic vision and at other times simply for the income it provided. Hopkinson was committed to international humanitarian work, but today there's an uneasiness involved in watching his films about the developing world. He criticised the paternalism evident in earlier documentaries like Terry Bishop's Oscar-winning Crown Film Unit story documentary *Daybreak in Udi* (1949), which indicated 'what *we* are doing for *them*', but his own films don't have entirely clean hands. As public-relations tools for large multinationals they implicitly support an agenda promoting commodity-based export economies friendly to first-world private industries. To modern eyes, they now more often seem to be in service of those aims than of Hopkinson's better intentions.

Peter Hopkinson died on 28 June 2007.

NOTES

1. This early enthusiasm is related in his first of two volumes of autobiography, *Split Focus: An Involvement in Two Decades* (London: Hart-Davis, 1969).
2. Peter Hopkinson, *Screen of Change: Lives Made Over by the Moving Image* (London: UKA Press, 2008), p. 241. The book was published posthumously.
3. Alan Whicker, *Whicker's War* (London: HarperCollins, 2005), p. 166.
4. Peter Hopkinson interviewed by Alan Lawson for the BECTU History Project, 24 November 1989.
5. This material is held at the BFI National Archive under the title *Russia 1946/47: Byelorussia and Ukraine* (1947).
6. Review in *Daily Worker*, 27 June 1947.
7. Review in *Daily Mail*, 27 June 1947.
8. Hopkinson, *Screen of Change*, p. 141.
9. Anon., 'Cinema: The Russians Nobody Knows', *Time*, 2 June 1947.
10. BECTU History Project Interview.
11. Kevin Brownlow, 'Peter Hopkinson', *The Independent*, 17 July 2007.
12. Peter Hopkinson, 'Facts out of Focus', *Films and Filming*, January 1958, pp. 13, 34.
13. Peter Hopkinson, 'The March of Time', letter published in *Sight & Sound* vol. 40 no. 4, Autumn 1971, p. 229.
14. A. H. Weiler, 'By Way of Report; De Rochemont Plans "Our Times"', *New York Times*, 17 May 1953, p. x5.
15. Peter Hopkinson, 'Facts out of Focus'.
16. Letter from George Seager of Film Centre to Peter Hopkinson Associates (25 May 1956) in Peter Hopkinson collection, BFI Special Collections, 'The Hopkinson Miscellany', Item 12, Box 9.
17. Letter from James Carr to Peter Hopkinson (24 October 1957) in Hopkinson collection, 'The Hopkinson Miscellany', Item 12, Box 9.
18. Hopkinson would always remain warmly disposed to Carr, whom he judged a genuine person and a film-maker at heart. Carr's obituary in *Film & TV Technician* was contributed by Hopkinson.
19. Elton apparently requested that all rushes for Shell Film Unit films be printed in colour, at great expense, rather than the standard practice of using black and white.
20. Hopkinson, *Screen of Change*, p. 318.
21. Letter from D. H. Buckle of the United Africa Company to chairmen and public relations managers of CWA, Unilever's holding company (19 April 1961), seeking their assistance in producing the film, in Hopkinson collection, 'The Hopkinson Miscellany', Item 12, Box 9.
22. See Peter Hopkinson, 'Obituary: Basil Wright', *Film & TV Technician*, December 1987/January 1988, p. 16.
23. Doncaster is a relatively neglected major figure of early British TV; she had been a pioneer producer of *This Week* and other Rediffusion current-affairs shows, and before that BBC 'documentaries' dramatised live.
24. BECTU History Project Interview.
25. Hopkinson, 'Facts out of Focus'.
26. Basil Wright, 'Film and the Third World', *Educational Broadcasting International* vol. 12 (1979), p. 58.
27. Birch-Hill was an offshoot of Editorial Film Productions, which had previously been Unilever's main film producer.

14 Science and Society: *Peter de Normanville, Sarah Erulkar*

ROS CRANSTON & KATY McGAHAN

Although Sarah Erulkar (born 1923) and Peter de Normanville (1922–1999) had long and successful careers, even by the modest standards of post-war documentary they are all but unknown today. Both commenced their careers working at the Shell Film Unit where their working relationship blossomed into marriage whence Shell's rigid policy on employing married couples compelled them to follow separate working paths. Their careers came to epitomise two different faces of the post-war documentary. While de Normanville refined a specialism in science and technology films,

Peter de Normanville and Sarah Erulkar

Erulkar focused more on human-interest stories but worked across genres and subjects. The spouses' professional paths would reconverge only towards the end of their careers.

'I was always so grateful when anyone employed me,' as Sarah Erulkar recalled, 'I always felt I must be such an oddity that they had to sell me to the sponsor as well.'[1] As an Indian-born female (and Jewish) documentary director, Erulkar was, if not an 'oddity', then certainly an extreme rarity in the realm of post-war British film-making. Although British documentary, and the Documentary Movement in particular, had spawned a number of talented and prolific female directors including Ruby and Marion Grierson, Jill Craigie, Margaret Thomson, Evelyn Spice and Kay Mander, when Sarah Erulkar joined the ranks in 1947 documentary directing, like many post-war professions, was rapidly becoming the preserve of men. While many women directors retired prematurely, Erulkar managed to negotiate the myriad obstructions she encountered across her forty-year career and made over eighty films.

Short-circuiting the usual gradual ascent from technician or scriptwriter to director, when Erulkar was hired into the Shell Film Unit by Alex Wolcough, her rise was meteoric. Having proven her visual and technical worth scripting and editing *Aircraft Today and Tomorrow* (1946) under the auspices of Geoffrey Bell, Sarah Erulkar's swift ascent at Shell was sealed with her direction of *Flight for Tomorrow* (1947). Respectively concerning the first post-war Radlett Airshow, and the repurposing of military aircraft for civilian use, this debut duo provided invaluable technical training to the young Erulkar. Then a trip to India with her father to witness the lead-up to Indian independence, gave rise to Erulkar's second directing role for Shell. While in India, she was asked to direct *Lord Siva Danced* (1946). Starring the celebrated Indian dancer, Ram Gopal, and mostly shot in Bombay, the film's introduction to classical Indian dance had a significant impact following its theatrical release, premiering at the Academy Cinema in London's West End. It also won accolades in India, where, in popularity terms, it was treasured on a par with Britain's *Night Mail* (1936). It was, in fact, the ever-influential *Night Mail* that had seeded Erulkar's passion for documentary when she first saw it as a fourteen-year-old schoolgirl. Her ardour was unwavering: unlike contemporaries happy to switch sectors and cross genres, Erulkar declined offers to work in feature films or television.

Sarah Erulkar directs *Lord Siva Danced*

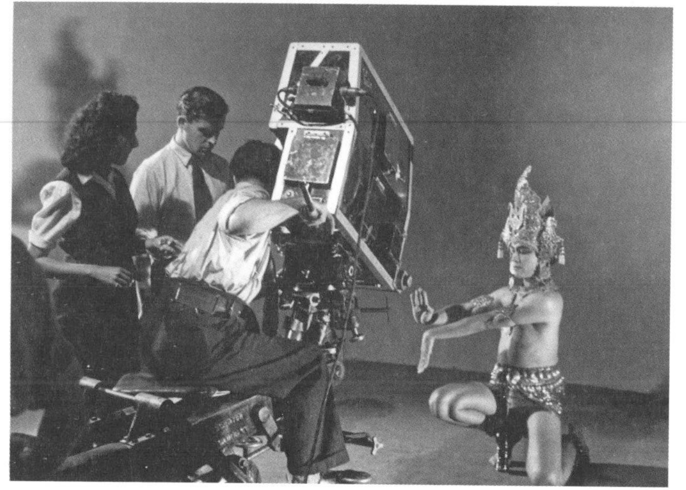

Although outwardly mild-mannered and self-effacing, Sarah Erulkar had an inner feistiness that frequently found expression in her work. That *Lord Siva Danced* demonstrated a vigour and singularity of voice was duly noted by a contemporary *Documentary Film News* review. Jointly penned by Pathé film-makers Peter Baylis and Jack Howells, the article compares and contrasts *Lord Siva Danced* with the similarly themed contemporary release, *Steps of the Dance* (1948), a three-reel Crown Film Unit production on the subject of British ballet:

> Two films on dancing. *Steps of the Dance* technically polished in production and content. *Lord Siva Danced*, production not as good, yet in content, more than polished. It had virility, something welling up from deep roots, speaking for and to the ordinary people.[2]

Perhaps the hardships associated with growing up as part of a, at the time very small, minority ethnic group and her academic engagement with sociology, informed the social conscience that Erulkar brought to her work.[3] In 1991, when interviewed about her career by John Taylor for the BECTU History Project, she discusses in no uncertain terms how as a twenty-three-year-old she had relished the opportunity to promote the culture of her motherland in the directing of *Lord Siva Danced* (1946): 'I wanted to do good for the world, the usual thing. I wanted to rescue India from the bloody British ... I saw myself on a white horse riding into Delhi.'

Such fervour was, of course, prudently kept in check during the directing of the apolitical pedagogical tribute to one of India's most ancient customs and lauded artists. The simple proscenium-arch style of the film both replicates and reveres the restraint and spiritual devotion exercised by the dancers. Pared and informative commentary (written by Erulkar) fuses with unobtrusive yet emotive lighting: all aptly deferring to the subject. In their article, Baylis and Howells smartly opined that, although 'well thought-out', 'neat' and 'well contrived', *Steps of the Dance* was unlikely to increase any viewer's enthusiasm for ballet. Despite featuring the dancers of Covent Garden and Sadlers Wells and an informative commentary by the famous ballet dancer, Robert Helpmann, it did not electrify critics. By comparison, *Lord Siva Danced* did spread enthusiasm and appreciation of Indian dance in the West, as well as becoming a cult classic in India. Ram Gopal had already done much to ignite British audiences to the wonder of Indian dance with his London debut in 1939 and went on to lead a successful career as a dancer in Britain, frequently returning to perform in his homeland. Combining religion, philosophy and folklore with a set of highly disciplined movements, the four great classical schools of Indian dance are illustrated by Erulkar's film together with Gopal's own 'Dance of the Setting Sun', in which he demonstrates how new dances evolve from classical traditions.

'No one knew why Shell wanted to make a film about Indian dance,' Erulkar retrospectively remarked. Evidently *Lord Siva Danced* fell somehow into Wolcough and Arthur Elton's belief that Shell's films should create general goodwill with perhaps no immediate or directly traceable return through its films. Ostensibly an educational short with entertainment value, it was no coincidence that the film was commissioned immediately ahead of India's independence from British rule. With the international spotlight on the emergent nation, to assimilate Shell into the widespread programme of flag-hoisting ceremonies and colourful cultural pageantry was the proverbial piece of enlightened public relations.

As well as the professional opportunities and creative freedom afforded to her, Erulkar welcomed the climate of interracial tolerance that she encountered at the oil company: 'Shell was very exciting. I suddenly felt that my colour didn't matter ... very different to my childhood.' If being a woman and Indian was no hindrance to advancement at Shell, being a woman and married definitely was. In 1952, after having directed three more films for Shell – *New Detergents* (1949), *Night Hop* (1950) and *The History of the Helicopter* (1951) – Erulkar found herself newly unemployed as a result of marrying de Normanville. Arthur Elton did not mince his words when advising Erulkar that, as a married woman, her role ought now to be 'to put out Peter's slippers'. The fact that it was her new husband who had the more junior role, and was earning £8 per week to Erulkar's £18, was evidently irrelevant in the face of ingrained convention. Gender discrimination, of course, pervaded British workplaces at this time. Fortunately de Normanville was entirely supportive of Erulkar's career ambitions and after the birth of their two daughters they both combined parenthood with their respective film-making. De Normanville's position on this was fixed: 'I married a film director and you're going to stay a film director!' They hired an au pair with the proviso that one or the other parent would be at home with their two daughters every evening. In the face of criticism from some of her male peers – and their wives – Erulkar progressed in her field as a career-long freelancer. As she later asserted: 'This was my life. It was what I'd wanted to do since I was fourteen. I just had to do it.' She recognised that de Normanville had taken on a lot more in his role as a husband and father than was normal in those days and she was, and remains, deeply grateful.

Until the war intervened, Peter de Normanville was heading for Oxford University after receiving an upper middle-class Catholic education at Ampleforth College. Instead, he joined the Royal Air Force, and, aged eighteen, he became the youngest four-engine bomber pilot in the world.[4] This was soon followed by a crash into a Scottish mountain in which most of his crew died. After six months in hospital, the young pilot was involved in another crash after an air-raid on Brest in 1942, and a year in hospital ensued.

While in the RAF, de Normanville had been impressed by the rudimentary training films he'd seen, and so decided – with some encouragement from a family friend working at Rank – to pursue a career in the film industry. Knowing nothing of the British Documentary Movement, he trekked fruitlessly around Soho until he ended up in DATA's offices. He was introduced to someone he later realised was a charming and sympathetic Donald Alexander, who explained that he couldn't afford just to take chaps off the streets and train them. Alexander recommended that de Normanville spend a year with the Shell Film Unit and that he would then guarantee him a job with DATA. De Normanville eagerly followed this advice and applied for a job as a Shell camera assistant. To his surprise, he was offered a more responsible post as a 'fully fledged assistant director at twice the salary' – £7. De Normanville already felt that technological literacy was his strength, as it was Shell's, and he appreciated the generous working conditions, whereby time and money were much more readily available than they would have been at an outfit like DATA. He later claimed to have spent most of his first year ensconced in libraries finding out the structure of molecules, presumably for the film *Atomisation* (1948), directed by Bill Mason, on which de Normanville is credited as assistant director. During his early years at Shell, de Normanville also worked as assistant director on a range of films about gasoline, motor racing, aeroplanes and locomotives. These included *Grand Prix* (1949), the seminal short showing the British Grand Prix at Silverstone, on which he was again assistant director to Mason. The following year he moved to another kind of motor racing – co-directing the film *Isle of Man TT 1950* with Geoffrey Hughes.

However, following in Sarah Erulkar's footsteps, Peter de Normanville's first film as a director was an aviation-themed commission. From the early 1950s onwards he became particularly prolific in this subject area, co-directing with Bill Mason two films called *Highlights of Farnborough*, released in 1951 and 1952, which de Normanville felt 'were great fun but not terribly important'. The second of these, however, was enthusiastically written up by a contemporary reviewer in *Scientific Film Review*:

> Many military and civil aircraft of advanced design show off their paces in an enthralling manner. The photography is sparkling, the camera work excellent, the commentary succinct and informative, and the musical accompaniment most apt. It will appeal to a wide audience, both as a factual record, and as a work of art.[5]

This crossover appeal to more than one type of audience, and a consideration of the ways in which scientific and technical films could marry art to fact, were subjects of active debate in scientific film circles at this time. Peter de Normanville was clearly finding his feet, and his form.

Soon after the Farnborough films de Normanville was directing solo, beginning with a series of short, detailed productions about aeroplanes, including the Valiant bomber, the de Havilland Comet and the Hawker Hunter jet fighter, which were 'record' films and designated 'Shell Aviation Library Material', from which extracts could be made available to use in other films. De Normanville's next two films, *Project 074* (1953) and *The Gas Turbine* (1954), were polished instructional films about industrial processes. The reviewer in *Scientific Film Review* wrote of *Project 074*:

> By excellent photography, clear diagrams and a concise commentary, the film describes this application [of] radioactivity to an industrial purpose in a straightforward and easily understood manner. An interesting and informative film.[6]

Another, or possibly the same, anonymous reviewer was similarly enthusiastic about *The Gas Turbine*, writing:

> A lucid, straightforward and accurate representation of the subject. The effective use of models and animated diagrams in conjunction with excellent photography and an adequate commentary succeed in making this a good instructional film.[7]

The recurrence evident in these reviews would prove relevant to a large proportion of de Normanville's later films. The admiration for the 'excellent photography' is slightly undermined in both reviews by the use of the word 'straightforward'. Likewise, the commentary of *The Gas Turbine* is described as 'adequate', reflecting its detailed yet at times pedestrian delivery. The reaction to these films suggests that early in de Normanville's career the key characteristics of his film-making style were in place: a fine visual awareness combined with recognition of the importance of explaining scientific fact via the commentary, a combination that could result in a tension between flatness of verbal explanation and genuinely striking visual artistry.

Sarah Erulkar and Peter de Normanville married in 1950. De Normanville's parents did not look favourably upon his choice of a wife, his mother advising her son, 'I understand the attraction but why can't you marry someone respectable and keep Sarah Erulkar as your mistress?' While mother and daughter-in-law were eventually reconciled, his father's bias was more entrenched and, according to Erulkar, he carried the resentment to his death. Erulkar recounted how, as a mixed-race couple, they had frequently been the target of abuse when out in public. Despite such experiences, Erulkar claimed: 'Being a woman caused me the most problems' – presumably because gender bias was a greater potential hindrance to her career progression.

Ironically, far from a hindrance, being a woman was almost requisite for her first commission as a freelance director. World Wide Pictures had recently been contracted by the Central Office of Information to produce a film about district nursing and, given that the subject area pertained to 'women's issues', a female director was deemed appropriate. *District Nurse* (1952) charts a day in the life of two nurses in the rural south east of England. It was one of the many government films made on behalf of the Foreign Office and Commonwealth Relations Office to promote Britain and its institutions to overseas audiences. The film's secondary function was to encourage applications to the nursing profession. The district nurses' encounters with people in need from all walks of life at clinics and in their homes suggest an attractive and rewarding profession. The film exudes warmth and humanity through the dedication of its subjects to helping people. A contemporary *Film User* reviewer described *District Nurse* as 'a very human film, beautifully photographed, it not only provides a lot of useful information about this part of the National Health Service, but should aid recruiting to the nursing service'. Erulkar would return to World Wide later in her career to direct a film of a very different order, *Physics and Chemistry of Water* (1965), produced by Peter Bradford, a multiple award-winning description of the atomic structure of water molecules. A feat of animation, it was one of a series on water sponsored by Unilever and designed for fourteen- to sixteen-year-old science students. When charged with subject matter that was unfamiliar to her, Erulkar would, like de Normanville, immerse herself in the subject, reading widely and even enlisting a private tutor on occasion.

Following this first directing stint with World Wide she joined Donald Alexander and his colleagues at the National Coal Board Film Unit as an editor. There she honed her cutting skills on a clutch of staff-training films produced between 1956 and 1958. During this time she also directed films for Leon Clore's two firms Graphic Films and Basic Films. After leaving the NCB, Erulkar worked almost exclusively as a director until she retired in the early 1980s. Her freelance career ran the gauntlet of post-war documentary commissioning bodies including the British Productivity Council, the COI, the Gas Council and the General Post Office, as well as the Children's Film Foundation. Adaptability was key, and Erulkar's choice of commissions yielded an oeuvre crossing the spectrum of genres from classic documentary, travelogue and 'trigger' films to children's features, medical training films and public information, as well as the customary swathe of promotional shorts for various commercial bodies.

With regard to subject matter, while around 20 per cent of the films Erulkar made pertain to themes conventionally associated with women, such as childcare, nursing and cooking (and this was increasingly the case in the latter part of her career), it did not entrap her reputation within the bounds of women's subject areas, nor indeed did it preclude her from being simultaneously assigned to films of a highly technical or industrial nature, albeit to a much lesser degree than her husband. In reviewing her career she conceded that to some extent she had felt pigeonholed as a woman director but had enjoyed the challenges of handling such wide-ranging subject matter, and had a personal passion for, for example, cookery, that she could bring to the treatment. She cited *Something Nice to Eat* (1967), a Gas Council-sponsored film celebrating the art of cooking, intended for housewives, as one of the most rewarding films she made (a film which eventually showed up on TV sets as one of the BBC2 trade-test films). Due dividends for her inventiveness came in the form of an award for the film that most imaginatively communicated its message at the Eighth International Industrial Film Festival at Lisbon in September 1967. A report in *The Times* noted Erulkar's unwavering ability to convey information in an engaging manner:

> The practice of the art of cooking by the professional and the amateur is presented in a way that holds the attention. The sequence on how to make a soufflé and Steak au Poivre is a typical example of the way in which originality in presentation, allied to fine photography, can turn the ordinary into the exquisite.[8]

Contrary to received wisdom, Erulkar felt that post-war documentary film-makers benefited from the lifting of restraints that had been imposed on sponsors during wartime and was astonished at the creative freedom that organisations like the Shell Film Unit afforded her and her contemporaries. While mindful that boundaries were built into the sponsored sphere, she felt that within these restrictions inventiveness was expressly encouraged.

> After the war was over and the subjects were more relaxed ... we were allowed to do things more our own way also to a certain extent. During the war you had to follow certain rules and the MOI was very tough. ... So it was a good feeling, apart from victory and peace, you could do subjects that were not so serious; that were not so complicated ... I mean I made films about food for God's sake. Apart from rationing that wouldn't have been a subject during the war.[9]

A temporal telescoping of her work across a two-year period midway into her career, between 1960 and 1961, illustrates the sheer diversity and quantity of projects that were then coming her way. *Land of the Dragon* (1960) was a Welsh travelogue for British Movietone. *Spat System* (1960), promoting its sponsor's GKN Screws and Fasteners products, was made at Rayant Pictures for a specialist industrial audience. The Ministry of Health-sponsored COI film *Mary Lewis – Student Nurse* (1961) is a slightly soapy personal story of a young girl's training to become a State Registered Nurse, also directed at Rayant, while *Anaesthesia with Methohexitone* (1961), made for Anne Balfour-Fraser's Samaritan Films, was a medical training film on the administration of anesthetic. From prestige to pedagogy, versatility and human interest characterise Erulkar's enormously eclectic output. This trend continued through the latter two decades of her career which yielded such diverse exemplars as *The Air My Enemy* (1971), a glossy and expensive Gas Council film concerning different types of pollution which received extensive cinema distribution, down to *Teenage Talk-In* (1977–82), a series of 16mm teenage 'trigger' films sponsored by the Scottish Health Education Unit on an array of emotive topics including relationships and alcohol abuse.

Erulkar stated that there was never any professional disharmony between husband and wife. Indeed, their mutual support helped sustain her career. As a mother of two, she periodically felt herself under pressure to sacrifice her career for her family and confessed that, given her work commitments, she might not always have been 'the best mother in the world'. But unfaltering encouragement and support from her husband coupled with a compulsion to keep making documentary films helped assuage the maternal guilt she sometimes felt: 'I was made to make films. I don't think there was anything else.'[10] Continuing in the spirit of her documentary forebears of the 1930s, she was also compelled by an underlying sense of social purpose, and this is possibly where Erulkar and de Normanville's approaches to film-making most notably differ. She related: 'I certainly hoped to be doing some good, to be justifying my existence. I never took on a subject I didn't want to do. I would just say "I'm sorry I'm busy". Every one of them I was involved in and I was part of it I think. I really did get involved in the subject and the people.'

Where de Normanville pursued his speciality in science, Erulkar embraced diversity. While she opted for more wide-ranging briefs, she refrained from crossing into other (possibly more lucrative) genres. As committed documentary film-makers they jointly decided not to make the leap into features or television. Erulkar – again in contrast with conventional wisdom – had the impression that television documentaries were 'more regulated': 'I think they had more rules', she surmised from the experiences of her peers who had crossed to the smaller screen. The latitude of the documentary world better befitted her professional persona and afforded ample scope for visual exploration: 'I think we were allowed to be more relaxed, not all the time trying to grab the audience. We were allowed to go outside the subject a bit in our films, and then come back to it.' Erulkar and de Normanville toyed with the idea of establishing their own production company, but after consideration they acknowledged that they both preferred the hands-on approach of directing and abandoned the notion.

After Erulkar had gone freelance de Normanville remained a prolific member of the SFU throughout the 1950s. Given his experience of aviation films, de Normanville was an apt choice of director for the ambitious film *High Speed Flight: Approaching the Speed of Sound* (1957) of which he was particularly proud – it became a standard training film on flying across the sound barrier for air forces around the world. This introduction to the principles and challenges of high-speed flight took advantage of Shell's ample budgets and has some spectacular aerial photography of planes performing dazzling feats. The SFU often incorporated animation techniques into predominantly live-action documentaries with great flair and the animated sequences used to demonstrate the repeating patterns of sound waves in *High Speed Flight* are particularly lively and stylish, reminiscent of Norman McLaren's avant-garde films. Ken Gay wrote that 'this is an exact (it is to the layman exacting) but never dull exposition of a problem in aerodynamics'.[11] For those who find the scientific background challenging, the film can instead be appreciated almost as an abstract work.

David Robinson wrote in praise of *High Speed Flight* that it demonstrates how 'Shell finds its own way to poetry, and in the process makes a real comment on its world.'[12] Edgar Anstey was equally enthusiastic, declaring that 'The series of films on *High Speed Flight* from Shell have not been equalled at any time in any country.'[13] Anstey went on, with a certain regret, to qualify his admiration of Shell films by alluding to the tension between the 'informational job in hand' of such films and expectations of 'originality of treatment'. Anstey says that the Shell films,

> and their now sometimes indistinguishable imitations from other sponsors still represent an important step in public information ... Yet many critics and international juries have got bored with their perfection. Critics seem to require something new in the style of treatment and particularly, perhaps, in the style of commentary.

Stuart Legg had earlier noted: 'It is perhaps not accidental that hardly a Shell film carries a credit to a commentary writer; it is one of the few units that still believe in the primacy of the visual.'[14] In de Normanville's films the uncredited writer and commentator is often de Normanville himself, and the sometimes earthbound tones do not always match the skyward visual delights. Legg also wrote: 'The SFU has little use for the accepted canons of showmanship' and perhaps de Normanville and the Unit would have deemed lively commentaries tantamount to flashiness. De Normanville wrote his scripts in the knowledge that they would be translated for international versions, and this also partly explains his tendency to functional language and delivery. In Shell films, Legg added finally, 'Showmanship is latent in the scientific approach itself.' This is likely to be a fair point for an audience already committed to, and well versed in, science, and de Normanville's films were often aimed at viewers who may have been less concerned by the sporadic flatness of delivery than those without an established knowledge of his subject matter.

Forming of Metals was released in 1957, the same year as *High Speed Flight*. It too makes startling use of the opportunity for spectacle 'latent' in its subject matter – the processing of red-hot metals in large-scale industrial works. This excellent film combines power and delicacy, aided by the stirring and soaring music composed by Edward Williams. The industrial processes are made clearly visible in such a way as to convey vital scientific information about them, while the remarkable camerawork (by Sidney Beadle and Eric Chamberlain) and music convey the beauty and rhythm of the hurtling red-hot sheets of metals. The production notes for the film report that 'for the close shots of huge red ingots, an asbestos blanket or steel sheet was used, where possible, to protect the camera and crew, yet sometimes the camera filter melted – and more than one member of the crew had their clothes set on fire or received burns from red hot flying scale'.[15] *Forming of Metals* won the Grand Prix at the Brussels World Festival in 1958. De Normanville's films often won awards at film festivals around the world and from the British Association of the Advancement of Science (now known as the British Science Association).

De Normanville's next major production, *Schlieren*, was released the following year, in 1958, and is another visual *tour de force*. It is an explanation of a technique used for photographing shockwaves in aerodynamic research. Schlieren photography is an eerily beautiful process which was invented by glassmakers to show up faults in their products, and the film fully exploits its visual potential right from the opening frames. The waves of rich colours sweeping across the frame again bring to mind the lively experimental films of McLaren. The technical ambitions of *Schlieren* meant that filming took place both in the laboratory and in a supersonic wind tunnel. The desired shots proved difficult to achieve in the wind tunnel and de Normanville had to ask Shell for two more weeks' filming time than had been scheduled, a request which was granted. In Peter de Normanville's interview as part of the BECTU History Project he recalls the challenges of making *Schlieren*, and his wife, Sarah Erulkar, interjects with a vivid anecdote. She tells of their visit to the Leipzig Film Festival (the year isn't mentioned) during which they had coffee with John Grierson, who told her husband that 'of course you're the Picasso of the documentary film world'. The bold and beautiful use of abstract shapes and colours in de Normanville's films, particularly in his work for Shell must have informed this flattering assessment. The print of the film viewed when researching this article has innumerable scratches and tramlines – it was clearly a much-seen film. The chief audience for such sponsored technical films was evidently a sizeable one and included those who used film for very practical purposes as a learning tool, a viewership seriously overlooked by film history.

De Normanville completed his career at Shell with a range of films made in the late 1950s and early '60s on topics such as fuels, lubricants and engines. The films include *Continuous Combustion* (1959), *Background to Performance* (1960), *Home Heating* (1962) ('a dreadful film' according to his wife), *Frontiers of Friction* (1962) and *Aviation Research Report* (1964). Gay, writing about *Frontiers of Friction*, perhaps summed up de Normanville's talents at the Shell Film Unit: 'this is a brilliant example of how a director with a clear mind and an extremely firm grasp of documentary technique can produce a technical subject film that satisfies any audience because of its clarity of exposition'.[16]

After fifteen years at the Shell Film Unit, de Normanville felt that he needed to make a choice to become 'a Shell man or a film man'. He opted for the latter. He said later that he felt lucky to leave when he did as he considered that the Unit subsequently went downhill. While de Normanville

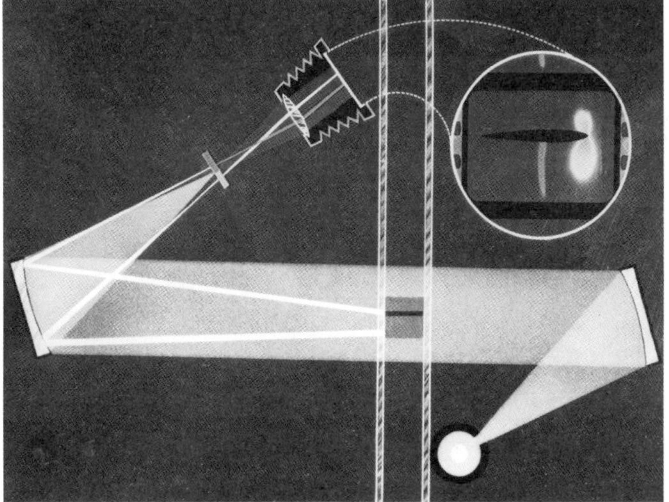

Peter de Normanville demonstrates *Schlieren*

was contemplating going freelance, Sarah Erulkar's own freelance career continued to flourish. Six years after making *District Nurse*, on the recommendation of Karel Reisz, Erulkar was sought by Anne Balfour-Fraser of Samaritan Films to make a film on Family Planning Services. 'A child's development as a person depends on many things, above all, whether he is wanted or not, loved or not, for that is his natural birthright.' These words of commentary resonantly delivered by acclaimed stage and screen actress Margaret Rawlings, convey the central premise of *Birthright* (1958), that birth control as advocated by the film's sponsor, the Family Planning Association (FPA), is conducive to 'happy family life'. Co-produced by Samaritan with Basic Films, when *Birthright* was released at the end of the 1950s, the FPA had been in existence for nearly three decades and the notion of contraception as a valid means by which to limit reproduction was by now generally accepted in Britain. The FPA's work in providing information, help and advice to people on a wide range of sexual-health issues, including controlling reproduction, infertility and sexually transmitted infections, is vaunted through dramatic enactments of visitors' experiences at some of the 300 FPA clinics that existed across Great Britain; by library footage of underprivileged women in India and Africa overburdened by their numerous offspring (who accompany their mothers to their factory jobs); and by an on-screen discussion on issues of birth control and population trends between three eminent members of the National Institute for Medical Research (NIMR): Sir Russell Brain, Prof. W. C. W. Nixon and Dr Alan Parkes.

In terms of charting attitudinal progress (or lack of) towards matters of sexuality in Britain, it is worth comparing *Birthright* with the first British film to advocate birth control, *Maisie's Marriage* (1923). Co-written by Dr Marie Stopes and based on her controversial best-selling publication *Married Love*, first published in 1918, *Maisie's Marriage* transmits, albeit more implicitly, the very

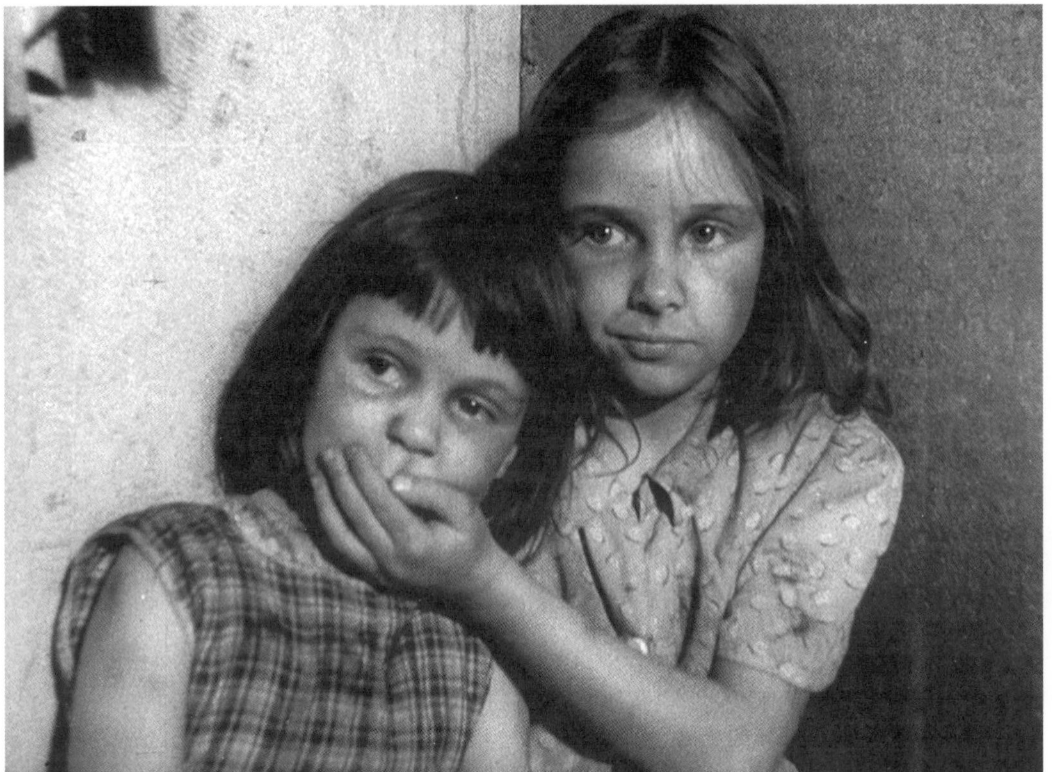

Birthright

same message propounded here. Both films graphically depict the misery associated with large families, especially when financial resources are limited, and advocate the use of contraception.

While birth control might have been commonplace in the late 1950s, it was subject to much demographic discrepancy. Scenes of large working-class families in their overcrowded domestic 'hell holes' are interlarded with more salubrious and tranquil depictions of small middle-class families dining together in harmony. The message is imparted with more bluntness than eloquence and is primarily directed at working-class women, among whom, we are told, fear and ignorance prevails: 'An unwanted child is an unhappy one. Unhappy children are the problem adults of the future.' The tripartite discussion between the NIMR scientists, intended to summarise intellectually the points suggested by the preceding sequences is stilted and interrupts the tonal flow of the film. The issues of unwanted pregnancy and illegal abortions, of which there are around '150 a day' and which can lead 'very often to sterility', are admittedly addressed with candour. Aside from this rather prolonged discussion, Erulkar's signature freshness of approach drives the essential points convincingly and the enactments are on a par with the 'kitchen-sink drama' trends in British feature film-making. Aptly matter-of-fact in tone, the film goes straight to the heart of the matter, opening on microscopic photographic images of sperm (apparently provided courtesy of cameraman, Wolfgang Suschitsky) as a backdrop for the opening titles, to be followed by graphic shots of a woman in the painful throes of labour. 'Family planning is a matter of great importance to the whole world ... I believe that the population of the world is growing so fast that by the time this film's finished there'll be a thousand more people alive than when it started,' pontificates one of the scientists. With the dawn of the 1960s, sexual attitudes radically changed. The pill was first prescribed in FPA clinics in 1961 and within ten years had become the contraceptive method of choice for over a million women.

The early 1960s saw further collaborations with Samaritan Films as disparately themed as *Woman's Work* (1961), charting the history of housework in England from the fourteenth century to present day; as editor on *Aircraft Fuelling* (1965), a demonstration of the sponsor, British Petroleum's, air fuelling and quality-control regulations (and Erulkar's first collaboration with de Normanville since she left Shell), as well as *Depression – Its Diagnosis in General Practice* (1963), on the importance of correct diagnosis of the mental affliction and its treatment. Also competing for Erulkar's expertise at this time was Rayant Pictures for whom she made a number of titles including the GPO classic *Ship to Shore* (1965), profiling the work of twelve GPO radio stations, with the added interest of the personal crises of officers at sea. So too was the Realist Film Unit, for whom, under the producership of J. B. Holmes, Erulkar directed *The Smoking Machine* (1963), a film for younger children which, through a Children's Film Foundation-style 'caper' narrative, served the Ministry of Health's first ever anti-smoking campaign. Erulkar addressed a similar age group, on two later major COI campaigns *Ready for the Road* (1970), about cycling proficiency, and the iconic *Never Go With Strangers* (1971).

Arnold Machin in *Picture to Post*

Among the scores of films she directed for various bodies in a freelance capacity through the next decade, Erulkar's directing and writing skills most notably effloresced in the visually immaculate *Picture to Post* (1969) and *The Air My Enemy*, which share the distinction, especially considering their relatively late dates, of being two of the most theatrically successful British documentary shorts ever. Produced by Rayant Pictures at the behest of the GPO, *Picture to Post* offers rare glimpses into the quiet vagaries of postage stamp design, but, like all good directors, Erulkar ensures that it works on multiple levels. Written and directed by Erulkar, *Picture to Post* delineates the differing techniques of three graphic designers: Arnold Machin, Jeffery Matthews and David Gentleman. Arnold Machin overcomes various design challenges in the construction of his definitive issue, a homage to Britain's inaugural adhesive stamp, the Penny Black, first issued in 1840. Primarily a sculptor, Machin first creates a Wedgwood-style clay relief of Elizabeth II, which is then painstakingly lit and photographed to achieve the requisite silhouetted effect. The result at once honours tradition and embraces modernity, as could also be said of the film, a delightful domestication of the more radical formalism of GPO design films of the 1930s. The film is also a valuable lesson in the principles of graphic design. In grappling with the miniaturist format all three designers gradually shed all superfluous detail in favour of increased abstraction.[17] Like the GPO Film Unit's best works, *Picture to Post* is as aesthetically triumphant as it is informative. It is also a fascinating prism through which to review the Britain into which it was released, in which scientific and technological achievement was the *leitmotif* of the era. Underlying Gentleman and Matthews' commemorative issues bearing such iconic symbols as Concorde, Jodrell Bank and the construction of the M4 viaduct, is a thinly veiled rapport with wider contemporary political objectives of the Wilson government's attempt to align the nation with technological and scientific advancement.

Erulkar's success in bringing universal appeal to such specialist subject matter was acclaimed in a contemporary *Film News* review: 'By use of the full range of colour-cinematographic techniques, the producers have made a film which will delight the cinephile as much as it will the philatelist.'[18] Innovative direction, aided by Douglas Ransom's adroitly constructed close-up photography and some judiciously used special effects, amplifies the miniaturist graphic assemblages to a theatrical scale. The film's high production value came to the attention of MGM who then selected *Picture to Post* for circuit release in ABC cinemas, and for world distribution in support of their feature release, *Alfred the Great* (1969), for which dubbed versions in German, Italian, Spanish and Japanese were prepared.[19] Gerald Boarer, the GPO's films officer, told Ken Gay: 'I think it is fairly safe to say that "Picture to Post" will be having about the biggest theatrical release afforded to a sponsored film since the war.'[20] Erulkar was clearly at the zenith of her career when she made *Picture to Post* and she later spoke of the personal and professional satisfaction she derived from this particular project: 'I remember it as being one of the happiest films I made really. I had a wonderful time. David Gentleman was a lovely man and I just enjoyed the subject as well.' The review already quoted from gives some insight into the respect that the quality of Erulkar's directing elicited:

> We have come to expect immaculate direction from Sarah Erulkar, and this film about the whole process of designing and producing recent British stamp issues does not disappoint us in a single detail. Not only has it a rich elegant surface, but it employs a number of technical rarities in a thoroughly justifiable way. ... I give this short top marks in the documentary class: indeed it is technically superior to most of the features that masquerade as entertainment these days.[21]

The 'technical rarities' he alludes to, most likely refer to the aforementioned special effects which include split screens (sometimes triple screens) and filtered-lens photography which do not distract but rather serve to facilitate audience understanding of complex design principles. *Picture to Post* won the 1969 Society of Film & Television Arts' Best Short Film award. (The same year, Peter de Normanville's physics film, *Let There Be Light*, sponsored by Joseph Lucas, won for Best Specialised

Film – one of several times that the husband and wife won awards in different categories of the same event.) *The Air My Enemy*, produced by Anthony Gilkinson Associates, transcends its remit in promoting the use of natural gas on behalf of the Gas Council, reaching an epic eeriness comparable with the previous year's similarly themed *Shadow of Progress*, though more modish in its technique. It secured a Silver Medal Award at the 1971 Venice Festival of Documentary and Short Films and, like *Picture to Post*, it was accepted for commercial distribution, in this case through Columbia Pictures.

If *Picture to Post* was a career high point, Erulkar's subsequent assignment *Korean Spring* (1969), a Rayant commission from Caltex Petroleum, was certainly the low point. She described the experience as 'the worst few weeks of my life'. The remit was to present a positive image of Korea through its landscape, life and culture in order to put the country back on the industrial and tourist map. A seven-week location shoot, the project promised a fascinating and challenging directing opportunity for Erulkar, but on arrival in Seoul she realised that the Korean production crew had been expecting a man and were not happy taking orders from a woman. As well as having to contend with such prejudice, the production was dogged with administrative obstacles, such as unanticipated demands for payments to shoot in certain locations. She felt that Rayant producer John Durst had made a mistake in sending her to Korea.

Since his departure from Shell, de Normanville had similarly gone on to make films for a range of different organisations, often on a freelance basis. De Normanville's film *Critical Path* (1963), made for the Costain Film Unit, allowed him to take the logical approach that underlay his film-making and apply it to a contemporary, 'scientific' management technique, namely critical-path analysis. Acquired for distribution by the Central Film Library, it went on to become one of the CFL's most frequently booked titles for several years. De Normanville also maintained his oilfield connections, making *78 Rivers* (1965) for the Burmah Oil Company. This film is about an ambitious venture – an oil pipeline which crosses the number of rivers in the title – in which he worked in India with an Indian crew. Still in the oil field, but moving to BP, de Normanville produced *Aircraft Fuelling* and directed *From Tanker to Fueller* (1966) both made by Samaritan Films with whom Erulkar also worked. He then made films for a range of organisations including the COI, IBM and Barclays Bank, at a number of production companies including World Wide, Millbank Films, Pelican Films and Anthony Gilkinson Associates.

Sadly, many of these items are no longer extant – or at any rate they are not held by the BFI National Archive. One of the exceptions is de Normanville's film *Carbon* (1968), produced by Gilkinson and made with cinematographer Wolfgang Suschitzky, whose lovely visuals make its 'dissertation on carbon', as de Normanville described it, almost into an abstract film. Fellow science film-maker and author Alex Strasser bracketed *Carbon* with John Armstrong's Unilever film *The Structure of Protein* (1969), and declared that 'these two factual films put many art films into the shade'.[22]

Stints working with British Transport Films followed, including directing *The Future Works* (1969) about the modernisation of railway workshops. For Barclays Bank at Millbank Productions, *GIGO – Garbage In, Garbage Out* (1969) covers the uses of computers. It was something of a pioneering film as computers were still a mystery to most people in the 1960s. It's likely that de Normanville would have relished the opportunity to grow his interest in the technical sphere from the more traditional aeronautics and engineering of his early career to the new, emerging realm of information technology. The film won awards, but unsurprisingly now appears highly dated, not only in the display of old-fashioned equipment, but also in the explanation on the commentary, which to computer-literate generations will seem heavy-handed. De Normanville's characteristically direct approach to the relaying of information also came to the fore in *Leprosy* (1974). Indeed, his very intention was 'not to wring our hearts like other leprosy films', but instead 'recruit 300 to be doctors, nurses, researchers'. His suspicion of feelings interfering with facts is exemplified by the way in which the atmospheric, bravura opening featuring shadowy lighting and dramatic music and a white-coated scientist looking into a microscope is quickly brought down to earth when the distinctly dry narration kicks in. While de Normanville claimed that the film's weakness was that it was too long, it is intriguing to speculate whether the film might have had greater propaganda value, and success as a recruitment film, if it combined the factual aspect with more of the heightened mood promised by the opening shots. In the late 1970s de Normanville continued to work as a freelance director, making *Islam and the Sciences* (1978) through Anne Balfour-Fraser's Inca Films, in which film-makers worked with objects in the collection of the Science Museum. De Normanville's final two works were released in 1983. *Coal, the Bridge*, a BP Film made at Balfour Films, demonstrates the intriguing prospect that (given the film's sponsor) coal might replace oil. *The Energy Problem – The Nuclear Solution*, an Antony Barrier production, concurs on the leading importance of coal, despite the implications of the title, though adding that uranium is also of vital importance. The film was sponsored by the UK Atomic Energy Authority. Both films were made as government policy was decisively shifting away from coal and towards the nuclear option.

Having worked together in 1965 on *Aircraft Fuelling*, a Samaritan Films/BP production that de Normanville produced and Erulkar edited, the pair's career paths would cross twice more. First, there was *The Living City* (1977), the BAFTA Best Factual Short-winning film that brought Erulkar back to her birthplace, Calcutta. Then there was *Toilers of the Deep* (1980), made for the Royal National Mission to Deep Sea Fishermen. Gay's *Films & Filming* review encapsulates the *Living City* project as 'a moving account of the human condition in the vast Indian city, well worth seeing'.[23] The film documents the physical improvement programme of the Calcutta Metropolitan Authority, particularly the modernisation of the 'bustees' (slums), and was intended to raise awareness among westerners of overseas development. Erulkar's final film saw another return to India, this time to direct *Disease Called Leprosy* (1984) for Graphic Films on behalf of the Leprosy Relief Association. Filmed in South India and New Delhi, it concerns the treatment and rehabilitation of patients suffering from the disease and includes footage of the work of the Kumbakonam Leprosy Hospital. De Normanville, of course, had gone to Africa ten years earlier to address very similar subject matter for the same sponsor in *Leprosy*. *The Living City* fittingly brings together the best of both their approaches: Erulkar's warmth, de Normanville's precision and the absorption of both in their subject matter.

Husband and wife more or less simultaneously ended their directing careers in the mid-1980s, Erulkar mainly on account of encroaching arthritis and her lack of enthusiasm for video. In 1999 her husband died of lung cancer. In her retirement Erulkar has pursued a lifelong passion for antiques and, in her late eighties, continues working as an antique seller in North London. Her inherent artistry and her passion for life, people and art remain. The films she and her late husband made were very widely seen and inspired and informed audiences around the world. As John Grierson recognised in his 'Picasso' accolade to de Normanville, the films are both works of art and pieces of historical record. The nearly 200 films made by Sarah Erulkar and Peter de Normanville convey between them nearly all the issues of the twentieth century – social and technological – which transformed the lives of their generation.

NOTES

1. BECTU History Project interview with Sarah Erulkar conducted by John Taylor, 28 February 1991. Other biographical details included in this piece are indebted to this source.
2. Peter Baylis and Jack Howells, 'Pas de Deux', *Documentary Film News* vol. 7 no. 68, p. 92.
3. During World War II, Erulkar read sociology at Bedford College for Women, a constituent School of the University of London. During wartime Erulkar and her fellow students were evacuated to Cambridge University.
4. BECTU History Project interview with Peter de Normanville (with interjections from Sarah Erulkar) by John Taylor, 28 February 1991. Other biographical details included in this piece are indebted to this source.
5. *Scientific Film Review*, April 1953, no. 1, p. 2.
6. *Scientific Film Review*, March 1955, no. 9, pp. 1–2.
7. *Scientific Film Review*, September 1955, no. 11, p. 2.
8. *The Times*, 2 October 1967, p. 24.
9. Interview with Sarah Erulkar by Katy McGahan, 8 December 2009.
10. Ibid.
11. Ken Gay, 'How Free Can We Be?', *Films and Filming*, September 1957, p. 33.
12. David Robinson, 'Looking for Documentary Part 2', *Sight & Sound* vol. 27 no. 2, Autumn 1957, p. 72.
13. Edgar Anstey, 'The Trend for Documentary', *Scientific Film Scientifique*, December 1964, p. 138.
14. Stuart Legg, 'Shell Film Unit: Twenty-One Years', *Sight & Sound* vol. 23 no. 4, April–June 1954, p. 210.
15. Publicity material held in the BFI National Library, *Forming of Metals*, 'Making the Film', p. 1.
16. Ken Gay, 'Has Britain Had It?', *Films and Filming*, August 1963, p. 34.
17. For further reading see Peter Jones's excellent article for the *Journal of Design History: Posting the Future: British Stamp Design and the 'White Heat' of a Technological Revolution* vol. 17 no. 2, 2004.
18. *Film News*, Spring 1970, no. 72, pp. 72–5.
19. Undated letter from the films officer of the GPO Publicity Branch to Ken Gay.
20. Letter to Ken Gay from Gerald F. Boarer, Films Officer at the Post Office Publicity Branch, dated 20 February 1970.
21. *Film News*, Ibid.
22. Alex Strasser, *The Work of the Science Film Maker* (London and New York: Focal Press, 1972), p. 67.
23. *Films and Filming* vol. 24 no. 12, September 1978, p. 36.

15 Shooting the Message: *John Krish*

PATRICK RUSSELL

'AN IDIOSYNCRATIC CAREER'

'It has been an idiosyncratic career, with children's films and documentaries and TV commercials interspersed with the odd feature.' So concludes a brief encyclopaedia entry on John Krish's thirty-seven years directing films.[1]

In the YouTube age, the pre-eminence of ninety-minute features over films of all other types and lengths is certainly in retreat: mixed careers will no longer seem so eccentric. Yet perhaps there may be more to Krish's idiosyncrasy than that: a resistance to fitting into the obvious pigeonholes; an equally refreshing refusal of cynicism.

Let's take a look ...

BEGINNINGS

John Krish was born in 1923, fourth and youngest son of a London Jewish family of quite recent Russian and Polish descent. Krish's father, Serge, had already lifted himself from total obscurity, to become a distinguished musician. His New Metropolitan Symphony Orchestra had brought classical music to the streets of the interwar East End, and he became a fixture, too, on national radio as leader of the Serge Krish Septet.

John, much younger than his brothers (though close to the middle brother, Felix) inherited his father's musicality, being able to play piano well by ear, but was prevented by him from learning to read sheet music. This was ostensibly to protect the younger Krish from the hardships and stresses of professional musicianship with which the older Krish was painfully familiar. The son suspects to this day that the father's jealousy was a subconscious motive. Whatever its cause, it profoundly affected him. More generally, Krish remembers having felt misunderstood as a child – common enough, in his generation as in others, but in his own case a sensation powerfully felt that, he now speculates, stimulated his later drive for firm control over his work. His formal education came to end in 1939 when he was fifteen and an evacuee. Returning to London in time for the blitz, his first job was in a local estate agents, his second as a clerk in a huge office of a biscuit factory. Then, in an unprompted act of adolescent pluck, he took the step on which his professional destiny would turn.

On a school visit, a screening of *Night Mail* in the Science Museum's cinema had enthralled Krish. Remembering it in 1941, and still restless, he resolved to work for the GPO Film Unit. Discovering it had been renamed and moved to Beaconsfield, he turned up, surprised to find guards at the gate. Thinking quick, he recalls, he told them he had an appointment with production manager Dora Wright. They let him in and Wright, perhaps out of sheer surprise at his gumption, brought him in to meet Ian Dalrymple. A week later, he was on the books, and in the midst of what

John Krish

is now legend. Then, it was merely a fresh world of good, hard work amid the sort of adult company the teenager had longed for, and an invaluable apprenticeship, at a paltry 17/6 a week, in the skills and joys of the medium.

It's significant that, almost without exception, in every article or interview from his later career, John Krish is at pains to point out how much he owes to the Crown Film Unit.

Krish found himself a junior assistant on Harry Watt's *Target for Tonight*, and went on to assist the editors and directors of films by Pat Jackson, J. B. Holmes, Jack Lee and (on *Listen to Britain*, no less) Jennings and McAllister. Krish found Watt abrupt and bullying, Jackson and Lee charming and kind. He quickly developed a deep affection for the chivalrous Holmes. And Jennings? Not the mythopoeic genius of cultural memory (invention not least of Lindsay Anderson, of whom, more later ...). For young Krish, Jennings was unmistakeably flesh-and-blood: an intimidating, inspiring, exhausting colleague. As we'll see in the second half of this chapter, his later screen-craft unconsciously blended the influences of the two father figures: Jennings's inventive, single-minded perfectionism tempered by Holmes's gentleness and professionalism. The premature deaths of both upset him greatly.[2]

Krish was called up in 1942, but in view of his Crown experience, after time in the Royal Artillery, and a life-threatening bout of meningitis, he was transferred into the Army Film and Photographic Unit, where he was one of the cutters on Carol Reed and Garson Kanin's *The True Glory* (1945). This in turn led to his being employed at the American War Office of Information's London office, editing official newsreel rushes – and to his being one of the first people to view, entirely unprepared for what was in the cans handed him that day, the dread images that confronted the first cameras at Dachau. To his newsreel period, Krish attributes a striving for 'simplicity and directness' in his later writing and direction. It also positioned him well to pick up editing work in a film industry adjusting to normality as war's dust settled.

Krish's brother Felix, who in the late 1930s had been considered a very promising stage actor, was among those who'd perished during the recent war.[3]

EDITOR TO DIRECTOR

Krish found employment at the growing Film Producers Guild, cutting films for several of its participating units, one of which, Ronald Riley's Technique Film Productions, offered him his first directing job. *Pattern for Progress* (1948) was filmed over two months at Richard Thomas & Baldwin's Ebbw Vale steelworks. Showcasing its modernised methods of steel-sheet production, the film runs for fifty minutes, replete with grand images of intricately spectacular metal fabrication: early signs of the compositional skill that would grace Krish's work.[4] But it never amounts to more than the over-extensive sum of its parts, which admittedly yield splendid stock footage.[5] The oft-clunking commentary (by Riley himself) replays the industrial film's 'man and machine' clichés without great care or conviction, while a sequence of cut-price Eisenstein has steelmen, shot from below, looking up, anticipating the conversion of iron to steel that climaxes in molten showers, while Krish the editor cuts back quicker and quicker to a barometer going off the scale. The novice director evidently learned two contrasting lessons from this production: neither to be content with treating familiar subject matter familiarly nor, conversely, to succumb to imposing 'art' onto craft.

The only Guild company Krish felt especially intrigued by was Greenpark, but its staff complement was full; he was happy to leave for Richard Massingham's Public Relationship Films, to edit and occasionally direct public-information shorts in Massingham's signature comic style. He also made his first important film there. *Health in our Time* (1948), for the Army, originated as a standard request for instructional material for soldiers. Krish lobbied to expand it into a kaleidoscopic treatment of health as a whole: the first time, of many, that Krish would challenge a sponsor. A portmanteau film, *Health in our Time*'s diverse sequences encapsulate many of the varied styles he would use in the films that followed, ending in an unexpectedly ambitious compressed reconstruction of the war in Burma. Hereon, human drama would prove particularly fundamental to Krish's conception of documentary.

In recent years, Massingham has acquired a loveable cult reputation, but Krish found him amateurish, soon joining instead the faltering documentary sector's great white hope. At the newly inaugurated British Transport Films, he made four shorts. Holmes was among his new colleagues, and they co-directed *This Year – London* (1951). One of the earliest and most agreeable entries in BTF's decades-long cycle of soft-sell enticements to travel, it was Krish's first fully realised piece. Covering a Leicester shoe factory's works outing to London, it was filmed by the two directors with six cameramen in seventeen hours flat, following the party to all the major tourist sites and filming their boat-trip down the Thames. They came up with the device of including a journalist covering the trip: the faintly bohemian bearded and check-jacketed fellow seen in the film is a genuine correspondent, not an actor as modern viewers might suspect. His end of the deal was to write the narration – but he disappeared into thin air, and so, deadline looming, Edgar Anstey pressed Krish into doing it: he had already written *Health in our Time* and from this point onwards, writing as well as directing was his usual dual role. Using a conversational multi-voice narration the script brings out the sincerity and sentiment implicit in the footage, affectionately kidding the foibles of the characters on screen, gently shading their sunny day out with moments of contemplation triggered by reminders everywhere of two world wars.

Inverting this happy experience, *Away for the Day* (1952) necessitated making a month's stressful shooting look like it had captured a single day's worth of relaxing countryside coach-trips round the country. Rigid notions of realism never burdened Krish's documentaries: more of a problem was that this film represented a lapse in Anstey's usually high technical standards. It was shot, late in the coaching season, in experimental 16mm Kodachrome,[6] sometimes lending it a pleasant home-movie quality but more often an unattractively muddy look, to which thin music was unfeelingly applied. For pretty much the last time, Krish allowed himself to get away with flat and clichéd words and visuals, even ending the film on the ultimate travelogue chestnut: a perfunctory shot of a sunset.

Krish's only internal film at BTF, *They Had an Idea* (1953), was better, a cheerful early contribution to the post-war productivity-at-work genre. It follows four reconstructed case studies of transport employees who'd ingeniously improved their workplace processes. Krish having honed the visual ambition of his debut, his directorial touches (close-ups on drills chiselling into wood, shadows falling behind machinery, long tracking shots down workshops) serve the subject instead of overwhelming it. Tellingly, though, when the film comes to *life* is when 'people' rather than 'things' are at centre stage.

Nothing in these three pleasant films suggests their director was about to make a small classic. One day, Anstey asked him to go out and take, for record purposes, a few shots of the ceremony marking the end of London's trams system. The most famous incident in Krish's career followed, and needn't be retold in detail here. Krish argued that they should make a proper film of it. Anstey refused. With a modicum of back-office connivance, Krish and a gang of fellow-renegades raided the stock cupboard, dragged their heavy equipment on the bus to south London and spent a week making the film anyway. *The Elephant Will Never Forget* (1953) sets its richly textured imagery of the doomed trams to an inspired soundtrack combination: nostalgic narration, melancholy Edward Williams score and an exuberant music-hall sing-song (recorded at a Darby and Joan Club). A faultless mixture of film-making poise with warm, pensive romanticism ... and as the oft-told story goes, no sooner was it finished than Anstey immediately fired Krish. The ostensible grounds were that (not yet thirty) he should make way for new blood. Was Anstey's truer motive a personal anger at Krish having proved his film-making instincts wrong, or a dispassionate civil service imposition of due penalty on his employee for having, undeniably, broken the rules, disobeyed a superior and allowed an otherwise tight ship to drift off-message?

Either way: it made theatrical release. It made the Edinburgh Film Festival. It eventually made it into British cinema's folk memory, becoming perhaps BTF's best-loved, and certainly Krish's most popularly remembered film (though it's not entirely typical of either's general output).

And its immediate effect on its director was to plunge him into a period of career uncertainty.

FREELANCING AND WORLD WIDE

Over the next three years Krish took freelance work from two companies with radically divergent film-making agendas but similarly miniscule budgets: DATA Film Productions and Republic Pictures. For the American studio's London outpost, Krish made a series of episodes of the *Stryker of the Yard* series of B-features. For DATA, he directed a handful of *Mining Review* stories. Playing to his emerging strengths as a director of people, they include some cracking items, like one covering a double-date weekend break on Barry Island, and another showcasing Rotherham FC's mascot comedy kazoo band.[7] Krish also made a longer film, *One Day in Perfect Health* (1955), about the London School for Tropical Hygiene. The picture element for this film hasn't survived but Krish reports that it was a disappointment on account of poor sound recording and editing. Like most DATA directors, he thoroughly enjoyed working with miners but, unlike the cooperative's members, he had no particular interest in its ideological navel-gazing, and felt it was inefficiently run.

In late 1955, the young director again found stable employment and a monthly salary at an established documentary unit by joining World Wide Pictures, whose other directors at the time included Paul Dickson, Peter Hopkinson and James Hill. Against the pattern of Krish's whole career, films from his World Wide period feel transitional, but it's important to be aware of the firm's set-up. At this point, James Carr was running it on the basis of bringing in as much work as possible, then farming out different stages of the numerous resulting productions to the multi-skilled people on his roster based on their availability. So they'd find themselves on four or five projects simultaneously, writing one while directing another and supervising editing of a third, seeing few through from start to finish. And lest the present account of Krish's career seems to veer towards auteurism, it's worth noting that among his World Wide films, the most-viewed at the time, certainly the one most fulsomely acclaimed by its own sponsor, was his first, and it's far from characteristic. *Under Your Bonnet* (1956), sponsored by Chloride Batteries, lay at the heart of its campaign 'against the cheap and unreliable batteries ... being encouraged by the post-war boom in cars'.[8] Screened up and down the country by a dedicated mobile projection unit, it formed the centrepiece to a full evening of sales-orientated entertainment. Krish's last industrial film is his most capable, and he pursues its sales mission with due diligence, but it again betrays his indifference to technical subjects, even if bringing disarming gentleness to an often-bombastic genre. Sublime Bruckner supplies the soundtrack to the industrial climaxes.

Krish's other World Wide productions enjoyed lower profiles, but had more in common with his future work, especially by their progressively more assured blending of fact with fiction – better put, their use of fiction technique to communicate matters of fact vividly. In *Instructional Technique* (1959, for the RAF) and *Consider Your Verdict* (1959, for the Milk Marketing Board!) Krish made his first contributions to that peculiar post-war form, the allegorical comedy-documentary. Perhaps Massingham's influence rubbed off on these enjoyable (if, by today's standards, overlong) fantasy courtroom comedies. But two other Armed Forces films made by Krish at the company were deadly serious in intent and approach. *Break-In* (1957) orchestrates an entirely professional cast, including Wilfred Brambell and Jim Dale, to enact a military police investigation, climaxing at a garrison theatre music-hall show.

The director's most ambitious production to date took a year to research and produce. The Army needed a film to make soldiers aware of the brainwashing techniques that could be used against British prisoners, as they had been in Korea. Writing and directing the hour-long *Captured* (1959), set in a Korean prisoner-of-war camp, Krish, on a budget minute in comparison to most films of its length, consummately establishes a claustrophobic ambience, delineates acrimonies among his group of confined characters, and ratchets up the suspense through a series of interrogation sequences climaxing in an agonising water-torture scene.

The director was lucky that his period at World Wide also coincided with its turn at contributing to the Children's Film Foundation's production programme, enabling him to make a splendidly streetwise shaggy-dog story called *The Salvage Gang* (1958), blessed with good performances, lovely London location footage, above all with the film-makers' respect for young audiences, as worthy of accomplished entertainment as any other (predictably, Krish did *not* get on with Children's Film Foundation head Mary Field; but Paul Rotha, no less, proclaimed the film 'better in all ways than many feature films in the same year though made for about a tenth of the cost'[9]). Still, it was *Captured* that he hoped would demonstrate his skill with scripts and actors to features producers.

Fortunately for this book, his graduation to feature films was to be deferred.

THE CLORE YEARS

Frances Cockburn was an editor at World Wide; Krish had been her assistant back in Crown days. In 1955, soon after Krish arrived at Carr's company, her career took a step up when she was appointed to the COI's Films Division. Leon Clore, increasingly successful in landing COI contracts, dealt with her frequently. Cockburn recommended John Krish to him as a film-maker to watch – one now growing restive. Carr's rota system had caused *Band Wagon* (1958), a witty musical treatment that he and fast friend Kevin Brownlow had worked out for a Ford Cars film, to end up being directed by Hopkinson (whose execution is a tad heavier-handed than the concept deserves). His being forced to shoot *Consider Your Verdict* in 16mm was a frustrating false economy (given the smaller gauge's restricted range of lenses). He was exasperated when his supervision of a film called *Every Drop To Drink* (1959) was stymied by the company's kid-gloves treatment of its sponsor.[10] The final frustration, this time not World Wide's fault, was when the MOD followed its delighted acclaim for *Captured* by slapping a 'Restricted' notice on it, because of its sensitive subject matter. Unviewable even by squaddies unless in the presence of a designated commanding officer,[11] no producer would ever be allowed to see Krish's calling card.

He was quick, then, to accept the offer of full-time employment by Clore. And it's Krish's work between 1959 and 1964, most of it done at Clore's principal companies, Basic and Graphic, that should secure his importance as a film-maker – and an instructive case study in the unique possibilities and constraints of post-war documentary.

New colleagues included older-generation documentarians like Sam Napier-Bell (the original head of Basic Films) but also (working mainly under the Graphic banner) freethinking film-makers of Krish's own generation: Lindsay Anderson, Karel Reisz, Anthony Simmons. Krish rather fell between the two stools, making his own those 'films geared to specialised or general audiences, but of general appeal dealing with or exposing a social problem'.[12] Though they had a certain brusqueness in common, Clore and Carr ran their companies quite differently. By all accounts, the producer was quick to support directors wanting to do interesting things with documentary and sponsorship. Hence his patronage of Anderson and Reisz's Free Cinema – to which Simmons reacted with ambivalence, Krish with contempt. Clore offered, rather than allocated, films to directors, meaning creative leadership of the entire project from treatment to final cut, and he would reliably back them whenever conflict with a sponsor loomed. Which in Krish's case wasn't uncommon.

The first one ran smoothly, though. *I Want to Go to School* (1959) was produced by Graphic for the National Union of Teachers, to publicise the ethos of modern primary schools. It was aimed especially,

> at showing to parents something of what happens to their children when they are working and playing at school, so that the two worlds of home and school can be brought closer together ... one of the first occasions on which a professional association has sponsored a film of social interest free from any sort of self-publicity.[13]

Shot over six weeks at a single school, the film brought to the waning social documentary an unexpected freshness noted by its many reviewers. Indeed it's arguably Krish's most successful film if judged by number of column inches generated. That was thanks especially to the BBC taking it up for no fewer than three transmissions, to the delight of the NUT (which also, as intended, made it available to its own local branches).

Krish's next project was *Counterpoint* (1959), by Basic for the GPO through the COI: his first film since *They Had an Idea* to deal with human relations in the workplace. Returning to the comedy-doc idiom, it was professionally acted throughout (though filmed in a real post office). Like the NUT film, it's shaped as a day-in-the-life narrative, but focused on a fictional

individual, a well-intentioned, slightly head-in-clouds clerk (the highlight sequence is his lunch-break day-dream). Unusually, it was targeted at employees and customers simultaneously – to trigger the employees to improve service, their clientele to appreciate the pressures they were under, as part of a nationwide counter-service campaign. In muted echo of *Captured*'s fate, this benign, fun little short was restricted. This time it was reputedly because the government's new postmaster general Reginald Bevins thought the lead character's name, Reg, was some sort of dig. If so, he was flattering himself: the scripting and filming were done when his predecessor Ernest Marples was in office.[14]

Krish would utilise comedy again, in two Basic films for the British Council, *What's the Time* and *What's the Price* (both 1961), distributed abroad to help with English teaching. But before then, on account of the NUT film's domestic impact, the COI had asked for Krish by name when commissioning Clore to produce the Foreign Office's big prestige production of 1959–60. Part of Britain's contribution to International Refugee Year, it was initially intended merely to extol her solid national record on the issue. Following tense debate with the sponsors, *Return to Life* (1960) became in Basic's hands an evocation of the emotional experience of the exile. Though not widely shown at home, it had the widest international reach of any of Krish's documentaries, translated into ten languages for cinema, non-theatrical and TV screenings. A scripted story documentary about a refugee family, it was filmed over four weeks, in just about the tensest circumstances imaginable, with actual (and unrelated) refugees as actors. It possesses an unusual, affecting mixture of tenderness and toughness.

Krish's reputation was burgeoning, as a singular director suited to humanistic briefs, and one with a rare talent for directing children. So when Clore was re-engaged by the National Society for the Prevention of Cruelty to Children (Anderson and Margaret Thomson having both directed NSPCC appeal films at Basic in the 1950s), Krish was an obvious match. This time he was faced with the challenge of making a piece for screening at schools to children from 'good homes', to prompt them to donate pocket money to the NSPCC's youth wing (named, with horrible Victorian pomp, the League of Pity) – but with a strict prohibition on depicting any cruelty. Initially flummoxed, the director discovered that the money was spent on day-trips for groups of deprived children – and remembered the shoemakers' outing of ten years before. With four cameras his unit filmed a trainful of children travelling from Birmingham to Weston Super Mare and then their day at the seaside. Graphic Films' *They Took Us to the Sea* (1961) was photographed, edited and scored with a true – but unobtrusive – lyricism, and a compassion that is gently handled but bittersweet (at several junctures, Krish fleetingly cuts away from the seaside to pithy glimpses of the Birmingham slums and wastelands momentarily left behind). The seemingly simple short film lingers long in viewers' memories.

Clore next offered Krish a project about youth employment, for the Department of Labour, via the COI – with whom the producer-director team won another battle, to make an anti-realist-scripted film with synch dialogue and even special effects. For Basic, *Mr Marsh Comes to School* (1961) features Reginald Marsh as a mysteriously magical Youth Employment Officer, breaking spatio-temporal barriers to reveal to a group of fifteen-year-olds the breadth of possible futures beckoned by the waiting working world. Next, the NUT was back, asking for a follow-up to its earlier collaboration with Graphic, to be made this time at a secondary modern school. Advancing but modifying its predecessor's technique, *Our School* (1962) was another life-in-the-day documentary swiftly taken up by the BBC, as well as non-theatrically, with great success.

In the same period as his paid work at Basic and Graphic, Krish helmed two independent documentaries in his own time. *Let My People Go* (1961) was produced for the Committee to Boycott South African Goods, on a similar basis to *March to Aldermaston* (1959), whose mastermind, Derrick Knight, was originally slated to direct it, but with involvement from a much wider public, following a national newspaper appeal. It was made a section at a time. Each time the money ran out, the producers ran screenings of the incomplete production, and passed the hat round. It was after production commenced, but before completion, that the Sharpeville massacre occurred: it was included in the film, ensuring a more attentive audience than it might otherwise have got. *Let My People Go* was photographed by Walter Lassally, with music contributed by Michael Tippett, and co-written by Krish and Napier-Bell with James Cameron (a significant selling point, Cameron having written well-regarded books about Africa). It combines studio dramatic reconstructions directed by Krish (based on incidents that Father Trevor Huddleston had written about) with rostrum work by Napier-Bell and incisively edited found – and smuggled – footage. The completed film was commended by such public figures as A. J. Ayer for making tangible to British viewers the hitherto abstract-seeming evils of apartheid. In addition to its expected outlets Granada Television broadcast it in North-west England (it wasn't televised elsewhere).[15]

Ever since BTF days (when filming *Away for the Day* and recording *The Elephant Will Never Forget*'s musical accompaniment brought him into rewarding contact with elderly people), Krish had thought of making a film on old age, urging viewers to do something about the plight of lonely pensioners in their midst. His industry reputation as a social documentarist now securely established, he felt it was time to press ahead with finding funding. Kevin Brownlow was now working for Anne Balfour-Fraser. Krish took the project to her, knowing the worthy intentions that informed her dablings in film. Sure enough, she secured relatively generous patronage from the Craignish Trust, a Scottish charity connected to her in-laws' distilling interests, for the production of a film by her company Samaritan Films. *I Think They Call Him John* (1964) is the austere, intense documentary of an old man, John Ronson, and his uneventful day at home in his flat. Its sounds and images marshalled with inconspicuous perfection, its pacing uncompromisingly deliberate and unswervingly sure, its meaning boldly direct, *I Think They Call Him John* is likely to prove (alongside *They Took Us to the Sea*) the most enduring item in Krish's filmography.

By this point, Krish's break into features was finally starting to happen, beginning with *Unearthly Stranger* (1963), a low-budget but sinisterly effective science-fiction fable in *Invasion of the Body Snatchers* (1956) vein, scored by his documentary friend Edward Williams. Through the rest of the decade, Krish's only brush with non-fiction was the making of the BBC2 series *Anatomy of the Film*, a six-part authored programme that he presented, exploring all aspects of film production. One episode was devoted to factual film, Krish advising his viewers, 'if you want to know how a film is put together from start to finish, I say start in Documentary', pragmatically defined as 'films made outside the accepted commercial set-up which try to reveal what we, the human race are, so that we can be more aware'.[16]

INTERMISSION

At this point, with our subject embarking on a feature-film career, it's worth pausing to sum up the remarkably productive preceding few years. Though John Krish's name wasn't well known to the public, within the industry he was its premier humanist-for-hire, virtually personifying (as Paul Dickson briefly had before him) the endurance of a social ethos in sponsored film-making.

In respect of their distribution, these films circulated mainly in three spaces, assuming slightly different meanings in each. Their principal life was non-theatrical, booked mainly for the various specialist purposes for which they were intended, but frequently too for groups of general viewers. Most of his films – not just the COI productions, but also the NUT and British Council ones – were hireable from the Central Films Library, while Contemporary managed the two independent productions. It's clear that some of them reached North American non-theatrical audiences. But the more ambitious films were also very visible on the festival circuit, in Britain and abroad – touted, and sometimes winning prizes, as artistic shorts.[17] Finally, as we've seen, a few made high-profile crossings to the living room, presented there as documentaries of general interest to television viewers.

Post-BTF, significant UK cinema distribution eluded all Krish's documentaries. *Return to Life* received a limited West End release, and Clore presumably, and plausibly, had theatrical ambitions for the accessible yet lushly cinematic *They Took Us to the Sea*: the prints he later donated to the BFI have censor certificates attached. There's no evidence he got very far with that. Contemporary managed to get *Let My People Go* into the prestigious art-house Academy Cinema, supporting *A Bout de souffle* (1960), no less. Krish was hopeful they might persuade cinemas to book *I Think They Call Him John*, an indelible experience when seen with an audience in a theatre. Exhibitors apparently judged it too bleak to risk with paying punters.[18]

It's also important to appreciate the economics of Krish's career, by introducing an element we've so far overlooked. A 1964 article reported that he 'has directed eight sponsored shorts over the past four years', which,

> would appear to have kept Krish and his family (he has three children) for about a year. Payment for a script, including all the research entailed, averages about £120, and the fee for direction, including supervision through the editing stages, about twice that, although it can be as low as £100. A shorts film-maker choosy about his subjects can only survive by also directing commercials, where £100 for a day's work is far from rare.[19]

When Krish joined Clore in 1959, television advertising was taking off. He had got himself on exclusive contract with J. Walter Thompson: Krish and Joseph Losey had an amicable pairing arrangement whereby if JWT needed one to direct an ad and he was busy with another project, the other would step up to the plate. Then when Clore formed Film Contracts to put his directors' advertising on a firmer footing Krish joined the company. Through the 1960s, Krish was making around half a dozen commercials most years. Without them it would have been impossible for him to direct the apartheid and old-age films, or to exercise a degree of choice over his Basic and Graphic work.

LATER CAREER

Krish's promising features career was beset by frustrations: the imposition of a seriously unsuitable lead actress on *The Wild Affair* (1964), forcible exclusion from the cutting-room of his contemporary adaptation of Waugh's *Decline and Fall* (1968) and on-set troubles and vicious studio politics descending upon *The Man Who Had Power Over Women* (1970), inherited at short notice.[20] None of these films is perfect, but they all have their moments, and compared with the feature-film legacies of Rotha, Watt, Jackson or Dickson, they're a solid trio. But it wasn't entirely without relief that, on the turn of the decade, Krish resumed making documentaries at Graphic (in the late 1960s, Krish had also taken on television assignments; he it was who directed *The Avengers*' iconic colour credits sequence). Krish's first 1970s documentary was *Maths With Everything* (1971), a twist on the education theme, being sponsored by the Nuffield Maths Project to show teachers being trained in its experimental maths teaching techniques before taking them back to their own schools. *What Are They Doing at College* (1973) returned Krish to the world of the teenager, revealing the value of Further Education Colleges via a group-discussion trigger film format. And for younger children, Krish made *Red Cross – That's Us* (1974), a recruiting aid for the British Red Cross youth wing, capturing the range of its work in a brisk, contemporary style.

Krish also made one film for the Rank Short Films Group, *Communicating with a Group* (1972), of which no copies appear to have survived, but which was an instance of modern management training of the sort that had been emergent since the end of the 1960s. But by now, he was busier than ever with those thirty- and forty-five-second spots that filled TV's programme breaks, freelancing for numerous advertising producers before being placed on exclusive contract by Sierra Productions. Krish not only made product advertisements but also became closely associated with COI public-information 'fillers'. If such films were the 1970s' equivalent of those made at Massingham's in the

1940s, by this point their industrial positioning was quite different: not miniaturised products of the film industry's documentary wing, but instead the public-service branch of the TV commercials business. Krish's COI specialisms acquired him unusual monikers, one 1975 trade-press article quoting him as saying that 'sometimes I feel more like a funeral director than a film-maker ... apart from labelling me "Dr Death" the trade is beginning to call me the "Conscience of Commercials" but it's certainly not how I see myself'.[21] Despite all this, provocative safety films like Krish's *The Sewing Machine* (1973, in which a young girl runs onto the road and is killed) and the shocking *Searching* (1974, in which a dead child's ghostly screams are heard as a camera pans around a burned-out house) are of a piece with his documentary work. No mere contractual engagements, they're taken every bit as seriously as the previous decade's feature films and documentary assignments – their purpose being, after all, to help save lives.[22]

In 1975, Krish made two longer road-safety 'documentaries'. Given their similar themes, stylistically speaking they couldn't make an odder couple. *I Stopped, I Looked and I Listened* (made at the Moving Picture Company, mainly an advertising producer) was a trigger film for OAPs, in which members of Lewisham's Darby and Joan Club talk freely about how to avoid danger when crossing roads. The simplest film Krish ever directed, it's yet an elegant, curiously poignant little film that somehow burrows right under the skin; whereas *Drive Carefully, Darling* (co-written with advertising colleague Michael Gilmour, and the last Krish film to be produced by Clore) is a wild semi-fantasy. Colin Baker, John Challis and Christopher Owen play Brain, Ego and Memory, bickering for control of the reckless, doomed driver's mind they inhabit.[23] It won the fourth annual Grierson Award – presented to Krish by none other than Edgar Anstey.

Anstey having retired from BTF, when the unit was asked for a film to lead a new campaign in schools against railway vandalism and trespass (the instances of which had doubled in the preceding decade, at costs to life, health and railway infrastructure), his replacement John Shepherd took a gamble on engaging the best-known director of public safety films of the day – though it meant his return, two decades on, to the parish he'd once departed in disgrace. If Krish was surprised, he and Gilmour were taken further aback when British Rail approved their daring treatment: a child imagines a fantasy school sports-day in which the events are all competitions in vandalism whose entrants get injured or killed in the process. The savagely humane *The Finishing Line* (1977) rapidly became a *cause célebre*, sparking fierce media controversy over its shockingly graphic imagery, before finally getting withdrawn and replaced by a softer and more conventional substitute.[24]

Krish's late 1970s also saw two longer, less unorthodox and less specialised documentaries. *HMP* (1976) was a COI Home Office film about prison officers, made for recruitment purposes as well as general public information, at James Garrett and Partners. Three trainees encounter the staff and inmates of Rochester and Holloway prisons – more importantly, they encounter the ethical issues those prisons pose. And for Westward Television, Krish directed his only small-screen documentary film. Made for a series called *Sunday, Sweet Sunday* (1979), his programme about how a Cornish family spends its weekend has remained unavailable since its only broadcast.

By the decade's end, Krish was unexpectedly back on a feature film, hastily parachuted in to replace the flailing director of a movie being made in Israel, based on Luke's Gospel. This was *Jesus* (1979). How an agnostic Jew came to play a central role in making a film about Christ which, several accounts claim, has been seen by more worldwide viewers in more languages than any other film ever made (yet isn't even mentioned in most respectable movie guides) is a question that doubtless deserves the close attention of a book some day – though not this one.

Advertising work, and a few more COI fillers, continued through the late 1970s and early '80s at a fairly steady pace (the director even made a handful of sex-education spots for German TV). And Krish's last long films brought him back to the Children's Film Foundation, under enlightened new management for whom he made *Friend or Foe* (1983) and *Out of the Darkness* (1985). Short features for kids with an understated, thought-provoking symbolism, they're as fitting a *finis* as any to an idiosyncratic career spent making movies for people of all sizes.

FILM-MAKER MEETS VIEWER

John Krish says: 'trying to connect up the diversity of what I have made has puzzled me sometimes and then I realised the answer is simple – I'm a pragmatic, jobbing filmmaker ... I do what I do as well as I can. Why? Because I'm there to do it.'

Fair enough, but with what tools, to what ends, for whom? Chasing patterns in the films isn't unproductive, but it's the wrong place to start. Better to begin by tracing the patterns that govern them off screen: the director's relationship not just with his material but with his sponsors and his audiences. Getting some grip on this not only provides the essential context for appraising the films themselves, it also tellingly positions them. Krish, we've seen, was a close, but sceptical, professional eyewitness to the Documentary Movement that preceded and nurtured him, and the Free Cinema of his own day. Temperamentally indifferent to movements, manifestos and coteries, apparently equally uninterested in upholding tradition and in overturning it, he forged a rather different path than either of these movements, leaving us a complementary witness to their life and times. The differences between Krish's record of the age and theirs hinge precisely upon a differing balance of interests between film-maker, subject, sponsor and viewer. And turning the usual scale of critical values on its head – it is the last of these that comes first.

Krish neither theorised his work, nor heavily promoted it, outside his own sector of the industry (where it was for practical more than cultural purposes). The closest he came to articulating views about film-making in writing was therefore via passing references in trade biographies and in the odd brief article. For instance, he penned a 1963 piece for the Journal of the Society of Film and Television Arts, a special issue on 'the new realism in British films' containing excitable articles by John Schlesinger, Michael Birkett and Kay Mander, Guy Hamilton, Donovan Winter – and from Krish, a contrarian end-piece:

> isn't it symptomatic of the present epidemic that not one of the contributors to this issue have mentioned the audience at all ... The job of the filmmaker is absolutely clear to me. His duty lies not in self-expression alone but in communication. ... He needs real understanding of how human beings behave, an adult judgement on values, a sound and flexible technique for putting all these things (and a large unit) together. But also a strong sense of responsibility to the audience and the economics of the industry which brings us our livelihood.[25]

These statements apply equally to Krish's recent documentaries as to his emerging feature-film work, and they place him, with much of his generation, on a busy if unloved spot of the cultural continuum. For such film-makers, documentary was not a vehicle for ideology or sociology (as for Grierson or Rotha), but nor for authorial expressionism (as for Anderson). The films may *have* an aesthetic and an ideology, as we'll see shortly, but they aren't motivated *by* them. Such motives couldn't, anyway, have survived being married to Krish's work ethic (spurning dilettantism in favour of professionalism) during the period in which he was busy. Krish's usual sponsors (those in the public and NGO sectors) were now specifying their purposes and audiences – and tightening their budgets – with a precision that had been rare in the 1940s.

So as twenty-first-century viewers we mustn't forget that these films weren't made for us, but for mid-twentieth-century target groups, groups differing markedly from one project to the next. It's no accident that *I Think They call Him John* is Krish's most timelessly moving production, for it's the only one whose target audience (the young and middle-aged at large, too many of them too quick to overlook their elders) largely still exists (though the 'subject' generation is now not the one that fought World War I, but Krish's own, which fought World War II). If films like *Under Your Bonnet*, *Mr Marsh Comes to School* and *Maths With Everything* lack such universal appeal, and are now of greater interest as social records of the moment in which they were made, that doesn't, of itself, tell us anything about how effective they may have been in influencing the target viewers who saw them then.

Some sense of context can prevent us from making false inferences or uninformed judgments about the films as they reach us today. If the technical detail in *Under Your Bonnet* seems excessive, that is probably because the demographic for its sales shows was the well-informed motor trader – not his clueless customer. *Return to Life*'s use of commentary in lieu of synch sound isn't merely a consequence of the COI's usual cost-cutting, still less of traditionalist observance of the Voice of God. On the other hand nor was it a creative attempt at distancing (a drama in which we see characters speak but do not hear their words, other than in the narration, incidentally spoken by Krish himself). Actually, it was a calculated choice predicated on practical necessities: of the film being translatable into numerous languages with minimal loss of force, and of its impact on its worldwide viewers not being dissipated by their being able to identify its characters' ethnicities too precisely. Much of the uproar over *The Finishing Line* failed to note the salient fact about its intended viewers – that they fell within a mere three-year age range. Schools were carefully advised that it was to be shown to eight- to eleven-year-olds. On the basis of psychological research, the producers assumed children of that age to be out of constant parental watch and influence, tempted therefore to try dangerous and irresponsible things – but not yet habituated to it.[26] They also judged them capable of recognising the use of metaphor – while still being impressionable enough to be strongly affected by it emotionally. The most common, conflicting, objections to the film, then, were off the mark. Younger children (potentially terrified, but to no good purpose) and older ones (who might conceivably be amused or even encouraged by the violence of the film) weren't expected to see it. And while the formatting of Krish's military films at World Wide suited his own professional agenda, limbering up for feature-film work, its principal aim was to conquer the audible groan likely to emerge from a platoon plonked in front of a screen for 'instruction', by unexpectedly giving them an absorbing drama. *Break-In* consciously takes cues from *Dragnet*, airing in the UK at the time, and *Captured* has the taut power of a fine 'B' war movie, reminiscent of low-budget American features by a Don Siegel or Sam Fuller (though its violence is psychological rather than physical).

Evidently, then, the films' exacting concern for their own effectiveness is most to blame for their puzzling, idiosyncratic diversity of style and tone. Planning *I Stopped, I Looked and I Listened* Krish advised the COI as follows:

> How do we reach an audience ... who have different levels of perception, hearing ability, varying capacities for understanding and therefore following the line of a film? ... we certainly can't treat them like kids. There's absolutely no point [*pace Finishing Line*] in piling on the horror and frightening them ... preaching from the screen is never a good idea – whatever the age of the audience. As for a teaching film – well, the old simply won't have the patience to watch and listen to a reel or two of HOW TO CROSS THE ROAD. And I wouldn't want to make it ... Nevertheless, something has to be done to save their lives and stop them getting hurt ... trust, so it seems to me, is the key word. It has, therefore, to be a film which shows unmistakably through its approach and technique that the people responsible for it, both sponsor and film maker, care about those for whom it is made. It has to be an affectionate film and it is that particular quality ... that is most likely to make this audience respond ... If the audience senses we understand (and *really* understand I mean) their special problems ... then when they're out next time they'll remember the film ... above all, this film, though serious in intent, must be an enjoyable experience for the over sixties, both while they're watching and later when they're remembering it.[27]

Thus his recommendation that the film should consist of spontaneous discussions about road safety between old people, the only ones at whom their viewers would be prepared to stop, look and listen without suspicion or impatience. However, when tasked the same year with addressing the drivers at risk of *causing* the accidents in which these pedestrians might get caught up, Krish took almost the opposite tack:

> The treatment of this subject is more theatrical than any other documentaries Krish has made and there is a very good reason for this. The audience for whom this film is made, he claims, is just about the most difficult one to get through to. It is made for everyone who drives a car – and just about all drivers think they're experts. After seeing this film, Krish believes, they will be shaken enough to be honest with themselves.[28]

Hence, *Drive Carefully, Darling* would take the form not just of fiction, but of fiction driven – literally driven – by the use of subjective camera. Krish's selling point for the Department of the Environment was that the driver at the centre of the story must not be shown: viewers would find excuses not to empathise with him. Instead the viewer is in the driving seat with him, seeing the same things he does but never seeing his face or clothes (they do know he's male, of course, the target viewer being male too).[29]

However, it doesn't follow from the director's outward focus that his own personality was clinically detached from the films or their subjects. Quite the opposite – their bond was oftentimes intense. Krish's method for determining what would move his audiences would seem to have been a matter more of emotional intuition than of cerebral calculation. It doesn't take too fanciful a reading of biography to detect the son of migrants in *Return to Life*, the high-school dropout in *Mr Marsh Comes to School* and *What Are They Doing at College*, the committed father in his many films about or for children. Nor is a crash-course in psychology needed repeatedly to sense Serge Krish's misunderstood son, and Felix Krish's bereaved brother, in his films' repeated tenacity in commanding their viewers' attention – usually to awaken their tenderness towards the vulnerable and the very young, their respect for their own and others' human potential, and a corresponding intolerance of its waste – whether brought by South Africa's apartheid brutality, North Korea's communist indoctrination or our own society's neglect of the lonely; by uninspired maths teaching, unfriendly counter service or reckless driving.[30]

To that extent, but to that extent only, is Krish (an extremely sensitive person) a maker of 'personal cinema'. If the channelling of private feelings was a factor in making these documentaries what they were, it was certainly never their governing purpose. And it's always properly concealed in the products that reached the screen, whose point isn't the expression of the self, but communication with the other. And on behalf of a third – the sponsor, to whom we turn.

FILM-MAKER MEETS SPONSOR

It's clear from the preceding account of Krish's career that his relationships with sponsors were frequently turbulent. He stated in *Anatomy of the Film* that 'if you have a producer who feels he must go along with the sponsor because he's afraid he won't get any more films, you're in trouble' – referring, undoubtedly, to Carr in comparison to Clore. Krish was something of a rebel, it's true – but not a subversive. To this extent, *The Elephant*'s a red herring. The story of its clandestine production may rather appeal to today's prevalent adolescent enjoyment of artistic disobedience as an end in itself, but if so it provides a misleading introduction to Krish's career. After all, the insurrection was in the cause of making an accessible, crowd-pleasing film about trams. And it was the *only* time Krish made a sponsored short that hadn't been requested, and was in dangerous tension with policy (which was to laud the upgrades to transport infrastructure and promote their use, not to mourn the loss of the decommissioned and unusable).[31] True, in the 1960s, Krish would again, twice, evade the standard mechanisms of sponsorship, via *Let My People Go* and *I Think They Call Him John*. But it's instructive that both times Krish sought to *stretch* sponsorship's boundaries, respectively over content and over form – not to break them. The first film still applies its makers' aptitude for dramatisation of information and their solid command of film form to the communication of a pre-defined message. It just happens to be one that no mainstream sponsor would have paid for. Meanwhile, Krish's one 'labour of love' project, *I Think They Call Him John*, involved his producer raising funds for the patronage not of a personal, experimental or radical work, but for the straightforward pursuit of civic responsibility. What was unusual about it was what it was pursued *with*: the film's uninterrupted stylistic rigour, which corrects the tamperings with their own efficacy that sponsors so often insisted upon. *Return to Life* had been momentarily interrupted by Foreign Office-approved lists of relevant British achievements and facilities – although, anxious to return to narrative, the film disposes of them as early in its running time as possible. The 16mm release of *They Took Us to the Sea* had added to it a prologue in which the League of Pity's head gives a direct-to-camera address whose unsubtlety and anti-cinematic quality is reminiscent of the preamble added, to Jennings's disgust, to *Listen to Britain*. Had *I Think They Call Him John* been funded either by government or by a more directly interested charity, it would likely have had comparable compromises forced on it.

Krish also turned some projects down. Though he did several Armed Forces productions, he refused any military films training soldiers in fighting, on moral grounds. Shell, intriguingly, once offered Krish a film about locusts, which he turned down mainly because it would mean several months away from family.[32] Thanks to his advertising income Krish was able to accept projects he felt some sympathy for – nonetheless he several times took a further risk with livelihood by challenging their sponsors to do some rethinking. However, this was almost the precise opposite of slyly undermining their goals: obstinately transparent attempts, instead, to persuade them to be better at *achieving* those goals, by convincing them that they could be better translated into the language of cinema – usually by bringing out more strongly the human dimension of their subject matter, often via a stronger emphasis on dramatisation.

Paradoxically, therefore, Krish's sometimes confrontational demeanour betrayed a real respect for the institution of sponsorship – for there was no bad faith involved. Krish feels that he was often dissuading sponsors (the COI, in particular) from wasting resources on approaches that ill suited the medium. However, such discussions *could* have the effect not only of inflecting the delivery of the message, but of subtly altering the message itself – crudely speaking, to make it more compassionate and slightly more liberal. *Red Cross – That's Us* inserts into its generally cosy and carefree scrapbook of Junior Red Cross activities a few more challenging sequences, the jumble sales and camping trips alternating with visits to autistic children and an old people's home – and most strikingly a visit to a supermarket interrupted by six sharp cuts, synched with low soundtrack thuds, to images of overseas famine. This is a surprising appearance, within a middle-class charity film, of the technique of 'deadly parallels' that Bert Hogenkamp has identified as the hallmark of leftist film-making in the 1930s (indeed, Krish also uses it in the more directly political *Let My People Go*, in which Sharpeville footage and stills are intercut with cheerful South African Tourist Board posters). While that may have been a bit more than the British Red Cross had bargained for, the sequence to which its officers openly objected at the approval screening was, far more shockingly, a warmly effective three-minute scene in which young volunteers kindly and confidently interact with the inmates of a mental institution they're visiting. Clore refused to budge, offering the budget back, unless the scene remained in the release and his sponsor gave in.[33] Twelve years earlier, a more trivial example of approval-show illiberalism had come from the NUT, otherwise an agreeable and progressive collaborator. Krish was asked to remove what he felt was the best scene in *Our School*, because the charismatic teacher giving the lesson in question wasn't wearing a jacket. That time, Graphic gave in.[34]

However, particularly in the COI's case, the sponsor usually proved pleased, even boastful, about the ultimate results of the collaboration. The COI's brief for *Return to Life* had been 'to further Britain's prestige by showing that this country is as much concerned today as she has been in the past with the plight of refugees'.[35] Compare against its summary of the finished product: 'Describes something of the health, educational, employment and welfare facilities available to the refugee arriving in Britain, and *conveys, in a human and moving way, the problems of adjustment which he must face.*'[36] This last, emerging from the film-maker's pressure on his sponsor, is the dominant impression left by the film, its liberal side-effect being to make it a less coarsely self-interested national contribution to the international project of which it was part. The film ends not on a sweet, but a sour-sweet moment, the viewer sensing that the young boy is ready to begin integrating into his new setting, but wondering what effect this will have on his family, who are too old to. Similarly, the stated purpose for commissioning *Mr Marsh Comes to School* was 'to encourage school leavers to adopt a right attitude to vocational guidance, and to make use of the Youth Employment Service'. But by the time of its press premiere (introduced by the Minister of Labour, John Hare), 'it is no mere documentary record of the facilities provided by this service. Its treatment is distinctly unorthodox'[37] – a positive selling point, presumably, despite apparently having been arrived at in the face of opposition from COI accountants concerned that dialogue scenes necessitated sound technicians, and professional actors meant Equity rates.

HMP quickly mutated from a film about the places in which a prison service recruit would likely find himself working, to one about what sort of work he will find himself doing and, implicitly, about the sort of employee such places call for. He will need, viewers infer, to be thoughtful as well as pragmatic, humane as well as dutiful, respectful of the necessity of prisons but sensitive to the shades of grey surrounding the ultimately insoluble issue of crime and punishment. The Director-General of the Prison Service wrote to Krish that, 'Lord Harris ... had been much impressed by the film ... and was very gratified by the general response. One MP has since written to him to say how "deeply impressed" he was by the film as "an admirable and imaginative recruiting aid".'[38]

Conversely, when the rough-cut *What Are They Doing at College* was previewed for a Department of Education official, the latter's enthusiasm was tempered by his fear that the Secretary of State might actually see it. Certain she'd chafe, he urged Krish to finish it fast so it could be released before she returned from foreign visits. She, of course, was Margaret Thatcher. The film-maker heeded the civil servant's advice, and the film, as he later put it, 'escaped the handbag'.

DOCUMENTARY FORM

With some sense in place of the films' interdependence with their audiences and sponsors off screen, we're better positioned to assess the ways in which the on-screen material has been put together. On one hand, we've seen that the assortment of styles is prompted by matching the sponsor's brief to a craftsman's assessment of what, within the available budget, can best bring it to life before its viewers. So, for instance, *They Took Us to the Sea* draws heavily on Jack Beaver's wondrous score to modulate its moods – from exuberantly jazzy vibraphone as the trip begins, through Western scoring of Krish's Fordian shots of the children on beach donkeys, and a musical motif, 'My Bonny Lies Over the Ocean'. Between this music, and occasional ambient sound, Krish sparingly inserts a child's first-person narration, in conversational Brummy: brief, descriptive, but somehow expressive phrases ('I'd never seen the sea before. It's got a funny smell to it. Alright really'). In direct contrast, *I Think They Call Him John* uses a single, disembodied commentary spoken by Victor Spinetti, but not one note of music, which would destroy its intense claustrophobia.[39]

On the other hand, Krish clearly had stylistic preferences. One of the most persistent predispositions in his documentaries is towards sturdy narrative design in preference to freeform. It's noticeable how many of Krish's documentaries have a 'circular' pattern: the NUT films, *They Took Us to the Sea*, *Let My People Go*, *The Finishing Line* and *HMP* all end on visuals echoing those with which they began, their meaning now changed by the journey the viewer has taken between them, posing the question of what the future will hold. In *I Think They Call Him John*, it is words that repeat: 'John Ronson. Retired. Old miner. Old soldier. Old gardener. Old-age pensioner. Widower, no children' – but by the end of the film, so much more than the set of vital statistics he is at its start. And to transport viewers between these points of opening and closure, a preference for firm pacing is often evident – even, or especially, in a film like *The Finishing Line*, one of Krish's few with a style superficially resembling chaotically 'free' documentaries shot with mobile cameras. A close viewing indicates a very tight structure, and a knowing orchestration of emotional effects – the deceptively offhand style of the film is almost a fictional pastiche of the 'documentary' spontaneity that Krish himself largely avoided.

For the director's most pronounced inclination is towards a highly, if often imperceptibly, controlled method of shooting, in strong-willed preference to improvisation and observation. These were, of course, Krish's principal aesthetic disagreements with Free Cinema, and it is here where his Crown roots most vividly show (even if, often, visibly outgrown). Krish's films make as good a case as any for – to coin a phrase – the creative treatment of actuality. We have seen that Krish's own psychology may have predisposed him to this. At the same time, the implicit assumption of the films is that in order to draw their spectators' attention to an underlying, overlooked truth about the world

– whatever particular truths about the film's subject the film-maker and his sponsor have agreed to communicate – then whatever manipulation of superficially perceptible reality is required is not only permissible but often unavoidable.

Given that licence, each of the films can be seen as sitting somewhere on a spectrum, with the scripted and professionally acted at one end, the spontaneous at the opposite. With respect to the first, it's notable that many of the films have a verbal prologue, in speech or text, which places the drama in a documentary context. *Captured* opens on an officer advising that the story to follow is 'based on our experiences and supervised by an officer who was with the battalion [in Korea] at the time so that you may know the practices of possible communist enemies and combat them successfully'. *Drive, Carefully Darling* starts with Frank Bough relaying road safety statistics and speculating on the place of reason in people's lives, frequently discarded as soon as they get behind a steering wheel. As late as 1975, this preface, and a public-information function, were enough to classify the fantasy-drama which followed as a documentary.

But the most intriguing points of the spectrum are those where the observed and the constructed more subtly interact. Next stop after the films with actors are those in which a script is played by a cast *mixing* actors with the non-professionals in whose setting the documentary takes place. In *Mr Marsh Comes to School*, everyone on screen is a pupil of the school in which Krish was shooting, except for Marsh himself and, less obviously, the two mouthy pupils with whom he has most of his dialogue: they are child actors. Then come the films peopled entirely by non-actors, but still performing to scripts. After Dickson's *The Undefeated* (1950), *Return to Life* is perhaps the second most significant example of the COI taking forward Crown's core creative strategem of directing non-actors in the playing of their 'types' into a post-war world. The difference is that in this world, disability and displacement (and, generally, the effect of the external world on the inner universe of people as individuals in their own right, rather than mere ciphers) are respectable public themes in a way they weren't in the early 1940s. The script was written in advance of the casting, translated so that the cast could understand it, Krish was taught a few phrases to assist his directing and the woman playing the grandmother knew enough English to help him translate for them (Krish has since recalled the extraordinary, even tragic circumstances to which the shooting of the film exposed him and his cast).[40]

At the next point along the continuum are films in which non-actors play themselves rather than similar people, but are heavily directed in doing so. *I Think They Call Him John*, a powerfully formalised though not an abstractly formalist film, is probably the purest case study in Krish's interpretation of realism. The film was shot entirely silent, though the first-time viewer never guesses, so much care having been given to sound design and synched effects (one of Balfour-Fraser's great achievements was in securing funding for a specialist sound editor, the talented Doug Turner, something few social documentaries could afford). Therefore, it was made rather as silent feature films once were, Krish using speech and action meticulously to direct Ronson's every move even as the camera whirred. Krish recalls one viewer commenting how lucky he must have felt to have had his camera running when Ronson fell asleep, though he was actually closing his eyes on command. The film also betrays a subconscious debt to the Crown tradition in general and to Jennings in particular: a respect for the carefully composed static shot, filmed with a tripod and then tellingly placed within a paced sequence, as a crucial unit of meaning in any creative documentary. In *I Think They Call Him John* not only are there oppressive medium long-shot compositions of Ronson's living room, carefully including all three visible walls surrounding Ronson and artfully emphasising his

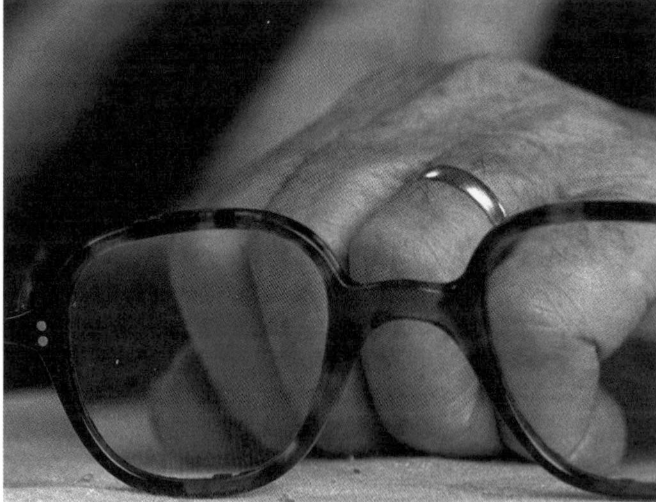

Calculated composition in *I Think They Call Him John*

isolation within the frame. There are also frequent pauses for close shots, just as tightly composed, of inanimate objects: treasured photos, World War I medals, a World War II Home Guard certificate. Of all documentarists of the day, probably the only other who so frequently deploys such imagery, not to further but to deepen the narrative, is Denis Mitchell – a television great whose films otherwise have little in common with Krish's.

In fact, Krish had been almost as exacting in his use of 'controlled documentary' in the NUT films, although to evoke quite different moods, and so indiscernibly that they're perhaps the best test of the validity of the approach. 'If you want', he argued then, 'to capture on film the feel, the atmosphere, the very spirit that can exist between a teacher and his class it's no use being on the outside. You've got to get in there.' Which didn't mean what a contemporary manifesto for 'pure' documentary might take it to: 'You need close shots, reaction shots, you need lots of shots that you must carry in your head and know how they're going to cut and where so that you can control the pace of the sequence.'[41] *I Want to Go To School* wasn't scripted in advance of filming: the crew arrived at Beechwood Primary School with only a one-page structural outline. But apart from that, it was made like a feature film, on a fraction of feature resources. Once a scene was worked out, all shots were listed, each set-up lit individually, all relevant business filmed there before the crew moved to the next set-up, regardless of the order in which the shots would eventually be assembled. To ensure every word was audible (the teachers and pupils being shot with live synch), the classrooms on either side were kept empty. Windows were kept tight shut, in high summer (1959's was a scorcher). Scenes took three or four days to shoot: the English lesson took six days, filling six minutes of screen time. Everyone had to wear the same clothes on different days, girls had to repeat hairstyles. If a close-up or two-shot were needed, children not in the shot were usually not in the room at the time. When the director observed in the school a spontaneous moment of interaction of value to the film, he reconstructed it with the camera running, directing as tightly as necessary to make it sparkle on screen as brightly as when it had happened in life. If needed, retakes were done. With *Our School*, complications were multiplied by the larger, more populous school running on intricate timetables based around streaming and the periods structure: the film has a slighter looser approach, an episodic structure in which the viewer is swiftly taken from classroom to classroom, with narration kicking in only in the final few minutes (one sequence, a maths lesson with humorous, quick exchanges between teacher and pupils, was shot using two cameras).[42] Nonetheless, classrooms were again turned into makeshift studios, the one-page treatment again broken down week by week into sequences planned then shot for clarity and impact: each of the episodes is like a little one-act documentary, rehearsed before the director called action.

With these circumstances in mind, consider two typical reviews. *Film User* remarked of the first film that 'the photography is brilliant, the direction so good that it is hard to believe that any of the cast were aware of the camera and microphone'.[43] *Teachers World*, the NUT's own journal, asked of the second, 'were the cameras unseen, and were they operated by the Invisible Man? Surely nobody was working from a script; surely it was quite unrehearsed ... so natural did it all seem.'[44] And given that Krish's shooting decisions were informed by several weeks' research, ensconced in the schools observing their workings closely, there is a lively debate to be had about whether he was misrepresenting that reality, or representing it better than it could have done by itself. It's worth noting that when Clore first asked Krish to direct *I Want To Go To School*, he appointed Karel Reisz to produce him. Probably Clore considered Krish, on his first project since leaving World Wide, an untested proposition; Reisz could keep an eye on him, providing help if needed. Now according to Krish, Reisz made one crucial contribution; the suggestion that 'Morning is Broken' be used in the morning assembly sequence was a radiant idea, the hymn encapsulating both the bloom of each new school day and the comforting cycle of its repetition. But while acknowledging that input, the director says the producer otherwise did very little producing, diplomatically disappearing as soon as – and precisely because – it became clear that the two men's thinking about how to direct attention-grabbing documentaries was incompatible. Reisz urged that Krish film his schoolboys and girls rather as *he'd* filmed his Lambeth boys: with an agitatedly kinetic camera prowling through a full classroom, as a real lesson proceeds, to zero in on whatever of interest might be going on, while recording wild sound on tape for later imaginative cutting to the most compelling images. Krish was unsurprised when Reisz, seeing the finished product, declared it 'too tidy'.

Similarly telling is comparison with a film called *The Happy Adventure* (1965), dealing with even younger children and completing the trilogy of NUT/Clore collaborations. Coincidentally this was made by John Fletcher, who'd performed sterling service as soundman on Krish's film but was more influenced, directorially, by Free Cinema, for which he'd been the regular audio technician. Being closer to what Reisz had presumably wanted from Krish, Fletcher's more improvisatory school film (made in 16mm colour) makes a pretty good test case. A likeable, informative short, some viewers might prefer it (arguing perhaps that Fletcher's five-year-olds, taught with less structure than Krish's nine-year-olds, lend themselves to a looser style). Others will miss those things that rarely infuse documentaries by chance: gripping tempo, easily comprehensible dialogue, set pieces that reveal rather than record, and a tiny touch of enchantment in gaining access to a world entirely real yet usually locked behind our children's school gates and in our own vanished childhoods.

Moving yet further from drama, films like *This Year – London*, *The Elephant Will Never Forget* and *They Took Us to the Sea* were shot largely off-the-cuff, sometimes with multiple cameras and with slightly higher shooting ratios than on other productions. But not only is the overall choice of sequences premeditated with a fair degree of logistical precision: the subsequent additions of music and commentary position them as essays on the events depicted, rather than records of them. Moreover, even these freely flowing films evince that enthusiasm for calculated composition mentioned above. *They Took Us to the Sea* includes many fine examples, notably in its final sequence, after the children have returned home, of forlorn images of deserted piers and the donkeys' shoe marks in the sand.

Finally, we arrive at the near-improvised films – mostly confined to Krish's later career. Indeed, if viewing Krish's films in chronological order, it becomes very striking how much more freewheeling the 1970s documentaries he was making shortly after his feature-films sojourn are than those he was making just before it. Was that solely because the subjects seemed to demand it, at a point at which affordable technology could now better deliver it? Or had something relaxed in the director himself? That point may remain moot, but *Maths With Everything*, *What Are They Doing at College*, *Red Cross – That's Us*, *I Stopped, I Looked and I Listened*, and *HMP*, when contrasted with the NUT films in particular, are as vivid an illustration as any of how, in their decade, the formal properties of sponsored factual films were increasingly coming to resemble those of television documentaries. That renders them, today, a more prosaic, earthbound experience than their more cinematic predecessors – again, irrelevant to assessing what their effect on their intended audiences may have been, but *I Stopped, I Looked and I Listened* is the only one that seems to speak quite so engagingly across the barriers of time. (It's significant that while Krish continued to win awards for some of these films, these were more often confined to the specialised communications field and, compared to the 1960s films, they certainly had less of an international film festival life.)

I Stopped, I Looked and I Listened

Like Paul Dickson, Krish has spent a chunk of his retirement lecturing to film students. In a 2003 London International Film School lecture, he warned them of a paradox he'd first sensed watching Watt direct *Target for Tonight* (1941), with its now cringingly stiff RAF men.

> By using real people you can, if you're not very careful, make your film seem less real ... I made a lot of documentaries and never thought of myself as being in the reality business. When you load a roll of film into a movie camera, use sound, scissors or the sophistication of Final Cut, I say you're in the world of magic.

One of his students wrote of Krish's seminars that,

> always there would be the comment that 'this is not a documentary'. After *Return to Life*, John informed us that the people in the film, although actual refugees, were not a real family and that the story we just saw was not their story but was scripted. In the midst of our protests, John said that although the family's story had not happened, stories like that were all too common, did the fact that the shadows on the white sheet weren't in fact a family make the truth of the situation any less? Was it our sense of truth that felt cheated, or in fact our sensationalism? Although my initial reaction ... was the same as those of some of my classmates, that is to say that they were brilliant but didn't remind me of documentaries very much, I slowly came to a realisation. I realised that my experience of documentaries originated from television ... I seem to have missed out on a basic premise of non-fiction film-making, the fact that *it is still film-making*.[45]

'AN IDIOSYNCRATIC CAREER?'

That Krish's films, with most of his generation's, are generally neglected clearly has something to do with the difficulty that standard historical accounts have in pigeonholing them. The extent of their divergence from Free Cinema, let alone from Direct Cinema, cinéma vérité and tele-journalism, is pretty obvious, while their demarcation from the older documentaries is less clear. They clearly remain part of a tradition in which sponsorship, public service, conventional decency and the 'message' film are bound up. And we have seen that they also advance some aspects of the Documentary Movement's style. However, they equally clearly retreat from certain of its aims. These are not films by artists using institutions to try to hasten the coming of social democracy. They are films by institutions using craftsmen to help manage the social democracy that is already there and taken for granted. To a Marxist, an anarchist – or indeed a Thatcherite – critic, that presumably makes them particularly suspect. But for the dispassionate historian, it is precisely because Krish was pursuing neither a personal nor a political agenda[46] – was instead *bringing to* institutional communications an intuitive, commonsense humanism, inflected by a professional sense of what audiences would be prepared to listen to, but also by a real and rare intensity – that his films leave us such thought-provoking evidence for the textures and assumptions of post-war British life.

The Britain of Krish's films is clearly a less politicised, but in most respects a more liberal place than the one his elders had documented in the 1930s. We have seen that its institutions, some enthusiastically, some more grudgingly, are embracing more forward-thinking notions of communication – and what needs communicating. We have seen that they are beginning to recognise the individual as a personality, instead of a mere personification of his class. This is evident when comparing *Pattern for Progress* and Krish's BTF films and *Mining Reviews* with those later works. The earlier films retain vestiges of sentimental condescension towards the working classes, quite absent from those of the Clore period (though suspiciously present in a number of the Free Cinema films made by Krish's

Clore contemporaries[47]). At the same time, like Free Cinema, mainstream social documentarists like Krish were able to turn their attention to the marginal and the dispossessed as interwar film-makers never could.

And how does Krish's Britain compare to today's? We'd expect it to be more conformist, conventional and conservative than our own. Sure enough, we have seen that 'progressive' sponsors were sometimes resistant even to minor relaxation of mid-century mores. On a broader canvas, so unassuming a short film as *Mr Marsh Comes to School* is a fascinating gauge of post-war possibility, but also of its limits. The eponymous youth employment officer is impassioned, almost shrill, in impressing upon his audience, on and off screen, that their futures are open if only they dare grasp them. At the same time he divides those futures up into categories, separating the children listening to him into neat groups: the 'makers and doers', the 'stayers', the 'office' group and 'people' group, although most of them fall into the '?' group. The kids answer back, the debate is heated and, via the magic of film, Marsh and his two loudest interlocutors (his two fellow professional players) enact eight little morality plays testing out the futures that might await them.

Yes, there is much missing from Krish's on-screen world, many debates and divisions unmentioned, suppositions unquestioned, possibilities delimited. Yet in many ways, these films tell a melancholy tale of how much *less* liberal society has since become. Is it likely that the Foreign Office of today would fund a half-hour cinema film promoting Britain as a place of kindness and protection for asylum seekers? Or that a film about customer service would be commissioned not to promote meeting targets, but customers and suppliers simply being nicer to one another? Above all, Krish's films encapsulate the post-war moment in which a full-fledged civic rapport with childhood emerged, in place of discarded Victorian values, and before itself being dissipated. *They Took Us to the Sea* invokes in viewers an empathy with the brief joys, and glimpsed hardships, of its subjects in place of mere pity. Krish's NUT films are far from the world of Basil Wright's *Children at School* (1937), made when Krish and his target audience were much the same age as Wright's subjects. It is not just that children are now at tables rather than desks. More fundamental is that the focus has shifted from educational infrastructure (warts and all: Wright's film, unlike Krish's, voices criticism of current provision[48]) to the *relationship* between teacher and pupils. It has since, perhaps, shifted back a little, under a welter of official targets.

Having emphasised the importance of seeing Krish's films in context, it must be admitted that hard evidence for their intended effects is hard to come by. Remembering that his films, though 'geared to specialised or general audiences' were still to be of 'general appeal' our contemporary emotional response is worth paying attention to, provided we try to remain empathetic with those original viewers. Krish's feeling for people is the link between us.

'Drive Carefully, Darling' is hardly a hip message, and the film of that name is likely to strike some modern, cynical viewers as slightly camp – but usually their laughter freezes half-way through the screening. They get caught up in its increasingly urgent pace, but, more importantly, in its mundane humanism. The script had directed not only that the driver not be seen but that 'to flesh him out, as it were, his home, his wife and ten year old son are introduced at the opening and she is seen for moments during his drive to point certain parallels of behaviour – and to underline what he's risking by his rule bending'.[49] The film's 'brain' sets may seem pretty cheap, courtesy COI budgets. What still reaches us is the silent cutaways from the dying brain to its fading images of the driver's wife returning from her grocery shopping. The same year, the deceptively artless *I Stopped, I Looked and I Listened* opened on faded photographs, enlivened (like *The Elephant Will Never Forget*) by a music-hall song. What follows is the Darby and Joans' lively, relaxed discussion of pedestrian safety rules, but a broader humanism again interjects. Edited into the film at this point, is the footage that resulted when Krish asked them to reminisce about the changes they'd witnessed in their long lives, the better to connect with their viewers – and, coincidentally and unintentionally, the better to connect with us. Memories stretching as far as the Boer War are shared with us on the screen – they can no longer be shared in person.

Then the film returns to road safety and, at the end of its eighteen minutes, articulates its overriding message as unambiguously as is possible, by putting the actual words on the screen, while a narrator simultaneously speaks them. In this distilled form that message is the same as *Drive Carefully, Darling*'s, and rather a lot of its director's work. If it's no more fashionable in 2010 than in 1975, it's still as applicable:

'Please: Take Care'

Idiosyncratic? You decide ...

NOTES

1. Brian McFarlane (ed.), *The Encyclopedia of British Film* (3rd edn, London: Methuen, 2008), p. 414.
2. Krish says today: 'Lindsay talked of Jennings being the only poet in British cinema – and, no doubt, he thought he was saying something terribly deep and important. He was talking bollocks. Having worked with Humphrey on *Listen to Britain* and knowing him outside that film, I can tell you there was nothing poetic in his thinking. He was an energetic, chaotic egoist.' Yet 'his ability ... to photograph things and make them very evocative deeply influenced me, unknowingly then but later on I was aware that something of his spirit had stayed with me.' Holmes was 'a mixture of Barry Fitzgerald and Jack Buchanan': 'a truer English gentleman you could not find'. Following Holmes's sudden death in 1969, aged sixty-eight, it was Krish who MC'd the memorial tribute to him held in the National Film Theatre.
3. The death was an avoidable one. Felix was flying a plane back to base that had just been refitted to carry heavier loads, when, the refitting having been faulty, a wing fell off, causing the plane to crash. One of the younger brother's treasured possessions, to this day, is a pencil drawing of himself as infant that his older brother drew when ten years old.
4. After completion, the Ebbw Vale steelworks expanded and wanted that new plant filmed. Cameraman Ray Elton went back to film it and his section was joined to Krish's finished film and a co-directing credit added. The film also includes a Halas & Batchelor animation sequence.
5. The same year, the Conservative and Unionist Film Association released *Common Sense About Steel* – a characteristically straight-talking two-minute screen attack on Attlee government plans to nationalise steel production, pictorially consisting entirely of reused footage from *Pattern for Progress*.
6. The system had been used for amateur film since 1935. *Away for the Day* was an unfortunate choice of guinea pig for its professional application: rendering the red of the buses accurately was all-important to the sponsor, incredibly tricky for the lab – and consequently inconvenient to the film-makers. To maintain colour control the lab had to grade the whole film in one go when it was finished, rendering the production team unable to view rushes.
7. These stories feature in *Mining Review 7th Year No 1* and *7th Year No 9*.

8. *Film User*.
9. Paul Rotha, *The Film Till Now* (4th edn, London: Vision Press, 1964), p. 736.
10. For the Metropolitan Water Board, Krish's job was to update the 1948 film of the same name (directed by Mary Francis) by blending it with more recently shot footage and a new commentary. In Krish's account, he settled on the shape of present first, then past, then future – but at the approval screening producer Hindle Edgar quite unnecessarily asked the sponsors if they thought it would work better in chronological order. He even suggested they put it to a vote, which went in favour of chronology but, in Krish's opinion, against a gripping narrative.
11. 'This film will be shown only under the supervision of an experienced officer (major/captain) who will use the lecture notes issued with the film. The film may not be shown to recruits.'
12. 'From Fact to Fiction', press biography, August 1969, John Krish collection (a collection of papers and ephemera donated by Krish to BFI Special Collections in 2009).
13. The NUT had only sponsored one film before, and that was back in 1935: *Citizens of the Future*, made by Donald Taylor at Strand.
14. The 'Reg' explanation is the one that Krish remembers having been given by the COI when he phoned to see how the film was doing – and was told it wasn't doing anything at all, for that reason. Some documentation survives at the Post Office Museum and Archives: it is clear that Bevins disliked the film but it is not specified that it was for this reason. Rather, there are indications that the film was felt not to have given a positive enough picture of GPO professionalism. Krish recalls a preview showing for GPO managers and trade union representatives at which they were extremely enthusiastic about it. The nature of the restriction was very similar to that of *Captured*: *Counterpoint* was only showable if a GPO official was present to introduce it and ask questions afterwards; otherwise, requests for a print would be refused. See: POST 122/448 and POST 122/996.
15. The South African embassy stupidly drew attention to the film by placing this notice in several newspapers: 'there is a film currently showing in London which will interest discerning people. It is an example of the modern technique of converting mass media or communication to a particular purpose – in this case, the discrediting of South Africa. It is somewhat obvious (*vide* the inclusion in a "documentary" of scenes reconstructed in Britain), but because of that it will alert the levelheaded observer to similar, though more subtle, treatment meted out by others from time to time via other media. Name of the film, "Let My People Go".'
16. *Anatomy of the Film*, Programme 9: 'The Documentary', 26 May 1965, transcript, p. 4; Krish collection. In keeping with the BBC's then policy, the programmes themselves were wiped after transmission.
17. For example, *Let My People Go* won the top prize at Leipzig and a special British Film Academy United Nations Award. The British Council films won the Venice Golden Lion. *I Think They Call Him John* won the Cracow Jury Prize for Humanitarianism and a similar award in California.
18. Krish admits that at its London Film Festival premiere a man jumped from his seat in the middle of the film yelling up at Ronson, 'why don't you *do* something!', and that it was subsequently heckled at the Odeon Haymarket.
19. Derek Hill, 'The Short Film Situation', *Sight & Sound* vol. 31 no. 3, Summer 1962, p. 110.
20. Along the way were lesser-known twists. Krish was due to direct the Cliff Richard vehicle *Summer Holiday*, but withdrew following disagreements with the producers; before *The Go-Between* was offered to Losey, Krish had turned it down, judging it snobbish and affected (unlike, presumably, his high-living would-be Marxist former colleague).
21. *Ad Weekly*, unidentified date, Krish collection.

22. A hyberbolic trade-press reaction to *Searching*: 'a shattering example of just how powerful film and television can be ... it made Hitchcock's *Psycho* look like Enid Blyton'. *Campaign*, 28 February 1975, unpaginated, Krish collection.
23. A couple of years later, Gilmour and Krish, with their advertising hats back on, weren't above plagiarising themselves, borrowing the personified 'brain' concept for a Lemsip advertisement, catalogued by the BFI National Archive under the title *Lemsip – Brain* (1977).
24. A selection of press cuttings is digitised and available to academic users on the BFI's *InView* website. The culmination of the controversy was a debate on the much-watched BBC current affairs programme *Nationwide*, which Krish refused to attend.
25. John Krish, untitled piece, *Journal* no. 11, Spring 1963, p. 14. Ironically, it was a philosophy that Krish shared with Edgar Anstey, who wrote later: 'If the young film-maker is concerned only to do what was recently called "his own thing", recognising no purpose outside himself, neither documentary nor the sponsored film is for him. Nor, perhaps is any medium requiring an audience to complete the artistic experience.' Edgar Anstey, 'Skill, Time and Money Needed if Audience is to be Impressed', *The Times*, 27 June 1974, p. 16.
26. The research was carried out by Dr Neil Thompson, and reported to a British Rail standing committee on the vandalism campaign, a committee on which BTF was heavily represented, via Shepherd and others.
27. John Krish, *Introduction and Shooting Treatment for the DOE's Film on Road Safety for the Old*, July 1974, unpaginated, Krish collection.
28. Unidentified trade press article, Krish collection.
29. In a good indication of how the post-war documentary, especially by now, was aimed at those affected by its subject rather than at film intelligentsia, the premiere screening was pitched not at film journalists but at newspaper motoring correspondents. One of them, the *Evening Standard*'s Ian Morton, wrote: 'I have never known a heavier silence imposed upon a group of cynical motoring writers than that reigning at the end of these 17 clever minutes' (Ian Morton, 'Mystery of Our Safer Roads', *Evening Standard*, 19 February 1975, p. 32).
30. The initial research for *They Took Us to the Sea*, before he came up with the seaside idea, involved Krish touring Birmingham slums with an NSPCC officer. They came upon one group of children languishing alone in an adult-less house. Straight after returning from Birmingham Krish wrote this raw verse:

    This afternoon
    Birmingham is too busy to know
    about the boy who sits in semi-darkness.
    The house lies behind the noise
    the row soon to be pulled down
    so they said ten years ago.
    This afternoon he sits, white faced
    breathing the urinated fog that passes for air,
    He seems alone, but behind him lying still
    a small sister
    sucks a teat latched to a bottle once full of disinfectant,
    supplied by the WVS, now half full of milk
    supplied by the NSPCC
    Upstairs, standing in a cot, a younger sister yellow and frightened.
    This trio's mother is out, as usual, until they shut.

It is afternoon in Birmingham
and in this front room the blue light
from their television is their warmth.
The boy's face has lost its boyish look,
in this house where his childhood counts against him.
I think only of that smell
and that Television
and that boy.
He and I are in Communion.

31. There is wistfulness aplenty in the BTF catalogue, but largely confined to the travelogues. Those dealing with transport developments are always forward-looking. Krish's political error was to have mixed the two modes.
32. The project was probably what became *The Ruthless One*, directed by Douglas Gordon in 1956. The internationalism of post-war documentary is largely missing from Krish's career: his focus on domestic as well as social subjects strengthens its resemblance to the earlier, Movement, phase.
33. In the BRC's monthly magazine, the premiere of the film was enthusiastically reported upon: 'That scene with the mentally-handicapped: they weren't at all put off, just deeply moved by the plight of the afflicted. "Your parents", we prompted – "would they mind your doing that sort of work?" Embarrassed we were at their reply; it made us feel how out of touch we were ... whether their parents minded or not, the children felt a need to get involved with those less fortunate than themselves ... And the observers, the young teachers? One had been in the Junior Red Cross and most thoroughly approved of what she'd seen. They thought us right to highlight the exciting bits in a film like this. The technique, too: very "trendy". "Besides, it's what kids are used to these days". As for working with the mentally-handicapped, well ...! "Children don't want to be cosseted, you know. They see far worse things in their own homes on telly."' 'JRC Film Smack on Target', *Cross Talk*, May 1974, p. 24.
34. Krish got on much less well with the headteacher at the secondary modern than he had with his primary-school predecessor. When the director discovered that the head was trying to control the production he booked the crew their return tickets and they began packing up their equipment. It took the intervention of the NUT to order the head to cease interference.
35. *Return to Life* COI Briefing Sheet, undated, Krish collection.
36. COI press release, undated, Ken Gay collection Box 2, emphasis added.
37. Ministry of Labour press release, 24 May 1961, Ken Gay collection, Box 2.
38. E. D. Wright to Krish, 17 February 1977, Krish collection. The most compelling moment, of several in the film, is the trainees' conversation with a prison chaplain, a charismatic and troubled man whose haunted disquisition on the role of the priest in prison is kept on screen for far longer than conventional documentary technique would say it should be.
39. Both soundtracks were of troubled gestation. Krish sacked Richard Rodney Bennett, the original composer for *They Took Us to the Sea*, objecting to what he felt was an inert, overly intellectualised response. Beaver, an immensely talented but largely washed-up veteran who had been scoring *Secrets of Nature* at the start of the 1930s, had scored *The Salvage Gang: They Took Us to the Sea* was his penultimate score, the last being another CFF/World Wide production, *The Rescue Squad* (1963).

    Krish had originally asked John Betjeman to write the words for *John* but after what he felt was a patronising response he did it himself – tersely poetic, it is one of his best scripts.

40. See: <www.bfi.org.uk/features/interviews/krish.html>
41. John Krish, 'Don't Look at the Camera', January 1960, unpublished Graphic Films document, Krish collection.
42. One review of the television broadcast made a comparison with Richard Cawston's *This is the BBC* (1961), similarly building up an impression of the institution by a series of 'cameos' of typical moments.
43. *Film User*, August 1960, p. 456.
44. Cinna, 'Viewpoint', *Teachers World*, 4 May 1962, p. 7.
45. 'From Antonis, Mature Student from Greece at LFS', Krish collection
46. Even the supporting literature for *Let My People Go* emphasised that its subject 'transcends party politics': programme notes 'The Academy Cinema Presents: Let My People Go', Krish collection.
47. Krish and Kevin Brownlow both remember that at some unrecorded point in the 1950s, Lindsay Anderson started 'The Sunday Group' at a London cinema (Krish thinks it may have been the Scala), intended to be a series of screenings for working film-makers followed by intellectual discussion, the inaugural screening being of his own *Wakefield Express*. Brownlow and Krish both recall that following the screening, the latter stood up to denounce the film for hijacking the sponsors' money (breaching trust between sponsor and film-maker, which could cost documentary dear) in order rottenly to patronise the working class. An acrimonious debate apparently ensued, in which all possible views were aired and the audience split down the middle, for Anderson's viewpoint or for Krish's. After which nothing further was heard of The Sunday Group ...
48. A number of reviews of the broadcast of *Our School* compared it to a BBC production broadcast the following day, 'Problems at School', part of a 'Children Under Stress' strand of a series called *Lifeline*. The tone of the NUT films is, by contrast with such TV reportage, inspirational more than critical.
49. Michael Gilmour and John Krish, 'Introductory Note to the Script', *Drive Carefully, Darling*, Shooting Script, July 1973, unpaginated, Krish collection. My thanks to Margaret Deriaz and Cal Skaggs for their insightful comments on drafts of this chapter. (Cal is producing *To Tell the Truth*, a major TV history of documentary, as this book goes to press [planned for 2012 release]. For his book, Cal has conducted interviews with many documentary veterans, including John Krish.) My greatest debt of thanks goes to my friends John and Carole Krish.

16 Who's Driving?: *Peter Pickering*

PATRICK RUSSELL

Other film-makers discussed here, moving from project to project, were moving from funder to funder: this firm to that charity, one government department to another. As studies in sponsorship, their careers are collages, their personalities and preferences by turns concealed or revealed in work speaking for a cluttered cross-section of many of the institutions shaping post-war lives. Other film-makers worked for the same concern over and again, yielding careers shaped predominantly by its interests. As studies in sponsorship, *these* careers are detailed excavations of the many facets of just one subject: the film-maker evolves in tune or in tension with its developing requirements. If, say, Peter Bradford's career, or Peter Hopkinson's, typifies the first type, then Peter Pickering's exemplifies the second. Pickering's four decades behind the camera were fuelled, mainly, by one industry, its post-war form a single elaborate national institution, its life-force a distinct, deep-rooted culture, founded on a particular, potent mineral. They were fuelled by coal.

For the National Coal Board, Pickering directed some 150 items between 1947 and 1983, making him the most longstanding, prolific NCB film-maker, and his career a good choice of case study.[1] In outline, it corroborates the traditional view of documentary's decline, amply demonstrating its downgrading to the status of a corporate tool. In detail (when we look closely at the films, with an informed grasp of their context), it proves that even downgraded it's far from uninteresting.

Pickering's film career neatly separates into two halves, divided by a couple of years away from professional film-making in the early 1960s. It's the comparison between these two periods that proves telling. There are continuities. Technical films were bread-and-butter in both phases of Pickering's career as they were for all the coal film-makers, whose work has left us unparalleled visual documentation of the nationalised industry's grand technological project. Over the decades, these accumulated works reveal the replacement of the hand-winning of coal, which dominated the pre-nationalised industry, by gradual, then rapid, then near-total mechanisation, indeed partial automation and computerisation (the dream of the totally automatic coalface died, in Britain, with the NCB itself). This ongoing process unfolds fairly seamlessly across the two periods of Pickering's film-making.

But there are also arresting contrasts between the director's 1940s and '50s films, and those he made in the 1960s and '70s. The earlier ones, mostly entries in the *Mining Review* series, are richly enjoyable but easily taken as pleasant postscripts to the more mainstream work of the wartime Documentary Movement, into which Pickering had unwittingly stumbled in his teens. By being about colliers and their communities they inherit some of the earlier Movement's favoured iconography pretty much by default. The deeper similarity is that they're proficient films micromanaging the home front while implicitly cheerleading for social democracy, now not forthcoming attraction but main feature.

After his return to both industries, film-making and coalmining, Pickering's productions had a markedly different character, reflecting a film-making climate at the NCB of the 1960s that was oddly adventurous for a decade of decidedly mixed fortunes in mining itself. Intriguingly, those of Pickering's films addressing directly (for strictly practical purposes) the radically altered circumstances in which the industry found itself are the very ones in which a pleasing personal style emerges with the fewest compromises. His film-making has no identifiable visual character, beyond a spare, effective technique instinctively honed by years of shooting in conditions as cramped technologically as they were physically. What *is* evident is a writer's interest in sound logical structure, and an appealing instinctive stance towards the recurring human subject matter of the industrial film-maker: decent, self-effacing, observant – but sceptical.

This last comes across most strongly in a peculiarly memorable sequence of particularly sour post-war docu-farces: internal NCB films with titles like *Who's Driving?* (1971). Tame if set against today's workplace satires, they are bracing if set against the documentary tradition from which they'd descended (its depictions of manual labour famously noble). Behind locked colliery gates, the negatives nagging and gnawing at the innards of the post-war settlement are let loose to fill the documentary screen: inefficiency, frustration, fruitless blame-positioning. Yes, an interesting case study.

ROTHA, AND DATA

Peter Pickering, who'd been born in 1924 into a lower middle-class London family, found himself in 1941 unhappily clerking at a Central London publisher's. At grammar school, he'd had an inspiring teacher named Harry Rée, later dropped into France to become a celebrated member of the Special Operations Executive (SOE).[2] Pickering had stayed in touch with, and now confided his frustration in, him. Rée, on the fringes of left-wing intelligentsia, had been at Cambridge with Donald Alexander: he put Pickering in contact with him. Their first meeting (in a Soho pub, inevitably: The Pillars of Hercules, which is still there) would determine the younger man's future career. Pickering became a fellow employee at Paul Rotha Productions. In one of those surprising opportunities so often thrown up by those unique times, he got given a directing job (a public-information trailer entitled *Sabotage!* [1942]) before his eighteenth birthday. Otherwise Pickering's role was, in his words, 'general factotum' to Rotha, whose talent he now appreciates but whose authoritarian self-importance, back then, rubbed him the wrong way.[3]

Pickering was called up. Demobbed in 1947, on getting back in touch with Rotha and hearing of the DATA breakaway he threw in with the new cooperative. DATA was still newish, spirits high, its portfolio still diverse. Pickering assisted on several productions including Francis Gysin's *Scottish Universities* (1949) and J. B. Holmes's *Probation Officer* (1950).[4] But directing opportunities came quickly to keen twentysomethings thanks to the company's exciting acquisition of the *Mining Review* contract. DATA's first issue of the series, *1st Year No 7* (1948), opens with a Pickering item, 'Living In' (about an Easington training centre) and closes with 'Coal on Ice' (about a Fife miner heading for the Winter Olympics as a member of the British ice hockey team), filmed, unusually, by two units, one directed by Pickering, the other by Mary Beales.[5] The following issue also opens with a Pickering piece, 'Pithead Nurse'. He remembers: 'I shot this with Su [Wolfgang Suschitzky] ... This was when he told me – a timid newcomer – "You're the director!" and insisted that I chose the shots.'

The BFI holds a largely complete set of DATA's *Mining Review* production files which provide the only reliable information on who filmed what (the series never included personal credits), and often contain fascinating ephemeral details. As a whole they communicate well what the experience of making the series must have been like. In keeping with the period's protocols, there's formality in DATA's external communications, banter behind the scenes. The impression given is of very nice folk with an effortless belief in the value of justifying public ownership and bringing positive imagery of miners into cinemas. The intensity of the belief evidently shrank with time; the informed affection for coalfield culture only grew.

The fun they had leaps from the screen. Still, watching many *Mining Review* stories with the volume down, it's easy to imagine more adventurous films in the directors' heads when shooting, than when cut to three minutes, John Slater's breezy commentary superimposed, music thickly pasted and everything formularised. 'The office was always buzzing with indignations,' Pickering says, citing the constraining influence of the series' longstanding editor Dick Storey, a talented former newsreel man of hard-won dexterity but hard-nosed disdain for any whiff of Art in the footage brought to him. Production schedules for the monthly series were kinder than the newsreel companies' (first cuts made on rush prints, whereas weekly newsreels usually got their sole edit on the camera negative), but it's fair to observe that *Mining Review* fuses 'documentary' matter with 'newsreel' manner.

Among other things, that makes it impossible to distinguish one director's work from another without the files' aid. Pickering's output, then, is highly representative of the rest. Most stories fell into a few categories. There were reports of community events (Pickering's 'Miners' Festival', say), personal portraits ('Geordie Browne'), technical items, naturally ('Lambton Worm', 'Gloster Getter'). And there were quirky interest stories ('Trawler', whose freelance cameraman was seasick throughout the stormy trip, merely loading the camera for Pickering to take the shots himself; 'Visit to Ayr', in which Scottish miners are visited by a group of Eton schoolboys, including a young Jonathan Aitken and several Cripps scions). Only coincidentally would all the stories in an issue be directed by the same person (as in *2nd Year No 11* [1949], for which Pickering supplied every item). Occasionally an important story would be given the whole issue. Pickering's first (closely supervised by Alexander, he recalls), was *2nd Year No 10* (1949), 'Replanning a Coalfield', about the NCB's planned migration of entire communities from increasingly worked-out Lanarkshire to coal-rich Fife. Important items like this were requested from the Board or specific departments. Mining communities themselves suggested others, like Pickering's likeable 'Downbeat', about a Kent miners' jazz band. Others were 'picked up' by the units when filming other stories. 'A Seat on A5' was about a group of retired miners whom Pickering's cameraman, John Reid, had chanced upon on his way to a shoot. The Geordie Browne story profiled another octogenarian ex-miner, an autodidact, in his Ashington study. Four issues later the touching 'Geordie Comes to Town' covered Browne's first visit to London in fifty-nine years (the 'young Londoner' accompanying Browne aboard the *Cutty Sark* is Pickering's daughter).

Close organisation was involved in setting up and bringing items in on time. They were investigated (usually by their eventual directors) a month or so before personnel, equipment and stock were shipped to the scene for filming. Often several recces or shoots were combined to make the most of train fares and hotel bills, like those for the three contrasting Pickering stories covered on one 1956 north-eastern trip: 'Winlaton Sword Dance' (a folk tradition which would give any modern safety planner a cardiac arrest!), 'Northumberland Dedication' (Ashington Cathedral's Rogation service) and 'Brass Bands'.[6]

Lovely as they are, compared to much 1950s documentary reportage these little films feel increasingly rather quaint. This is a function of the equipment with which they were made (mainly for NCB safety reasons, DATA was stuck, much longer than most, with wartime camera and sound technology) but also of a stylistic atrophy descending on DATA's productions, not coincidentally overlapping with the increasingly inescapable obviousness of the fact that post-war Britain wasn't quite the utopia its prophets had imagined. Covering the Lanark to Fife story (the biggest internal migration in Scotland's history), Alexander and Pickering still have a foot in Rotha's world, one of tumultuous change, where exciting futures might grandly emerge from smoky industry's churning pasts, where 'the difference between plan and chaos' is still something to get excited about; where Slater's talk of past closures is met by a shot of a man walking away from the camera, where his rhetorical question about the future is answered by a *group* of men walking towards it. But their other foot is in a more prosaic world where policy-makers must try to square rationalism with compassion, evidently leaving their official film-makers feeling conflicted. Pickering is obliged to give the NCB's Scottish head Lord Balfour centre stage, while finding room for the reservations of union reps at a meeting. After filming them (with superb facial close-ups, and touchingly awkward line-readings) Pickering retired to the bar with them and got very drunk on wee halfs and heavies. He comments that the shooting of *Mining Review* stories typically ended in a miners' pub on a Friday night with everyone in a state of euphoria – and that he would often find himself feeling pangs of middle-class guilt about having descended into their world with his crew before disappearing back to London. Yet, he also remembers, his hosts always met him with enthusiasm, grace and hospitality.

Within a few years, such tensions have worked themselves off the screen, the urgency has dissipated, and Rotha's pupils, liking it or not, have relaxed into sunny bulletins from inside the Butskellite consensus. The point is substantiated by a look at DATA's output other than *Mining Review*: minus Storey's punchy editing its increasing sluggishness is less well disguised. For starters, DATA made a few NCB films besides the regular series. Though Alexander had left DATA, and as the Board's new films officer had founded the NCB Technical Film Unit, for several years a proportion of technical commissions remained outsourced, some of them to his former company. These practical films shouldn't be dismissed: they were important. At a time when Britain's entire economic policy was predicated in part upon its miners winning as much coal as feasible, these films were intended significantly to aid their facility with transformative technology, or indeed their colliery managers or area directors' prior commitment to investing in it. For instance, Peter Pickering's *The Trepanner* (1956) provided many miners' introduction to the eponymous coal-cutter whose nationwide supply, vital to mechanised faces with thin seams, would increase tenfold within six years of the film's release. Pickering's *Installation of an Armoured Face Conveyer* (1958) reconstructs (to teach by example) one pit installing, over the weekend, a still more important handmaiden of modernised mining: virtually every longwall face in Britain would soon be equipped with its own armoured face conveyor (AFC). However, Pickering personally wasn't a mechanics man, and it shows, while DATA's films, generally, lack the incisive lucidity that Alexander's new unit had begun impressively displaying. In the AFC film, a meeting between the colliery manager and area mechanisation engineer is unconvincingly staged, badly post-synched and surrounded by heavy slabs of exposition suggesting the director hadn't entirely understand what he'd filmed them talking about. *Wagon Handling at Dalkeith* (1953) is so boring it's trance-inducing, although recut as 'Wagon Wheels' it's a perfectly peppy *Mining Review* item (similarly, Pickering's painstaking account of mechanised haulage on a Lanarkshire colliery's grounds – *Surface Mechanisation (Kingshill Colliery)* [1952] – yielded the more digestible 'Rope Trick').

Pickering's DATA films for other sponsors are also, too often, muddy and old fashioned. Much the most ambitious and surprising was a pair of films made with his then closest DATA friend John Ingram for, of all sponsors, the Anglo-Iranian Oil Company: *The Island* (1952) and *The Tower* (1954).[7] These films trace the construction, opening and initial operation of the new refinery and port on Kent's Isle of Grain which significantly assisted BP's penetration of the newly competitive British fuel market, ironically aided by the coal shortages the NCB was busy battling. Though credited to both men, Pickering states that they were directed by him but written by Ingram. This was a slow-burn project, shot over several years during which the film-makers kept in touch with site managers and about once a month went down to Kent for a week's research and shooting. *The Tower*, focused on the refinery itself, especially the erection of the distillation unit at its heart, slots easily alongside DATA's films for other industries. Low-angle shots and suspenseful music inject doses of heroism and romance into an essentially process-based story with a technocratic message (actors, including Slater, providing off-screen voices for construction workers, draftsmen, trainees: everyone neatly fitting into the master plan). *The Island* is more complex, fascinating and problematic. Covering earlier stages, it depicts tensions between the Isle's long-entrenched rural community and environment and the incoming oilmen, adopting a dual perspective that its sequel stripped away. Acted voices of the engineers narrate scenes of the site being surveyed, drained and built upon – scenes similar to *The Tower*'s operational content – but alternate with a local voice representing the besieged community, philosophically musing upon time and change. These conflicting forces are reconciled, but so conveniently and perfunctorily as to leave the viewer with the strong impression that resolution hadn't been achieved at all. *Monthly Film Bulletin*'s review referred to a 'slightly pretentious 'poetic' quality, where the film might have profited from a more down to earth technique'.[8] The theme (rural timelessness harmonised with necessary modernity) feels like a Documentary Movement throwback, plus distant home counties echoes of Robert Flaherty, while stylistically, too, Ingrams and Pickering seem to be fighting a previous war. The high-contrast cinematography of noble landscape compositions is exceptionally attractive, suitably accompanied by a Malcolm Arnold score. The film-makers evidently thought they were bringing a lyrical touch to DATA's increasingly formulaic output while breathing creativity and even political enlightenment into the sponsor's brief. Their direct sponsor, Ronald Tritton, doubtless felt in turn that he was applying their ambition so as to enable his employer to win over viewers more subtly and cleverly than many in the company might have been inclined to – while getting the more conventional *The Tower* thrown into the bargain. If so, Tritton's view was probably closer to the truth than the directors'. What they actually *made* was pretty good middlebrow oil-company propaganda very much in the style of a Greenpark production of a few years earlier, though leaving some intriguing unanswered questions hanging in the air around it. *The Island* remains an absorbing case study in the shifting post-war relationships between artist and sponsor, films officer and Board of Directors.

DATA had originally expected a core activity to be making films for the Cooperative movement, seeing as it was itself a formally affiliated co-op. This never panned out: the Cooperative Wholesale Society notoriously failed to formulate a rigorous film policy. But Pickering did direct three Cooperative films: *It's Up to You!* (1954), *It's All Yours* (1956) and *Your Business* (1956). In the last, identical twins (not, as it at first appears, double exposure) are used to visualise a housewife as both CWS customer and owner. The gender stereotyping is predictable, but the film has a pleasantly light touch. *It's All Yours*, for the London CWS's Education Department, makes the same points about common ownership, but by far more basic expositional means. What is more interesting is that it makes a much more ideological pitch than most CWS films of the 1950s, which usually emphasised product advertising over political rationale. DATA's film openly attacks audience apathy: '*Her* shop. *His* society. Owned and controlled by *them*. How often do they forget it?'

The British Productivity Council twice engaged DATA, and on one of these projects Pickering was the allotted director. *All Over the Shop* (1955) is capably produced, but one of the plainest films in the BPC catalogue (which is saying something ...). Consisting of accounts of work study's successful introduction at a Dartford pharmaceutical company, a Sydenham electronics firm and a Leicester clothes factory, it notes the common factors. These firms were all agreeable to exposing complex, specialised processes to objective logical analysis; and at all three, management and staff shared sensible motives and proceeded positively and collaboratively. Although actors (Slater again included) are used to voice various people on screen, their lines are written and delivered matter-of-factly, and the corresponding visual content is, overwhelmingly, of minimally staged on-site footage of the workplaces. DATA's other BPC film, *Method Study in the Office* (1958) was directed by Leslie Shepherd, and produced by Pickering. Mostly it is made in a similar style. DATA's phlegmatic approach to the productivity genre reflects a certain double Puritanism: rather spartan, stylistically, while, politically, being willing to commend scientific management to workforces only if minus gimmickry and guile.

There is the hint of a different sensibility in the bridging sequences that Pickering imposed on Shepherd's film, featuring comedians Eric Barker and Pearl Hackney epitomising *in*efficiency. In this context, it's also worth mentioning a bizarre 1956 side-project for DATA, a speculative theatrical 'B' feature film that was an offshoot of a *Mining Review* story shot at Skegness' Miners' Holiday Camp. Pickering directed its music-hall cast in an improvised farce about a disaster-prone show, ending with the theatre going up in flames. Called *We Never Opened*, it never did. Distributors turned it down; Pickering and *Mining Review*'s then-editor Robert Kruger added a narration by Deryck Guyler (who voiced many DATA documentaries, including *The Trepanner*), only to see it spurned again. It was presumably laboured and rather amateurish: we'll never know since no copies have survived. Pickering recalls that 'off-stage the acting of the "cast" (and/or my direction of them!) was ... well!!!' Yet, a decade later and back underground, the concept of directing non-professionals in semi-doc low comedy would furnish his most characterful films.

Pickering's last DATA production was *Learning in Slow Motion* (1961), 'a record of research into subnormality' filmed at Epsom Manor Hospital, in collaboration with psychologists Alan and Anne Clarke. The Clarkes pioneered there the vocational training of the learning-disabled, to international acclaim in the psychiatric community. So the film has some historical importance. One of DATA's first forays into 16mm production, it's a hybrid of scientific research-and-teaching film with social documentary, and the Central Film Library picked it up for wide distribution. Its technique is static and stodgy, and its message couched in terms sounding less enlightened today than they were then ('these patients can never hope to lead independent lives but ... they can nevertheless achieve in a restricted sphere on simple industrial tasks levels similar to those of normally intelligent people'). Still, it's the sort of socially progressive film-making that DATA was founded in the expectation of doing much more of. As things had developed, it now rarely worked on anything but *Mining Review*. The contract renewal became an annual cliffhanger. In Pickering's own caustic recollection, DATA's story was a small-scale retelling of an ancient story, the journey 'from idealism to apathy to a kind of corruption'. He'd never exercised a leadership role, always more an attentive observer, and frequent intermediary between factions, eventually finding himself on DATA's managing committee. Before the cooperative's downfall, he jumped ship. He'd already been taking on outside work, as a scriptwriter for schools television, then in its infancy. Freelancing for Associated-Rediffusion, he wrote scripts for *The British Isles* (1960–1), *Looking About* (1961–2) and virtually every episode of *Finding Out* (1964–5), the first UK television series for infant schools. His interest in solid construction and clear communication was perhaps ideally matched to this new genre.

At DATA, Pickering was almost the youngest person around, at Associated-Rediffusion practically the oldest. Increasingly turned on by education, he retrained as a schoolteacher, but, after a couple of terms on the job, got an offer to come back to film-making at the NCB, which he accepted. Teaching at a London primary had proved a tougher way to earn a living than directing films.

BACK AT THE COALFACE

In 1964, Pickering became for the first time an NCB employee, remaining so until 1975. Thereafter he was freelance, still working mainly for the Board. In his brief absence, plenty had changed. On the grand scale, the 1960s, for coal, was a mammoth tragi-comedy. At the very moment years of reinvestment kicked in, speedily spreading a modernised infrastructure and technical philosophy across every coalfield, into every colliery, upturned market conditions and fickle government policies conspired to cause dramatic, rapid downsizing. At the margins of this puzzle sat a smaller one: the NCB's film section, now firmly ensconced inside this traumatically shrinking industry, was newly minded, and surprisingly able, to *expand* its horizons.

DATA had folded. Alexander had brought *Mining Review* into the renamed NCB Film Unit. In 1963, he'd resigned as films officer and producer, having first head-hunted his replacement: Gysin, abroad since 1958 heading Shell's Venezuelan film operations. Gysin's period running the NCB's film programme has been undervalued. He's easily seen in the shadow of his illustrious first-generation predecessor, perhaps contrasted with him as a lighter-weight character and nonchalant producer. Whatever their merits as film-makers or managers (difficult, at this distance, to assess), the range of films produced under Gysin is less coherent, but just as impressive. Inheriting several DATA staff and existing Film Unit employees, he supplemented them with new hires, like Alexander becoming known as a good employer to go to for valuable camera or cutting experience plus union card, before moving to mainstream film or TV. So two generations mixed: one cradled in Soho Square twenty-five years before, another fresh, freer-spirited, owing nothing to Rotha's or Grierson's doctrinal purities. Middle-aged, Pickering fell somewhere in between. Some of his later output suggests a certain creative restlessness had been inhibited hitherto, its only outlet the ultimately flawed *The Island*.

The NCB's predicaments were paradoxically propitious. Lord Alfred Robens was its first twentieth-century-born, media-conscious chairman, the first personally interested in its own use of film. For general distribution, *Mining Review* still needed making, but coal's new need to compete prompted the Unit into previously closed-off genres: sales and prestige films, respectively pursuing hard and soft sell. For internal distribution, technical instruction remained in high demand, but the stresses on the corporation prompted films facing the bigger picture more directly. Looking, in turn, at Peter Pickering's *external*, *internal* and *non-NCB* work, the dynamics of these sponsor–film-maker relationships appear yet more multifaceted.

EXTROVERSION

The everyday work continued to be *Mining Review*, renamed *Review* in 1973. Just as before, directors covered local interest (Pickering's 'Children's Band', filmed at Cotgrave, Nottingham), touching social stories ('Helping Hand', about Lea Hall Colliery, Staffordshire miners' involvement with a local C of E orphanage) and jovial eccentricities ('Dogs Allowed', about a menagerie of pomeranians who line up for their food on a 'shift' basis; 'Lucy's Table', about Barnsley billiard-players' parrot mascot).[9] The technical coverage became yet more extraordinary: 'Phoenix', about reopened Lynemouth Colliery, Europe's largest undersea mine, depicts a vast, futuristic treadmill of machines, miners and conveyors.

The 1960s issues use music more sensitively than DATA's, and employ a more spontaneous camera style including judicious use of the zoom lens. In the 1970s, all editions became single-story issues, and their house style became blander (not helped by increasingly terrible accompanying library music), but the choices of content were revealing. On one hand, many issues nostalgically looked back. For example, Pickering's 'The Art of Mining' reuses footage from his 1950s coverage of the Ashington painters group in a summary of the history of miners' art. Yet alongside this sat an increasingly obsessive attention to *contemporary* energy crises, and propaganda for coal as the cavalry that could ride to the nation's rescue. These films' repeated sideswiping of oil and nuclear is remarkably strident, given that governments committed to fuel diversity had indirectly funded them. For *24th Year No 12*, subtitled 'Energy on Earth', Pickering interviewed the outgoing Robens and his incoming, cerebral successor Derek Ezra. An uncharacteristically reflective, if self-justificatory, Robens comments of governments that 'their error' had been to underestimate the growth of affluence and the place of coal in sustaining it. The production team throws in montages of the pastoral, urban and even third world, using plenty of bought-in footage, culminating with a still of Earth from space. In 1979's *32nd Year No 11* ('The Race Is On'), 'we stand between a future that has not arrived and a past that has gone forever'. The off-screen voice (now Gysin's, incidentally) has become more pressing, the on-screen crosscutting of heavy industry, eerie power stations, newspaper headlines, even famine scenes, swifter and more insistent. Thinking of Pickering's CV, and Gysin's, it's hard not to hear tinny echoes of Rotha: the repressed returning, though returning enfeebled. These montages are cut to dire contemporary library music (rock guitar in 1971; by '79, cheap synths), and the rhetoric's urgency smacks more of desperation than drive – though perhaps only in hindsight. 'The prize for winning the race may well be survival': faith is urged in NCB scientists' world-beating ingenuity, the clout of British Coal International (global trading arm, since 1977, for the NCB and its various subsidiaries and partners), and the 'one thing we can be sure of', that 'coal is beneath our feet'. Britain *was* at the cutting edge of mining research; BCI had a degree of success; and the coal's still down there. But history tells us that a treble bet on corporatism, collectivism and coal is one spectacularly ill advised, if placed in the year of 1979.

'The Race Is On' had been made simultaneously in two versions: the ten-minute *Review* for the British public, and a thirty-minute global BCI promotional tool, distributed to France, China and Latin America. Replete with technical and organisational detail, it's essentially a different, much less heady film. Pickering's other sales films are all (to say the least) less heady still. NCB subsidiary National Smokeless Fuels sponsored *Getting the Best out of Sunbrite* (1977), whose efforts to prove that the eponymous coke 'will burn evenly, steadily, night after night, day after day' with maximum convenience rather backfire on explanations of how air-vent controls have to be fiddled with.

Even non-coal collaborators with briefly coinciding interests were courted: *Conversions* magazine had input into Pickering's *Home and Warm* (1967). A young family start doing up a large Surrey Victorian house, installing, of course, solid central heating. Facetiously seen through the daughter's eyes ('Mummy says Daddy's always right! Well ... usually ... don't you Mummy?'), with 'magic' jump-cuts for before-and-afters, it's pleasant kitsch which, abridged and reprinted in black and white, became a story in *Mining Review 20th Year No 10*. More often, Pickering found himself working for the mainly Scottish firms that supplied mining equipment to its sole UK buyer, the NCB. *Up To Date with Anderson Maver* (1971) was, for sending to sales territories behind the Iron Curtain, translated into Polish and Chinese. *The Modern Mine* (1965) originated as a multi-screen colour film installation at the 1965 Confederation of Underground Machinery Manufacturers' London exhibition, then was repurposed as a regular film for general distribution. Shot at a colliery, two years from full production, planned as a test-bed for a generation of remotely operated longwall faces (ROLFs), it none-too-compellingly depicts a science-fiction environment in which the central controller sits at his console of monitors and calibrators surveying his domain. But the ROLF strategy proved premature, electronics still being too imprecise (Bevercotes, the flagship Nottinghamshire colliery where this film was shot, reconverted to standard operation six years later).

Pickering's most ambitious project, probably the Board's costliest film ever, was the fifty-minute *Longwall USA* (1970), jointly sponsored by the NCB's Production Department and suppliers Dowty and Gullick Dobson. Seeking to boast of and to boost the market inroads that British equipment was making into the USA's capitalist coal business, it proved an object lesson in affably awful British project management meeting transatlantic culture clash. Filming at collieries in Pennsylvania, Illinois and Utah using American technicians, each time they turned up to find no one expecting them, each time necessitating hasty negotiations with perplexed or suspicious managers, but within minutes of which they were underground filming their first and only takes – US health and safety being infinitely laxer than Britain's (where an indispensable part of the process was getting an Exemption to Film Underground form countersigned weeks before shooting). Pickering's preference for structured exposition survived the chaotic production circumstances: each of the three geographical chapters intercuts above-ground explanation, below-ground visual coverage and a more discursive section using location photography and interviews to evoke an unfamiliar coalmining culture and sociology. Standard-of-living comparisons are emphasised. A descending dayshift leaves behind a carparkful of spanking new autos; the narration later lists typical earnings which (though the film needn't make the comparison explicit) are some four times greater than British mineworkers'. Some interviewees have British connections. One miner's father had come from 'Durham County, England'; another says the English did better than many migrant mining communities because they worked hard and 'spoke better American'. Such sociological details are incidental to the film's function, but provide its only gripping content. In the pits themselves, their infrastructure so unfamiliar to him, and having been given little briefing, Pickering simply couldn't understand what he was asking his crew to shoot. And as *they* were New Yorkers, they had no clue either. To make the footage comprehensible and keep the managers sweet he felt obliged to film them in their offices, speaking to camera describing their pits' layouts. The film thrice grinds to a standstill as these men explicate sitemaps in impenetrable detail.

Pickering evidently approached these jobs with weary professionalism mixed with cheerful cynicism. More promising was the NCB's newfound enthusiasm for prestige production. Gysin's team turned out a mixed bag of productions loosely falling into the category: *The Big Meeting* (1963); Robert Vas's *The Master Singers – Two Choirs and a Valley* (1965); David Pitt's *Coals! Coals!* (1967); Robin Carruthers' *The Cathedral in a Village* (1969); and, most memorable of all, visiting Australian director Richard Mason's *Portrait of a Miner* (1966). Pickering's contribution, 1965's twenty-minute colour film *Two Worlds*, is a different proposition: botched, but illuminatingly so, leaving a fascinating and telling impression of director and sponsor both repositioning themselves, a little too anxiously (making up for lost time?) and a little too pretentiously (suggesting it's too late).

Two Worlds was marketed as a documentary about 'the parallel between the mining and using of coal in new ways and teaching young people new skills for the modern world'.[10] It's certainly on comfortable ground celebrating preceding years' mechanical advances, and the newer remote control of faces. Cue large monochrome chunks of Film Unit library footage, including shots and outtakes from *The Team on 204s* (Pickering's mechanisation training film of the previous year). But the technical revolution is rhymed with wider social progress, especially in education – illustrated by vivid Eastmancolor footage of colleges and schools in the North East, Nottingham and Devon, as well as Hexham Abbey, which places everything in a longer historical continuum. The link being that they all use solid fuel heating systems.

In many ways, *Two Worlds* is the counterpart, in the director's second period, of *The Island* in his first. According to Pickering, the regular NCB directors were intensely jealous of Mason and *Portrait of a Miner* – the NCB's 'art film', stylistically modelled on the British New Wave. *Two Worlds*, competing instead with other sponsored film-making, is a studied pastiche of more assured, expensive prestige essays: Jennings's *Family Portrait* (1950), the more florid BTF historical travelogues and, most blatantly, the oil-sponsored prestige film. Its opening lines set the mood: 'Beneath this English soil – lies energy. Down there, the sunlight of primeval time crumbles in the hand, and the forest of layered centuries that no man saw now crumble beneath our machines.' Cue shots of a shearer busily slicing through a face.

After decades' obscurity, *Two Worlds* was revived by the BFI for a 2007 screening. Seeing it again, Pickering wrote about it with refreshing honesty:

> I can vaguely remember ... that the brief offered the possibility of making something other than ... technical expositions and didactic managerial assertions ... [but] it seems to me now ... pretentious and vapidly 'poetic'. ... Wool from a third-rate sheep pulled over the eyes of the NCB Marketing Department, who surely needed, if they needed a film at all, something to convince or mislead their customers into buying solid fuel installations rather than the alternatives offered by their oil, gas and electricity competitors.[11]

The NCB of *Two Worlds* is a corporation too insecure to rest its case on its truly impressive technical record without groping for momentarily fashionable Wilson-era rhetoric rather at odds with its temperamental conservatism. The narrator speaks about 'radical times', 'the spirit of our times', 'bright new flames', while the director duly supplies footage of laboratories, new university architecture, telescopes and, well, bright new flames. Unfortunately, it takes at least two viewings to make proper sense of all this. That second or third viewing reveals a film as schematic in its underlying design as it is confusing on the surface, built on a painstaking series of conceptual contrasts. Underground/overground, monochrome/colour, past/present, present/future. brawn/brain, men/machines (in the mine), art/science (in the classroom), male/female, adulthood/youth: the film ends, in classic social documentary vein, with fresh-faced children in a primary school playground.

Binary oppositions all but, the film argues, actually symbiotic pairings: two worlds composed of the one energy. Unfortunately, Pickering's no Schopenhauer.[12] He anyway can't escape his two worlds' dreary connecting portal, being obliged constantly to cut back to basement boiler rooms. This is necessary, to remind bemused viewers (and a perhaps equally bemused sponsor) of the pretext for his cerebral meanderings. Yet the contractual obligation also feels like a visual Freudian slip, the film, and nationalised mining itself, not so much bridging two worlds as inescapably sandwiched between them. It would have been improved had the NCB been able to afford a luscious score by a Lutyens or Williams (instead, it's coarsened by Kenneth Morrison's tinkly efforts), but had Pickering spent ten years working on prestige films like his BTF and private-sector counterparts, he might have turned out something surer-footed in the first place. He further confuses his prestige pitch by switching into different modes of address entirely, including a modish sequence about Newcastle University students containing vox pops and self-consciously 'with-it' jump-cuts.

Two Worlds received a big press screening, but its beautifully unscratched archival film elements suggest that it wasn't booked often, and never needed reprinting, though NCB catalogues highlighted its suitability for colleges and for 'film societies and adult groups'. So too Pickering's next major NCB external film – which, made a decade later, couldn't be more different. Unself-conscious, understated, affecting, *Miners* (1976) is like *Two Worlds* a film mindful of more esteemed models for documentary. But the model is not the (now steeply declining) sponsored prestige film but its usurper: television. Happily, this time the film-makers aren't straining to keep up with it, instead breathing a sigh of relief that television technology has belatedly caught up with *their* original mission, so long ago proclaimed by Donald Alexander: to humanise 'The Miner'. Indeed, the request for the film, by Geoff Kirk, Head of Public Relations (and Gysin's line-manager), was couched in terms of the Board's film history: that the 1970s needed their equivalent to the previous decade's *Portrait of a Miner*, itself replacing *The Miner* made for the NCB by J. B. Holmes at World Wide in 1950.

Commissioned in October 1974, *Miners* wasn't released until June 1976, having been derailed by tragedy. Pickering found at Daw Mill Colliery, Warwickshire, a respected, engagingly eloquent machine operator with whom he spent many hours, taping their conversations to inform the shape of the film to be based around him. The day before shooting was to start, he was killed in a car accident. Sequences of the tapes where he talked of career plans, family, forthcoming holidays immediately acquired unbearable poignancy.[13] Distraught, the director closed down then restarted the project, moving it to Bagworth Colliery, Leicestershire, focusing not on an individual but on a whole shift, and some of its spouses. This enables a far better-grounded 'two worlds' concept to be integrated fully with the film's method. Underground and overground footage, speech and sounds, voices and faces, men and women: each subtly reinforces what's stated or implied by the other. Below the surface, lightweight, blimpless 16mm cameras, containing fast stock, are used. So, cleverly and crucially, are miners' lamps in place of the heavy flameproof lighting with which the NCB's film-makers had long been encumbered. The excitement of cameraman Jim Howlett at being able to prowl around the pit, track down corridors, is palpable: a shooting style that's almost literally a breath of fresh air. But although the men there are heard as well as seen, their verbal contributions to the film ('Down there, it's a different world'; 'Everyone's the same, down the pit'; 'Years ago it was cloth and cap, pick and shovel ... it's a skilled job, now') are from tape-recorded interviews played over that footage of them at work. It's the wives whom we simultaneously see and hear speak, interviewed in their lounges and kitchens, Pickering and Howlett occasionally picking up details like ironing being done by the interviewee, or family photos behind.

So the film's voice, essentially, is female: a politically important point. This isn't, of course, an oppositional film, but it does need to soften harder edges of the miners' modern case, made as it now was in light of two major national strikes and the resulting Wilberforce pay settlement, far from universally popular with the public. 'How many people when they have to go to the toilet do what a miner has to do, and go back and eat his food. Not many men would put up with that,' says one wife. 'They say the miners are always wanting this, that, more money. But would they do it? No.' Pickering's first cut included some grim safety statistics being cited by an off-screen voice – shades of the facts on death and injury more urgently intoned by the narrator of *Coal Face* in 1935. Kirk politely, firmly, insisted this must be removed. The women do, though, talk about their worries for their men.

Meanwhile, social changes tracked from the earlier films are significant. One wife says that after years of renting, she and her husband bought a house seven years previously. Another comments on the differences between Leicestershire and the tight-knit Durham coal community she'd come from. *These* miners aren't huddled in shared necessity near the bottom of the national salary-scale in rows of houses clustered round their collieries. Like many Midlands mining families (more than those in Wales, Scotland, and England further north), they've dispersed into mixed housing estates. Embracing private ownership, they're at the early stages of resembling the Americans Pickering had filmed in 1969. 'Scab' Bagworth, like most of Leicestershire and Nottinghamshire, remained open throughout the 1984 strike. Back in 1976, when the NCB paid for the whole face team and all their wives (not just interviewees) to come to the premiere at Hobart House (the NCB's London HQ), the Film Unit itself had seven years' life left. This would prove its last major production for the public; it now assumes an unmistakably elegiac tenor, which might well have been invisible to its subjects and its makers that day in Hobart House. There's a lovely shot near the end, a gentle pan round the cage taking in all the faces of all the men ascending from the shift – faces which then break, all of them, into smiles. Soon, the men are back out, returning their lamps, the shift's over and the film has closed on them leaving the grounds at dusk.

Besides late *Reviews*, Pickering made only one further NCB film for non-mineworkers, a curiosity worth mentioning. *A Dangerous Playground* (1980) was made to discourage schoolchildren from colliery vandalism, graphically illustrating its hazards. At Bolsover Colliery, Pickering interviewed the safety officer to ascertain likely accidents, worked with Bolsover School's headmaster to find pupils of various ages to enact such scenarios, then on the colliery grounds hastily committed to 16mm their improvised performances. The result makes a good addition to any cult retro programme of the period's gory safety films, alongside better-remembered shorts like John Krish's *The Finishing Line* (1977), and especially John MacKenzie's *Apaches* (1977), distributed to rural schools and local television to discourage children from wandering onto farms equipped with lethal modern machinery. An expensively mounted half-hour parable with genuinely creepy dreamlike ambience, *Apaches* received quite extensive trade press attention. *A Dangerous Playground* – which didn't – is a squat, earthy, no-frills, working-class, heavy-industry counterpart weirdly devoid of narrative: strung-together episodes of energetic but bored kids, on half-term perhaps, mucking about under dusky-brown early autumn sunshine before they (or nearby surface workers) meet violent ends under coal trucks or slagheaps. Only at the end does any story surface: the Derbyshire Constabulary fishes one victim from the mud, then brings his father home to break the news to his wife. Pickering shock-cuts her distraught reaction with flashbacks to the various corpses who've littered the preceding quarter-hour. Though this feels a wee bit exploitative now, the intention is sincere, if the execution rather gauche. Without extant data measuring its deterrent effect, *A Dangerous Playground* is hard to evaluate except as a period piece incidentally capturing smatterings of the conversational culture of coalfield childhoods on the eve of the industry's *Gotterdämerung*.

INTROSPECTION

Turning to Pickering's internal films, the one prolific production line to which he made scant contribution was films for the annual cycle of nationwide safety campaigns that followed Robens's appointment. He supplied his continued share of other staff training. *Powered Supports '72* (1972) prefaces a survey of contemporary advanced support systems and a lucid explanation of the novel technical principles they're based on, with a history of the 'three-shift' cycle whose long-familiar stranglehold on mining had loosened. To train deputies, *Eyes on 80s* (1981) reconstructs a new appointee's first shift, ending with a nicely staged shot of him writing his end-of-shift report in an alcove from which the camera slowly tracks back, the light receding until it's a mere mid-screen flicker surrounded by black tunnel.[14]

Far richer were Pickering's 'state-of-the-industry' films. At DATA the director had felt more than usually engaged by the human dimension of *Mining Review* stories hinging on the triangular relationship of business demands to logistical challenge and group psychology. In 1949, making 'Success Story', Pickering had been impressed by the manager and men at Yorkshire's Wentworth Silkstone and their authentically collaborative accomplishment in doubling productivity. For 1955's 'Short Lease' he'd visited Wentworth Drift (a different Yorkshire mine), reporting similar good news. But Slater had narrated then that Wentworth Drift was one of those short-lived collieries winning 'badly needed coal in a hurry ... while the big new collieries are being sunk'. At the NCB of ten years later, meeting overall output targets remained desperately important, but it was no longer a question of throwing everything into extracting every lump of coal. Instead, prefiguring future terminology, 'market forces' had to be come to terms with, pits had to be 'economic'. Men taught for ten years to think one way were now to redouble their efforts in a different direction, while witnessing half their industry disappear around them. In the NCB official historian's words, it was 'a severe test of human nature', impressively passed, with costs that mounted later (when the industry's future brightened again but it was no longer so well equipped to capitalise).[15]

Film-makers like Pickering, aware documentary was evolving and equipped with lighter-weight gear than DATA had ever used, felt well placed to interpret on the screen the more sophisticated industrial psychology now required. In a career full of binaries, a crucial pair of opposites is the two sets of films Pickering made on such topics, in completely opposite registers. *The Team on 204s* (1964) and *The Longhirst Story* (1968) have a hopeful stance, rendered in a sober, modern documentary style. The cycle of films beginning with *Nobody's Face* (1966) revealed Pickering's truer metier to have been sarcastic comic fiction.

The Team on 204s was commissioned (under working title 'Mine Efficiency'), under joint sponsorship from the Board's Production and Staff departments for screenings at mechanisation courses, though bookable by anyone in the industry pursuing its two objectives: to convey the principles of organising power-loaded faces effectively, and to demonstrate that for teams working them, remarkable outputs were achievable.

By virtue of the first, *The Team on 204s* is valuable evidence for how a mid-1960s mechanised shift was intended to operate, taking viewers through several major steps (especially trepanning, stable-cutting and loading) and elucidating their interrelationships. Of broader interest is its tone: low-key, no brash *Mining Review*-style bluster. The unidentified colliery at which it's filmed (actually Lea Hall, Staffordshire) is, it's mentioned, unremarkable as regards geology and equipment, but is achieving a 14 tons per manshift output (the national average was then just above 5 tons, but the film, leaving inferences to viewers, deliberately doesn't quote that figure).

The ambient sound seems very natural. There is a narrator and his diction is clear, though northern-accented and conversational. But it alternates with those of the deputy, chargeman, loader and other men on the shift explaining what's happening as it unfolds in the present tense. The lessons are that each man's role in relation to each process and tool is always unambiguous; but the fundamental principle of teamwork and camaraderie still applies. 'It's the machine cutting the face that's going to make their money', but: 'The men behind the machines are the key.' The 'good shift' shown, and the whole face's good organisation, is the result of 'teamwork, initiative, confidence, craftsmanship, trust between men working together towards a common aim'. The film-makers assume their discreetly contemporary 1964 technique, allied to careful underplaying of the optimism, will make it much more likely to take.[16]

It's taken further by *The Longhirst Story*, filmed at M4's face, Longhirst Colliery, Northumberland (like the second Wentworth, and Lea Hall, a drift rather than a deep mine). M4's had been mandated a 'spearhead' face by Robens, selected to meet huge output targets: 1,000 tons per face-shift. The preface of Pickering's treatment argued that the film was 'largely about attitudes – the argument is that what was done at Longhirst can be done at many other places', so 'a straightforward, exhortatory film, with a commentary ... over re-created scenes, would be unlikely to convince. Attitudes ... must be demonstrated rather than described ... for this reason the Longhirst story should be told by the people who made it. The cumulative impression of a number of people, *no different in essence* from their audience, can communicate something of the "feel" of what lies behind M4's.'[17]

Pickering uses only one line of introductory narration. Thereafter the voices of Longhirst's protagonists carry the film's meaning. It is in two halves. In the second, more narrative-driven section these voices are off screen, as in *The Team on 204s* describing processes illustrated by highly technical footage. Odder is the first half, which consists largely of portrait 'cameos' of many of the people involved – from Northumberland's area director in his office through the method study engineer and the colliery manager to two miners, Consultative Committee members, in the canteen, all synopsising their part in the story – cut together, a patchwork of attitudes. Pickering's treatment had laid out a rough framework, leaving verbal detail open for shaping from the best bits of long interviews. Nonetheless, the treatment's expectations of what would broadly be said at which point fairly closely predicted the final balance. For instance, Pickering wrote that 'the consultative committee members' would express 'initial scepticism – but prepared to give it a try *because of attitude and atmosphere engendered*'.

These people all have wonderfully characterful, lived-in faces, communicating a lot about their place and ease in their specialised world by their brief presence on the screen, but none is identified other than by generic on-screen captions: 'Area Director', 'Chief Mining Engineer' or, even more gnomically, 'DDO' (which stood for Deputy Director of Operations) or 'Area IR Officer' (Industrial Relations). Another peculiarity is that they are often filmed facing the viewer, rather than in orthodox over-the-shoulder style. It's important not to misunderstand this approach: pragmatic, rather than experimental.[18] To contemporary mining audiences job titles were all that was needed to explain each individual's role, and because the point of the film is that their experience is generally applicable, Pickering avoids all distraction from its 'essence'. But that's precisely what makes *The Longhirst Story*, for anyone *outside* its original target audience, such a weird hybrid: half TV journalism customised for NCB use, half abstract meditation on the 'essence' of 1960s coalmining. The abstraction is emphasised by the conclusion, in which we revisit these faces and voices, as vox pops crosscut with a shearer moving closer and closer to the camera. Key political points are made in this final sequence. The DDO voices the most familiar, that Longhirst's successes are a 'compound' of 'consultation, organisation, supervision and enthusiasm' but above all 'determination'. A miner, staring straight at the camera, states that 'in future the pit, in order to exist, *must* adopt this type of face'. It is the area director who makes the most exacting point: Longhirst 'exploded a myth'. It proved that men would work without the 'carrot' of piecework, under the National Power Loading Agreement – this being 1966's crucial negotiated settlement that rationalised and standardised day rates for different classes of workers across the coalfields.

Soon after completion, a truncated 35mm blow-up version was put out as a regular *Mining*

Area director, colliery manager and miner explain their part in *The Longhirst Story*

Review. Removing the most esoteric content and adding a Slater narration rendered Longhirst's story generally intelligible while reworking its message for public consumption. 'In coalmining breaking the 1,000-ton barrier is like breaking the four-minute mile!' Longhirst is now more than merely a model for other collieries to aspire to, but *proof* of where they're all heading. 'In an industry already far ahead of the rest of Britain in productivity and output per-man, Longhirst is making a new pattern for the future of coalmining ... As the spearhead-face bandwagon really gets rolling, the benefits are to the industry and the nation as a whole – more coal off more efficiently planned faces, and ever-more competitive in cost!'

Off screen, Longhirst's story ended fast. Nearing exhaustion, it closed in 1969 – dying with its boots on as Wentworth Drift had, its namesake film long outliving it.

The Team on 204s reflects the NCB film-makers' intricate familiarity with the mining industry's technological set-up. *The Longhirst Story* reflects more their familiarity with its intricate structures of organisation. Specialist films, they're oddly intriguing to non-specialists precisely because of their strange sealed-off, airtight ambience. But there's more fun to be had on the flipside ... Between these two productions, in October 1965, Pickering was commissioned to make a film with the working title *Machine Utilisation on the Face*. Completed the following March, as *Nobody's Face* (1966), it proved the central film in the director's career.

Good shift/bad shift

The Production Department had requested a piece tackling shortfalls caused by inefficient machinery deployment at faces. Gysin allocated the project to Pickering, whose fact-finding commenced by interviewing Norman Siddall, a well-respected area manager in the East Midlands division (ironically, Britain's *most* efficiently productive). Siddall presumably expected another *The Team on 204s*. Pickering wanted to try a different tack, a comic parable of a hopeless, allegorical coalface – *Nobody's* Face. But to work it had to be shot at a real working face. Siddall bit, turning Markham No 4, Derbyshire, over to Pickering for one week. Installed 'on set' the director selected from the available miners the most promising partners in crime, ones who'd help him sketch a storyline knitting likely incidents together into one hapless shift – then perform it on camera with the right mix of veracity and exaggeration to connect with viewers 'no different in essence' from them. The film opened and closed with Robens addressing the audience, at length, direct from a viewing theatre, analysing the industry's challenges, drawing lessons from the story, and (as *The Team on 204s* had) explicitly connecting the industry's competence with its employees' personal prosperity.

The lineage of film-makers directing working-class people acting as 'themselves' or their 'types' to dramatise a 'documentary' account of the national state-of-play was of course eminent indeed. So the first thing to say is that the acting in *Nobody's Face* is great: believable *and* entertaining, nothing like Crown's stiff airmen or chirpy cockneys. In the lead, irascible machine man Johnny plays himself with glee, barely hampered by the necessary post-synching (the footage having been taken by the faithful hand-wound Newman Sinclair silent camera). Pickering remembers that Johnny came up with the line 'No wonder Lord Robens wants to close th' bloody pits!', which as director he seized on as the film's central talking point 'knowing Robens would love it'. In his outro, Robens rejoinders that '*I* don't want to close pits. The people who close pits are *customers*, the people who forsake us if our coal is not competitive in price.'

Pacy camerawork captures all the familiar images: cutters, the coal along the conveyor, the props, the cables, the telephone. But the props are falling over, the conveyor constantly grinding to a halt, the cables are always in the way and the phone's for bitching more than communicating. Pickering had wanted the story to speak for itself, but by providing a present-tense running commentary on what's happening, totting up the accumulated delays ('The machine is cutting. So far they have lost fifteen minutes ... Five minutes lost there ... Nearing the end of the first strip, they've lost fifty-seven minutes') the narration, improbably provided by Ewan MacColl, works well as an inversion of the po-faced, positive present-tense accounts littering Pickering and colleagues' technocrat process films since the 1950s.

Nobody's Face was listed in library catalogues as among the dozen or so films unsurprisingly 'restricted to NCB audiences', yet bizarrely became the basis of *Mining Review 23rd Year No 11*, subtitled 'Men and Machines – Let's Work Together'. It's easy to see how rapidly repurposing Longhirst's story had met the series' ongoing brief. What it was doing, five years late, with *Nobody's Face* is mystifying. Most of the play is left in, mildly coarse dialogue included (*Nobody's Face* was littered with the 'b' word: 'We shall never do two strips at this bloody rate!' 'Get the bloody stuff open and don't bloody argue!' 'I'll screw 'is bloody neck off when I get in that gate!'). But it carefully excises telling dialogue like the Robens reference, and ends on coal finally coming off the face (swiftly followed in the original by a final breakdown, a raging argument and the shift calling it a day). Whence Slater labels what we've just seen 'a fantasy, but based on real-life facts that could have happened, *not only in mining but in most industries*'. Robens's equivalent statement had been that Johnny's was 'a shift that I'm sure we all agree nobody works on; perhaps now you would like to consider another shift on which people *do* work, and that's your own', following which he'd urged viewers to do everything possible to get an extra half-hour cutting time out of each future shift. Which in the re-release becomes Slater's more detached, cheerful,

> just 1 per cent greater output from all our coalfaces would mean an extra million and a half tons' output a year ... the more that everyone in a mine knows what's going on, the better. It's good industrial relations, it's

> good communication. Today at British mines men and management are reaping the benefits of regular get-togethers, talking over man to man the sensible ways of beating those delays ... more continuous use of expensive machinery and skilled labour. That way lies enhanced security in the future, for mining and the nation!

Robens had ended the original staring straight at his audience, Kitchener-like, asking 'Will *you*, members of your consultative committee, representatives of your power-loading teams and under-officials discuss what can be done at *your* pit to get better machine utilisation?' Even to viewers unfamiliar with the off-screen economics, the feeling's inescapable: pressure's on. But the problem's being shared.

Nobody's Face was indeed judged helpful. Siddall's career progressing, by 1971 he was Director General of Production.[19] He asked Pickering to make a sequel, applied to the specific problem of face re-engineering delays. If *Nobody's Face* can be positioned as *The Team on 204s*' mirror image, then its sequel, *Who's Driving?* is a deconstruction of *The Longhirst Story*. Pickering's treatment, much more literate and ambitious than the finished piece (which suggests the backroom frustrations channelled into his characters?), is set in 'Hulldown, North Blankshire', peopled by essentially the same cast of symbolic, depersonalised administrators as Longhirst's, only remodelled as comic archetypes whose personalities are part of the *problem*. Pickering describes the area planner as 'an extremely diffident man with a conscientious, if cautious, mind' who 'has risen as far as he has because of the conscientiousness, and no further because of the diffidence ... a man who is used to not being heard', who 'irritates by bringing a martyred gloom to all proceedings'. The colliery planner has 'the look of a man determined to say nothing', while the mechanical engineer has 'the look of a man determined to say little very forcefully'. The deputy manager 'wishes he could remember the intricacies of what he'd learned on that course about "Accountability" '.[20]

The fifteen-minute film Pickering wound up with has fewer, far less nuanced characters and a greatly simplified storyline – but retains its unhappy milieu of insecure men who'd rather get through meetings in one piece than get decent decisions from them. The faulty planning depicted had been deemed by Siddall more a managerial than a coalface problem, and *Who's Driving?* was screened at managerial level only. The other, related and substantial, difference between *Who's Driving?* and *Nobody's Face* is technical: it was mostly shot above ground using 16mm synch. Pickering retains from his treatment an atmospheric attention to drizzle falling on the colliery car park (filmed through the office window-pane): in grainy 16mm, this evokes a descending dreariness with great economy. Indoors, he adeptly orchestrates rapid-fire, overlapping, often shouted dialogue, busy compositions and frequent movement within the frame, engendering a convincing impression of work processes descending faster, faster into chaos. Dramatic reconstruction aping Direct Cinema is common today – but not what you'd expect of a 1971 training film. This said, *Who's Driving?* isn't a 'pure' trigger film. Between scenes, it cuts to a timeline showing the weeks mounting up as the project gets further behind schedule. In an early scene, this chart is shown being mounted on the wall, to which the manager comments: 'That's alright as a chart, Will. Whether we'll actually achieve what it bloody shows, I don't know.' He quite lacks Johnny's charisma and wit but is believable as a dour, hard-boiled, hard-bitten fellow drifting out of his depth (it's perhaps apt that Siddall takes the Robens role opening and closing the film: if Robens loomed larger than life, the earnest, trustworthy Siddall seems smaller).

Even better were seven small throwaway pieces made between these two major NCB-wide releases, under series umbrella *Case Studies for Management* in 1970. 16mm, all under ten minutes long, they were shot at a training face (Kemball, Derbyshire), for screening at the NCB's Staff Training College, pure triggers to group discussion. These have no Robens or Siddall telegraphing their sarcasm's purpose, just pokerfaced narration by Pickering himself, and further terrific miners' acting. *What About That Job* counterpoints umpteen upbeat recruitment films, with a new miner sitting in a drab pub with a mate, lamenting his career choice. *Won't Do at All* is like a compressed *Nobody's Face* and ends on a zoom in to a hand-lamp (the logo for all the 1950s technical films: symbol *there* of clarity and purpose), as complaint and recrimination are heard dissipating into 'surrounding gloom'. The pick of the bunch is *It's Up To You*. At Black Hole Colliery, a failing face's luckless, defensive overman gets bollocked by his colliery manager: an uncomfortable, expertly acted, well-directed scene. Fred Gamage's camera tracks steadily closer as the man shifts in his seat under the tirade. 'You haven't achieved your bloody objective ... you'll get more bloody trouble than you've bloody known': method study and all! In the next set-up, we're below ground. Blame duly transmitted, two miners moan that it's all management's fault, closing this dispatch from a Sisyphean cycle of despondency. Considered too dark to risk being shown out of context, these films' distribution was, uniquely, strictly under the Staff College's direct control, not the NCB Film Library's.

With the self-reflexive, less-than-sparkling *Black Friday* (1978), the last of Pickering's 'negative' films, and the only one filmed in colour, we reach *reductio ad absurdam*.[21] It opens with a training officer being advised that a crew is coming later that day to make a safety film, closes with a jovial miner telling him the film unit's outside his room waiting to see him. In between, staff visit him with various problems, each vague conversation petering into procrastination. The training officer is a Mr Gamage, his visitors named Pitt, Morgan and Pearson: all surnames of NCB Film Unit directors. The acting's once again non-professional and semi-improvised. But the story this time revolves entirely around one protagonist, in an undramatic white (if grubby white) collar above-ground setting. Coaxing naturalism from him is more challenging and Pickering pulls it off only at the cost of filming him in unsettlingly long, static takes. Such cold formalism, applied to teeth-grindingly humorous content intensifies the dismal atmosphere and sense of pointlessness beyond what's bearable. Gamage's entire job apparently consists of sitting at his desk or pacing his dishevelled office in mounting annoyance at interruptions to a day spent mislaying documents, ducking files falling off untidy shelves and telephoning half-hearted excuses for never delivering anything on time because he's been so busy. Even more than its predecessors, this weird little film might almost have been commissioned as a Thatcherite satire.

Except it wasn't. These downbeat, deadpan films are still trying to help: civic cinema merely adjusting to twists of history that its departed founders never envisaged. Keeping the show on the road, rather than drawing the curtain, such films strive in their sardonic way for statements as honest and humane as *Miners*'.

AWAY FROM THE COALFACE

As at DATA, Pickering's later mining output is shadowed by a smaller number of films on other topics. A glance at these usefully demonstrates that he indeed remained in the civic-education tradition, but might have preferred a less middle-of-the-road interpretation than coal sponsorship generally allowed for.

In 1973, Francis Gysin found an ingenious solution to the reduction of funding, revenue and distribution for *Mining Review*, namely that it would secure outside sponsorship for 50 per cent of future issues, continuing to make the remainder directly for the NCB. Although some of the new sponsors were commercial firms, most were NGOs, and the jobs taken were ones consistent with a public-service remit. Several sponsors were pleased enough to become repeat clients, usually paired up with the same directors who'd worked with them before. For Pickering, one such sponsor was National Girobank, for whom his trim, diagrammatic explanations of savings drew on the Redifussion experience of writing for schoolchildren. The other was the Spastics Society, for whom he turned out simple, gentle studies slightly marred by naff musical accompaniments. Another *Review* occasioned the sole career instance of the even-tempered director's relationship with a sponsor breaking down. *27th Year No 8* (1974) was commissioned by the Health Education Council (HEC) to present a vaguely environmentalist message about responsibility to the planet, paralleled with individuals' responsibility to their bodies. Pickering rough-cut an experimental compilation film with a radical anti-corporate message and original music, flatly rejected by the HEC. The cutting copy was junked, and the director angrily walked off the production.

An extracurricular project, running throughout the director's second period in film, provided a better outlet for his leftfield inclinations, taking forward a strand of his work started by his collaboration with the Clarkes at Epsom. In 1964 Pickering and Robert Kruger, by then *Mining Review*'s producer, set up, with Charles Griffiths, a company called ie Films – Images for Education – to make in their own time zero-budget 16mm, films, portably lit and using tape-recorded sound, for causes they sympathised with. Pickering directed many, but at other times ie made its equipment and advice available for their collaborators to make the films themselves. Gysin turned a blind eye to Kruger using the NCB's cutting-rooms in downtime. Distribution of all ie's work was managed by the Concord Film Council.

Child development proved a specialism, arising from associations with noted developmental psychologists. With Elinor Goldschmied (inventor of heuristic play, a concept later influential on childrearing theory, especially as applied to institutional daycare), ie made the *Growth Through Play* series (1969–71), some films directed by Pickering, some by Goldschmied. They chart the formative journey from tactile solipsism to full-fledged interaction with the outer world, via purely observational record footage (yielding clinical data), mixed with curious, cheap experimentation with 16mm image and sound (suggesting the blurry subjectivity of early consciousness – helped by particularly coarse print-stock). *Hand to Mouth* (1970), for instance, evokes the four- to eight-month period of five observed babies using jarring, deliberately carelessly framed, often unfocused shots of their home surroundings, and narration alternating factual description with oddly worded, childlike yet portentously philosophical phrases ('Touch is outwards: from ... The warmth of all the worlds: towards, towards ...'). A climactic sequence has several such axioms intoned over intercutting of calm, familiar domestic interiors with a noisy street-market symbolising 'the world ... a cornucopia spinning its strangeness, a treasure basket of wealth to be touched and fingered ... its sharpness, its softness, its roughness, its smoothness, its silken radiance'.

ie eventually pulled a higher-profile client. Pickering's last ie directing job was for Save the Children (STC): *Our Centres in Northern Ireland* (1983). Being an appeal to 'mainland' STC sympathisers (humanitarian but apolitical) it isn't about the Ulster troubles as such. Glumly familiar exteriors of Belfast wastelands provide backdrop for a more domesticated, hopeful account of a children's centre working in a difficult area. Scenes of committed staff interacting with disadvantaged kids are accompanied by their unscripted tape-recorded comments, describing aims and working methods. One reports that the centre has escaped violence because STC is seen locally as a 'neutral' organisation. Belfast's tensions aren't alluded to any more directly: we're aware this is a deprived community, but not advised its allegiances.[22] The film ends on a plea for funds over closing credits (the same year, Pickering's final NCB job had also been a charity film, an Oxfam-sponsored *Review* featuring Jonathan Dimbleby).

ie's last venture brought it onto more controversial territory, and into direct counterpoint with Kruger and Pickering's disappearing day job. Not having come off, it's an intriguing nugget of what-if history. Within weeks of Margaret Thatcher's 1983 re-election, ie formally approached Arthur Scargill with a proposal dubbed *An Alternative Voice*, a programme of video production and coal-field distribution for the NUM. Their suggestion derived, they explained, from 'a complex experience of the mining industry and the media and a deep conviction of the need for a radical approach ... to the communication of the socialist and trade union case'. They recommended Low-Band U-Matic as the production format, VHS for distribution.

> The impingement of new technology and the diffusion in some areas of miners among the general community [as at Bagworth] may have had some effect on this unity of dependence and community, and perhaps should not be underrated as a potential threat to it, but it still remains unique in the industrial world. (That it is threatened is a major argument, we believe, for making use of that same technology to defend it) ... today, now, for the time being, many of them are paid enough, for long enough, to own their houses, to own cars, refrigerators, washing-machines, television sets – AND VIDEO RECORDERS ... the NUM is uniquely placed to set up a network for the distribution of video cassettes among its membership ... Such a network would have the same unifying and exciting effect in local communities as political education had in the heroic past ... would be weapons in the hands of union members, instantly available in situations where public misunderstanding had to be combated. In a strike situation, for example.[23]

When the 'strike situation' came, it spawned *The Miners' Campaign Tapes*, six agitprop films distributed on VHS in 1984 to mining communities nationwide, made, on U-Matic, by younger film-makers, from the 1970s film collectives and 1980s video workshops, with scant connection to the sponsored documentary tradition and none to the NCB's ex-*cinéastes*. Half-hearted discussions between Pickering and the NUM's education officer had tailed off in late 1983. Looking back he considers the idea of a much larger alternative channel 'pretty fatuous ... the internet offers what we were ridiculously imagining could be done by snail mail!'.

The 'alternative voice' of Kruger and Pickering's proposal isn't easily heard in the films they'd spent thirty-five years making to order. And few commentators have acclaimed such films, precisely because they prefer working life to be represented on screen by campaigners, or by journalists. Yet neither group is better placed to capture many important particulars of workplace life the industrial film-maker inevitably will. Moreover, he works in circumstances far more similar to those of the workers he films, especially if they work for the same organisation.[24] His motives, mood, creative drive, sense of direction, his company loyalty, his simple suitability for the tasks in hand, are in similarly constant fluctuation.

His films will usually be modest, as Peter Pickering's mostly are. It doesn't follow that they can't, sometimes, be absorbing or smart – but their testimony will, often, be unwitting. Reflecting on *Nobody's Face* and its successors, their director says:

> That's the irony ... because for once we were trying to make a mickey-taking film *with* miners (they like teachers and all other working groups were happily ironic about their own industry) we ignored the fact that its

purpose was still to further the usual 'efficiency', the propagation of which, if not with Robens, at its Blairthatcherite extreme can lead to ... we all know what![25]

NOTES

1. This introduction oversimplifies the nature of NCB sponsorship inasmuch as NCB films had *several internal* sponsors, namely different departments of the Board.
2. Rée featured in the official film about SOE agents in France, *Now It Can be Told* (1944), later re-edited as *School for Danger* (1946).
3. Though film-making became his profession, Pickering feels that writing was his vocation. In recent years, under the pen-name of Alan Hubbard, he has self-published novels and stories with satirical, surreal and erotic elements not necessarily to be expected from a retired maker of industrial films! I mention this here, because Hubbard's short story *Young Hobbled Goes to War* contains a heavily fictionalised version of Pickering's entry into the film industry, in which Grierson is mentioned by name but Alexander inspires a character named 'O'Riordan' ('O'Riordan was a romantic, down from Cambridge, who dreamed of Celtic Kings and Joseph Stalin') and Rotha a producer called 'Bennifer'. Alan Hubbard's writings are available from their author.
4. Pickering recalls that *Scottish Universities* entailed his only direct encounter with Grierson, who didn't impress him any more in person than his writings had: Pickering witnessed him, in his COI role, bawling out Gysin for imagined deficiencies in his direction.
5. Pickering remembers: 'In those days, immediately after the war, the "Moles" (Mole-Richardson lights and electricians) still travelled up to locations by rail and were met by transport at the other end ... all well known to us and very often "characters". I think it either happened on the ice-rink item, or I heard of it on that item – but a "Mole" certainly once died on the location, and the I'm sure *not* apocryphal story goes that out of respect his fellows played poker on his coffin in the luggage van on its long journey back to London from the north.' (Where unattributed, all quotes from Peter Pickering in this essay are sourced from the author's conservations with him, from Pickering's interview by Emily Fuller (now Crosby) of the British Universities Film & Video Council in 2006, or emails or notes supplied by Pickering to the author. I am grateful to both Peter and to Emily.
6. Details of which *Mining Review* issues contain particular stories can be found on the BFI Film and TV Database at http://www.bfi.org.uk/filmtvinfo/ftvdb/ and in the *Mining Review* annual release listings on screenonline. It should be remembered that the attribution of stories to directors is usually reliant on a single surviving piece of paperwork, or on the vagaries of human memories; Pickering recalls having directed some of the items mentioned in this essay, while having no recollection of others.
7. They were followed by the anonymously put together compilation film, *The Kent Oil Refinery* (1954). After leaving DATA, John Ingram directed a number of other sponsored films, including the successful Greenpark/BP production *Mikhali* (1960), before moving into television where, among other things, he directed many episodes of John Pilger's campaigning *Pilger* series in the 1970s.
8. *Monthly Film Bulletin* vol. 19 no. 226, November 1952, p. 160.
9. 'I came back from "Dogs Allowed" with a Pomeranian as a present for my young second daughter. I must have been mad, we already had a poodle. It was a champion but no longer showable and going cheap as it had broken both legs. It proved to be a disaster, aggressively attacking dogs of any and all sizes. "Lucy's Table" was shot, without asking for or obtaining permission, on the way back from another story. We stopped at a pub where some miners happened to be playing billiards with parrot mascot beside them ... got the camera out of the van and we filmed them.'

10. This wording was reused in several editions of the NCB Film Library catalogue.
11. From Pickering's blog, <bearincupboardpress.blogspot.com>. His thoughts on the film are followed by fascinating, sceptical comments on the Documentary Movement in general.
12. Neither am I, and yes, I'm being a bit facetious. All the same: Rotha, Pickering's old employer and fellow autodidact, had precociously cherry-picked the structures for films like *World of Plenty* and *Land of Promise* from German metaphysics – the dialectics of Hegel and Marx. His *Face of Britain*, especially, makes an instructive screening partner for *Two Worlds*. Both contrive grand historical statements from contemporary technological developments, in Rotha's case the 1930s expansion of the electricity grid. As 'philosophy', Rotha's vision is inconsequential, passing too few tests for logical rigour. But, further helped by Soviet montage, in screen terms it's exciting. *Two Worlds* rather less so.
13. The film, commissioned under the title *A Miner's Life*, was originally intended as the 'social' companion piece to the largely technical *Winning the Coal* (1975), directed by David Pitt, but the subject's death put paid to this plan.
14. *Eyes on 80s* was a remake/update of Philip Owtram's film *Report on 60's* (1961), in light of the technical and procedural changes that had rendered the earlier short redundant.
15. William Ashworth, *The History of the British Coal Industry, Vol. 5: 1946–1982, The Nationalized Industry* (Oxford: Oxford University Press, 1986), p. 669. Ashworth's masterful history is out of print, but remains an essential source for anyone interested in coalmining history. Incidentally, its nearly 700 pages include no reference to the NCB's film activities.
16. *The Team on 204s* was selected by BIFA, on behalf of the Federation of British Industry, as one of the films representing Britain at 1964's International Industrial Film Festival. (Others included BTF's *Snow* and *All That Mighty Heart*, Shell's *Mekong* and *Frontiers of Friction* and Costain's *Critical Path*.) It was, in fact, shot before Gysin invited Pickering to the NCB, commissioned by Donald Alexander before his resignation, as a gesture of financial help to Pickering. Pickering remembers Alexander having strongly praised Pickering's decision to abandon film-making in favour of teaching (as, in a sense, Alexander himself was to do soon). 'I didn't see him after that I don't think, so what he thought of my reneging on that decision I'll never know!'
17. Treatment for *The Longhirst Story*, held in BFI Special Collections file for *Mining Review 21st Year No 11*, based on the earlier film. For reasons lost to the history of the NCB Film Unit's dying days, few production files for individual films such as *The Longhirst Story* survived alongside the *Mining Review* files.
18. In *Portrait of a Miner*, a similar technique had been used: there, it *was* for experimental effect.
19. Siddall would later briefly become chairman, a stopgap before Ian MacGregor's fateful appointment.
20. All quotes taken from *Who's Driving?* treatment, deposited with BFI Special Collections as part of the Pickering collection.
21. Pickering's draft treatment was entitled *Who's Dreaming?* and was, characteristically, much more complicated and artistic than the finished film. There were some discussions between the film branch and the IR department of showing *Black Friday* at a staff-training conference following which attendees would improvise a re-enactment of its scenarios under Pickering's direction and be videotaped doing so. However, Pickering recalls that this never came off.
22. Attentive viewers will pick up a few visual and verbal clues that the centre is in a Protestant neighbourhood.
23. ie Films, *An Alternative Voice*, Pickering collection. Despite the calculatedly fiery rhetoric of the document, Pickering is not a conventional left-winger, professing himself an admirer of the more

existentialist Andre Gorz. On coal, he believes Scargill based the strike on the wrong premises by pressing the debatable long-term viability of the industry ahead of compassion for its communities. More generally, he says: 'I think the one thing that unified Brit Doc was political belief. In the century of delusion it was possible to believe in a different future. Marxist and Labour supporters could at least hold hands when they weren't spitting at one another. The confident delusion of a defeated capitalism crumbled finally I suppose after the Hungarian revolution.'

24. Pickering estimates that over the course of his film career he accumulated a year underground.
25. Even after such close analysis (which the modest director finds 'excruciatingly embarrassing') Pickering's career remains a little mysterious: the worthily ambitious but patchily achieved *The Island* and *Two Worlds*, and the less grandiose but more genuinely noble *Miners* surrounded by large numbers of historically interesting, artistically nondescript productions and that intriguing handful of 'negative' films, almost all of them based on treatments too ambitious to be executable. The gap between intentions and objectives is the theme that the latter share with Hubbard's much more freethinking fiction writing; Pickering's other published work is *Uncle Norman* (1968), a children's story in the *Nippers* series devised and edited by Leila Berg as a realist working-class alternative to the infamously suburban *Peter and Jane* Ladybird books, and Pickering's contribution is informed by much the same spirit as *Nobody's Face* et al. That gap between plans and achievements seems almost the motif for Pickering's own career in films, and perhaps ultimately it was the absence in him of the intense, even ruthless drive that a film director needs to impose himself on his circumstances that prevented him from doing so more often. He also speculates that his fateful encounter with Donald Alexander brought him into an artistic culture, that of British documentary, that he wasn't, ultimately, in tune with, though he remained with it until near its end. 'The idea that the human race is much more loveable when seen as clumsily incapable rather than "lazily" inefficient asks surely for fictional expression rather than documentary exposition. Grierson, it seems to me, talked of poetry but didn't know much about it. Rotha did, and his practice always – even if sometimes sentimentally – puts him for me up with Basil Wright and Jennings. ... I often think myself that I should have taken the plunge and left DATA to freelance for World Wide or wherever, and that my obsession with DATA's politics may have lost me any chance I might have had of marrying my own fictional imagination with the film medium. Water under bridges anyway!'

17 The Passing Stranger: *Anthony Simmons*

MICHAEL BROOKE

The films of Anthony Simmons run in parallel with, but often distinctly apart from, many of the other British post-war documentaries discussed in this book. At a time when many of his peers were producing industrial films or other sponsored work, he made personal, independently financed pieces such as *Sunday by the Sea* (1953) and *Bow Bells* (1954), non-narrative studies of the people he grew up with in London's East End. By the time Free Cinema had taken wing a few years later, despite a sensibility that would seem, on the face of things, perfectly attuned to it (on top of a long-standing creative association with Free Cinema's favoured technicians Walter Lassally and John Fletcher), he was alternating COI-sponsored films and commercials. As the British New Wave was blazing a new trail for feature films, Simmons was to be found directing an old-fashioned farce, and by the time he finally made a distinctive fiction feature in the form of *Four in the Morning* (1965), the 1960s had begun to swing in earnest, offering far gaudier distractions. Simmons is one of the most avowedly independent of British film-makers, and although this resulted in a peripatetic career spent working across various media (film, television, literature) and modes (fiction, documentary, advertising) there are undeniably thematic and tonal threads running through much of his work. He claims that he finds it very hard to tell a story that isn't personal in some way, and in the context of post-war documentary, not notably conducive to the cinema of free expression, this makes him an interesting anomaly, though he moved among the same circles of producers and sponsors as his peers.

Hailing from working-class immigrant roots and very active in student politics before turning to film, Simmons's background and political preoccupations set him apart from many of his industry colleagues. Internationalist in outlook, he shot his first film in Bulgaria and edited it in Rome, and his early output betrays the influence of 1920s/30s Soviet cinema, Italian neo-realism and documentaries by people such as the Americans Robert Flaherty, Herbert Kline and Joseph Strick, the Czech Alexander Hackenschmied (later Hammid) and the Dutchman Joris Ivens. It was through his politics that Simmons made his first connections with the film industry: Ralph Bond at the union, and such socialist-sympathising film-makers as Donald Alexander to be found in and around the short-lived Federation of Documentary Film Units. Entirely self-taught as a film-maker, Simmons was particularly fortunate to meet Leon Clore before he turned professional, as this brought him a highly sympathetic producer who guided and nurtured his documentary career while ensuring that he retained some creative independence. From the start, Simmons's films showed a strong interest in the lives of individuals and communities, whether at work or play, allied to an unfashionably upbeat, cheerfully optimistic attitude towards life's many vicissitudes. Sympathy for the underdog is a theme common to his documentary shorts and fiction features, but this is rarely idealised or sentimentalised.

London looms large, with the Thames and its immediate environs a particularly favoured locale – Simmons once planned to make a documentary entitled *People on the Thames*, and while it was never completed, ideas and even shot-on-spec footage found their way into other projects.

Simmons first came to public attention with *Sunday by the Sea*, in which assorted East Londoners travel to Southend (the film opens with a steam train haring out of London) for what British Rail's long-running ticket promotion used to call an Awayday. Their carefree, unself-conscious frolicking on the sands and in arcades is given a cultural anchor by the use of old-time music-hall songs, to which the footage has been cut with surgical precision. 'Where Did You Get That Hat' sets the tone, underscoring a montage of amusing titfers, candyfloss and naughty post-cards, while photographers and preachers ply their trade side by side. Groups are transported by pleasure-cruiser and narrow-gauge railway, and there's much daytime drinking, dancing and revelry ('A Little of What You Fancy'), charmingly mimicked by the children. Drinking gives way to eating ('My Wife's Cake'), before a piano glissando follows a young man sliding down into a swimming pool to the strains of 'Rule, Britannia', the waves ruled over on this occasion being manufactured by the swimmers and divers themselves. Children cheer on a Punch and Judy show, sail model boats or survey the horizon with a telescope (when their father hasn't commandeered it to stare at pretty girls). 'Yip-I-Addy-I-Ay' takes us to the fairground, the camera mounted on the rides themselves, the cutting matching the circular motions of Ferris wheels, dodgems and helter skelters. Finally, 'My Flo from Pimlico' is sung as the sun goes down, lovers kiss in silhouette and the seafront's nocturnal illuminations are switched on. While John Taylor's later *Holiday* (1957), a conventionally sponsored film (being a British Transport Films production), made much use of a hidden camera, Simmons and Lassally went down on the beach among their subjects, who were clearly aware of their presence, some visibly so. It's a joyous, effervescent film (at one point the music

Moments of reflection and cheer in *Sunday by the Sea*

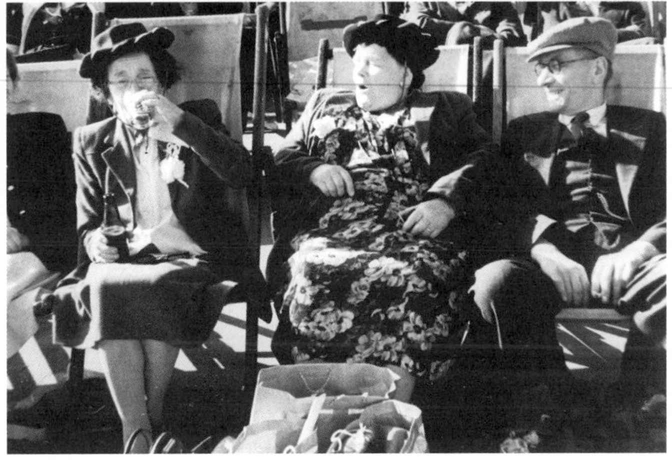

pauses for an outbreak of laughter) that retains its great charm over half a century on – it set Simmons apart from his contemporaries from the start of his career.

On the opposite side of the documentary spectrum from BTF, a direct contrast can also be drawn between *Sunday by the Sea* and Lindsay Anderson's *O Dreamland* (also 1953), which shares a cinematographer, an approximate length and a desire to capture the essence of a seaside resort largely favoured by the working classes. But through Anderson's eyes, they're gloomily despondent, trudging along the sea front, and reduced to watching sideshow recreations of famous torture and murder cases because there seems to be little else to do. Both films feature at least one cackling puppet, but while *Sunday by the Sea*'s is cheerfully convivial, the ones in *O Dreamland* range from mocking to downright sinister. Simmons acknowledges that each film reflected their directors' highly individual personalities:

> We had totally different points of view about humanity. Lindsay's was desperate and hostile, and mine was ... I won't say caring, but I like people. ... I came from the East End, I liked the East End, and that's what we went and filmed. Lindsay didn't like the East End, or any end, and that's what he went out and filmed.[1]

Whereas Anderson's East Enders are victims of their oppressive circumstances, Simmons's are survivors, enjoying themselves against the odds – which is not a bad description of Simmons himself. Himself a native of London's East End, a location he would constantly revisit in his films, he was born in West Ham on 16 December 1922.[2] The son of traders at the Queens Road street market (his father was a Polish Jewish immigrant who followed his brothers to Britain at the turn of the twentieth century), he grew up in an authentically multicultural environment, living among market traders whose first language frequently wasn't English – as was the case with his parents.

Simmons was educated at West Ham Secondary School (later West Ham Grammar) before being evacuated to Brentwood with the onset of war in 1939, a year that he regards as pivotal for personal as well as historical reasons. His Latin teacher Peter Hewitt, a young left-wing poet, encouraged Simmons's early writing efforts and helped get him sufficiently good A-level results to go to the London School of Economics, which was then occupying buildings at Peterhouse College, Cambridge, following its own wartime relocation. There, he read law, but also pursued his writing and became increasingly involved in left-wing political activism, becoming President of the Union. In 1942, he became liable for call-up, but spent many of the subsequent months intercepting German radio broadcasts on the Isle of Man before finally being sent to Arundel on the South Coast in 1944 to protect airfields against German paratroops who never actually landed. The following year, he went to India, where he ran war newspapers and taught recruits at an Indian Army signals camp. Released from the Army on New Year's Day 1946, Simmons returned to the UK, the LSE (which had since returned to London) and his degree.

The young man was still undecided about whether to work as a writer or a barrister, but the generous grant provided for his legal studies helped subsidise other activities. Still very active in student politics, he forged links with equivalent organisations in Eastern Europe during that brief period between the end of the war and the definitive descent of the Iron Curtain, travelling to Czechoslovakia, Hungary, Yugoslavia and finally Bulgaria, meeting many of the countries' leaders thanks to his NUS connections. He wrote a book about his travels, *History Goes On Holiday*, but it never appeared thanks to its prospective publisher's bankruptcy – an early example of the bad luck that would dog much of Anthony Simmons's career.

Simmons completed his degree in 1947, but between that and beginning training as a barrister in 1948, he returned to Bulgaria. His original plan was to recreate the journey that the reporter Negley Farson took along various European rivers as recounted in *Sailing Across Europe* (1926). Despite having had no experience in film, he decided to take a cameraman with him (Charles Heath, the brother of a fellow student), but the boat only got as far as the Humber before it sank off Spurn Point. So Simmons and his colleagues went to Prague instead, intending to film its 1947 youth festival as part of the NUS delegation; but when they saw how many professional camera crews were doing the same thing, they quickly altered their plans again. They decided to go to Bulgaria to film a ten-year-old male dancer who had been spotted by Simmons's friend Owen Ambrose.

On arrival in Bulgaria, after disentangling themselves from official red tape (they were initially arrested for trying to enter the country illegally), the group's plans changed yet again: instead of focusing on a single figure, Simmons recalled watching Herbert Kline and Alexander Hammid's documentary *Forgotten Village* (1941), about Santiago in Mexico, and decided to attempt a similar study of the village of Krushuna in north-central Bulgaria. What attracted Simmons was both its history and its mixed community of Bulgarians, Turks, communists and non-communists. Simmons initially saw himself as a writer-producer (and retained that credit on the film), but took over as director after Heath confessed that he had no experience of directing people. Under the influence of *Forgotten Village* and assorted Soviet classics, Simmons shot his first film, later to be titled *Bulgarian Village* (1948).

When he returned to Britain, all he had to show for his trip were reels of silent, unedited 35mm footage. The director screened it to various people in the industry, including Alexander at DATA Film Productions, George Hoellering (the Hungarian-born owner of the famous Academy Cinema in Oxford Street) and Phil Hyams (Eros Films), to a mixed reception. Interestingly, DATA, being a very socialistically inclined film unit, liked Simmons's rushes enough to agree to fund the processing, but failed to see any commercial future for it. Determined to finish the film on his own terms, Simmons turned down an offer from *March of Time* for access to the raw footage (on the grounds that it was the only 35mm footage of Bulgaria available in the West), and instead raised £200 to enable him to accept an offer to finish post-production in Rome.

After qualifying at the Bar and beginning a stint as a pupil in chambers, Simmons travelled to Italy in the summer of 1949, where he edited the film with the help of Italians steeped in neo-realism, who understood Simmons's ambitions for the film in a way that his British counterparts had failed to grasp. Simmons returned to Britain having left detailed instructions for the completion of the soundtrack. But disaster struck when the Italian government refused permission for it to be screened on the grounds that it was overtly left-wing propaganda, and yet at the same time the film was also banned in Bulgaria for being too right-wing – which is to say that it was not a paean of praise to Stalin and his lackeys.

It took six years for Simmons to retrieve a silent dupe of the cutting copy from the Italians, by which time the completed film had vanished. The original 35mm negative survived at Humphries Film Lab in London, but was legally DATA's property until Simmons reimbursed their expenses, which he was never able to do. On DATA's closure, its unclaimed negs found their way into the film vaults of the National Coal Board, and there they stayed, together with all the *Mining Reviews* and colliery technical films, until the whole collection was transferred to the BFI on the NCB Film Unit's closure. So the film remained in its silent form, occasionally screened with Simmons's commentary read out loud, but never given a formal release. This is a shame, because on the evidence of the new 35mm print recently struck by the BFI National Archive from the ex-DATA mute negative, it's a striking piece of work for a total beginner, not least in the quality of the photography. Whatever Charles Heath's self-perceived limitations as a director, the Associateship of the Royal Photographic Society highlighted by the opening credits was amply justified by his evocative images.

Bulgarian Village combines a general study of life in Krushuna with a more specific look at the effects of the encroachment of modern technology. The first few minutes create a calculatedly timeless impression: transport and industry are exclusively powered by peasant, horse, ox or donkey, and the most advanced equipment initially appears to be the looms operated by a group of bare-footed women. Bread is baked, concrete is mixed, a school dance is accompanied by a small boy on a harmonica (in the presumed absence of a radio or gramophone) and, in a shot that makes one grateful for the absence of location sound, a dentist uses pliers to extract a woman's tooth.

After this overture, a lorry arrives, laden with men, who are greeted effusively by the villagers. At the same time, Simmons begins revealing other evidence of the twentieth century: a low-angle shot shows a man up a pole adjusting wiring of some kind. The truck is parked by a tractor, and repairs are carried out with the aid of a blowtorch. Later, Simmons will cut between the tractor pulling a mechanical plough with several blades as it passes horse- and ox-drawn equivalents: more picturesque, certainly, but much less efficient. New buildings are under construction, their uniform architecture suggesting the influence of a planning committee from outside the village.

In parallel with this, Simmons examines the progress of the harvest, as water begins to irrigate parched fields (both naturally and with the aid of a waterwheel) and cotton and sweetcorn are grown, harvested and processed by large groups of huddled women using (inescapably symbolic) sickles. Throughout, as one might expect both from Simmons's influences and his own political views, there's a strong sense of community, with meetings of the local peasants' organisation held in the open air, and one assumes that the finished film would have made more explicit links between a sequence in which villagers queue (enthusiastically) to sign some kind of document and subsequent evidence of collective labour. The film was also intended to feature traditional Bulgarian music on the soundtrack, several decades before the album *Le Mystère des voix Bulgares* became a pioneering world-music hit in the 1980s.

However, it was not to be, and the salutary experience, familiar to all film-makers, of putting in vast amounts of work for little (or, in this case, no) reward sent Simmons back to the Bar for much of the early 1950s. He continued to dabble in film, working with various left-wing groups to produce *May Day 1950*, a sort of no-budget forerunner of the making of *March to Aldermaston* (1958) by film-makers like Anderson and Derrick Knight a few years later. Simmons recalls:

> In 1950 May Day had been banned. We weren't allowed to demonstrate in Hyde Park, because it had been banned. And I organised – me and, I think, Peter Brinson ... went round all the left-wing film directors and cameramen, and we knew where the Trades Council was organising demonstrations. For example, they were all going to be in Whitehall and they were going to march down towards Trafalgar Square, and the police were obviously going to stop them. So we organised about six teams of camera crew on 16mm and 8mm – we were actually using an 8mm camera that Ivor Montagu had used in Spain. It was all we could get our hands on. But somehow, we kind of guessed, or I had information from the Trades Council, of places where there was likely to be trouble with the police. We knew where the police were coming to, and we filmed *May Day 1950*, and it became a big celebration for the London Trades Council, because it was a march that had been banned. But they couldn't ban the movie, and so it played at every Trades Council up and down the country. It was an act of defiance of that period.[3]

Simmons also directed two films, *We Who Are Young* (1952) and *One Great Vision* (1953) under the pseudonym 'Andrew Taylor', a disguise deemed necessary because he felt that it was unwise to become publicly identified with left-wing propaganda films at a time when he was still trying to establish himself as a barrister. However, this side of his career was faltering. His wife disapproved of his decision to specialise in divorce, but a switch to town planning law resulted in six months' unemployment.

Effectively subsidised by his spouse, whose career as an architect had been somewhat more successful, Simmons wrote a play, developed links with the Players Theatre, and discussed with their pianist Betty Lawrence the notion of a film set in an Essex resort like Southend or Westcliff (the latter being the favoured holiday destination for the East End Jewish community), with the only verbal commentary provided by the lyrics of music-hall songs, to be arranged by Lawrence and performed by her with associates John Hewer and Joan Sterndale Bennett. Inspired by Joseph Strick's non-narrative observational study *Muscle Beach* (1948), and with Jennings and McAllister's *Listen to Britain* also in mind, Simmons set about trying to turn his idea into a film:

> I prepared a script, I'd found all the songs, and I went round all the people like Max Anderson, Sam Napier-Bell, all the people working for Leon [Clore, at Basic Films] who were proper directors and said 'Would you do it?' And none of them were prepared to go without a very strong script. I said, 'Well, here's a list of all the things you're likely to find, I've been there for two days, this is what you're going to get.' None of them would do it. So Leon said, 'You do it'. I said 'Fine, but who's going to pay for it?' He said 'You are.'[4]

So Simmons borrowed the money from the Midland Bank (his wife's bank manager had been active in ENSA during the war, and so was surprisingly sympathetic to the project) and shot the film over two weekends in 1951 with Walter Lassally, Derek York, John Fletcher and a lightweight 35mm Arriflex camera on loan from Clore. The 'script' consisted of the written-out song lyrics annotated with ideas as to the kind of images that they inspired. The soundtrack was recorded later, but Simmons had the songs in his head throughout shooting, as a kind of mental guide track.

The film was cut in a rented room in Wardour Street, and a local preview theatre owner, Mr Frost, allowed them to screen work in progress outside normal working hours. Simmons and editor Luisa Krakowska painstakingly calculated the synchronisation of music and image to what Simmons calculated was a ninety-sixth of a second (i.e., individual sprocket holes, with four making up the standard twenty-four-frames-per-second film speed). Since neither of them was being paid (the bank loan only covered film stock and associated lab costs), it was a true labour of love:

> Luisa was a tremendous editor. She was at that stage already retired, in the sense that she'd married and had kids, though I didn't know her before we did *Sunday by the Sea*: it was through Leon who knew her. She'd worked at UNESCO and Leon said 'Let me introduce you to her, and she will come and do it with you.' And at that stage we thought we were just going to work a normal eight-hour day, but we'd become so involved in making the sprocket hole match up to that point on the track, you could actually be there for hours – because if you made one shift, you were affecting six other shots further back and further forward. Everything had to shift. And unless you've actually sat down and done it, you don't realise the kind of devotion to duty. The amount of black that was in the film was amazing. We couldn't afford to go and reprint, we just had to do without the image. It was black. Everyone forgets all that.[5]

Simmons had no plans for the film beyond completion, so was as surprised as anyone to discover, on returning to Britain with Lassally after shooting a student festival in Romania for *One Great Vision*, that his wife was waiting for them on the station platform with the news that it had won the Grand Prix at the Venice Film Festival: Clore had submitted it without his knowledge. This secured it commercial distribution in British cinemas via Republic Pictures, an unexpected bonus. For ongoing distribution after this theatrical release, it was handled by Charles and Kitty Cooper's Contemporary Films (a company strongly inclined towards left-wing and Eastern European films).

The director's next project, *Bow Bells*, was both a sequel to and a development of *Sunday by the Sea*. Running almost the same length (just over thirteen minutes apiece), and using the same formula of silent footage accompanied by and cut to recordings of East End music-hall songs, the difference here is that the portrayal is of East Enders on their own (and Simmons's) home territory. The film also needed more planning at the script stage, thanks to a considerably larger canvas making it less likely that Simmons would chance upon the perfect image in the same way. However, he did relatively little advance research, preferring instead to turn up at places like Billingsgate Fish Market at times when he knew that there would be plenty going on.

Screened back to back (as, following initial release, they often were, since they shared a distributor as well as many thematic and technical points in common), it quickly becomes clear that *Sunday by the Sea* and *Bow Bells* have as many differences as similarities. While the first film is all hustle, bustle and bubbling enthusiasm, from the opening piano burst of 'Oh, I Do Like To Be Beside the Seaside', *Bow Bells* opens with a ship slowly gliding down the Thames and empty lorries entering a depot before the first 'musical number' starts with 'They're All Very Fine And Large' over Billingsgate porters, fish and wriggling eels. A brief aside in which a porter is distracted by a pretty girl is followed by a full-scale East End market sequence, with wrapped packages tossed into the crowd, and all manner of goods on sale including pets, cooed over by assorted children and accompanied by the inevitable 'Daddy Wouldn't Buy Me a Bow-Wow'.

With the next number, 'If It Wasn't For The 'Ouses In Between', the tone becomes more explicitly elegiac. East Enders are shown at home, scrubbing steps, growing vegetables on allotments and playing games in cramped backyards in the middle of long lines of terraced houses ('Wiv a ladder and some glasses/You could see to 'Ackney Marshes/If it wasn't for the 'ouses in between'). In this partial landscape of the imagination, gasworks stand in for mountains, and a donkey can be turned into a dead ringer for a cow with the addition of some 'artificial 'orns'. Back in the workplace, 'We All Got To Work But Father' is wittily accompanied by shots of a male supervisor watching a group of young women, before a fade-out leads into the film's second section.

This is the first of Simmons's many portraits of the eastern end of the Thames, with overlapping vocals on 'Row, Row, Row Your Boat' mimicking the water rippling on the shoreline. Children play on the banks and splash in the water as though they were at an upmarket seaside resort, or they stand and watch the ships go by. Outside the Tower of London, a busby-wearing guard is greeted with a cheerful 'wotcher!' by the lyrics of 'Knocked 'Em in the Old Kent Road' and lines of marching and saluting children. This segues into a fashion parade, nattily dressed men and behatted women out in public to see and be seen – while at the other end of the income spectrum, an old man shuffles through rubbish-strewn streets to 'Poor Robin'. In a sequence that most explicitly recalls *Sunday by the Sea*, it's off to the races – greyhounds and bikes, respectively, accompanied by a jaunty glissando-strewn piano solo, before the film returns to Tower Bridge for a wistful, open-ended conclusion as a wife and child ('played' by Simmons's own wife and child) bid farewell to their breadwinner as he sets out into the open river heading eastwards, presumably to the sea.

By the mid-1950s, Simmons had started dabbling in feature-film production through Harlequin, the company he had founded with Clore and John Arnold, initially to produce *Sunday by the Sea* and *Bow Bells*. Simmons wrote the 1954 feature *The Passing Stranger* (directed by Arnold), and Harlequin also made *Time Without Pity* (1957), directed by Joseph Losey under his real name for the first time since his blacklisting by the House Un-American Activities Committee. However, Simmons continued to make documentaries, usually for Leon Clore, which included work for both government (the COI) and commercial (Ford) sponsors – as well as films destined to remain unmade because of Simmons's refusal to compromise on what he felt was the best (usually instinctive and unscripted) approach for the material.

The Gentle Corsican (1956), Simmons's first film in colour, would have seemed to a contemporary viewer like a change of direction, though it's at least partly a return to the territory first marked out by *Bulgarian Village* and also continues Simmons's run of films about places whose homespun approach contrasts with the polished texture of the (splendid) travelogues made by contemporaries at units like BTF, or for sponsors like BP. As with the earlier film, it arose from pure opportunism: Vladimir Raitz, one of Simmons's LSE acquaintances, had founded Horizon Holidays, Britain's first mass package holiday company in 1949, and so was in a position to offer Simmons, Walter Lassally and John Fletcher free flights to and accommodation on Corsica, where they would shoot a film that would incidentally promote the island as an attractive destination. As with *Bulgarian Village*, Simmons had no prior notion of exactly what he would film, but given that his costs were negligible (film stock aside, which he had to supply himself), he was confident that he'd find something.

After considering a possible feature-film story about a Dutch nurse travelling to Corsica and falling in love, he eventually came across father and son Toussain and Jackie Maraninchi, living together in a makeshift shelter just off the beach, but embodying different generations. They were rechristened 'Maurin' and 'Nico' for the film, but it was inspired directly by their lives. Maurin lives a traditional life, fishing for food and exchanging the surplus in the nearby town of Calvi for bread, fruit, vegetables and wine. He is happy to coexist with the tourist hordes who descend upon the island (not least for the ogling opportunities offered by the female bikini-clad variety), but is concerned that Nico might succumb to temptation and abandon him – his ninety-three-year-old cousin Roger's various descendants have already decamped for Marseilles and further afield. Eventually, with several misgivings about both its cost and purpose, he buys Nico a diving mask in a small concession to modern technology.

It's a slight tale, over-reliant on the narrator's explanations (script by Ted Allan, delivery by Nigel Stock) in lieu of purely visual expression, and while Lassally's 16mm Kodachrome photography apparently looked more than acceptable in the original, Simmons was never able to produce a satisfactory 35mm blow-up. *Monthly Film Bulletin* complained about the harsh colour of the British release print and, more seriously, a Paris-based film distributor refused to handle it, for the same reason.

Blood is Life (1957) was Simmons's first directly sponsored film, made under the auspices of Clore's main company Basic, and so is interesting as the outcome of him working to a tightly specified brief as in the films of his contemporaries. This partly dramatised documentary was made through the COI to promote the work of the National Blood Transfusion Service, specifically through the South Western Regional Transfusion Centre in Bristol. It's a film of two halves, each with a didactic introduction followed by a dramatised illustration. After an opening sequence in which low brass chords thrum a heartbeat over the credits, we are given a lecture, via the commentary, on different blood groups and an under-the-microscope demonstration of what happens when the wrong types are mixed. Simmons's humanist concerns assert themselves when we're told that the bottles of blood are given personalised labels because they 'contain lives, lives that can be saved by blood', but it isn't until the film's mid-section that this is developed into involving drama.

When the narrative shifts from a detached look at the work of the transfusion service to an individual case study, so too does the style. We are first introduced to the child protagonist Jimmy via an almost Expressionist shot in which a black cat prowls the foreground while the combination of a wide-angle lens and a chequerboard floor pattern serves to exaggerate perspective and create a sense of foreboding even before anything happens. Simmons then cuts to a high angle, with a pan of simmering water dominating the frame, its handle pointing towards the child as if reaching out to it – while the cat, the implied threat in the earlier shot, is now tiny and insignificant in the background. He places the cat in an empty pan, reaches up for the other one, and three rapid cuts to his mother (previously gossiping outside), the cat quickly fleeing the pan and a speeding ambulance, accompanied by a scream, tell us all we need to know. We then return to the process of plasma preparation, but this time with a highly personalised note of urgency, the opening heartbeat motif returning on the soundtrack. The operation on the child is shown at a discreet distance, but the narration spares us little, with its references to 'fluid from the blood leaking from a young body to the blisters on the surface of the skin'.

Having tugged at the viewer's heartstrings, the film then moves into its second, more directly polemical half, by showing us examples of selfless young men volunteering to donate blood. (In a detail that charmingly dates the film, one volunteer offers another a cigarette.) Clearly aware that this section might seem tediously moralising compared with the high drama that preceded it (he originally intended for the film to have more dramatised material), Simmons peppers these shots with witty visual touches: a statue of a nurse dissolves to her contemporary counterpart, an arm connected to the transfusion equipment flexes its biceps to make a pair of tattooed women appear to dance.

The dramatic element at the end of this second half is the story of regular donor Charles Wright, approaching the statutory cut-off age of sixty-five and about to give blood for the last time. Arriving early, he strikes up a conversation with a little girl, Susan, who is waiting for her mother to finish giving blood herself. But this is merely a prelude to the scene's real meat: Mr Wright's own reminiscences of his wife's hospitalisation following a German bombing raid in 1942. The transfusion saved her life, compelling him to become a regular donor. The film concludes by showing how his blood saves the life of a young mother, while at the same time emphasising Simmons's view of human civilisation as a fundamentally interconnected entity, with age, gender or class distinctions rendered irrelevant by far more straightforward biological links – as emphasised by a shot of the newborn infant suckling at its mother's breast. Although far from the 'free' style of the Harlequin productions, *Blood is Life* has some of the same strengths (a gift for evoking atmosphere) and weaknesses (a wayward grasp of structure).

In the late 1950s, Simmons began to make commercials on a regular basis for another Leon Clore venture, Film Contracts, which provided him with his main source of income throughout the next two decades.[6] As *The Gentle Corsican* and *Blood is Life* had already hinted, he was becoming increasingly interested in pre-scripted drama, and his next documentary was Basic's entirely dramatised *Dispute* (1960), sponsored by the British Productivity Council. Simmons was very proud of the script and originally intended to direct it, but scheduling issues intervened and the job was ultimately taken on by industrial film-maker (and BPC regular) Fred Moore, a fellow Clore associate.

Simmons's script was jointly inspired by Akira Kurosawa's *Rashomon* (1950) in its depiction of a contentious incident seen from four divergent viewpoints, and by Reginald Rose's play *Twelve Angry Men* (best known in its 1957 film incarnation, directed by Sidney Lumet) in its insistence that the viewer look again at what initially appears to be an open-and-shut case of workplace insubordination. It works very well in its own right as a three-reel drama, but it was actually commissioned by the BPC for workplace screenings, to demonstrate the delicate diplomacy required on the part of managers, supervisors and union reps in establishing the truth behind disputed incidents that might affect productivity through poor workplace morale. It proved an outstanding success, winning the Society of Film and Television Arts' award for the best specialised film of its year, and becoming one of the most heavily booked films in the Central Film Library for several years thereafter.

True to the *Rashomon* model, the chronology goes back and forth, fleshing out initially obscure details surrounding the peremptory sacking of machine operator Charlie Wilson for insolence. The four principal characters – Wilson, his foreman Sid Turner, shop steward Joe Cooper and works manager Lloyd Mitchell (the actors are uncredited) – are given complex and believable psychological motivations for their behaviour. Wilson, for instance, has learned over breakfast that morning that his son-in-law has had his hours cut, and suspects that a newly introduced machine monitoring system at his own factory has a more sinister application than simply making maintenance more efficient. Whether his suspicions are correct is an open question, but Cooper explains that the new monitoring system was approved by the union on condition that certain workplace amenities and perks were improved, which they hadn't been. Turner is nearing retirement and wants a quiet life, while Mitchell is acutely conscious that his youth and inexperience make him vulnerable in the eyes of colleagues who feel he's been appointed above his station.

The film incidentally reveals a great deal about how small independent firms had to operate in an increasingly international environment. The company at the heart of the dispute, a precision toolmaker called Campbell's, is supplying gearboxes for Sanderson Tractors, which is about to close a deal with a Swedish agent. If the dispute is not resolved in time (sequences of Sanderson sales rep Geoffrey Davidson waiting for the go-ahead to board a Stockholm flight are threaded throughout the narrative to add a note of urgency), at least two British firms will suffer financially, and possibly more. At one point, Davidson refers to the deal being kept afloat by the 'Old Pal's Act', and later agrees to a temporary solution whereby he flies to Stockholm with the aim of stalling contractual negotiations for forty-eight hours in the hope that the dispute might be resolved in the interim. Crucially, the film proffers no solutions itself: the BPC clearly intended it as a 'trigger', to stimulate debate following 16mm screenings.

Dispute was entirely pre-scripted, but with many other documentary projects Simmons remained a fervent champion of 'finding the story' during the shooting, as he had previously done with *Sunday by the Sea*, *Bow Bells* and especially *The Gentle Corsican*. Unsurprisingly, this caused problems when he moved into the sphere of sponsored documentary, especially with the COI, a stickler not merely for scripting in advance but for its contractees delivering precisely what was planned. In the late 1950s, Simmons proposed a project about the then relatively young Heathrow Airport called *Zero at 1500* (the level at which one first entered the airport), which would portray the place from top to bottom as an organic entity. The COI was very keen on the idea, but the problem was, according to Simmons:

> that the COI wanted a script, and I wouldn't do a script. I said the whole point if you want to film what goes on at night is 'let's go and find out what goes on at night'. If I give you a script, it would be people doing their jobs in the old-fashioned way. I want to go round and find what's happening at night, where the work is going on, rebuilding engines, where the dustcart was going, but we won't know until we do it. They loved the idea, but no way could they finance it: they had to have a script.[7]

Simmons also discussed the project with Edgar Anstey, who was equally keen, but although he verbally agreed to a deal whereby he would write a script in advance but would be allowed to shoot the actual film in his own way, Simmons suspected that this would not be the situation in practice. His regular collaborator John Arnold eventually made the film for the COI (at Basic Films) as the entirely pre-scripted *Air Crossroads* (1958). Watching it, one can understand Simmons's qualms: it's a perfectly competent study of a day in the life of Heathrow Airport, but it's entirely led by its omniscient narrator. Though individuals are occasionally singled out for attention and sometimes even named, the abiding impression is that they were primarily chosen to illustrate a predetermined point (a recurring one being the airport's growing importance as an international hub, as reflected by the huge range of nationalities passing through), and they are never allowed a voice of their own. One brief moment, in which a Chinese student is given a message at the information desk and her expression rapidly segues from delight to apprehension, hints at the more personalised treatment that Simmons envisaged, but otherwise the COI remains firmly in control.

Other sponsors were more easy-going. *From First To Last* (1962) was made by Clore's Graphic Films on the back of a verbal agreement with Norman Vigars, films officer at the Ford Motor Company, to produce a film illustrating every stage in the process of creating a car from blueprint to test drive. It's an engaging spin on industrial film-making. With the film's structure implicitly predetermined by this straightforward pitch (and indeed its very title), Simmons was left free to visit the factory and to film operations there without a script. Ford clearly intended the end result to be used primarily as a promotional film in the vein of, for example, *First on the Road* (made by Simmons's erstwhile colleague Joseph Losey in 1960), but Simmons himself regarded it as 'a bit of Free Cinema by accident'. In giving individual factory workers a voice on the soundtrack, *From First To Last* also harks back to a much older British documentary tradition, sharing with Paul Rotha's *Shipyard* (1935) a soundtrack that is partly constructed from the anonymous reminiscences of the workers involved.

The scene is set by a quality control inspector describing the company's overall aims, while an engineer discusses the various conditions in which the cars will be expected to perform if Ford is to maintain its position in the global marketplace (substandard roads in Australia, high-speed autobahns in Germany, ice and snow in Finland). The film then explores the various raw materials that eventually comprise a car, the casting process and the tolerances required. Precision measurements of an order impossible for a human craftsman to match ensure that any one Ford car part will be completely compatible with another, regardless of whether the two were made in the same factory or even country. To fit this theme of the dominance of technology, at several points in the film the voices provide the only evidence of human activity, with many shots consisting of almost abstract

close-ups of factory processes as the car components are moulded, stamped and drilled into their final shape (their natural rhythms augmented by Les Condon's jazz score), before a visible human element is reintroduced during the inspection process. Individual contributions are mostly on-message (i.e., stressing the importance of what the factory workers are doing in terms of quality, efficiency and marketability), but more anecdotal material sometimes peeks through, especially when older methods are contrasted with then-current ones. The elaborate testing process on finished vehicles also offers opportunities for brief quasi-surrealist flourishes such as a disembodied shoe pressing repeatedly on the pedals.

No Short Cut (1964), another COI commission, made on behalf of the Ministry of Transport, went in the opposite direction, being thoroughly pre-scripted in advance. However, this fitted the material: it's a cautionary tale (made to support the work of the Royal Society for the Prevention of Accidents, and aimed at schoolchildren) and, like *Dispute*, it plays most successfully as a short didactic drama, this time with some comic inflections. An opening montage intercutting the fragile wheels of a child's bicycle with a lorry's far more rugged equivalent sets the tone, with the moralistic voiceover once the bike has inevitably been crushed quickly usurped by snippets of unsympathetic vox pops ('I always said he'd come to a bad end, that one'). As the wrecked bike is unceremoniously shoved into a dustcart, the narrator constructs an anthropomorphic Cain-and-Abel metaphor about two bikes growing up together but turning out markedly differently. One is sold to Jimmy, whose neatly knotted tie and immaculately parted hair establishes him as the goody-two-shoes even before this is reinforced with the information that his father is a keen advocate of the National Cycling Proficiency scheme. By contrast, Les, with his rumpled hair and lack of adult supervision when buying the bike (not to mention cheeking the salesman), is the flawed but vastly more interesting 'bad guy'.

Jimmy, naturally, is taking cycling lessons while the untrained Les takes to the road, initially carefree, but rapidly overtaken by children who have been properly trained in efficient body-weight distribution to assist their pedalling effectiveness. A lecture on puncture repair is accompanied by images of a forlorn Les standing by the roadside as it starts to rain, a cawing crow in the trees implicitly mocking him. Traffic management is illustrated by the kids gleefully staging a multiple pile-up on 'roads' outlined in the training ground, following which the film cuts to the equally busy but far more regulated Piccadilly Circus. The point is rammed home with a sequence in which Les weaves wildly down a road, into the path of a car and then, alarmingly, a bus doing the same thing. Les can't win: even when he reluctantly enrols in cycling classes himself, he starts off being far behind the others, and has to watch from the sidelines as Jimmy takes and passes his proficiency test. Desperately jealous, Les agrees to accompany Jimmy and his victorious colleagues to a favoured countryside spot, but decides to take a short cut through heavy traffic, the bike's own misgivings given guttural, occasionally panicky voice.

Throughout the film one feels that Simmons has more than a little sympathy for the hapless Les, who is given far more screen time than Jimmy. For all his inability to think things through, Les is a believer in diving into the deep end when it comes to ambition, and it's easy to see how this might have struck a chord with his creator. Fortunately, *No Short Cut* was made well before the shock-horror COI road-safety campaigns of the 1970s, so Les ultimately escapes with barely a scratch, albeit leaving a heap of mangled bars and twisted spokes in his wake. But he bounces back: a coda sees Jimmy and Les, the latter presumably having learned his lesson, cycling calmly (and *safely*) along a country road.

Simmons spent the next decade making feature films, planning unmade ones (an association with James Bond producer Harry Saltzman came to nothing) and shooting commercials. In 1972, Simmons, Arnold and Karel Reisz were invited to address that year's BISFA Festival of Industrial Films, as feature film-makers who had started in documentary shorts, now invited to look in and comment on their old line of business. Simmons's final out-and-out documentary was the COI commission *Greenwich: A People's Heritage* (1976). This turned out to be his most conventional sponsored film, a thoroughly professional but almost entirely anonymous trot through the borough's history, art and architecture. Keen Simmons-watchers might note a quick detour to the banks of his beloved Thames, but this is comfortably his most impersonal documentary, mainly of interest as a serviceable contribution to the plethora of sponsored films then being made on urban conservation subjects. Produced by Graphic, Simmons directed it as a favour to Clore, and quickly recognised that the brief offered next to no scope for innovation, and so he decided to treat it as an extended commercial, scrupulously meeting the sponsor's detailed requirements.[8]

Simmons' fiction features are nominally outside the scope of this study, yet once the routine Donald Sinden-Peggy Cummins potboiler *Your Money or Your Wife* (1960) is discounted, the remaining three offer plenty of evidence of his non-fiction roots, as does the BBC TV play *On Giants' Shoulders* (1979). Indeed, *Four in the Morning* (1965) grew organically out of Simmons's uncompleted *People on the Thames* documentary project. It was developed in collaboration with Larry Pizer (the Clore employee who by then had taken over from Walter Lassally as Simmons's regular cinematographer) and funded by their earnings from making commercials. They initially hired a tugboat to film evocative sequences of the Thames in the early morning fog (these found their way into the film's credit sequence), and Simmons's plan was to travel down the Thames offering brief portraits of the various people who earned a living off the river. Once again Edgar Anstey had liked the idea of making a BTF film using Simmons's concept, but once again requested a script.[9] This time, Simmons decided that if a story was going to be imposed on this material it might as well be conceived as fiction from the outset, so he devised three short stories, all set around the Thames. He developed the final script in collaboration with his actors (who included Judi Dench, Ann Lynn, Brian Phelan and Norman Rodway), encouraging them to improvise around pre-established core themes in a manner that anticipated Mike Leigh's work. Although the final film was shot to a fully worked-out screenplay, much of it chimes with his earlier work, especially the episode in which the lovers (Lynn and Phelan) spontaneously take off on a speedboat on the Thames.

The long-gestating *The Optimists of Nine Elms* (1973) gives off an even stronger whiff of authenticity, in part because the film was originally conceived in the late 1950s as a feature-film expansion of the spirit that animated *Sunday by the Sea* and especially *Bow Bells*. The sentimental story of Peter Sellers' elderly busker being befriended by two children is enhanced if not usurped outright by its vivid portrait of the Wandsworth district of Nine Elms and environs (including Battersea Dogs Home and a southern stretch of the river whose various activities are depicted in sufficient detail to suggest that Simmons still hadn't got his *People on the Thames* project out of his system) before it was redeveloped. Even in the early 1970s, people are shown living in slum dwellings that have barely changed since Anstey and Arthur Elton's classic *Housing Problems* (1935), aspiring to little more than being rehoused in high-rise tower blocks on the other side of the river. Simmons also harks back to his earlier films in the use of music-hall songs, albeit here filtered through Lionel Bart's compositions and Sellers' often on-screen performance. *Black Joy* (1977) also makes very effective use of its Brixton locations, the milieu established just as often through hand-held, quasi-vérité shots of everyday life in the streets, markets and pubs, offering a more convincing depiction of the district than the conventionally dramatised material that tended towards stereotype.

Despite excellent reviews, none of Simmons's features achieved any significant box-office income – *Four in the Morning* and *The Optimists of Nine Elms* both fell victim to the age-old curse of film distribution: opening in a week full of higher-profile alternative distractions. In particular, *The Optimists of Nine Elms* was up against William Friedkin's horror blockbuster *The Exorcist* (1973) and never stood a chance – Simmons ruefully quipped that the only money he made on the entire project was the publisher's advance on the novel, and even that had appeared in 1964, when it seemed unlikely that it would ever become a film. *Black Joy*, intended from the outset as a more commercially attractive proposition, looked set to be a modest yet solid success until music-rights complications pulled it from circulation for four years.

By then, following an abortive trip to Hollywood (he was replaced as director of the thriller *Green Ice* [1981] shortly after shooting began) Simmons had embarked on a sixteen-year stint directing for television, alternating episodes of *The Professionals* and *A Touch of Frost*, even of *Supergran* and *Inspector Morse*, with more distinctive one-off work such as *On Giants' Shoulders*, broadcast in the BBC's *Play of the Week* slot on 28 March 1979. Although pre-scripted and largely performed by actors, in several respects this is Simmons's final documentary, since it was based on the real-life story of thalidomide victim Terry Wiles, and Simmons decided that the nature of his disability (he had no arms and virtually no legs) made the role unperformable except by Wiles himself. Verisimilitude is further enhanced by the use of real names, and genuinely disabled children in the hospital classroom scenes, although the other main speaking roles are all played by actors (notably Judi Dench and Bryan Pringle as Wiles's adoptive parents) and Wiles himself had to have his dialogue dubbed by a younger actor in order convincingly to reincarnate his ten-year-old self. Physically, this was surprisingly straightforward, since he had only grown an inch in the seven intervening years.

Wiles was the subject of two follow-up films, straight documentaries this time, broadcast in 1980 and 1997. Simmons was supposed to direct the second, which would look at Wiles's story since the 1970s (following a big compensation payment for thalidomide victims, he emigrated to New Zealand, married and worked as a counsellor), but although Channel 4 agreed to back the project, they were unwilling to allow Simmons, by then in his late seventies, to direct it. So he was bought out and the film *Fight For Love* was eventually made by Sarah Boston and broadcast on 3 August 1997. By then, albeit not through choice, Simmons's directing career was effectively over, though he continues to write and to pitch to this day.

It's hard to know how best to sum up Anthony Simmons's career: to celebrate his undoubted achievements or lament the fact that his obvious talent and independence of spirit rarely led to the critical and popular recognition enjoyed by many of his contemporaries. However, since Simmons himself has doggedly maintained an upbeat and cheerful outlook both through his films and in person, one should look on the bright side: an output that includes *Sunday by the Sea*, *Bow Bells*, *Four in the Morning*, *The Optimists of Nine Elms* and *On Giants' Shoulders* is by any yardstick a legacy to be proud of – and Simmons's origin in documentary is the key to understanding much of his work, in factual and fictional film-making alike.

NOTES

1. Interview with Michael Brooke, 10 November 2009.
2. The most detailed account of Anthony Simmons's early life is found in the BECTU History Project interview conducted by Rodney Giesler on 25 September 1997, with supplementary details obtained by Michael Brooke in an interview with Simmons conducted on 23 February 2010.
3. Interview with Michael Brooke, 23 February 2010.
4. Interview with Michael Brooke, 23 February 2010.
5. Interview with Michael Brooke, 23 February 2010.
6. Clients included Players Cigarettes (1960), Kraft (1970), Martini (1970), Mothercare (1971), Embassy Cigars (1972) and Findus (1974).
7. Interview with Michael Brooke, 10 November 2009.
8. Interview with Michael Brooke, 23 February 2010.
9. Interview with Michael Brooke, 10 November 2009.

18 Meet the Pioneers: *Early Lindsay Anderson*

ERIK HEDLING

There is a little-known side to the work of British film director Lindsay Anderson, the maker of classic feature films like *This Sporting Life* (1963), *If...* (1968) and *O Lucky Man* (1973): namely, the bulk of his work as a documentary film-maker. This may seem an odd statement, for Anderson the documentarist has been internationally recognised for over fifty years. *Thursday's Children* (1953) won an Academy Award and *Every Day Except Christmas* (1957) a Venice Grand Prix. Above all there were the famous Free Cinema programmes staged at the National Film Theatre in London between 1956 and 1959. As well as *Every Day Except Christmas*, and alongside documentaries by other film-makers, Free Cinema included Anderson's *Wakefield Express* (1952), his cinematic tribute to Humphrey Jennings, and the vitriolic short *O Dreamland* (1953), which has gained much critical attention in the literature on documentary for what some argue is a patronising approach to the leisure habits of the British working class.[1] But in roughly the same period as these last two films, the late 1940s and early 1950s, Anderson made some other documentaries. These were all sponsored films, for private companies, charities or government agencies and, more or less, are 'unknown' Anderson films.

Until recently, most of the 'unknowns' have been hard to get hold of and to study, but they are now becoming more available, and it is my object in this chapter to say something about them. They represent an interesting case study, which could be set against two very different backgrounds: one, Anderson's own later career, subject of books in its own right; the other, the busy world of sponsored documentary film-making in Britain in the early post-war period, the subject of this book. One of the questions raised by the 'unknowns' is whether they are more usefully placed in the first context (Anderson the auteur) or in the second (British post-war documentary)

In a recently published anthology on industrial films, *Films that Work*, the editors Vinzenz Hediger and Patrick Vonderau claim that this largely neglected area of film history constitutes 'the next big chunk of unchartered territory in cinema studies'. If so, they maintain, along with collector-archivist Rick Prelinger, that 'it would be a great leap forward for cinema studies if we were able to avoid the auteur theory this time'.[2] This would suggest that Anderson's industrial films are best understood in relation to the other sponsored documentaries of the time. However, since Anderson is – unlike others covered in this volume – a well-known film-maker, an auteurist assessment is not an unreasonable way to begin looking at his least-known works. Provided it is open-minded, it doesn't preclude other approaches, and may ultimately bolster the case for them. In this chapter the main parameter will therefore be the personal dimension of the films: how Anderson's unknown films may be connected to his authorial reputation, and what is perceived as his particular style of film-making, as well as whether these films might add to our historical understanding of Lindsay Anderson the documentarist and engineer of Free Cinema.

ANDERSON THE FILM CRITIC

It is well known that Anderson made a name for himself as a film critic in *Sequence*, the journal of the Oxford University Film Society.[3] Here, he published some very ambitious articles on film from 1947 to 1952; he continued this critical mission in *Sight & Sound* between 1952 and 1957. Over his ten years as a film critic, he developed something of an aesthetic ideal, which put particular emphasis on cinema as primarily being an art form, and which brought forward the director as the principal artist working in film.[4] This influential aesthetic had wider consequences for British film criticism of the 1950s and '60s.

The only articles by Anderson in *Sequence* or *Sight & Sound* that dealt exclusively with documentary were about Robert Flaherty and Anderson's particular hero, Humphrey Jennings.[5] John Grierson and Paul Rotha had criticised Flaherty for the lack of political and social analysis in his films. Anderson, on the other hand, was typically enchanted by the sheer artistry of Flaherty and Richard Leacock's *Louisiana Story* (1948), reaching for comparisons with masterly painters like Paul Klee and Marc Chagall. Similarly, Anderson analysed Humphrey Jennings in purely aesthetic terms and he praised the aspects of Jennings that had been criticised by Jennings's fellow documentarists. Jennings's biographer Kevin Jackson claims that the relationship between Grierson and Jennings had been characterised by 'long-standing antagonism'.[6] Grierson's utilitarian view of the film medium became the target of some of Anderson's critical polemics and when he wrote an introduction to a projected reprint of *Sequence* in the 1990s, he explicitly stated that 'John Grierson himself, though a great producer, was more interested in social propaganda than in art. This did not appeal to us.'[7]

Even if Anderson has, mostly by word of mouth, become known as one of Grierson's fiercest critics, he did not actually mention Grierson's name particularly often, either in *Sequence*, or in *Sight & Sound*. Jack C. Ellis has scrutinised their respective arguments more closely, and has underlined Grierson's generally condescending attitude when, for instance, calling Free Cinema 'baby stuff'.[8] Much of Anderson's criticism against Grierson was in reality articulated much later, at the beginning of the 1970s, when Anderson himself was a famous film-maker (though no longer specialising in documentary) and was accordingly interviewed frequently by scholars and film journals.[9]

One point Anderson did make in the 1940s was to deny the documentarists sole credit for having inspired the introduction of realism in British feature films: 'It was inevitable that British features should become more realistic as a result of the war, but whether as a result it is legitimate to associate them with the movement which started with *Drifters* [1929], and during the war gave us many feature-influenced documentaries, is questionable,' Anderson wrote in his 'British Cinema: The Descending Spiral'.[10] Later, he would scorn the 'anti-art impatience that, from Grierson down, seemed so often and so unnecessarily to reflect documentary thinking'.[11]

Grierson himself initially gave the editors of *Sequence* his 'blessing'.[12] He soon, however, discovered the aesthetic bias in Anderson's writings, and counterattacked, talking of Anderson in terms of: 'those intellectual teddy boys who have recently been in the ascendant'.[13] There is no question, however, that much of Anderson's film criticism, aesthetically inclined as it was, took aim at the respected position of the Griersonian documentarists in British film culture. With its auteurist approach, its artistic flavour and, indeed, its elitist pretensions, *Sequence* sought to reform this film culture. Very importantly, however, during his years at *Sight & Sound*, Anderson modified his outlook so as to maintain a demand for social responsibility, alongside artistic commitment, from both critics and film artists alike.

This bias towards ideological commitment, which necessarily involved a slight detour from the pure *Sequence* aesthetic, can also be noticed in the first Free Cinema Manifesto, published as a printed programme in the first Free Cinema screenings in February 1956:

> No film can be too personal. The image speaks. Sound amplifies and comments. Size is irrelevant. Perfection is not an aim. An attitude means a style. A style means an attitude. Implicit in our attitude is a belief in freedom, in the importance of people and in the significance of the everyday. [14]

Much of Anderson's later cinematic style is best described as falling somewhere in the middle of the tension between *Sequence* and the Free Cinema movement.[15] But what about the films he was making at the same time he was writing criticism – the 'unknown' films? Did they express a similar aesthetic?

THE INDUSTRIAL FILMS

Lindsay Anderson made his debut as a film director in 1948. As mentioned, the films he made have been little written about. Among the secondary sources that do exist are Anderson's own commentary for Paul Ryan's collection of his writings,[16] Anderson's brief comments on the early films in the published diaries,[17] Gavin Lambert's biography,[18] and a substantial fourteen-page, unpublished statement by Lois Smith, written in 1997.[19]

It was Lois Smith who, under the name of Lois Sutcliffe, commissioned Anderson to make what became four documentary films for the big Wakefield company – Richard Sutcliffe Limited – run by her husband, Desmond Sutcliffe. These films were *Meet the Pioneers* (1948, thirty-three minutes), *Idlers that Work* (1949, seventeen minutes), *Three Installations* (1952, twenty-eight minutes) and *Trunk Conveyor* (1952, thirty-eight minutes).

According to Lois Smith's narrative, the most thorough account of these four films, it was she who had the idea of hiring Anderson, whom she, a fellow film buff, knew personally and as an editor of *Sequence*.[20] Smith and Anderson had initially met at a gathering of British film societies at Oxford, and had discovered their mutual admiration for American cinema. Her husband had decided to make a promotional film for his company to be shown at the Industrial Exhibition at Earls Court in London in July 1948. The Sutcliffes rejected a script made by a London film company, and decided to produce the film themselves. Lois Sutcliffe thought of Anderson and her husband readily agreed. She managed to get Anderson to Horbury, outside Wakefield, Yorkshire, where the Sutcliffe plant was situated. Along with her, Anderson set up the Sutcliffe Film Unit, which also contained the cinematographer John Jones (a local school master and amateur photographer) and Edward Brendon, a friend of Gavin Lambert's with some experience of film shooting. Lois Smith's recollections are meticulously detailed:

> Lindsay decided that our first shot should be a tracking shot; maybe he wanted to test us all out, including the commitment of the Works itself, as we needed their help. We had to have a 'dolly' made – tracks and a stand on wheels for the camera; none of it very stable. I seem to remember that the camera wobbled as it moved along the rails; one of the many improvisations we had to invent from time to time. And we needed workers. There were eight operatives on this small production line and they were all women. *Meet the Pioneers* shows that even in quite heavy industry women had replaced men in the work place. After all, this was not so long after the end of the war during which women were trained to make up for the loss of the men who went into the forces.[21]

Beside the interesting remark on the use of women in the traditionally all-male work force, Lois Smith catches something of the spirit of the production: ambitious, artistic, inexperienced and innocent – all at once. On the other hand, at odds with *Sequence*'s rhetoric, it was certainly not independent. The films were all on the Sutcliffe Company and its employment, manufacture and sales (even encompassing exports to Malaya) of conveyor belts, an industrial device introduced at the beginning of the twentieth century into Britain by the Irish engineer Richard Sutcliffe, the founder of the firm and the grandfather of the current owner.

It is interesting that Anderson's first venture into practical cinema should have been in the field of the regionally produced semi-professional industrial film (albeit the Sutcliffe films were made on 35mm) – not an obvious destination for a critic of Anderson's views, but also a world entirely separate from London's established documentary industry. The very idea of filming conveyor belts was somewhat ironically commented on in a contemporary letter to Anderson from his close friend and co-publisher of *Sequence* (and later biographer) Gavin Lambert: 'Conveyor belts: they do not sound you or us, of course.'[22] One senses an anti-capitalist ethos in Lambert's remark, an ethos which Anderson probably shared, but which he had to disregard against the background of actually being able to make a film.

Still, Anderson himself arrived at a rather low opinion of *Meet the Pioneers*, later expressed as, 'today, it looks very amateurish'.[23] Lambert even added some derogatory remarks regarding Lois and Desmond Sutcliffe, the financiers, as being the kind of people who were 'entirely non-creative'.[24] *Sequence* had been (and remained) very hostile towards the role of big business in film-making. In fact, Anderson came to be close friends with Lois Sutcliffe – later, of course, Lois Smith – for the rest of his life. He died while visiting her in France in 1994. This all said, as the diaries make clear, the opportunity to make a film was at the time very important to Anderson. He writes:

> Oddly enough, I feel that as regards a career in films this experience has left me pretty much where I was. I never seriously doubted my ability to produce something, once my feet were set on the track and I was given a shove. I suppose I have gained in self-confidence. Apart from the photography, after all, I did the whole thing myself – editing, writing and speaking the commentary, arranging the music. Yet all this has not exactly convinced me that I can or even want to get a job in a studio – or even make another film for Sutcliffes. Although I suppose I *shall* do the latter.[25]

Working again for the Sutcliffes was, of course, exactly what he did.

In fact, Anderson's artistic contribution doesn't look particularly amateurish in any of these films, although he was initially working with cameramen of very limited experience. Instead, one is struck by the unobtrusive qualities of the editing as well as the surprisingly mobile camerawork. Also, the didactic voiceover – in all Sutcliffe films provided by Anderson himself – feels very well timed in relation to the flow of images. The factual description of the technology behind the conveyor belts feels convincing. *Meet the Pioneers* is more professional than one would expect from someone who had never made films before.

Nevertheless, if one compares Anderson's films to the industrial documentaries of the period, made by professional documentarists, there are certainly differences. The latter are self-evidently superior in terms of cinematography, narrative flow and editing. The very first edition of the National Coal Board's long-running newsreel – *Mining Review 1st Year No 1* (1947), made by the Crown Film Unit – makes an instructive comparison. Here, there are several conveyor belts at work, albeit appearing in the film very briefly, but still quite sufficiently for the audience to grasp the basic principle of what they do. The film, which also enjoys the luxury of some synchronised sound, includes at the beginning an interesting collage of superimposed images with the forward run of the belts contrasted with workers descending down the pit stairs. Such technical bravado was simply beyond Anderson's editorial skills at the time. The industrial documentaries that came from the likes of the NCB are often edited so as to mix close-ups and long shots in an artistically convincing way that seems strikingly effective when compared to Anderson's admirable attempts. The fact remains that I can find very little in these films that can be connected to Anderson's individual style, or to his theoretical stipulations of a film aesthetic, in spite of his own remarks in the diaries:

> To this extent, the films are truly personal. I refuse to indulge in the flashy for its own sake, and try to avoid the more notorious clichés; but in their place can be found only an utterly conventional conception, proceeding in a number of unadventurous, if tastefully arranged, set-ups. I suppose, it's still possible that *Three Installations* will constitute an advance; but I feel that any progression in it is comparative – no liberation.[26]

There is little personal intervention from the director in the films; personal intervention being one of the things that would characterise all Anderson's works from the mid-1950s onwards.[27] There is, for example, really nothing that could be argued as constituting an alternative approach to the Griersonian documentary that Anderson had criticised, even if it could be claimed that he achieved this in some of his Free Cinema work such as *O Dreamland*. His industrial films even appear to be partly modelled on the standard documentary modes at the time, as in, for instance, the role of the elevated narrator (Anderson) speaking in received pronunciation and arguably expressing a socially superior point of view. Lois Smith remarks: 'his pronunciation was very much like the style of the old BBC newsreaders, which fact would date the film accurately as sometime in the Forties'.[28]

Moreover, in accordance with Griersonian social democracy, much of the focus is placed on the well-being of the workers, who are enjoying their lunches, and also transporting themselves in a leisurely and relaxed manner on the conveyor belts. The films are all concerned with the welfare of labour and how much the conveyor belts have contributed to the improvement of working conditions (and also, not least, how the employers have been able to cut labour costs).

In a sequence somewhat longer than two minutes in *Meet the Pioneers*, the film dwells on the three different ways in which the workers choose to spend their lunchtime: some go home, some sit by their machine reading a paper, enjoying a sandwich and a pot of tea, and some visit the canteen. Here, the tone is tender, particularly in the shots of some young male workers playing with a rope swinging from a tree over a tiny creek. This is indeed an idyllic place for the working class. Charles Silet commented on these images as follows: 'there are scenes characteristic of Anderson's later work, for right in the middle of the film he caught the factory workers during their lunch break in images reminiscent of the best war documentaries of Humphrey Jennings'.[29] Among the voluminous literature on Anderson, Elizabeth Sussex is one of the few writers beside Silet to have seen the films and to really reflect on them in much depth. She maintains:

> More particular to Anderson, however, is a sequence showing the lunch break at the conveyor factory. The commentary has just described how much the factory has expanded from its original row of cottages and single weaving shed. Now there are more than five hundred people to break for lunch ... To find this unstressed series of shots inserted here is like finding the beginning of Anderson's style.[30]

The images were certainly relevant to Anderson's later style, but I would not say that they distinguished Anderson from other film-makers at the time.[31] Images of a collective spirit suffusing the lunch break seem to have been a standard part of the industrial film's repertoire. British Transport Films' spectacular Technicolor featurette *They Take the High Road* (James Ritchie, 1960), to give a later example, was produced by Edgar Anstey and Stewart McAllister, exactly the sort of documentarists that Anderson would have decried. The Sutcliffe films do, however, feature one image that could fit into Anderson's later predilection for the expression of cinematic self-consciousness. In *Trunk Conveyor*, the last of the conveyor belt films, made in 1952, there is a shot of the extremely complex path of the conveyor belt. Sitting at a Steenbeck watching the film running through the multiple machine rollers, the possibility of an allusion to an editing table does not seem too fanciful, considering Anderson's sense of humour. But to reiterate, I cannot really agree with Anderson's own claim that 'all the documentary films I made were, I hope, personal and subjective'.[32] These early ones, albeit technically more proficient than Anderson described them, were a bit too mainstream for that. But Anderson seemed to be quite pleased with his work on *Trunk Conveyor*, the last in the series, at the time. In *The Diaries*, he concludes:

> It is pleasant, and healthy to return with a sense of achievement behind one. However minor one's efforts. And I find that I am really quite proud and even affectionate towards this film (though the pretentious ambitions I had for it are hardly realised. Humanity ... poetry, etc.).[33]

Later, in another note in *The Diaries*, he states regarding his ambitions in *Trunk Conveyor* that the ideas: 'went straight away – probably rightly for, after all, the film was intended to be instructional, and there would have been no point in artying it up until one was left with nothing but atmosphere'.[34] However, it would today be very interesting know how, exactly, he had planned to 'arty' things up, since there is not much art in *Trunk Conveyor*.

MUSICAL AESTHETICS

There is one undeniable example of authorial intervention in all Anderson's Sutcliffe films. That is the choice of music, which later would become a distinguishing feature of Anderson's films. Already in the Sutcliffe films are traces of an individual sensibility guiding the music. Although Lois Smith mentions a musical arranger, Len Scott, who was also credited on *Meet the Pioneers*, Anderson himself chose the music for the film.[35] The *Sequence*-style art lover can be discerned in Smith's reminiscences of a visit to Anderson at the end of the 1980s, when she was shown *Meet the Pioneers* again for the first time in forty years: 'I was not prepared for the flood of emotion I felt as the titles came up over the Henry Moore drawing and the music – *Appalachian Spring* – began.'[36] Here, the use of Moore's stylised drawing of a coalmine and the music from Aaron Copland's 1944 ballet echoes Anderson's future techniques, making meaningful and carefully planned intertextual allusions. Copland's music is usually understood as celebrating American nineteenth-century pioneers, a historical aspect of great interest to Anderson (i.e., his adoration for John Ford). Besides Copland, Anderson employed Antonin Dvořák's *New World Symphony* (1893), another work adding an American flavour in keeping with Anderson's artistic tastes at the time.

This touch of Americana is also present in the other Sutcliffe films. Copland reappears in *Idlers that Work*, where there is exactly the same sequence from *Appalachian Spring* at the beginning. Copland's music is also used at the end of the film, accompanying the steady roll of the idlers. In *Three*

On location for *Three Installations*

Installations, the music is more daring. Besides music by Aaron Copland and southern composer Don Gillis, among others, there is a distinctive boogie woogie performed by Alan Clare on piano and Johnny Flanagan on drums (according to G. Roy Levin, this piece is named 'Conveyor Boogie'[37]). The blues-based piano seems particularly apt for accompanying the forward slide of the conveyor belt. Finally, in *Trunk Conveyor*, Anderson employs a concertina (Alf Edwards) and acoustic guitar (Fitzroy Coleman) to accompany songs collated by Bert Lloyd (a famous folksong collector). The songs are 'Sixteen Tons' and 'The Collier's Song'.[38] In fact, Lloyd's work formed the basis for some issues of the NCB's *Mining Review*, but in the context of Anderson's film criticism their Celtic-and-Western mixture fittingly suggests the presence of Irish-American director John Ford, Anderson's favourite film-maker.[39]

SCREENING THE FILMS

Predictably, there is little material accounting for the reception of the Sutcliffe films. *Meet the Pioneers* was, as mentioned, made for an industrial fair at Earls Court. However, it was also shown locally, and on this there is further reminiscence from Lois Smith: 'We booked the Savoy at Lupset for an evening. Lindsay had decided that we should show *Cover Girl* to accompany our *Pioneers*. He thought that the men would enjoy Rita Heyworth [sic] and that their wives would like the extravagant clothes that she wore.'[40] The story does not disclose whether *Cover Girl* (Charles Vidor, 1944) was actually shown, but *Meet the Pioneers* certainly was, and Lois Smith concludes:

> After it was all finished it was no better. No spontaneous round of applause came as the lights went up and it was all over. No one, not a single person, congratulated us. Not a word was said and Lindsay rightly never forgot this. He felt that it showed the worst side of all the people present. Yorkshire reticence taken to its graceless conclusion. It was bleak.[41]

Thus was launched the cinema career of Lindsay Anderson.

Things did improve. Regarding a screening a few years later of *Idlers that Work*, again at the Savoy cinema, Anderson notes in his diaries: 'Strengthened by a viewing on Thursday of *Idlers that Work* – shown at the Savoy to the proprietor of the *Wakefield Gazette*, who is considering the celebration of his paper's centenary with the production of a film.'[42] The screening was successful at least to the extent that Anderson, on the strength of *Idlers that Work*, was commissioned to make *Wakefield Express*.

Despite this, there are some indications that Anderson actively prevented the public screening of Sutcliffe films later in his career. In a letter to Lois Smith, written in 1959 and after the breakthrough of Free Cinema, he made it clear that: '[T]hey were proposing to show *Meet the Pioneers* at the National Film Theatre as an early example of my work!!! I have given a firm veto to *that* idea.'[43] Possibly, Anderson wanted these films to remain unknown, once he had some more personal works to display.

OTHER SPONSORED DOCUMENTARIES

The next group of documentary films directed by Anderson was more closely connected to the ongoing project of embedding the welfare state in post-war British life – a project to which, of course, much of Soho's documentary industry was co-opted. Indeed, these films were professionally produced by Leon Clore at Basic Films, with Walter Lassally usually photographing them.[44] Clore would later produce, and Lassally photograph, some of the Free Cinema films – and Lassally later shot several of the British New Wave films of the early 1960s.

Anderson now made films for various governmental agencies: *£20 a Ton* (1955, five minutes) and *Energy First* (1955, five minutes) for the National Fuel Efficiency Service and *Foot and Mouth* (1955, twenty minutes) for the Central Office of Information on behalf of the Ministry of Agriculture, Fisheries and Food. Anderson also directed four five-minute films for the National Society for the Prevention of Cruelty to Children (NSPCC), a charity with a long history but now evolving in the light of the national welfare project. Anderson's NSPCC films were *Green and Pleasant Land* (1955), *Henry* (1955), *The Children Upstairs* (1955) and *A Hundred Thousand Children* (1955).

One of these films that really stands out is *£20 a Ton* (shot by Larry Pizer). Here, an accountant is confronted with the wastage of coal at the plant he controls, which is causing spending on fuel to be four times higher than it should be. The wastage is due to uneven distribution in the furnaces, faulty insulation of the pipes and the unnecessary leakage of precious steam. The didactic narrator tells the story of this misuse in a matter-of-fact manner. The narration is gradually and interestingly juxtaposed with increasingly comic acting from the accountant, neatly attired in hat, gloves, umbrella, overcoat and a handkerchief that he pulls out every time he encounters surplus steam or smoke. He becomes more and more agitated, bullies the workers and reluctantly pulls out his big wallet to pay for the coal at the end of the film. A shot/reverse shot structure dominates the final sequence. The accountant brings out a banknote, a pipe is seen blowing steam, and this is repeated several times. This is clearly a moment of Andersonian irony. He was to be attacked severely for ridiculing the working class in *O Dreamland*; here his target is much further up the class ladder and prefigures the satirising of the bourgeoisie in his later work. Although a farcical approach to dramatised documentary is not unique to Anderson, in this context the interest of *£20 a Ton* is that it is the director's first attempt at the kind of satirical comedy (*O Dreamland* was certainly satire, but certainly not comedy) which he would later employ in films such as *O Lucky Man!*.

Foot and Mouth also contains some personal touches. One of the few who has commented on the film, Patrick Russell, writes that: 'Lindsay Anderson's *Foot and Mouth* (1955) is a succinct government information film: effective, but not easy to square with the Anderson of later Free Cinema fame.'[45] On the other hand David Robinson, who saw the film more or less when it came out, characterised it as:

> A key example of how a film made to a sponsor's exact requirements can, by its truth and artistry, achieve much more. The film contains some of the best evocations of the English countryside in the cinema, and often recalls the opening scenes of Franju's *Le Sang des Betes* [1949].[46]

To these remarks, I would add a few comments. *Foot and Mouth* does represent Anderson's first attempt at creating a more complex narrative, in this case twenty linear minutes in strict continuity and less impressionistically than in, say, *Meet the Pioneers*. As I see it, he also chose to do *Foot and Mouth* as a horror film, just as he would later make parts of *Britannia Hospital* (1982) in that particular mode. In the story of how foot and mouth disease strikes a British farm, Anderson is happy to turn to gory detail. We watch slaughter, carcasses, injection needles repeatedly inserted into a cow's tongue, cow droppings in a close-up of the cow's backside, rats and the preparation of pyres for the burning of the dead animals. Anderson also uses montage to show a succession of horrible carcasses, each accompanied by the sound of the gunshot that, the viewer presumes, has killed the animals.

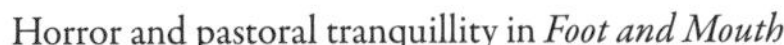

Horror and pastoral tranquillity in *Foot and Mouth*

In one particularly interesting sequence the camera pans along a shelf with animal body parts in glass jars. The Anderson aficionado will instantly remember the famous scene in *If* of the rebels finding a conserved foetus in the school basement (and *Britannia Hospital* has a similar image too). The good agency deployed in this battle is the veterinary service – the welfare state authority presence entering the second part of the film, reassuring spectators that the havoc can be limited and that there is a cure in the shape of disinfection and thorough infection control.

I will not go so far in my analysis of *Foot and Mouth* as to regard its many images of tractors, trucks, cars, trains and even a boat as an allusion to Humphrey Jennings's symbolically charged use of such motifs. It is enough to state that there are quite a few for a Lindsay Anderson film. The film is certainly impressive, but despite everything I have said I cannot see anything particularly personal in it, not even its pleasing images of the English countryside, for these do not seem unusual when compared to other documentaries of the period.

INSPIRED TRAILERS

At Basic, Anderson also wrote and directed four short films, photographed by Lassally, more directly in the cause of social welfare. These were commissioned by a charity, the NSPCC. Ranging from four to five minutes in length, they do show Anderson developing as a film-maker. And in the last two, Anderson's interest in the creative treatment of music is again evident.

The first two of Anderson's NSPCC films, *A Hundred Thousand Children* and *The Children Upstairs*, were more or less standard charity appeals, the first urging its audience to contribute financially to the NSPCC. The other two, however, were surprisingly personal and very Andersonian in their approach. *Henry* tells the story of young boy who runs away from home while his parents are quarrelling fiercely. He goes on the Piccadilly Line to Piccadilly Circus and then straight out into the nightlife. Charles Silet has described the world Henry encounters as: 'sex shops, neon signs, crowds, shop windows, film posters, newspaper sellers, litter-strewn pavements, and, finally two close-ups of Henry who is taking all this in'.[47] Henry is even enjoying a cigarette and he enters a pool hall, from which he is thrown out. I cannot resist comparing the montage representing urban decay to Ingmar Bergman's contemporary classic *Summer with Monica* (1953), where the heroine (or, as it were, anti-heroine as played by Harriet Andersson) enters a seedy world that eventually leads to her infidelity. Anderson and Bergman both depict popular leisure habits as potentially devastating, and both imaginatively employ jazz to illustrate the decline. But the most obvious intertextual move would, of course, be to relate *Henry* to *O Dreamland*, Anderson's earlier, non-sponsored, condemnation of working-class people senselessly enjoying the pleasures of gruesomely tortured wax figures at the amusement park in Margate. Behind all this lurks the shadow of Humphrey Jennings and the romantic-ironic presentation of working-class leisure traditions in his documentary *Spare Time* (1939), plus a touch of French surrealist Jean Vigo, another director in Anderson's pantheon. But even the Jennings-inspired touch of popular leisure habits is not the most remarkable aspect of *Henry*. Henry goes to a railway station, intending to travel even further away, but a railway officer picks him up. The railway officer makes a telephone call and a uniformed inspector of the NSPCC swiftly arrives. This man is played by none other than Lindsay Anderson himself, who self-consciously twinkles his eye towards the camera.

Of course, Anderson was not particularly well known in 1955. Still, this cameo appearance is most Andersonian, prefiguring his appearance in, for instance, *O Lucky Man!*, in the television production *The Old Crowd* (1978, voice only) and in his last film, *Is That All There Is* (1993). There is actually a clue to understanding the cameo in *Henry* in *The Diaries*, where Anderson writes:

> I am a great one for looking for symbols that may mark the beginning of new periods: new leaves turned, abandonment of old ways ... Of course, life isn't like this. But can't it be? The cardinal rule is surely that

> anything can happen; and not only the unpleasant things. The traditional things, the clichés can happen too. Those NSPCC inspectors: upstanding, enlightened Christians ... Not embittered, and certainly not doing the job only for some sort of morbid fascination. Well, why shouldn't I turn over a new leaf.[48]

The do-gooding NSPCC inspector, Anderson seems to say, is generally a cliché. But the cliché can also be 'true': the inspector really can be the Good Samaritan who wishes to do the morally right thing, to 'turn over a new leaf'. The twinkling eye, as I read it, catches this ambiguity in the character. And Anderson's appearance can be regarded in the same self-ironic mode as the one he was to do in *O Lucky Man!*.[49]

It is equally possible to relate *Green and Pleasant Land* to the later work of Lindsay Anderson, particularly due to the strong influence of Humphrey Jennings's aesthetic on the film. Jennings often turned to the poetry of William Blake to express his themes. Thus, in Anderson's *Green and Pleasant Land*, a children's choir performs Blake's 'Jerusalem' (or, more correctly, the lyrics from the 'Preface' to *Milton*, 1804, set to twentieth-century music). The imagery is initially lyrical with its magnificent English countryside (to my mind, superior to the images in *Foot and Mouth*) gradually closing in, as Elizabeth Sussex describes it, on: 'the other face of England, the filth, disorder, dirt and hunger that exists "not only where the smoke of industry darkens the sky"'.[50] And the title itself refers to the very last line in Blake's poem: 'England's green and pleasant land'. The Humphrey Jennings film that comes primarily to mind is *Words for Battle* (1941), according to Anderson himself one of Jennings's masterpieces, or as he would put it in his *Sight & Sound* article: '*Words for Battle, Listen to Britain, Fires Were Started, A Diary for Timothy*. To the enthusiast for Jennings these titles have a ring which makes it a pleasure simply to speak them.'[51]

In *Words for Battle*, documentary footage is juxtaposed with verbal quotations from English poetry and prose, read by Laurence Olivier. In the first sequence, in which Olivier reads from William Camden's *Britannia*, beautiful images of an English landscape appear, and they are very reminiscent of the footage in *Green and Pleasant Land*. There is also one specific section of Jennings's film alluded to by Anderson's, the Blake sequence in which Olivier quotes 'Jerusalem' verbatim. In *Words for Battle*, the sequence starts in a London haunted by the terror of war. Then the children are evacuated by train to the countryside and finally they reach the 'green and pleasant land': trees, water and pastoral beauty. In *Green and Pleasant Land* the equivalent sequence runs in reverse. As Elizabeth Sussex points out, it is when 'the hymn reaches the words "dark satanic mills"' that the film starts to focus on its very object: the suffering of children in the squalor of modern society (the 'dark satanic mills', of course, being Blake's description of the horrors of industrialisation).[52] The film ends with an appeal and a call for contributions to the NSPCC. Of all of the films discussed in this article, *Green and Pleasant Land* is, I think, the one that took Anderson closest to personal expression. And as a movie trailer it was certainly on a par with the narrative skills of the contemporary newsreels.

ARE THE UNKNOWNS FREE?

As we have seen, Lindsay Anderson's industrial films for Sutcliffe, albeit not as technically poor as he would later claim, are hard to connect to the *Sequence* or Free Cinema projects. But some of the later unknown Anderson films – *Green and Pleasant Land, £20 a Ton* and *Henry* – could be related to them, and also resonate with his other work. *Green and Pleasant Land*, in particular, clearly derives something from the artistic credo of *Sequence*. But it is once again important to emphasise that *Sequence* and Free Cinema, in spite of their common denominators, including Lindsay Anderson himself, had somewhat different agendas. The latter had a political outlook, while the former often suppressed the workings of ideology in its *l'art pour l'art* approach.[53]

From what I can see, Anderson only made one personal documentary with a clear-cut 'attitude', and that was his controversial Free Cinema classic *O Dreamland*, a film that deliberately set itself apart from any mainstream of British documentary film. Its stance also differed very much from the general celebration of the welfare state that was the object of so much post-war documentary film-making in Britain and Western Europe. *O Dreamland* was witty but also nasty: not only did it criticise working-class culture but also the working-class *people* consuming this culture.[54] It had very little to do with Grierson and not much to do with the other of his own documentary films that Anderson presented in the Free Cinema programme. But it was genuine Free Cinema as stated by the manifesto; few other Anderson films were, in the strictest of senses. The National Coal Board's *Mining Review* yet again offers an instructive comparison: it is very interesting to compare Anderson's outlook on working-class leisure pursuits with the enthusiastically propagandist description of a Yorkshire holiday camp to be found in *Mining Review 2nd Year No 12* (Patricia Spielman, 1949). Here, there is no doubt about the qualities of collective vacationing for the working classes.

Most of Anderson's unknown films appear not to be particularly Free Cinema. They were all the result of external financing from either business or the government, although *Thursday's Children* (1953), Anderson's beautiful depiction of a school for deaf children, originated as an independent production.[55] This film, together with *Wakefield Express* and *Every Day Except Christmas*, would seem to fall somewhere between the industrial films and the entirely unconstrained *O Dreamland*. As well as being sponsored they adhere to certain notions of good craftsmanship.

I have found the unknown films very interesting, and their study worthwhile, but I still find that the four films just mentioned, the documentaries already established as Anderson classics, are the aesthetically superior ones, and they did undoubtedly inspire many other film-makers in Britain and elsewhere. Hence, there is not much reason to rewrite the canon and, after all, a less auteurist approach to these films, one that considers them in their industrial context as much as their authorial one, may have as much to recommend it.

In his *Sight & Sound* analysis of the development of British documentary from the Grierson years to the 1950s, David Robinson placed great emphasis on Anderson's significance for the period: 'Lindsay Anderson is one of the most articulate and individual artists working in the British cinema today; and so far his work has been entirely in documentary.'[56] Still, neither the 'unknown Andersons' nor even the Free Cinema films managed to establish Anderson as a maker of feature films. That came through his subsequent work in theatre, which is another story.

NOTES

1. I thank Christophe Dupin for his many useful comments on this chapter. For a discussion of *O Dreamland* and Free Cinema, see Erik Hedling, *Lindsay Anderson: Maverick Film-Maker* (London: Continuum, 1998), pp. 41–6. For some recent writing on Free Cinema, see Dupin's entry on the subject on *screenonline*: <www.screenonline.org.uk/film/id/444789/index.html>. The most recent research on Lindsay Anderson and Free Cinema has been presented by Danish documentary scholar Søren Birkvad in his Norwegian PhD-thesis, 'At ofre sig eller være offer: En kritisk gensyn med den internationale dokumentarfilms kanon 1930–60, Diss'. (Trondheim: Norwegian University of Science and Technology, 2008). Here, Birkvad devotes a substantial part of his work to *O Dreamland* and *Every*

Day Except Christmas. A rough translation of the title of the thesis would be: 'To Sacrifice Oneself or to be a Victim: A Critical Study of the Canon of International Documentary 1930–60.'

2. Vinzenz Hediger and Patrick Vonderau, 'Introduction', in Vinzenz Hediger and Patrick Vonderau (eds), *Films that Work: Industrial Film and the Productivity of Media* (Amsterdam: Amsterdam University Press, 2009), p. 10.
3. An interesting question is the extent to which *Sequence* was actually read. At the most, they printed 5,000 copies. I was myself given several editions by Gösta Werner, a prominent Swedish film director in the 1940s, who accordingly had been a subscriber and admirer. On the other hand, Charles Barr, who was involved in a quite similar journal project in the 1960s, claims that he, along with the other writers in *Movie*, had never heard of *Sequence* when they started their journal.
4. For a study dealing specifically with Anderson's film criticism, see Erik Hedling, 'Lindsay Anderson: *Sequence* and the Rise of Auteurism in 1950s Britain', in Ian MacKillop and Neil Sinyard (eds) *British Cinema of the 1950s: A Celebration* (Manchester: Manchester University Press, 2003), pp. 23–31.
5. The articles were 'Louisiana Story', *Sequence* vol. 6, Winter 1949, pp. 38–40, and 'Only Connect: Some Aspects of the Work of Humphrey Jennings', *Sight & Sound* vol. 2, April–June 1953, pp. 180–3, 186.
6. Kevin Jackson, *Humphrey Jennings* (London: Picador, 2004), p. 348.
7. Lindsay Anderson, 'Sequence: Introduction to a Reprint' in Lindsay Anderson, *Never Apologise: The Collected Writings*, ed. Paul Ryan (London: Plexus, 2004), p. 41.
8. Jack C. Ellis, 'Changing of the Guard: From the Grierson Documentary to Free Cinema', *Quarterly Review of Film Studies*, Winter 1982, p. 33.
9. See, for example, G. Roy Levin, *Documentary Explorations: 15 Interviews with Film-Makers* (New York: Anchor, 1971), p. 64, and Eva Orbanz (ed.), *Journey to a Legend and Back: The British Realistic Film* (Berlin: Zeotrope, 1977), pp. 40, 43.
10. Lindsay Anderson, 'British Cinema: The Descending Spiral', *Sequence* vol. 7, Spring, 1949, p. 6.
11. Lindsay Anderson, 'Going it Alone: The British Documentarists', in Anderson, *Never Apologise*, p. 353.
12. John Grierson and Philip Mackie, 'Welcome Stranger!', *Sight & Sound*, Spring 1949, p. 51.
13. Quoted from Lindsay Anderson, 'Correspondence – Straight Questions', *Sight & Sound* vol. 2, October–December, 1954, p. 108.
14. Hedling, *Lindsay Anderson*, p. 41.
15. The notion of a 'movement' in relation to Free Cinema is of course problematic. In a very interesting study, Alan Lovell has wittily suggested the term 'dwarf movement'. See Alan Lovell, 'Free Cinema', in Alan Lovell and Jim Hillier, *Studies in Documentary*, Cinema 1 Series (New York, 1972), p. 145.
16. Lindsay Anderson, 'Starting in Films', in Anderson, *Never Apologise*, pp. 50–5.
17. Lindsay Anderson, *The Diaries*, ed. Paul Sutton (London: Methuen, 2004), pp. 53–64.
18. Gavin Lambert, *Mainly About Lindsay Anderson: A Memoir* (London: Faber and Faber, 2000), pp. 45–7.
19. Lois Smith, 'Discovering Lindsay', unpublished manuscript, The Lindsay Anderson Collection, University of Stirling, Scotland.
20. Smith, 'Discovering Lindsay', pp. 1–13.
21. Smith, 'Discovering Lindsay', p. 6.
22. Gavin Lambert, 'Letter to Lindsay Anderson', 27 January 1948, The Lindsay Anderson Collection, University of Stirling, Scotland.
23. Anderson, 'Starting in Films', p. 51.
24. Lambert, 'Letter to Lindsay Anderson'.

25. Anderson, *The Diaries*, p. 53.
26. Anderson, *The Diaries*, p. 57.
27. In fact, Anderson's blunt refusal to 'indulge in the flashy for its own sake' is highly remiscent of his critique of Hitchcock's American films. See Lindsay Anderson, 'Alfred Hitchcock', *Sequence* vol. 9, Autumn 1949, pp. 113–24. Cf. also the Free Cinema manifesto.
28. Smith, 'Discovering Lindsay', p. 10.
29. Charles L. P. Silet, *Lindsay Anderson: A Guide to References and Resources* (London: Prior, 1979), p. 18.
30. Elizabeth Sussex, *Lindsay Anderson* (London: Studio Vista, 1969), p. 16.
31. As interesting, really, as the lunch shots are the final shots of the ship picking up limestone, freighted on a Sutcliffe conveyor belt from the quarry on the northern shore of Wales. The personal connotations could here be claimed to be Fordian, taking into consideration Anderson's admiration for Ford's naval concerns.
32. Anderson, 'Starting in Films', p. 51.
33. Anderson, *The Diaries*, p. 60.
34. Anderson, *The Diaries*, p. 61.
35. Smith, 'Discovering Lindsay', p. 11.
36. Smith, 'Discovering Lindsay', p. 13.
37. Levin, *Documentary Explorations*, p. 58.
38. Silet, *Lindsay Anderson*, p. 37.
39. See *Songs of the Coalfields* (1964), which includes a rendition of '16 Tons' by Ewan MacColl, on the BFI DVD release *National Coal Board Collection Volume One: Portrait of a Miner*.
40. Smith, 'Discovering Lindsay', p. 11.
41. Smith, 'Discovering Lindsay', p. 12.
42. Anderson, *The Diaries*, p. 57.
43. Smith, 'Discovering Lindsay', p. 14.
44. Anderson was also a founding member of Clore's advertising production company, Film Contracts. Clients for whom he apparently worked included Mackesons, Guinness, Persil, Kelloggs and Ronson Razor.
45. Patrick Russell, 'Leon Clore', <www.screenonline.org.uk/people/id/534016/index.html>.
46. David Robinson, 'Looking for Documentary', Part Two, *Sight & Sound*, Autumn 1957, p. 74.
47. Silet, *Lindsay Anderson*, p. 41.
48. Anderson, *The Diaries*, p. 64.
49. According to a private conversation he had with Walter Lassally, Christophe Dupin has informed me that the reason for Anderson's appearence was financial. One had so little money for the production that an actor could not be hired. To me, there is certainly no coincidence in Anderson himself choosing to do the part. And it still carries semiotic meaning, whatever the initial reasons.
50. Sussex, *Lindsay Anderson*, p. 26.
51. Anderson, 'Only Connect: Some Aspects of the Work of Humphrey Jennings', p. 182.
52. Sussex, *Lindsay Anderson*, p. 26.
53. Cf. Lovell, 'Free Cinema', pp. 150–6.
54. In the earlier-quoted thesis, Søren Birkvad devotes a full chapter to Anderson's relations to an ideological approach, particularly common in Scandinavia, that is called 'cultural radicalism'. Anderson was a typical exponent, albeit the fact that he was certainly no Scandinavian, with his ambiguous view of the working class. Birkvad particularly stresses *O Dreamland*, claiming it to be 'the master narrative'

for a certain current in later documentary: from Emile de Antonio and Erroll Morris to Michael Moore. Birkvad, 'To Sacrifice ...', pp. 359–68.

55. Normally, one gives Anderson as well as Guy Brenton directorial credit for *Thursday's Children*. Cinematographer Walter Lassally has, however, told my colleague Christophe Dupin that Anderson did 95 per cent of the work on the film. The film, generally hailed by film history, appears, however, more problematic today. The education of the deaf in the film is based on the learning of verbal speech in spite of handicap. Most people who are hearing-impaired today prefer sign language.
56. Robinson, 'Looking for Documentary', p. 73.

19 A Person Apart: *Guy Brenton*

ROS CRANSTON

> I am continually amazed that any warmth or tenderness, any sanity at all, can appear in what exists. That life may be experienced as a daily wonder, it is the duty of insight to foster with every energy and invention it can command.[1]

Guy Brenton's career encompassed a diverse cultural range. He was a film critic, theatre director and actor, a scholar of anthropology and psychology – as well as a television director and producer, and a maker of documentary films. His film work allowed him a very sensitive communication of his perceptions of the tensions between society and the individual in the western world. This conflict was expressed in greatest detail in his major written work, a substantial volume called *The Uses of Extremity: An Inquiry into Man's Malfunction and Discontent* (1974), in which Brenton enlarges on the duality of western culture and within individuals, a duality apparently fundamental to his world view. In the book, he interpreted it bleakly: 'Personal unhappiness ... is in fact entailed in the logic of the contemporary culture.'[2] A sense of tragedy at the heart of modern western civilisation led Brenton to the conclusion: 'I do not think it too strong to say that many go through life without encountering or experiencing a single generous outgoing spontaneous emotion.'[3] With very little consolation to be found in Brenton's analysis of the western psyche, the closest thing to solace comes in his suggestion that: 'the antidote to despair is wonder'.[4] In his writing, he doesn't enlarge on this more positive prospect, but it is exactly what comes so beautifully into view in some of his films.

In light of this brief character sketch, it is perhaps not surprising that Brenton's film career was such a short one. It may be more surprising that it took place, in large measure, within the field of sponsored film-making. Beyond his footnote status as the co-director, with the much better-known Lindsay Anderson, of *Thursday's Children* (1954), Brenton's interest as a 'case study' in post-war documentary rests on his apparent attempt to reconcile working within the conventional, sponsored London documentary industry, albeit mostly at its margins, with the sort of sensibility to be found in his other work. Under the sponsorship of charities rather than of the state, this led him to a form of social documentary very different from that of the Grierson generation but equally distinctive when set against most of the output of the documentary industry around him, sponsored mostly by the state or by industry. Brenton claimed 'I am a deviant in this society.'[5] His interest in how society deals with those who don't easily fit into conventional patterns is at the heart of his best film work, and happily for him it was largely consistent with the interests of his most suitable sponsors. The title of his film about people with epilepsy – *People Apart* (1957) – could stand for nearly all the subjects of these films. They were people on the margins in one way or another, just as he certainly seems to have seen

Lindsay Anderson and Guy Brenton with the cast of *Thursday's Children* (Lindsay Anderson Collection, University of Stirling)

himself as a person apart from the bulk of society, and must have seen himself as a documentarist apart from the bulk of the sponsored films scene.

Born in 1927, Brenton grew up, an only child, in London, in a 'dormitory suburb of irretrievable respectability'.[6] His father was a junior civil servant who, his son felt, 'loathed his occupation for forty years; thwarted, from within and without, of satisfaction in every area of being – work, marriage, pleasure, God and man'.[7] Nor was his mother much happier, in the recollections of her son: 'My mother died when I was seventeen from a sense of uselessness.'[8] This stark summing up is telling of the manner in which Brenton assessed people; he believed that he had 'developed at the very outset a marked natural ability, a real flair for assessing what people felt and thought ... I could tell what they were *like*.'[9] A strong aspect of his view of life as expressed in *The Uses of Extremity* is how self-deluded are most people. Perhaps in keeping with his own sense of himself as an artist, and with his later involvement with 'psychical research', he doesn't appear to have considered that there could have been any delusion on his own part – and his writing duly expresses many outlandish certainties. Likewise he had little concern with other people's views of him – he was happy to swim against the mainstream. This suggests an affinity with the visionary, William Blake, whose deeply held personal beliefs were very much at odds with his contemporary society, and about whom Brenton made an experimental film, *The Vision of William Blake* (1958).

Brenton's father was in no doubt of the importance of his son 'getting on' and ensured that he attended the prestigious Westminster School, from which he won a scholarship to Christ Church, Oxford. He won prizes at school and broadly conformed to the system though he later resented the discipline, competitiveness and 'calculated emotional void'.[10] At Oxford, Brenton became heavily involved in the Experimental Theatre Club with Kenneth Tynan, and the Oxford University Dramatic Society, both as an actor and director. Some of his earliest performances and directorial attempts were reviewed in *The Times* and *The Observer*, including a production of *Othello* in in which Brenton, then in his early twenties, appeared. The theatre reviewer in *The Times* reported, 'There is a good Iago. Mr Guy Brenton has the clearest intellectual appreciation of the Machiavellian but he lets him take little joy in his villainy.'[11]

After leaving Oxford, Brenton sought opportunities to work at the BBC, arranging to meet Norman Collins, Controller of Television, following a letter of introduction from his Oxford tutor. Collins wrote in a memo after the meeting: 'he struck me as an unusually lively and promising young man ... He turned to television because he regards it as having replaced the films ... I think that we should be able to arrange some trial period of, say, three months.'[12] Brenton did not take up this opportunity due to 'an unfortunate set of circumstances' as he wrote in another letter to the BBC in June 1951. This letter resulted in an interview with Leslie Page, Assistant Head of Television Administration. Following their meeting, Page sent a memo:

> He came down in June 1950, and forthwith teamed up with a friend to make a 10-minute documentary film about Regents Park. It appears they ran out of money before they got to the stage of adding the soundtrack, and so that was that. He then went to Norwich and worked there under Nugent Monk as his assistant. Because of the bad pay he then joined Instructional Films Ltd, with whom he acted as a Script Writer and Cutter. This firm has now been liquidated, and he is out of a job. He is trying to make a living by tutoring small boys, but is finding things a little tough.[13]

Page's recommendation led to Brenton securing a number of consecutive short-term contracts, first as an ad hoc stage manager and then in the last couple of months of 1951 as a scriptwriter for the *BBC Television Newsreel*. Perhaps the '10-minute documentary film' mentioned by Page, was later completed and became *The Jason's Trip* (1952), Brenton's earliest recorded credit. It does not appear to have survived and little is known about it. It follows canal-boat excursions from London's Maida Vale and as the same canal goes through Regent's Park it is plausible that it is the same film.

In contrast, Brenton's next film is by far the best known he ever worked on, *Thursday's Children* – made in 1953 and released in 1954. The film's interest in people on the margins of society, in this case young children attending the Royal School for the Deaf in Margate, who share moments of communication and warmth in the face of their separation from the mainstream world, may now be outdated in terms of the modern politics of deafness, but is undeniably affecting. It was Brenton who had the idea for the film and, probably in 1951, approached Anderson, an Oxford acqaintance, to suggest that they make it together. Brenton was then working at the BBC and his job had led him to visit the school. He and Anderson began filming on an independent basis with their own and friends' money. Cinematographer Walter Lassally completed the film crew. It was shot on 35mm, although on a tiny budget which ran out before the soundtrack was completed. At this point one of the giants of the documentary industry, James Carr's World Wide Pictures, stepped in and agreed to fund the film's completion. Anderson then asked Richard Burton – who was performing at the Old Vic – to record the commentary without payment. Burton agreed, and the film was duly completed and a distributor sought. Anderson recalled 'we hawked it about in the traditional way, and everyone was very moved, and all the distributors cried, but said of course it wasn't entertainment, and they were very sorry.'[14]

Guy Brenton with teacher in the *Thursday's Children* classroom (Lindsay Anderson Collection, University of Stirling)

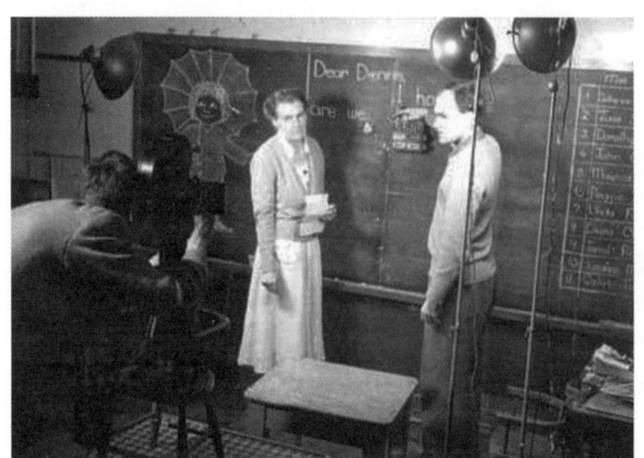

The film was unable to gain distribution in the UK until it won an Oscar, almost out of the blue, for Best Short Subject in 1954. It was then advertised by its distributors MGM in *Sight & Sound* under the headline 'Tribute after tribute, honour upon honour have been heaped on this, the world's most highly praised documentary.'[15] These tributes include the *Monthly Film Bulletin*'s praise for 'the remarkable intimacy with which the camera has caught the children at their lessons and in their social life together'.[16] Likewise, the *Kinematograph Weekly*

reviewer found the film 'an inexpressibly moving insight into tots of four and upwards learning by lipreading to overcome their exile from the hearing world'.[17]

In *Thursday's Children* the approach to suffering is more optimistic than Brenton's later work such as *People Apart*. This has been put forward by Gavin Lambert as evidence for Anderson's greater involvement in the film than Anderson himself claimed. However, optimism is hardly the dominant characteristic of Lindsay Anderson's film-making. *Thursday's Children* certainly epitomises Brenton's philosophy that 'life may be experienced as a daily wonder' amid its bleakness. The 'daily wonder' is exemplified by the film's charming vignettes of young children striving to follow their sympathetic teachers' instruction and their mutual affection and delight in their hard-won progress. Anderson himself recorded these thoughts in his diary about his experience of working on the film:

> We have worked hard at it, and I am tired. Exhausted too by nervous strain. Working with Guy is not exactly a holiday: no doubt I plague him as he plagues me. Also fatal is his terrible conviction of moral superiority, past which nothing can get. Humourless too. The film is his creation of course, as a project completely his. After that – I suppose pretty well 50–50 his and mine. On his own he'd almost certainly have made a mess of it – buggered it up with his 'theoretical' ideas. And on my own, I'd never even have begun.[18]

Brenton was the sole director of *Birthday*, also apparently released in 1954, and his first sponsored film: made for the National Fund for Polio Research. Having more of a fictional character, this is the story of four children spending the day looking for birthday presents for their little brother Christopher, who, as is revealed only towards the end of the film, 'is paralysed in the legs from polio', then still one of the most feared of childhood diseases. Christopher's four young siblings set off on their own to go shopping in London, instructed by their mother merely 'to be back in time for tea'.

Beautifully photographed by Billy Williams, *Birthday* contains some lovely street scenes and is also notable for the freedom with which the youngsters roam the city unaccompanied. They have lively encounters with market stallholders, and the eldest boy Robert, aged about eight, ventures into the British Museum and inside a pet shop, both of which provide camera-observational opportunities from unusual vantage points – such as the close-up shot of the heels of Robert's shoes as he stands on tiptoe to peer inside a cage at a snake. There is no synchronised sound and overlaid dialogue is intercut with, unusually, harpsichord music, which manages to add both a jaunty and a lyrical mood to the film at the same time. Youngest girl Fiona, aged about three, sets off on her own to the pond to spend her sixpence. On losing her coin in the water she is approached by a man who gives her sweeties to console her. The scene has a striking innocence; despite Brenton's tendency to bleakness, he sees no cause for concern here.

Birthday has a lightness of touch, as well as an optimism that is much in the spirit of *Thursday's Children*. Idyllic scenes of the children with their mother create an impression of a model family – though there is no father in sight, he presumably being at work in the city. The uncredited children give engaging and charming performances, and Christopher, the little boy with polio, has a delighted expression on his face almost constantly. The audience's heartstrings are well tugged as the narration, which was delivered by Deborah Kerr, concludes: 'What do you suppose would be Christopher's wish on his birthday this year?' Details of where to send contributions to the National Fund for Polio Research follow. Brenton's own personality has blended well with the film's direct aim and it succeeds as a moving appeal for funds. Its success in financial terms for its sponsoring charity is not recorded.

Both these films were made by Morse Films, a production company set up by Guy Brenton while still in his twenties (Morse and World Wide are co-credited on *Thursday's Children*). Unsurprisingly, he set up his own independent company rather than choosing to join an existing organisation like World Wide, which would entail the necessity of fitting in. As Derek Hill puts it, Brenton 'found it psychologically impossible to work within the film industry on whatever subjects were offered him, and instead set up his own company'.[19] This was no easy option, as Robin Denniston noted in his obituary of Brenton: 'his vigorous standards together with lack of resources and financial acumen made the production of high quality films a hazardous affair'.[20]

People Apart was made by Morse for the British Epilepsy Association and in many ways epitomises Brenton's attitude to the world. The opening titles announce that 'This film is about people who have an affliction of a special kind ... The aim of this film is not in the first place to tell what can be done for such people – primarily, it is to let you see into the lives of those who, in some degree, are set apart.' The film consists largely of people who have epilepsy talking straight to camera (or rather to an off-camera interviewer) – which is suggestive of televisual technique; however, this is offset by the exaggerated lighting of the interiors more reminiscent of film noir, with its highlighted contrasts between shadow and light. The cameraman is credited as W. D. Williams – quite possibly the admired cinematographer Billy Williams who had shot *Birthday*, Brenton's previous film. The balance between the televisual style of the interviews and the filmic use of framing and lighting is sustained to the end of the film, which closes on carefully posed portrait shots, reminiscent of old master paintings, of the interviewees sitting together.

The interviewer (Brenton himself? It's not apparent) had clearly gained the confidence of the interviewees who speak openly of their experiences, with dignity, determination, humour and grace. The use of interior locations throughout, combined with the shadowy ambience conveys a sense of relentless claustrophobia, in keeping with the participants' own sense of being unable to escape other people's perceptions of their illness.

Brenton's films were not widely reviewed and the details of his filmography are incomplete – even the release dates of some his films are uncertain. According to Derek Hill, he made four films between 1957 and 1962: *People Apart*, *The Vision of William Blake*, *Four People* and *Via Crucis*. Alan Lovell noted that latter two titles were his 'latest films' in 1962 at the time of the NFT season, *Anarchism Today*.[21] Neither Hill nor Lovell, however, mentioned that Brenton had also made two industrially sponsored films – *The Three Brothers* and *See For Yourself* – commissioned by British Petroleum and the British Productivity Council respectively and both apparently released in

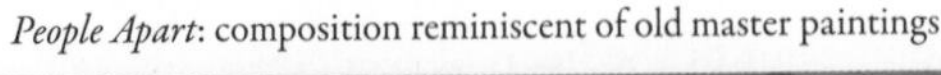

People Apart: composition reminiscent of old master paintings

1957. These were not produced by Morse, but were instead made under the auspices of Greenpark Productions. Perhaps Brenton's lack of financial acumen and resources, mentioned by Denniston in his obituary, meant that cashflow was an issue and that some reliable income generated by working for one of the major production companies was an appealing prospect. *The Three Brothers* is the story of a Sumatran farmer's three sons – a trainee teacher, an agricultural student and a worker in the oil-fields – which provides the background for the theme of the impact of modern patterns of industry on traditional patterns of life. This theme recurs in Brenton's later television programme *A Step out of Time: The Story of Tristan da Cunha* (3 September 1966). The subject matter of *See for Yourself* is untypical of Brenton – several employers explain how their firms have benefited from the exchange of ideas made possible by the Circuit Scheme run by the local productivity committees which were a core component of the national productivity campaign.

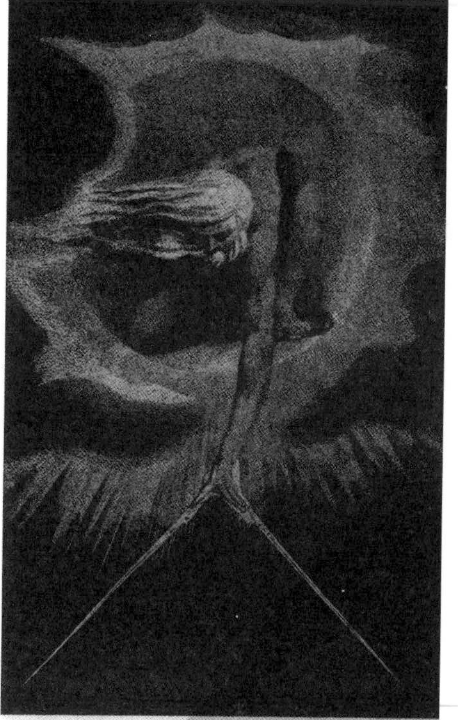

Neither of the Greenpark films appears still to be extant: a great pity, as it would be fascinating to see the products of Brenton's work with the production company that most epitomised tasteful, relatively expensive and, its critics would argue, conformist post-war sponsored film, on projects commissioned by two of the post-war period's major sponsors. Brenton returned to a conspicuously personal choice of subject the following year with *The Vision of William Blake*, an experimental short which was funded by the BFI and produced by Morse Films. It was shown at the Academy Cinema in London. An anonymous reviewer in *The Times* was impressed by the match between Blake's poetry and Brenton's film-making style:

> Blake's flamelike bodies, writhing, strenuous, ecstatic, stream across the screen with a sense of movement beautifully liberated by the camera's ability to prowl about a picture and detail after detail fastened upon in the terrifying enlargement of close-up remains obstinately bitten into the memory. What they all mean within the detailed system of the artist-poet's metaphysical symbolism is more problematical. Mr Brenton rightly avoids anything but the most generalised interpretation.[22]

The extensive use of the camera panning across Blake's paintings is a technique that retains the focus on the subject matter, rather than the more conventional use of speech to elucidate the paintings. The soundtrack consists chiefly of Blake's verse set to music by Vaughan Williams. Both Brenton and Blake had their own very personal, semi-mystical beliefs (Brenton enlarged on his own beliefs in depth in *The Uses of Extremity*) and their admirers described them as visionaries. Blake's talents became widely recognised only after his death and Brenton's work certainly deserves to become better appreciated, at least, than its current neglected status.

Also during his fertile years of film-making between 1957 and 1962, Brenton made the little-known *Via Crucis*, described by Derek Hill as a 'short on the nature of suffering' which was commissioned by Group Captain Leonard Cheshire and is not held in the BFI National Archive. It is referred to in an unusual undated document in the BFI National Library entitled 'British Anarchism' (probably tying in with the NFT season of that title in 1962). The anonymous author (likely to be Alan Lovell who curated the NFT season) writes:

> *Via Crucis* is a kind of summing up of Brenton's preoccupations. Starting from the mystery of the shroud which appears to have a photograph of Christ in it, Brenton moves to Lourdes and looks at the mystery there. An attitude to pain and suffering emerges clearly from this exploration. Brenton sees suffering as an essential part of life, as a stimulus to growth. In so far as we suffer, we grow.

There is a note appended to the document: '*Via Crucis* was sponsored by Group Captain Cheshire. He wishes to point out that the views expressed in the film are not necessarily his.'

A few years later, *Four People: A Ballad Film* was released. Slightly better known than *Via Crucis*, it too was not reviewed in the film journals of the time. It tells the stories of four people with polio and its subtitle reflects the dominance of the music and words of Ewan MacColl and Peggy Seeger on the soundtrack. These are combined with delicate, even lyrical photography of scenes in the lives of the four people featured. Much of the film takes place in a light and airy hospital. There is very little spoken commentary and polio is referred to in the sung ballads as the 'hidden enemy lurking': it strikes the four adults suddenly as they go about their daily lives. The film is presumably mostly staged, putting it more in line with *Birthday* than with *People Apart*, but, in a musical reinvention of the wartime 'story documentary', features non-actors. In hospital, the four patients struggle to learn to walk again and to come to terms with their new dependency on others – even to the extent of having an itchy nose scratched by a nurse.

Like *Thursday's Children* and *Birthday*, *Four People* is full of subtle moments, with a light touch in both image and sound that is delicately achieved. There are unusual visual angles – the ambulance swerving through traffic and filmed from the driver's perspective; the under-the-bed shot as the occupant's feet reach for the floor for the first time in weeks. Neither shot is necessary to the narrative of the film, but both add vividness and a sense of looking at the world from an unusual perspective – an appealing side of Brenton's avoidance of the mainstream. A new angle on the world is just what the polio patients have had thrust upon them and they also learn greater control over their perspective and how to widen it as they reach out to the life around them, having been cut off for some time. Guy Brenton's own experience of having tuberculosis 'which put him out of circulation for a year'[23] when he was at university, must have heightened his awareness of the effects of the isolation of patients in a long-term hospital ward.

Made eight years after *Birthday* – about a child with polio – *Four People* is an adult version of that childhood film with a darker undercurrent as well as flashes of happiness. With its suggestion of the possibility of longer-term contentment its mood is more optimistic than *People Apart* – and its photographic lighting much brighter.

Four People inspired a BBC *Radio Ballad*, entitled *The Body Blow*, when MacColl and Seeger approached Charles Parker, their producer and regular collaborator on that famous series. A MacColl biographer writes of the *The Body Blow* that:

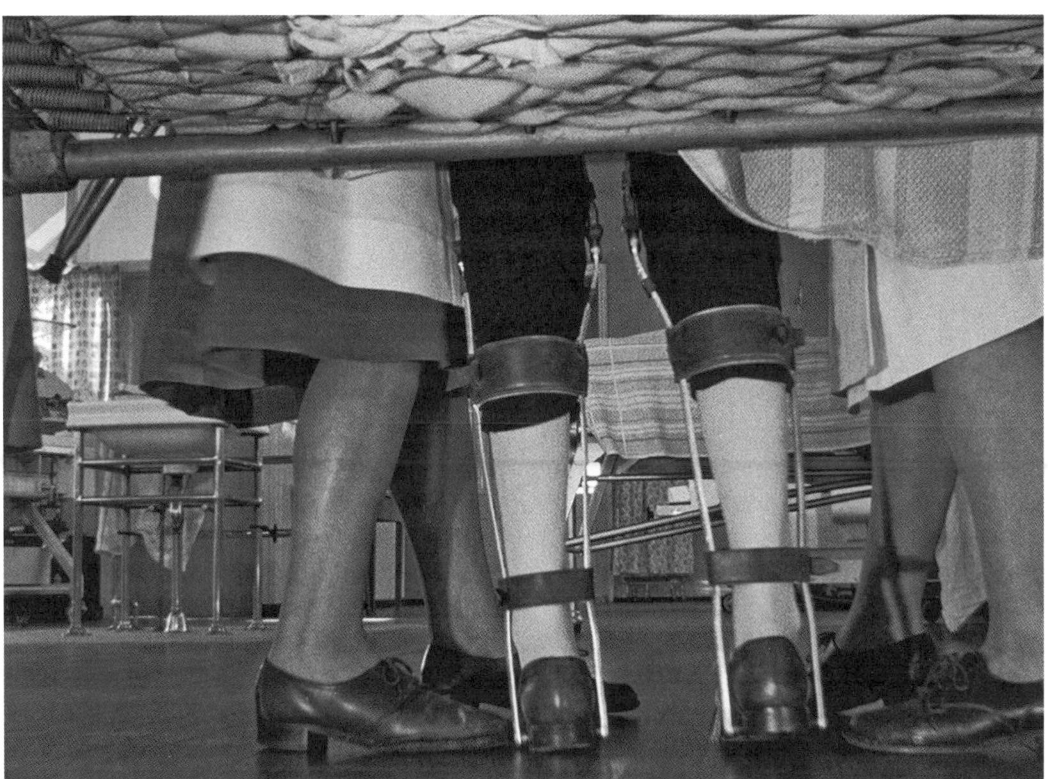

Four People

> The year before, they had written and sung some songs for a half-hour television feature about polio sufferers, *Four People*. They hadn't particularly liked the result, largely because of the 'stagey' dialogue, and the sufferers' own words hadn't been heard, but thought it would be an interesting vehicle for a radio ballad.[2]

The description of *Four People* as a television feature is intriguing, given that the BBC's contibutor index does not include the programme under Brenton and no television company is mentioned in the credits on the print held at the BFI National Archive. It might also seem unusual to make a radio programme on the same subject with the same contributors so soon after a television programme. The *Radio Ballad* featured the same four people and generated widespread comment, mostly very favourable.

In 1962, Alan Lovell programmed an evening of Brenton's films at the National Film Theatre. These were included in his 'British Anarchism' season and Lovell described Brenton in his introductory text as 'one of the most ignored of British short and documentary film-makers'.[25] The films shown were *The Vision of William Blake*, *Via Crucis* and *Four People*.

In the mid-1960s Brenton worked for the BBC again. In 1965 he directed two programmes for the series, *The Group*, which the opening titles describe as 'A series of Documentary Films about Small Groups of People. Their Attitudes to Themselves, their Work, and their Place in Society'. Brenton's first contribution was *Fancy Dressers* (5 October 1965) about the London fashion world, featuring designers Mary Quant and Jean Muir, and model Jeanne de Sousa. The mood and style of the programme captures a spirit of the 1960s, with Beatles music and stylishly dressed women shopping in Quant's shop in London. Quant and Muir speak about their fashion work and beliefs, though it is Jeanne de Sousa who makes the most striking points, and who concludes the programme with the comment that clothes show the state of mind of groups of people – whether they are feeling tough, arrogant or happy and relaxed. This closing note of the programme hints at Brenton's belief in the differences between people often being more influential than any sense of shared humanity.

Brenton followed *Fancy Dressers* with *Parish Priests* (19 October 1965) about five priests in Woolwich, London. The *Radio Times* noted 'The priests ... were fighting a battle to find themselves a meaningful social context. They felt, very strongly, that they were losing, that there was no place for them.'[26] This sense of feeling beyond the mainstream is of course much in keeping with Brenton's own outlook. Brenton was also commissioned a few years later to make another programme for the BBC – with TV documentary greats Norman Swallow and Denis Mitchell for the *Report from Britain* series. However, the programme was then cancelled.[27] The BBC had agreed to pay Brenton £1,000 for this commission, and on its cancellation he suggested that the money be used instead to pay his salary for a film which he was keen to make about the islanders of Tristan da Cunha. There followed lengthy negotiations and complex arrangements about transport and budgets. At one point it looked likely that the project would fall through – when Brenton was offered a feature to direct, which then itself failed to get off the ground, and about which very little is known.

A Step Out of Time: The Story of Tristan da Cunha was broadcast on 3 September 1966. The tiny population of the South Atlantic island – which has been described as the remotest island in the world – had experienced little change in its way of life until 1961, when a volcano erupted and the community was evacuated to the UK. The programme follows their reactions to twentieth-century civilisation and the repercussions after they returned to the island. The subject matter reflects Brenton's interest in non-western societies and his belief that their lifestyles are likely to be preferable to those of the West. He describes in an article in the *Radio Times* how the islanders had evolved their community:

> What came to be prized and valued above all other virtues was good feeling. On that level Tristan was, and is, one of civilisation's successes. With no violence, no crime, no divorce, no neighbours to fear, no taxes, no wars, next to no money problems, and no disease to speak of, it has a unique record.[28]

The BBC's Audience Research Report on the programme reported that it,

> was hailed by the majority of the sample audience as a documentary of quite exceptional interest and unsurpassed brilliance ... The story of this unique community ... had been told in moving and telling terms, according to most viewers. Superb pictorial material and an excellent commentary had revealed the islanders as people of great dignity and sincerity.[29]

The subject was clearly close to Brenton's heart, and the programme conveys a sense of a distinctive authorial voice that *Fancy Dressers* makes little attempt to aspire to (though it possesses other lively charms). The correspondence held in the BBC Written Archives suggests that Brenton's approach to programme-making did not always sit comfortably with the BBC bureaucracy, and indeed David Attenborough, then controller of BBC2, would have called off the project but for the fact that

Brenton had already been paid £1,000 for the cancelled programme.[30] It seems that television would not, any more than the sponsored film, provide the ideal home for an individualist director of social documentaries that Brenton may have hoped for. *A Step Out of Time* is apparently the last television programme to have been made by him.

Brenton's BBC file concludes with two letters he sent from Western Samoa (in June 1967) and Hawaii (in September 1967) and these missives suggest that Brenton was putting his beliefs into practice and was keen to experience life outside the conventional western world. One substantial result of his experiment with living abroad was his book *The Uses of Extremity*, and he wrote in his introductory comments about his travels: 'I was trying to set in perspective the paradox of my own culture.' He became increasingly interested in the fields of anthropology and religion and also became involved in the Society of Psychical Research. Denniston noted in his obituary that Brenton 'would have liked to become a guru ... but his abrasive style, concealing strong and unexpected feelings of tenderness and benignity ... made this impossible'.[31]

This combination of contrasting qualities is characteristic of Brenton's work in which the focus on the harshness of the world is often shot through with shafts of gentleness. His personality was not ideally suited to the collaborative nature of film-making, and his non-conformist beliefs also meant that working in sponsored film-making, and then later in television documentary, could be an uncomfortable position for Brenton. And as Alan Lovell has recently commented 'I wouldn't be so harsh about Guy as Lindsay Anderson was – I liked him – but he did have a certain precious, vulnerable quality which didn't help with the politics of documentary film-making.'[32]

Brenton does not fit neatly into film history – becoming neither an established sponsored documentary film-maker nor associating with any alternative group, such as the Free Cinema of his one-time collaborator Lindsay Anderson. Though ultimately unfulfilled as a film-maker in terms of achieving a long-term career, and unsatisfied too with many other aspects of his life, he made a small number of remarkably vivid, like-affirming films, that illuminate both the harshness and the wonder of life – and raised awareness and money for good causes.

NOTES

1. Daniel Tallis (pseudonym of Guy Brenton), *The Uses of Extremity: An Inquiry into Man's Malfunction and Discontent* (London: Hodder & Stoughton, 1974) p. 22.
2. Ibid., p. 36,
3. Ibid., p. 61,
4. Ibid., p. 66.
5. Ibid., p. 66.
6. Ibid., p. 79.
7. Ibid., p. 82.
8. Ibid., p. 83.
9. Ibid., p. 90.
10. Ibid., p. 121.
11. *The Times*, 1 March 1950.,
12. Norman Collins, BBC Memo to H. D., 23 June 1950, in BBC Written Archives File No. R94/1015.
13. Leslie Page, BBC Memo to Assistant Head of Drama, Television, 25 June 1951, in BBC Written Archives File No. R94/1015.
14. Quoted in Elizabeth Sussex, *Lindsay Anderson* (London: Studio Vista, 1969), p. 21.

15. *Sight & Sound*, Spring 1956, p. 221.
16. *Monthly Film Bulletin*, October 1954, p. 151.
17. *Kinematograph Weekly*, 3 March 1955, p. 20.
18. Lindsay Anderson, *The Diaries*, ed Paul Sutton (London: Methuen, 2004), p. 59.
19. Derek Hill, 'The Short Film Situation', *Sight & Sound*, Summer 1962, p. 110.
20. Robin Denniston, 'Guy Brenton', obituary, *The Independent*, 5 August 1994.
21. Alan Lovell, *National Film Theatre June/July 1962* (BFI), p. 17.
22. 'Film Study of the Art of Blake', *The Times*, 1 October 1958.
23. Denniston, 'Guy Brenton'.
24. Peter Cox, *Set into Song: Ewan MacColl, Charles Parker, Peggy Seeger and the Radio Ballads* (London: Labatie, 2008), p. 121. *The Body Blow* was broadcast on 27 March 1962.
25. Lovell, *National Film Theatre*, p. 17.
26. *Radio Times*, 21 October 1965, p. 36.
27. Various correspondence in BBC Written Archives File No. WE21/6/1 to Guy Brenton from Desmond Hawkins and others, 16 June 1965–18 August 1965.
28. Guy Brenton, 'Tristan da Cunha – A Step Out of Time', *Radio Times*, 1 September 1966, p. 3.
29. *Tristan da Cunha: A Step Out of Time – An Audience Research Report*, BBC Written Archives.
30. David Attenborough, BBC Memo, c. July 1965 in BBC Written Archives File No. WE21/6/1.
31. Tallis, *The Uses of Extremity*, p. 11.
32. Denniston, 'Guy Brenton'.
33. Alan Lovell, email to Ros Cranston, 23 March 2010.

20 Tracts of Time: *Derek Williams*

PATRICK RUSSELL

PROLOGUE – OIL AND WATER

Beginning on the hills overlooking Hadrian's Wall, the moors in its shadow, ending above the mountains, on the dunes and beaches, of Oman, it was a successful career by several measures. Derek Williams spent forty years shooting prestigious films in some fifty countries on every continent. Demonstrably, millions worldwide saw them. Demonstrably, too, they were acclaimed by their industry, accumulating fifty-eight international gold prizes. No fewer than four of those that Williams wrote and directed (plus one written by him for another director) were nominated for short-subject Academy Awards: surely one of Britain's greater Oscar successes. Yet you'd search in vain for reference to them in the journals and reference books documenting our national cinema.

Typical of his generation in suffering critical neglect, he also typifies some of the reasons for it. First, there was the source of his funding. Two-thirds of Williams's films were sponsored by private industry, mostly UK concerns with widening post-war horizons. His work was lubricated especially by the quickening flow of oil into the western economies: the colossus bestriding his career was British Petroleum. Williams represents that part of his documentary generation that consisted of *cinéastes* comfortably drawn to corporate patronage, enthused by the international subject matter it offered, at ease with modes of film-making it cultivated. Stacked against such a career are the modern assumptions that creativity and corporatism can mix no better than oil and water, that film-making drenched in oil (however well-perfumed) will inevitably reek of it.

Second, the technique in Williams's films is an unfashionable one. At the peak of his success, however (between 1964 and 1977), Williams perfected this admittedly conservative style of film-making, tailored to industrial prestige, and applied it to the one important subject that sponsored documentary was then making its own. With his landmark film *The Shadow of Progress* (1970), arguably the last momentous production to emerge from the entire tradition, Williams became the leading exponent of environmental documentaries. And a third reason for his neglect: his misfortune was to hit this stride, in mid-career, just as the climate for prestige sponsorship was itself becoming unsustainable, as television advanced and recession bit.

In this chapter, these themes are explored first by describing the progress of Williams's career, then by examining more closely the main groupings into which his more important films fall.

BITS OF DOING

Derek Williams was born in 1929 to a middle-class family, on the right side of the tracks of proletarian Newcastle upon Tyne. Educated at the city's Royal Grammar School, following National Service he went up to Corpus Christi, Cambridge, to read history. In 1950, Corpus alumnus Basil

Wright (accompanied by Henry Cornelius) returned to lecture at his alma mater. Williams had seen and admired *Song of Ceylon* (1934). Now Wright's zealous promulgation of documentary aesthetics inspired his purchase, using money saved from Army pay, of a 16mm cine-camera that had seen better days. With it he made one of the more ambitious amateur films of its day, about Hadrian's Wall near where he had grown up. 'The idea of filming the Roman Wall came to me in a daydream, early in the summer of 1950. For the next six months I studied the subject, explored the country, gradually acquired the necessary minimum of apparatus and did my best to learn how to use it.'[1] Williams photographed the locations during the vacations of 1951. With parental financing, he was able to record a commentary and music to go with these images: words written and spoken by himself, music composed by a fellow undergraduate, Raymond Warren, and performed by six Cambridge musicians under Warren's direction.[2] The twenty-four-minute *Hadrian's Wall* was premiered at the Newcastle News Theatre, then prints (as well as a filmstrip) made available to schools, with accompanying teaching notes, despatched from the director's parental address. Besides making Williams a fleeting local hero, the film won some acclaim on the growing national amateur and educational film scenes. The *Times Educational Supplement* declared it 'of more than usual significance in the world of amateur film making ... with some fine photography and well devised sequences so often absent in the amateur film'.[3] *Visual Education* proclaimed: 'Oscar for the best amateur film goes to Mr Derek Williams ... a genuine contribution to the most vexed of all school subjects, the teaching of history. Mr Williams is one of the very few amateurs who, tempering zeal with humility and vision, graduate into professionals.'[4]

So it proved. On the strength of the film's reception Williams entered the industry, as trainee assistant in World Wide Pictures' Old Compton Street cutting-rooms. Once in, he quickly grasped that his new milieu bore scant resemblance to that of the Cambridge University Film Society, or to the milieu Wright had inhabited twenty years earlier. In post-war Soho's school-of-hard-knocks, Williams's degree, courtly demeanour and greenhorn enthusiasm for his newfound medium were not social advantages. Nevertheless, within months, he was hand-picked for a substantial assignment. Put another way, he was handed down a lengthy, lonely sentence, already declined by everyone else in the company. George Wimpey and Co. had secured a major contract, building a BP port at Aden to serve a nearby refinery (marking BP's Middle East fight-back, after ejection from Iran). Anxious to publicise one of the biggest civil engineering schemes ever initiated, the firm engaged World Wide for an exhaustive record of progress. This would be on 16mm Kodachrome, though World Wide was still almost exclusively a 35mm company. James Carr selected for the job the young fellow who'd come to him with a background in shooting, unaccompanied, on the smaller gauge (albeit in black and white).

In return, Carr (an honorary ACT steward) held out the promise of a union ticket. Hence, the twenty-three-year-old spent the next two years in Little Aden, a one-man unit filming every major stage of a development involving 200 acres of land reclamation, £1.5 million worth of plant and the construction of berths to take 32,000-ton tankers. *Oil Harbour, Aden*, released to the non-theatrical market in 1955, remains a valuable industrial record (Aden would briefly become the biggest oil port on the globe). Uncomfortably long at forty minutes, it looks today no cinematic triumph. At the time, it picked up solid trade press reviews. In view of its implications for outward-looking national achievement and overseas collaboration between British industries, the COI took prints for domestic and overseas dissemination.[5] It belatedly won the major prize at the first Harrogate festival, though not without controversy.[6]

Aden had paid well: Williams started a personal, self-financed project, *The Wheel of Islands*, about the Cyclades. Script completed, he had already begun shooting when an intriguing letter from Carr arrived for him on Santorini. World Wide had attained BP's sponsorship for filming the first stage of the Commonwealth Trans-Antarctic Expedition under Dr Vivian Fuchs. Carr was writing to Williams 'to query whether or not you would be interested in a trip to an extremely cold place, as a change from Aden and Greece', advising his protégé that 'you would fit in with the sort of people involved in this expedition better than any other character I know. You will appreciate that the men involved, as well as being adventurous are all of a high intelligence level and expert at a variety of branches of science.'[7] *The Wheel of Islands* was abandoned. As official cameraman, Williams became a full member of the sixteen-man party that sailed to Weddell Sea, and spent Christmas 1955 trapped in ice before setting up a base for the main expedition.[8] After five months, Williams returned to London to assemble a twenty-one-minute account of the venture. *Foothold on Antarctica* (1956) received nationwide cinema release on the Odeon circuit, attracting applause for its stirring proof of stiff-lipped modern heroism and as an exemplary renewal of Britain's strength in documentary.[9] It was given a private screening at Buckingham Palace and went on to receive an Oscar nomination, before settling into long life as a popular 16mm booking from the Petroleum Films Bureau.

Williams's career was ascending spectacularly, but to Carr's chagrin he now left World Wide. By chance, while making *Oil Harbour, Aden*, Williams had crossed desert paths with writer Jack Howells, cameraman Roly Stafford and director Humphrey Swingler: the production team for *We Found a Valley* (1955), Greenpark's film for BP about the Aden refinery itself. Swingler doubtless sensed that World Wide's young director-cameraman – soft-spoken, erudite, willing to travel, good at filming scenery – suited his house style better than Carr's. From early 1957, Williams was on the Guild's books, as Greenpark's director-in-residence.

Oxford (1956) was an anodyne sketch commissioned by the COI for use within its overseas distribution programme to attract Commonwealth students. *From the Good Earth* (1957), for Hovis, was Williams's first fiction-style directing, of a Sussex-set farming story scripted by John and Anne Krish, Williams's neighbours at the time. Two other projects were more ambitious. *There Was a Door* (1957) was written and produced by G. Buckland-Smith, and (like both the previous productions) photographed by Fred Gamage. Investigating care of the severely

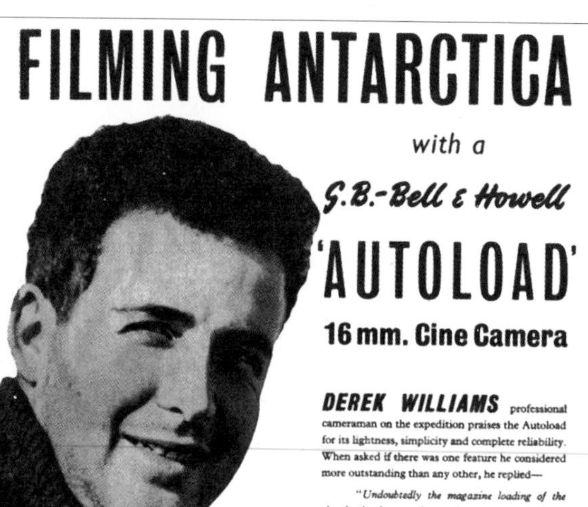

learning-disabled, it was sponsored by the Manchester Regional Hospital Board. For Williams, it broke new ground, being his first social subject. It was also his last film to attract any notice from British intellectual film culture (its waning interest in documentary momentarily spiked). *Monthly Film Bulletin* praised 'a wholly adult and uncompromising approach to a problem rarely brought before the public ... a sad film, but a positive, constructive one; and an unusually distinguished British documentary'.[10] Two months after non-theatrical release it was televised by the BBC, gaining admiring overnight reviews.[11] 1958–9 saw Williams back globetrotting for the private sector, meeting Greenpark's brief to mark BP's fiftieth anniversary with a celebratory self-portrait, designed first for shareholders and staff, thence for general 16mm distribution. Williams gathered material in Australia, Canada and Denmark with cameraman Wolfgang Suschitzky; in France, with Jean Forgue; and, doing his own camerawork, in Germany, Greenland, Iraq and Kuwait, and his own native Northumberland. *The Road to MIS* (1959) is a patchwork of these sketches.[12] This format – though a function of the corporate narrative the sponsor wanted – yielded a bitty, overlong viewing experience.

After this, Williams left Greenpark, on amicable terms, freelancing for the next ten years, under several producers including Swingler. His next employer was none other than Ian Dalrymple, for whose Wessex Films he directed *Bank of England* (1960), a thirty-four-minute non-theatrical film sponsored by the Bank as a self-conscious, if diffident, experiment in modernisation – allowing cameras in for the first time, to reveal arcane functions to a largely ignorant public. The film's strong reviews read puzzlingly today.[13] Williams himself scorns the film.[14] While for the producer this was a rare post-Jennings return to documentary, the director, conversely, was restless to pick up some feature-film experience. Under Dalrymple's wing he took that well-trodden path for young documentarians with itchy feet: directing a short feature for the Children's Film Foundation. *Hunted in Holland* (1961), co-written by Williams and Dalrymple, had middling success, but started for Williams a run of dramatised films: a misstep, in retrospect.

The Cattle Carters (1962), made next, has some significance in the annals of oil-industry filmmaking: it was the first time BP's London and Melbourne offices had co-sponsored a film. It was made by Greenpark, who commissioned Williams to write and direct, in association with Cinesound Productions of Sydney, who provided his unit. The film's theme allowed Williams's dabblings in drama to blend with his formative fluency: shooting marathon factual films in remote locations. Documentary supplied the subject: the use of road-trains – giant diesel trucks, fuelled by a BP agent – to transport cattle 800 miles across the Outback. But the story was told fictionally, via the odd-couple tale of a hard-nosed Aussie and a tenderfoot Cockney undertaking the arduous drive, both played by actors. Cinema-released in both countries, the resulting short initially drew more attention in Australia than in its director's homeland (where *Kinematograph Weekly* not unreasonably dubbed it 'fair to middling quota').[15] Pleasantly reminiscent of B-Westerns, it retains, thanks to later trade-test transmissions, a minor nostalgic cult among fiftysomethings.

Next, Williams was in Malta directing, for Anvil, his second Children's Film Foundation production, a six-part serial, *Treasure in Malta* (1963). This proved wildly successful on Maltese cinema release (reputedly yielding the biggest box office in Maltese history, bar *Ben Hur* [1959]). In Britain it slipped unnoticed into Saturday morning children's screenings, then onto TV.[16] The same year, Williams picked up a few days' work directing *A Bit of Doing* (1963) at Merton Park Studios for the Guild's Technical and Scientific Films. He was replacement for David Villiers, who'd scripted it before his tragic death (an on-screen credit pays tribute). Again mixing documentary motive with fictional means, this conscience-pricking short, for the Royal British Legion, takes the form of a supernatural vignette in which a war memorial's statues come to life one foggy night. A rather weird curiosity, it brought Williams's present cycle of semi-fictional films to an end. His next project brought him into contact, and conflict, with the very fount of documentary Calvinism.

Williams accepted Films of Scotland's offer to direct a film marking the centenary of Glasgow's installation of a Medical Officer of Health. Spending the notorious 1962–3 winter (the one that gave rise to Geoffrey Jones's *Snow*) in pokey lodgings, shaken by the severity of Glasgow's social problems, Williams gauchely attempted frank coverage, drawing him into inexorable conflict with the Films of Scotland Committee and its most prominent member John Grierson. Grierson to this day has left a negative impression on his intimidated director. Williams persisted but was removed from post-production after his first cut. Ostensibly this was for budgetary reasons, but the pressure had been for the more upbeat portrayal of Glasgow offered by the finished film, *Health of a City* (1965).

After such a bumpy political ride, Williams embraced extreme *physical* discomforts like a familiar friend. Back freelancing for Greenpark under BP sponsorship, with cameraman James Allen and an assistant, he spent six months following and filming a team of oil contractors barging supplies down the Mackenzie river system from Alberta to Arctic Alaska, trekking across tundra to a well location where the three-man crew filmed drilling in freezing conditions under the Alaskan North Slope's cloak of permanent night. This significant occasion – Britain's first American and first Arctic oil search – yielded a strong record. Allen's glacial camerawork (plus shooting by Williams himself) combined well with Williams's script, lacing a spare realism with romantic but clipped and convincing evocations of heroism, and a musical score by Edward Williams better than any of his namesake's earlier films had enjoyed. For three years, the twenty-one-minute *North Slope – Alaska* (1964) was a frequent PFB booking, and an unusually popular supporting short in UK cinemas.

For its director, it was a turning point, a splendid climax to his cycle of adventures but also the start of a new sequence of films into which – encouraged by *North Slope*'s success and sombre mood – he quietly insinuated more of himself. Where, hitherto, he had been offered assignments by producers, after *North Slope* sponsors frequently sought him out direct. His most persistent patron would be Roly Stafford, the fellow-cameraman he'd met in Aden, who had recently been appointed to head BP's films programme.[17] Williams's next BP films were contrasting examples of small-scale, intelligently sponsored film-making. As an extension of its participation in the Conference on Mathematics in Education and Industry, BP provided funding for *I Do – And I Understand* (1964) on behalf of the Nuffield Maths Project. This involved Williams directing a 16mm shoot at a Blackpool primary school. It won the Society of Film & Television Arts award for best specialised film. Unsuited to Greenpark's polished style, it was made at Leon Clore's Graphic Films. BP also had a Turkish subsidiary, on whose behalf the multinational's London HQ sponsored a tourist film to awaken western viewers to its then little-known past and undiscovered beauty. The schedule would be short by London standards, and the budget modest. The contract was accepted by Anne Balfour-Fraser's small Samaritan Films, which hired Williams and Allen. The former, with his love of the ancient world, embraced the chance to make a film about past instead of present exploits. *Turkey – The Bridge* (1966) accordingly lingered on shots of splendid ruins, over which, for the first time since *Foothold on Antarctica*, Williams spoke the English commentary himself. Skilfully edited by Kevin Brownlow, it was Oscar-nominated.

Around this time, Stafford asked Williams to salvage a rudderless World Wide production, about North Sea gas and oil search. 'I was in an awkward situation, fuelled by James Carr's pique that

I had left him, seven or eight years earlier; and by his and Clifford Parris's guilt that they had neglected completion for so long.' It was a moot point who should have the director's credit. After discharging his duties Williams left without accepting any credit, which went instead to World Wide's veteran cameraman Ronnie Anscombe. *North Sea Quest* (1967) had no great non-theatrical success but was a frequent trade-test choice: 'millions saw it at home; and one could scarcely pass a TV shop without seeing it on screens in the window … a credit would have done me good. So it taught me a lesson: not to be proud.'

Williams was next in Algeria, on a coverage film made by Greenpark for Constructors John Brown, of the laying of a gas pipeline from the Sahara to the Mediterranean. Williams remembers newly independent Algeria as a ruined and traumatised country. Despite attracting praise on the industrial scene, *Algerian Pipeline* (1967) is a flat affair, especially compared to Williams's next, the justly well-regarded *Indus Waters* (1967). Made by the Guild's international arm, Interfilm, and reuniting Williams with producer Buckland-Smith (and with Wilfred Josephs, who had scored *Oxford*), this documentary examined the project which, under treaty between India and Pakistan, provided shared access to the Punjabi rivers, vital to both feuding nations. The film was funded by the treaty's third signatory: the World Bank, characterised by Buckland-Smith as 'the ideal sponsor: it has left the film judgements and decisions to us'.[18] *Indus Waters* earned more awards than any of Williams's films so far, another SFTA Award included (this time, in the main Short Film category).

At this point, the director went back to salaried employment, rejoining Greenpark. His first two films on his return determined his attitude to the second half of his career, crystallising lessons of the varied freelance period. First came *The Taking Mood* (1969), a throwback to the hybrid form of *The Cattle Carters*, and more precisely a pallid imitation of Pirelli Tyres' recent smash *The Tortoise and*

Contrasting faces of British Petroleum

the Hare (1966). Made at the suggestion of BP New Zealand, using an NZ crew, its plot concerns a fishing bet between a craggy South Island fisherman and an urbane North Island motorist and playboy. UK circuit release notwithstanding, this short's lack of recognition finally brought home to Williams that he was no dramatist, still less a comedian. That realisation was thrown into sharper relief by his next undertaking, the film that seemed finally to synchronise directorial style and personality with enlightened sponsorial self-interest and deeply serious subject matter, to world success. That film was *The Shadow of Progress*.

Environmental issues began bubbling under the late 1960s. The Shell Film Unit had been successful with *The River Must Live* (1966). Now European Conservation Year loomed. As BP's contribution, Stafford commissioned Swingler and Williams for a film given the banal working title 'Pollution', soon widened to 'Environment', the term swiftly assuming its modern meaning as its topicality surged. *The Shadow of Progress*, released in 1970, rendered a cerebral yet mournful, haunting study of the subject on a broader canvas than ever attempted, thanks to BP's (by documentary standards) blockbusting budget. Vast distribution figures were soon claimed: 6,000 PFB bookings in Britain, where the BBC broadcast *The Shadow of Progress* not only as trade-test, but twice in primetime; 1,900 copies distributed in fifteen languages, and in time over 50 million viewers worldwide. Acclamation and awards poured in, fixing in Williams a determination to pursue similar subjects in comparable style.

Since Williams had filmed on the North Slope, Alaskan oil had finally been struck, at Prudhoe Bay by the American firm ARCO.[19] No movie cameras were present then, but it swiftly dawned on Wall Street that ARCO's tiny Alaskan bloc was hemmed in by the massive holdings BP had been quietly building up around it (and had been on the verge of abandoning prior to ARCO's discovery). The British giant, hitherto scarcely known in the USA, urgently needed prestige publicity to cement its bond with Alaska, by way of tribute to her heritage and scenery. Williams delivered a film expertly pulling together historical, geographical and ethnological facets of the state's character. The beauty and craftsmanship of *Alaska – The Great Land* (1971) was again enhanced by Edward Williams's first-class musical accompaniment, and the initiation of a productive partnership with cinematographer Maurice Picot, who would shoot the director's next five films. Worldwide awards included Williams's final SFTA prize and a BISFA Gold.

By this point, the three ascendant curves – of BP Films, Greenpark and Williams himself – must, within their specialised world, have seemed unassailable. In hindsight, they were running on empty.

For now, however, Williams felt able to press the advantage on his friend and sponsor Stafford, and for the first time since his amateur debut found himself directing a documentary of his own devising. Williams's proposition – a sequel to *The Shadow of Progress*, whose focus turned on the narrower topic of escalating traffic levels – was well timed, for in 1972 the UN would stage a major international conference on the environment (and an environmental film festival in Montreal would follow). BP saw that such a film could be premiered there, the perfect launch pad for worldwide release. The director, meanwhile, had in his words 'become emotionally involved with the early green movement'. Seeking to ally *The Shadow of Progress*'s stately technique to a sharper message, *The Tide of Traffic* (1972) got a more tepid response than its predecessor, despite a third Oscar nomination, a Venice Golden Mercury (doubtless helped by Williams's prominent use of Venice as a symbolic location) and further impressive viewing statistics.

Since Williams had helped document 1967's budding North Sea investigations, the strategic importance of Scotland had loomed ever larger in the boardrooms of the UK oil industry. Screen sponsorship was certain to follow. Thus, BP's motives for having commissioned *Alaska* were the same ones that now prompted the less exotic *Scotland* (1973). They enabled its director to paint another evocative oil portrait of a place and its history. Understandably, Scotland's smaller size commanded a smaller budget, but this also portended the shrinkage of Williams's sector of the industry. Indeed, his next, *A Heritage to Build On* (1975) was the final film made by the original Greenpark Productions, the last ever produced by Swingler – and a middling project to go out on. The Cement and Concrete Association's contribution to European Architectural Heritage Year lacked the dignity of Greenpark-BP's conservationist film-making. The truth is, no one loves concrete (especially the British who've used so much of it).

Happily, Williams's second freelance period started on a high note. For Shetland, North Sea developments represented an opportunity for greater wealth, but also a threat to wildlife and way of life. The Shetland Islands Council formed the Sullom Voe Assocation with the interested petroleum companies to devise a settlement balancing rural with industrial interests. This body commissioned a film: a conservationist work to be inflected with an acute sense of history and a feeling for the remoteness of Britain's own miniaturised Alaska. Among petroleum's favourite film-makers, Williams was an obvious choice. Balfour Films (as Samaritan had been renamed) was the chosen production company, Picot the cameraman, Douglas Gordon producing. Shot on a generous schedule (in both summer and winter) and tying together every strand of Williams's best directing and writing, *The Shetland Experience* (1977) is perhaps his most characteristic single film, and among the last really special products of documentary sponsorship. It was Oscar-nominated and, for the first time, Williams attended the Academy ceremony. Afterwards, he recalls, 'I chatted for several minutes to the chairman of the Short Subjects jury, who sought me out. He suggested I pass the word to British sponsors that "petroleum blockbusters" ... could never hope to win. Juries were focused upon compassionate, socially aware or green "underdog subjects" and these stood the best – perhaps the only – chance of winning.'[20]

If Williams's Shetland experience brought hope of more, then it was prolonging an illusion fostered by *The Shadow of Progress*. Sponsorship's better days were fast fading: when the same production team next worked for BP, a truer precedent was set. *Planet Water* (1979), an unofficial follow-up to *The Shadow of Progress* and *The Tide of Traffic*, focused now on the ocean, with sadly diminished sweep. The unit had been allowed four months on Shetland, the better to weave minute threads of nature and culture into an intricate narrative. Now, facing the relationship of land and sea, a vast and potentially profound global subject to which Williams sought to bring something of *The Shadow of Progress*'s contemplative outlook, they had to make do with six weeks and a single camera. The result was an adequate classroom film that failed to achieve substantial distribution or press impact. Williams's corner of the film business had thrived in good times in the shadow of PR departments flourishing in turn in the shadow of big industry. Under these shadows, Williams had been able, as he puts it, 'to scavenge spin-off topics, like culture, history and environment'. Now times were tougher. Even the mightiest sponsors would not consider investment in film without a watertight economic case. Meanwhile, over the previous fifteen years, Williams had sensed the incursion of documentary television onto film's historic territory, though his worldwide travels and professional successes had distracted him from its full extent. Now sharply aware, he knew it was too late to jump ship.[21]

> Launching a film used to be like dropping a pebble into a pool – there was a splash, an audible and visible splash, and ripples. But now: it was as if you dropped the stone into a bowl of treacle ... no splash, no sound and no ripples, after a year's work! ... What went wrong?[22]

Williams now found himself in a decade-long drift: following work from unit to unit, on films fulfilling rigid functions, his interest in their subjects occasionally flickering to life. *The Science of Art* (1976), promoting Winsor and Newton's new range of oil colours, was his first overt sales film since that 1957 job for Hovis. *South East Pipeline* (1982) was Williams's only Esso film, about the construction of a pipeline through the Home Counties, echoing his Algerian subject on home ground (albeit in pleasant, low-key register, and with extensive reference to environmental implications). Williams's final BP short, *Fair Wear and Tear* (1982), was about the maintenance of a North Sea platform, and proved his wisdom in having earlier avoided the technical subjects at which some film-makers (like Peter de Normanville at Shell) excelled. *Army Cadet* (1980), *Configuration Management* (1985) and *Replenishment at Sea* (1986) reflected a respect for, but betrayed limited empathy with, the Armed Forces. Amid these small, focused efforts a couple of productions evidenced the occasional willingness of global firms to sink large sums into multi-location, promotional documentaries. *The Chemistry of India* (1979), one of two films Williams made under David Evans at Millbank, portrayed the range of work of ICI's Indian subsidiary – prints were screened in cinemas across India but unseen in Britain. The Central Selling Organisation (a London ancillary of De Beers) sponsored *Diamond Day* (1982), a day-in-the life of the world diamond industry, shot (shades of old BP films) in twelve countries on 35mm stock – but principally distributed on VHS and Betamax to CSO staff (or given as a 'freebie' to clients).

Throughout the period, some of Williams's earnings came through writing commentaries for other directors – notably Pelican Films' Alan Pendry and John Armstrong, whose Williams-scripted BP film *The End of the Road* (1976), about Alaska, was Oscar-nominated.[23] Only in Williams's final two films could the character of his better directorial work resurface. Williams relates that from the beginning he had admired the Shell Film Unit and had long wanted to work there, but that *The Shadow of Progress*'s success had put paid to these hopes. It not only outshone Shell's contemporaneous releases, but shattered the unwritten agreement between the companies' film departments, that Shell could corner the market in concerned statesmanship and popular science, while BP concentrated on exotic locales and human stories. 'Hearsay had it that Shell's long-time films officer, Dora Thomas, never forgave me. Certainly she avoided me and did not answer my letters.' So it was with surprise that in mid-1988 Williams received in the post, from Thomas's successor Max Michie, an invitation to 'tender for writing a script and treatment for a major new Shell film' on 'Soil as a Resource'[24] (Williams had secured the contract to make *Diamond Day* on a similar competitive basis). His principal rival was none other than Douglas Gordon, twice his producer and steeped in Shell tradition. A summons from Shell automatically implied internationalism: Gordon focused on China, Williams on Russia. Unconnected events conspired to swing judgment decisively against Gordon (the Chinese government's increasingly reviled human rights record) and in favour of Williams (the week his treatment arrived, Shell had opened an office in *glasnost* Moscow, to corporate fanfare). Williams became the first western corporate film-maker to shoot in the USSR. His first production for many years shot on 16mm stock, indicating the constricted audiences that even a pricey Shell film now expected, *A Stake in the Soil* (1990) nevertheless returned Williams to his beloved 'spin-off topics'. The brief was broad enough to allow a scientific subject to be taken in an historical, even mildly philosophical, direction, and Williams to resume his blend of the thoughtfully didactic with the curtly poetic. The film topped Shell's distribution charts for the next two years, and Michie re-engaged its director for *Oman – Tracts of Time* (1992). This study of a key Shell territory's diverse geology had been requested by the Sultan of Oman, to whom the film is dedicated. Narrower in scope, more sternly pedagogical in tone, it nevertheless played to Williams's strengths in filming the inanimate world, and had high production values – considering its humble outlets. Poignantly symbolising a dying tradition, Williams's last film was shot in 35mm Eastmancolor but edited on video (traditional London cutting-rooms themselves dying on their feet), before being put back onto both 35mm neg stock and master videotape. The first was to strike prints for screening in Oman, including the Sultan's private viewing theatre. The second was to generate VHS copies, for circulating between British classrooms, screening, presumably, to fifth- and sixth-formers with varied attention levels.

> Looking back, as I left the short film industry (which I had joined, with high hopes, over 40 years before) it seemed a sadly diminished ruin ... Nonetheless, our small films, edited in the Soho back rooms of what we called our 'cottage industry', produced its moments of distinction and gained considerable respect for Britain abroad.

VOYAGES AND VENTURES

Plainly, the career just outlined was shaped by shifting fiscal forces and by fluctuating fashions in public relations. It's in the work's texture, less tightly bounded, that scope remained for talent and temperament, most clearly revealed when we sort these films into categories. Many of Williams's shorts – and all the important ones – fall into four loose groupings, all spawned by PR politics but each variously inflected. The first consists of films on which Williams's initial reputation was established, expressing industry in action more than in thought. Kevin Brownlow comments: 'I was in awe of Derek Williams ... He was the pioneering 1920s type that I admire so much – very modest, very brave, and produced good stuff.'[25] Williams's modesty reflected this standing as adventurer-cameraman having been accrued accidentally and incongruously, for his own inclinations were pensive rather than athletic.

Williams's most successful and best 'venture' films were *Foothold on Antarctica* and *North Slope – Alaska*, and they share several features, besides the bitter cold. Both were shot in chaotic conditions; both depend on subsequent editing and imposition of commentary to bring coherence and to supply a viewpoint.[26] Pictorially, Williams seeks striking, purposeful compositions whenever possible to set them up, but the tersely poetic commentaries are entirely under the writer-director's control: emotion recollected in tranquillity. Its main elements are awe for the strange beauty of the backgrounds, and deep regard for the unassuming, valiant characters in their foregrounds, but both the awe and the admiration are expressed at a certain reserved distance from their objects. *Foothold on Antarctica* has a greater wistfulness than to be found in, say, George Lowe's deadpan sequel (Lowe, a photographer on the Everest ascent, replaced Williams on the main expedition: his longer film *Antarctic Crossing* [1958] picking up where Williams left off). And both Williams's films possess a peculiar repose missing from, say, the colourful, virile adventures of a James Hill. *North Slope* and Hill's *The New Explorers* are indeed equally born of BP's post-Abadan policy: never again to sink investment in a single territory, instead to seek reserves in unproven places worldwide. Yet the two films could not be more different: a matter of temper as much as of temperature. Williams admires adventurers but is not really one himself: he is there with them by circumstance more than by instinct.

Both films document incomplete missions: both end on a falling note. The *Theron* departs, Williams and camera onboard, leaving the advance party of eight to prepare the base for the return of the main mission that Lowe would cover. The Alaskan well at which Williams and Allen filmed proved dry: narrative stops mid-drilling, emotion climaxes instead on a paean to the men. The coda is a lonesome long shot over which Edward Williams lays a harmonica lament. However, the films are differently related to their common sponsorship, which explains their one sharp divergence. Though *Foothold on Antarctica* was paid for by BP, it was as an extension of the company's patriotic contribution to the expedition itself (which can't, mind you, have harmed business). Besides credit acknowledgment, the paymaster's screen presence is fleeting, a barrel glimpsed as the party's meagre supplies are unloaded – 'oil, coal, a picture of the Queen, a case of rum ...'.

North Slope, by contrast, documents a mission in the service of BP's commercial objectives. The company had been putting significant investment into Alaska from the late 1950s, gambling on exploring the north of the state while most American competitors worked its south. This background clarifies the PR function of Williams's film: to educate the public about the uncertainties and risks on which BP's business is founded, while instilling in viewers an excited feeling for the rugged romance of oil searching. Just as Brownlow's remark implies, this brings to both films (as to Hill's) a spirit of derring-do, shared with those silent epics of non-fiction cinema that similarly chronicled perilous journeys and set them against vignettes of base-camp life. In *Foothold on Antarctica*, the long voyage culminates in a month trapped in pack-ice, while *North Slope* has its own extended trips by water then by land, before both arrive at base and a remote, rudimentary day-to-day existence is sketched. However, BP's public education motive brings the latter parts of *North Slope* closer to a very different brand of documentary. As the Guild's journal *Imagery* had it:

> to make industrial films, film men have to go where industry goes, stand alongside the men on the job wherever they are, however dangerous or unpleasant the job is – so that audiences all over the world may understand a little better what *modern industrial enterprise really means*.[27]

Many seminal EMB and GPO films had sought to awaken the public's imagination to the unseen physical work, and primeval natural resources, underlying their own rising living standards. Thus, *North Slope* unexpectedly transposes a Grierson project to exotic Eastmancolor settings, to the service of adventurous capitalism, to making humble heroes not of stalwart Scots fishermen or Welsh colliers but of rootless Canadians toiling for Britain's overseas interests in infinite Arctic wilderness. The superb final sequence of fruitless drilling, shot in mythic silhouette at the very edge of the colour stock's tolerance,[28] find a harsh beauty in industrial processes, while the accompanying words exalt the dignity in manual labour. The score pulses and surges in discordant couplets as the braying drills are turned and twist, and steam rises from the frozen borehole:

> So now it's up to the truckers and the cat-skinners, the motor-men and the derrick-men, the drillers and the tool-pushers and roughnecks, working on and on through the long winter where the wind cuts and the cold aches ... They don't talk tough or act big ... but in their way – they are giants.

The director resents the sudden curtailment, around 1967, of *North Slope*'s considerable success, as anti-establishment anti-capitalism captured youthful imagination: 'Heaven knows, if those lotus-eating hippies had spent a winter working through the total darkness and killing cold of the Arctic night, they might have been less ready to mock my admiration for those brave men.'[29]

Williams's other voyages and ventures are less compelling. Prompted by a very different set of BP commercial activities, *The Cattle Carters* is a corruption of *North Slope*, into laid-back, fictional mode. That said, despite being set in less extreme physical conditions, the director's own responsibility for negotiating those conditions was greater. This time Williams was not eyewitness but leader: head of the six-week-long expedition required to film a story occupying (as it would in 'documentary' reality) a forty-hour timeframe. The same regard for the characters' rugged individualism shines through the dramatic contrivances, laboured comedy, badly dubbed dialogue and game but amateurish performances. Emphasising its place in the cinema of action, *The Cattle Carters*' several cowboy (or overlander) motifs add to its agreeable tone: a lazy small town (complete with BP filling-station); a ballad (sung by Frank Ifield: 'Cattlemen, Cattlemen/Rolling on our way ...'); riders silhouetted against sunsets – and even Aborigines in 'friendly Indian' role.

By the time of Williams's other antipodean story, the synthetic *The Taking Mood*, any such shards of romance have scattered, and what's left behind is a trivial film. Meanwhile Williams's 'pure' documentary coverage of unquestionably major engineering feats in Aden and Algeria are, in their formulaic triumphalism, equally far from his stirring, but melancholy, elegies to Antarctica and Alaska. Wimpey and John Brown probably insisted on excessive technical detail, but the films' weaknesses also testify to the film-maker's own inflexibility, in the face of impressive collective enterprises devoid of individual heroism. Similarly, in *The Road to MIS*, excitement flickers on and off, depending on which of that film's portmanteau episodes are on screen at the time. Certain other of Williams's films evince weaknesses of the entire filming tradition of which they're part: so proud of its prowess in documenting *process*, it was confounded when confronting processes resistant to its technique, especially as its budgets fell. Witness *Fair Wear and Tear*, Williams's contribution to the plethora of repetitive North Sea films turned out in later years. Its sound-synched television style of reporting is a distinct comedown if viewed after the silent-film style of *Foothold on Antarctica* or *North Slope*. And its message? 'There may be no profit in maintenance but without it there would be one hell of a loss.' Such fiscal facts, of real importance to national prosperity, are hard to express in cinematic terms, suggesting the creative, and now financial, limitations of the documentary school to which Williams belonged.[30] On a much higher budget, Williams's *Bank of England* had similarly failed to take flight. The *Financial Times*, acclaiming the film, astutely observed that 'the producer has wisely pinned his flag to the graceful and endearing "basket weaving in Norfolk" tradition'.[31] But the Bank's processes were monotonous, self-regarding and devoid of visual appeal. Notwithstanding Williams's temperamental conservatism, his sympathies, and British documentary's cinematic powers, were more easily roused by the coalface than the colliery office, by the oil well than by the boardroom: a drawback for any project purporting to map 'reality'.

SOCIAL PROBLEMS

Unlike some, Williams was entirely sanguine about post-war documentary's uncoupling from ideology, in which Wright's generation had been steeped. His apolitical professionalism suited him to employment by the likes of the Guild, in willing receipt of sponsorship from any institution for any purpose. In the post-war era, that implied filming on foreign soil as often as on domestic: spatially, temporally, spiritually remote from the world of *Housing Problems*, *Enough to Eat?* or *Land of Promise*. Williams further admits to being 'a natural conservative, educated – perhaps overeducated – in the classics of English and Latin literature', adding that 'coming from Tyneside, the Kitchen Sink, all too familiar and never far distant, was less magnetic than it might seem from Hampstead'.

Williams's output *does*, nonetheless, exemplify documentary's lingering, carefully non-partisan, aspirations to statesmanship. In the first half of his career, Williams thrice accepted commissions to enquire into British social conditions, with mixed success. The first, *There Was a Door*, was hailed precisely for replenishing the social documentary tradition (not yet fully migrated to television), by applying to fresh post-war subject matter a favoured wartime form. David Robinson, in *Sight & Sound*, observed that 'documentaries on social themes have become so unusual in this country', that the production 'would be important in itself, even were it not an exceptionally coherent and well-made film'.[32] Released soon after the publication of the report of the 1954–7 Royal Commission on Mental Illness and Mental Deficiency, from which its opening and closing titles quote, the film, chiming with a broader shift of attitude towards institutionalisation of the mentally handicapped, was initiated before the report was released. In 1955, the Manchester Regional Hospital Board conducted a survey suggesting that 500 in-patients could be discharged if suitable day centres existed. In January of that year, one such experimental Industrial Occupation Centre for adult males was opened in Oldham. Spurred by its success, the Board began considering a film on the whole subject. As its secretary subsequently recalled,

> members ... recollected some documentary films they had seen and by which they had been much impressed. Further enquiries led them to The Film Producers Guild and to a very interesting meeting with the Guild's Secretary, Mr H. G. Jessop – interesting because whilst the Board were in no doubt about the need to stimulate public thinking on this important matter there was still, at that stage, something of a question mark in their minds as to the suitability of their subject for the film medium. Mr Jessop's confident view was that the subject was one which presented the film maker with a wonderful opportunity.[33]

Jessop's view was presumably a compound of compassionate and business motives, but he would have had little doubt that among Guild members, Greenpark had the necessary breadth of outlook and subtlety of touch.

The film's objective was precise: an address from one layer of officialdom to another, seeking to persuade local authorities, on both humanitarian and fiscal grounds, to open more facilities like Oldham's. But sponsor and film-makers alike were aware of the broader social potential of 'stimulating public thinking'. On completion, *There Was a Door* was screened to the Minister of Health and his senior officials. It was then premiered at the Lord Mayor's reception for the National Association for Mental Health's 1957 Conference at Manchester Town Hall. It was the Association that recommended the film to the BBC. Following its broadcast, *Radio Times* published this letter from 'Mrs P. L., Haywards Heath':

> I should like to voice my appreciation of the film ... a wonderful insight into a world quite unknown to the majority of people. As the mother of a mentally handicapped child I was, needless to say, intensely interested, as my child is in an institution. However, as she was on holiday at the time, I definitely noticed a more friendly and helpful look on people's faces the next day. This alone is a good thing. That extra bit of sympathy and understanding certainly helps.[34]

In respect of its form, the film was novel for Williams: a refinement of the World War II story documentary, in which characters are played by non-actors, not so much replicating their specific circumstances, as drawing on them to recreate a factually based morality play.[35] The film centres on a doctor who has taken on the case of the Harris family, who have a mentally defective nineteen-year-old son, and his investigation of existing facilities. Buckland-Smith's impressive, self-possessed script falls, almost imperceptibly, into sections, across which he shades his theme with exemplary dexterity: alternating, balancing and reinforcing information with drama, the general with the particular, the troubling with the hopeful. More surprising, in a sponsored communication of the time, is the maturity with which the writer eschews pat answers, ending on the doctor confessing both to having had little choice but to place Johnny in the institution and to his equal certainty that the choice was wrong. As we witness the boy being walked into the building by officials, the film ends on its door closing before us.

Williams's contribution was to embody and amplify Buckland-Smith's words. He succeeds by directing from the same sympathetic standpoint, but at similar emotional distance, as in his best adventure films.[36] *Film User*'s review eloquently lauded the film's 'piercing but wounding clarity', which its attention to its own formal properties greatly assists.[37] The one weakness in Williams's direction is his handling of Johnny's mother, particularly in a scene in the doctor's office requiring her to simulate breakdown, with hanky in hand. Unlike people in, say, the best Dickson or Krish films, she's stagy and unconvincing: Williams secures much greater impact from carefully framed shots of her husband, staring pensively ahead, and her impassive son, dignified and isolated in his mysterious world. The film's best sequence follows immediately, as, the family departing, the doctor looks down on a playground full of 'normal' girls, from which Williams cuts (remaining in long shot) to a single lonely girl, shadowed in the background, then sees the Harrises passing two chatting women who look askance at them, as the doctor and his wife continue observing from above. His off-screen voice remarks: 'how thoughtless people are'. Then Williams cuts back to a single shot of the chattering ladies and their accompanying 'normal' child. In narrative terms this sequence merely bridges two more substantive ones, but its influence on the viewer's mood is important. The scene plays on the concept of *distance* as having both physical and emotional meanings. It seems to reflect the director's stance, as much as the doctor's, when surveying the film's harrowing subject – compassionate and respectful rather than empathetic and distraught. Formally, the scene's strength lies in eloquent *staging*, not in performance.

Later, when Templar Films' head, Robert Riddell Black recommended Williams to Films of Scotland's Forsyth Hardy, at the head of a shortlist including Peter de Normanville and Margaret

Thomson,[38] it was because of his 'ability to work with people and give them character and credibility'. He was making a mistake: as we have just seen, Williams's strength is pictorial, not dramatic. Hardy, advising Grierson that de Normanville (whom Grierson might well have preferred) was unavailable, further cited *There Was a Door* and *The Cattle Carters* as having impressed him, on similar grounds. Williams, perhaps sensing his miscasting, then compounded it by groping for ill-fitting stylistic clothes:

> This treatment is based on the idea of a series of 'interviews' with a cross-section of real people ... encouraged to speak for themselves, direction largely consisting of agreement on the general lines of subject matter to be followed ... apart from introductory and closing passages of commentary, it is anticipated that the dialogue spoken during the interviews will be sufficient to carry the film's meaning ... The past is the key to Glasgow's problems and we must think of problems before solutions. But briefly, for the past has no major place in a film which looks forward ... Our final image is of a smashed tenement window, seen from inside. The jagged, star-shaped hole in its centre allows a glimpse of a bright sky outside and admits a beam of sunlight.[39]

The tortuous twists of the resulting protracted production of *Health of a City* are documented in its fat surviving production file. In essence, it was subject, throughout, to mutual misunderstandings and clashing political forces: Glasgow Corporation, sceptical of the film's value; Films of Scotland, anxious to prove it and thus to sweeten its sponsor; Templar Films, still riding high on its Oscar for *Seawards the Great Ships* (1960) but nervous about risking future income; and Grierson, to whom everyone's forelocks were primed for tugging, and who at several stages took Williams 'under his wing' for cajoling in the right direction. Williams remembers,

> After an initial tour of the tenements of many a mean district – accompanied by brave and dedicated social workers – I decided that Glasgow was Britain's most deprived, sordid city. Dr Grierson, who described *Seawards* (in his usual drunken, shouting manner) as 'one hell of a fighting film' was surprisingly defensive when it came to criticism of matters north of the border (especially by someone from south of it!) ... when the first cut was complete and a first draft of commentary written, I was packed off, on the grounds that the budget could no longer be stretched to paying and accommodating me ... Robert Black, with 'the Doc' breathing down his neck, proceeded to remove uncomplimentary material.

The file corroborates this recollection, and reveals Black as having been in an acutely uncomfortable position.

Williams's efforts to balance congratulatory content with doses of grim realism were trebly ill advised: conflicting with his sponsorship, with his own personality and with national sensitivities. On seeing his treatment, William Ballantine at the Scottish Information Service reminded Hardy that the film would,

> determine for a long time ... the Corporation's attitude to the Films of Scotland ... this document turned into black and white celluloid ... will torpedo us ... I don't care very much for the condescension of this script. I find myself resenting the lack of understanding which seems to motivate the writer. I can assure you that it will take no tricks with the men and women it's supposed to be about ... they'll need another film to go out at the same time for industrialists thinking of coming this way and perhaps entitled 'Glasgow Isn't As Bad As All This.'[40]

Hardy replied, in Williams's defence, that 'your conception of him as a condescending, superior individual is well wide of the mark. He is rather shy, sensitive and self-effacing, altogether sincere, and desperately anxious to make a success of the film,' but as treatment progressed to shooting and post-production, he joined the naysayers.[41] Scenes shot in the Gorbals (window-smashings included), were among the material excised from the production, while, in late summer '63, Williams was conveniently embarking for the more congenial climate of Arctic Alaska. Williams, innocent abroad amid circuitous civic affairs, was ill prepared for their being much more liable than multinational businesses to turn 'political'. Before and after his departure, single shots and lines were subject to rounds of detailed scrutiny that Williams's private-sector films were spared (in his recollection, most discussions with corporate films officers were verbal, and were relaxed). The project went through further such contortions before the twenty-three-minute final cut was premiered in August 1965 for 1966 release, well over three years after its genesis! No director was credited. The film is fair but bland, feeling, as it was, the work of a committee: blended Scotch more than single malt.

The lesson of these contrasting exercises in municipal cinema was that an oil-schooled film-maker like Williams, when on the unfamiliar ground of the social documentary, needed congenial sponsorship to play to his strengths. The success of Williams's last social documentary, *I Do – And I Understand* may be ascribed to three factors it had in common with the otherwise very different *There Was a Door*. First, it similarly articulated newly prevalent, specifically *post*-war thinking: that primary-age children learn better maths from concrete practice than from abstract theory, a sensible liberalism to which Williams was a convert. Second, it was again the product of organisational structures specific to post-war Britain, this time an alliance of industry with NGOs and state education. In BP's in-house journal, *BP Shield*, Williams argued that,

> if mathematics, the sick man of the syllabus, cannot be cured, then it will go badly for us as a competitive nation in a rapidly developing world ... it is in the light of this reasoning that BP's interest in the project can be understood. No major improvement in mathematics teaching could fail, in the end, to be felt in industry. Aiding such work is a far-sighted, far-reaching investment ... At last ... with the Ministry's blessing and with the Nuffield Foundation's assistance ... an organised campaign for a revision in maths teaching methods will begin. This is where our film can help. A speaker can give excellent reasons for the changes he is advocating, but only the eye-witness media of camera and tape recorder can show his theories in action.[42]

The third common factor was stylistic. The 'free' observational style of *I Do* was as far from Williams's *metier* as the drama of *There Was a Door*, but again it gained from a cooler technique than other film-makers might have brought. The Graphic crew included Brian Probyn, who had shot some of the Direct Cinema-influenced social documentaries at Derrick Knight's company, and had even worked on Peter Watkins's *The War Game* (1965) (on *I Do*, he was assisted by Peter Suschitzky, son of Wolfgang). 'Filming was unexpectedly easy in such an atmosphere. Even where there were lights to be pointed and microphones placed, the children were able to perform without undue self-consciousness, because they were doing things which absorbed them, things which they enjoyed.'[43] However, the film depends on the juxtaposition of this fly-on-the-wall imagery with its considered commentary, spoken by two of the teachers. Where many classroom observation films are simply sloppy, *I Do* nicely balances friendly spontaneity with unobtrusive control – much as a skilled school-teacher does.

ENVIRONMENTAL ENIGMAS

> We told ourselves that we made them with the greatest sincerity – and even that they were sponsored with the greatest sincerity, but the question is: were they?[44]

We should beware of too categorical an answer. In any case, Williams found his voice as an 'issues' film-maker when dealing with topics calling for more abstract engagement, from a more aloof perspective. In retrospect, *Indus Waters* was an important transitional film. Its ostensible subject, the diversion and damming of three Indus Basin rivers to irrigate both India and West Pakistan under the auspices of the eponymous treaty, was said to be the biggest civil engineering project in world history. Williams's early experience as official cinematographer for such schemes doubtless helped secure him the job. Yet the film spends mere minutes on logistics. Its sponsorship, being not from the project's contractor but from its funder, enabled many more to be devoted to setting and context.[45] Reunited with Buckland-Smith, but now scriptwriting himself, Williams embraced a caste of social documentary far better fitting him. Its stance is sober and sincere, internationalist, magisterial. Its fixations not on human individuals but on nations and destinies, it communicates them not through physical performance but through careful alignment of image and written speech. The film's final lines read:

> If people matter, and if many people matter much, then those one and a quarter billion dollars, which would not meet the cost of one week of modern war, are surely not too high a price to secure their futures and to remove a source of conflict between nations.

Further, the subject prompted an intricate structure through which two further strands were laced. Ultimate causes (water, drought, cyclical seasons) gifted the film's more poetic passages, bringing out the writer's metaphysical mindset. Proximate causes (the story of the region since the end of British rule, culminating in the Treaty's negotiation) engaged his private passion: for history. Visually, the film is strongest in compositions implying nature and history at work, weakest when mimicking Shell-style humanism in formulaic shots of children waving and of people at work and play. Politically, the film is limited by its brief, mentioning in passing that while the 'water problem' has been solved, the Kashmir problem has not. John Chittock's *FT* review applauded the film's convincingly 'statesmanlike' qualities. Another journalist told *Imagery* that 'its sponsorship has been so carefully interwoven that you have to watch the credits to see if you picked up the right clues'[46] – the ultimate aim of patronage which, for whatever reason, prioritises the message ahead of the brand.

The positioning of Williams's most successful film was different. By spreading a thoughtful global message it yet bolstered and cleansed its sponsor's brand. As Sir Eric Drake, BP Chairman, wrote to Williams:

> During 1970 BP received a number of international film awards, but none gave me more personal pleasure than those earned by *The Shadow of Progress*. I recall our discussion in the theatre earlier this year [at the internal approval showing] and the spirited way in which you defended the film against criticism; clearly you had put a great deal of imagination and skill into the making of the film, and the subject is one about which you feel deeply. You will be aware that the film has been shown very widely throughout the world, but I would

> also like you to know that it has received the highest praise from our overseas associates, and despite the passing of European Conservation Year, we feel confident that the film will continue to serve the cause of conservation and of BP for many years to come.[47]

To the film's premiere in London, senior politicians of all parties, civil servants and conservationists as well as journalists were invited: a late high point for industrial film-making's claim to a progressive role in public affairs.[48] Drake addressed the assembled dignitaries:

> we have made this film because we are deeply concerned about the state of the world we live in. We believe that as many people as possible should realise the problems that technological progress has created; and we hope that this film will make them pause and think.[49]

Williams applauds the 'sponsorial courage' of Roly Stafford, who gambled his career on *The Shadow of Progress*. For his part, Stafford recollects that while it was intended, in part, to put BP 'ahead of the game' that environmentalism's sudden rise to respectability had kicked off, nevertheless:

> It was not a film, when completed, that many of the senior ducks in the company liked. It showed how the industrial nations were in fact polluting very heavily in their manufacturing processes and of course these were clients of the company – we were busy selling them fuels, and oils, and lubricants ... it was not considered very good news to point a finger at processes where we were involved ... the film initially didn't go down at all well with the company itself. In fact the marketing director of Shell-Mex/BP ... banned its use by Shell-Mex and BP in the UK, and it was also banned by BP Germany and BP France! However, it did have the backing of my chairman and in time wiser counsel prevailed ... the company itself took on the mantle of environmental responsibility to a far greater extent as a result of that film ... you can't be making a film, showing it round the world, when people can point a finger at you ... it meant the refinery people were looking at their refinery processes, and so on – and this was done through the hierarchy of the company. It was recognised that this created a slightly different mental state within the company. So, I think if I had a monument it would be that I helped, a little bit, in the environmental cause – and a great debt, I think, was owed to Derek Williams.[50]

Here is a genuine documentary dilemma. Activist film-making, unsullied and preaching radical change, risks preaching to the converted. Is it automatically superior to corporate film-making, necessarily guarded, which manages to convert its own apprehensive sponsor to modest, yet measurable and real, change? In any case, *The Shadow of Progress* was Williams's coming-of-age as a director of first-rate cinema of a peculiar kind, devoid of conventional drama. *The Shadow of Progress*, like the adventure films, is constructed of 100 per cent mute footage: the silence of its shooting is (once combined with Wilfred Josephs' musical score, accentuating the glassy splendour of the camera's compositions, filmed on four continents) essential both to its industrial purpose and to its emotional effect. It is one of several Williams films whose opening title is translated, on screen, into several tongues. Built into BP films' very purpose was their distribution across language barriers. Thus shots of ominous, voiceless crowds and menacing, mute vehicles take on the same eerie aspect as those of beautiful nature and ugly detritus alike (some critics accused the film-makers of having made their belching chimneys and stagnant rivers beautiful, belying their message). Williams is on record as regretting the film's later sections, in which several mundane, rapidly outdated 'solutions' to the problems, posed earlier, are presented. The saving grace is

Industry and idyll in *The Shadow of Progress*

that a hypnotic mood, descending from the film's opening shots, of headlights coming into focus, is maintained. Moreover, in the long run, the film's compromised origins have, ironically, worked in its favour. *The Shadow of Progress* is less political than philosophical. It blames environmental damage on deep dilemmas arising from humanity's ascent, more than on specific cause-and-effect: a broad analysis, which, if it could be accused of being evasive on the part of BP, remains applicable and provocative.

The sequel, *The Tide of Traffic*, is more problematic, precisely for taking a step closer, but just *one* step closer, to the oppositional school of film-making. On the subject of cars, Williams found himself on the same side as the deepest Greens: 'my own opinions favoured swingeing taxation and other measures to promote the birth control of the motor vehicle'. Of course, had he gone that far, BP's board would have pulled the film: so its punches were pulled instead. They are nonetheless there. The narrator's ruminations sound increasingly bitter:

> A world dazzled by the car, dazed by the scale of its usage ... Surely no invention has been permitted to so close a partnership with mankind ... Most men covet it: it is the dream of most families to own one, or a better one, or a second one ... The parked vehicle: tyrant of the townscape ... the city street ... a place of conflict and pollution; a denial of civilised standards.

And so on. Unable to press on to radical, logical, but unacceptable solutions, but having already strayed from *The Shadow of Progress*'s steady sobriety, such repeated lamentations sound shrill. In particular, they clash with the pictorial style that had served the earlier film so well. The film (which opens and closes on the motif of car-free Venice, surrounded by Europe's tide of traffic) contains visual sequences equal to its predecessor's (though Humphrey Searle's musical accompaniment, albeit derived from Venetian baroque music, is weaker). Yet the tart message would better suit the rough grain of agitprop than the lush texture of the prestige documentary.[51]

Williams's proposal that BP complete the environmental trilogy with a film called *The Push of People* was shelved (re-emerging much later, as John Armstrong's Williams-scripted 1988 production with that title). We've seen that later environment films were either less ambitious in intent (Williams's next sponsor requested that the breadth of the treatment for what became *A Heritage to Build On* be narrowed before production commenced) or less capable in execution (as on the underbudgeted *Planet Water* where Williams's characteristically brooding script lacks the grand visuals it calls for, making potentially thought-provoking phrases sound facile). In this previous 'era of recession', Williams's better late films retreated from the towering perspective of the two BP blockbusters, to recreate more closely the *Indus Waters* pattern in which case studies in civil engineering and conservationist theory are tightly interwoven with local histories and ecosystems.

North Sea questing had disclosed numerous fields in the East Shetland Basin. A dozen companies, including BP, Shell and Esso, had interests. All fully expected to develop their own onshore installations. Shetland's council, with remarkable pluck and foresight, secured Westminster legislation granting powers to prevent such proliferation, and entered into partnership with these hungry firms. In a landmark for Environmental Impact Assessment, the resulting Sullom Voe Association devised a settlement whereby conservation effects would be continually monitored, while a single unobtrusive terminal would be built for *all* oil from the Brent and Ninian pipelines (associated respectively with Shell/Esso and BP), brought ashore for onward transhipment to tankers. The film was thus commissioned by the whole of this group, including the council, with BP, via Stafford's successor Ian Brundle, facilitating it (while producer Gordon brought his Shell background to the project). Prints were then available to all participating companies – each one affixing its logo to the end of prints, as if it were solely 'their' film.

Therefore, although allocated to it on the strength of their BP experience, Williams and crew can truthfully be said to be telling the story not from BP's perspective but from that of the public good, as refracted through a complex, innovative public–private partnership. The deceptively simple, and at times breathtakingly beautiful, film that resulted is knitted of overlapping movements, continually, carefully shifting focus from scenery, geology, nature, through archaeology and history, economic and ecological analysis, to coverage of the engineering project and back again. Further, *The Shetland Experience* is the rare Williams film integrating *people* into the bigger picture without strain. A lovely scene is based around fiddle-playing and knitting in crofters' cottages. A montage of Shetland faces set to music is a gentle riposte to TV vox pops (pops minus vox). Each subject-sketch reverberates with the others: their sequencing suggests a year's seasons passing simultaneously with the dawn-to-dusk of a single day. The symbiosis of industry with idyll, symbolised by Picot's rapid reverse zoom from an offshore platform to a smallholding onshore, has a long lineage in British documentary's history. The film's conclusion is optimistic if subdued, speculating about a future founded on similar benign partnerships. The hopeful prognosis has remained valid for Shetland itself, at least.[52] The film's emotional climax lies in twilit scenes of silhouetted Viking helmets against fire: Shetland's Up Helly Aa festival, 'an expression of identity: an assertion that these are not the sons of Saxons, or of Celts, but of Norsemen'. Though a romantic exaggeration, such impassioned ethnology, married to elemental imagery, is clearly what set the film-makers' pulses racing: and their viewers' too.[53]

South East Pipeline is an altogether more domesticated, superficial story of British environmental planning ('Spring in Surrey and Kent, once the wild land beyond the North Downs and therefore called the Weald: this will be the pipeline's setting, a shy landscape'). But Williams's penultimate film, *A Stake in the Soil*, revisited the intricate construction of *Indus Waters* and *The Shetland Experience*. Shell's invitation to tender had positioned the project as,

> part of a series of films that examine in depth some of the major social and humanitarian problems facing mankind ... The intended audience is a broad international one, mainly, but not exclusively, educational. It is expected that the film will also have a wide appeal and be of value to UN organisations, NGO's and others.

Noting that the tendering process itself was a novel practice for Shell, it further observed that 'although "the Shell Film" is a highly respected animal, it has also, perhaps, become a little staid and

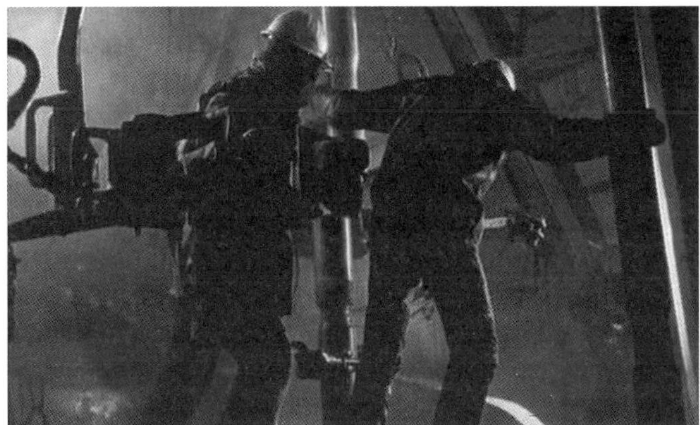

Heroic silhouette: *North Slope – Alaska* and *The Shetland Experience*

in need of some rejuvenation. Nevertheless, we are a conservative organisation and would not relish anything too avant garde!'[54] Williams's treatment, *A Sense of the Soil*, fitted the bill. It noted 'how evocative is our theme, how fertile for symbolism and poetry, how rich in contrasts, ironies and opportunities for comment ... our interpretation of soil will seek a balance between four aspects ... soil as a science, soil as a symbol, soil as a resource and soil as a problem'.[55]

If the music (synthesiser backing small ensemble, incorporating suggestions of the places shown) isn't up to the work of a Williams or Josephs, its pastiche is effective enough, a distinct improvement on several years of trite library music. To its accompaniment, a persuasive argument is built for mixed planting and vigilance against soil erosion. The entire first sequence consists of landscape shots, under descriptive narration. Hands sifting through earth launch a second movement, taking up the history of soil science, introducing its pioneer Vasily Dokuchaev – the film's presiding figure – and prompting extensive Russian location work. Further sequences, fruits of a shooting schedule harking back to BP glory days, spread across the globe to rhyme Russian steppe with Midwest prairie and Tunisian wilderness, the technical study of soil with its social effects. Along the way, Williams characteristically takes opportunity to picture the forlorn (rain, dust and wind across an unpeopled vista; an abandoned jalopy, shacks and broken wheels; empty huts in derelict, Sahara-threatened villages), and to verbalise paradox ('the least prestigious of our resources, though the most precious: locally common, collectively rich beyond measure ... soil has a deep emotional meaning. Millions died for it. The bond is basic'). Writing in *Shell World* (*BP Shield*'s counterpart), Williams commented that the theme was,

> full of fascinating contradiction and promise ... well suited to the Shell tradition ... the prestige class of documentary for 'thinking' audiences on questions of general or world concern ... a genre in which, over a 50-year period, the Shell Film Unit has won incomparable laurels.[56]

That genre sought always to evade controversy. Nine years before, Brundle had commissioned, but BP management had then rejected, Williams's treatment for a half-hour film entitled *Inner City*, on the grounds that it was 'too political'. The surviving second draft was submitted in September 1981, just as several multiracial cities were cooling after a sweltering summer of infamous riots: 'The film opens with a series of LONG SHOTS of maximum pathos: sad, grey landscapes of semi-dereliction, each with a solitary figure, perhaps an aged or disabled man or woman, at least one of whom is coloured.' The impressively ambitious treatment then moves through history (British cities' growth and decline since the industrial revolution), to a bleak, deft dissertation on the modern cityscape and its dispossessed population, by way of 'glimpses of inner city environments seen – as middle-class people tend to see them – through the windows of moving cars or trains' to a final meditation on the nature, and possible futures, of cities, ending with:

> A final montage of black, brown and white faces, filmed in inner city settings. Wasteland, with floating thistle-down. Dandelion, groundsel, willow herb, seeding. Ominous slogans on crumbling walls. Waste land, waste people. Places most of us prefer to forget. But this ground grows bitter flowers; and violence seeds in these sour spaces. The cure may be costly, but there are ills we cannot afford to neglect.[57]

Their cure isn't, of course, specified: the Achilles' heel of *The Shadow of Progress* and *The Tide of Traffic*. The treatment is anachronistic, politically naive, but in earnest. *Inner City* might have sounded a moving grace note on the part of its genre (as well, perhaps, as paying Williams's penance for his part in the botched *Health of a City*). It's impossible to imagine any firm, in 1981, seriously contemplating its sponsorship.

PLACE-HISTORIES

The Shetland Experience and *A Stake in the Soil* cross into the final grouping of films, concerned with the character and history of particular places. These are much the least problematic of Williams's films, being those in which the aims of maker and sponsor are most deeply compatible. Williams's very first film, *Hadrian's Wall*, had been characterised by a continual, patient interchange between 'silent' (with music) passages, and those illustrating words. The commentary script in turn alternates fact with evocation. In the programme notes for the amateur film's first screening, Williams rehearsed thinking which he would apply, repeatedly, in professional life:

> There seemed to be two approaches ... the 'instructive' film of historical and educational value, and the vaguely emotional 'travelogue'. I wished to avoid both ... I chose to attempt what I then called a 'mood-poem' in film ... to seek ... the atmosphere of the northern frontier of an Italian civilisation; the atmosphere of a remarkable ruin; and the sense of contrast between past and present implicit in it ... through camera and music ... Put to the test, the plan failed ... to give body to the film I was forced to ... adopt an unhappy compromise between a 'mood-poem' and a lecturette on Romano-British history.[58]

The COI's *Oxford* was certainly lecturette more than mood-poem. It was for BP that Williams began replicating almost exactly the *Hadrian's Wall* formula, balancing the two. The quasi-mystical mingling of past and present was a long-established currency of sponsored travelogue, to which BP's film-making template was particularly friendly. Yet Williams took to it naturally, given his background, his eye for landscape composition and his propensity for matching it to text carefully honed and weighed.[59] *Turkey – The Bridge*, *Alaska – The Great Land* and *Scotland* – all history films – are undoubtedly Williams's most purely enjoyable works. Petroleum's purpose in funding them isn't difficult to discern (manifesting itself in *Alaska* and *Scotland* as brief, late sequences introducing oil to the territories' sweeping histories, once again predicting a smooth integration into national life and land). But the films are otherwise free, in the equal interests of both sponsor and film-maker, to concentrate on evoking an apolitical, artistic response to geography and history. Structurally, the three films are similar, following a largely chronological narrative (book-ended by prologue and epilogue). History is compressed into mere minutes without seeming rushed, through the use of curt half-poetic voiceover summary (there is an immense difference between these short, tightly written essays and the long-form, presenter-led television history pioneered by the BBC's *Civilisation* [1969]). Earlier sequences emphasise natural features, and archaeological survivals, while stills and ruins help advance the histories related by the narrator. Significantly, *people* only appear (once again, filmed silent) as the films reach the present day, well over midway through the running time. Indeed, *Turkey* (Williams's personal favourite) has a bifurcated structure. The director's feeling for Asia Minor's earlier history and surviving remains evidently runs deeper than his response to present Turkey. Also, the sheer density of Turkish history ('bridge' between East and West) gives the film a compacted feeling. *Alaska*, with its sparser source material, is the strongest film in the trilogy, binding its poetics to a sturdy structure supplied by its past: fur rush, gold rush,

Derek Williams on location in Turkey

defence rush, oil rush. The film's other advance is technical, Williams and Picot making extensive, subtle use (as had *The Shadow of Progress*) of the zoom lens and of selective focusing, enabling a broader range of effects. The static, telling composition (a broken wheel on Nome beach, a pioneer's gravestone, the US flag posed against a child of Russian Orthodox heritage) remains the core of the repertoire. Yet almost as important are moments in which the camera pulls back from the close-up to the wider vista (in a cinematic era ridden with fast zoom-ins, this director favoured medium-speed zoom-outs). The film pictures a paradoxical Alaska, desolate yet rich, once in gold, now in nature and history as well as oil.

Evidently it did the job. Within the UK the film's main viewership was the catch-all 'general audience', to whom it was presented, like many of the British Transport Films, as a civilised entertainment. Concurrently, BP's Alaskan office advised London that it was being used to open Alaska Travel Association conventions, in place of keynote addresses, and that many US airlines and tour operators had also requested copies (it was even used during induction of US servicemen posted to the state). When *Scotland* premiered at the Dominion, Edinburgh, it generated a wee bit more scepticism, judging by *The Scotsman*'s review:

> cynics might say it is a public relations exercise, designed to placate those who object to the way that North sea oil is being exploited. It might appear that the flowering of the Forties Field was some kind of recompense for the withering of Flodden Field. But the film ... does not give undue emphasis to the oil exploration. It occupies only a brief sequence in this skilfully compiled and compressed record of a nation's triumphs and disasters.[60]

The film is, anyway, solidly patterned on its Alaskan predecessor. Both benefit greatly from Edward Williams's luxurious, sometimes heroic, often sad musical scoring adroitly incorporating local elements (Flora MacNeill's Gaelic singing for Highland sequences, fiddles for the Lowlands, banjo and harmonica for Alaska). Some years later Shell's *Oman – Tracts of Time*, returning Williams to the model of these films after years working with lesser material, styles itself 'a portrait of the Sultanate of Oman, seen through the eyes of geology ... shaped and reshaped through prodigious tracts of time ... her present enriched by the knowledge of her distant past'. Reflecting its high budget, *Oman* has richly textured chamber music, heavy on trumpets, harp and wordless female voice. The film's concern is mineral rather than human history, animated graphics replace the maps used in the earlier films, and by this point experiments with focus and zoom were passé: the immobile tableaux are instead, as with *Turkey*, mixed with fluent, careful pans, together with a profusion of aerial shots (the Sultan provided a police helicopter, Shell a geologist-guide). Tonally, however, the film is strongly reminiscent of its BP precursors, and of *Hadrian's Wall*.

Besides *The Wheel of Islands* Williams took several 'place-histories' to treatment stage but no further. In 1976, National Benzole humiliated him by rejecting *Bath – an English Masterpiece* as an addition to the *Our National Heritage* series, in favour of a cheaper PR strategy: free drinking glasses! Much earlier, five treatments that Williams had written on his own initiative covered the Highland Clearances (*The Year of the Sheep*); the history of Japan, revealed in Hiroshige's art (*The Fifty Three Stages of the Tokaido*); the American War of Independence (*The Family Quarrel*); a biography of Kemal Ataturk (*Grey Wolf*); and a study of Welsh castles (*James of St George – Architect of Oppression*). None secured sponsorship – or broadcast commissions. Williams had hopefully submitted the first and last of them to an uninterested BBC (*The Year of the Sheep* was partially retrieved later, as *Scotland*'s best sequence, dealing with the Clearances). Of his generation, Williams seems the most disappointed by the lost opportunity that television represented, despite his reputation having been built on a style owing much to cinema tradition, little to TV innovation.

CODA: TRACTS OF TIME

In retirement, Williams has written three history books: *The Reach of Rome* (1996), *Romans and Barbarians* (1998) and *Rome and the Imperial Message* (as yet unpublished).[61] The first one's subject is the Empire's frontiers: 'having begun, forty-five years earlier, with my amateur film on Hadrian's Wall, the wheel had, in a very real sense, come full circle'. An occupational psychologist's diagnosis of Williams's intervening career might well cast him in the role of the closet scholar trapped in a worldly trade. There's a grain of truth in that. Yet the evidence on screen is of an effective, journeyman film-maker at work, and in love with his medium.

Directors whose strengths and weaknesses are enmeshed with those of their film genres, are enabled and simultaneously constrained by their conventions, have long been familiar, even cherished objects of film appreciation (and their having, as in Hollywood, a capitalist financial base is apparently no barrier). Film culture began rescuing them from disrepute over forty years ago. Its smaller documentary branch, driven by dissimilar values, largely declined to follow the trend. But the comparison remains. In Williams's field, his friend and Guild colleague Eric Marquis (or, in a different way, Geoffrey Jones) resembles directors who wrung the changes on feature-film genres by injecting an excitingly flamboyant stylisation. Williams resembles those less assertive film-makers in whose work personal and generic elements are more subtly compounded. They may falter when least equipped to deliver what convention requires (as in Williams's industrial-process films, lacking the excitement that a Marquis or Jones, or the technical precision that a de Normanville, might have brought them); or, conversely, when their ambition overstretches their genre's capacity (as in *The Tide of Traffic*). They usually work best when personality and genre are in closest alignment, as in Williams's place-histories.

A recurring feature of Derek Williams's films is the scripted, single-voice, authoritative commentary – the much-maligned 'Voice of God' – accompanying the visually (if sometimes bleakly) picturesque. We have seen that this both conformed to conventions of the prestige and travel films in which Williams specialised *and* chimed with personal inclinations. Karel Reisz's attack on spiritually aloof, verbally trite, visually ornamental tools for sponsors was squarely aimed at films more-or-less of the Williams type.[62] Reisz's critique didn't, however, account for the possibility that idioms such as Voice of God weren't inherently invalid, merely sometimes badly used, and able to bring pleasure when used well.[63] They were also of recognisable documentary lineage: Humphrey Jennings's *Family Portrait* (1950) and Basil Wright's *Waters of Time* (1951) being among immediate antecedents, and themselves descended from the purer 'poetry' of *Listen to Britain* (1942) or *Song of Ceylon*, now translated to prose. It's true that at their worst, the commentary tracks on prestige films suggest jumped-up *Reader's Digest* articles, but at their best they suggest delicately crafted, semi-poetic tracts. The dividing line could be perilously fine. Williams's commentaries typically alternate neutral, informative prose with bolder cadenced phrases. Verging occasionally on florid pomp, they usually stop short of it – just. Witness this word-montage, culled from a selection of his scripts:

> Her sailors had circumnavigated the world, her poets had circumnavigated the soul ...
>
> ... from nowhere to nowhere, following a pencilled line across an empty map ...

... July: the wheel at the bottom of its turn, the sun, a blowlamp, peeling the earth like old paint ...

... this place is a kind of frontier, between the world as it was and as it is now coming to be ...

... commuter homewards, pleasure-seeker citywards; tide and undertow, current and counter-current, evening into night ...

... the short days of winter. The crofter's life goes quieter and whispers of loneliness louder. Farming marks time. Nature hangs on, awaiting the sun's return. Life contracts to cottage and chimney corner ...

... so timeless landscapes are reduced, by time. But for man, whose view is shorter, rock is the most permanent thing he knows ...

... soil is the matrix of mankind which generates, sustains and, in the end, enfolds us all.[64]

Taking the long view, the genre documentaries in which such lines are uttered have a personality of recognisably English, middlebrow, cultural ancestry. In disposition: civilised, sober, deceptively dispassionate. In manner: literate yet visual, logical yet lyrical. Disdaining expressionism, it is a paradoxical personality: most clearly exposed when using *im*personal modes of address.[65] Classical form safely shelters furtive, fervent, romantic feeling. In cinema, we've seen, such a personality was readily recruited to meeting the needs of post-war industries that (whatever view one takes of them) have shaped today's world. Yet it also remains (whatever view one takes of it) an authentic facet of national character.

A measure of its constancy – and sincerity – in this individual case, is the stylistic similarity between Derek Williams's last film, made under contract in Oman, and his first, made in his spare time at Hadrian's Wall – in whose shadow he has instructed his sons to scatter his ashes, when the time comes.

NOTES

1. Souvenir programme for the premiere screening of *Hadrian's Wall*, 20 December 1951, Derek Williams Collection (this small collection of papers and ephemera was donated to BFI Special Collections in 2009).
2. At the film's premiere, the sound was presented in the rudimentary form of a vinyl record, played as the mute 16mm camera reversal print was projected; subsequently, further funds were found for its rerecording onto optical track married to the picture of dupe prints.
3. 'Fine Amateur Film', *Times Educational Supplement*, 29 August 1952.
4. Quoted in unidentified newspaper cutting, Williams collection.
5. Other Williams titles that would be distributed by the COI included *North Slope – Alaska* and *Algerian Pipeline*.
6. According to one unidentified cutting in the Williams collection, 'A few eyebrows were raised when the competent but modest *Oil Harbour – Aden* ... took the award for Public Relations and Prestige films in the face of strong competition': competition including Williams's own next film, Maxwell Anderson and United Steel's *Steel Rhythm*, John Armstrong's Shell opus *Song of the Clouds* and Ford and Lindsay Anderson's *Every Day Except Christmas*.

7. Carr to Williams, 28 July 1955, Williams collection.
8. Williams was filming with both 35mm and 16mm cameras (containing Eastmancolor and Kodachrome stock respectively, the latter later blown up) subjected to cold-chamber tests before departure to satisfy him that they could withstand the conditions, chemically treated and re-engineered so mittened hands could more easily operate them. However, the testing proved unnecessary. Pack ice, not excessive cold, was the true menace to expedition and shoot alike.
9. *Kinematograph Weekly*, 5 November 1956, referred to 'thrills and beauty ... a historic and important record. Brilliantly photographed and edited ... a very special offering for showmen ... A superb documentary for any audience.'
10. *Monthly Film Bulletin* vol. 25 no. 288, January 1958, p. 12.
11. It also had a certain impact overseas, winning 1960's Blue Ribbon Award from the American Educational Film Library Association, having previously won a bronze medal at the Brussels World Fair.
12. The title refers to Mesjit-I-Sulaiman, where the Anglo-Persian Oil Company's most productive early well was drilled.
13. *The Economist* proclaimed it 'excellent ... it is impossible to be unmoved by the sheer force of tradition and procedure in the daily life of the staff of the Bank', 'Old Leading Lady', *The Economist*, 30 July 1960, p. 27.
14. Williams remained in touch with 'Dal' until the death of the older man, of whom he says that he was 'a forceful, even a domineering producer, who sought to have a hand in the writing, to sit on the director's shoulder during shooting and ... he would not hesitate to take over in the cutting room ... While liking and respecting him personally; and while it was encouraging to be chosen as – so to speak – Jennings' successor, I was thoroughly unhappy with the Bank film ... Here ... was a smug and pompous sponsor, and a highly conservative producer, deferential to the sponsor and patronising to me. I have often thought about the Dalrymple-Jennings relationship and wondered that there was room in *Family Portrait* for two such personalities. Jennings was by then a decade dead and, of course, I should have questioned Dal on the matter; but I was young, on tiptoe and felt it impolitic to pry.' These recollections are quoted from correspondence between Williams and the author, sent on various dates between 2008 and 2010, as are all unattributed quotations from Williams used in this essay. I am very grateful to Derek Williams for his erudite and unfailingly courteous assistance.
15. *Kinematograph Weekly*, 9 August 1962, p. 19.
16. Williams remembers the film having been badly received by the CFF committee, on which Michael Powell was an imperious presence and who savaged it for amateurish performances. Williams submitted a third treatment to the CFF but it was rejected, though a copy survives in the collection of papers he has donated to the BFI. *Mystery of the Mist* (1962) is a Lake District-set atmospheric caper, for which Williams drew on memories of his World War II evacuation to Cumbria.
17. They are also relatives by marriage: Williams's wife and Stafford's are sisters.
18. John Chittock and Jill Sykes, 'Don't Tell Me – Show Me', *Imagery* vol. 18 no. 2, p. 23.
19. Atlantic Richfield Company (later bought by BP).
20. 'On a different occasion a senior official of the National Film Board of Canada told me that it was almost essential for Oscar nominees to emply an LA lobbyist, and confided that *they* always did so. The idea had never occurred to me, or my sponsors.'
21. A mere three years after *Planet Water*, the BBC televised David Attenborough's *Life on Earth* series, incidentally scored by Edward Williams, and bringing a far richer study of the natural world into people's very living rooms. At this point, with documentary film's remaining advantages over television

– budgets, schedules and cinematic aesthetics – having slipped from its grip, only to assert themselves so triumphantly in the rival medium, the scale of the young pretender's rout of its elder must finally have become inescapable.

22. Williams, BECTU History Project interview conducted by (fellow maker of sponsored films) Glyn Jones, 1 May 2002.
23. Williams effectively took over from the retired Stuart Legg as Armstrong's scriptwright.
24. Williams, *A Sense of the Soil: An Outline Treatment and Discussion submitted as a Tender for a Shell Film on the subject of Soil*, June 1988, Williams collection.
25. Email to author, 14 May 2008.
26. At one of the regular screening nights run by the ACT documentary branch, on 19 February 1957, Williams introduced *Foothold* to his fellow members, by saying 'he thought that films came into two categories: "films that you control and films that control you" ', *Foothold* of course falling into the latter category (Steve Cox, 'Shorts & Documentary Section', *Film & TV Technician*, March 1957, p. 37). Williams's natural bias is equally clearly to the former, perhaps best exemplified by *Shadow of Progress* and *Alaska – The Great Land.*
27. 'North Slope – Alaska', *Imagery* vol. 18 no. 1, Summer 1965, p. 9 (emphasis added). The article is subtitled '7,700 miles from Guild House'.
28. The director remembers: 'Our large, 5kw lamps were hired from LA and brought in by an intrepid bush pilot who ventured to land the two cargoes on a nearby, small frozen lake, in the almost total dark. These now glared balefully across the drilling floor, revealing a Walpurgisnight dance of toiling men ...'
29. Williams was first notified of this cultural change when sitting in a public cinema in which *North Slope* was playing: 'the film's final line played out, "But in their way, they are giants"; and I heard a whisper behind me: "But in their way, they like the dough". I thought, "did I spend a winter in the frozen tundra to hear that?"'. BP's sponsorship rebounded more quickly within Alaska. Due to the film's release, Alaskans discovered that Canadian contractors had been used. The film thus underscored the necessity of BP counting local affection. Robert Beatty speaks the commentary with distinctively Canadian vowel pronounciation.
30. Earlier, Williams's salvage-job on *North Sea Quest* had taken the characteristic route of overlaying romantic history onto modern development: 'the lonely coast; the quiet coast ... once it was the noisy coast, the raider's coast, the invader's coast, where Saxon and Viking waded ashore'.
31. Lombard, 'Drama In and Out of Court', *Financial Times*, 2 August 1960, p. 3.
32. David Robinson, 'Two Documentaries', *Sight & Sound* vol. 27 no. 3, Winter 1957/8, p. 149. The other documentary discussed by Robinson is Anthony Simmons' *Blood is Life*: 'a less satisfactory film'.
33. J. Gibbon, 'There Was a Door', *Imagery* vol. 1 no. 1, Summer 1958, p. 19.
34. Mrs P. L., 'There Was a Door', *Radio Times*, 9–5 February 1958, p. 9.
35. 'with one exception all the "actors" in this film, including all the "leads" are true life characters ... As to the exception – a professional actor who had to be brought in to substitute for a "player" who was ill – finding him can be an interesting diversion but you will need to be very shrewd to succeed': Gibbon, 'There Was a Door', p. 20. Gibbon does not reveal the answer to his puzzle: the actor, a local rep performer, plays the character Neville, one of the beneficiaries of industrial training. Locations are also 'real'. As well as the Occupational Centre, the film was shot mainly at the Royal Albert Hospital, Lancaster – which supplies the imposing exteriors and grounds, in which the almost gothic opening scene of the film is shot – and at the Brockhall Hospital, Blackburn. Their subsequent fates are telling.

Both closed in the 1990s, following the first really concerted (and controversial) push for 'care in the community' (the legislation following the Commission report had not been backed up with extensive funding; the Royal Albert, indeed, grew even more overcrowded in the interim).

36. Something of the film's character – drama with an icy mood – reappears in *A Bit of Doing*, which is after all another film with a social motive (in that case – the promotion of Poppy Day and a respect for military sacrifice – one accepted throughout the political mainstream though applauded most enthusiastically by conservatives).
37. *Film User*, December 1957, p. 581.
38. 'has the desirable qualities of experience and competence, but possibly not quite the spark to lift this film out of the rut. Her fees lie outside the scope of the budget'. National Library of Scotland SSA: 4/11/464.
39. *Treatment for MOH Centenary Film*, 8 February 1963, Scottish Screen Archive special collections: SSA: 4/11/464.
40. Ballantine to Hardy, 17 March 1963, SSA: 4/11/464.
41. Hardy to Ballantine, 19 March 1963, SSA: 4/11/464.
42. Williams, 'I Do – And I Understand', *BP Shield*, issue unidentified, p. 4.
43. Ibid. Stafford presented the film at the British Federation of Film Societies' 'Best sponsored films of 1965' event at the NFT where, *Film User* reported, he gave a 'lengthy discourse ... on the sponsor/producer relationship' (other films screened on this occasion, indicating the sheer variety of current sponsored output, included *The River Must Live* and Derrick Knight and Partners' *Stress*). Gloria Tessler, 'Sponsors or Patrons – Is There a Difference?', *Film User*, January 1967, p. 26.
44. BECTU History Project interview.
45. Grants and loans from several western states augmented the funds provided by the Bank: those pledged by the USA and UK contributed to breaking deadlock within the Treaty talks. The scale of the British funding, together with the reputation of British documentary, still high abroad, were factors in the World Bank's decision to send its sponsorship the Guild's way.
46. Chittock and Sykes, 'Don't Tell Me', pp. 12–13, 23–4.
47. Drake to Williams, 4 January 1971, Williams collection.
48. BP branches overseas arranged similar events.
49. Unidentified magazine report, Williams collection.
50. BECTU History Project interview with Stafford, conducted by Rodney Giesler, 20 July 2001. Williams further notes that Stafford 'was aware that industry's secrect compact, never to mention its own responsibility in this matter, must at last be threatened ... hearing of the approach of European Conservation Year he took it upon himself to act. When I had written an Outline Treatment – consisting of a summary of the subject's pros and cons, backed with references from environmental literature, such as it then was ... mainly American and rather emotional – he did in fact form a scientific committee, partly as an act of self-protection and partly to grill me and scutinise my document. They were severely critical, and somewhat scathing of my sources, but Roly somehow got me through ... It may certainly be said that *Shadow*, the world's first comprehensive account of the cost of progress, is *his* monument as much as mine.' Stafford adds that he took the precaution of screening the film to Sir Eric, with whom he had a good relationship, before showing it to the rest of BP's board. Had the film not gone on to be a success, Stafford's continued employment by BP would have been unlikely. As this book went to press, Williams sadly advised the author: 'Surprising that I should ever say it, but as events in the Gulf of Mexico went from bad to worse I actually began to feel embarrassed to have made *Shadow*

and other BP films with environmental promise ... Documentary is linked to life. The advantages, in terms of strength and conviction, are obvious. But there are disadvantages too. The link can only be as strong as the sponsorial chain.'

51. A snapshot indication of how both films were being discussed within BP Films while still at treatment stage is given by this surviving memo from G. R. Sharp to Stafford: 'the usual masterly exposition of a modern problem ... Like *TSOP* as originally conceived, however, I do not think that the story gives sufficient indication of what we should do about the very real problem of the car ... *TSOP* in its final form certainly encourages the man in the street to do something about pollution, even if only to take his own litter home. *TTOT* presents an admittedly pretty terrible problem but is rather weak on the positive side. In its present form it might deter a motorist from taking his car into town, but I do not know what other practical step the man in the street could take. The author is certainly a master of the combination of words and picture, but is he in this draft really telling us anything we do not know already?', Sharp to Stafford, 23 March 1971, BP Video Library production files collection.
52. On the film's release, the director wrote to *The Shetland Times*: 'I cannot recall a place or a people for whom I came to feel greater affection or higher regard ... [in the 1970s] national scrutiny turned to North Sea oil. Here was a magical solution, an Aladdin's lamp which Britain was impatient to rub ... But a mere 18,000 people refused to be knocked down in the rush ... a triumph of sense and steadfastness ... All who hope that our national strategies should be shaped not to impress bankers, nor for the approval of economics correspondents, nor for prestige, but simply for people, will always be in Shetland's debt.' Williams, 'Double Debt', *Shetland Times*, 24 June 1977, p. 12.
53. Up Helly Aa was a nineteenth-century invention – and by then, many mainlanders were migrating to Shetland. Recent genetic study indicates that a plurality, but not quite the majority, of Shetland genes are Scandinavian (admittedly, the population has been further diversified since the film's making, thanks largely to the growth that has followed the oil developments).
54. Michie to Williams, tender invitation, 16 June 1988, Williams collection.
55. All quotes from Williams, *A Sense of the Soil: An Outline Treatment and Discussion submitted as a Tender for a Shell Film on the subject of Soil*, June 1988, Williams collection.
56. Williams, 'At the Root of it All', *Shell World*, June 1990, p. 18.
57. Williams, *Inner City: A Treatment for a Thirty Minute BP film on Inner City Decay and its Associated Problems*, September 1981, Williams collection.
58. *Hadrian's Wall* souvenir programme.
59. Although Williams's films would suggest a preference for writing over directing, a letter from him, published by *Film User* in 1957, suggests otherwise: 'the discipline of a writer's plan is often essential and everyone has seen films which are poorer for starting without it. But ... the script is not so much the writer's blueprint for the director, as the producer's compact with his sponsor'. During the war, 'the documentary branch which bore the choicest fruit was that in which directors started with a couple of thoughts and a dash of vision and *felt* their way to a film, shaping it as they went ... This method might have been common today. But the post-war boom of industrial sponsorship reversed the trend ... the sponsor wanted to know what he was getting; and producers became infected with script-fever.' Williams, 'Realism and Spontaneity', *Film User*, March 1958, p. 123.
60. Allen Wright, 'Films', *The Scotsman*, 6 July 1973.
61. Derek Williams, *The Reach of Rome* (London: Constable, 1996); Derek Williams, *Romans and Barbarians* (New York: St Martins Press, 1998).

62. 'those who make colour films with immaculately photographed landscapes, expensive-sounding commentaries and symphonic musical backgrounds ... the prestige merchants'. Karel Reisz, 'A Use for Documentary', *Universities & Left Review* no. 3, Winter 1958, p. 24.
63. Counterfactual history: what if Williams had found himself in the public sector? It's very hard to visualise him fitting into the NCB Film Unit but easy to see him making something of BTF's lusher cinema releases: the likes of John Taylor's *The England of Elizabeth* or Tony Thompson's *Any Man's Kingdom*. However, Williams says: 'I recall turning down a film offered by Edgar Anstey about an English county. He showed me one, already made in the same series, about Sussex [this must have been *Down to Sussex* (1964), directed by Kenneth Fairbairn]: how twee and trivial I thought it. I remembered a line in its commentary about 'the dying art of the thatcher' and hi-jacked the phrase to describe little, decorative films of slight relevance to our times, such as should be left for the likes of *Pathe Pictorial*. Alas Edgar, who had made far better films, never contacted me again.' How Voice-of-God gets used is indeed a more interesting question than whether it is used or not.
64. The quotes are, respectively, from *Scotland*, *North Slope Alaska*, *Indus Waters*, two from *The Tide of Traffic*, *The Shetland Experience*, *Oman – Tracts of Time* and *A Stake in the Soil*.
65. It may be revealing that Williams had a weakness for inserting Hitchcockian cameos into his decidedly unflamboyant films: to list but a few, Williams can be spotted sleeping on a park bench outside the filling-station in *The Cattle Carters*, chatting to an Istanbul shoeshiner in *Turkey – The Bridge*, smoking a cigar while being shaved in *North Slope – Alaska*, birdwatching in *The Shetland Experience*, sifting soil in *South East Pipeline*.

21 Savage Voyages: *Eric Marquis*

REBECCA VICK

The Savage Voyage (1971) begins with highly stylised scenes of copulation, ejaculation, conception, embryonic development and then, in a single close-up, an opening vulva, the crown of an emerging head, the rush of blood and breaking waters, the shoulders, the umbilical cord untangled, the girl-child slithering out to be laid in a pool of blood and the detritus of birth, the mother's vulva closing with relief from pain. Two unblinking minutes of film that dare their spectators to look away. A female voiceover says:

> I came out of a kind of violence. A million years of genetic memory may have crippled me from conception – programmed my growing cells struggling to expand my mother's virgin uterus. After nine centuries of growth and adaptation, 'they' made the first vicious assault upon my total security; made me make a bloody, savage voyage down the birth canal; thrust and crushed me out through the strangulating way whence half myself had come with such lubricious ease.

Brutal words and graphic images are the distinctive motifs of this film's distinct creator, Eric Marquis. His is not a name that readily springs into the minds of those who have studied British documentary. Yet his output in post-war sponsored film-making was considerable, and his version of 'documentary' a fascinating one. Marquis's career of scripting, directing and producing spanned the 1950s through to the 1980s, totalling some sixty titles. A versatile film-maker, Marquis made public- information documentaries, industrial films and corporately sponsored promotional pictures. In all of these, he was particularly skilled at adding humour and excitement, sometimes surprising depths and, now and again, a certain savagery. Although his films have little in common with the canonic social documentaries of the 1930s and '40s, still less with TV current affairs, they often amount to 'social documentary' of a different and compelling sort. Marquis frequently constructed a vivid, unflinching representation of reality, informed by a detailed understanding of his subjects – this is particularly true of his works relating to mental illness, a theme rarely covered in the non-fiction films of earlier epochs. In histories of documentary, however, his presence is elusive and rarely referenced. Many of Marquis's best films were commissioned to highly specific briefs, and were intended mainly for showing to professional or educational organisations, whereas the best work of talented sponsored film-makers was more often distributed publicly. This contributed to Marquis's lack of profile within general film culture – even further out of sight, out of mind, than many of the others (themselves not exactly household names) profiled in this book. Yet one of the most impressive features of these films is that they refuse to allow their imaginative scope to be limited by these circumstances: Marquis assumes that their 'specialised' audiences have the right to be

Eric Marquis

entertained, excited or provoked, as well as informed, by first-rate cinema. If the film-maker has an important message for them from his sponsor, he has all the more responsibility to give them such cinema.

This chapter recalls and reappraises Eric Marquis's contribution to the field of documentary film-making. Although mentioning every stage of his career, it focuses most upon his 1960s and early 1970s work, during the later years of the Film Producers Guild. Incidentally proving that it was possible to do very interesting work in this commercial set-up, it demonstrates that this talented but unjustly neglected film-maker's choices of subject and approach to them were often brave, and the results he achieved thought-provoking and stylish. Perhaps, long after his retirement, Eric Marquis may yet become a cult film-maker.

A foundling, born on Guernsey in 1928, Eric Marquis was taken to the slums of Stockport in the 1940s. There, he found distraction from its squalid conditions, in what he describes as the 'womb-like venues' of the library and the picture-house, where, as a boy, he was able to educate himself and to escape from the grim reality of daily life through film. At fourteen, Marquis left school and spent all of his days in the warm and darkened comfort of Stockport's cinemas, earning his wages rewinding 35mm prints.[1] Two years later he ventured to the metropolis in search of film-related work:

> I travelled to London for the first time, and slept on a park bench in Hammersmith (I had no money), as I tried to storm the gates of Riverside Studios to get to see Sydney Box and join his (then) Company of Youth, which included technicians. I couldn't get past the gatekeeper and returned whence I came, defeated.[2]

Undeterred, Marquis wrote to Box to make an appointment and, to his surprise, was offered an interview. His film aspirations were put on hold, however, when he received a less than welcome invitation to complete two years' national service.[3] Once this was over, Marquis was free to pursue his film goals and got a job as a chief dubbing projectionist at the Mancunian Film Studios. Founded by John E. Blakeley, the man who had put George Formby on the road to film comedy stardom, these studios, in Dickenson Road, Rusholme, had successfully brought 'Hollywood to Manchester', turning out a particular brand of Lancashire comedy.[4]

Marquis then became a trainee photographer at the Forestry Commission, based in Hampshire. Having passed all his British Institute of Professional Photographers exams, Marquis was the only member of his small department qualified to make a film. So, aged twenty-four, he gained his first opportunity to direct and edit, making *The Culbin Story* (1954), a factual film exploring the reforestation of the Barony of Culbin on the Moray Firth coastline. It did not go unnoticed and was programmed in that year's Edinburgh Film Festival.[5]

Marquis, now a camera operator for ATV, used the film as a calling card to approach many documentary companies. Eventually he caught the eye of producer, director and scriptwriter John Haggarty who was currently at British Films, where he offered Marquis his commercial directorial debut, *To The Four Corners* (1957). Targeting mothers and their children, this charming but overly long colour travelogue, strangely reminiscent of the travel films of the 1920s, examined four picturesque parts of the British Isles: Ulster, Cardiff, the Hebridian island of Lewis and Lincoln. The Cardiff section stands out as a particularly interesting social record, illustrating something of what life was like for children playing in the backstreets of Tiger Bay and reflecting the city's multicultural society, with its inclusion of a West Indian sailor's perspective. Sponsored by Brooke Bond Tea, *To The Four Corners* cheerfully embraced product placement to demonstrate that despite contrasting geography and lifestyles, the nation was united by this brand of its favourite beverage. Marquis's rather clumsy first attempt at professional film-making may have reached large numbers of viewers. It was part of a big programme of roadshows 'that operated throughout the country through the company's fourteen regional sales offices, each with its own mobile unit, consisting of a 16mm Bell & Howell projector, a Ford 7cwt van and a driver/projectionist'.[6] Prints of the film would also have been hired out to Women's Institute branches and similar organisations, through film libraries. The relatively large-scale promotion and backing by its sponsor meant that *To The Four Corners* had its fair share of exposure. It was a very respectable place for Marquis to begin honing his skills for a professional life in sponsored documentary.

His next project, however, was a comedy drama, *Shamus* (1958), which he scripted as well as directed, under the auspices of the low-budget production company Border Films. Featuring a cheeky Irish orphan, who captures a leprechaun (played by a dwarf performer, 'Tiny Littler'), and is then cursed for stealing the mythical creature's pot of gold, this adventure film was shot using a Newman Sinclair 35mm camera, with no guide track, despite being all dialogue! It benefited from the British quota system and was distributed as a second feature rather than being pitched only at children. Received positively in the press, it was described in *Kinematograph Weekly* as a 'novel story' of 'wholesome sentiment' and 'clean comedy'.[7] However, Marquis, who had dreamed of making features as a youth, was not offered any more fiction and instead went on to direct the first of many careers-guidance films. However, his creative writing and his appreciation for drama and comedy would often be applied to his later documentary work, the better to communicate with and win over his audiences.

Marquis's next film was *They Chose the Sea* (1960), produced by Jack Howells at his production company and sponsored by BP for use in technical colleges. According to one reviewer:

> This is an attractive film that gains stature from the choice of the voyage after which the Commodore of BP Tanker fleet retired; his farewell party not only established authenticity and adds human interest; it emphasises the continuity of the fleet and, of course, shows youngsters the heights to which they can reach.[8]

By no means the first picture to explore the possibility of a career at sea, it was, however, complimented by *The Times* as: 'certainly one of the best to date'.[9] This well-composed and appealing piece of filmcraft lavishly illustrated the experiences of a modern-day mariner aboard BP's flagship 50,000 tonne oil carrier. The daily routine of its star, *British Queen*, with her 'wondrous heritage', is fully mapped by the director for the curiosity of potential young recruits. The commentator's promise is that if they did choose the sea, 'Their future is as broad as the horizon.' Counterpointing the main narrator, the additional commentary representing Jim, the recruit, successfully conveys the voice of youth, and makes a connection to the audience to which it is designed to appeal. Marquis had already realised he could only capture the imaginations of those he was tasked with addressing by telling credible human stories containing convincing characterisation to which his intended viewers could relate. For the young men watching *They Chose the Sea*, he turned a potentially tedious subject into a genuine and attractive prospect.

Increased confidence and reputation led to this adaptable director applying to join the Film Producers Guild in 1960, rotating between several of its member production companies. Marquis's first job was at Greenpark Productions, to script and oversee, under producer G. Buckland Smith, a safety film sponsored by the Central Electricity Generating Board. Starkly named *Survival* (1961), this dramatised documentary highlighted the dangers of ignoring safety regulations and misusing equipment on power-station building sites. As Marquis said at the time:

> There are several deep-rooted convictions to be overcome. A man's unshatterable belief in his own longevity. The belief that avoidance of accidents depends solely on the skill of the individual. The belief that the adoption of safety precautions is somehow antimasculine and that one would lose the respect of one's own hormones.[10]

When an operative is permanently disabled as a consequence of not being 'safety-conscious' a safety officer is employed, but treated with contempt by the old hands on the site. Consequently another accident occurs, this time fatal. Buckland-Smith intended to 'hold up a mirror to the audience, a convex mirror, with its wide angle of acceptance with, at the same time, certain things exaggerated',[11] but critics seemed not to understand this dual aim. *The Times* saw a 'certain lack of conviction in the portrayal of some of the incidents',[12] while, conversely, *Film User* found it 'over-dramatic'[13] (some of Marquis's later mental health films were similarly criticised by the medical profession).[14] *Monthly Film Bulletin* provided a more balanced view, labelling *Survival* a 'well-intentioned and capable short which doesn't pull its punches, yet doesn't altogether succeed'.[15] This is never an easy balance to strike, but, to anyone familiar with Marquis's canon, it is clear he often preferred to confront, horrify or unsettle his viewers, to fix their attention on what they believed to be a familiar subject. A number of his films have something of a B-horror-movie, or exploitation-pic, quality to them and are delivered with unusually high aesthetic ingenuity, belying their small budgets. The effect is achieved visually, with gruesome imagery and snappy editing, and in this case the grim accident. These 'horrors' drive home the film's point, despite the obvious use of a dummy (even Greenpark's relatively good budgets did not stretch to feature film special effects).

1962 saw Marquis working with a lower-rent Guild outfit, Harold Goodwin Productions, to make two much more lighthearted and straightforward promotional films, which were positively received. *Headline Hovis* featured a zealous journalist, who goes to examine all parts of the eponymous bread company's operation. *Handle with Care*, sponsored by Domestos, was directed at shopkeepers, to promote their 'Stergene' germ-killing steriliser, which guaranteed a 'completely safe and satisfactory standard of hygiene' in shops.[16] In the film, John Ross Senior, owner of a grocery shop, is suddenly taken ill and his inexperienced son John Junior has to step into the breach. He's seen struggling to cope until his Uncle Bob, a modern grocer, arrives and shows him how poor cleanliness is endangering the family business. The message is uncomplicated: 'The shop which looks clean is not necessarily safe' and good hygiene encourages the 'keepability' of food and therefore ensures greater profit.[17] No doubt due to Domestos wanting to stamp authenticity on the piece, a north London grocer was appointed as technical advisor. Present for every sequence of the film, the aptly named Mr R. Haddock even instructed the actors in such matters as how to slice cheese and bone bacon.[18] Such attention to detail, married to the family drama, meant that Marquis was able to construct an accomplished and lively, entertaining and persuasive piece. That the film itself, not just the products it advocates, was backed by glossy promotional material reflected the sponsor's belief in its effectiveness. The power of marketing was not lost on Marquis, who produced very lavish booklets for some of his later productions, notably the films he made for another big corporation, Roche Products.

The pace picked up from 1964, when Marquis made three films: *A Sound of Living*, *Plutonic Attachments* and *Worthy of Their Wings*. The first two were with Verity Films whose founder had been none other than his childhood hero, Sydney Box. Commissioned by the General Post Office, the first of these industrial films explored the labyrinthine manual and mechanical operations behind making a telephone call. A contemporary write-up in *The Times* praised *A Sound of Living* for its use of effective imagery in place of reliance on patronising commentary. It was also complimented on 'some nice touches of humour'.[19] Marquis never missed an opportunity to engage his crowd through adding a laugh, when it was appropriate: his contemporary and friend, the Greenpark film-maker Derek Williams, remembers him as: 'ever the humorist, of the tongue-in-cheek, twinkle-in-the-eye kind'.[20]

Oswald Skilbeck, who had produced the GPO film, also worked with Marquis on *Plutonic Achievement*, commissioned by Shell-Mex and BP. Written by Skilbeck and Richard Taylor, this fifteen-minute short extolled the benefits of oil-fired heating to the British public. Bill Megarry edited the film and, like Skilbeck, would have a role to play in Marquis's later projects. *Worthy of Their Wings*, in comparison, was for distribution to overseas audiences via the British Information Services, and was set in part in the North African desert. Focusing on the Royal Air Force, this military recruiting film was produced by Greenpark for the Air Ministry through the COI. Marquis did not complete the project after difficulties shooting in Libya and has never seen the finished film.[21] However, this range of productions underscored the director's adaptability and helped establish relationships with future collaborators.

The accommodating director now maintained a consistent level of employment and, though not yet at its peak, Marquis's increasingly unique style crept further and further into his creations. His two best films yet materialised in 1965 – though they're as different from one another as could be imagined. Very much of its time, *Out Shopping* (1965) is a guidance film for the uninitiated purchaser – a fable of consumer rights.[22] In it we see newly wed Mrs A.'s excessive supermarket sweep of exotic okra and aubergine, juxtaposed with shots of the purchases of the seasoned but overcautious housewife Mrs B., who only stocks up on the essentials, while offering Mrs A. sage advice on her statutory rights. This potentially very boring subject was tackled with real comic panache by Mr Marquis, who was commended by John Chittock for opting for black-and-white film when using pixilation:

> A technique by which movement is speeded up into the jerky action of a silent comedy. Yet there is nothing naive about it and few audiences will fail to be highly delighted (and convinced). The point is, of course that such a style reminiscent of the Keystone Cops – would be hopeless in the realistic world of colour. In black-and-white it looks just right.[23]

Marquis's distinctly unusual conception and approach to the making of *Out Shopping* gave it genuine entertainment value. Funny and visually memorable, it stood apart from the crowd and got its sponsor's message noticed. Fabulous 1960s organ music, devised by Gerald Shaw, is played enthusiastically throughout, and slots in perfectly with the 'Keystone Cops' visuals, while joyously bringing it bang up to date.[24] The film was produced for the Consumer Council, a body campaigning for a fairer deal for consumers, especially the more vulnerable. Concerned with the dangers of indiscriminate consumerism, for them this was a significant first moving-image commission, and noteworthy for Marquis as being his first collaboration with scriptwriter Anthony Short. Having targeted housewives, the sponsor spent time and money identifying possible audiences and distribution mechanisms: advice often given to sponsors by the likes of *Film User*, but not always taken by them. The National Council for Women, the Townswomen's Guild, the Mothers' Union, the National Association of Women's Clubs, the Women's Institute, the Cooperative Women's Guild and the Women's Gas Federation were all pinpointed as organisations to be approached. In an article in *Imagery*, the Film Producers Guild journal, the sponsor acknowledges the power of Short and Marquis's humour in helping to convey their message: 'From the start the audience is laughing, not at Mrs A. or Mrs B., but at the fixes they get themselves into at one time or another – so we understand, and take note.'[25] It's still a distinctively funny and stylish short, and one its director should be recognised for.

And Then There Was One ... (1965), in contrast, marks a really serious moment in Marquis's career, being the first of his medical films, and one that received much praise in its field. For this Verity production, Marquis had teamed up with cameraman Josef Ambor, with whom he frequently worked thereafter, and once again, with producer Oswald Skilbeck. Sponsored by home-grown pharmaceutical manufacturer, Allen and Hanburys, it is a consistently fascinating dramatised documentary, looking at the diagnosis and treatment of clinical depression, and the chemistry of the drugs on offer from its sponsor. It manages to be a conscientious, incisive study of the subject. *And Then There Was One ...*, won a silver award in the 1966 British Medical Association Film Competition and was nominated to represent the UK at the Seventh International Industrial Film Festival in Venice, having already gained from BISFA a British Industrial Film Award in the category of health.[26]

Intended for general practitioners, the narration is delivered by Dr David Stafford-Clark, giving the piece a sense of medical authority. A physician who helped change the face of psychiatry in Britain during the post-war era, Stafford-Clark's gift for communication and the celebrity he gained as one of the first television doctors helped him change prevailing attitudes to mental illness. For him the purpose of medicine was to relieve suffering, and therefore the needs of the patient were paramount. He felt the doctor's job was to comfort as well as to cure; to explain as well as to treat. This attitude is evident in this film and in Marquis's later works examining psychological disorders. Stafford-Clark had written the book *Psychiatry Today* in 1951 and, a year before the Marquis film, the seminal textbook, *Psychiatry For Students*. Having been on radio in the 1950s, the psychiatrist had moved into television, appearing on the BBC's groundbreaking series *Lifeline*. According to his son, film and television producer Nigel Stafford-Clark, the area outside his specialised field that gave him the greatest pleasure was his work in film. He loved the cinema, and was happy for it to make use of his expertise, which Marquis effectively showcased here.[27]

Marquis's tense and characteristically unflinching dramatised documentary revolves around four fictional characters suffering from varying degrees of anxiety, who on visiting their doctors, receive differing levels of sympathy and dissimilar treatments. The general practitioner in the third of the four case studies overlooks the severity of the patient's mental turmoil and, in this compelling portrayal of crisis, Marquis takes the opportunity to give his audience of medical professionals an abrupt jolt with a realistically grim depiction of the suicide of this tortured soul, the 'one' referred to in the film's title. This is doubly horrifying because the respectable, bowler-hatted and stiff upper-lipped character seems initially the least likely to go through with such an act. At the end of this bleak film, the audience is left in suspense, with the fourth and last patient's course of medication up for debate, the outcome unknown. This suspended ending is cleverly used to underline the fact that a patient's destiny is so often dependent on a clinician's actions – or lack of – in the case of mental illness as much as any physical affliction. This picture succeeds because by combining a clever concept, believable human scenarios, unshakably tough visual realism and sharp editing, its audience is given no option but to confront the issues. A brave gamble for Marquis, it was one that paid off, gaining awards from those it addressed – the medical community – as well as recognition from the film industry. Significantly, too, parallels can be drawn between this and his later documentaries on mental disorders. Unlike the distressed characters of the narrative, the film-maker was, for once, not overlooked by his own sponsored film community and he was critically applauded for his efforts. His talent had not, however, been recognised by the British film industry as a whole.

Also released in 1965, *People Like Us* was a Technical & Scientific Films production for the sponsor Freemans, concerned with the cost of mistakes made at work, and the consequences of those errors on customer care. This was the dullest of Marquis's projects, in what had been an amazingly varied year. Rather randomly, he had also written the commentary for an episode of a travelogue series, *Wonderful Switzerland* (1965). Unashamedly a jobbing film-maker, he did, after all, have a mortgage and family to support. The high volume of work that year may in part also account for its inconsistencies. What is important to stress, however, is that Marquis was at this time producing his most diverse work, and sometimes deploying his already well-developed tongue-in-cheek sense of humour to converse successfully with the general viewer, while at other times using an evolving brutal, abrupt and uniquely challenging style to catch the eye of his more specialised audiences.

In a much more relaxed vein, *Vision in the High Street* (1966), as with *Handle with Care*, promoted the idea that shop modernisation would lead to 'profitability'. Intended for the Chamber of Commerce and Trade, the National Association of Shopkeepers and Shopfitters, and produced for the Glass Advisory Council by Cecil Musk, this thirty-minute film was designed to inform and instruct the independent trader on how he might increase turnover. Topics on rejuvenating independent shops included interior and exterior design, how to apply for planning permission, and guidance on the managing of finances associated with modernisation.[28] Marquis also now made an advert for ICI that incorporated an animated sequence: this was his first and only film to use a cartoon. *Canary Islands Cable* (1966) was yet another contrast: an internal short for the staff of Standard Telephones & Cables. Made again with Skilbeck and Ambor, this self-promotional commission outlined the company's background, highlighting the difficulties of telephone communication between Spain and the Canaries, demonstrating how the laying of the sponsor's cables solved the problem.[29] Having been distributed only through the companies themselves, there seems, unfortunately, to have been little written response to these films, and in neither case does the BFI National Archive hold any of the film elements.

In 1967, Marquis directed a 'beautifully presented impression' (as opposed to a scientific account) of the creative effort involved in oil-industry research and product testing.[30] As so often, Marquis's unusual take on a topic set him apart from his contemporaries. *Search and Research* was intended to explain the range of BP's activities to uninitiated audiences overseas, and included claims (in keeping with Shell's more famous films about famine) that the company's studies were in part helping to prevent starvation. Here, BP's Research Centre in Sunbury-on-Thames is seen to be 'sometimes making zero – more often making tomorrow'. This visually rich prestige film successfully illustrates a 'melting pot of progress', with colourful close-ups of bubbling test tubes and other scientific processes interspersed with black-and-white photomontages of eccentric scientists and their experiments. Marquis's visually stimulating approach depicts a weird and wonderful world that comes alive for its viewers, far more accessible and exciting than it would have been otherwise. Despite the 'fine' photography, however, critics raised objections to the film's 'light-weight approach'.[31] As it was pitched at lay audiences, coming afresh to the subject, these comments seem a little unfair. Both the lyrical commentary and Johnny Hawksworth's library music were attacked further in *Film User* for 'getting the better of the commentator – whose delivery, incidentally, may strike some as too "poetic"'.[32] Again, a harsh assessment for this film dealing with a dry topic, and one that needed to use all the means at its disposal to engage its uninitiated audience. Successful in conveying its message, in that year *Search and Research* claimed a silver award at the Eleventh International Industrial Film Festival, in Florence. 'Company portrait' films are all too often boring for non-employees – and sometimes even to the intended audience – but Marquis's attempt was, at least, uniquely stylish. Furthermore, what a contrast in quality *Search and Research* makes with Marquis's last attempt at a pure prestige film, *To the Four Corners*, back in 1957. In 1970, Marquis directed another short for BP, called *Food From Oil*, produced by Verity Films' managing director Seafield Head. It illustrated, like its predecessor, improvements in the refinery process and showed how it was possible to produce protein from oil to help solve world food shortages.

Marquis was subsequently involved in a couple of minor productions[33] before really coming into his own with *Time Out of Mind* (1968), one of his most compelling, dynamic and (albeit again only within the industrial films field) acclaimed cinematic works, winning as it did the Industrial Film Correspondents Director's Award, a Silver Award from the British Medical Association and a much sought-after BISFA Gold Award. According to the sponsor, the transnational pharmaceutical company Roche Products:

> *Time Out of Mind* projects the academic and clinical knowledge of a consultant psychiatrist through the creative skill and talent of a writer and film director. This marriage of two disciplines enables the audience to share in a disturbing, but clinically illuminating way, the psychiatric patient's whole experience of breakdown, treatment and recovery.[34]

Marquis was now the director of Verity Films and this was the first of four Guild productions he devised for Roche. It was a trusting and winning collaboration, whereby Marquis was able to push forward the creative boundaries of his projects without fear of interference. Continuing the established creative/clinical partnership, Stafford-Clark is again the advisor and commentator. As with its predecessor, three emotionally disturbed patients' case histories are dramatically reconstructed,

Severed foot (aka toilet roll), in *Time of Terror*

although this time in vivid colour and with more striking effects. On reviewing *Time Out of Mind*, Ken Gay positioned it as a social documentary: 'not in any sense a sales film for its sponsor but a fairly successful attempt, despite some of the loose ends and some measure of failure to create absolute credibility with the actors, to win sympathy for people in extreme psychological states'.[35] The film illuminates in a visually brazen and experimental way the debilitating effect of mental illness. Imaginatively but discreetly conveying the message of its sponsor, it shows real insight and sensitivity towards its subjects. On restricted loan to those working in the field of psychiatry, it apparently reached 26 per cent of the profession within the first six months of its release.[36] The brutally graphic opening depiction of an elderly lady slitting her wrists brings mental turmoil sharply into focus. This visceral, even gruesome, shock tactic is similar to the first sequence of Marquis's later work *Time of Terror* (1975), which features a child's severed foot. At a fast pace, a series of human stories now unravel like the psychological states of the characters. We feel the pain of a concerned wife, and that of her husband, a stressed businessman. We experience the fear of a damaged young woman unable to leave the house, a condition in part induced by a troubled upbringing, and we witness the escape from reality of a panic-stricken gentleman, no longer able to cope with the everyday. Stanley Bowler described the overall affect of this film succinctly when he stated:

> *Time Out of Mind* is a remarkable film. It begins with a suicide sequence that would stand up in any collection of classic film-openings and continues in an atmosphere of terrifying, distorted realism ... As a document, its value is in the sensitive portrayal of the victim's sensations; as a film it is masterly.[37]

Contrary to this view, P. G. Jones stated that it 'Will probably achieve its object but is over-dramatised. Some sequences are out of place in a scientific exercise.'[38] Marquis was doing things differently. His visual, brutal, upfront way of tackling serious issues, and his engagement of target viewers through communication of the human story (rather than through the stating of scientific truths) was unorthodox and not always going to be popular. However, so successful was Marquis in his approach that Roche commissioned a whole series of comparable productions, from film-makers outside Britain, that according to Roche's archivist: 'albeit interesting and experimental – did never quite reach Marquis' brazen but nevertheless elegant style'.[39]

In 2002 *Time Out of Mind* had an unexpected new lease of life when its visual content was plundered for a promotional video to accompany the appropriately named song 'There Goes the Fear', by indie band Doves.[40] Described by the video's design and production company, Intro, as a 'fractured

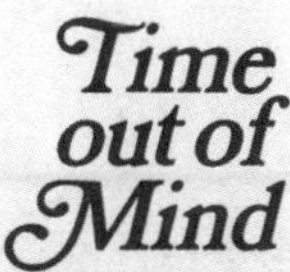

This is a film that adds depth and insight to the general practitioner's view of psychiatric disorders. Relevant and significant in content, it is both original and compelling in style and represents an entirely new approach to the filmed presentation of case studies in a field which contains many intricate problems for the general practitioner.

tale of a man losing his mind and running off to Brazil', it was constructed entirely of pre-existing footage, primarily from *Time Out of Mind*. This skilful repurposing was not overlooked, with Intro's Julian House and Julian Gibbs honoured for 'outstanding direction' in the 2003 D&AD awards. Using this footage, the directors, consciously or not, paid homage to the continuing effectiveness of Marquis's trippy, troubled mindscapes. And through this reinvention, images from *Time Out of Mind* have been seen and acclaimed by much larger audiences than were ever intended for the original film. The video is globally distributed on moving-image sites such as YouTube.[41] The 'second life' of *Time Out of Mind* perhaps indicates how far removed is Marquis's style from Griersonian earnestness – having more in common with the frenetic, accessible experimentalism of today's pop video, though still having deeply 'documentary' aims.

Marquis's second Roche film, *Fighting Back* (1969) saw *Time Out of Mind* cameraman Josef Ambor and editor Bill Megarry collaborating with the film-maker once more. This was Marquis's first attempt at producing: his associate Anthony Short directed. The film won several awards: the Screenwriters Guild's Award for Best British Documentary and Best Short Script for Peter Goodman, the British Medical Association's Certificate of Merit and, like Marquis's previous health film, BISFA's Gold Prize.[42] In the *Financial Times*, Chittock declared:

> This film brilliantly grasps the human problem – relating it to the traditional instruction. And it does so in a way where director, cameraman, sound mixer and editor have used a rare blend of cinematic art – to a stark and coldly practical end.[43]

Demonstrating how physiotherapy is used to manage chronic bronchitis and other respiratory ailments, *Fighting Back* was made in cooperation with the Brompton Hospital. A functional, factual and potentially life-saving film, it was made the more memorable and effective because of its cinematic approach, but in a lower key than Marquis's films about psychiatric illness. It certainly was not as savage in its representation as the films that were to define Marquis's later style. In 1970 he wrote and directed a further film intended for medical audiences, which promoted a new sedative for surgical procedures, *The Gentle Persuader* or *Intravenous Valium Roche*. Though this third commission from the pharmaceutical company won a Certificate of Merit from BISFA, it was the slightest of the Roche films.

Thanks to his success, in 1969 and 1970 Marquis was in high demand. He was involved in directing *Geigy UK* (1969), a company-sponsored film, and directing *Policeman* (1970) for the Metropolitan Police. He also produced Short's film *Guinness For You* (1971) (also known as *A Bottle of Guinness*)[44] and *Asbestos*, also known as *Why Asbestos*? (1970). Ironically (knowing what we do now), this last item, sponsored by the Asbestos Information Committee, examined the product's indispensable benefits to such social goods as fire prevention and vehicle safety.

Frustrated after ten years of having 'suffered' many producers, Marquis threatened to leave the Guild unless he was given complete autonomy.[45] A deal was struck and on 6 April 1970 a press release announced that, at the age of forty-one, Marquis, who had recently been appointed to the Guild's Board, was also to become Managing Director of a newly formed production company, Unit 7 Film Productions Limited.[46] Marquis was now undoubtedly at his peak, working to full capacity and gaining the independence that he had grafted for, but he continued to devote his efforts to his sponsors' messages. The rewards and recognition continued to pick up pace: and Marquis had both creative freedom and his sponsors' trust.

In the 1970s, Marquis was getting to grips again with serious subjects, reflecting his sense of civic duty. *Policeman*, a careers film for the Metropolitan Police by Verity Films, was for Gay 'easily one of the best sponsored short films we have seen for some time'.[47] Marquis had established a good rapport with the Met's Head of Public Relations, Jack Courtney, and this led to further collaborations with the law enforcement agency. His films are realistic because real officers of the law were used and he never attempted to glamorise them or their jobs. *Policeman* showed a job full of variety and pace, where material rewards and personal satisfaction could be gained from protecting society. Distribution was held up when, tragically, after filming the featured recruit was murdered. On the advice of his widow, however, the film was released to restricted audiences, and went on to win another BISFA Gold Award and was also honoured at an American Film Festival.[48]

1971 saw Marquis script, produce and direct what was perhaps his most expensive and certainly his most important film, the internationally praised *The Savage Voyage*.

This genuinely experimental mental health prestige title illustrated the research and development of benzodiazepines. Through his film, Marquis pressed for the correct diagnosis and treatment of anxiety, while subtly suggesting that Roche's latest psychotropic compound, nobrium, might aid recovery. *The Savage Voyage* received a Bronze Award in the medical research shortlist of the New York Film Festival, Best of Category at the San Francisco Festival and a Stella Award for Best Specialised Film from the Society of Film and Television Arts in 1972, the ultimate in home-grown accolades for such a piece. In a year when Chicago awarded no Gold Hugos, it won one of three Silvers, and was the only non-American film to gain an award in the Business and Industry Category. Peter Rigg wrote from Chicago of its compelling effect:

> Only twice in a long life of watching sponsored films have I felt an audience really sit on the edge of its seat. And at the end of the film they applauded twice, once after the visuals and the second time after the technical credits. This was the only film so applauded. The film really stood out from the other films in the competition, because it really uses cinematic techniques to condition the mind of the audience to receive the sponsor's message.

An outstanding success with its critics, the film was shown to 3,200 doctors within six weeks of its release and generated much debate around the treatment of nervous conditions. At the time Marquis was quoted as saying: 'I think there will be some among them who will think it controversial. But perhaps it will make GPs think twice about the treatment of anxiety.'[49] Marquis had skilfully made it impossible for these physicians to escape the horrors of their patients' terrifying experiences.

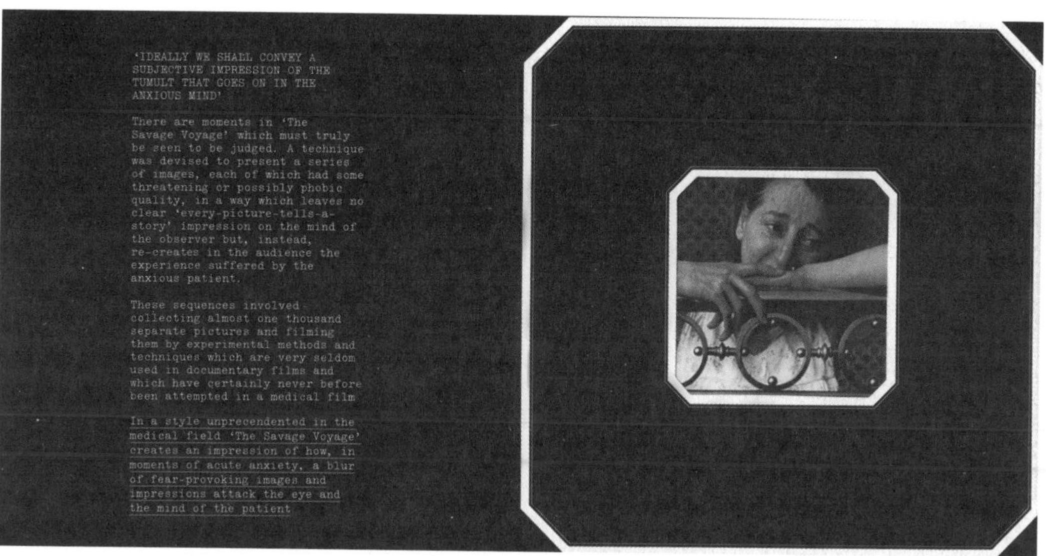
'IDEALLY WE SHALL CONVEY A SUBJECTIVE IMPRESSION OF THE TUMULT THAT GOES ON IN THE ANXIOUS MIND'

There are moments in 'The Savage Voyage' which must truly be seen to be judged. A technique was devised to present a series of images, each of which had some threatening or possibly phobic quality, in a way which leaves no clear 'every-picture-tells-a-story' impression on the mind of the observer but, instead, re-creates in the audience the experience suffered by the anxious patient.

These sequences involved collecting almost one thousand separate pictures and filming them by experimental methods and techniques which are very seldom used in documentary films and which have certainly never before been attempted in a medical film

In a style unprecendented in the medical field 'The Savage Voyage' creates an impression of how, in moments of acute anxiety, a blur of fear-provoking images and impressions attack the eye and the mind of the patient

A page from the lavish promotional brochure for *The Savage Voyage*

Through this scientifically probing, savage and strangely poetic film Marquis employs a wider range of techniques than ever before to create a cogently clear expression of the vague fears and apprehensions of the haunted victims of anxiety and depression. The tension of the pacing, combined with the experimental aspects, makes the film both gripping and mesmerising. *The Savage Voyage* had a practical purpose, and yet it met it with a powerful expression of art, drawing its audiences into visual turmoil. Marquis was also particularly successful in juxtaposing the trauma of the individual's experience with the research and development of the drug. For example, an account of what can be learned from testing lab rats and monitoring aggression in primates is followed by a discussion of how emotions can be measured, and then more importantly of how complex and debilitating emotions might *feel*. A particularly triumphant aspect of the film is its brutal, gruelling and abrupt timeline of life (beginning with the 'savage voyage' – birth). In one sequence thousands of threatening images of memories and thoughts are swiftly and cleverly edited together to illustrate the fractured nature of a troubled mind (relatively easy, if fiddly, to do in the era of Final Cut Pro – really quite something for a 35mm sponsored film made in 1971). Marquis recollects that his long-term collaborator, cameraman Josef Ambor (who, unbeknown to the rest of the crew, was dying during the filming) felt worried that it might not make sense to the viewers.[50] Undeterred by the difficult and serious subject matter, this bold – but by now very experienced – director maintained and executed his strong vision for the film, adding the noted experimental composer Tristram Cary's grating and complementary avant-garde sounds to great effect.[51] In Cary's previous projects, *Narcissus* (1968), a flautist and a tape operator had aurally reflected each other's performances (hence the title), and *Trios* (1971) had employed the VCS3 synthesiser and two turntable operators, whose actions were directed by dice. Cary's dynamic sounds and performances therefore seemed a perfect fit.[52] In the medical field, this experimentalism was 'unprecedented'.[53] But the unsettling effect on its audiences was by now a Marquis trademark.

After this triumph, two further film commissions from the Met came Unit 7's way: *Police Cadet* (1972) and *A Ten Letter Word* (1972). *Police Cadet* came with a booklet for careers officers, and was designed to encourage school leavers to enrol for a rewarding, exciting, but responsible public-service job in the force. The film followed a cadet on his comprehensive training at the Met's 'ultra-modern' Hendon facility, from his attachment to a division, through to his first arrest. The sponsor asked for a candid portrayal and in many ways the film's strength lies in its less than glamorous depiction of the force. Not a job for everyone, according to the Met's press release, the intention was to show that: 'It's man's work ... important work' with the need for 'tact, intelligence, patience and guts'.[54] Reflecting the sexist attitude of the then establishment, it was very much a film of its *Life on Mars* times. Flash-forwards allowed the potential recruit to visualise life beyond the training academy and one critic said its style was 'very reminiscent' of *Top of the Pops*. With no scripted narration, only spontaneous conversations between the instructors and pupils, it was suitably pitched at youthful viewers.[55] David Wilson of *Monthly Film Bulletin* was not convinced of its usefulness claiming, 'it avoids controversy, and barely touches on the social role of the police, or the changing public attitudes which partly explain the need to promote recruitment'.[56] There is truth in this but the objective was not to question the role, rather it was to endorse the benefits of a career in the force to the sorts of recruits that the Met of 1972 wanted.

'Prevention' is the subject of *A Ten Letter Word*, produced and directed by Marquis, its mission, to make society more aware of the possibility of a crime occurring, while simultaneously directing homeowners to seek advice from New Scotland Yard's crime prevention service. This short benefited from a series of fear-generating reconstructed crimes, the most savage being a scene of senseless vandalism, the chilling effect of which would not have been lost on the most complacent of audiences.

A world away from grimy London streets, Marquis's third BP commission, *Go Mocamp* (1972), employed images of an unspoiled landscape with poetic narration to lull the audience into a state of relaxation. Winning the Gold Award at the Tourist Film Festival, this was a promotional film for the sponsor's campsites in Turkey. Although nothing to write home about, it nevertheless fulfilled BP's brief pleasantly enough. In a different register again, that same year, John Player & Sons sponsored Marquis's filming of the John Player Grand Prix, at Brands Hatch, with a behind-the-scenes look at race preparations. That year, the Brazilian Emerson Fittipaldi won for the British Team-Lotus, driving a revised Lotus 72.

The motoring theme recurred for Marquis, in a more unusual way, when in October 1973 the Metropolitan Police publicly screened *Without Due Care* at the International Motor Show, in London's Earls Court. Their award-winning film-maker was asked to devise a road-safety movie with a slightly different aim than most: to bring about a better understanding between motorists and the traffic police, while at the same time visually communicating a broader picture of the officers' work.[57] This characteristically impressionistic documentary won a Bronze Hugo at the Chicago International Film Festival, but was less favourably reviewed by Kenneth Myer in *Audio Visual*, who, despite considering it 'eminently watchable', complained that it projected the view that 'nearly all bad drivers are men' and contained a lack of courtroom scenes.[58] This project was followed by the Ministry of Defence and COI-sponsored *Skill-At-Arms: The RAF Regiment Gunner* (1973).[59] Both these films were, for Marquis, routine commissions; but thankfully, even as the sponsored films industry was undoubtedly declining, there were still projects ahead that would grab more attention.

Anthony Short and Eric Marquis teamed up again as director and producer to make *Certified Accountants – Springboard to Success*, which premiered in January 1974. Made for the Association of Certified Accountants, this careers film was designed to give a lively representation of the range and scope of this field of work, and followed on from a successful television advertising campaign. Descriptions provided in reviews and the press release suggested, however, that it was radically different in tone from the experimental, stylish and slick *Guinness For You*, developed by the same creative partnership some years previously.[60] Ever versatile, in 1974 Marquis also made an amusing four-and-a-half-minute animated film 'loop' for projecting behind shop counters, advertising ICI's new wallpaper product, Novamura.

The most exceptional film devised by Marquis in 1974 was *Tomorrow's Merseysiders*, produced on behalf of the *Liverpool Daily Post and Echo*. In a press release Marquis claimed that it was: 'in no way intended as a severe exercise in social commentary'; instead he had answered a brief to be: 'aware, objective, interesting and constructively critical' about the Merseyside environment – which, in fact, meant that the film contained a little more social commentary than was usually to be found in sponsored films by this late stage.[61] Notwithstanding Lindsay Anderson's *Wakefield Express* (1952), this film was one of the few sponsored by British newspaper groups not just to highlight the mechanics of production, but to explore newspapers' relationships with the communities they serve. With narration proudly proclaiming: 'Liverpool, more than most, is a city held in trust for tomorrow's Merseysiders, who are growing up today', the paper saw itself as the responsible 'guardians of the trust it will inherit'.

This non-theatrical 16mm film sketched a picture of 1970s regional journalism, in which class and gender segregate newspaper staff. More importantly, *Tomorrow's Merseysiders* delved into Liverpool's history and wondered about its future. Just as a journalist might, Marquis questions why the civic destruction of scores of back-to-back terraces is not 'balanced with the compensation of construction', and why lost youth can only proclaim their existence through graffiti and vandalism. Having experienced the intolerable slums of Stockport, Marquis shows great sympathy for the lives of those he films. A bleak depiction of burning rubble is juxtaposed with shots of the university settlement, where positive energy is channelled. The documentary's strength lies in its unassuming but complex visual interweaving of series of scenes. Patrick Russell has observed and praised 'how associations and contrasts, sometimes subliminal, are built up by careful use of picture and sound. Walker Art Gallery paintings recall Toxeth graffiti. A Punch-and-Judy show echoes youthful vandalism.'[62] The subtly cinematic style of editing and of shooting scenery, contrasted with the vérité trappings with which people are filmed (including the now commonplace fly-on-the-wall sequence of the newspaper's editorial conference) gives the piece an authentic and unusual edge.[63] Finally, the aerial shots succeed in providing a sense of the scale of a damaged cityscape and the real challenges ahead for the next generation of scousers (whose city would become poorer before it got richer).

This was the most serious phrase of Marquis's career. His next film was far from light entertainment. In the often-gruesome sponsored film, *Time of Terror*, images of ravaged limbs and devastating destruction are commonplace, as bomb victims are apparently being resuscitated in an ambulance, while a crime prevention officer stands in the front of the frame lecturing his audience about the devastating effects of terrorism. According to the director, *Time of Terror* was not meant for consumption outside the four walls of its commissioners, the Metropolitan Police.[64] Produced in the midst of a decade of Provisional IRA violence in mainland Britain as well as Northern Ireland, it was filmed a year before the targeting of the Houses of Parliament and after there had already been several London car and letter bombings and the bombing of the BT Tower. This was, indeed, a time of terror, and the effects of acts of violence are particularly well conveyed by this documentary through the use of eyewitness accounts. One cannot help but shudder as a bystander, exclaims through angry tears that the 'bastards have done it'. The film implores its viewers to be 'vigilant' and to take collective responsibility for the prevention of such horrors. Unfortunately for us, Marquis was right when his script suggested 'Terrorism is here to stay.'[65] An impressive aspect of the film, given the temper of its own times, is that while it is hard hitting, it is also apolitical and unprejudiced, emphasising that most of those in the communities from which terrorists come are innocent of any wrongdoing.

Seven Green Bottles (1976) another Met Police commission, is a story of seven truants who collectively commit a series of criminal offences, which at a fast filmic pace escalate in severity. Its realistic and hard-hitting portrayal of juvenile delinquents gained critical acclaim with a Silver Award from the BISFA Festival and a nomination for the British Academy Flaherty Documentary Award (losing out to Alan Pendry's Shell Film Unit history film *The Early Americans*, which according to Marquis cost seven times as much, and took seven times as long to shoot).[66] The film premiered at Scotland Yard, shortly after the Film Producers Guild, including Marquis's Unit 7, had been sold to Cygnet Films. A distinctive strength of this gritty and accomplished social documentary – there is no better label for it, though it takes purely dramatised form – is its believable protagonists, whom Marquis had insisted should not be trained actors. (One of them was a very young Danny John-Jules, later famous as 'The Cat' in television's *Red Dwarf*.) Suspending disbelief was essential for the director but he found the Met initially resistant to his stipulation. Officers were even less amused when, at the station's screening, it became apparent to them that they already knew some of the starring gang members! Ironically, despite involvement with this 'crime doesn't pay' production, a few of these 'characters' continued to tread similar paths and eventually found themselves in the slammer.[67]

Marquis, who had always been creative at 'making a silk purse out of a sow's ear of a budget', had worked mainly with non-professional actors, and, amazingly, says that he had never had more than three weeks to shoot a film. He never believed in shouting 'action!' as it would send the novice into a 'stuttering panic', and instead employed a technique of the trade known as 'board on end', shooting when the relaxed non-professional thought it was only a rehearsal. In the case of this low-budget film, however, the lads never bothered to learn their lines and Marquis resorted to reading them out before every take.[68] Point-of-view shots from the troublemaker's perspective were frequently and effectively used and, as with *Tomorrow's Merseysiders*, this study of disillusioned youth goes to more lengths than it might have to explore the reasons why these vulnerable 'green bottles' go about shattering their lives with crime. While subtly pointing out that it's always possible to take a less dangerous path, the grim, and in one case fatal, consequence of their misdemeanors is smashed home.

This 'sit up and listen' title, shot as well as distributed on 16mm, was aimed at eight- to fifteen-year-olds, parents, teachers, social workers and those at risk of committing offences. Though his long-term sponsors had come to trust him, on this occasion they needed some convincing. Persuasive characterisation, big scenes including a grisly joy-riding accident with a pounding heart sound effect, combined with more subtle details like the boys' use of strong language to give the film a streetwise authenticity that is rare indeed for the sponsored documentary form. With *Seven Green Bottles*, Marquis created a viewing experience so believably tense that even the most hardened of youngsters couldn't fail to see that juvenile delinquency was no laughing matter. It would represent a benchmark of style and effectiveness for Marquis.

Declining an offer to join the new Cygnet Guild conglomerate, Marquis made one last film under the Guild umbrella (a British Gas promotional film, called *Customer Service* [1976]); he continued to pursue various commissions on a freelance basis before later setting up his own company, to pursue further contracts independently. Marquis continued to make award-winning documentaries with the sponsors he had collaborated with over the years until he retired from film-making in 1984. Notable titles produced by his own company included: *Dentistry Today* (1977), a recruitment film that stressed the importance of dental hygiene; and the accomplished, BISFA Gold Award-winning, Metropolitan Police film *Police Station* (1979), covering a day in the life of the Gypsy Hill station. A BISFA Silver Award winner, *Selling By Post* (1980) was the Post Office's introduction for traders to mail-order marketing. The Abu Dhabi Petroleum Company's contribution to the development of the United Arab Emirates was explored in *Road To Progress* (1980). *Better Than Cure* (1981) was a health and safety film about occupational health; and, a little ahead of its time in tackling obesity, *Too Fat To Fight* (1982) – the only film narrated by the director – won Marquis the Best Director Craft Award and a Silver Award for the picture from the BISFA Film Festival.[69] Then came *Thieves Junction* (1982), the sole production of a new, short-lived company Marquis Productions. According to Marquis the triumvirate forming the company fell out even before finalising the film, with one of the trio credited with being producer, although he was in effect only the unit driver! Gerry Boarer as its films officer was the direct sponsor on behalf of the Post Office, and wouldn't allow what Marquis considered a worthy film to be entered for any film awards on the basis of 'security'.[70] Marquis then freelanced under the trading name of Eric Marquis Films. He was particularly proud of his intelligence and security films *Operation Intercept* (1984) and *I Cannot Answer That Question* (1985), intended to illustrate enemy methods of interrogation, both produced for the Ministry of Defence and screened only to restricted audiences.[71] The last film that he wrote and directed, *Listen*, produced in 1984 for the Army, examined the dangers of hearing loss as a result of not using adequate noise protection and won a Bronze Award from BISFA. Having fallen out with the Post Office over money, his final project, *Men of Letters* (1985), which he was meant to script and direct, ended on bad terms. His contemporary, Derek Williams, suggests that by this point Marquis might have felt like many of the generation who had entered the big-screen documentary industry of the 1950s: 'discouraged, doubtless, by the lack of attention that afflicted us all'.[72]

After a distinguished career in films, Eric Marquis chose to leave the stresses of producing, directing and scriptwriting behind, setting up a self-catering hotel with his wife on his beloved island of Guernsey. They have been happily retired there since 1999.[73]

NOTES

1. Information provided by Eric Marquis in email, 28 January 2010.
2. Correspondence from Eric Marquis to Patrick Russell, c. September 2006.
3. He was stationed in a Wiltshire barracks and this was where he met his wife, with whom he has two children. One of them, also called Eric Marquis, currently works in the industry as a freelance cameraman.
4. The cinematographic expertise developed there would form the foundations of Granada Television. The studio was sold to the BBC in 1954 making it the first regional BBC TV studio outside London. It was demolished in 1975 when operations were transferred to Oxford Road. See <www.itsahotun.com/history.html> for a history of the Studio by Professor C. P. Lee of the University of Salford.
5. Marquis also edited an Olive Negus travelogue, *Exploring in Dalmatia* (1957), aimed at juvenile and family audiences.
6. Harold Rose, 'Two Kinds of Sponsored Film for Tea: Brooke Bond Road Shows for Britain's Housewives – and their Children', *Film User*, February 1963, pp. 70–2.
7. *Kinematograph Weekly* no. 2679, 18 December 1958, p. 136.

8. *Film User* vol. 15 no. 174, April 1961, p. 192.
9. *The Times*, 31 October 1960, undated cutting in the Ken Gay Collection, Box 2.
10. G. Buckland-Smith, 'Survival', *Imagery* vol. 5 no. 1, Winter 1962, p. 19.
11. Ibid., p. 21.
12. *The Times*, 1961, undated cutting, Ken Gay Collection, Box 2.
13. *Film User* vol. 16 no. 183, January 1962, p. 30.
14. P. G. Jones, 'Time Out of Mind', *Information from the Department of Audio Visual Communications* no. 2, 1 November 1969, p. 4.
15. *Monthly Film Bulletin* vol. 28 no. 335, December 1961.
16. Press release from Domestos Limited, Newcastle Upon Tyne, issued by S. & B. Public Relations Ltd, Ken Gay Collection, Box 3.
17. Ibid.
18. Ibid.
19. 'Humorous Touches by Telephone', *The Times*, 8 June 1964, p. 17.
20. Correspondence from Derek Williams to Patrick Russell, 23 June 2008.
21. Information provided by Eric Marquis in email, 12 April 2010.
22. The film is featured in the *Shop 'til You Drop* Collection of the BFI Mediatheque.
23. *Financial Times*, 24 August 1965, p. 13.
24. Since 1958, Gerald Shaw had been the popular resident organist in the Odeon Leicester Square. This composer and performer had a hit with his LP *Fanfare* and worked in and around cinema until his death in 1974. Ken Russell's *Tommy* (1975) featured Shaw playing the organ.
25. *Imagery* vol. 18 no. 2, 1965, p. 9.
26. Film Producers Guild Press Release: 'Silver Award for Guild Film', Ken Gay Collection, Box 12, file 29.
27. Before Marquis, Michael Powell had consulted Stafford-Clark when preparing *Peeping Tom* (1960) and Alfred Hitchcock, whose films, of course, often contained a strong element of the psychological case study, had him brought to Los Angeles. In 1961, his favourite director, John Huston, asked him to be the consultant on *Freud*, starring Montgomery Clift and Susannah York. For more of Stafford-Clark, see the obituary written by his son in *The Independent*, 14 September 1999.
28. *Vision in the High Street* (1966), press release from the Film Producers Guild, Ken Gay Collection, Box 4.
29. 'The Film Producers Guild Ltd Information Sheet', Ken Gay Collection, Box 15.
30. *Film User* vol. 22 no. 259, May 1968, p. 39.
31. *Film User* vol. 21 no. 250, August 1967, p. 41.
32. *Film User* vol. 22 no. 259, May 1968, p. 39.
33. These were *Computer Aided Design* (1968), about developments in the British computer industry for an overseas audience, and *A Guide to Goodness*, a promotional film for Guinness stout. Marquis produced a subsequent, more stylish film for the same brewery: *Guinness For You* (1971).
34. Roche Products Limited publicity, printed February 1969, Ken Gay Collection, Box 18.
35. Ken Gay, 'Views of Reality', *Films & Filming* vol. 15 no. 10, July 1969, p. 88.
36. Tim Ewbank, 'Films in Industry: Here's Food for Medical Thought', *Today's Cinema* no. 9953, 2 November 1971, p. 3.
37. Stanley Bowler, *Film User*, June 1969, p. 17.
38. Jones, 'Time Out of Mind'.
39. Email correspondence, 27 November 2009, from Alexander Bieri of Roche Products to Patrick Russell.

40. Intro website: <www.introwebsite.com/index2.asp>
41. Doves' *There Goes the Fear* (2002) can (at the time of writing) be seen at: <www.youtube.com/watch?v=GZgBKVBduQg>
42. Film Producers Guild Limited press release, issued 13 March 1970, Ken Gay Collection, Box 21.
43. From an information sheet supplied by the film-maker himself.
44. For an assessment, see Patrick Russell, *100 British Documentaries* (London: BFI, 2007), pp. 78–9.
45. Email correspondence with Eric Marquis, 28 January 2010.
46. Film Producers Guild Limited press release, 'New Production Company Formed By The Film Producers Guild', Ken Gay Collection, Box 20.
47. A film that this modest director is himself particularly proud of.
48. Ken Gay, 'Over the Fence', *Films & Filming* vol. 16 no. 10, July 1970, p. 81.
49. Ewbank, 'Films in Industry'.
50. Email correspondence with Eric Marquis, 28 January 2010.
51. He also scored *Guinness For You*.
52. For more information on Cary, see the obituary 'Tristram Cary: Pioneer of Electronic Music', written by John Riley in *The Independent*, 28 April 2008.
53. Roche Products publicity, Ken Gay Collection, Box 28.
54. New Scotland Yard press release, 'A Career in the Metropolitan Police Cadets Has Everything', Ken Gay Collection, Box 30.
55. *Audio Visual* vol. 1 no. 3, March 1972, p. 18.
56. *Monthly Film Bulletin* vol. 39 no. 458, March 1972, p. 61.
57. For more information, see the Metropolitan Police press release, 'Without Due Care', Ken Gay Collection, Box 40.
58. Kenneth Myer, 'The Traffic Cop's Lot is Not a Pretty One', *Audio Visual* vol. 2 no. 23, November 1973, p. 32.
59. A copy survives in the Imperial War Museum's Film and Video Archive.
60. Press release: Premiere of *Certified Accountants – Springboard to Success*, Ken Gay Collection, Box 41, file 88.
61. Ken Gay Collection, Box 43.
62. Patrick Russell, *Tomorrow's Merseysiders*, <www.sceenonline.org.uk>
63. The fly-on-the-wall technique is again successfully employed in *Police Station* (1979), devised to help the public arrive at a better understanding of the force's everyday work.
64. Correspondence from Eric Marquis to Patrick Russell, 3 September 2006.
65. For more, see Rebecca Vick, *Time of Terror*, <www.bfi.org.uk/inview>
66. Eric Marquis to Ken Gay, 5 April 1976, Ken Gay Collection, Box 23.
67. Information supplied by director and a member of the cast, who attended a public screening (part of the *Flipside* strand), at the BFI Southbank, January 2010.
68. Information supplied by Eric Marquis in conversations and in email, 28 January 2010.
69. Ken Gay, 'Canada and Brighton', *Films* vol. 3 no. 11, November 1983, p. 45.
70. Email to the author from Eric Marquis, 12 April 2010.
71. Copies of both are held at the Imperial War Museum Film & Video Archive.
72. Correspondence from Derek Williams to Patrick Russell, 23 May 2008.
73. A big thank you to my colleagues and friends for their advice, assistance and support during the research and writing of this chapter: Ros Cranston, Margaret Deriaz, Sam Dunn, William Fowler

Alison Kirwan, Catherine McGahan, Vic Pratt, John Riley, Ben Thompson and Kieron Webb. I owe special thanks to Eric Marquis, without whose assistance (despite his description of himself as a 'cantankerous old bastard') this piece could not have been written and to whom I am very grateful. I had always been engaged by his work but my appreciation of his talent has grown even greater through this process.

22 Between Two Worlds: *Derrick Knight*

BERT HOGENKAMP

'It seems to me quite clear that, while film-makers of documentary and shorts have been going through a period of easy prosperity, they have allowed themselves to be lulled into creative idleness.'[1] Undoubtedly, Derrick Knight must have been aware that he was not making friends when this statement of his was published in the autumn of 1957. He had started his article 'The Captive Cinema' with another controversial observation, stating that Free Cinema, which had received a lot of praise in certain circles, 'has, in my opinion, shown us no real innovations in content, technique, style or approach'.[2] Instead he was impressed with the documentaries which television, in particular the much-maligned commercial television company Associated-Rediffusion, had been offering. He hailed 'the direct speaking-to-camera by people in all walks of life' as an important innovation, for it 'has an impact which we filmgoers are not used to. It is documentary with the gloves off once more.'[3]

When 'The Captive Cinema' was published, Derrick Knight had yet to make a name for himself in the world of documentary and short films. He had been working for a couple of years as a writer and director at Technical & Scientific Films, one of the Film Producers Guild companies, that, as its name suggests, concentrated on making straightforward 'nuts-and-bolts' films for a wide variety of sponsors. The qualifications 'easy prosperity' and 'creative idleness' seemed eminently applicable to Technical & Scientific Films. But in all fairness, it must be said that Knight would always stress that the years he spent at T&S enabled him to learn the basics of film-making. Ten years later, in 1967, the situation was completely different. Spearheading the film technicians' union ACTT's campaign for short films, Knight had become a household name in the whole British film industry. He was the co-author of an ACTT report on the Short Entertainment and Factual Film, *A Long Look at Short Films*. It was a culmination of the frantic efforts he had undertaken to create opportunities for young film-makers and to find support for producing films that were of social and aesthetic value (films 'with the gloves off'). Yet another ten years later, Knight had been forced out of the film industry, taking on the job of researcher at Christian Aid, for whom he mainly wrote reports and books.

Although it was only during a relatively short time span (between 1957 and 1972), Derrick Knight made his presence very firmly felt in the British film industry. His contribution has since been largely forgotten and deserves to be revisited. Coming at the end of this book, Knight is a particularly enlightening figure. He straddled the world of mainstream state, industrial and – particularly – charitable sponsorship of documentary (the world in which most of the film-makers covered here were so firmly entrenched), and a parallel universe (one which some of them might have wished they could inhabit) of independent, experimental and oppositional film-making. Knight apparently saw no contradiction in keeping one foot in each camp simultaneously. His career is thus an interesting study in the possibilities that the 1960s seemed to be opening up – and the intractable nature of film financing which eventually closed them down again. This chapter will look at the films that he directed or produced, the film-makers that he offered an opportunity to master the trade, the campaigns that he was involved in, and the organisations that he set up – chief among them, his production company Derrick Knight & Partners.

Born in 1929 and raised on a yacht that had been transformed into a floating home in Poole harbour, Derrick Knight's earliest recollections of the cinema are the 9.5mm screenings of silent films held on board by his father. Later, during his time at Canford Public School near Bournemouth, he learned to appreciate the best of the film society fare. Canford had its own 35mm projection equipment and regularly presented feature films to its pupils.[4] In the school's projection box Knight had his 'first love affair with carbon tetrachloride cleaning fluid and acetate cement', a foretaste of what he would later encounter in the cutting-room.[5] Thanks to film buff and collector Dudley Shaw Ashton who had his own projection room in the basement of his house overlooking Poole harbour, Knight was able to see the key avant-garde works by European artists such as Walter Ruttmann, Man Ray, Moholy-Nagy, René Clair, Cavalcanti, Joris Ivens and others.[6] He was much impressed by a visit to Canford by Roger Manvell and devoured Manvell's *Film* (1944). As he would later recall, the Pelican edition of this volume was the only cheap book on film around.[7] Moreover, it contained almost 200 film stills, which made a vivid impression on the teenager.

As a student, reading modern history at Oriel College, Knight wrote film reviews for *Isis* and became active in the Oxford University Film Society. A handful of society members formed an Experimental Film Group with the idea of making their own films, as a supplement to those shown by the society. The American artist Sam Kaner who had come over in 1951 from Paris to Oxford to develop new engraving techniques, presented the members with an idea for a film based on an abstract ballet. Professional ballet-dancer Tutte Lemkow – the Norwegian husband of Swedish film-star Mai Zetterling – supported the idea and was prepared to appear in the film together with his dancing partner Sara Luzita. The film was shot during a five-week period in a makeshift studio in the gymnasium of Cheltenham College. The costumes and sets were designed and painted by Kaner. Canadian research student Guy Coté – later to make a career as a director and producer with the National Film Board of Canada – acted as director. As the film's producer Derrick Knight was responsible for keeping the shooting costs of this 16mm colour production within its £700 budget limit, largely by begging for equipment and services at reduced rates.[8] *Between Two Worlds* was a study in colour, movement and music, without any spoken word. The film reflected the views on the cinema that were prevalent in the film society movement. *Between Two Worlds* was released in 1952 and won top awards for amateur films, such as the Amateur Cine World Ten Best for 1952 and the special prize of the Scottish Amateur Film Festival 1953.

Next, the Experimental Film Group produced *Just in Case* (1952), a piece that was quite different from *Between Two Worlds*. It was an enacted documentary with a direct function: recruiting volunteer nursing staff for the Oxford hospitals. Using two voiceovers (a subjective, female voice and an 'objective', male one), the film shows two cases to demonstrate the need for volunteers: that of Bobby, a young boy who undergoes a successful operation after a life-threatening accident, and of a woman who has become a volunteer after she had visited the hospital with a cut finger. Derrick Knight can briefly be seen as a patient with his arm in plaster. *Just in Case* was very much his film. As the most senior and experienced member of the Group he took on its commission from the

Oxford Regional Hospital Board, producing, directing and editing it. In a way the two films produced by Oxford's Experimental Film Group presage the dual focus of Knight's later professional film career: *Between Two Worlds* being independent and experimental and *Just in Case* sponsored for a practical social purpose.

After coming down from Oxford with an Honours Degree in 1953, Knight got a job at Technical & Scientific Films. Starting as an assistant in the cutting-room and ending up as a writer and director, he was involved in productions for Esso, the Mitchell Construction Company and other sponsors. He was also responsible for the monthly screen magazine *Home and Away* about the achievements of the Renfrew-based big-boiler manufacturer Babcock and Wilcox, which was shown in some thirty local cinemas around Glasgow. In 1957 Knight worked for six months on *Home Farm*, a COI film about tenant farmers produced by the Realist Film Unit, bringing him into direct contact with the pioneering days of British documentary, in the form of Realist's managing director Basil Wright. When asked whether he would care to join the unit, Knight told Wright that he had to decline the offer as he was going to start his own company. Still a genuine film buff, Knight 'moonlighted' in his spare time by writing film reviews for British and French journals that were connected to the film society movement.

By the end of 1957 Knight had set up his own company, Derrick Knight & Partners (DKP). The issued share capital was modest and consisted of 500 £1 shares. Knight held the majority of the one hundred voting shares. Apart from Knight, cameraman William Smeaton-Russell and American film-maker Allan Forbes were directors of the company – but only for a short time. In 1959 both resigned: Smeaton-Russell over differences of opinion about cinematography and Forbes because he returned to the USA. In 1960 Knight's wife Brenda and Charles Hodgson joined Knight as directors. The main objective of DKP was 'to promote by every means possible the image of a company highly skilled, intelligent, strongly humanist, socially conscious, technically adventurous, young in spirit and flexible'.[9] To begin with, DKP found it difficult to obtain work: there was no lack of companies trading in the sponsored film sector. A serious problem was the absence of a portfolio film that could be shown to prospective clients in order to convince them that DKP could deliver the kind of film that they were after. In order to survive, DKP took on various editing and post-production jobs. Right at the start in 1958 Derrick Knight was also heavily involved in a volunteer job for the ACT.

Together with his DKP partner Allan Forbes and writer Bernice Rubens, Knight had cooked up the idea to make a film of the march from London to the Atomic Weapons Research Establishment at Aldermaston at Easter 1958, which was organised by the newly established Campaign for Nuclear Disarmament (CND). Helped by the adoption of a resolution on the renunciation of nuclear weapons moved by former National Coal Board films officer Kurt Lewenhak at the ACT's AGM, which had taken place very early in the year, on 8–9 March 1958, Knight, who had long been an active union man – a shop steward at T&S – was able to appeal to the members of the union at large to volunteer. For this purpose a Film and TV Committee for Nuclear Disarmament was formed, with Knight as its honorary secretary. Some thirty members and non-members were involved in the shooting of the film. Feuds were temporarily set aside as Free Cinema luminaries Lindsay Anderson and Karl Reisz worked side by side with Derrick Knight despite his derogatory comments on their work, published only a few months earlier in *Film*. However, the positive spirit that had characterised the Easter weekend proved difficult to sustain afterwards. Although Knight was generally considered to be the 'Generalissimo' leading the film-making volunteers, Lindsay Anderson apparently hijacked the material in order to impose his ideas on it; there is no doubt that Anderson and Mary Beales spent considerable time in the cutting-room putting the film into shape.[10] Richard Burton was coaxed to be the film's narrator. It was not until February 1959 that Contemporary Films, whose managing director Charles Cooper had been involved from the start, was able to release *March to Aldermaston* theatrically and non-theatrically.[11] It is still undoubtedly the most famous film Knight was involved in, although his pivotal role in it is not always remembered.

In the meantime DKP had released a first production of its own, *To End with a Curtsy* (1959). This was a twenty-minute film for theatrical distribution, the start of a series that the company hoped to produce, in a search for direct revenue. *To End with a Curtsy* dealt with the last presentation of the debutantes at Buckingham Palace. In 1958 this tradition of more than 200 years came to an end. It was cameraman Smeaton-Russell who had come up with a contact ('a middle-aged lady', as Derrick Knight recalled) who put up a sum and helped DKP with the right contacts to film the ceremony. The film follows a number of the debs before the ceremony and deals with the problems that the girls have finding work after the season of balls and cocktail parties has finished. *To End with a Curtsy* was made on a small budget but the main problem was that the film lacked a clear view on the phenomenon of the debutantes: should their lifestyle be taken seriously (as the sponsor maintained) or were they a relic of the past (as Knight felt)? The latter view comes closest to the surface in the film's most enjoyable sequence, set to a specially composed, slightly satirical song 'Debutante's Blues', while too much of the rest of the film suffers from enforced cheer.

To End with a Curtsy was distributed by Contemporary but failed to make any money for DKP. This did not prevent the company from venturing to produce a self-financed film about the 1959 Aldermaston March. Although there was only one camera crew on hand, it did cover the second march – now starting in Aldermaston and ending in London – in the way that Derrick Knight preferred, with plenty of big close-ups of marchers and onlookers. Tod Greenaway wrote a script for the film, demonstrating what living in the shadow of the Bomb meant for citizens of every walk of life. *No Place to Hide* (1959) was distributed both by Contemporary Films and by Concord Film Council, the new film distribution outfit with close links to CND and

Promotion for Derrick Knight & Partners' fledgling film, somewhat more exciting than the film itself …

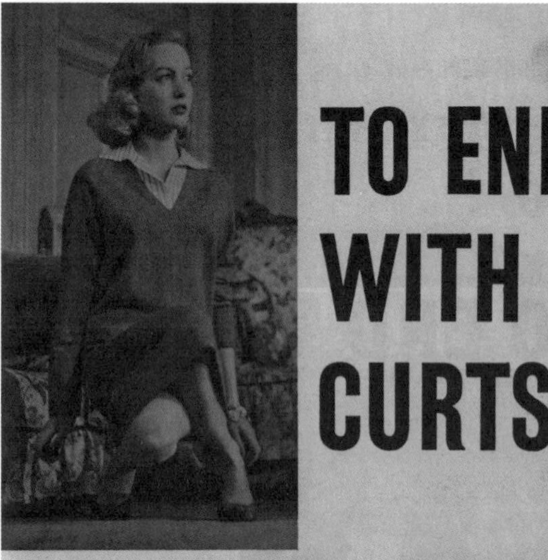

Quaker groups that had been set up by Eric Walker and his wife Lydia Vulliamy.[12] For its next anti-nuclear film DKP at least found a sponsor, the Friends Peace Committee. It needed a film for the Schoolboys Exhibition at Olympia in early 1962. In view of the fact that almost half of all British scientists were working on military projects, it was felt that the younger generation should be made aware of scientists' choices and responsibilities for life – or death. Scripted and directed by Tod Greenaway, *Science for Life* (1961) presented the fable of a boy who aspires to be a scientist. While he is dissecting a frog in his classroom, he first meets a scientist who as a typically idealistic academic does research for the benefit of mankind and then one who has a well-paid job working in a government establishment on nerve gases. The boy questions both of them on the fundamental choices that scientists have to face: working for life or for death. The film had its premiere at one of the film viewing sessions organised by the Quakers at Friends House in London, in November 1961, with a record attendance of 850 persons. *Science for Life* was distributed by Concord, while the (Labour-run) London County Council acquired a number of prints for screening in its schools.

Science for Life makes an interesting contrast with other films about the place of science in society made for school distribution, by more mainstream sponsors such as ICI. However, it is important to point out that DKP was more than willing to work for such conventional clients provided it was on commissions with which it was not out of sympathy. For Smedleys it produced *The Good Things of Life* (1960) about the care that was taken in the company's food processing plants over the quality of food. *Room for Hygiene* (1961) was made for Unilever as an educational film for secondary-school audiences and junior catering colleges about the need for cleanliness in the home and the risk of food poisoning. For the Patent Glazing Conference DKP produced *Broad Daylight* (1963), a half-hour colour film designed to give a positive image of the traditional patent glazing system. *Marketing is the Link* (1964) was sponsored by the British Productivity Council. Using the example of two marketing directors with differing attitudes to problems in their respective industries, this film, which was distributed by the Central Film Library, was aimed at management. Its contemporary pro-marketing philosophy (when compared to the more inwardly facing films that the BPC had sponsored in the previous decade) was in keeping with the youthful, forward-looking personality that DKP sought to project when courting potential sponsors.

From a Derrick Knight & Partners promotional booklet

"Since the Company began ten years ago, I have favoured films which I felt could further man's understanding of contemporary society, and where possible, to provoke his awareness and concern.

In a world where technological innovation can change society in a flash; in a world where all the hitherto separable media of communications, even within this Company's short lifetime, have fused into a giant instantaneous and global information system, the creative film maker has been placed in a position of terrible responsibility as interpreter of the social scene. He can either opt out of this responsibility, or he can choose to use his influence as a catalyst of ideas and as provoker of change. I have sought to encourage clients and film makers alike to choose the second.

As far as subject matter is concerned, I have always been discriminate in the work the Company has undertaken. I have turned down films on weapon systems and re-armament programmes; I have refused commercials for television; my acceptance or rejection of film offers is prompted by my concern with the use and abuse of film as a medium.

We will not, for instance, make a film that propagates war, or that generates sympathy for a cause in which we do not believe. But we do have our causes for which we gladly give our talents.

I have produced films supporting the struggle in South Africa and for the anti-apartheid movement.

I have produced films on the dangers of smoking and the abuse of harmful drugs, but I would not make a film to propagate the sale of either.

Over the last ten years, I have found it possible to satisfy my own principles and at the same time, to build a profitable business. My primary aim remains the satisfaction of my clients".

Derrick Knight.

Thanks to Charles Cooper at Contemporary, early in 1960 Derrick Knight got in touch with Dai Francis and Dai Dan Evans, respectively secretary and president of the National Union of Mineworkers (South Wales Area). Although they were short of money, Francis and Evans were keen for their union to have a film. Evans told Knight with enthusiasm how he had assisted Humphrey Jennings in the making of

The Silent Village (1943), in which the massacre that the Nazis had brought about in the Czech mining village of Lidice was 're-enacted' in Wales. With the ultra-low budget that the union could provide, there was no way that such an elaborate work could be produced by DKP – particularly since Francis and Evans insisted on having their film on 35mm, in colour and on one reel, so that it could be screened as a short in the Miners' Institutes and Welfare Halls. It was agreed that the Miners' Gala in Cardiff offered the best subject for the proposed film. Unlike other British coalfields where Galas had a long history (the most famous one, in Durham, was first held in 1871), in South Wales it was a tradition that had only recently (in1953) been 'invented'. All the more reason for a film about this 'great show of solidarity', thought Dai Dan Evans.[13] On this occasion, however, Knight did not have dozens of technicians at his disposal, as on the Aldermaston March. He could only afford one crew consisting of the experienced cameraman David Holmes with assistant Brian Probyn. They hoped that the weather on June 1960's Gala Day would be bright, as the Eastmancolor stock that they were using needed good light. On the day it rained intermittently, but there were enough dry spells for the crew to cover the main aspects of the event. Evans had persuaded Gwyn Thomas to write and read the commentary. For this, the well-known Welsh writer and broadcaster travelled to London and saw the film twice, making a few notes. After he had had a few pints for lunch, Thomas read an extempore commentary live to the projected images. As Knight later recalled: 'He did it once and it was fine, not just technically good but the words were strong, good humoured and right.'[14] Distributed by Contemporary Films, *Miners' Gala Day* was not only shown extensively in South Wales but also internationally, for example at the International Labour Film Festival in Tel Aviv and the Leipzig Shorts and Documentary Film Festival. Moreover, DKP found it a most useful film to screen to prospective clients. With its energy and warmth, it perfectly embodied the virtues of the company.[15]

Miners' Gala Day had whetted the appetite of both Derrick Knight and Dai Dan Evans for more films. As a possible subject Evans proposed the work being done at the Talygarn Miners' Rehabilitation Centre, of which he was the chairman. The miners often chose not to make the best use of the centre out of superstition or fear. A film might help to break through these barriers. Evans devised a cunning plan to use his personal connections with National Coal Board chairman Lord Robens to have the Board put up the finances for the film. Normally this meant that it would have to be made by the NCB Film Unit. But thanks to some further scheming by Evans, a good film script by Knight and a flexible attitude by Donald Alexander, the NCB's films officer and head of its unit, DKP was allowed to produce the film. The Coal Industry Social Welfare Organisation (CISWO) provided further financial support. Before this positive decision had been made, Knight had spent considerable time in South Wales, at Talygarn in particular, doing research for the film. The resulting script envisaged a (mock) pit accident at the Cambrian Colliery, followed by an operation on the victim in Bridgend Hospital and his rehabilitation at Talygarn.

Derrick Knight felt that the Talygarn film, entitled *A Time to Heal*, warranted a new approach that was breaking with the classic documentary mould: an experiment in 'direct cinema'. He admired the spontaneity that American, Canadian and French colleagues of his had managed to capture in their films, using 16mm blimped cameras with synch sound. But it proved very difficult to find the right equipment in the UK. In the end the cameramen Peter Jessop and Ian McMillan made use of an Arriflex with a rather cumbersome blimp consisting of a fibreglass case that was padded inside. Synch sound was recorded by means of an umbilical cord from the camera to the sound recorder. It took time for the protagonists to get used to the presence of the camera, but after a while it worked.

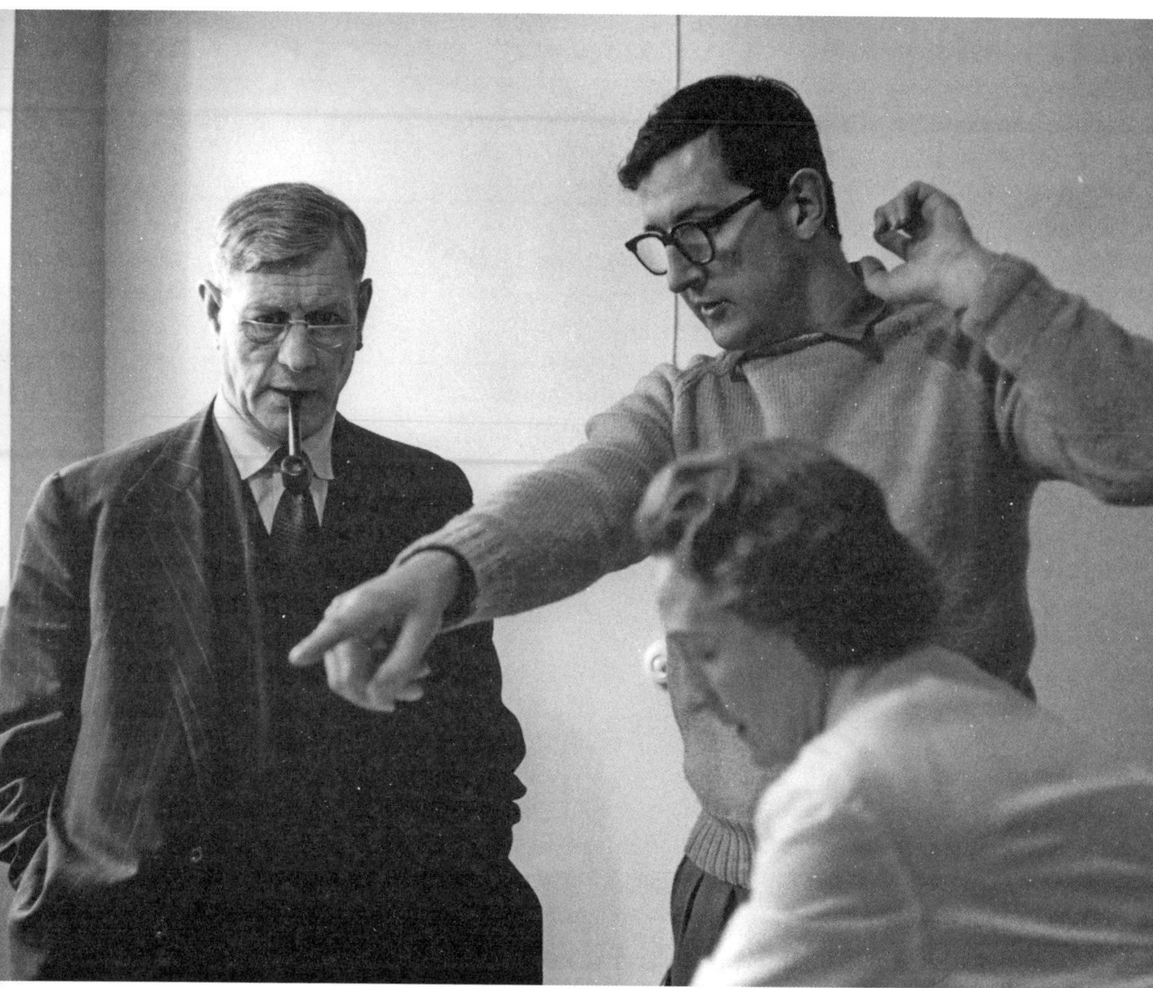

Derrick Knight directing a doctor in *A Time to Heal*

Although the fact that the accident sequence at the start of *A Time To Heal* was enacted makes this film inadmissible as vérité proper, it contains some good examples of the kind of spontaneity and authenticity that could only be achieved by using this approach. Thus the spectator is made aware of the strenuous exercise that is needed for the men to recover their physical strength thanks to the proximity of the camera, when they are playing a competitive ball game on the gym floor (with the cameraman sitting in the middle on the floor). The camera also manages to capture some special moments, like the man who ignores the singing of grace at lunchtime and starts liberally sprinkling salt over his plate.

A Time to Heal is a forty-minute film without narration. The soundtrack consists of the voices of the miners and the nursing staff, in synch or off, plus a couple of songs performed by folksinger Bob Davenport. The film was released in 1963. It was distributed as part of the NCB's film library and seen by the mining audiences for which it was intended.[16] Thanks to Tyne-Tees in the North East and TWW in Wales it also reached a wider television audience. *A Time to Heal* was also, blown

Shooting *A Time to Heal*

up to 35mm, shown at festivals in Leipzig, Tours, Edinburgh and Cork. For DKP there was an extra bonus that the film caught the attention of potential sponsors of future productions in the social welfare sector.[17]

Despite the support of NUM General Secretary Will Paynter, it proved impossible to raise the money for a third production that DKP and the South Wales NUM had agreed on. This was to be a film about the Miners' Eistedfodd in Porthcawl, celebrating the miners' love for and ability with music. Knight had been envisaging 'a cinéma vérité style which would expand outwards into hotels, bars, journeys and homes'.[18] With the abandonment of this project the collaboration between DKP and the South Wales NUM came to an end. Efforts to interest other trade unions into commissioning their own film failed. Likewise a joint attempt by DKP, the left-wing film distributor ETV, managed by Stanley Forman, and Ken Sprague's publicity agency Mountain and Molehill to use Centre 42 – a cultural centre that had been founded in 1961 by playwright Arnold Wesker to promote 'a greater participation by the Trade Union movement in all cultural activities'[19] – as a platform for the production of trade union films came to nothing.[20]

DKP would make a name for itself with a handful of films on health issues. For the Ministry of Health, via the COI, the company produced a short colour film which made clear that 'smoking, far from being glamorous or manly, is a rather dirty habit'.[21] This was done by graphically showing the damage done to the lungs by smoking. A heavy smoker, for example, gets out of breath after he has only walked a few steps, while a scientist collects the tar left by cigarettes in the tubes of an artificial lung. *Smoking and You* (1963) was commissioned as part of an anti-smoking campaign aimed at children aged twelve to seventeen. At its premiere the film was personally introduced by the Minister of Health, Enoch Powell. Available on free loan from the Central Film Library, *Smoking and You* received the highest number of bookings for any film in 1963, reaching an estimated total audience of 100,000.[22] Financially, however, such government commissions did not bring a great deal. The COI, as Knight himself was later to make a point of saying, was known in the industry for its stringency and petty bureaucracy.[23] Fortunately DKP had found other, more profitable sources of income. Early in 1961 it had moved to new premises (8–12 Broadwick Street), with sufficient space to offer editing and cutting-room services for hire. At times demand was such that customers had to be turned away. In 1964 Derrick Knight estimated that 'the [three] cutting rooms produce an average income of £2000 per annum'.[24]

Helped by the examples of *A Time to Heal* and *Smoking and You*, DKP was able to attract new clients from the health sector. The Spastics Society wanted a film that looked at the problems that parents with children suffering from different kinds of spasticity were faced with. The Parents Relief

Centre in Nottingham, run by the Society, was one of the features of *One of the Family* (1964). It was distributed by the commissioning body itself as well as by Concord. Bernice Rubens, the director of *One of the Family*, was a friend of Derrick Knight and had contributed to *To End with a Curtsy*. She was a tactful interviewer who could win the complete confidence of the persons who were being filmed. Although she had published a few novels by this time, it was not until Rubens won the Booker Prize for *The Elected Member* in 1970 that she would become a well-known author. That Knight did not direct *One of the Family* himself was the result of a painful decision that he would be a producer in the first place. As one of DKP's directors Charles Hodgson explained a few years later:

> From the beginning it became clear that clients were asking for films not so much from the company as from the directorial hand of Derrick himself and this presented us with one of our most difficult problems. As long as Derrick alone made the pictures, we could not grow to the size where we could become really profitable.[25]

Although Knight continued to direct one or two films annually, because their subjects mattered to him, the decision that he should concentrate on producing and leave directing to others worked well. He trained a team of young directors, writers, cinematographers and/or editors, including Bernice Rubens, David Gladwell, Chris Menges, Dai Vaughan, Peter Neal and Paul Joyce. They worked with freelance technicians whose approach fitted into what Hodgson called the 'company style'.[26] It must be said, though, that this comprised a wide range of different film styles, from cinéma vérité to classic documentary with 'Voice of God' commentary to short entertainment films for theatrical release.

In 1965, a few years after it had been proven that the birth of babies with physical defects was caused by the use of the drug Thalidomide during pregnancy, DKP was commissioned by the Society for the Aid of Thalidomide Children to make a film that would support its campaign work. It was decided to single out one victim, the four-year-old boy Brett Nielsen who was born without arms. *One of Them is Brett* (1965) shows him at home with his family (he has two healthy brothers), at school and getting an artificial arm adjusted. His parents pay a visit to the Lady Hoare Experimental Workshop and to the factory where artificial limbs are made, deriving some hope for their son's future. The film was shot in cinéma vérité style by director Roger Graef who was at the start of a long career in this kind of documentary film-making, and cameraman Peter Jessop who had the experience of *A Time to Heal* behind him. *One of Them is Brett* is a compassionate film. As Ken Gay put it: 'There is no self pity or recrimination in this film. It is positive and factual, even inspiring.'[27] *Monthly Film Bulletin* described it as 'a television rather than a cinema film'. Usually, such a characterisation meant a reproach, implying that a film was not up to the desired cinematographic standards, but *Monthly Film Bulletin* was otherwise extremely positive, praising among other qualities the film's 'tact and reticence'.[28] In fact, *One of Them is Brett* did have a very successful television career. Broadcast first by the BBC on 16 July 1965, it was later transmitted in a dozen countries, giving the Thalidomide campaign a huge boost.

One of Them is Brett was followed by DKP productions for the Mental Health Film Council (*Stress – Parents with a Handicapped Child*, 1966, directed by Bernice Rubens), for the Spastics Society (*A Place Like Home*, 1966, directed by Peter Neal) and the National Society for Mentally Handicapped Children (*New Way at Northgate*, 1969, directed by David Gladwell). Each film was preceded by careful research, during which a basic relationship with the protagonists was built up. Still, awkward moments might arise during the shooting – on 16mm in black and white, using vérité

Film User covers *One of Them is Brett*

techniques – demanding reticence from director and crew. As Bernice Rubens pointed out: 'There are moments in such filming when you have to decide to go on shooting or whether a film, however good, is worth the distress it causes.'[29] Before the film was released it was shown to the families concerned. In the case of *Stress* this led each of them to conclude that other families were worse off than themselves. All the health films produced by DKP were distributed by Concord which had a very effective network for this type of production.

In parallel with its sponsored work, DKP was still intent on producing self-financed short films for theatrical release, hoping to make a small profit in the end. But it discovered that television, too, offered revenue opportunities. In some cases the rights to transmit a DKP film were sold to TV, for example *28b Camden Street* (1966), directed by David Gladwell, was bought by the BBC. This was a 16mm film which was 'made in odd moments over 3 years about a group of artists in studios due to be demolished in a St Pancras clearing scheme'.[30] It had cost approximately £1,000 to make, with the BBC deal returning a part of this investment. The narration of *28b Camden Street* was spoken by one of the artists concerned, Peter Peri (1899–1967), a sculptor of Hungarian origin who would pass away shortly afterwards. In other cases, a co-production agreement was reached. Thus, *The Pied Pipers of Harlow* (1965), a celebration of the thriving musical activities in this New Town, in particular the stimulating presence of teachers and musical personalities (such as the Alberni Quartet), was a co-production between DKP and the BBC. Again demonstrating the company's flexibility in jumping from one type of project to another, this independently produced film was a spin-off of an earlier DKP production, *Faces of Harlow* (1964). In fact, the making of the music to this colour film was taken up in *The Pied Pipers of Harlow*, showing Derrick Knight discussing the soundtrack with composer Alan Jellen who also was the director of the Harlow Musical Society. *Faces of Harlow* had been commissioned by the Harlow Development Corporation and was meant both as a boost in local self-esteem and as an introduction to general audiences, and industrialists contemplating moving there, of the excellent amenities which this New Town had to offer. In a rapid succession of shots with plenty of camera movements (but not in a cinéma vérité style), *Faces of Harlow* holds up Harlow as the epitome of the post-war idea that a properly planned town will benefit its inhabitants, not only economically but also socially and culturally. (Following completion the COI took prints for distribution at home and abroad: it was the sort of film that, Knight felt, the COI should be commissioning more of in the first place. As well as the COI, it was also available from Sound-Services.)

The Pied Pipers of Harlow was not the only DKP production about music. In 1961 a concert given by the famous American folksinger Pete Seeger in the London pub The Feathers was filmed, resulting in two shorts, directed by Kurt Lewenhak: *An Evening with Pete Seeger* and *Pete Seeger and Friends*. In 1966, DKP got the BBC interested in co-producing a film about a leading group of the British folk revival, The Watersons. In *Travelling for a Living* (which The Watersons baptised 'Grovelling for a Pittance') the members of the group are seen at their home in Hull, on the road in their van and performing in a number of folk venues. Filmed in a grainy black-and-white cinéma vérité style, with a sparse commentary and plenty of close shots, it gives an intimate portrait of the folk group. The Watersons are given the opportunity to talk about the roots of their music and illustrate their arguments by means of a number of songs. The forty-minute film, directed by Knight himself, was transmitted by BBC2 on 16 May 1966. As folksinger Louis Killen (who himself appeared in the film) recalled thirty years later, 'everybody in Britain on the folk scene saw that transmission'.[31] In 2003 *Travelling for a Living* was rereleased in a box set with four decades of music of The Watersons. Music of an entirely different character was the subject matter of *Dance* (1967), directed by Gladwell, which was also transmitted by the BBC. This short film follows Ernest Berk, who had written the music for *28b Camden Street*, developing the score and choreography for his new ballet 'Les Amis'.

In the late 1960s DKP developed yet another product line, by making a number of 'featurettes' for television, film reports on the making of contemporary feature films. *Work is That What it's Called* (1968) showed impresario and theatre producer Peter Hall directing his first feature film *Work is a Four-Letter Word*. *The Youth Wave* (1968) dealt with the work of a number of 'young' Paramount directors: Peter Collison (*Up the Junction*), Christopher Morahan (*Diamonds for Breakfast*), David Green (*The Strange Affair*) and Joe McGrath (*The Bliss of Mrs Blossom*). *Barbarella City* (1968) was shot at Cinecitta in Rome and the home of Roger Vadim and Jane Fonda, dealing with Vadim's *Barbarella*, in which Fonda played the lead. *Pancho Villa – Myth or Man* (1968) dealt with *Villa Rides*, directed by Buzz Kulik, making effective use of the still pictures that the Hollywood director had collected for the film. *Walking with Love and Death* (1968) showed how a film unit went about creating a period atmosphere in Austria for the John Huston feature *A Walk with Love and Death*. Lastly, *The Chairman in Taiwan* (1968) was made during the shooting of *The Chairman or the Most Dangerous Man in the World*, featuring Gregory Peck.

With the 35mm colour short *The Great Steam Fair* (1965) DKP finally hoped to get a theatrical release that would make a profit for the company. This seventeen-minute film gives an impression of a fair of old steam-powered merry-go-rounds and scenic organs, together with all sorts of sideshows, assembled for a weekend in the grounds of the country estate of John Lindsay Smith at White Waltham in Berkshire. Smith, a director of Coutts Bank, Rolls Royce and the *Financial Times*, was a fairground enthusiast. He agreed to pay all net costs of a 35mm Techniscope production, filmed by DKP. Revenue from the distribution was shared between Smith and DKP on a 75–25 per cent basis. Once the original costs had been recouped, the ownership of all rights reverted to DKP.[32] However, despite a convenient length and a U-certificate, the film did not get sufficient bookings for it to provide the extra income DKP had hoped for.

In 1966, DKP invested in its only fiction film, *Jemima and Johnny*, for which Peter Sellers and friends had already put up some money. Scripted and directed by exiled South African film-maker

Lionel Ngakane, and shot on location in the Notting Hill area, this thirty-minute film told the story of an adventurous afternoon spent by two five-year-olds, a Jamaican girl and an English boy. Although *Jemima and Johnny* was screened at many foreign film festivals and was even awarded the Golden Lion at the Venice Film Festival for the best short fiction film, like *The Great Steam Fair*, its financial returns from theatrical exhibition were disappointing.

There was obviously a structural deficiency that made it 'virtually impossible to exhibit an independent short film profitably in Britain'.[33] The big cinema circuits in the UK preferred to schedule their own films in their supporting programmes to the detriment of independently produced, or indeed sponsored, shorts. Not only DKP but other companies too were confronted with this problem. Given the important role that shorts played in the training of young film technicians, the ACTT was concerned too. The union had a Shorts and Documentary Branch which regularly held meetings where short films were screened and discussions among members were held. Derrick Knight offered to organise a survey and write a report with recommendations on how to improve the chances for the theatrical exhibition of shorts and documentaries. He was joined by Vincent Porter, an assistant director in the Shell Film Unit (he would later become a lecturer and then professor at the Polytechnic of London). In the autumn of 1966, *A Long Look at Short Films: An ACTT Report on the Short Entertainment and Factual Film* was published.

The authors of the report noted two basic problems. One was the Eady Levy, a kind of tax included in the price of a cinema ticket. This Levy was paid into a fund, out of which producers were given a percentage on their box-office receipts. Given the fact that British film production in the 1960s was predominantly financed with American capital, it was overseas investors rather than British independent producers who benefited most from the Levy. The second problem was the near monopoly held by the major circuits Rank and ABC, which preferred to book their own, cheaply produced shorts such as Rank's *Look at Life* or the *Pathé Pictorial*. What Knight and Porter proposed was to earmark £200,000 from the Eady Levy for shorts. It would be up to a selection board to place a hundred British shorts annually in the 'category for compulsory screening'. Each film in this category would automatically receive £1,000. If a voluntary agreement guaranteeing the exhibition of the hundred shorts against an acceptable allowance could not be reached with the major circuits, it was proposed to introduce legislation. The authors, bemoaning the demise of the Crown Film Unit as so many film-makers had for so long, further stressed the need to replace the COI with a National Film Board of Great Britain, based on the Canadian model and therefore with a remit to initiate films of its own.

With the Film Act expiring in 1967 and a Report of the Monopolies Commission, in which the circuits were told in guarded terms that they were not always operating 'in the public interest', it was hoped that some of the changes demanded in *A Long Look at Short Films* could be realised, especially since the ACTT's natural ally the Labour Party had extended its majority in Parliament in spring 1966's general elections.

A Long Look at Short Films was less radical than some of the Left's earlier proposals with regard to the film industry. There was, for example, no mention of nationalisation nor of the need to establish a state-owned cinema circuit. Still, the report sparked off a lively debate, in the first place on the pages of the ACTT's journal *Film & Television Technician*.[34] There was support for the report from surprising quarters. The *Financial Times*, for example, considered *A Long Look at Short Films* 'an essential book ... for the filmgoer who wonders why the supporting programmes at his local cinema are as deadly as they are, and for politicians and producers'.[35] But there was opposition too. *Film*

User, which had regularly and positively reported on the activities of DKP, devoted an editorial to the report. It warned that Knight and Porter were making a mistake by proclaiming that the average standard of sponsored films had fallen in the last decade: 'if sponsors have their confidence in the medium destroyed, their enthusiasm for films – whether made by one-man bands or ACTT professionals – will indeed wither away. This is why it is a pity that the authors have taken their long look at short films through a lens that distorts.'[36]

Under the auspices of the union a Short Film Makers Campaign was started, advertising itself in the ACTT journal as 'the industry's radical voice'.[37] Not for the first time, however, the Labour Party shirked the opportunity of bringing about radical changes in the film industry. It simply extended the existing legislation until 1970.[38] After a year the Campaign had therefore very little to show. As ACTT organiser Caroline Heller admitted in the *Film & Television Technician*: 'In theory it is obviously a good thing that we have been putting our case to the right people at the right time, though in practice the returns are not yet evident.'[39] Rank announced that it had stopped making its own *Look at Life*. So theoretically there was now room for thirteen independently made shorts per year. Disappointingly, though, Rank laid the blame with the Campaign for the redundancy of the technicians who had been responsible for *Look at Life*. As further returns failed to materialise the Campaign slowly petered out.

Despite the many hours that Derrick Knight put into the report and the Campaign that followed it, production activities at DKP continued unabatedly, many of them from industrial firms which did not regularly sponsor films. They included commissions from companies like Thomson Provincial Newspapers (*All the News*, 1965), Smedleys Food (*The Harvest is Yours*, 1967), Aer Lingus (*Shamrock Sky High*, 1968), British Gypsum (*Self Portraits*, 1968), IBM 100 Per Cent Club (*A Time to Be Bold*, 1979) and Astral Marketing for Dodge Trucks (*A Power of Difference*, 1969). Of those films, *Self Portraits* – directed by Stephen Cross and one in a series that DKP made for this plasterboard manufacturing company – was, as Knight later recalled, 'one of the most innovative industrial films the company made'.[40] Using a cinéma vérité style, *Self Portraits* shows (in black and white) workers and managers on the factory floor talking directly to the camera about their work. The film links these mini-portraits with footage of their domestic lives (in colour).

The tradition of campaign films that had started with *March to Aldermaston* (although strictly speaking not a DKP film) was also continued. In 1961 DKP was forced to abandon its production of a campaign film in support of the South

"From an industry distinguished by its ability to make terrible films."

The bricks that get heaved at the building industry are usually concerned with housing.

But John Chittock in the Financial Times of May 7 found a new line of attack.

He had a dig at the films the industry makes.

Then he turned his attention to our latest effort. (An epic of life in a Midlands plasterboard factory.)

Mr. Chittock didn't mince his words.

"Praise indeed to British Gypsum for at last breaking the vicious circle with a really refreshing approach to the use of industrial film....

In 'Self Portraits' they have sponsored a film that will, I am sure, do more to sell their plasterboard than a dozen tedious exercises in manufacturing technology....

It is an oddly unpolished film – professional always, but without glitter. To some extent, this is meant as a slight criticism because it gives the film a low key effect which leaves me a little uneasy.

But a human principle emerges with a clarity and force that will stay with me for years."

If you'd like to see this film, which Derrick Knight made for us, you've only to ask.

Just ring June Warner at 01-486 1282. Or write to her at British Gypsum Limited, Ferguson House, 15-17 Marylebone Road, London N.W.1.

British Gypsum Limited.

(A member of the BPB Industries Group.)

African Boycott Committee, to be based on a script written by Knight and Tod Greenaway that was inspired by Paul Strand's Frontier Films production *Native Land* (1941). As *Let My People Go*, the film was subsequently realised by John Krish.[41] As a positive outcome, however, Knight got to know the exiled South African poet and activist Raymond Kunene, who persuaded DKP to film the funeral of the communist black activist Claudia Jones, also known as the 'Mother of the Notting Hill Carnival', in December 1964. In 1966 Derrick Knight personally helped out with the making of a film for Medical Aid for Vietnam, *A Message from Vietnam*, produced by ETV. In 1967 the company produced two party political broadcasts for the Labour Party. Although Knight had been a member of the Party's TV advisory group for some time, the request came out of the blue. *Education for the Future* dealt with comprehensive education: it was filmed at the David Lister School in Hull, with its charismatic headmaster Albert Rowe, and made good use of Knight's trademark naturalism. *Second Chance*, directed by Robert Kitts, focused on the retraining of workers made redundant as a result of technological change, the 'White Heat' that had been so ardently advocated by Tony Benn. For the International Defence and Aid Fund for South Africa DKP produced, in 1970, *Witnesses*, in which the effects of Apartheid were shown, using among other sources the stills of Ernest Cole.

In 1968 DKP made its first film for Christian Aid. This organisation had been set up after World War II to help reconstruction in Europe but under the charismatic leadership of Janet Lacey had shifted focus to the poorest regions in the world, particularly in Africa and Asia. The first DKP production for Christian Aid, *Reaching Out*, looked at the difficulties of grassroots agricultural development and social welfare in Africa. It was followed in 1970 by *The Migrant Way*, which was largely shot in the sertao, the barren countryside in North East Brazil, with its feudal conditions. Both films were not only used as campaign films by the commissioning body (and distributed by Concord) but also transmitted by the BBC.

In the meantime the production company had started a major film series, *The World Without*, for the United Nations, to mark the beginning of the Second UN Development Decade. The UN had a reputation for churning out rather bland if not completely dull documentaries, even if such well-known film-makers as Thorold Dickinson, Paul Rotha and Basil Wright had once been involved. So it was a challenge for DKP to come up with something different. Derrick Knight visited numerous locations over the world, was confronted by the enormous contrast in lifestyle between UN officials and local population and decided in the end on three communities (Java, Peru and Senegal) that had enough to offer for three stories, that of the peasants, the workers and the students. In each of the individual films – *The Villagers*, *The Newcomers* and *The Inheritors* – the developments in the three countries are compared.

The contract that the UN had 'imposed' on DKP left absolutely no room for eventualities. As there were delays – some inherent in the logistics of such a major international production and others caused by UN bureaucracy – the budget for *The World Without* spiralled out of control. By the time that the films were delivered to the UN, DKP was so deep in debt that the bank was no longer willing to support it. So the company, which had never had more than five people on its payroll and had been unable to build up financial reserves, went into voluntary liquidation. To make matters even worse, the UN decided to recut *The World Without*, because they did not consider the films 'upbeat' enough. The directors (Derrick Knight, Bernice Rubens and Peter Neal) asked to have their names removed.

For a time a sister organisation of DKP, Knight Film Distribution, kept at least most of the films in circulation. It was run by Derrick Knight's wife Brenda, operating from a new address. Apart from a great number of DKP productions, it also distributed films produced by Thames Television, the National Film Board of Canada and Seminar Films. Seminar was a new company that Knight had set up with Edward de Bono, the lecturer, management consultant and guru of lateral thinking, fascinated by ideas about creativity. A five-part course by De Bono on organised creativity was recorded by Seminar Films on videotape and distributed by Knight Film Distribution, both on half-inch video and 16mm film. Knight Film Distribution merged with Film Forum (DBW), run by David Burns Windsor who had been Knight Film Distribution's general manager. Brenda and Derrick Knight were bought out. On the suggestion of De Bono, Knight opened a games shop in Soho, which he had to abandon after a few years as the result of an altercation with the owner of the premises of the shop. It was Christian Aid that came to the rescue in 1977. Surprisingly, given that he was a convinced atheist, he got a job as a research journalist with the public relations department of this organisation. One of the conditions was that he was not to interfere with the work of the officer responsible for films at Christian Aid. So during his seventeen years with the organisation Knight was only involved in the production of two films, *Exiles in Their Own Land* (1980) and *No Time for Crying* (1986).

During the short period of its existence Derrick Knight and Partners was unusually productive, more than many other independent production companies. It has left a legacy of films that are in its own words 'strongly humanist, socially conscious, technically adventurous, young in spirit'. Some can now been seen on DVD (e.g., *Travelling for a Living, A Time to Heal*), others deserve a second career (*One of Them is Brett*). Because Derrick Knight – again, unusually among those who had entered the film industry in the early 1950s – did not look down upon the medium, DKP was a pioneer in working for television, either through sales or co-production. As such it was ahead of its time – and it makes one wonder how the company might have fared in the 1980s with the coming of Channel 4 and with the BBC commissioning a growing percentage of its programmes from external producers. Although the Short Film Makers Campaign did not achieve its aims, it did play an important role in raising the consciousness of both politicians and the industry regarding the vulnerability of a certain kind of film that was internationally highly regarded, as was witnessed by the many awards it won at foreign film festivals. Last but not least DKP was an important meeting place, where anyone with a query or a problem could turn up and be assured of a sympathetic ear and sensible advice. Often, one of the editing tables would be put at the disposal of a promising young film-maker during the night, when they were not needed. Examples are journalist and television commentator Danny Schechter, who used the cutting-room at DKP to shape up the footage that he had shot of the student unrest at the London School of Economics, resulting in *Student Power* (1968), and a young documentary film-maker by the name of Nick Broomfield, who was able to do the same for his very first film *Who Cares* (1970).[42]

NOTES

1. Derrick Knight, 'The Captive Cinema', *Film* no. 13, September–October 1957, p. 16.
2. Ibid., p. 14.
3. Ibid.
4. The programmes can be consulted in the issues of *The Canfordian*: the years 1923–63 are online. See <canfordschool.websds.net/>
5. Derrick Knight, 'Draft Reply to Bert Hogenkamp about DK Film Work', February 2010, p. 2.
6. Ashton was later best known for his films about the arts, made for the BFI or, at Samaritan Films and Balfour Films, for the Arts Council.
7. Derrick Knight, Interview with the author, 21–2 October 1996.
8. David Mitchell, 'Between Two Worlds', *Picture Post*, 15 December 1951. A copy of the programme booklet, *Between Two Worlds*, at Scala Cinema, 9 November 1952, is in the possession of the author.
9. Derrick Knight, 'Progress Report (1964)', personal archive of Derrick Knight, Banbury.
10. 'Generalissimo' was a designation used by Morton Lewis, 'The Road to Aldermaston', *Film & TV Technician*, May 1958, p. 274.
11. Charles Cooper was the Honorary Treasurer of the Film and TV Committee for Nuclear Disarmament. Bert Hogenkamp, *Film, Television and the Left in Britain 1950 to 1970* (London: Lawrence & Wishart, 2000), pp. 56–60.
12. Alan Lovell, 'The Growth of Concord Films', *Peace News*, 1 December 1961, p. 9.
13. Derrick Knight, *The Miners*, typescript (section of Knight's draft memoirs), p. 197.
14. Ibid., p. 202.
15. Ibid., p. 203.
16. *Films on Coal: A Catalogue of Titles Available in June 1964* (London: National Coal Board, 1964), p. 9.
17. Knight, *The Miners*, p. 221.
18. Derrick Knight, 'Films that Never got Made', unpublished manuscript, 1996, p. 3.
19. Bert Craik, 'Centre 42', *Film & Television Technician*, May 1963, p. 113.
20. Hogenkamp, *Film, Television and the Left in Britain*, pp. 86, 118.
21. *Film User*, September 1963, p. 484.
22. *Film User*, June 1964, p. 292.
23. See Derrick Knight and Vincent Porter, *A Long Look at Short Films. An ACTT Report on the Short Entertainment and Factual Film* (Oxford: ACTT, 1967), pp.108–31.
24. Knight, 'Progress Report (1964)'.
25. Charles Hodgson, 'Voice Over ... A Personal Reminiscence on the Growth of Knight Films', in: *Knight Films: The First 10 Years*, supplement to *Film User*, 1968, pp. iv–v.
26. Cameramen: David Holmes, Peter Jessop, Ian McMillan, David Macdonald, Brian Probyn, Louis Wolfers; editor: Terry Twigg.
27. *Films & Filming*, September 1965, p. 39.
28. *Monthly Film Bulletin*, August 1965, p. 127.
29. Bernice Rubens, 'Face to Face with Stress', in *Knight Films: The First 10 Years*, p. xii.
30. Knight, 'Progress Report (1964)'.
31. Booklet accompanying the CD/DVD set *Mighty River of Song*, Topic Records, 2003, TSFCD4002, p. 19.
32. Knight, 'Progress Report (1964)'.
33. Knight and Porter, *A Long Look at Short Films*, p. 139.

34. This debate was kicked off by a review of the report by Sir Arthur Elton ('Several Ways Ahead', *Film & Television Technician*, December 1966, pp. 505–9), followed by reply by Knight and Porter ('Rejoinder', *Film & Television Technician*, January 1967, pp. 12–13). Later Maxwell Munden made a case for non-theatrical exhibition ('So You want to People to See Your Films?', *Film & Television Technician*, March 1967, pp. 61–3 and 'This is Where the Film Audiences Are', *Film & Television Technician*, April 1967, pp. 108–12).
35. *Financial Times*, 13 January 1967.
36. *Film User*, January 1967, p. 13. In a lengthy review in a different section of the same issue Robinson P. Rigg came to a similar conclusion: 'But like many reformers, they have tended to stress the "ills" and permitted themselves to be carried away by enthusiasm rather than to offer a really constructive solution', p. 6.
37. *Film & Television Technician*, February 1968, p. 7.
38. Margaret Dickinson and Sarah Street, *Cinema and State: The Film Industry and the British Government 1927–84* (London: BFI, 1985), p. 230.
39. Caroline Heller, 'Campaign with a Case', in *Film & Television Technician*, February 1968, p. 7.
40. Derrick Knight, 'List of Knight Films, Where They Were Processed and Where Copies May Exist', 1996.
41. Hogenkamp, *Film, Television and the Left in Britain*, p. 65.
42. Derrick Knight, 'Draft Reply to Bert Hogenkamp about DK Film Work,' February 2010, p. 8; Jason Wood, *Nick Broomfield. Documenting Icons* (London: Faber and Faber, 2005), p. 17.

Last Words ...

... go to our anonymous bard at Millbank Films:

Popular Misconceptions, Or: Don't Confuse Us With the Feature Boys[1]

Myth

1. Directors wear green eye-shields and sit on canvas chairs with their names on the back.
2. Producers affect fat Havanas and shapely mistresses.
3. Locations mean Corfu, Bangkok, Martinique and Pacific Prawns for elevenses.
4. Actors are jet-set hell-raisers with their own Press agents.
5. Making movies is a great big warm-hearted razzmatazz job, done by irresponsible broths of boys.

Truth

1. Directors collect green shield stamps and sit on assistant directors.
2. Producers affect fat overdrafts and have dreams like anyone else.
3. Locations – well we haven't done Scunthorpe yet, but Runcorn, Wallsend, Dalston – you name them. Elevenses – yuk!
4. Actors are nice lads from Esher who go to bed after *News At Ten*; they have a poor memory for lines, and incipient baldness.
5. Making short films is serious, difficult work, done by worried administrators with artists inside them who – luckily – quite often break out.

NOTE

1. *Take 11*, April 1975, back page (unpaginated).

Index

Page numbers in **bold** indicate the main focus of an article/section; those in *italic* denote illustrations. *n* = endnote.

B

D

E

G

H

I

N

Q

R

LIST OF ILLUSTRATIONS

Whilst considerable effort has been made to correctly identify the copyright holders this has not been possible in all cases. We apologise for any apparent negligence and any omissions or corrections brought to our attention will be remedied in any future editions

Children Learning By Experience, Realist Film Unit/Film Centre; *Blue Pullman*, British Transport Films; *Every Valley*, British Transport Films; *Dylan Thomas*, Jack Howells Productions/TWW; *The Undefeated*, World Wide Pictures; *David*, British Film Institute/Regent Film Distributors/ World Wide Pictures; *The Film That Never Was*, World Wide Pictures; *Dodging the Column*, British Transport Films; *Portrait of Queenie*, Eyeline Films; *Arabia the Fortunate*, Film Drama; *Elizabethan Express*, British Transport Films; *The New Explorers*, World Wide Pictures; *A Sunday in September*, Granada Television; *African Awakening*, World Wide Pictures; *Today in Britain*, World Wide Pictures; *Lord Siva Danced*, Shell Film Unit; *Schlieren*, Shell Film Unit; *Birthright*, Samaritan Films/Basic Films; *Picture to Post*, Rayant Pictures; *I Think They Call Him John*, Samaritan Films; *I Stopped, I Looked and Listened*, Moving Picture Company; *The Longhirst Story*, National Coal Board Film Unit; *The Team on 204s*, National Coal Board Film Unit; *Sunday by the Sea*, Harlequin Productions; *From First to Last*, Graphic Films; *Three Installations*, Sutcliffe Film Unit; *Foot and Mouth*, Basic Films; *Thursday's Children*, World Wide Pictures/Morse Films; *People Apart*, Morse Films; *Four People*, Morse Films; *The Shadow of Progress*, British Petroleum Company/Greenpark Productions; *North Slope – Alaska*, Greenpark Productions/Film Producers Guild; *The Shetland Experience*, Balfour Films; *A Time to Heal*, Derrick Knight & Partners.